Delucia Survalance photo

Published in 2016 by HoseHead Productions

ISBN 978-0-9851169-1-0
Library of Congress Control Number 2015960619

Typesetting & Cover Design by Frank Menolsino
Manufactured and Printed in the United States of America

First Edition 2016
10 9 8 7 6 5 4 3 2 1

Mob Boss:

Chicago Mob Bosses
Paul Ricca and Tony Accardo

Tony Dark

Contents

Chapter 1

Paul Ricca

One person once described Paul Ricca as a formidable and imposing individual. His demeanor; his build; his conversation; were all of a legitimate business man. Famous mobsters like John Gotti and Al Capone were not afraid to show their gangster sides, each wanted you to know he was the boss and the emperor of organized crime. Where as men like Paul Ricca and Tony Accardo prided themselves on being legitimate businessmen rather than racketeers. At least out in public, behind the masks, were men who would end a man's life with just a nod or a certain look and had no problem doing it. After awhile, it became second nature to them.

As one government agent once said, next to New York City, Chicago was perhaps the greatest melting pot of different kinds of people in the United States. At the end of the nineteenth century most of its population was born on foreign shores arriving as immigrants. Herbert Asbury wrote Chicago started in 1779 when a Santo Domingan Negro built a cabin at the junction of the north and south branches of the Chicago River which gave the city its starting point. The first white man to build a shelter in Chicago was a known criminal, a French trapper who sold liquor and other illegal goods to the Indians. A county sheriff had jurisdiction over the city until the first Chicago police department was formed in 1835. By 1850 the Chicago Police Department had about nine officers to control around 80,000 in population.

The great Chicago fire in 1871 devastated the city, burning over 1,450 acres and around 13,300 buildings, leaving some 500 still standing. Chicago was rebuilt in a more organized manner but still gave way to gangs of hoodlums running gambling, prostitution and used killing as a main tool.

Between 1890 to about 1910 Chicago grew in size almost 200 square miles. With this new territory came more than a million inhabitants all searching for the American dream. The Swedes, Lithuanians, Poles, Croatians, Dutch, Norwegians, Danes, Greeks and Slovaks poured into Chicago, bringing the good and bad from Europe. The city's boundaries filled with the third largest gatherings of Norwegians and Swedes, the forth largest of Poles, fifth largest of Germans and the second largest Bohemians in the world.

Chicago at that time was an overgrown village with the machinery of a small town that struggled to govern its 3,000,000 inhabitants. Townships, wards, and county governments were set up to control the vast amount of people pouring into the city. Each group settled into self-claimed areas made up of its own nationality. John Landeace once wrote Chicago was handicapped in that, after all, it was a subordinate municipality governed principally by the legislature, deprived of the right to self-government in many material matters, and subjected to the restrictions of a constitution which was created for an agricultural state.

Suburban areas around Chicago began to form with over a million immigrants looking to settle. Meat packing plants, furniture building shop and clothing stores were the major form of non-government jobs in the city.

Mob Boss

After 1910 Chicago was swarmed by Italian immigrants and the rise of old Italian gangs from the old country surfaced on the streets. After World War I printing and publishing replaced furniture building, while steel and iron assumed the role of Chicago's most important industry. Many of the lucky and smarter criminals gained control of these businesses which began a substantial money flow. By the middle 1920s it seemed crime in Chicago trumped them all as gangsters focused on supply and demand of illegal booze. Religion and the ever-changing wind of politics won its hand in the formation of Prohibition, making the consumption and production of alcohol illegal, and a sin. It handed the gangsters the greatest prize imaginable, a prize that made killers millionaires.

By the 1930s organized crime came into its own and stabilized into a single organization lead by one boss with many little gangs that played ball with the bosses. Instead of knocking off the top boss and moving up the ladder to become head of a gang, the little gangs simply gave a small percentage of their spoils to the boss which stopped most of the violence and killings.

In Chicago, few have assumed the roll of top boss, commander, emperor, leader, whatever title you wish to use, but in order for a criminal organization to run efficiently there had to be that one person to lead, or chaos would control the operations. After Chicago and the world had seen an organized crime boss like no other in Al "Scarface" Capone, with the spotlight, celebrity status and flaunting of wealth, many Chicago gangsters knew what did not work and did not want another Capone exposing their enterprises. One man under Capone fit that bill perfectly; someone who enjoyed the shadows, who did not have to sit in the front row to show everyone he was a somebody; someone who did not need a blond girl on each arm as he walked the night in a big city; someone with the brains of a banker or lawyer who understood when to order a killing for the right reason. That person was Paul "The Waiter" Ricca, Chicago Mob boss.

Though history knows him under the name Paul Ricca, as in every book, article, movie and many government reports he will always be known as Paul Ricca, but his real name was Paul DeLucia, and it is the name I will use to explain the story of Paul Ricca. Paul Ricca was just a name he made up to tell the police when he was arrested in the 1920s. He never intended it to be the name he would be known for but the Chicago newspapers picked it up and it became history as the name he would always be known as. His family, friends and many associates never called him Paul Ricca. He was always referred to as DeLucia. Even most of the FBI's files on him, which range between 50,000 and 100,000 pages, refer to him as "Paul DeLucia, aka Paul Ricca."

Much of this book is written from a law enforcement view of Paul DeLucia. Much of the information and stories came from law enforcement, informants and newspaper articles which may or many not be the real complete story. There is a section with stories from actual people who knew Paul DeLucia or from members of the DeLucia family. I have always believed you take law enforcement's version and then the version outside of law enforcement and where you meet in the middle is closer to the truth.

Map of Italy showing Naples, Apricena and the Puglia Region

The story of Paul DeLucia's life is told by Paul DeLucia himself. However, the story may be only half the truth. He told the government his beginnings began in Apricena, a town in northeastern Puglia, Italy. However, the government investigation determined that DeLucia was born in or around Naples, Italy. Some reports state he was born on July 10, 1898, some say January 14, 1897 and others say November 14, 1897. Some say he was born under the name of Felice Maglio but his real last name was Felice DeLucia.

The reasoning for this is that in 1915 and 1917 he signed prison and military papers in Italy using the name of Felice DeLucia. In 1925 and 1928 he filed a petition for naturalization in the U.S. claiming his name was Paul Maglio. In 1947 he told the FBI that his real name was Paul Maglio. By 1932 every form he filled out he said his real name was Paul DeLucia. In 1959 J. Edgar Hoover of the FBI received a letter about DeLucia stating that DeLucia had literally stolen another man's identity, to which in April 1957 the real Paul Maglio testified in DeLucia's court case that DeLucia had used his name to gain entrance into the United States.

The facts discovered were that in August 1920, Paul DeLucia boarded the S. S. Ryndam steam liner boat in Boulogne, France under the name Paul Maglio setting sail to escape Italy. You may ask, escape from what? Before we get to that, let's look at DeLucia's life growing up in Italy.

Paul DeLucia lived with his mother, who he said was named Nunzio Maria Torelli but who the U.S. Government later said was really Maria Annunziata, and his four sisters Emily (Amelia), Anna, Clementina and Luisa. DeLucia told the government his father was Enrico Maglio but the Immigration and Naturalization Department believed his fathers name was Antonio DeLucia. When Paul married in 1927 in Chicago he wrote on his marriage license that his father and mother were Anthony DeLucia and Mary Annunziata from Naples, Italy.

In 1944 Paul DeLucia told the government that his mother died of blood poisoning in 1917 at the age of 39. He said his father was a contractor and wine merchant who died of a heart attack in 1924 in Italy.

DeLucia told the investigators that he had a better-than-average life growing up in Italy. He lived in a 12-room house that was owned by his father. He claimed to be the older of two living children after two twins his mother gave birth to died. He claimed to have started school in 1906 and quit after completing the fourth year of high school to enlist in the Italian Army. Years later he was known to tell people that he had three years of high school.

The climate in Italy around 1916 was that of war. Europe was in the midst of its greatest war ever seen. DeLucia himself told the FBI that he was just out of Italy's equivalent of high school when he joined the Royal Italian Army and went off to fight in World War I. He was assigned to the Italian Signal Corps and saw horrible combat action. His valiant action during combat gained him the honor of being awarded Italy's Good Conduct Citation. He was honorably discharged on January 2, 1920 and he received a monetary bonus from the Italian government as a result of his war service. However, other records list him as a World War I draft dodger.

Much of this seems to be not truth and could have been a great story told to the FBI. What is known for sure is the following story which makes DeLucia's version of growing up more believable.

In 1915 his sister Amelia became engaged to a young man named Emilio Perillo whose family was powerful and had a very good reputation in the city of Ottaino, near Naples, Italy. Angered by the engagement, the boys family, thinking their son deserved better than Amelia, ordered him to break off the engagement and relationship. Upset by the breakup, Amelia turned to her brother Felice for help. Felice instructed his sister to invite this young man over to the family house one more time to say good bye. Once the young man arrived Felice killed him and dumped his body in the street.

Paul DeLucia was arrested and charged with voluntary murder. On May 18, 1917 in the Common Assize court of Naples, his fate was handed down. Since he was only 17 years old, he was given a sentence of two years, six months and 16 days for his crime and served his time at the S. Eframo prison in Naples.

After serving two of those years, he was released, only to kill yet again. While DeLucia was in prison, a Vincenzo Capasso fired a bullet from a pistol at DeLucia's father Antonio which hit him, causing only a slight wound. Capasso was arrested but won his release and had his name cleared of any wrongdoing. However, just because the Italian government said Capasso was not guilty, Paul DeLucia rendered his own guilty verdict.

On June 17, 1920 DeLucia, out of prison, walked into a saddle maker's shop where he found Capasso and shot him to death. Before being caught, DeLucia went into hiding, then fled Italy for America. He found a travel agent who gave him a passport belonging to a man named Paul Maglio to use to get into America. Capasso's murder was linked back to the feud between the DeLucia's and the Perillo's.

Back in Naples four years later on June 30, 1924, judges held a trial without DeLucia and found him guilty, sentencing him to 21 years in prison. But it did not matter because DeLucia had fled the country successfully.

In 1924 Paul DeLucia's father Antonio and his sister Amelia were also found guilty, with four others, in the robbery and extortion murder of Raffaele Perillo, Emilio's only other brother, and served jail time for the slaying. Antonio received 2 years, 9 months and 10 days while Amelia received 4 years, 7 months and 16 days in prison for supplying the weapon used for the killing. In all, 14 members of the two families were killed in this feud. Whoever said love did not hurt?

In 1920 the Holland Line Steamship sailed from France to America and docked at Ellis Island. Later the U.S. Government decided that this was a lie and Paul DeLucia entered the U.S. illegally on August 10, 1920. Once on the mainland in New York City, Paul DeLucia knew almost no one and could speak very little English so he headed for Manhattan's Little Italy. There he blended into the Italian colony since most of the occupants spoke Italian. After a month in New York City, Paul DeLucia met a powerful member of the Chicago Black Hand who was there visiting relatives. The Chicago Black Hand was the organized crime organization of the time made up of Mafia members from Italy. This man would change DeLucia's life forever. His name was Johnny Torrio, who at the time had just become the leader of the Chicago criminal organization that his uncle once held. His uncle, James "Big Jim" Colosimo, refused to enter into the business of making alcohol after it had become illegal in the United States in early 1920. So Torrio had Colosimo killed to take over as boss and escort Chicago into bootlegging alcohol.

Paul DeLucia had mentioned to Torrio that he was looking for work, and according to an FBI informant years later, Torrio noticed that DeLucia had potential as a leader and enforcer which Torrio needed in Chicago. So Torrio told DeLucia to pack his things and move to Chicago which he did to start his new life.

In September of that year he landed on Chicago's near west side, known as Chicago's Little Italy. There he had no trouble at all finding a job at a local coffee shop and later worked for William Cosironi (one report spells his name Coseran) at his restaurant located at 901 South Halsted. There he worked as a waiter, or so the story goes. It was not known for sure if or what kind of work he did for Torrio once in Chicago, but according to DeLucia himself he denied doing anything for

Torrio. It is possible Paul DeLucia did come to Chicago because of Torrio but very little evidence of him actually working for or performing illegal acts for Torrio has ever been proven.

He finally found steady work at a place known as the Dante Theater, an Italian show house located at the corner of Taylor and Halsted Streets, 905 Halsted to be exact. He quickly became friends with the owner, Joseph Vicedomini. Later he would say that a man named Ralph Vicedomini was one of the first people he met in Chicago when he arrived. During the three years he worked at the Dante he managed to learn the English language and worked his way up to assistant manager.

In 1923 his life would change once again. He began to meet members of the Torrio, Genna, and Aiello Gangs who were in a engaged in a battle for the streets of Chicago. One of the gangsters was named Joseph "Diamond Joe" Esposito who controlled much of Chicago's Little Italy.

Diamond Joe Esposito was a union boss in the Chicago Hod Carriers Union who owned an Italian restaurant located at the corner of Forquer and Halsted Streets. Esposito gave DeLucia a job waiting on the tables of the political big shots, gangsters, and Italian Black-Hand members who came in for a meal. However, in some reports it suggests that DeLucia actually worked in a restaurant across the street from Esposito but it was not known for sure. Either way, being the waiter to the most important clientele, DeLucia became friendly with them, something which would come in handy down the line.

His job as "the waiter" would stick with him the rest of his life as it would become what he was known as, Paul "The Waiter". One story says the name "The Waiter" came from his mannerism of saying "sir" in almost every sentence and his penchant for dark ties and suits. Many years later Paul DeLucia denied he was ever a "waiter" at anytime and was always above that position, being a manager.

The story does say that he became so respected that Diamond Joe made DeLucia the manager of the restaurant. Between 1923 and 1926 Paul DeLucia became close friends with gangsters Phil D'Andrea, Louis "Little New York" Campagna, Charles

A 1920's Chicago P. D. arrest photo of Paul DeLucia

and Rocco Fischetti and the three who would become most important people in his life; Frank "The Enforcer" Nitti, Anthony "Joe Batters" Accardo and the top boss him self, Al "Scarface" Capone. One FBI informant years later said that DeLucia actually was considered a member of the Genna Gang who was allied with the Capone Gang. However, no proof of that had been found.

The DeLucia wedding photo that is maintained in the DEA's files. Al Capone is standing to the left (second from left) of Paul DeLucia (center)

In 1928 when Diamond Joe Esposito was shot and killed, DeLucia found himself out of a job. He was still working part time at the Dante Theater but decided to open his own restaurant, a small Italian restaurant near Taylor and Halsted streets in Chicago's Little Italy. However, after a few months DeLucia decided to close the business which was not profitable.

It was around this time that old Chicago Police detectives began to notice Paul DeLucia mostly in the presence of Frank Nitti, Frank Rio, Jake Guzik, Charles and Rocco Fischetti, Frank Diamond, Hymie Levin, William Heeney, Tony "Caps" Capezio, Carl Torraco, aka Charlie Carr, Rocco DeStefano and Joe Fusco. DeLucia was observed attending many social functions given by Al Capone at the New Lexington Hotel at 22nd and Michigan, which was Capone's headquarters.

Frank Nitti was drawn to DeLucia's intelligence and inducted him to work at Capone's headquarters at the Lexington Hotel as a confidential aid to Nitti. Frank Nitti became DeLucia's sponsor in the Capone Gang. Years later DeLucia admitted to authorities that he worked for Al Capone. He said, *"Capone would bet as much* *as $10,000 on a horse and I would book the bets. I made a lot of money from gambling, horses, dice and all that. I put all the cash in safety deposit boxes."*

Paul DeLucia soon found himself on the "strategic" committee of the Capone Gang with Frank Nitti, Murray Humphreys and Louis Campagna.

In 1928 DeLucia claimed he had married his wife Annunciata "Nancy" Gigante on January 3, 1927 in Chicago in a civil ceremony. Later the two held a Catholic Church wedding at Holy Guardian Angels Roman Catholic Church at 717 W. Arthington in Chicago. In a photo from the wedding it was believed that his groom mates were Frank Nitti, Louis Campagna and Tony Accardo, with his best man being Al Capone. However, this fact has never been verified, though Al Capone and his sister Mafalda did sign as the witnesses on the marriage certificate. Nancy Gigante was said to be born in Naples, Italy on October 2, 1905 and brought to the United States by her parents when she was seven years old.

The two would have three children; their daughter Marianna DeLucia, who attended Trinity High School in River Forest Illinois and the University of Illinois; son, Anthony Paul DeLucia who attended Purdue University as an agricultural student; and the youngest son, Paul Richard DeLucia.

When the FBI went looking for the marriage license certificate they found the number of the certificate but the actual papers were missing and the index card to the file system was altered to cover up their names. The name Nancy Gigante was changed to the name Mary Gerola and the name Paul DeLucia was changed to the name Peter DelRosa. It also listed them as being married on June 15, 1927. When the FBI went to the church they found the marriage license under the name of Paolo DeLucia, son of Anthony and Maria Annunziata from Napoli, Italy.

It was said that Tony Accardo was the one who convinced Paul DeLucia to become a full time gambler. He began taking bets for himself but years later said he never owned a handbook or gambling establishment, he would just walk around the streets of Chicago making personal bets with people in different cafés and restaurants.

September 27, 1928 saw Paul DeLucia naturalized in U.S. District Court. His witnesses were Frank Meo and Michael James Lopiscilo, other wise known as Mike Fish, who would own the well known Mike Fish's Restaurant on Ontario Street in Chicago, which became known as a mob headquarters in the 1950s.

D 420
Family name: De Lucia (Maglio) | Given name or names: Paul
Address: 905 S. Halsted St. Chicago, Ill 3
Certificate no. (or vol. and page): P-55072 CN-2827322 | Title and location of court: U S Dist. Chgo
Country of birth or allegiance: Italy | When born (or age): July 10, 1898
Date and port of arrival in U.S.: Aug. 10, 1920 New York | Date of naturalization: Sept 27, 1928
Names and addresses of witnesses:
Frank Meo, 905 S. Halsted St. Chgo
Michael J. Fish, 4920 Monroe St., Chgo.
U.S. Department of Labor, Immigration and Naturalization Service   Form No. I-P.

PaulDeLucia's naturalization card

Qc14 (1917) Felice De Lucia
Qc15 (1915) Felice De Lucia

Qc23 not comp. [sig is Paul Maglio)
Qc24 (1928) Paul De Lucia
Qc25 not comp. [sig is Paul Maglio)
Qc26 not comp [" " "]
Qc27 Paul De Lucia (1935)
Qc28 (1944 Paul De Lucia
Qc16 (1928) Paul De Lucia
Qc17 (1927) Paul De Lucia
Qc18 (1932) Paul De Lucia
Qc19 (1934 Paul De Lucia

No concl because:
(1) not suff comp
(2) not at all comp
(3) time lag.

Qc23,c24,25 in name Paul Maglio
Qc28,c27,c17,c18,c19 in name Paul De Lucia } no concl not enuf of same letts & letter combs

KC11 + Qc21 Paul Maglio Paul Maglio

Qc16, c23→c26
c16 Paul De Lucia [no concl KC11 & Qc21 not suff comp. diffs noted
19 c23→c26 Paul Maglio [no ident KC11 & Qc21)

Signatures of Paul DeLucia compiled by the FBI

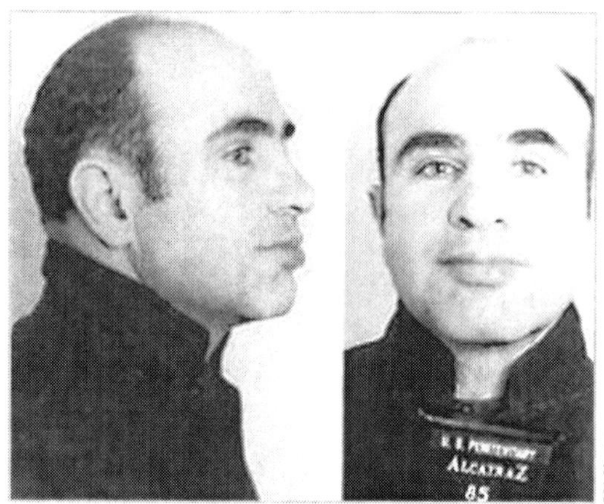

FBI Photo

Al "Scarface" Capone

Paul DeLucia once told the FBI that between 1929 and 1939 he was an unusually lucky gambler which he said was his main business. Capone Gangster Phil D'Andrea once said that around the early 1930s Paul DeLucia started showing up all the time at Capone's Lexington Hotel. When D'Andrea was asked at the time whether DeLucia was a big shot he said no, DeLucia was very, very quiet. Years later the FBI interviewed Dan Serritella, a political figure and race track sheet publisher, who told the agents that he attended many meetings with Al Capone at the New Lexington Hotel in Chicago during the late 1920s and early 30s, and that Paul DeLucia was present on many occasions to make decisions on mob business. Years later DeLucia would tell an interviewer that he was involved in buying distressed stocks of goods and other available items for resale in addition to importing merchandise for resale. He gave the example when being interviewed that he had just purchased a lot of marble from a firm which was financially distressed and was going to sell it for twice what he purchased it for.

Paul DeLucia's name began appearing in Chicago newspapers around 1930. In June 1930 Chicago police were on the hunt for the killer of Chicago Tribune Newspaper reporter Alfred J. Lingle, known as Jack Lingle, who was shot in the back of the head while he walked in the subway at Michigan Avenue and Randolph Street.

The killing sparked outrage in the Chicago papers and by its clergymen. Chicago police responded by arresting 664 prisoners in a 24-hour period. Many arrested were common thugs, robbers, small time hoodlums who would have never been considered to be involved in the Lingle murder. Big time gangsters like Peter Genna, James Belcastro and Rocco Fanelli were picked up and tossed in jail while ambitious police lieutenants staged raids on gangster's hideouts such as the Aiello Gang's headquarters at 473 West Division Street in Chicago. The leader of the Aiello Gang, Joseph Aiello, was not there so his brothers Carl and Dominick were arrested and charged with possessing fire arms.

After the arrest the then police chief of detectives said to the press, *"I am confident that Chicago right now is rid of the worst of its criminal element. We shall see whether they dare come back to face our squads of police marksmen."*

The Chicago Police received some interesting news. Ten Capone Gang members were arrested from a train entering New York City. The men arrested were Paul Ricca (DeLucia), Ted Newberry, Edward Vogel, Peter Fosco, Jake Guzik, Dennis Cooney, Frank LaPorte, Joseph Corngold, Ralph J. Carroll (Capone) and Agostino Loverde. Found on DeLucia was a bag containing $60,000 in cash. When police asked why he was carrying all that money, he said he and his friends were on their way to New York City to watch and place a bet on the Sharkey-Schmeling boxing match.

Just the Facts

On November 4, 1930 Chicago police raided the building at 901 S. Halsted and found Paul DeLucia, Murray Humphreys, Sam Tannenbaum, Frank Rio, Ralph Pierce, Mike Castella, Tony Pintozzi, Anthony Scargo, August Demore, Tony Prignano and Republican candidate Roland V. Libonati sitting around a table listing to election returns. Police found five loaded revolvers laying on a piano next to the table. No one there would admit to ownership of the weapons. All were released.

In April 1932 Paul DeLucia was arrested with top New York City mob bosses Charles "Lucky" Luciano and Meyer Lansky outside a Chicago hotel. Police noticed right away when Luciano and Lansky arrived at the Chicago train station and followed them through the city. First they went to a night club on Chicago's South side under Capone's control; then they were driven to their hotel room where Luciano received more than 30 phone calls in a two-hour period. The policemen following the two rented the room next door to listen in and heard Luciano's conversations. Most of the conversations concerned Detroit, shipments, steamboats and airplanes and the name of Joe Fusco, then one of Al Capone's right hand men in booze, was mentioned as the contact. When Luciano and Lansky went down to the street from their room, police noticed a car pull up and four men exited to greet the New Yorkers. The four men were Sylvester Agoglia, then a former Genna Gang gangster, Harry Brown, a race track owner, John Senna, a one-time Moran Gang member and Paul DeLucia.

The police swarmed in and arrested all six men. Police found on Luciano a paper statement that read "accounts receivable" amounting of $46,655. He also had $900 in his pocket.

Paul DeLucia had very strong ties with New York mob bosses. For example, DeLucia was very close to Vito Genovese. An incident involving Genovese occurred when Sarveria Pollaci, then the consiglieri of New York mob boss Joseph Masseria, had disrespected Genovese, then a vice-capo of Lucky Luciano, and Genovese wanted to avenge himself from what he called an "abuse" by Pollaci. Genovese invited Pollaci to accompany him to Chicago. Once the two were in

Chicago they met with Paul DeLucia, then DeLucia and Genovese killed Pollaci and buried his body somewhere in the city. The story came from an FBI informant in Pittsburgh where Genovese and Pollaci had stopped on their way to Chicago and Genovese informed this informant that Pollaci was on a "one way trip."

Chicago Police Department arrest photo from April 1932 of Paul DeLucia (1st on left) Charles "Lucky" Luciano (3rd from left) and Meyer Lansky (4th from left)

Vito Genevese

Tony Dark

On November 2, 1932 Paul DeLucia, using the name Paul Ricca, was arrested with Frank Rio, Phil D'Andrea and Michael Costello at the Planters Hotel. They were charged with disorderly conduct but all told the police they had met at the hotel to arrange a trip to Florida.

Chicago P. D. arrest photo Frank Rio, Michael Costello, Phil D'Andrea and Paul DeLucia (last on right).

By 1933 Paul DeLucia, under the name Ricca, was listed as Chicago Public Enemy number 152 on the Public Enemy list produced by the Chicago PD and the Chicago FBI office. Even though he was not in the lower numbers on the list he was still high enough for law enforcement to take notice. One example was when law enforcement gathered information that Paul DeLucia was the messenger sent to New York City to hold meetings with mob boss from the five families of organized crime there. One thing learned was DeLucia always insisted on eating at Henricis Restaurant in New York.

One incident involving DeLucia happened when he was a sponsor for the Italian Village Restaurant at the 1933 Century of Progress Exposition in Chicago. Architect Hugh Garden had come up with the idea of opening the restaurant at the fair and the leader of the group of investors he had found, named Paul Salvi, was actually Paul DeLucia. Garden said that he would call DeLucia on the phone and say that the contractor needed money to keep working. DeLucia would show up and pay the contractors by laying out large sums of money on a table in the office. He would have the contractors sign a receipt in an adjoining room and then leave the contractors to pick up their money off the table themselves. The venture turned out to be a $180,000 bust of a money pit.

Capone gangster Charles "Cherry Nose" Gioe testified that Paul DeLucia owned a restaurant around 1934 called the Blue Grotto at either Wabash Avenue and Congress Street or Wabash Avenue and Van Buren Street and another restaurant on Market Drive in Chicago. Gioe said he would go to the Blue Grotto to purchase champagne for his own restaurant before prohibition ended. Gioe said that DeLucia's place was run by a man named Ralph and this Ralph claimed that DeLucia and he made the champagne themselves.

On September 30, 1934 the FBI office in Chicago received an anonymous letter signed "A Poor Banker" stating that Paul Ricca was wanted in Naples, Italy for murder. This letter also stated that Ricca was a Capone gangster and was in control of the Italian Bakers Association in Chicago. He was stealing one-half cent on every pound of bread made under the threats of burning their trucks and other acts of terrorism.

Dear Mr. Purvis

As I read in the Papers, you mean business with the gangesters, I have a good job for you, for a man worst than Dillinger.

This man real name is De Lucia, wanted in Naples, Italy for murder, his alias are Poul Viela, Paul Salvi, Paul Ricca and he is a Capone gagester, you will find this man in the Italian Village at the World Fair, because the Village is owned by them.

I am a Italian Baker, this man control the Italin Bakers Ass. we have to pay half cent for every pound of bread we make and if we do not do what they say they burn our truks and all kinds of damages. I wish you will take kare of this criminal and send him back to Italy

Hope to hear soon some good news,

very truly yours
a poor Baker

Chapter 2

Walk in Capone's Shoes

Many informants told the FBI that around the time Al Capone was encountering the many difficulties that lead to his downfall in the early 1930s, he called a meeting of his top and trusted mobsters. There he named his top trusted men who he called "leaders", namely Frank Rio, Frank Nitti, Paul DeLucia, Charles Fischetti, Jake Guzik and Louis Campagna, so there would be no confusion when he went away to prison. He then named his top field marshals, Nicholas Circella, Charles Gioe and Tony "Joe Batters" Accardo, to carry out the business activities of the gang. Accardo, Circella, Frank Diamond, Lawrence Imburgio and Louis Romano were also said to be picked to see that order was kept in the gang.

Once Al Capone was sent to prison Frank Nitti took over as top boss of the Capone Gang. His real name was Frank Nitto who came to America in 1891 with his mother Rose and elder sister Anna. Their father, Louis, had died two years after Frank Nitto was born. First they lived in Harrison, New Jersey before moving to Brooklyn, New York where his mother re-married. Frank Nitto went to school until the 7th grade. After school he learned the baker's trade but would work other jobs on and off, around Brooklyn in factories, such as the time he worked in a shoe factory for pennies. His new stepfather and a young Frank Nitto did not get along very well, forcing him to flee home.

Nitto left New York in 1919 and headed to Chicago where he claimed he worked as a baker until 1925. He said he worked for two bakers named R. Russo and Louis Esposito.

However, one of the stories was that back in Brooklyn he was a member of the Five Points Gang with his pal Al Capone before 1920. When Capone made his way to Chicago he sent for his pal Frank Nitto to come to Chicago and work for Johnny Torrio in bootlegging and gambling. Nitto had been arrested many times but always managed to have the records and photos destroyed by a court order.

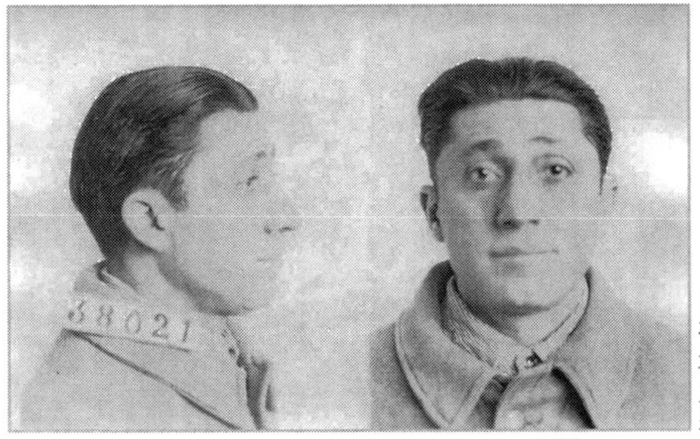

National Archives

Frank Nitto

Mob Boss

File Card

Frank Nitti
Real Name Frank Ralph Nitto, Francesco Raffele Nitto
AKA The Enforcer
AKA Frank Novelli, Frank Raddo
Born January 27, 1886 Angri, Italy
Arrived in America Spring 1891
Died March 1943 (Committed suicide)
Naturalized U.S. Citizen February 1925

Family

Father Louis "Luigi" Nitto (From the town of Angri, died in Italy 1888)
Mother Rose "Rosina" Fezza (Died in Brooklyn, New York 1913)
First wife Rose Levitt (Married Dallas Texas, divorced 1927)
Second wife Anna Ronga (Married February 16, 1929 in St. Louis, Missouri)
Third wife Annette Caravetta
Sister Anna "Giovannina" Vollaro (Lived at 104 Garfield Place, Brooklyn, New York)
Son Joseph Nitto (Adopted 1934)

Known Addresses

Harrison, New Jersey (1891-1893)
Brooklyn New York (1893-1907)
148 Navy Street, Brooklyn, New York (1907-1911)
104 Garfield Place, Brooklyn, New York (1900's)
Dallas, Texas (1917)
914 Halsted Street, Chicago (1918)
2653 North Halsted Street, Chicago (1919-1923)
833 South Marshfield Avenue, Chicago (1925-1927)
1801-50th Avenue, Cicero, Illinois (1927-1928)
1200 McAllister Place, Chicago (1929-1930)
3201 South Clinton Street, Berwyn, Illinois (1930)
714 West Di Lido Island Drive, near Miami, Florida (1936-1940's)
1208 Lexington, Chicago (1941)

Known Businesses

Manhattan Distributing Company, Miami, Florida (1930's)
F. R. Nitti Company, New DuPont Building, Miami, Florida (1939)

Known Arrest Record of Frank Nitti

Date	Charge	Agency	Result
4-6-1925	Disorderly Conduct	Chicago PD	Released
4-23-1925	U/K	Chicago PD	Discharged
10-30-1930	General Principles	Chicago PD	Released
11-7-1930	Vagrancy	Chicago PD	Released
9-7-1930	Warrant	U.S. Marshal	U/K
12-3-1930	Vagrancy	Chicago PD	$10,000 Bond
3-9-1931	U/K	Chicago PD	Nolle Process
1-11-1931	Tax Evasion	Leavenworth	18 Months
12-19-1932	Investigation	Chicago PD	Released
4-6-1933	Attempted Murder	Chicago PD	Not Guilty
8-12-1936	Bolton Murder	Chicago PD	Released
8-1936	Prignano Murder	Chicago PD	Released
8-13-1939	Bribery	Chicago PD	Bond Out
10-18-1940	Conspiracy	Chicago PD	Grand Jury

Chicago Police Department arrest photo of Frank Nitti in the early 1930's

UNITED STATES PENITENTIARY
LEAVENWORTH, KANSAS

RECORD OF Frank R. Nitto NO 38021

Alias Frank Nitto, Frank Nitti Color White

Crime Vio Revenue Act(Failure to File Income Tax Return) Military or Civil Civil

Sentence -- years 18 months -- days.

Fine $10,000 Com. Yes. Cost xx

Received at Penitentiary Jan. 11, 1931 From ND Illinois, Chicago.

Date of Sentence Dec. 20, 1930 Sentence begins Jan. 11, 1931.

Maximum term ends July 10, 1932 Minimum term ends March 24, 1932

Good time allowed 108 days, Occupation Clerk Age 45 Years.

Eligible to parole July 10, 1931 --

Action of parole board Filed - June 18, 1931, JULY 3, 1931, DENIED, Page 21.

Trusty Appointment and Grades	Criminal History
Appd.Trusty 4/11/31 Outer East Gate Trustyship revoked 7/14/1931.	12/3/30 As Frank Nitto #C-26115, arr. Chicago, Ill. Vag. held under $10,000 bond. (RCZ 1-22-31)

(OVER)

DATE	VIOLATIONS	days lost
	A TRUE COPY, September 15, 1931. N R Timmons N. R. TIMMONS Parole Officer.	

Following pages Frank Nitti's arrest and prison reports

JOHN EDGAR HOOVER 38021-P

Federal Bureau of Investigation
United States Department of Justice
Washington, D. C.

Form T-2

April 10, 1943 753 hg

The following is the record of FBI number 328934

J. E. Hoover
Director.

CONTRIBUTOR OF FINGERPRINTS	NAME AND NUMBER	ARRESTED OR RECEIVED	CHARGE	DISPOSITION
	As Frank Nitto, #C-25924, Chicago, Ill., 10/30/30, chg., G.P. - theft; for Gov't.			
USM, Chicago, Ill.	Frank Nitto #	10/31/30	Int. Rev. Act	1/10/31, sent. 18 mos. Leavenworth Pen. and $10,000. fine.
PD, Chicago, Ill.	Frank Nitti #C-26115	arr. date not given (prt. rec. 12/3/30)	vag.	C.C., $10,000.
USP, Leavenworth, Kans.	Frank R. Nitto #38021	1/11/31	viol. Rev. Act	18 mos. - 3/24/32 rel. exp. short term.
SO, Racine, Wis.	Frank Raddo #2596	8/13/39	attempting to bribe officer - traffic viol.	posted $210. bond
PD, Chicago, Ill.	Frank Nitto #	found dead 3-19-43		

* Represents notations unsupported by fingerprints in FBI files.

NOTICE: THIS RECORD IS FURNISHED FOR OFFICIAL USE ONLY

Frank Nitti's FBI Arrest Sheet

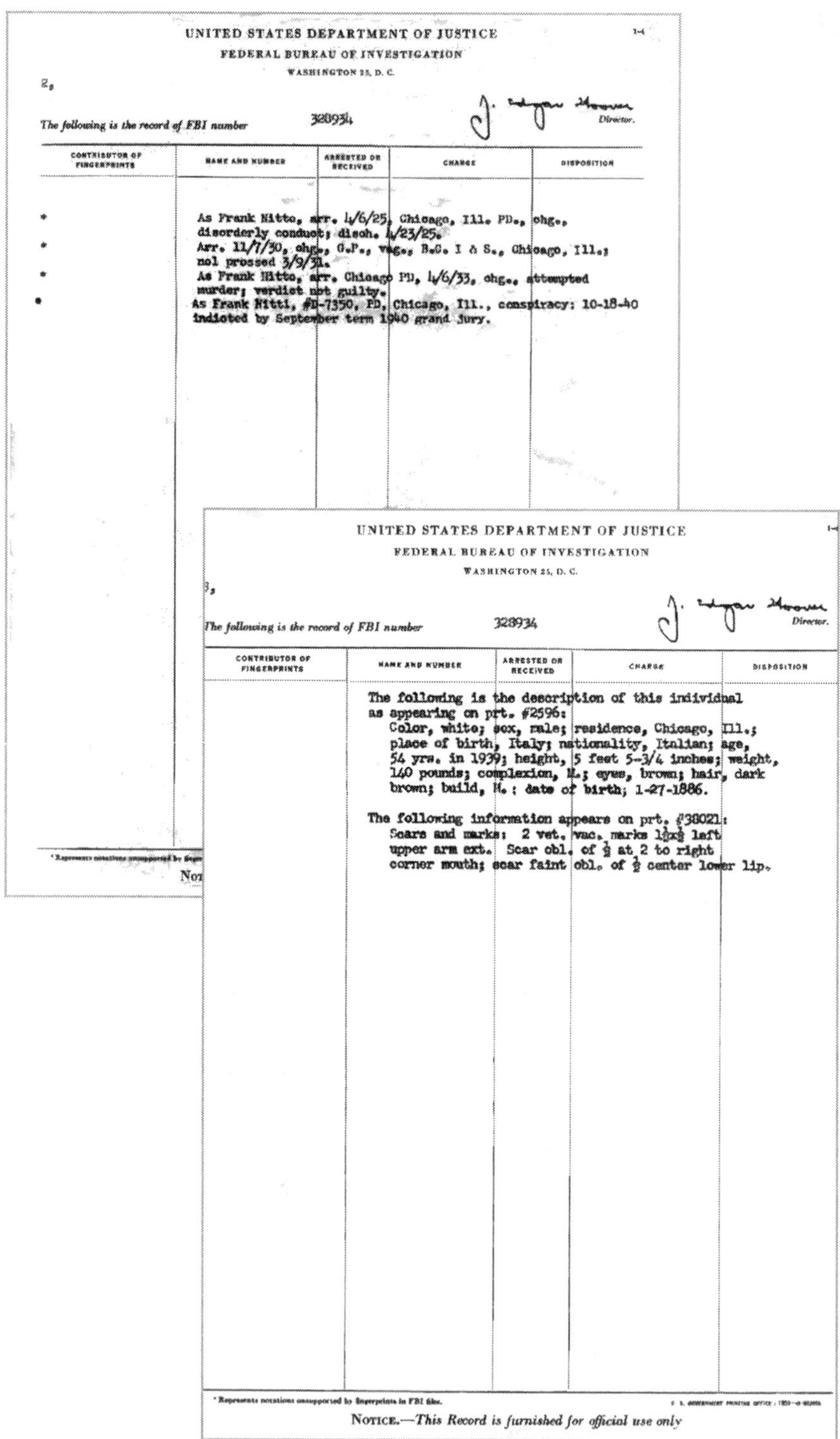

UNITED STATES DEPARTMENT OF JUSTICE
FEDERAL BUREAU OF INVESTIGATION
WASHINGTON 25, D. C.

2,

The following is the record of FBI number 328934

J. Edgar Hoover, Director.

CONTRIBUTOR OF FINGERPRINTS	NAME AND NUMBER	ARRESTED OR RECEIVED	CHARGE	DISPOSITION
*	As Frank Nitto, arr. 4/6/25, Chicago, Ill. PD., chg., disorderly conduct; disch. 4/23/25.			
*	Arr. 11/7/30, chg., G.P., vag., B.C. I & S., Chicago, Ill.; nol prossed 3/9/31.			
*	As Frank Nitto, arr. Chicago PD, 4/6/33, chg., attempted murder; verdict not guilty.			
*	As Frank Nitti, #D-7350, PD, Chicago, Ill., conspiracy: 10-18-40 indicted by September term 1940 grand jury.			

UNITED STATES DEPARTMENT OF JUSTICE
FEDERAL BUREAU OF INVESTIGATION
WASHINGTON 25, D. C.

3,

The following is the record of FBI number 328934

J. Edgar Hoover, Director.

CONTRIBUTOR OF FINGERPRINTS	NAME AND NUMBER	ARRESTED OR RECEIVED	CHARGE	DISPOSITION

The following is the description of this individual as appearing on prt. #2596:
Color, white; sex, male; residence, Chicago, Ill.; place of birth, Italy; nationality, Italian; age, 54 yrs. in 1939; height, 5 feet 5-3/4 inches; weight, 140 pounds; complexion, M.; eyes, brown; hair, dark brown; build, M.; date of birth; 1-27-1886.

The following information appears on prt. #38021:
Scars and marks: 2 vct. vac. marks 1½x½ left upper arm ext. Scar obl. of ½ at 2 to right corner mouth; scar faint obl. of ½ center lower lip.

* Represents notations unsupported by fingerprints in FBI files.

NOTICE.—*This Record is furnished for official use only*

In October 1930 Frank Nitti was sleeping in his bed at his richly furnished apartment at 3201 S. Clinton in Berwyn, Illinois when twenty police officers arrested him and his wife for tax evasion in the amount of $278,000 for the years 1925-1927.

Frank Nitti was married to Anna Ronga then, the daughter of Dr. Gaetano Ronga. One FBI report said that Frank Nitti had caught his wife cheating on him in Florida which caused a divorce. Later it was said by an informant that Anna went on to marry one of the members of the Chesrow family, a politically powerful family in Chicago. A Frank Chesrow became the president of the Chicago Sanitary District and had strong political clout in the city of Chicago. However, this could not be true since Anna Nitti died in 1940 with Frank Nitti at her side listing him as a widower. Frank Nitti did go on to marry his third wife, another Italian girl named Annette Caravetta, who was the secretary of mob associate Edward O'Hare shortly before his death.

On December 30, 1930, Frank Nitti was sentenced to eighteen months in prison for falling to file an income tax return. His sentence began January 11, 1931 at the U.S. penitentiary at Leavenworth, Kansas. During his prison time his wife Anna tried desperately to have the parole board grant Nitti early parole promising them that she and her husband would move "south" away from Chicago and not associate with any Capone Gang connections. Frank Nitti himself also promised the parole board he would leave Chicago and lead a useful, upright life. He was discharged on March 24, 1932 after serving only fifteen months.

There were reports published in the newspapers that when Nitti was released from prison open warfare was going to erupt on the streets of Chicago because Nitti wanted to take over Al Capone's spot as top boss. Reports said that the person leading the revolt against Nitti was Murray Humphreys.

Perhaps the truth came from a known hoodlum who was around during this time and told the FBI that when Al Capone went away to prison there was great turmoil and lack of control. Al, his brother Ralph, and Frank Nitti were all going away to prison around the same period of time and it became a challenge to hold the Capone Gang together. This informant said that Charles Fischetti and Jake "Greasy Thumb" Guzik were able to bring the organization back into a profitable business by supervising all their enterprises. When Frank Nitti returned he moved into the spot as boss after Capone.

Authors Collection ©

Author's collection ©

Frank Nitti's grave at Mount Carmel Cemetery in Hillside, Illinois

Authors collection ©

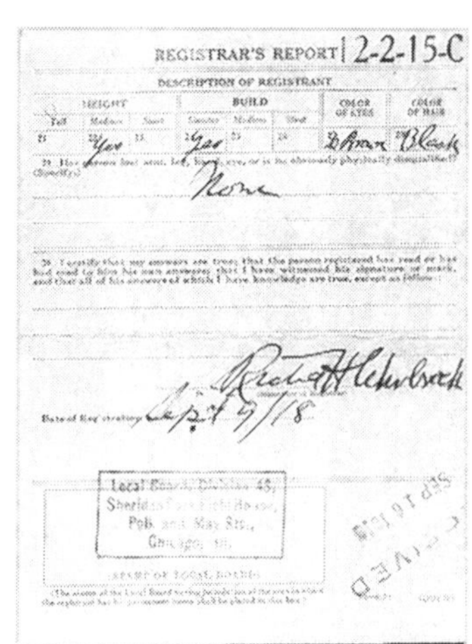

REGISTRAR'S REPORT 2-2-15-C

DESCRIPTION OF REGISTRANT

HEIGHT			BUILD			COLOR OF EYES	COLOR OF HAIR
Tall	Medium	Short	Slender	Medium	Stout		
	Yes		Yes			Brown	Black

None

Date of Registration Sept 9/18

Local Board, Division 45, Sheridan, Polk and May Sts., Chicago, Ill.

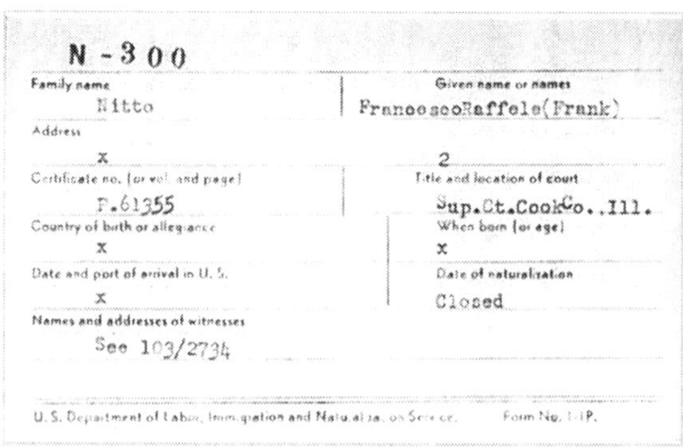

N -300

Family name	Given name or names
Nitto	FrancescoRaffele(Frank)

Address	
x	2
Certificate no. (or vol. and page)	Title and location of court
P.61355	Sup.Ct.CookCo.,Ill.
Country of birth or allegiance	When born (or age)
x	x
Date and port of arrival in U.S.	Date of naturalization
x	Closed

Names and addresses of witnesses

See 103/2734

U.S. Department of Labor, Immigration and Naturalization Service. Form No. 1-IP.

REGISTRATION CARD

SERIAL NUMBER 4599 | ORDER NUMBER A4404

1 Frank Ralph Nitto (First name) (Middle name) (Last name)

2 PERMANENT HOME ADDRESS: 914 S. Halsted St Chicago Ill (No.) (Street or R. F. D. No.) (City or town) (County) (State)

Age in Years 3: 32 | Date of Birth 4: Jan 27 1886 (Month) (Day) (Year)

RACE

White	Negro	Oriental	Indian: Citizen	Indian: Noncitizen
5 Yes	6	7	8	9

U. S. CITIZEN: Native Born	U. S. CITIZEN: Naturalized	U. S. CITIZEN: Citizen by Father's Naturalization Before Registrant's Majority	ALIEN: Declarant	ALIEN: Non-declarant
10	11	12	13	14 Yes

15 If not a citizen of the U. S., of what nation are you a citizen or subject? Italy

PRESENT OCCUPATION 16: Broker in Grocery | EMPLOYER'S NAME 17: Self

18 PLACE OF EMPLOYMENT OR BUSINESS: Traveling Chicago to New York (No.) (Street or R. F. D. No.) (City or town) (County) (State)

NEAREST RELATIVE: Name 19: Rose Nitto; Address 20: 914 S Halsted St Chicago Ill (No.) (Street or R. F. D. No.) (City or town) (County) (State)

I AFFIRM THAT I HAVE VERIFIED ABOVE ANSWERS AND THAT THEY ARE TRUE.

Frank Ralph Nitto (Registrant's signature or mark)

P. M. G. O. Form No. 1 (Red) (OVER)

B-43 914 So Halsted St Chicago Ill.

REGISTRATION CARD—(Men born on or after April 28, 1877 and on or before February 16, 1897)

SERIAL NUMBER U 2138 | 1. NAME (Print) FRANK NITTO (First) (Middle) (Last) | ORDER NUMBER

2 PLACE OF RESIDENCE (Print) ~~1208 Lexington St~~ Chicago Ill. (Number and street) (Town, township, village, or city) (County) (State)

[THE PLACE OF RESIDENCE GIVEN ON THE LINE ABOVE WILL DETERMINE LOCAL BOARD JURISDICTION; LINE 2 OF REGISTRATION CERTIFICATE WILL BE IDENTICAL]

3. MAILING ADDRESS: Same [Mailing address if other than place indicated on line 2. If same insert word same]

4. TELEPHONE: Mon. 0220 (Exchange) (Number) | 5. AGE IN YEARS — DATE OF BIRTH: Jan. 27, 1886 (Mo.) (Day) (Yr.) | 6. PLACE OF BIRTH: Salerno (Town or county) Italy (State or country)

7. NAME AND ADDRESS OF PERSON WHO WILL ALWAYS KNOW YOUR ADDRESS: Lucy Ronga - 1208 Lexington

8. EMPLOYER'S NAME AND ADDRESS: None

9. PLACE OF ~~EMPLOYMENT~~ OR BUSINESS: 1208 Lexington - own boss (Number and street or R. F. D. number) (Town) (County) (State)

I AFFIRM THAT I HAVE VERIFIED ABOVE ANSWERS AND THAT THEY ARE TRUE.

D. S. S. Form 1 (Revised 4-1-42) (over) 16—21630-2 Frank Nitto (Registrant's signature)

(Previous Page Frank Nitti's Naturalization Card) (Top Frank Nitti Registration Card) (Bottom Frank Nitti's World War I Registration Cards)

Chapter 3

Paul's Rise Under Nitti

Around 1935 Paul DeLucia listed himself as vice president of the World Amusement Corporation which operated the World Play House, a theater and movie house at 410 South Michigan Avenue right in the heart of Chicago. This play house showed foreign made pictures not ordinarily run in other theaters. He claimed to be the vice president since 1930.

DeLucia listing in the Chicago Police Department was moving up the list. Chicago Police noticed that Paul DeLucia was accompanying mobsters Charles Fischetti and Frank Nitti to the Riverside home of Harry Hochstein who then was listed as a Syndicate leader. These meetings were said to be very sensitive and were for the top boss ears only.

In the middle 1930s Paul DeLucia was now acting as Frank Nitti's right hand man and continued to be the emissary between Chicago and New York bosses. Paul DeLucia was also taking over duties such as handling other Chicago big shots like Mike "Dago Mike" Carrozzo who had control of all the street cleaners unions and the paving unions. Actually Carrozzo's right hand man, Frank "Frankie X" Esposito, met with Nitti's right hand man Paul DeLucia when certain business had to be worked out. The close friendship between Esposito and DeLucia would last another 35 years until their deaths.

In 1939 word on the streets that Paul DeLucia was becoming one of the under bosses in the Outfit came as a surprise to many of Chicago's hoodlums. One report stated, *"DeLucia fronted for various gambling enterprises for the syndicate in Chicago. Under the regime of the Kelly-Nash political machine in Chicago, DeLucia received recognition as the head of the syndicate formerly headed by Al Capone. He is said to be a member of the Grand Council of the International Mafia Society."*

He was beginning to be called or subpoenaed to appear before federal grand juries. One case he was subpoenaed in was investigating income taxes for a collector in the Chicago gambling syndicate named Billy Skidmore. His name was appearing more and more in police files as a top boss in the Capone Gang. One report in 1939 actually named Paul DeLucia as moving ahead of Frank Nitti as the top boss. Nitti had been spending much of his time away from Chicago, leaving Paul DeLucia to handle the day-to-day operations in Chicago. Nitti, as his mentor Al Capone had done, had trust in his appointed underboss which may have made it seem like DeLucia was now the boss. Nitti was focusing on the overall position as to where the Outfit had to go, while DeLucia handled Chicago's rackets that were already in play. In some views it was true and in others it was not. What was known was that both Frank Nitti and Paul DeLucia were among the top powerful people running Chicago.

By 1940 the Chicago syndicate was described as being made up of a hierarchy that apportioned districts of the city to its lower members. These district leaders known as "Capo's" controlled all the gamblers in their area, taking drastic measures if they proved to be untrustworthy. The hierarchy then received a certain percentage of the profits for all gambling in their districts. They were then required to pay an assessment to the top bosses.

In June 1940 Paul DeLucia was named in an injunction restraining Capone gangsters from looting the treasury of the Bartenders and Beverage Dispensers Union, Chicago Local 278. DeLucia, Frank Nitti and Louis Romano made a bid to forcefully take over the Chicago Bartenders Union Local 278 back in 1935 but failed.

Frank "The Enforcer" Nitti, Murray Humphreys, Louis Campagna, Louis Greenberg, and Frank Evens were the other Capone members named with DeLucia in the injunction. It began in 1939 when Paul DeLucia was instrumental in placing Louis Romano as head of the Bartenders Union in Chicago. Romano was organizing the union so he could become its czar to control the union's treasury collecting $125,000 in yearly dues from its members.

During the investigation Paul DeLucia was named as Frank Nitti's secretary of war for the Capone Gang. It was DeLucia's responsibility to make sure people who got in the way were killed.

List of union officers Local 278

Louis Romano President
James Crowley, Secretary Treasurer
Tom Panton, Business Reprehensive

In October 1940 the indictment was issued for the arrest of DeLucia, Campagna, Humphreys, Nitti, Evens, Romano and Thomas Panton, then assistant business agent of the union, for attempting to pirate the union treasury. Nitti, Panton, Humphreys and Romano all surrendered but DeLucia, Campagna and Evans refused and remained at-large.

George B. McLane, one time president and business agent of local 278 told the story of how the Capone Gang took over his union. He said it all began in 1935 when Capone gangster Danny Stanton called McLane and wanted $500 so he could make a trip to the Kentucky Derby in Kentucky. McLane said it was impossible but Stanton ignored him and sent two hoodlums to collect. When these hoodlums arrived and McLane refused to hand over the money, they telephoned Stanton and gave the phone to McLane. Stanton told McLane, *"You son of a bitch, we'll get the money and take the union over."*

Three weeks later McLane had a meeting with Frank Nitti and Nitti told McLane that the only way to overcome the problem was to put one of Nitti's boys in the union as an officer and he wouldn't have any more problems like the Stanton situation. When McLane told Nitti that it would be impossible because he needed the executive board and ratification by the membership, Nitti replied by saying that he had taken over other unions before and all McLane had to do was give him the name of those who opposed Nitti and he would have them taken care of. Nitti finished with, *"We want no more playing around. If you don't do as we say, you'll get a shot in the head. How would your wife look in black?"*

Weeks later McLane was summoned to the Capri Restaurant at 123 North Clark Street for another face to face. There Frank Nitti, Murray Humphreys, Fred Evens and Louis Campagna were sitting and wanted answers from McLane about why he had not placed one of their men in the union yet. The week prior, Nitti's men had sent sluggers to the picket lines and intimidated the union officials. Labor trouble had doubled and the locals members were being harassed left and right. Nitti informed McLane that if he would just place the Capone Gang's man in the union all his troubles would stop and Nitti promised that he would give McLane a man with no police record to place in the union. He said all the syndicate places would join the union and there would be no reason for any pick lines, everyone wins. McLane informed Nitti about the last union meeting he attended and when he informed the other union officers that a Capone man was going to be placed in the union they all refused to allow it. Both Nitti and Humphreys demanded that McLane provide the names of those who opposed, but McLane refused. Humphreys assured McLane that, *"we'll take care of that"* referring to the members who had a problem with the Capone Gang. Nitti said in one last attempt, *"This is your last chance. This is the only way we'll stand for anything. Put in our man or wind up in an alley."*

So McLane went back to his fellow union officers and told them how he would be killed if they did not accept. Reluctantly, with their backs against the wall, they agreed. A month later McLane was summoned to the Capri Restaurant where Nitti, Paul DeLucia, Louis Campagna and Murry Humphreys were seated. Nitti introduced Louis Romano to McLane and informed him that this was the man that would be placed in the union as an officer and that Romano had no police record. Once Romano was in the union all labor trouble stopped.

Then Nitti informed McLane that he had to have the bartenders in the union push syndicate beer. He told Nitti that he was afraid the organization would get in trouble with the Fair Trade Practice act which Nitti replied, "*See that your men do this, and let us worry about fair trade. The bartenders don't push it they'll get their legs broken."*

Then in June 1938 McLane went to meet with Nitti, George Browne, Nick Circella and William Bioff where they discussed McLane's candidacy for general president at the international convention coming up. The goal was to have the presidency for at least two years because in those two years they would make enough money and would give the union back to McLane to do with it as he pleased. McLane informed Nitti that it would be a fight to get control of the international. Nitti informed McLane that they, the syndicate, had made other international presidents and why couldn't they make him one. Nitti said they "made" Browne, George Scalise and Mike "Dago Mike" Carrozzo presidents with no problems. McLane refused and went out of his way telling other labor union officials not to elect him and to keep them selves neutral.

Nitti got what he wanted; Murray Humphreys, Louis Romano and Fred Evens walked into the union office with guns and informed McLane they were taking over the union completely.

In the end the indictments against the Capone mobsters were dismissed when George McLane became in fear of his life. Word had reached McLane that he would not live long if he testified and on grounds he may have incriminated himself. As a result, the union was thrown into receivership and taken over by Roy D. Keehn. Soon after a free election was held.

In 1940 Chicago Police observed Paul DeLucia in the constant company of Charles Spizzeri, who was in control of a gambling operation, Rocco DeGrazio, Robert McCullough, then a muscle and trigger man of the Capone Gang, Francis "Slim" Curry and Ralph Pierce. When police discovered that Paul DeLucia was still associating with mobsters Lepke Buchalter and New York mob boss Charles "Lucky" Luciano in various labor extortion rackets on a nation-wide scale, authorities placed together a list of Paul DeLucia's 1940 associates. The list was:

New York Associates

Vincent Mangano
Phillip Mangano (Brooklyn N.Y.)
Charles Luciano (New York City)
Meyer Lansky (New York City)
Joseph Bonanno (Brooklyn N.Y.)
Joseph Profaci (Brooklyn N.Y.)
Joe Traina (Brooklyn N.Y.)
Stefano Magaddino (Niagara Falls N.Y.)

Cleveland Ohio

Al Polissi
Frank Milano

Los Angles California

Johnny Roselli

Chicago

Sylvester Agoglia
Harry Brown
Louis Campagna
William Cosironi
Michael Costello
Philip D'Andrea
Frank Diamond
Michael J. Fish
Rocco Fischetti
Joe Fischetti
Charles Fischetti
Charles Gioe
Frank Meo
Frank Nitti
Ralph Pierce
Frank Rio
Ralph Vicedomini

Chapter 4

Paul's Kingdom's

Once Paul DeLucia was in the position of Capo in the Capone Gang, the money came pouring in like a water faucet. In the early 1930s Paul DeLucia bought a farm in Michigan for around $23,000. He had also owned a home in Michigan City, Indiana.

He purchased his first home in River Forest, Illinois around the middle 1930s for $25,000. He quickly made improvements, adding another $30,000 to the house to make it a mansion. When investigators went looking at the mortgage on the house, they found it in the name of a Mr. Matrlrone, who was a spaghetti manufacturer in Chicago.

In 1941 DeLucia purchased a 1,104 acre farm in Kendall County near Joliet, Illinois for $145,000 with a down payment of $35,000. The farm, known as the Hog Farm to locals, grew wheat, corn and soy beans on almost 900 acres of the farm. The remaining 200 acres maintained a herd of 105 steers, 200 pigs and 30 cows. In the late 1940s, the farm was bringing in a $50,000-a-year profit. He sold the farm in 1951 to a New York attorney for $600,000. One of the realtors who dealt with the sale of the farm said he heard rumors through the years about DeLucia and his farm. He said strangers from the Chicago area would often appear and disappear, never mixing with any of the locals or other farms in the area. One rumor he recalled was that DeLucia was only operating the farm as a front for the purpose of evading military service when America entered World War II. He also heard rumors that DeLucia was using the farm as a base for black market butchering operations during the early 1940s because of the war. None of the allegations were ever confirmed.

In 1942 Paul DeLucia himself said he was unemployed and listed his occupation as a speculator. He told the Selective Service office that he made $68,000-a-year income. He was living in a mansion at 812 N. Lathrop Street with his wife Nancy and their three children since 1938. The mansion had five bedrooms, a huge basement and large attic (to hide his money in), four fireplaces, a library, sun room and a three car garage.

DeLucia told the Selective Service Board of Cook County in 1942 that he was disabled and could not work because of diabetes.

He also had a lawsuit pending in court against the tenant and owner of a downtown building for personal injuries suffered when an elevator fell, in the building fracturing DeLucia's left hip and right foot. This injury would cause DeLucia to walk with a slight limp the rest of his life. DeLucia had been in the building at the time to purchase an oil painting with Robert Carnahan and the Fischetti brothers, Charles and Joseph.

In March 1943 Frank Nitti, Louis Campagna and Paul DeLucia were credited with completely cleaning out the treasury of the Retail Clerk's International Protective Association, Local 1248 with the help of Max Pollack, also known as Max Caldwell, an ex-convict and ex-bootlegger. The group reportedly robbed $910,000 from its treasury.

Paul DeLucia's house at 812 N. Lathrop Street in River Forest as it stood in 2014

Mob Boss

Authors Collection 2016 ©

Paul DeLucia

From the Collection of T.M.

Chapter 5

Hollywood Millions

In May 1941 Chicago and Los Angeles gangster union business agent William Bioff was indicted along with his crony George E. Browne, then the president of the International Alliance of Theatrical Stage Employees and Moving Picture Machine Operators of the United States. Both were charged with extorting $550,000 from four Hollywood motion picture studios in California. The case was filed in the New York City court system. Browne and Bioff used their corrupt power to call strikes using their 35,000 union followers for their own gain.

Government agents were aware of this racket dating back to 1935. The FBI started receiving letters and reports about the movie operators unions in large cities being under the control of gangsters and stealing all the unions' money. Letters sent from Chicago in the early days of this investigation were mailed to the head of the FBI, J. Edgar Hoover, wondering why the FBI was not doing anything to stop these men. Portions of these letters are listed on the next page.

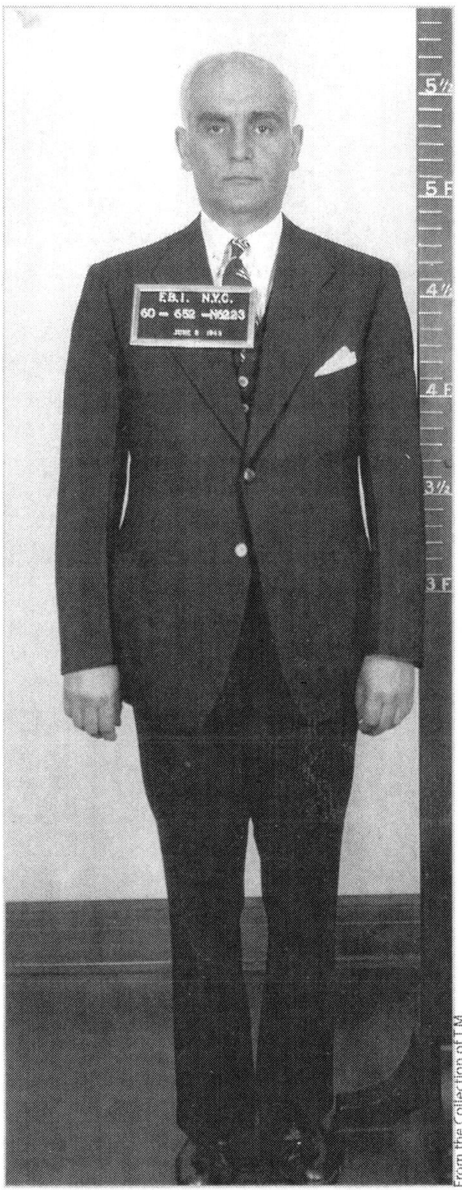

From the Collection of T.M.

Paul DeLucia's arrest photo in 1943

Chicago, Ill., Nov. 23rd, 1936.

Attention of Attorney General Cummings,
Also Edgar Hoover.

Gentlemen:

I feel it is my duty as a citizen of these great United States to inform you of the invisible government that exists in Chicago today.

When Federal government placed Al Capone in Alcatraz they figured that this gang was materially weakened and that a ship without a rudder would eventually die out. Well Gentlemen, you are very much mistaken, as the newspapers state the remnants of the Capone gang, is a lot of hooey and the remnants is a 1000% stronger now than it ever was. They have as their capable leader none other than the ex convict, Frank Nitti, and when they say the enforcer, they don't mean maybe. As his able assistants he has, Louie Campagna, known as little New York, also a Paul Russo. This constitutes the governing body of this powerful gang. Then the killers come in the following rotation, Jack Mcgurn, Ralph Pierce, Sam Hunt, Tony Accodo alias Joe Batters Willie Heeney, Ralph Capone, Mike Kelly, Nick Kelly George King and so many others that it would take me all nite to write their names but these are the well known ones. They also have front men or office men which are able to contact politicians and businessmen such as Eddie O'Hare, John Patton, Joe Fusco, Ed Vogel Harry Hochstein, Harry Hyms and a few others. This gang is the invisible government of Chicago and they are gradually taking over all unions and gambling of all descriptions. They killed Tom Maloy of the Moving picture operators union and thru their George Brown are deriving the proceeds of that union today. They also killed Louis Alterie and took over his union the janitors theatrical union. They didn't have to kill the officials of the waiters and bartenders union, after what happened to Maloy and Alterie, the officials of these two unions figured it would be better to live and gave them up without a fight. They are gradually taking over every union in Chicago and you can rest assurred that any union existing in Chicago is paying tribute to this gang of cutthroats today. Their gambling regresentatives, the Fischetti brothers, Charles and Rocco, have levied a monthly charge against all books in the town, pay or get bombed and get putout of business. They are in every kind of business imaginable and anyone who tries to give them competition is leaving himself to getting killed. You haven't got a chance to fight them, as they have a network of gangsters and killers that [illegible] from New [illegible] San Francesco. What chance has an individual? When the whole Chicago police force openly admit that if you kill one you will have to kill five thousand and even the police department is deadly afraid of this gang. They have the Unione Siciliano, they have placed at the head of this organization that covers every large city in this country, none other than Phil D'Andrea, of Capone Court day fame, who was convicted of carrying a revolver in the federal Building. This gang is directly connected up with the Luck, Luciano Gang in New York, and they take orders from none other than the enforcer, Frank Nitti, They control all the gambling in Cicero, Chicago Heights, Gary, Hammond, and all small towns bordering Chicago, they also control the following brewries, The Manhattan, the Great Lakes, the Hammond and the Thornton Brewries. They also control the Sportsman Racetrack. They are in partnership with Mike Carrozzo, head of thestreet cleaners union and also with D'Andrea in the Hod Carriers union. They meet every monday afternoon directly across the street of the Chicago City Hall on Clark street in Mike Carrozzo's restaurant The New Capri. They also meet in The Club Royal, 428 So. Wabash Ave., and Valentine Barbershop, at Michigan & 22nd st., just west of Mich

On November 6, 1941 Bioff and Browne were found guilty on three counts of violating the Federal Anti-Racketeering Statute. They were fined $20,000 each and sentenced to 8 to 10 years in prison. That's when it was learned that Bioff and Browne had "others" involved in this extortion plot and the "others" were from the Chicago Syndicate.

On March 18, 1943, the U.S. Grand Jury in Southern New York filed two indictments charging violations of the Anti-Racketeering Act and of the Mail Fraud Statute. The first indictment named nine defendants; Frank Nitto (Nitti), Louis Campagna, Paul DeLucia (Ricca), Phil D'Andrea, Charles Gioe, John Roselli, Ralph Pierce, Francis Maritote (Frank Diamond) and Louis Kaufman together with defendants George E. Browne, William Bioff, Nick Circella and Isadore Zevin. The nine defendants were charged with conspiring to defraud the members of the International Alliance of Theatrical Stage Employees and Moving Picture Machine Operators of the United States, a labor union with which only Browne, Bioff, Circella and Zevin were officially connected.

The second indictment charged mail fraud relating to a union two percent assessment fund named all the foregoing individuals as defendants except Kaufman. The two percent assessment was against the workers weekly wages and the purposes represented to be bona fide union activities, whereas it was the plan and intention of the defendants and confederates throughout to appropriate the funds so assessed to their own use and benefit. The defendants and their agents extorted over $1 million dollars from Hollywood movie producers and exhibitors engaged in the motion picture business and looted the union in that industry of its funds.

Since the indictments could not be tried together, the government elected to try the anti-racketeering indictment first. On March 24, 1943 Paul DeLucia and Louis Campagna turned themselves in to U.S. Marshals. DeLucia dressed in a blue suit with a red tie, oxford grey topcoat and brown hat, and Campagna in a pencil-striped blue suit with a dark top coat and red and blue tie, each made bond. The trial never went the Capone gangster's way and the case was successfully prosecuted with a conviction obtained on December 21, 1943.

Chicago mobsters involved in this case:

Paul DeLucia
Louis Campagna
Phil D'Andrea
Charles Gioe
Frank Maritote (AKA Frank Diamond)
Ralph Pierce
Frank Nitti
Johnny Roselli
Louis Kaufman (Newark, New Jersey mobster was involved)
Nick Circella
Isadore Zevin

Mobsters who were not charged but were said to have slight participation in this crime were:

Tony Accardo
Charles Fischetti
Lawrence "Charles" Imburgio
Robert McCullough
Louis Romano
Ralph Capone
Louis "Lepke" Buchalter

The International Alliance of Theatrical Stage Employees and Moving Picture Machine Operators of the United States and Canada, (IATSE for short) had a membership of approximately 42,000 members in the 1930s. The union was also affiliated with the American Federation of Labor.

Frank Nitto (Nitti) could not handle going to prison again and it was possible he was dying of cancer. On the day the indictments were returned he committed suicide by shooting himself in the head along railroad tracks. Louis Kaufman was found guilty and sentenced to seven years in prison and fined $10,000. The indictment against Ralph Pierce was dismissed by the court at the end of the government's case. Lawrence Charles Imburgio was suffering from Buerger's Disease and was hospitalized in 1943 when the FBI wanted to question him about the extortion. He managed to not get indicted. He was the brother of mob lawyer Joseph I. Bulger. Al Capone's brother Ralph "Bottles" Capone was said to be involved in the Hollywood extortion after the arrests were made. Reports were that Nick Circella, William Bioff and George Browne had flown to Miami, Florida to have a meeting with Ralph and Al Capone concerning the shake down. One report listed the incident as the three men were "getting orders" from the Capone's. One report said that Ralph Capone took over the Chicago management and collection for Nick Circella after Circella was arrested. Ralph was called to testify in the case but nothing ever came from it. No charges were filed against him.

The indictment against the Capone gangsters came from William Bioff and George Browne who turned government witnesses against the Capone Gang, testifying that the Chicago mobsters were the ones that made Bioff and Browne extort the movie industry.

After a lengthy trial in the U.S. District Court of the Southern District of New York, Paul DeLucia was sentenced on December 31, 1943, to 10 years imprisonment and fined $10,000 for conspiracy to interfere with trade and commerce by coercion, threats and violence. That same day DeLucia appealed the verdict but elected to enter upon service of his sentence on March 8, 1944. He was taken to Atlanta Federal Prison in Georgia. He was eligible for parole on July 7, 1947, and would have been eligible for conditional release on November 23, 1950.

If there is one way to sum up William Bioff it would be calling him a "compulsive liar." Bioff had lied under oath many, many, times. He lied on insurance polices, a marriage license, to government authorities, other gangsters, and the only one person to know the truth about William Bioff was William Bioff. However, some truthful information on William Bioff came from the time he was a very young boy.

William Bioff's father, Louis Lazar Bioffsky, was born in Russia as a Jew, came to America in 1907, and made a living as a glass beveller. He legally changed his name from Bioffsky to Bioff before being naturalized as an American citizen in 1916. He died of throat cancer in 1925. His mother Freda Pollack was born in Russia and died while giving birth to twins who both died with their mother. Louis re-married a woman named Millard Nelson a year after the death of Freda and the family lived in a house at Kostner and Archer Avenue in Chicago.

William Bioff and his mother Freda came to America around 1908 and settled in Chicago with his father. He attended a Chicago Hebrew school and later transferred to the Gladstone School but dropped out after the third grade and spent most of his time playing hooky running around the streets of Chicago trying to score a fast buck.

At the age of 14 and after the death of his mother Freda, William and his older siblings did not get along with the new stepmother Millard so William went out and found a job delivering ice in hopes of getting away from her. When that job ended he found a job in a printing company working in the ink-making department. With money coming in, William moved into a cheap hotel until he turned 18 and became interested in the labor movement.

His life in crime started as a teenager with one of his first arrests in January 1919. He was arrested with local gang members Paul Battaglia, Leo Cheritenson, Nick Ciculla, Joe Dass, Ernest Fontana, Frank Miller and Felix Salzo. This group attempted to break into a commission house on Eagle Street between Halsted and Union Streets. Another arrest came on May 4, 1921 when William was charged with burglary.

In February 1922 Bioff was sentenced to six months in prison doing hard labor stemming from his arrest on a pandering charge on January 14, 1922. Bioff claimed he "took the rap" for his employer (gangster Jack Zuta) who was operating a house of prostitution in the same building at 210 South Halsted in Chicago while Bioff worked as a bartender. However, police painted a different story saying Bioff was the collector who collected the house's share of the money from the prostitutes. The women involved, named Bobbie, Dottie, Pearl and Sarah were all dismissed but the charge of accepting $29 from a Bernice "Rosie" Thomas, one of the popular prostitutes, was the charge the authorities were pursuing. He was released on a $500 bond while he waited for his case to be appealed and never did serve his prison sentence.

In 1924 William Bioff was arrested with Torrio gangsters Frank Rio and Frank Pope. Both Rio and Pope were high ranking members in the Torrio Gang. It was through these associations that William Bioff got his chance in the labor field. Bioff was placed in a union as an organizer with the Truck Driver's Teamster's Union located at the offices at Ashland Blvd. and Jackson Blvd. and the Packing House Teamster Union in Chicago. He was also associated with the Kosher Jewish Butchers Association in Chicago.

Mob Boss

On October 19, 1931 Bioff was arrested with Capone gangster Frank Laino, aka James Mundo. Once again Bioff had failed to appear in court for this arrest and his bonds were forfeited. However, no other action was mentioned. The day after he was released on this bond, October 20, he was arrested again, only this time he used the name Henry Martin. Bioff was in the company of gangsters Paul Mango and James Adduci. Reports said that Adduci disposed of two guns before he was arrested. This was before James Adduci became a political power figure in the West Side Bloc legislative group in Chicago's government. All three were released without being charged.

In November 1932 William Bioff and James Adduci were wanted in connection with the kidnapping of John Touhy, the 13 year old son of John J. Touhy, then a member of the Chicago Sanitary District. Bioff was labeled then as a Chicago 27th Ward hoodlum.

Despite his continued arrests in 1932 he was hired by George Browne and placed in the Stage Employees Labor Union, Local 2. In 1934 he was made the International Representative of the Alliance of Theatrical and Stage Employees and Movie Operators Union in the United States and Canada with there offices in New York City. With this new position he placed his two brothers, Allen and Hyman, in jobs in Chicago as movie projectionists.

In 1933 William Bioff, Phillip Mangano and James Adduci were running a taxi dance hall racket together in Chicago. After some time they lost the racket to rivals. All three were arrested together and taken to a Chicago police station in February 1933 where they were photographed and released. The three had been charged with trying to muscle their way into the Poultry Handlers Union in Chicago. Five days later Bioff was charged with burglary from this arrest.

In June 1934 William Bioff acted as a body guard for George Browne at the I.A.T.S.E. convention in Louisville, Kentucky. Also acting as bodyguards that night with Bioff were mobsters Jack Zuta and Lawrence "Dago" Mangano.

In 1935, on two occasions, William Bioff was wanted for questioning in the gangland killings of Clyde Osterberg, who attempted to start a rival union against Bioff, and the killing of gangster "Two-Gun" Louie Alterie, who was the boss of the Theatrical Janitors Union. Each time William Bioff's name came up as one of the first suspects but detectives failed to link Bioff to the killings.

By 1937 Bioff was the "shake down" man for the Chicago mob. During a trial in 1951, Harry M. Warner, owner of Warner Brothers Studios, testified that in 1937 Bioff approached him and asked him for $20,000. When Warner asked Bioff why he had to pay that money, Bioff told him that the boys in Chicago were expecting their money or else. In fear of his life, Warner paid Bioff.

Paul DeLucia and Phil D'Andrea had gone to California to see Bioff concerning the cash flow of money that was not coming in as expected. DeLucia told Bioff that the money situation coming into the Capone Gang was low and they needed him to start shaking down producers again. Bioff did as he was told. He continued to perform this job until 1939. It came to a stop when in November 1939 Bioff was arrested in Los Angeles. He was returned to Chicago in February 1940 and placed in jail.

The reason for this was that Bioff was never cleared from his January 14, 1922 arrest and had been a fugitive for 17 years. Bioff had been arrested many times since the 1922 arrest but for some reason the Chicago police never "caught on" about Bioff being a fugitive or he was able to "pay off the right people" for 17 years to stay out of prison. The truth has not been discovered. This time Bioff could not get out of it and was sent to serve 7 months in Bridewell Prison in Chicago. While in prison not too much changed. He was voted by the Board of Directors of the Theatrical Union to keep his union job and was given a pay raise once out. Years later Bioff told authorities he was successful in his appeal and he believed all the charges had been dropped.

Classification Form 1a
Rev. January 1939

UNITED STATES PENITENTIARY
LEAVENWORTH, KANS.

ADMISSION SUMMARY

Committed Name B I O F F, William   Reg. No. 5 8 9 4 4-L   Classified Feb. 11, 1942

Inst.   SD-New York-New York City

True Name   Oct. 12, 1900   Judicial District See Notation below for Offense-****

Date of Birth   41   Offense See Below** Yes $20,000.00   5 Yrs*

Age   White   Sentence Nov. 18, 1941   Committed Fine   Probation

Race   Russia   Sentence begins   Jan. 9, 1942

Country of Birth   USA   Committed   July 17, 1948

Citizenship   Married   Eligible for Parole   Apr. 23, 1955

Marital Status   California   Conditional Release Date   Nov. 17, 1961

Legal Residence   Expires Full Term, SEE BELOW***

Detainers

REPORTS REC'D FROM: F. B. I. Received   U. S. ATTY. Not Received   PROSECUTING AGENCY Received

1. PREVIOUS CRIMINAL RECORD: Source

**Date   Place   Offense   Disposition

OFFENSE: Anti Racketeering Act: (Interference with trade & Commerce, by Violence).

\- - - - - - - - -

***

SENTENCE: Count #1-10 Yrs & $10,000.00 Fine "Comm.-Yes".
Count #2-10 Yrs - Concurrent with Count #1.
Count #3-10 Yrs - Consecutive to Count #1 & #2.
Execution of prison sentence on count #3 suspended as a condition of payment of fines of $20,000.00 & placed on probation for 5-Yrs, consecutive. FINES NOT PAID TO DATE RECEIVED.

\- - - - - - - - -

*PROBATION: TO BE PLACED ON PROBATION FOR A FIVE YEAR PERIOD AFTER COM-Pletion of Prisons sentence.

\- - - - - - - - -

DATE	PLACE	OFFENSE	DISPOSITION	SOURCE
3-7-21	Chicago, Ill. Burglary	& Receiving Stol. Prop.	Case Dismissed	F. B.I.U.
2-23-22	Chicago, Ill.	Pandering	$300.00 & Costs & 6 Mos H. of C.	F.B.I.U.
3-28-32	Chicago, Ill.	Gen. Pick-up	Released	F.B.I.
11-24-39	Los Angles, Cal.	Fug. from Ill. & Income Tax Evas.	Cases Dismissed, on Fug. Charge-Detainer Filed on 2nd charge	F.BI.
5-25-41	Los Angles, Cal.	Anti - Racketeering Act: Interference with trade & Commerce by Violance.	Present Case	F.B.I.

PPI Ad. Sn. 5-24-40 25M

Mob Boss

File Card

William Bioff
Last name changed legally on January 28, 1916 from Bioffsky to Bioff (He had his name legally changed to William Nelson once out of prison in the late 1940's)
AKA Fat, Morris, Henry Martin, William Berg, Link, Bill Bronson, Bill Berger, William Byoff, Morris Bioff, Berger, William Bronson, Morris W, Bioff, L. L. Berg, Morris Beoff, Will Wioff,
Born October 12, 1899 Odessa, Russia / Told the FBI he was born October 12, 1900, Illinois / Wrote October 12, 1893 on marriage certificate / Father naturalization papers listed him as being born on July 25, 1900 in Russia.
Died November 4, 1955 (Killed in Phoenix, Arizona)
I.Q. 87 (Dull Normal)
Chicago PD # C-37305
FBI# 553811
Height 5' 6-1/2"
Weight 195
Build Medium Heavy
Hair Dark Chestnut
Eyes Hazel

Family

First Wife Mary Christofferson (Died of heart trouble on April 15, 1924)
Second Wife Lauria A. Nelson (Married May 25, 1925) (Born in Illinois)
Father Louis Lazar Bioff (Died 1925)
Mother Freda Palikov Bioff (Died 1914)
Brother Hyman Bioff (Lived on Chicago's North Side) (1940's)
Brother Allen Bioff (Lived at 1011 Washington Blvd. Oak Park, Illinois) (1942)
Buby Bioff (Died in 1914 of diabetes)
Sister Sylvia Russo (Lived at 1122 Washington Blvd, Oak Park, Illinois) (1942)
Sister Sarah Bioff (Died in 1914 from heart trouble at the age of 18)

Known Arrest Record of William Bioff

Date	Charge	Agency	Result
1-25-1919	Burglary	Chicago PD	U/K
3-7-1921	Burglary	Chicago PD	Dismissed
3-7-1921	Receiving Stolen Prop.	Chicago PD	Dismissed
4-2-1921	Burglary under Morris	Chicago PD	Dismissed
5-4-1921	Burglary under Morris	Chicago PD	Dismissed
6-30-1921	Conspiracy under Berger	Chicago PD	Noelle Processed

Tony Dark

Date	Charge	Agency	Result
1-14-1922	Pandering	Chicago PD	$300 Fine
2-23-1922	Pandering	Chicago PD	6 Months Prison
10-23-1923	Conspiracy	Chicago PD	Dismissed
1-25-1924	Larceny	Chicago PD	Discharged
11-16-1924	U/K	Chicago PD	U/K
10-19-1931	Section 2655	Chicago PD	Bond
10-20-1931	General Purposes	Chicago PD	Released
3-23-1932	Investigation G.P.	Chicago PD	Released
11-11-1932	Touhy Kidnapping	Chicago PD	Released
2-3-1933	Disorderly Conduct	Chicago PD	Discharged
3-3-1933	With J. Adduci / Invest.	Chicago PD	Released
3-21-1933	Disorderly Conduct	Chicago PD	Discharged
10-31-1933	Vagabond Warrant	Chicago PD	Warrant
May1935	Osterberg Murder	Chicago PD	Released
7-19-1935	Questing Alterie Murder	Chicago PD	Released
11-24-1939	Fugitive / Pandering	LAPD	Dismissed
1-11-1940	Tax Evasion	US Marshall	U/K
2-20-1940	Pandering / Fugitive	Chicago PD	7 Months Jail
5-25-1941	Anti-Racketeering	L.A.P.D.	8 Years Prison
6-12-1941	Conspiracy	N.Y. Marshall	U/K
11-6-1941	Anti-Racketeering	Fed's	10 Years Prison

Prisons Characteristics of William Bioff

"From a very humble beginning and with scarcely any formal schooling, through taking advantage of every opportunity offered to him (oftentimes an unfair advantage) had pushed himself to the top of the labor union movement. He is a self-made man in the worst sense of the word. By always looking after the selfish interest of William Bioff he succeeded in gaining a position whereby he could live comfortably and provide lucrative employment for his brothers. He is an unscrupulous individual whose desire for wealth caused him to promote some of the most notorious racketeering schemes this country had known." "Reports reveal that William Bioff is an untruthful and unreliable in many respects and that he is inclined to make excuses for himself."

Known Professions

Ice delivery boy for Chevrolet Company (1915)
Van Hossen Printing Company, Ink Maker / Delivery Boy (1915-1917)
Chauffeurs and Teamster's Labor Union / Chauffeur to Mike Galvin (1917-1922)
Organizer for the Truck Driver's and Teamster's Union (1922-1932)
Jewish Butchers Union of Chicago / Organizer, 1137 Fulton Street, Chicago (1933)
Organizer for the Chicago Stage Handlers Employees Union Local 2 (1932-1934)

Mob Boss

International Representative of the Alliance of Theatrical and Stage Employees and Movie Operators Union for the U.S. and Canada (1934-1941)

Known Addresses of William Bioff

Kostner & Archer Avenue, Chicago (1907-1920's)
3254 Ogden Avenue, Chicago (1921)
329 S. San Francisco Avenue, Chicago (1921)
216 S. Halsted Street, Chicago (1922)
1700 Madison Street, Chicago (1932)
1549 Jackson Boulevard, Chicago (1924)
1220 Washington Boulevard, Chicago (1933)
1920 Jackson Boulevard, Chicago (1933)
10552 Wyton Drive, Westwood, California (June 2, 1936-1939)
5975 Shoup Drive, Canoga Park, San Fernando Valley, California (1939-1940's)
(80-acre farm in Los Angeles County with a 6-room modern home and an additional attached home for the servants. The entire grounds were surrounded by a brick wall and a guarded gate. Alfalfa was produced on the farm. He had Warner Brothers Studio trees and shrubs used for filming delivered his this property and planted.)

National Archives

JOHN EDGAR HOOVER

Federal Bureau of Investigation
United States Department of Justice
Washington, D. C.

Form T-2

May 31, 1944 1765 dm

The following is the record of FBI number 559821

J. E. Hoover
Director.

CONTRIBUTOR OF FINGERPRINTS	NAME AND NUMBER	ARRESTED OR RECEIVED	CHARGE	DISPOSITION
PD, Chicago, Ill.	William Bioff C-37305	[illegible]	D.P.	* rel.
PD, Los Angeles, Calif.	William Bioff 38084	11-24-39	susp. fug. (Ill.) pandering	* $1,000. bond dism. DA 12-12-39
USM, Los Angeles, Calif.	William Bioff #7952	[illegible]	Income Tax Evasion	
USM, Los Angeles, Calif.	William Bioff, #9311	5-24-41	consp. to violate anti-racketeering Law	on $25,000 bail for appearance S Dist. New York
USM, N.Y., N.Y.	William Bioff, #C0-226	6-12-41	obtain money and interfence with trade commerce by violence	
Fed. Det. Hdq. NYC NY	William Bioff, #33520	11-6-41	vio. Anti-Racketeering Act of 6-18-34	11-12-41, U.S.D.C., S.D.N.Y., actual sent., 10 yrs. on 2 cts. to run concurr. and $10,000 fine on 1st ct.; susp. sent. imposed 10 yrs. on 3rd count and fine of $10,000; prob. 5 yrs. from 11-13-51 to 11-12-56, susp. upon payment of fines of $20,000. (prob. effective upon completion of sent. on cts. 1 and 2)
U. S. Pen., Leavenworth, Kans.	William Bioff #58944	1-8-42	Anti-Racketeering Act; interfer. with trade and commerce by violence	20 yrs.
Fed. Det. Hdqrts. New York City, N.Y.	William Bioff #34958	4-30-42	anti-racketeering Act.	

* Represents notations unsupported by fingerprints in FBI files.

NOTICE: THIS RECORD IS FURNISHED FOR OFFICIAL USE ONLY

William Bioff's FBI Arrest Sheet

UNITED STATES DEPARTMENT OF JUSTICE
FEDERAL BUREAU OF INVESTIGATION
WASHINGTON 25, D. C.

2

1-4

J. Edgar Hoover
Director.

The following FBI record, NUMBER 552811, is furnished FOR OFFICIAL USE ONLY.

CONTRIBUTOR OF FINGERPRINTS	NAME AND NUMBER	ARRESTED OR RECEIVED	CHARGE	DISPOSITION
...d. Det. Hdqrts. ..., NY	William Bioff #34958	4-30-42	Anti-racketeering Act	5-7-44, to FCI, Sandstone, Minn.
...I ...ndstone, Minn.	William Bioff #2150	5-9-44	Anti Racketeering Act, Interference with Trade and Commerce by vio.	10 yrs. - disch. 12-26-44, exp. of amended sent.
Phoenix Ariz	Willie Bioff #Morgue File #400	DECEASED 11-4-55		

...otations indicated
...rnished this Burea...
...NVESTIGATIVE

UNITED STATES DEPARTMENT OF JUSTICE
FEDERAL BUREAU OF INVESTIGATION
WASHINGTON 25, D. C.

3

1-4

J. Edgar Hoover
Director.

The following FBI record, NUMBER 552811, is furnished FOR OFFICIAL USE ONLY.

CONTRIBUTOR OF FINGERPRINTS	NAME AND NUMBER	ARRESTED OR RECEIVED	CHARGE	DISPOSITION
*	As Willie Bioff, #82140, PD, Chicago, Ill., 3-7-21, burg.			
*	#82140, PD, Chicago, Ill., Morris Bioff, 5-4-21, stricken off, burg. and R.S.P.			
*	#85637, PD, Chicago Ill., William Bioff, 2-23-22, 6 mos. H. of C., and $300 and costs, pandering.			
*	As William Bioff, #38084, PD, Los Angeles, Calif., 1-11-40, fugitive Ill., dism. D4 2-20-40.			
*	As William Bioff, if appre. during period of prob. from 11-13-51 to 11-12-56, notify US Prob. Off., N.Y., N. Y., per inf. rec. 12-16-41.			

Address:
5975 Shoup Ave Canova Pk Calif
(As on prt #C9-226 USM NYC NY)
Date and place of birth:
9-12-1900 Russia
(As on prt #2150 Fed Corr Inst Sandstone Minn)

US Prob Officer
NYC NY

...tations indicated by * ARE NOT BASED ON FINGERPRINTS IN FBI files. The notations are based on data ...nished this Bureau concerning individuals of the same or similar names or aliases and ARE LISTED ONLY AS ...VESTIGATIVE LEADS.

16—15780-3 U. S. GOVERNMENT PRINTING OFFICE

As for George E. Browne, his rise was along the same lines as Bioff's. In 1932 Browne was with the Chicago Chicken Killers Union on Fulton Street and a business agent of the Stagehands Union Local 2 in Chicago when he ran unsuccessfully as a candidate for the presidency of the union. In the following years a bitter Browne joined forces with William Bioff as they formed an association with the help of the Chicago mob. Bioff was a panderer who had organized a protection association of Jewish butchers.

George Browne's childhood was difficult growing up in Woodstock, Illinois since his mother died when he was 9 and his father, who was an electrician, died when he was 14. He was raised by an aunt in Chicago. At the age of 17 he left home and went to work as a stage hand. He soon became acquainted with Chicago hoodlums through various people connected to shows which lead to a March 9, 1924 arrest. Browne was arrested by the Chicago police with mob associate Ralph O'Hare for fighting with a Harold Fletcher. When police handcuffed Browne they found two guns in his coat, believing O'Hara slipped his gun into Browne's pocket.

In another incident in January 1925, Browne was rushed to the hospital after being shot in the hip. When police tried to question him as to who shot him he refused to speak. However, years later he said he was shot as a result of a brawl in which he was not a participant.

With the new found power of his association with Bioff, Browne and Bioff shook down Barney Balaban, an owner of a chain of movie theaters, for $20,000. Both Bioff and Browne would go to a club owned by gangster Nick Circella and spend their money wildly. When Circella asked the two where and how they had gotten all their money they told Circella about the shake down. That turned out to be a mistake as Circella ordered the two men to the home of Frank Nitti. At the meeting Nitti, Circella, and gangster Frank Rio informed Bioff and Browne that the Chicago mob was now in business with the two men and demanded fifty percent of the shake down money. Nitti then informed Browne that Circella was now a union representative in Browne's union and Circella spoke for Nitti.

After that meeting Frank Nitti called another meeting at the Riverside, Illinois home of Harry Hochstein. There Frank Nitti, Frank Rio, William Bioff, Louis "Lepke" Buchalter, Paul DeLucia, Nick Circella, George Browne, Louis Campagna and Charles Fischetti listened to plans on how they were going to control the stage handlers union's convention which was being held in June 1934 in Louisville, Kentucky.

During the meeting Frank Nitti and Frank Rio did most of the talking, asking Bioff and Browne where the weak spots were throughout the country that defeated Browne in his 1932 election. Nitti told Bioff that he had connections that would make it possible for Browne to change those opposition delegations in his favor. Bioff said that when the discussion about which cites were against Browne in his election bid Campagna, DeLucia and Rio all said they had the connections to "make things go their way." Frank Nitti said, *"We will take care of Jersey and New York; we will take care of Jersey through Longie Zwillman."* Bioff added that Nitti said Zwillman would take care of New York through Lucky Luciano and Louis Buchalter; he would take care of Cleveland through Al Polissi; and he would take care of St. Louis through Johnny Dougherty.

Frank Nitti ordered that Capone mobsters Louis Romano, Hindu Imburgio and Tony Accardo be the Chicago delegation. The group discussed the rigging of the election for the International Stage Hand Union at the convention and decided that George Browne would hold the presidency.

At the delegation Browne was named International President of the union with Bioff as his personal representative with full power to act, call strikes and settle them. Nick Circella was named the Chicago representative of the union to keep an eye on the two. The plan was that the conspirators were to receive 50 percent from future activities and Bioff and Browne were to receive the remaining 50 percent. Later on the Capone Gang demanded and received 2/3 of the income and Bioff and Brown were allowed to keep only 1/3 of the shakedowns and extortions.

A year later Tommy Malloy, then head of Chicago Local 110, of the Motion Picture Operators Union was killed when Frank Nitti ordered Nick Circella to take over the presidency of that local. It was then that Frank Nitti planned the extortion of over a million dollars from the motion picture industry. The money came from producers and exhibitors in various parts of the U.S., mainly New York, Chicago, Newark and Los Angeles. Most of the payoffs were made in the southern part of New York where most of the producing offices were located. It was then that Frank Nitti informed Browne and Bioff that the Capone Gang was going to change the deal and be taking 66 % of the profit.

Browne, Bioff and Nick Circella produced 2% of the assessment fund from the union right into the greedy hands of the Capone Gang. To make that 2% fund grow they flooded the membership with inexperienced operators which resulted in a operators pay lowered from $2,500 per year to $1,200 per year. But the larger amount of members in the union, the more that 2% number grew and the more money was paid to the hoodlums. This assessment was in effect on two separate occasions totaling $1,513,338.78 which was all deposited in a bank.

Some of the money was used to extend the jurisdiction of the International Alliance of Theatrical Stage Employees and Moving Picture Machine Operators, Local 37 of Hollywood, on the west coast. The idea was to make the Hollywood local the most powerful under the control of gangsters.

In 1939 screen actor Robert Montgomery, then President of the Screen Actor's Guild, and Joseph W. Carpenter, then president of Local 37 of the I.A.T.S.E. in Hollywood, made a complaint against Browne, Bioff and the I.A.T.S.E. The complaint was received by the FBI which conducted an investigation. Information was discovered that George Browne had threatened to call a nationwide strike of the projectionists in an attempt to give movie producers an excuse to exert pressure on local authorities to drop a Grand Jury Investigation of labor racketeering against him and his union. There were reports of bribes ranging from $5,000 to $100,000 being paid to stop legislative investigations of the I.A.T.S.E. However, the investigation failed to indicate any federal violation had occurred.

Evidence found was a 1937 check that was deposited in William Bioff's bank account for $100,000. The money had been given to William and his wife Lauria by Joseph Schenck, who at the time represented the Motion Picture Producers, as a "gift" for settling a strike in the motion picture industry. Schenck actually used his nephew Arthur Stebbins to deliver the check to Bioff. The Attorney General found three ways to go after Bioff. One was income tax evasion; the second was prosecution under the collective bargaining agreement and third was an antitrust racketeering charge. However, all three failed with insufficient evidence.

By 1941 all of the I.A.T.S.E.'s money was gone. Bioff and Browne claimed that a large fund in currency was needed for union purposes. With the aid of the officials of the union, fictitious disbursements were made to international representatives who, upon each receipt of the reported salary, kicked back all his portion of the receipt in the form of currency to certain officials of the union who in turn transmitted the currency by registered mail to a man named Isadore Zevin in Chicago. Zevin was Browne's secretary and bookkeeper of the 2% fund.

The money received through extortions and through misuse of union funds was divided pursuant to an agreement which went 1/3 to Bioff and Browne and 2/3 to the Capone Gang. A man named Louis Krause who was a member of the International Union served as a collector for the mob, traveling around the country collecting the shake down money. The syndicate demanded the money to prevent them from obstructing the production of movies being made.

It all lead to the May 1941 arrest of William Bioff and George E. Browne and their convictions on November 6, 1941. By May 1943 a rumor had reached the press that angered many people. The rumor was that Bioff and Browne were not in federal prison but were serving their time in a Federal House of Detention in Hoboken, New Jersey which was considered to be an "easy ride" and nothing like prison. It turned out to be true which led to Bioff and Browne being sent to Leavenworth Prison and then transferred to the Federal Correction Institution at Sandstone, Minnesota.

William Bioff and George Browne were paroled on December 22, 1944.

National Archives

Mob Boss

File Card

George E. Browne
Born October 22, 1893, Woodstock, Illinois
Died Believed to be in the mid 1950's
I.Q. 117
Wife Margaret Brown
Daughter's Colleen Browne and 2-twin girls Margo and Marylyn
Mistress Margie Malone

Known Addresses

Woodstock, Illinois (Early 1900's)
328 Selborne Road, Riverside Illinois (1933)
212 South Maples, Oak Park, Illinois (1935-1938)
340-acre Farm at Route #3 Woodstock, Illinois (1938-1940's)
200 W. 47th Street, Hotel Edison, New York City (1940's)
Burlington, Iowa (1950's)

Known Arrest Record of George E. Browne

Date	Charge	Agency	Result
8-29-1929	Section 2655	Chicago PD	Fined $50
3-9-1924	Aggravated Battery	Chicago PD	Dismissed
3-9-1924	Concealed Weapon	Chicago PD	Dismissed
12-4-1933	Disorderly Conduct	Cicero PD	Released
5-27-1941	Anti-racketeering	US Marshall	Guilty
6-20-1941	Anti-racketeering	US Marshall	Guilty

Known Professions

Messenger at Western Union Telephone Company Chicago (1905-1906)
Messenger at Marshalle Jackson Company, Chicago (1906-1907)
Oiler maintenance man at Riverview Amusement Park, Chicago (1907-1910)
Stage Employee for many theater and motion picture studios in Chicago (1910-1922)
Business Agent for the Stage Employees Union of Chicago (1922-1934)
President of the I.A.P.S.E. in New York City (1934-1941)

(Signed) George E. Browne

JOHN EDGAR HOOVER

Federal Bureau of Investigation
U[illegible]ited States Department of Jus[illegible]e
Washington, D. C.

Form T-2

The following is the record of FBI number 2348761

J. E. Hoover
Director.

CONTRIBUTOR OF FINGERPRINTS	NAME AND NUMBER	ARRESTED OR RECEIVED	CHARGE	DISPOSITION
USM, Chicago, Ill.	George E. Browne #3205	5-27-41	Anti, racketeer ing Sec. 88 Title 18	
USM, N.Y., N.Y.	George E. Browne, #	6-20-41	Anti-racketeering Sec. 420a- Title 18	
Federal Detention Hdqtrs., New York, N. Y.	George E. Browne, #33519	11-6-41	vio. anti-racketeering Act; of 6-18-34	8 yrs. on 2 cts. t run concurr. and $10,000. fine on first ct; susp sent imposed of 10 yrs. on 3 rd ct. and fir of $10,000. prob. imposed, 5 yrs; susp. on payment of fines of $20,000. from 11-13-49 to 11-12-54 (prob. effective upon completion of sent. on cts. 1 and 2, 1-7-42. trans. to USP Leavenworth
USP, Le venworth, Kans.	George E. Browne, #58945	1-8-42	Anti-racketeering Act; interfering with trade and commerce by vio.	8 yrs.
Fed. Det. Headquarters N.Y.C., N.Y.	George E. Browne #34959	4-30-42	Anti-racketeering Act	
Fed. Correctional Institution, Sandstone, Minn.	George E. Browne #2151	5-9-44	Anti-Racketeering Act; interfering with trade and commerce by viol.	8 yrs.

COPY FOR BUREAU OF PRISONS

SANDSTONE
2151-SS
MAY 9 1944

NAME BROWNE, George E. NO. 2151-SS

United States Department of Justice
Washington, D. C.

The following is the record of FBI number 2348761 . J. E. Hoover
Director.

CONTRIBUTOR OF FINGERPRINTS	NAME AND NUMBER	ARRESTED OR RECEIVED	CHARGE	DISPOSITION

As George E. Bro. e, if appr. during period of prob. from 11-13-49 to 11-12-54, notify BFD, NYC, NY their file 60-652, per inf. rec. therefrom 12-16-41, Bu. file 60-2149.

As George E. Browne, chg. Anti-Racketeering; 11-12-41, USDC SDNY, sent. 8 yrs. on 2 counts to run concurr. and $10,000. fine on 1st count; susp. sent. imposed of 10 yrs. on 3rd ct. and fine of $10,000. probation imposed 5 yrs., suspended on payment of fines of $20,000. from 11-13-49 to 11-12-54 (probation effective upon completion of sent. on Counts 1 and 2) per inf. rec. 12-16-41.

National Archives

Record Form No. 1a
(Revised Feb., 1936)

This Copy for
Bu. of Prisons
Wash., D. C.

RECORD OF COURT COMMITMENT

Department of Justice

PE[illegible]AL AND CORRECTIONAL INSTITU[illegible]NS

Federal Correctional Institution
(Institution)

Sandstone, Minnesota
(Location)

Revised 12-27-44 to conform with order amending sentence.

Inst. Name BROWNE, George E. — No. 2151-SS

Alias None — Color White — Age 51 (10-21-93)

True Name Inst. Name — Name and number of prior commitments to Fed. Inst. 39519-N.Y 58945-L. 34959-N.Y.

Offense Anti Racketeering Act: Interfering with trade & commerce by violence

District S.N.Y-N.Y.City (Cr.No.110/2) Judge Knox

Sentence 8 Yrs. (2cts. conc) — Costs / Fine $20,000.00 — Committed Paid — Not Committed — Paid

Sentence changed Dec. 22, 1944 — New term 3 yrs. 28 das. to expire forthwith. — Reason therefor Judge amended sentence.

Sentenced Nov. 12, 1941 - Appealed — When arrested May - 1941

Committed to Fed. Inst. Nov. 12, 1941 - N. Y. — Where arrested Chicago, Ill.

Sentence begins Nov. 20, 1941 -Elected to serve. — Residence Woodstock, Ill.

Eligible for parole — Time in jail before trial None - Made Bond

Eligible for conditional release with good time — Rate per mo. good time 0 — Total good time possible 0

Eligible for con. rel. with extra good time

Forfeited good time — Amount forfeited

Restoration good time — Amount restored

Expires full term Amended Sentence Dec. 17, 1944 *

Former Com. on Sentence to Other Institutions			Co-defendants in Present Case	
No.	Name of Institution	Location	Names	Action of Board

* Order amending sentence entered 12-22-44 received at Inst. 12-26-44, changed sentence to read as follows: "Three yrs. and 28 das. on cts. 1 & 2 to run concurrently, to expire forthwith. Count 3 - Ten yrs. to run consecutive to concurrent sentences on cts. 1 & 2. Execution of sentence on ct. 3 suspended. Prohibition for 5 yrs. to begin after service of sentence on cts 1 & 2, subject to terms of Probation as set forth in Order filed 12-22-44.

Reports Received	[illegible]	[illegible]	[illegible]	[illegible]	[illegible]	Nat.	Imm.	Cus.	Post	S. S.	Vet.	Ind.	Pen.	War	Others

ACTION OF BOARD										
Date	No. app.	Parole: Forth.	Effect.	Rel.	Den.	Cont.	War. is.	Rev.	Dis. from par.
June '44						✓			
7-6-44					D				

Releases and recommitments on present sentence other than parole	
Date	Method
12-28-44	Exp. Amended Sentence
	Retained in custody until 12-28-44 as per [illegible] attached

George Browne Prison Records

Mob Boss

On April 4, 1944 Paul DeLucia was transferred from the New York House of Corrections and arrived at the United States Penitentiary at Atlanta, Georgia. After he settled in to his cell prison officials interviewed him. They told him he was there because he was found guilty of interfering with trade and commerce by coercion, threats and violence. DeLucia replied, *"They claim we got money from movie executives for protection by threats in Chicago and New York. I pleaded not guilty."*

The admission summary to the prison called DeLucia lazy, evades work, was unconcerned and indifferent, just got along, needed occasional checking up on as to cleanliness and tended to be emotional and moody. He appeared to be older-looking than his actual age; that he had a dejected facial expression; slowly responsive and exhibited very little emotions. It ended by saying DeLucia was cooperative, his attitude appeared to be satisfactory during the interview, but his quarantine adjustment had been unsatisfactory and indicated he had little inclination toward honest employment. Other impressions were that he had rather close family ties and required close supervision.

He spent much of his time reading newspapers, magazines and books on agriculture, history and travel. He was assigned to General Maintenance in the clothing issue department and the tailor shop to pass the time for 17 months. His time at Atlanta was not too bad; he did spend some time in isolation and in the special treatment unit for some kind of conniving.

While her husband was in prison, Nancy DeLucia hired mob lawyer Eugene Bernstein on a suggestion from the wife of mobster Louis Campagna. Bernstein had been successful in handling the IRS suit against Campagna for evasion of income taxes on money supposedly obtained in the extortion conspiracy. First Bernstein met with Paul DeLucia at the prison in Atlanta who was in complete disagreement with Bernstein's strategy in handling the income tax matter. Bernstein desired to have DeLucia offer a settlement of the income tax evasion case but DeLucia feeling that he had never realized any money from the extortion scheme should not pay any taxes on money he never received.

In the end DeLucia did what Bernstein wanted. Bernstein settled all of the back taxes owed by DeLucia and Campagna. When FBI agents interviewed Bernstein about this, he told them that unknown men would walk into his law office and leave large sums of cash with his secretary Geneva Cox until enough was there to settle with the IRS. Bernstein was paid $190,000 to settle both DeLucia and Campagna's tax settlements.

Paul DeLucia and Louis Campagna after their arrest

Tony Dark

Many years later Paul DeLucia himself told FBI agents during an interview that he made up his mind when he was sent to the Atlanta Prison that the best plan for him was to follow prison rules and behave himself in such a manner so that when parole was to be considered, his exemplary prison record would act in his favor toward the granting of an early parole. DeLucia said when he and the others were brought to Atlanta they were interviewed by the warden and were told in a confidential talk that they were going to be considered and treated like any other prisoner. The way for them to behave was for them to "keep their nose clean" and they would thus be eligible for the same parole as anyone else. Not all of the Chicago men convicted in the extortion case agreed with DeLucia's ideas but in spite of adverse conditions at Atlanta, DeLucia attempted to be a model prisoner.

The conditions in the penitentiary at Atlanta were not very good. The cell blocks were infested with rats, mice and bugs. It was not considered a desirable penitentiary. He truly believed that he did not belong in Atlanta since he was a Chicago guy and that he belonged in a federal penitentiary adjacent to Chicago.

Years later, DeLucia told an investigator that when it came time for him to go off to prison he took all the cash he had been hiding in safety deposit boxes that he had made from gambling dating back to the 1920's while under Al Capone, and placed it all in a trunk. Actually DeLucia and mob lawyer Joseph Bulger together on Christmas Day 1943 took all the money, counted it, and placed it in a metal trunk. The trunk contained $30,000 in $500 bills, $250,000 in $100 bills, and the remainder in $1,000 bills. Oh, there was a $10 gold note mixed in with the larger bills. He then took the trunk with over $300,000 in cash and nailed it to the rafters in a dark corner of the attic of his Lathrop Avenue mansion in River Forest. They then boarded up a fake wall and DeLucia gave the key to Bulger. In an affidavit filed by Paul DeLucia in 1957 he said he hid the money because he was afraid his wife might make away with the money while he was gone by either divorcing him or spending it. He told Bulger that if he died in prison he wanted the money to go to his kids so they would not "be out on the streets."

DeLucia, D'Andrea, Gioe, Campagna and Roselli were all in Atlanta Federal Prison together. Campagna and Gioe were the first to be transferred out of Atlanta on July 27, 1945 to Leavenworth Prison in Kansas City. D'Andrea and DeLucia followed the next day while Roselli had to wait a year until September 29, 1946 when he was transferred to Terre Haute Prison in Indiana.

DeLucia was transferred to Leavenworth Prison in Kansas which was closer to Chicago so his wife, family and more important business associates could visit him. He was listed as a normal individual who showed no change in his mental status since being incarcerated and was listed as having a good chance to make an adequate social adjustment outside the prison when released. The only difficulties he had a Leavenworth were that he required a daily injection of insulin for his diabetes, suffered from chronic hemorrhoids and had a deformity of the foot from his elevator accident that required a special pair of shoes. He worked in the kitchen and as an orderly in the medical unit. His cellmate was Harry Russell Winkelblack.

The visitor seen the most at Leavenworth was DeLucia's lawyer, Eugene Bernstein. Every time Bernstein came for a visit he was accompanied by the same man. That man was DeLucia's second in company, Tony "JB" Accardo. The purpose of those visits were one, to keep DeLucia up-to-date on syndicate matters in Chicago and second, for Accardo to convince DeLucia that he should make a settlement of the income tax case and "wipe the slate clean."

Accardo was able to explain the various angles of the case to him better than Bernstein could. Some time later, as DeLucia once told the feds, while sitting in jail he was informed that a settlement was reached in his income tax case and that according to DeLucia, *"persons unknown to him had contributed money to cover this settlement."* He added that he did not know that it was Bernstein who delivered the money to the IRS for the settlement nor that receipts were made out to the persons who gave the money without their names.

When Accardo came to visit, he did not sign his real name in the register book to enter the prison, but used the name of mob lawyer Joseph Bulger. Bulger, who was one-time mayor of the mob-plagued town of Melrose Park, Illinois and who had offices in Chicago's City Hall on LaSalle Street, had represented DeLucia in the past and had been in the "internal circle" of many of the Outfit's big decisions concerning money matters.

In 1947 the FBI went to Louis Campagna's home to interview him about the incident. Campagna told the agents that Eugene Bernstein and Tony Accardo had come to visit him, and Paul DeLucia, on several occasions. Campagna said that Accardo, Bernstein, Paul DeLucia and himself would sit around a round table to discuss stuff with one guard watching. When agents pressed him to answer why Accardo was there, he said he had no idea since he had no business with Accardo so he claimed. He added that maybe Accardo was there to help Bernstein and DeLucia communicate since Campagna claimed DeLucia spoke very broken English.

Eugene Bernstein was asked by FBI agents why Accardo signed his name as Joseph Bulger. Bernstein said he did not pay attention to what name Accardo signed and denied knowing anything about it.

Later in 1948 Accardo and Bernstein were indicted by a Federal Grand Jury and charged with conspiracy stemming from signing a fake name in a federal prison. Both were found not guilty.

In 1947 Paul DeLucia told the FBI that he recalled he had become acquainted with William Maloy of the Moving Picture Operators Union during the time he was connected with Diamond Joe Esposito. Somewhere around that time he also became acquainted with Browne and Bioff, who where also connected in some way with the union. DeLucia said that as a result of his acquaintanceship with Maloy he was able at different times to secure jobs for a few of his friends and in this manner placed both of his wife's brothers in the union.

DeLucia told the FBI he was convicted in New York City on testimony which was very hazy and indefinite. He also added that neither Browne nor Bioff could mention when or where money passed hands between them and that the thing was definitely a "bad rap."

When FBI agents went back to Atlanta prison to ask the warden why the hoodlums were transferred, he did not have an answer. The warden recalled that

Campagna, D'Andrea and DeLucia were very talkative people and were constantly bragging about their exploits to other inmates. He did recall that Gioe was a tough, quiet, ruthless individual while Roselli never had much to say. The warden said one of the inmates came up to him to inform him that Campagna, DeLucia and D'Andrea had been telling other inmates that they had paid $10,000 each to be transferred to Leavenworth because it was closer to Chicago. The warden added that it was not unheard of that prisoners paid their lawyers large sum of money to arrange a transfer. The attorney would contact a U.S. Congressman who in turn would call the Bureau of Prisons requesting the particular favor and push the request to such an extent that the favor was frequently granted. Then the attorney would report back to the inmate that he had a hard fight on his behalf but finally succeeded, when in reality the favor was performed by the Congressman.

The warden added that DeLucia, Campagna and D'Andrea had caused disturbances among the prison population. The three would continually brag and throw their weight around which caused the other prisoners to look up to them and try to imitate their actions, thereby tending to lower prison morale. Because of their gang leader position and wide publicity, some of the other prisoners thought anything they said was right. Because of this the warden wanted to take one-hundred and fifty days of good time away from D'Andrea and two-hundred and four days away from DeLucia but the disciplinary board overruled him.

D'Andrea had three known disciplinary reports against him. First on May 27, 1944, D'Andrea had an inmate in the prison laboratory return a positive report showing sugar in Paul DeLucia's urine so he could get on the diet line. Second on September 10, 1944, D'Andrea was cited for violating his diet restriction when he was found drinking coffee which he specifically was instructed not to do. Third on July 26, 1945, he refused to mop the floor which he tracked after being ordered to do so by an officer. He told the officer that because of his physical condition he was unable to do this type of work.

John Roselli was transferred to Terre Haute Prison in Indiana on October 7, 1946. Louis Kaufman died in May 1955. Once William Bioff was released from prison he headed straight back to Hollywood, California. He was seen staying at a millionaire movie executive home while meeting with big shot movie producers.

By 1955 only Paul DeLucia, Ralph Pierce and Johnny Roselli were still alive. George Browne had moved to Burlington, Iowa and chose to drop off the face of the earth. The FBI did try to warn him after bodies were piling up of those involved in the extortion case. No one knew what really happened to Browne or if he was alive or dead at the end of the 1950's.

Who were the men that were convicted with Paul DeLucia in the movie extortion case? They were Capone Gangsters who had different stories.

Louis Campagna

Some would say Louis Campagna was one of the most powerful gangsters Chicago had produced. Some say he was very powerful but never actually served as a "boss" in the Outfit. Some reports state he was Frank Nitti's and Paul DeLucia's Consiglieri, which means top adviser to the top mob boss. No matter what his position or his ranking. Louis Campagna was a leader in the Chicago organized crime family.

Louis Campagna's father, Luigi Campagna Sr., was born in 1852 in Italy under the name Luigi Campani. His mother, Marie A. Scardini, was also born in Italy around 1872 and both were listed as illiterate. Just before 1900, Luigi left Italy with his wife and headed for America, landing in New York.

They made a home at 286 16th Street in Brooklyn, New York and had seven children together; Raymond born around 1896, Anthony born around 1898, Louis Jr. born September 23, 1900, Mary born around 1911, Louise born around 1913 (who married Frank Speranze), and Rose born around 1915.

A young Louis was raised on the streets of Brooklyn and was somewhat of a bad seed being highly excitable, wild and headstrong. He was given the nick name "Lefty Louie" by the other wild kids. His father made his living as a shoemaker and owned a shoe shop in the neighborhood. The Campagna's were not considered a poor family, after a few years they purchased a very nice home living in an eight-room, two-story house at 1118 57th Street, Brooklyn, New York.

Louis stayed in school until the 8th grade before heading to the streets causing mischief. He told authorities years later that he left his home at the age of 15 to escape being whipped and beat by his father.

While his brothers Raymond and Anthony became painters and moved to Brookfield, New York, the rest of his family stayed in Brooklyn. Louis became a transient traveling through state after state before winding up in Chicago. There is an FBI report in which one of their trusted informants, who always gave accurate information, said that Louis Campagna was brought to Chicago by Johnny Torrio around the same time as Al Capone was brought in. This informant said Campagna was a member of the old "Five Corner Mob" in New York City and was brought to Chicago with his fellow gang member Tony "Mops" Folti. However, this information was never verified.

The scares of an abusive father prevented him from going back to see his family until he was 24-years-old. His father Luigi died of a stroke in 1936 and in 1947 his mother Marie Campagna, was listed as having cancer and was confined to a bed for five years in her Brooklyn home.

According to Louis himself, he married Elizabeth "Charlotte" Shikany on October 6, 1919 in Chicago. Charlotte was said to be born around 1902 in Chicago and having a 6th grade education. There is one marriage license in Cook County, Illinois with Charlotte Shikany listed as being married on September 23, 1919, age 19 years old; however, the groom is listed as Albert Elleckson, age 26. It could not be determined if this was the correct Charlotte Shikany or if Louis Campagna was using an alias on the marriage certificate.

Form 44

842427

State of Illinois, Cook County, } ss.

Marriage License

To any Person Legally Authorized to Solemnize Marriage,

GREETING:

Marriage may be Celebrated, in the County of Cook and State of Illinois, between Mr. Albert Elleckson of Chicago, in the County of Cook and State of Illinois, of the age of 26 years, and Miss Charlotte Shikany of Chicago, in the County of Cook and State of Illinois, of the age of 19 years.

Witness, Robert M. Sweitzer, County Clerk of the County of Cook, and the Seal thereof, at my office in Chicago, this 13 day of Sept A.D. 1919

Robert M. Sweitzer County Clerk.

The Person who Solemnizes Marriage is cautioned against making any change in this License.

STATE OF ILLINOIS, } ss. I, Arthur H. C. Both [illegible]
COUNTY OF COOK.

hereby certify that Mr. Albert Elleckson and Miss Charlotte Shikany were united in Marriage by me at Chicago in the County of Cook and State of Illinois, on the 23rd day of September 1919

Arthur H. C. Both [illegible]

(The Names in this certificate must be identical with Names in above License)

Address 3110 [illegible] Chicago Ill.

N. B.— This License, with certificate of marriage properly made, must (within 30 days) be returned to the COUNTY CLERK, by the person who performed the marriage ceremony.

Possiably Louis Campagna's marriage certificate (above) dated September 23, 1919. Louise entered prison in April 1919 so if it is his marrage certificate he was married while in prison. Louis's children's birth certificates (below and the next page)

H. D. V. 125A 50M. 1-20 500

1. PLACE OF BIRTH

Registration Dist. No. 3104

Primary Dist. No.

STATE OF ILLINOIS
DEPARTMENT OF PUBLIC HEALTH
Division of Vital Statistics

Certificate of Birth

HEALTH DEPARTMENT'S RECORD
CITY OF CHICAGO

County of COOK

Registered No. 27866

City of CHICAGO †No. 517 No. Morgan Street St.; Ward

2. FULL NAME OF CHILD JOSEPH FRANCIS Campagna (If child is not yet named, make supplemental report, as directed.)

3. Sex of Child M. | 4. Twin, triplets, or other? | Number in order of birth (To be answered only in event of plural births) | 5. Date of birth July (Month) 5th (Day) 1920 (Year)

FATHER		MOTHER	
6. FULL NAME	Louis Campagna	12. FULL MAIDEN NAME	Charlotte Shikany
7. RESIDENCE	517 No. Morgan St.	13. RESIDENCE	517 No. Morgan St.
8. COLOR	White	14. COLOR	White
9. AGE AT LAST BIRTHDAY	26 Years	15. AGE AT LAST BIRTHDAY	20 Years
10. BIRTHPLACE (State or Country)	Brooklyn, N.Y.	16. BIRTHPLACE (State or Country)	Chicago
11. OCCUPATION	Laborer	17. OCCUPATION	Housekeeper
18. Number of children born to this mother, including present birth	1	19. Number of children of this mother now living	1

20. CERTIFICATE OF ATTENDING PHYSICIAN OR MIDWIFE.*

I hereby certify that I attended the birth of this child, who was born alive at 6:45 A.M., on the date above stated.

* When there was no attending physician or midwife, then the father, mother, householder, etc., shall make this return. See Sec. 12 of vital statistics law.

21. (Signature) Dr. Vincent Filetti M. D. / Midwife (Physician or Midwife)

22. Give name added from a supplemental report ......, 19...... Registrar

Address 2354 Grand Ave Telephone See-2164

23. Filed AUG 1920 Registrar

† If birth occurred in hospital or institution, give its name instead of street and number. [signature]

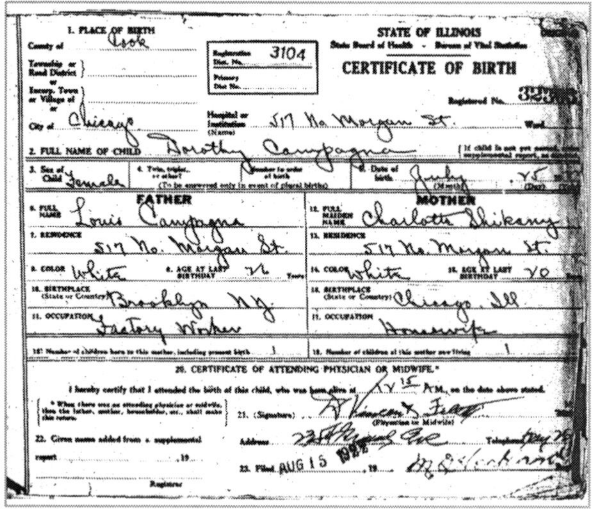

STATE OF ILLINOIS
State Board of Health - Bureau of Vital Statistics
CERTIFICATE OF BIRTH

1. PLACE OF BIRTH
County of Cook
Registration Dist. No. 3104
City of Chicago
Hospital or Institution (Name) 517 No. Morgan St.

2. FULL NAME OF CHILD Dorothy Campagna

3. Sex of Child Female
Date of birth July 25

FATHER
Full name Louis Campagna
Residence 517 No. Morgan St.
Color White
Age at last birthday [illegible] Years
Birthplace (State or Country) Brooklyn N.Y.
Occupation Factory Worker

MOTHER
Full maiden name Charlotte Shikany
Residence 517 No. Morgan St.
Color White
Age at last birthday 20
Birthplace (State or Country) Chicago, Ill
Occupation Housewife

Number of children born to this mother, including present birth 1
Number of children of this mother now living 1

20. CERTIFICATE OF ATTENDING PHYSICIAN OR MIDWIFE.*
I hereby certify that I attended the birth of this child, who was born alive at [illegible] P.M., on the date above stated.
21. (Signature) [illegible] (Physician or Midwife)
Address [illegible]
22. Given name added from a supplemental report, 19
23. Filed AUG 15 [illegible], 19

Louis Campagna's 1920's Chicago Police Arrest Photo

Louis Campagna first came to the attention of law enforcement in 1917 when he was arrested for armed robbery. His confidence grew when the jury found him not guilty.

In October 1918 Louis Campagna was arrested with William Taglia, aka John Fredericks, Gus Saunders and James Knight for robbing the Argo Bank in Argo, Illinois. The four men made away with between $105,000 and $135,000. Saunders turned state's witness and ratted on his fellow gang members. On March 29, 1919 Campagna and Taglia entered a plea of guilty and were sentenced to fourteen years at the Pontiac Prison in Illinois. He entered prison on April 9, 1919 and went to work in the print shop for over 3 years and spent a year working in the chair shop as a weaver. He served just less than five years and was paroled on April 8, 1924. William Taglia, aka Federicks, was later killed as he tried to escape from prison. The following pages contain a copy of Campagna's Joliet Prison record.

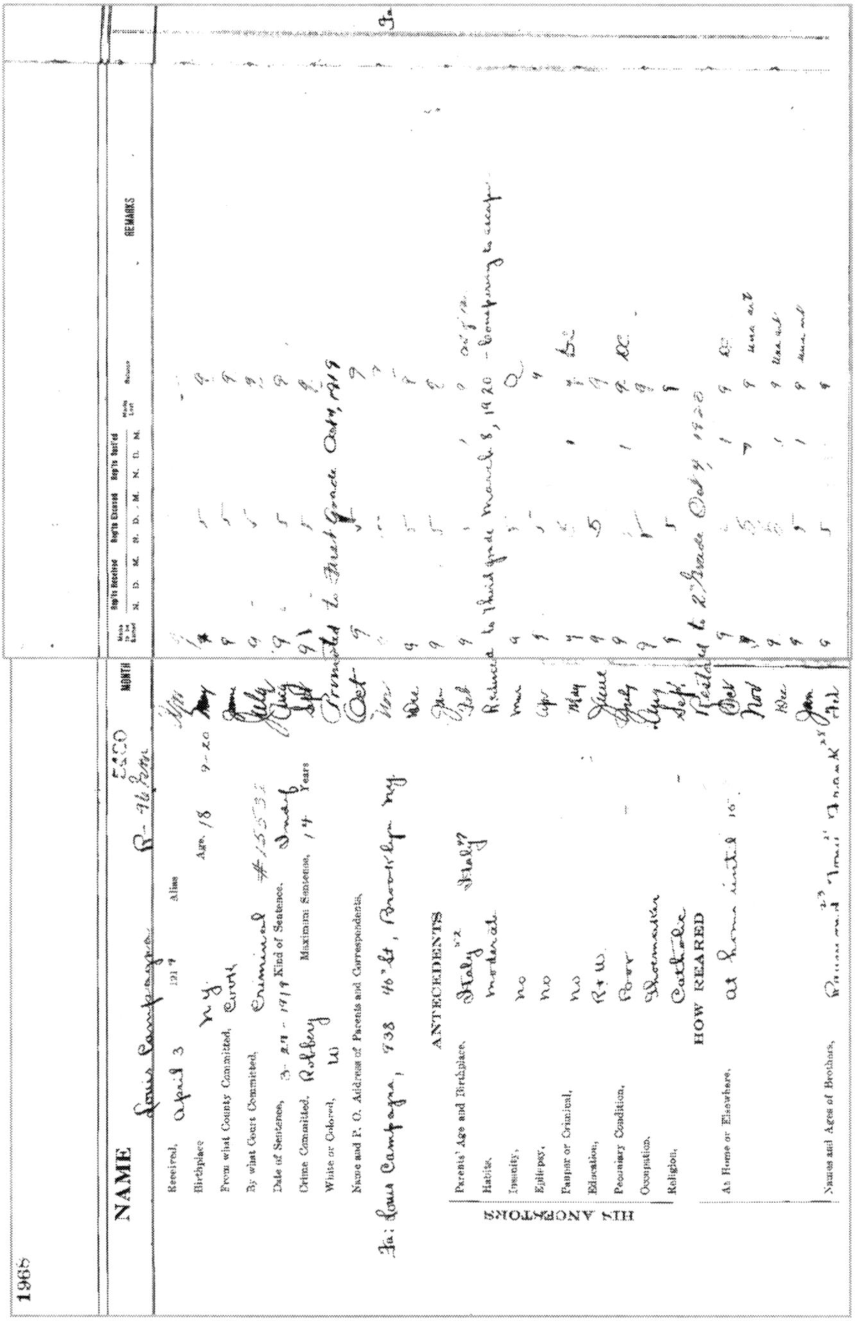

1965

NAME Louis Campagna Alias

Received, April 3 1919 Age 18

Birthplace N.Y.

From what County Committed, Kings

By what Court Committed, Criminal #15533

Date of Sentence, 3-24-1919 Kind of Sentence, Indef.

Crime Committed, Robbery Maximum Sentence, 14 Years

White or Colored, W

Name and P. O. Address of Parents and Correspondents,

Fa: Louis Campagna, 738 46th St, Brooklyn NY

HIS ANCESTORS

ANTECEDENTS

Parents' Age and Birthplace, Italy 42 Italy 37

Habits, moderate

Insanity, no

Epilepsy, no

Pauper or Criminal, no

Education, R+W

Pecuniary Condition, Poor

Occupation, Shoemaker

Religion, Catholic

HOW REARED

At Home or Elsewhere, at home until 16

Names and Ages of Brothers,

MONTH — REMARKS

Promoted to First Grade Oct 1, 1919

Reduced to Third grade March 8, 1920 — Conspiracy to escape

Restored to 2nd Grade Oct 4, 1920

Louis Campagna's 1919 Prison Record

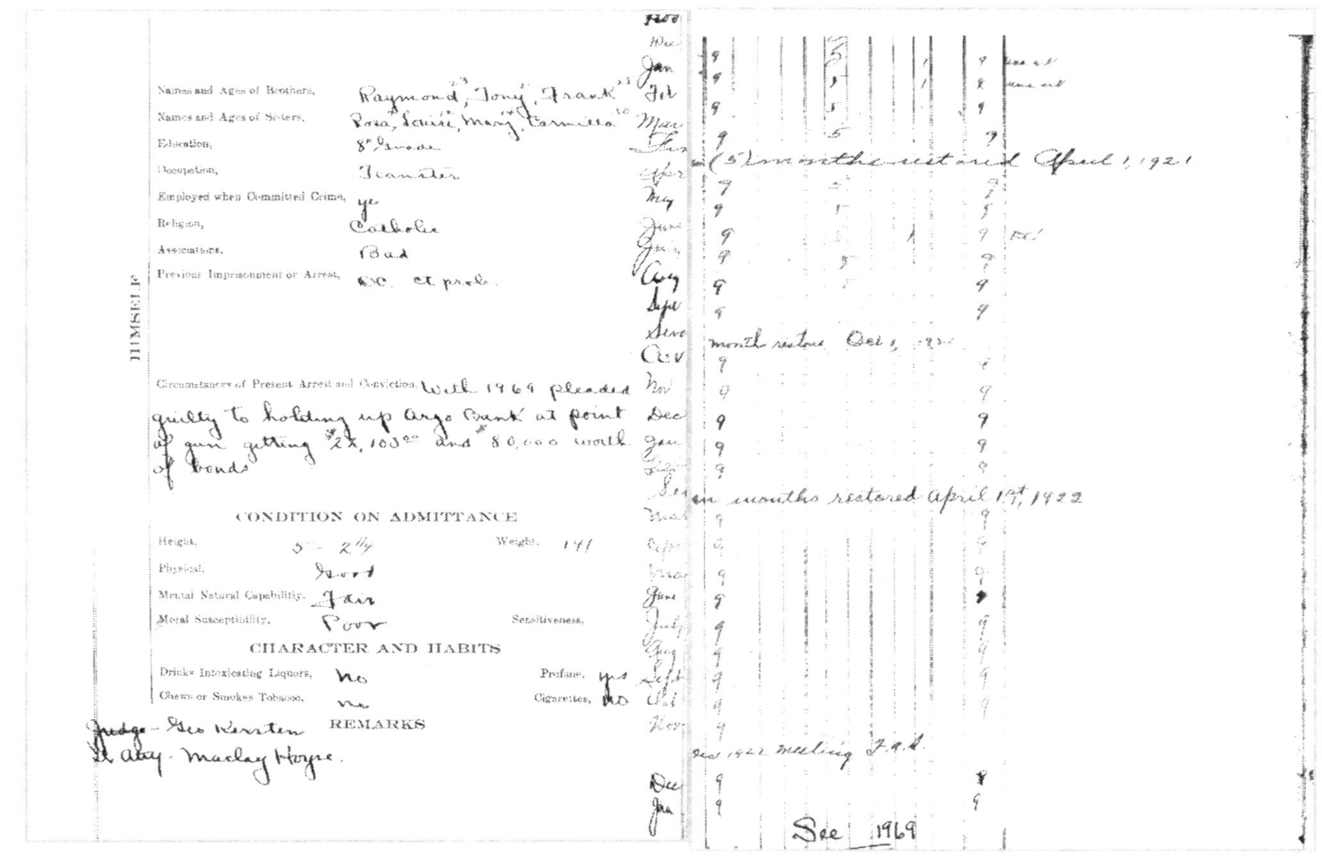

HIMSELF

Names and Ages of Brothers, Raymond 23, Tony, Frank 13

Names and Ages of Sisters, Rosa, Louise, Mary, Carmella 10

Education, 8th Grade

Occupation, Teamster

Employed when Committed Crime, yes

Religion, Catholic

Associations, Bad

Previous Imprisonment or Arrest, No. ex prob.

Circumstances of Present Arrest and Conviction. With 1969 pleaded guilty to holding up Argo Bank at point of gun getting $27,103.00 and $80,000 worth of bonds

CONDITION ON ADMITTANCE

Height, 5' 2¼ Weight, 141

Physical, Good

Mental Natural Capability, Fair

Moral Susceptibility, Poor Sensitiveness,

CHARACTER AND HABITS

Drinks Intoxicating Liquors, No Profane, yes

Chews or Smokes Tobacco, No Cigarettes, No

REMARKS

Judge - Geo Kersten

St. Atty. - Maclay Hoyne.

(5) months restored April 1, 1921

month restored Oct 1, 1921

months restored April 1st, 1922

Dec 1922 meeting

See 1969

Louis Campagna's 1919 Prison Record Part 2

Tony Dark

Charlotte had given birth to the couple's first child, Joseph Frank Campagna, born on July 5, 1920 while Louis was in prison. Once Louis was out of prison in 1924, the two moved into a three-room apartment in Chicago. Campagna admittedly said he went to work running gambling for the Torrio-Capone gang once out of prison. He spent time acting as Al Capone's bodyguard and chauffeur. It was then that Al Capone began to call him "Little New York," a nickname that he would take to the grave.

On April 19, 1925 he was arrested by Chicago police at 12:30 a.m. at a soft drink parlor located at 727 West Park Street in Chicago which was owned by gangster James Adduci. He was one of fifteen men arrested that night including ex-convicts Edwin Lattyak and Joe Novelli, aka Tony Campagna. Campagna and Novelli were turned over to parole agents.

Later that year Louis was injured, the left side of his body paralyzed, but he made a full recovery. He refused to tell authorities how it happened.

By 1927 business was so good that Campagna bought the house at 2927 South Maple Avenue in Berwyn, Illinois. The house was a seven-room brick building with a two car garage in what was listed as a middle class neighborhood in the 1930's.

Louis Campagna was arrested on November 21, 1927 with Sam Marcus and Frank Perry while walking on North Clark Street in Chicago. Apparently all three men had loaded .45 revolvers on them. The next day Louis Cowan, aka Louis McCowan, then the editor of the Cicero Tribune Newspaper, paid the bond for their release. McCowan had driven Al Capone to court that day when Capone had to appear on a vagrancy and disorderly conduct charge. A month later when Campagna court case was to be heard he and his fellow gangsters did not show up in court and their bond was forfeited. Days later Campagna showed up to court stating that he failed to appear that day because they were in a car accident. The court believed him and charges were set aside. Al Capone, himself, explained to a reporter at the time why Campagna was arrested. Whether it was the actual truth or the truth Al wanted him to believe, he told him, *"Want to know the truth about what the police call my attempt to kill Chief O'Connor? Why it's ridiculous, I'm not such a fool. Two of my men were picked up. They had guns for their protection. They were dragged into the Chief's office and one of them was punched in the stomach so that the gun in his belt slipped. It was about to fall, and naturally he reached to catch it. So O'Connor calls that an attempt to kill him in his own office."* All men in this case walked free.

On March 31, 1928 Chicago police were out in force because they were expecting trouble since a war had broken out between the Capone Gang and the Aiello Gang. A tip came in to the police that a machine gun nest was being set up on the opposite side of Mike Kenna's smoke house shop on Clark Street. Kenna was one of Chicago's corrupt politicians in Capone's pocket. Police were on the lookout in the vicinity when they noticed two Capone hoodlums on the street. Louis Campagna and Anthony Ricci, aka Tony Gobels, were arrested on State Street in Chicago's Loop area while looking in store windows. The police officer, the infamous William Drury, asked them what they were doing there. Campagna replied that they were business agents for the Newsboys Union. Drury found each carrying a .45 revolver and both were arrested. It was mentioned that Tony Gobels was wanted in connection with an unknown charge. However, the charge from this arrest was later dismissed after the evidence was suppressed. The police report listed Tony "The King" Gobels as a "great big fellow" about 6'3" in height and weighing 240 pounds. After they fingerprinted Gobels, no record could be found but the police did discover that he was a so-called "big wig" from New York with lots of "power" behind him.

In 1931 Campagna had become very wealthy and reached a high point in the Capone Gang. He purchased an 880-acre working farm and listed thirty-five acres of corn, ten acres of oats and 110 hogs. He was also named as the "traffic manager" for the Capone Gang around this time, just as Al Capone was going away to prison for tax evasion. His advice was always asked for when making Capone Gang decisions which eventually lead to Campagna's role as adviser to future mob bosses.

One report mentions that around 1932 Al Capone was arrested for vagrancy and three of Capone's bodyguards, one being Campagna, waited in front of the police headquarters at 11th and State Streets for Capone to be released. Police, who were not going to allow Capone gangsters in front of their home base, went out and arrested all three. Found on all three were loaded .45 caliber pistols.

December 20, 1932 a crazy incident was reported stating that Louis Campagna was listed as being in court with John Pope, Louis Messessa, Martin Sanders, Joseph Parrillo and Charles McGee. The charge stemmed from an incident where all the men were in the office of Frank Nitti on December 19, 1932 when Nitti was shot by a Chicago police officer. Nitti lived and all were released on habeas corpus.

A setback occurred in 1934 when Louis Campagna was incapacitated for several months with a nervous disorder characterized by irritability, headache, and hot flashes. He recovered from this illness and resumed his roll in the Capone Gang.

In July 1936, Louis Campagna was listed with gangster Frank "The Enforcer" Nitti and Illinois State Representative James J. Adduci as the head of the Sicilian Camorra in Chicago controlling all illegal operations in that city and its surrounding areas. That lead to both Nitti and Campagna being arrested on August 12, 1936 to be questioned in the murder of Illinois State Representative John M. Bolton. Bolton was killed on July 4, 1936. After being released both were again picked up by police and questioned about the murder of Albert J. Prignano, but were released on writ of habeas corpus.

By 1939 Louis Campagna had been Frank Nitti's bodyguard and one of his advisers. He had been given a new assignment by Nitti; he now was in charge of cracking down on bookie joints in Chicago forcing the proprietors to agree to a cut for the Capone Gang or else. As a result, one-third of the profits were turned over to the Capone Gang's representative, adding a new flow of cash to the Outfit.

Around this time Campagna also opened his own bookie joint with Sheeny Yario at 161 North Wabash Avenue in Chicago. He also became partners with Joseph "Fifkie" Corngold and Willie Heeney in the El Patio Tavern at 5914 Cermak Road in Cicero, Illinois. The El Patio, a very profitable gambling house was the headquarters of Anthony "Mops" Volpe in 1944, a Capone gunman. Campagna was also a partner with Capone gangsters Joseph Corngold and Willie Heeney in another gambling joint known as the Austin Club located on the second floor at 5941 West Roosevelt Road in Cicero.

After the United States was attacked by Japan and the country entered World War II, Louis Campagna got caught lying on his questionnaire for the Selective Service Board. He had failed to mention that in December 1941 he purchased a $100,000 farm near Berrien Springs, Michigan. The property contained a tennis court, swimming pool and an underground waterway system which was rare in those days.

When Campagna arrived at Leavenworth prison for his conviction in the Hollywood extortion case his official statement was, *"I was supposed to have taken money from a movie union by threats. I pleaded not guilty."*

The Leavenworth report read, *"In regard to the instant offense, like his codefendants he pleads not guilty. He says he was implicated only by association and is bitter against the individual who involved him and his codefendants, claiming that this individual lied. When he said that he and the subject were partners, the subject claims that they were not and this individual did not tell the truth."*

Campagna told the prison authorities he was a gambler and speculator most of his life and his work record was very irregular. The prison summary of impression was, *"During the interview he was evasive and parried questions in an effort to avoid giving information. He has a prior record of bank robbery and claims clear conduct record while incarcerated. His quarantine adjustment has been unsatisfactory and unless his attitude and outlook changes he will become involved in difficulties here. The instant offense indicates a vicious nature and in view of this, his gang connections, and possible detainer, he should be given careful supervision."*

Life in Leavenworth was not pleasant for Campagna. His prison record said he was lazy and went to great lengths to avoid any kind of work. He was very unconcerned and indifferent and was said to "just get along" with his fellow inmates. Prison guards said that Campagna needed occasional checking up on as to his cleanliness and had a pattern of being emotional and moody.

While Louis was in prison, his wife Charlotte was said to own a flower shop in Chicago while watching over the 880-acre farm through an overseer. Louis claimed that his wife was financially independent. Investigators frequently observed Charlotte's car at the house of deceased mob boss Frank Nitti in 1944.

An investigation disclosed that in the 1940's the flower shop known as Orchid Flower Shop was owned by Charlotte Campagna and Marie Capezio, wife of top mobster Tony "Caps" Capezio who died in 1955 when struck by lightning while playing golf. They had a man by the name of Louis Ancarola run the flower shop for them. The flower shop's top buyer of flowers was Chicago Local 777 and mobster Joey Glimco.

Campagna was still considered a top boss in Chicago. He never expressed an interest in taking the top seat from DeLucia or Accardo but he did still control certain areas. He controlled Arthur X. Elrod who was the ward committeeman of the old 24th Ward and county commissioner in Chicago. He had mobster Willie Heeney giving him 60 % of the "take" in Cicero, Illinois with 25% going to Heeney and the other 15% going to Joseph Corngold to take care of public officials and himself. Campagna did have a mail fraud incitement against him but it was nolle processed on May 6, 1947.

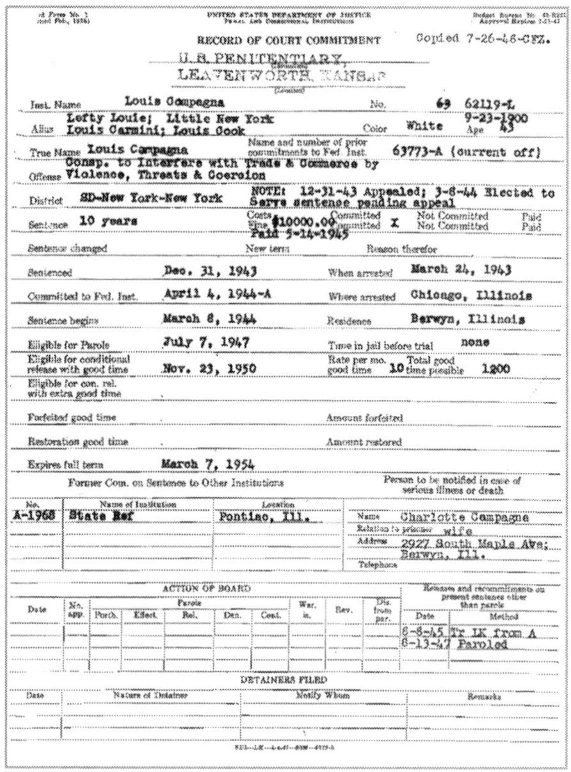

UNITED STATES DEPARTMENT OF JUSTICE
PENAL AND CORRECTIONAL INSTITUTIONS

RECORD OF COURT COMMITMENT   Copied 7-26-46-CFZ.

U.S. PENITENTIARY,
LEAVENWORTH, KANSAS

Inst. Name: Louis Campagna   No. 63 62119-L
Alias: Lefty Louie; Little New York; Louis Carmini; Louis Cook   Color: White   Age: 43 (9-23-1900)
True Name: Louis Campagna   Name and number of prior commitments to Fed. Inst.: 63773-A (current off)
Offense: Consp. to Interfere with Trade & Commerce by Violence, Threats & Coercion
District: SD-New York-New York   NOTE: 12-31-43 Appealed; 3-8-44 Elected to Serve sentence pending appeal
Sentence: 10 years   Costs / Fine: $10000.00 Committed X; Paid 5-14-1945
Sentence changed   New term   Reason therefor
Sentenced: Dec. 31, 1943   When arrested: March 24, 1943
Committed to Fed. Inst.: April 4, 1944-A   Where arrested: Chicago, Illinois
Sentence begins: March 8, 1944   Residence: Berwyn, Illinois
Eligible for Parole: July 7, 1947   Time in jail before trial: none
Eligible for conditional release with good time: Nov. 23, 1950   Rate per mo. good time: 10   Total good time possible: 1200
Eligible for con. rel. with extra good time
Forfeited good time   Amount forfeited
Restoration good time   Amount restored
Expires full term: March 7, 1954

Former Com. on Sentence to Other Institutions

No.	Name of Institution	Location
A-1968	State Ref	Pontiac, Ill.

Person to be notified in case of serious illness or death
Name: Charlotte Campagne
Relation to prisoner: wife
Address: 2927 South Maple Ave; Berwyn, Ill.
Telephone

ACTION OF BOARD

Releases and recommitments on present sentence other than parole

Date	Method
8-8-45	Tr LK from A
8-13-47	Paroled

DETAINERS FILED

Date	Nature of Detainer	Notify Whom	Remarks

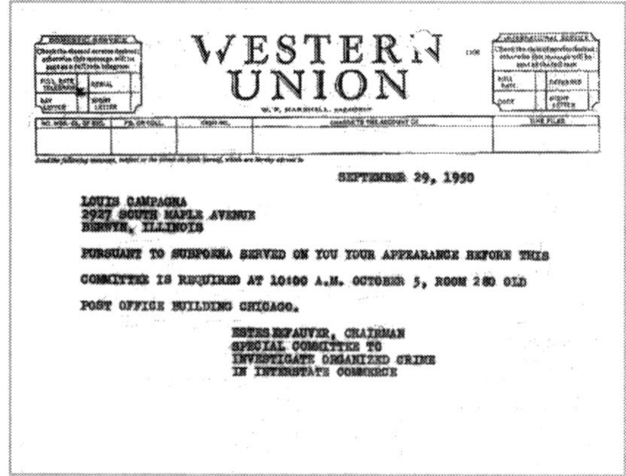

WESTERN UNION

SEPTEMBER 29, 1950

LOUIS CAMPAGNA
2927 SOUTH MAPLE AVENUE
BERWYN, ILLINOIS

PURSUANT TO SUBPOENA SERVED ON YOU YOUR APPEARANCE BEFORE THIS COMMITTEE IS REQUIRED AT 10:00 A.M. OCTOBER 5, ROOM 280 OLD POST OFFICE BUILDING CHICAGO.

ESTES KEFAUVER, CHAIRMAN
SPECIAL COMMITTEE TO
INVESTIGATE ORGANIZED CRIME
IN INTERSTATE COMMERCE

Louis Campagna telegram to appear before the Senate Committee

Tony Dark

Transcripts of Louis Campagna being question by the committee

62 ORGANIZED CRIME IN INTERSTATE COMMERCE

Mr. ROBINSON. For how long?
Mr. CAMPAGNA. 15 or 18 years.
Mr. ROBINSON. Do you know him intimately?
Mr. CAMPAGNA. I would say yes.
Mr. ROBINSON. Do you know Mr. DeLucia?
Mr. CAMPAGNA. I do.
Mr. ROBINSON. You have known him intimately?
Mr. CAMPAGNA. That is right.
Mr. ROBINSON. For how long?
Mr. CAMPAGNA. I would say about the same.
Mr. ROBINSON. How about Gioe?
Mr. CAMPAGNA. I have known him for quite a while, too.
Mr. ROBINSON. Where did you come from originally?
Mr. CAMPAGNA. Originally?
Mr. ROBINSON. Yes.
Mr. CAMPAGNA. Well, I hit, I think, Chicago in 1915. I was all over the country. I left home.
Mr. ROBINSON. What were you doing at that time?
Mr. CAMPAGNA. Just bumming around.
Mr. ROBINSON. You had no source of income at that time?
Mr. CAMPAGNA. No; I was just working and getting a little money and bumming around.
Mr. ROBINSON. How would you get the money?
Mr. CAMPAGNA. Working.
Mr. ROBINSON. Did you get it any other way?
Mr. CAMPAGNA. No, sir.
Mr. ROBINSON. Were you convicted of robbery at one time?
Mr. CAMPAGNA. I was; in 1919.
Mr. ROBINSON. You served time for that?
Mr. CAMPAGNA. I did, sir.
Mr. ROBINSON. How old were you then?
Mr. CAMPAGNA. About 17, 18.
Mr. ROBINSON. How come you settled in Chicago?
Mr. CAMPAGNA. Well, I guess it was a good city to live in.
Mr. ROBINSON. What was that?
Mr. CAMPAGNA. I guess it was a good city to live in. I liked it.
Mr. ROBINSON. What made up your mind on that score?
Mr. CAMPAGNA. Well, the first thing I had to do my parole there. Then I got working there and I stayed there.
Mr. ROBINSON. Where were you working?
Mr. CAMPAGNA. A print shop. I think it is Van Buren and Market, or Van Buren and Wells.
Mr. ROBINSON. How long did you work there?
Mr. CAMPAGNA. I worked there, I would say, about a year.
Mr. ROBINSON. Then what did you do?
Mr. CAMPAGNA. Just took odd-and-end jobs.
Mr. ROBINSON. When did you start working for Al Capone?
Mr. CAMPAGNA. Well, let's see. I would say I was with him for a couple of years around 1927.
Mr. ROBINSON. When?
Mr. CAMPAGNA. 1927.
Mr. ROBINSON. He brought you to Chicago, didn't he?
Mr. CAMPAGNA. No, sir; he did not.

ORGANIZED CRIME IN INTERSTATE COMMERCE 63

Mr. ROBINSON. Who brought you there?
Mr. CAMPAGNA. I brought myself there.
Mr. ROBINSON. How did you first meet him?
Mr. CAMPAGNA. I was hanging around the saloon where he was delivering.
Mr. ROBINSON. Where he was what?
Mr. CAMPAGNA. Delivering.
Mr. ROBINSON. What?
Mr. CAMPAGNA. Delivering beer, I guess.
Mr. ROBINSON. That was during prohibition?
Mr. CAMPAGNA. That is right, sir.
Mr. ROBINSON. Tell us how you happened to meet him.
Mr. CAMPAGNA. That is the way I met him in the saloon. I asked him for a job and went to work for him.
Mr. ROBINSON. What kind of a job?
Mr. CAMPAGNA. Just "tailing" merchandise.
Mr. ROBINSON. Tailing merchandise?
Mr. CAMPAGNA. That is right.
Mr. ROBINSON. What does that mean?
Mr. CAMPAGNA. Like alcohol and beer.
Mr. ROBINSON. I don't understand. Tailing it?
Mr. CAMPAGNA. That is right.
Mr. ROBINSON. How do you tail it?
Mr. CAMPAGNA. Just watching it, seeing nobody robs it.
Mr. ROBINSON. Were you armed?
Mr. CAMPAGNA. No, sir.
Mr. ROBINSON. Never was?
Mr. CAMPAGNA. Well, yes, I have been armed.
Mr. ROBINSON. When did you first start putting on arms?
Mr. CAMPAGNA. When I got in that trouble in 1919.
Mr. ROBINSON. Did you start after you had formed this acquaintance with Capone and started working for him?
Mr. CAMPAGNA. No, I didn't. I stopped after I come out.
Mr. ROBINSON. You never had a gun on while you were working for Capone?
Mr. CAMPAGNA. I was arrested and accused of having a gun on me in 1927 or 1928, I am sure.
Mr. ROBINSON. Did you have a gun on?
Mr. CAMPAGNA. Yes.
Mr. ROBINSON. So you did have a gun on at one time while you were working for Capone?
Mr. CAMPAGNA. That is right.
Mr. ROBINSON. That is while you were tailing?
Mr. CAMPAGNA. No, I wasn't doing nothing. I got arrested in the morning downtown.
Mr. ROBINSON. Did you also drive for Capone, chauffeur?
Mr. CAMPAGNA. No, I drove several times out to the dog track with him, but I wouldn't say I was a chauffeur. I mean there were other people around that were chauffeurs, but sometimes he asked me to drive and I drove him out.
Mr. ROBINSON. You were one of his bodyguards, weren't you?
Mr. CAMPAGNA. I wouldn't say that.
Mr. ROBINSON. Well, were you or weren't you?
Mr. CAMPAGNA. No.

64 ORGANIZED CRIME IN INTERSTATE COMMERCE

Mr. Robinson. Never was?
Mr. Campagna. No. I may be accused of a lot of things.
Mr. Robinson. How many times were you arrested?
Mr. Campagna. On numerous times. I just don't recall about how many.
Mr. Robinson. Do you know Greenberg?
Mr. Campagna. Yes; I know him.
Mr. Robinson. How long have you known him?
Mr. Campagna. Oh, I have known him, I would say, a few years.
Mr. Robinson. About the time you met Capone?
Mr. Campagna. No, it was away after that.
Mr. Robinson. What was your actual business with Capone?
Mr. Campagna. I just explained, just working for him.
Mr. Robinson. How much did you get for that?
Mr. Campagna. About $50 a week.
Mr. Robinson. Did you get anything else from any other source at that time?
Mr. Campagna. No; I did not.
Mr. Robinson. What have been your union activities?
Mr. Campagna. None.
Mr. Robinson. No connection with any union?
Mr. Campagna. No, sir.
Mr. Robinson. Never at any time?
Mr. Campagna. No, sir.
Mr. Robinson. Were you involved in any union litigation?
Mr. Campagna. Well, yes; in this extortion of 1943, I was.
Mr. Robinson. Prior to that?
Mr. Campagna. Prior to that, I was not. It goes back. It is a conspiracy, they say, to 1934–35.
Mr. Robinson. Do you know Frank Nitti?
Mr. Campagna. Yes.
Mr. Robinson. When did you meet him?
Mr. Campagna. I met Frank around 1928 or 1929, something like that.
Mr. Robinson. And you stated you know Paul Ricca?
Mr. Campagna. That is right.
Mr. Robinson. What was Paul Ricca's connection with Al Capone?
Mr. Campagna. That I never did know.
Mr. Robinson. You never did know that?
Mr. Campagna. That is right.
Mr. Robinson. Well, you knew it was a close association?
Mr. Campagna. No; I wouldn't say that. To me the man was close with a lot of people. I couldn't say which one was close and which wasn't.
Mr. Robinson. Name some he was close to.
Mr. Campagna. I don't know them.
Mr. Robinson. Well, he was close to Ricca?
Mr. Campagna. Not that I know of.
Mr. Robinson. How about Murray Humphreys?
Mr. Campagna. I don't know him.
Mr. Robinson. You don't know him?
Mr. Campagna. I say I don't know. You say was he close to Al. I don't know.

ORGANIZED CRIME IN INTERSTATE COMMERCE 65

Mr. Robinson. How long have you known him?
Mr. Campagna. I have known Humphreys for a few years.
Mr. Robinson. How long?
Mr. Campagna. Eight or seven years.
Mr. Robinson. Were you ever associated in business with him?
Mr. Campagna. None whatever.
Mr. Robinson. What business was he in?
Mr. Campagna. I don't know.
Mr. Robinson. Have you ever had any knowledge of what business he was in?
Mr. Campagna. No, sir; I do not.
Mr. Robinson. Or what his source of income was?
Mr. Campagna. No; I did not.
Mr. Robinson. How about Jack Guzik?
Mr. Campagna. I know him.
Mr. Robinson. How long?
Mr. Campagna. Ten or 12 years.
Mr. Robinson. What business is he in?
Mr. Campagna. I don't know.
Mr. Robinson. Were you ever associated with him?
Mr. Campagna. Before? If you call associated meeting him in the cafe for dinner——
Mr. Robinson. Let me put it this way. Were you ever associated with him in any business activity in connection with gambling?
Mr. Campagna. No, sir.
Mr. Robinson. Never at any time?
Mr. Campagna. No, sir.
Mr. Robinson. Fred Evans?
Mr. Campagna. Fred Evans, I have known him for quite a few years.
Mr. Robinson. What business was he in?
Mr. Campagna. That I don't know.
Mr. Robinson. Were you ever associated in business with him?
Mr. Campagna. No, sir.
Mr. Robinson. Louis Romano?
Mr. Campagna. No, sir.
Mr. Robinson. You knew him?
Mr. Campagna. Yes; I do.
Mr. Robinson. You don't know what business?
Mr. Campagna. No.
Mr. Robinson. Danny Stanton?
Mr. Campagna. No.
Mr. Robinson. Joe Fusco?
Mr. Campagna. No, sir.
Mr. Robinson. You know Pete Fosco?
Mr. Campagna. I know him.
Mr. Robinson. Who is he?
Mr. Campagna. Committeeman, first ward.
Mr. Robinson. How about Joe Fusco?
Mr. Campagna. I know him.
Mr. Robinson. That is the committeeman?
Mr. Campagna. No.
Mr. Robinson. Who is Joe Fusco?

Tony Dark

66 ORGANIZED CRIME IN INTERSTATE COMMERCE

Mr. CAMPAGNA. I think he is in the liquor business if I am not mistaken. I am not positive of that, what he is, but that is what I think it is.

Mr. ROBINSON. You were never in business with him?

Mr. CAMPAGNA. No; I was not.

Mr. ROBINSON. How about Johnny Patton?

Mr. CAMPAGNA. No; I was not.

Mr. ROBINSON. Do you know him?

Mr. CAMPAGNA. Know of him.

Mr. ROBINSON. Never met him?

Mr. CAMPAGNA. I don't know whether I did or not.

Mr. ROBINSON. Phil D'Andrea?

Mr. CAMPAGNA. Yes, I know him.

Mr. ROBINSON. How long have you know him?

Mr. CAMPAGNA. I have known him for a few years previous to this trouble.

Mr. ROBINSON. What business was he in?

Mr. CAMPAGNA. I don't know.

Mr. ROBINSON. Ralph Pearce?

Mr. CAMPAGNA. I know him.

Mr. ROBINSON. How long have you known him?

Mr. CAMPAGNA. A few years before this trouble.

Mr. ROBINSON. Have you ever been associated in business with him?

Mr. CAMPAGNA. No, sir; I was not.

Mr. ROBINSON. Did you ever work for the Fischettis?

Mr. CAMPAGNA. No, sir.

Mr. ROBINSON. Do you know them?

Mr. CAMPAGNA. Know of them.

Mr. ROBINSON. Know of them?

Mr. CAMPAGNA. Yes.

Mr. ROBINSON. Ever met them?

Mr. CAMPAGNA. I know Charles.

Mr. ROBINSON. What was your connection with Charles?

Mr. CAMPAGNA. Dinner, no connection at all.

Mr. ROBINSON. When did you first meet him?

Mr. CAMPAGNA. That I don't know. I think it was at the Chez Paree at one time having dinner.

Mr. ROBINSON. Was it at the time you were working for Capone?

Mr. CAMPAGNA. No; I don't think so. I think it was after that.

Mr. ROBINSON. Did your first meeting of any of these people occur while you were working for Capone?

Mr. CAMPAGNA. Some may have.

Mr. ROBINSON. In fact, it was most of them; wasn't it?

Mr. CAMPAGNA. No; I wouldn't say most of them.

Mr. ROBINSON. Did you ever go under the name of Carmini?

Mr. CAMPAGNA. Yes; I did.

Mr. ROBINSON. When?

Mr. CAMPAGNA. I judge around 1930. I used it once or twice.

Mr. ROBINSON. What other names have you gone under?

Mr. CAMPAGNA. I just can't recall offhand. Many times I would stop in the hotel and give a fictitious name.

The CHAIRMAN. What did you go under the name of Carmini for?

Mr. CAMPAGNA. I don't know.

ORGANIZED CRIME IN INTERSTATE COMMERCE 67

Mr. ROBINSON. What would you change your name for?

Mr. CAMPAGNA. I would do it many times when I stopped at the hotel and just give my name.

Mr. ROBINSON. Some particular reason for it?

Mr. CAMPAGNA. No; there was no reason for it.

Mr. ROBINSON. Where did you acquire the name "Little New York"?

Mr. CAMPAGNA. That was pinned on me by the newspapers.

Mr. ROBINSON. Because you originally came from New York?

Mr. CAMPAGNA. From Brooklyn; that is right.

Mr. ROBINSON. Do you know Jack McGurn?

Mr. CAMPAGNA. I did know him; yes.

Mr. ROBINSON. What did he do?

Mr. CAMPAGNA. That I don't know.

Mr. ROBINSON. You have no knowledge of what Jack McGurn did?

Mr. CAMPAGNA. No.

Mr. ROBINSON. Did he work for Capone?

Mr. CAMPAGNA. I don't know.

Mr. ROBINSON. How about Frankie and Mike Kelly?

Mr. CAMPAGNA. I know of them.

Mr. ROBINSON. When did you first learn about them or meet them?

Mr. CAMPAGNA. I don't know. Casually being in the booking game at that time, you met a lot of people. I guess every one of them played horses or liked to play horses.

Mr. ROBINSON. Did you meet them while working with Capone?

Mr. CAMPAGNA. I didn't work with Capone very long, so I don't know.

Mr. ROBINSON. How long did you work for Capone?

Mr. CAMPAGNA. A couple of years at tops. I don't think it was even a couple of years.

Mr. ROBINSON. Always at the same pay?

Mr. CAMPAGNA. That is all I ever got from him.

Mr. ROBINSON. $50 a week?

Mr. CAMPAGNA. That is right, and that is why I left.

Mr. ROBINSON. Ernie Rossick?

Mr. CAMPAGNA. I never knew him.

Mr. ROBINSON. James and Rocco Belcastro?

Mr. CAMPAGNA. No.

Mr. ROBINSON. Rocco Finelli?

Mr. CAMPAGNA. No.

Mr. ROBINSON. Frank Diamond?

Mr. CAMPAGNA. Yes; I know him.

Mr. ROBINSON. What did he do?

Mr. CAMPAGNA. I don't know.

The CHAIRMAN. Mr. Campagna, how is it that you know these people, and you know some of them pretty well, and you do not know what they do?

Mr. CAMPAGNA. Well, usually you don't ask people their business, how they make their money, or religion, or politics. If they volunteered, the only thing I could say is what they told me. If you meet a man in the cafe or book, you are not sociable with him.

The CHAIRMAN. If you know them, you know what they do.

Mr. CAMPAGNA. A fellow could surmise that they are bookmaking, but it would be foolish for me to say what I surmised.

Mr. ROBINSON. Let us have your surmise of what Jack McGurn did.
Mr. CAMPAGNA. I don't know.
Mr. ROBINSON. What was his nickname?
Mr. CAMPAGNA. I never did know his nickname.
Mr. ROBINSON. Do you know whether he had a nickname?
Mr. CAMPAGNA. That I never asked. I don't know.
Mr. ROBINSON. You know it was "Machine Gun" Jack McGurn.
Mr. CAMPAGNA. If you say so. That is what the papers say. I will have to say "Yes," because I read that, but I don't know.
Mr. ROBINSON. Do you know Claude Maddox?
Mr. CAMPAGNA. Yes.
Mr. ROBINSON. How long?
Mr. CAMPAGNA. A few years.
Mr. ROBINSON. What business is he in?
Mr. CAMPAGNA. What I know, I think he was interested in some kind of saloon out there in Cicero. I don't know. That is just hearsay.
Mr. ROBINSON. Sam Hunt.
Mr. CAMPAGNA. I know of him.
Mr. ROBINSON. You say you know of him?
Mr. CAMPAGNA. That is right.
Mr. ROBINSON. You never met him?
Mr. CAMPAGNA. Not to my knowledge.
Mr. ROBINSON. Do you know James Ragen?
Mr. CAMPAGNA. No, sir.
Mr. ROBINSON. Patrick Burns?
Mr. CAMPAGNA. No, sir.
Mr. ROBINSON. Do you know any people connected with the wire service business?
Mr. CAMPAGNA. No, sir.
Mr. ROBINSON. Hymie Levin?
Mr. CAMPAGNA. I know Hymie; yes.
Mr. ROBINSON. How long have you known him?
Mr. CAMPAGNA. I know Hymie for quite a few years. I met him at Mayo Bros.
Mr. ROBINSON. What business is he in?
Mr. CAMPAGNA. Bookmaking. I surmise. I cannot positively say. You are asking me to surmise. I am just giving you that.
Mr. ROBINSON. Roy Jones?
Mr. CAMPAGNA. No.
Mr. ROBINSON. You don't know him?
Mr. CAMPAGNA. No, sir.
Mr. ROBINSON. Do you know any of the Kellys of the wire service business?
Mr. CAMPAGNA. No, sir; I do not.
The CHAIRMAN. How about this fellow Curry?
Mr. CAMPAGNA. I know of him.
The CHAIRMAN. You know him personally?
Mr. CAMPAGNA. Yes; I met him.
The CHAIRMAN. He was in the wire service business, was he not?
Mr. CAMPAGNA. Not that I know of. I read about this wire stuff while I was in the penitentiary. I never heard about it before.
Mr. ROBINSON. Who visited you in the penitentiary?
Mr. CAMPAGNA. My wife, my children, my lawyer, Mr. Bernstein.

Mr. CAMPAGNA. I supposed through court. I don't know the process.
Mr. ROBINSON. You knew there was money owed.
Mr. CAMPAGNA. Yes, that is right.
Mr. ROBINSON. Did you ask him, "Well, did my wife give you the money?"
Mr. CAMPAGNA. No, I didn't ask him anything. To the best of my knowledge, I didn't. I just took it for granted it was taken care of.
Mr. ROBINSON. By being taken care of, it was paid?
Mr. CAMPAGNA. That is right.
Mr. ROBINSON. And you didn't ask where he got the money to pay it?
Mr. CAMPAGNA. That is right.
Mr. ROBINSON. From your wife or somebody else?
Mr. CAMPAGNA. That is right.
Mr. ROBINSON. You didn't ask him about that?
Mr. CAMPAGNA. That is right.
The CHAIRMAN. Did you have a big amount of money put away at that time?
Mr. CAMPAGNA. I wouldn't say a big amount. I had some money.
The CHAIRMAN. How much?
Mr. CAMPAGNA. I judge around $30,000.
The CHAIRMAN. Did you ask him whether he used that money?
Mr. CAMPAGNA. He wouldn't know where to get it and nobody else would.
Mr. ROBINSON. Where did you have it?
Mr. CAMPAGNA. I had it hidden.
Mr. ROBINSON. I asked you if you had any money around the house and you said the most you had was seven or eight thousand dollars.
Mr. CAMPAGNA. That is right.
Mr. ROBINSON. That was in your house.
Mr. CAMPAGNA. That is right.
Mr. ROBINSON. Apparently you had some at some place outside of the house that was not in a bank or safe deposit.
Mr. CAMPAGNA. That is right.
Mr. ROBINSON. Where was that?
Mr. CAMPAGNA. It was in some fellow's house.
Mr. ROBINSON. Who was the fellow?
(No response.)
The CHAIRMAN. That is a proper question.
Mr. CAMPAGNA. Well, I will be frank, I had it at home. I didn't want my wife or nobody to know about it. I was going to go away for quite a while and I didn't know——
Mr. ROBINSON. You had it hidden in your own home?
Mr. CAMPAGNA. That is right.
Mr. HALLEY. Now, you are either lying now or you were before. You said it was in another fellow's house. You said it was not in your house. You are trying not to tell the committee where you had it. As counsel for the committee, I would advise the committee not to accept the answer.
The CHAIRMAN. You said it was in somebody's house.
Mr. HALLEY. You were definite about it.
Mr. CAMPAGNA. I would like to retract the statement.
Mr. HALLEY. Your retraction has no effect at all, because the way you testified, it is quite clear it was not in your own house, that it was

in somebody else's house, and after the chairman told you you had to answer the question, and say in whose house it was, you changed your testimony. You are lying either now or then. Which way do you want to have it. Either way you are committing perjury. Which way do you want it?

Mr. CAMPAGNA. I had it at home.

Mr. HALLEY. You mean you were lying when you told the committee it was in somebody else's house?

Mr. CAMPAGNA. I wasn't lying. I just said somebody else's house.

Mr. HALLEY. That was a lie, wasn't it? It was untrue, was it not?

Mr. CAMPAGNA. I wouldn't say it was untrue.

Mr. HALLEY. I would say it was untrue. You said it. You used those words, did you not?

Mr. CAMPAGNA. I did.

Mr. HALLEY. And you knew what you were saying?

Mr. CAMPAGNA. No I didn't know what I was saying.

Mr. HALLEY. You didn't know what you were saying when you said it was in somebody else's house?

Mr. CAMPAGNA. No.

Mr. HALLEY. You are lying again. This is the third lie when you say that you didn't know what you were saying.

Mr. CAMPAGNA. I just told you that I had it home. I didn't want anybody to know where I had it.

Mr. HALLEY. You told Mr. Robinson quite definitely that you didn't have it home. Then you had it in somebody's house. Then he asked whose house, and you hesitated to answer, and the chairman said you had to answer. Then you changed your testimony and you said you had it in your own house. Now, one or the other statement was untrue, is that not so?

Mr. CAMPAGNA. I suppose.

Mr. HALLEY. Well, isn't it?

The CHAIRMAN. Where did you have the money?

Mr. CAMPAGNA. I had it home.

Mr. ROBINSON. I asked you a short while ago how much money you had in your house and you told me, I believe, seven or eight thousand dollars.

Mr. CAMPAGNA. That is right.

Mr. ROBINSON. Now you are telling me that you had $30,000 in your house.

Mr. CAMPAGNA. I said around $30,000, I am not sure.

Mr. ROBINSON. So when I asked you how much you had in the house previously, you didn't tell me the total amount that you had in the house.

Mr. CAMPAGNA. Well, that is what I meant.

Mr. ROBINSON. In other words, you didn't intend to say anything about the $30,000 that you had hidden somewhere.

Mr. CAMPAGNA. No; I would say something. The question would come up about the income, and I would tell you about it, and I would tell the truth about it.

Mr. HALLEY. You realize you perjured yourself with one answer or the other.

Mr. CAMPAGNA. I am telling you the truth. You are asking questions and I am giving you the best of my knowledge.

Mr. HALLEY. I think you are doing the opposite.

Mr. CAMPAGNA. I don't think so. You misunderstand me in a lot of things.

The CHAIRMAN. I think it might be very well for the committee to go back over this record and review the questions and answers, and see if this witness has perjured himself. After all, he is on parole. I think we might have a short recess for that purpose.

Mr. HALLEY. I agree.

The CHAIRMAN. Will you wait outside, Mr. Campagna, while we go over this matter?

Mr. CAMPAGNA. Yes, sir.

(A short recess was taken.)

The CHAIRMAN. Mr. Campagna, the committee is not satisfied with the answers you have given to this question about where the money was. You have given two different answers. So that unless you have some further statement you want to make about anything, we will have no further questions to ask you at this time.

Mr. CAMPAGNA. That is the only thing. I told you the truth. I had it at home. I just didn't want to divulge I had it at home. Not that I made any wrong statements here or anything else. A lot of things you asked me naturally a person cannot remember 15 or 18 years ago, 7 or 8 or 10 years ago. I am trying to do the best I can. I am not here to lie to you or hurt anybody.

The CHAIRMAN. Do you have any other statement you want to make?

Mr. CAMPAGNA. Well, that is all I can say. I have answered truthfully everything I have known. I have tried my best to the best of my knowledge.

The CHAIRMAN. We will take this matter under advisement for future action, but I see no reason for going on. You will remain under subpena, Mr. Campagna.

Mr. CAMPAGNA. Do I have to stay here in town?

The CHAIRMAN. You do not have to stay in town, but when you are notified to come back or subject to any further action of the Senate, you will appear.

Mr. CAMPAGNA. That is right.

The CHAIRMAN. That is all.

Mr. CAMPAGNA. I hope I done the best I could for you.

The CHAIRMAN. Mr. Gioe, will you hold up your right hand?

Do you solemnly swear that the testimony you give this committee will be the truth, the whole truth, and nothing but the truth, so help you God?

Mr. GIOE. I do.

The CHAIRMAN. All right, Mr. Robinson.

TESTIMONY OF CHARLES GIOE, CHICAGO, ILL.

Mr. ROBINSON. Will you state your full name?

Mr. GIOE. Charles Gioe.

Mr. ROBINSON. Is that spelled G-i-o-e?

Mr. GIOE. Yes, sir.

Mr. ROBINSON. What is your residence?

Mr. GIOE. 200 East Chestnut Street.

Mr. ROBINSON. Chicago?

Mr. GIOE. Yes, sir.

Mob Boss

On December 29, 1952 FBI agents interviewed Louis Campagna at his home. Campagna denied he had any contact with any underworld figures since his release from prison in 1947. He told the FBI his only income was from his farms, one in Fowler, Indiana and the other in Berrien Springs, Michigan. He did admit he had a "private cash reserve" which he said he acquired before the extortion case in 1943.

In 1954 Louis Campagna became the subject of an FBI investigation. Campagna had put up half of the money to fund the construction of a new four-million-dollar-shopping center and a Howard Johnson Restaurant at Irving Park Road and Harlem Avenue in Norridge, Illinois.

The corporation that purchased the land, Lonny and Associates of Chicago, had been promised that they would have no problems of any kind in the building and operations of the shopping center. Another Howard Johnson Restaurant at 4240 North Harlem Avenue in Norridge, Illinois had been bombed and then burned down when the new Howard Johnson was reported to be opening.

On January 10, 1955 Illinois Sheriff's Police raided Campagna's gambling joint known as the Hilltop at 4819 West 65th Street. They arrested 100 gamblers but Campagna was nowhere to be found. Law enforcement detectives labeled Louis Campagna as the mob's main strategist. He was fifth in line of succession by 1955. One FBI agent reported that Louis Campagna had a secret home in Ironwood, Michigan, where he had been living under a surname. It was reported that he had a relative named Frank Campagna who lived in Ironwood and this "hideaway" was actually his brother's house. Informants in 1954 did mention to police that Louis Campagna arrived in Northern Wisconsin a few days before Frank Maritote "Frank Diamond" was killed in Chicago. It was also mentioned that Campagna would occasionally stop by Ralph Capone's home in Mercer, Wisconsin when going to see his brother.

Miami FBI agents would take note as Louis Campagna spent his winters in Miami. He would stay in a villa at the old Golden Strand Hotel at Miami Beach between December and April under the name of Louis Shakiny. Agents would often see Paul DeLucia, Tony Accardo, Joe Fischetti, John "Mimi" Capone and Martin Guilfoyle visit the villa. Investigators noticed that during the 1953-54 and 1954-55 winter season Campagna was always accompanied by mobster William Daddono acting as body guard and driver.

On May 30, 1955 Louis Campagna was 16 miles off the coast of Miami Beach, Florida fishing on a yacht owned by a wealthy Chicago attorney named William Scott Stewart. On board the yacht, named "Nellie", which used to be owned by Tony Accardo who called it the "Clair-Jo," were his brother Anthony Campagna, mobsters Joe Fischetti, Paul DeLucia, Tony Gobels and John Capone, Al Capone's brother, and William Stewart. In the middle of the trip Louis Campagna suffered a heart attack. A Coast Guard helicopter was called and before the helicopter could reach the mainland and Miami's Mercy Hospital, Campagna was dead.

Anthony Campagna told the press that he, his brother and Stewart were aboard. He said Louis had just caught a large fish and began to reel it in and once the fish was aboard Louis cried out and collapsed. Anthony told the press his brother had been having heart problems for over a year and that he had been in Miami for only one week.

His body arrived at Chicago's Midway Airport in a plain wooden box. No one was there to pick up the body so it had to be stored in a freight hanger until his body was retrieved. Once picked up, his body was placed in a solid bronze casket worth thousands of dollars.

His two-night wake was held at 2921 South Harlem Avenue in Berwyn by the Rago Brothers. An investigation report said that Tony Accardo stood at the door of the funeral parlor and would only admit family and senior mobsters into the wake.

Investigators noted the following mobsters who were allowed in:

Joey "Doves" Aiuppa
Gus and Sam Alex
William "Smokes" Aloisio
Joe Amato
Sam Battaglia
James Catuara
Jackie The Lackey" Cerone
William Daddono
Sam Drago
Jim Emery
Ben "Foggie" Fillichio
Rocco and Joe Fischetti
Sam Giancana
Joey Glimco
Fred Grieco
Jake Guzik
Murray Humphreys
Sam Hunt
Lester Kruse
Frank LaPorte
John Lardino
Claude Maddox
Ralph Pierce
Dominic Sibilano

Investigators sat at Mt. Carmel Cemetery in Hillside, Illinois and watched as scores of cars and people arrived at the grave site to watch Campagna lowered into the ground. His casket was made of solid bronze and took ten men to move it even though the little mobster was only 5'2" in height.

Investigators noticed that standing around were Rocco Fischetti, Joey Aiuppa, Sam Hunt, Claude Maddox, William Aloisio and Joey Glimco. Standing in another group surrounded by twenty-five other men was Tony Accardo who used the group of men as cover from reporters. Accardo, dressed in sports clothes and dark sunglasses, stood out of earshot from the final prayer waiting to make his exit. Once the praying was over, Accardo began to walk as fast as he could to his car with about ten of his bodyguards following him, 10 to 15 feet behind. Accardo entered the only non-Cadillac in the cemetery, a Ford automobile, and waited for his wife and driver. While waiting, Accardo glared and hollered at reporters while one of his body guards punched a camera out of the way.

William Scott Stewart, the mob attorney who was with Campagna when he died, told a reporter *"Lou wasn't a bad guy. He wasn't a bad guy at all. He had a good heart."* Absent from the service were judges, city officials and top ranking policemen on order from the boss.

Days after the funeral a search for Campagna's millions was launched, including a search for hidden safety deposit boxes. In his will his estate was estimated at

$55,000 and he left each of his three children $10 each. When Louis Campagna died, other mob figures learned a lesson on what not to do. When both Louis Campagna and Frank "The Enforcer" Nitti died, their "hoodlum" financial interests were so concealed that the relatives of both families could not find all of their hidden money. Not all of Nitti's money was found and very little of Campagna's money was found. It was a lesson to other mobsters that "outfit" members should always put stocks, houses and bank accounts in their wives' names so the money could be accessible to the relatives when the mobster died.

After the funeral the Campagna family attempted to move on but Louis's wife Charlotte was heartbroken. Four months after the death of her husband Charlotte died on August 12, 1955. Years later in an investigation into mobster Joey Glimco it was discovered that when the will and testament of the Campagna's was found, it had been witnessed by Jennie LeBrun, Andrew Cuzzino and Lena Glimco, the wife of Joey Glimco.

STATE OF FLORIDA

OFFICE of VITAL STATISTICS

CERTIFICATE OF DEATH

FLORIDA

STATE BOARD OF HEALTH
BUREAU OF VITAL STATISTICS

STATE FILE NO. 12935
REGISTRAR'S NO. 2787

1. PLACE OF DEATH a. COUNTY — CODE NO. 23-XX
c. LENGTH OF STAY: 1 day
d. FULL NAME OF HOSPITAL OR INSTITUTION: At Sea

2. USUAL RESIDENCE a. STATE: Illinois b. COUNTY: Cook
c. CITY OR TOWN: Berwyn
d. STREET ADDRESS: 2927 South Maple Avenue

3. NAME OF DECEASED a. (First) Louis c. (Last) Campagna
4. DATE OF DEATH: May 30 1955
5. SEX: Male 6. COLOR OR RACE: White 7. MARRIED, NEVER MARRIED, WIDOWED, DIVORCED: Married
8. DATE OF BIRTH: Sept. 23, 1900 9. AGE: 54
10a. USUAL OCCUPATION: Farm Owner 10b. KIND OF BUSINESS OR INDUSTRY: Farming
11. BIRTHPLACE: New York 12. CITIZEN OF WHAT COUNTRY? USA
13. FATHER'S NAME: Louis Campagna
14. MOTHER'S MAIDEN NAME: Marie Campagna
15. WAS DECEASED EVER IN U. S. ARMED FORCES? no
17. INFORMANT'S SIGNATURE: K. E. Gordon
ADDRESS: 710 S.W. 12th Avenue, Miami

18. CAUSE OF DEATH — MEDICAL CERTIFICATION
I. DISEASE OR CONDITION DIRECTLY LEADING TO DEATH (a) Acute Coronary Occlusion
4201-25
20. AUTOPSY? YES [X] NO

22. I hereby certify that I attended the deceased from did not attend D.O.A. ... that I last saw the deceased alive on never ... and that death occurred at 3:50 P.m., from the causes and on the date stated above.
23a. SIGNATURE: David L. Crane, M.D. 23b. ADDRESS: Dade County Court House 23c. DATE SIGNED: 5-31-55
24a. BURIAL, CREMATION, REMOVAL: Removal 24b. DATE: 31 May 1955 24c. NAME OF CEMETERY OR CREMATORY: Mt. Carmel 24d. LOCATION: Hillside Cook Illinois
DATE REC'D BY LOCAL REG.: 5-31-55
25. FUNERAL DIRECTOR'S SIGNATURE: K. E. Gordon — GORDON Funeral Home, Miami

VOID IF ALTERED OR ERASED

Louis Campagna Death Certificate

Authors Collection 2016 ©

Louis and Charlotte Campagna's Graves at Mt. Carmel Cemetery in Hillside, Illinois

Authors Collection 2016 ©

Authors Collection 2016 ©

Mob Boss

Years after Louis Campagna died, his nephew, Frank Campagna, was called as a witness in the tax fraud trial on mob boss Tony Accardo. Frank Campagna was part owner in a Calumet City Illinois liquor store with Mrs. Connie Franzy, a sister of mob boss Frank LaPorte and wife to Tony Franzy. Franzy purchased the Owl Club from Accardo and LaPorte. Frank LaPorte was said to have been moved up through the ranks after Campagna's death to fill the role Campagna held in the Outfit.

Frank Campagna's brother, Rudolph "Rudy" Campagna, resided in Hammond, Indiana and was employed as a horseman for a bookmaking and poker racket run out of Poor Eddie's club in Burnham, Illinois. He was assisted in this operation by a former high-ranking police official in the town of Burnham. This game was under the wing of Frank LaPorte. Rudolph and his brother Frank also owned City Liquors store and Whitey's Lounge, a bail bonds business in Calumet City, Illinois. For some unknown reason, a disagreement developed between Frank LaPorte and the Campagna's so the bail bonds business was turned over to LaPorte's nephew Frank Luzi. In turn, the Campagna's were allowed to continue operating gambling in the Calumet City area.

Rudy Campagna's wife was once married to one of Frank LaPorte's "boys" named Phil Musganero before marrying Campagna. When Mrs. Campagna was interviewed by investigators she said that Rudy was the kind of guy that would gamble only if he knew if the game was rigged or fixed. She even told investigators that she had employed a private detective to find out if Rudy was chasing other women. By 1963 Rudy was living with another woman and had gone legit because he found out the FBI was investigating him and he had an overwhelming fear of being prosecuted and going to prison.

File Card

Louis Campagna
Name on birth certificate Louis Campani
Aka: Little New York (Given to him by Al Capone), Little Old New York, Lefty Louie (New York City nick name), Louis Cook, Louis Carmini, Lugi Compagna, Louis Campagnia, Louis Campagni, Louis LeBrun, Morino C. Cook, Louis Shakiny, Louis Shikany
Born September 23, 1900 (Brooklyn, New York)
Died May 30, 1955 in Miami, Florida
FBI # 618863
Chicago PD # C44831
Weight 161 Pounds
Height 5'2"
Complexion Ruddy
Hair Black, receding hairline

Tony Dark

Family

Father Luigi Campani, Aka Louis
Mother Maria Scardini
Wife Charlotte Shikany, one report says Elizabeth (Died August 12, 1955)
Children: Joseph F. born July 5, 1920 *(College graduate of Notre Dame who joined the Armed Forces and became a war hero in World War II. Once back he married Margaret Hans and went to work for his father-in-law Marin Hans in the Burton Auto Spring Corporation in Chicago)*
Mrs. Dorothy Charles, born July 25, 1922, Chicago. Married Frank Koch, 2927 Maple Avenue, Berwyn, Illinois. *(Listed in 1949 as an intern at Presbyterian Hospital in Chicago)*
Jo Ann Campagna born April 29, 1933 in Chicago
Brother-in-law John Cook. *(A 1951 FBI report listed John Cook as the brother-in-law of Louis Campagna working as an "outside man" for the Illinois Sports News wire)*
Brother-in-law Neil Bishop (Listed as a brother-in-law of Campagna's in 1959)
Brother-in-law George Shikany *(In 1935 George was placed in Chicago labor local 110 of the movie projector operators union. In the 1950's he was listed as living at 3837 Winside Avenue in Hollywood, Illinois)*
Buried with Lucille (1898-1960) and Sigismond (1894-1955)

Known Addresses

286 16TH Street, Brooklyn, New York (1900)
1118 57th Street, Brooklyn, New York. (1900-1915) *(In 1943 Louis Campagna listed his mother living with him in Chicago and receiving $400-a-month for renting this building)*
Pontiac Prison, City of Pontiac, Livingston, Illinois (1920)
517 North Morgan Street, Chicago Illinois (1920's)
2927 Maple Avenue, Chicago (1930's-1943) (A bungalow house)
800-arce farm - Route 1, Berrien Springs, Berrien, Michigan (1937-1950's) *(Officially listed as Section 1, Township 6S, Range 17W, all in town ship of Oronoka at the North end of Kerhard Lane, 1 mile north of Berrien Springs, Michigan)*
2927 South Maple Avenue, Berwyn Illinois (1943-1950's) *(Telephone number Berwyn 3417)*
800 Acre Farm near Fowler, Indiana (1950's)
Ironwood, Michigan (1950's) (Alleged)
Golden Strand Hotel, Miami Beach Florida (1953-1955)

Government Analysis of Louis Campagna in 1945

"He is a pleasant and agreeable, wiry, alert little man, pleasant and agreeable in conversation, but not at all cooperative in talking about his case."

Known Occupation

Labor (1918-1920) (Listed on sons birth certificate)
Factory Worker (1922) *(Listed as his job on daughters birth certificate)*
Gambling Joint at 161 North Wabash, Chicago (1930's)
Operated an 88-acre farm in Berrien Springs, Michigan (1940's)
Operated an 800-acre farm in Fowler, Indiana (1940's)
El Patio Tavern, 5914 West Cermak Road, Cicero, Illinois (Partner) (1940's)
Austin Club Gambling Joint, 5941 West Roosevelt Road, Cicero (1940's)
Farmer, 80 acre farm at Berrien Springs Michigan and 900 acre farm in Fowler, Indiana (1950) (What he told police)

Known Arrest Record of Louis Campagna

Date	Charge	Agency	Result
1917	Armed Robbery	Chicago PD	Not Guilty
10-1-1918	Robbery	Chicago PD	14 Years Prison
3-27-1919	Enter Prison	Pontiac	14 Years
4-8-1924	Paroled	Pontiac	Released
10-10-1924	Parole Violation	Chicago PD	1 Month
11-11-1924	Paroled	Pontiac	Released
4-19-1925	Parole Violation	Chicago PD	U/K
4-4-1928	Vagrancy	Chicago PD	Discharged
4-4-1928	Conspiracy	Chicago PD	Discharged
5-2-1931	Vagrancy	Chicago PD	Discharged
12-19-1932	General Princables	Chicago PD	Released
1-13-1933	Vagrancy	Chicago PD	Discharged
2-14-1933	Vagrancy	Chicago PD	Discharged
10-31-1933	Vagabond Warr.	Chicago PD	Warrant Arrest
2-14-1934	Vagrancy	State's Attorney	Discharged
2-14-1934	Disorderly Conduct	State's Attorney	Dismissed
6-11-1934	Conspiracy	Sheriff Office	Nolle Processe
8- 12-1936	Bolton Murder	Chicago PD	Released
8-1936	Prignano Murder	Chicago PD	Released
12-2-1940	Conspiracy	Unknown	Stricken Off
6-23-1941	Reinstated	Unknown	Nolle Processed
5-6-1947	Mail Fraud	New York	Nolle Processed
10-3-1950	Drury Murder	Chicago PD	Released

UNITED STATES DEPARTMENT OF JUSTICE
FEDERAL BUREAU OF INVESTIGATION
WASHINGTON 25, D. C.

1900.M.W. Louis Campagna J. Edgar Hoover, Director.

The following is the record of FBI number 618 863

CONTRIBUTOR OF FINGERPRINTS	NAME AND NUMBER	ARRESTED OR RECEIVED	CHARGE	DISPOSITION
	#75173, PD, Chgo., Ill.,		arr. 10-1-18, bank robbery.	
* SRef., Pontiac, Ill. *	Louis Campagna #A-1968	4-3-19	robbery	1 to 14 yrs. *paroled 4-8-24
	As Louis Campagna, 10-10-24, vio. of parole; TOT Parole Officer and rel. on parole 11-11-24; disch. 11-1-25.			
PD, Chgo.,Ill.	Louis Carmini #C-44831	12-19-32	G.P.	
USM, Chgo.,Ill.	Louis Campagna #6879	3-24-43	extortion and postal fraud	
USM, Chicago, Ill.	Louis Campagna #6989	4-7-43	extortion	
USM, NYC, N.Y.	Louis Campagna #--	6-8-43	mail fraud	5-6-47 nolle prosequi
FDH, New York, N.Y.	Louis Compagna #41918	2-15-44	Anti-Racketeering Act	10 yrs. 3-25-44 disch. to USP Atlanta
USP, Atlanta, Ga.	Louis Compagna #63773	4-4-44	consp. to interfere with trade and comm by violence, threats and coercion	10 yrs.
USP, Leavenworth, Kans.	Louis Compagna #62119	8-8-45 in trans from USP Atlanta Ga.	Consp. to interfere with trade and Commerce by violence Threats and Coercion	10 yrs.; appealed elected to serve; 8-13-47 paroled

* Represents notations unsupported by fingerprints in FBI files.

NOTICE.—*This Record is furnished for official use only*

Louis Campagna's FBI Rap Sheet of Arrest

UNITED STATES DEPARTMENT OF JUSTICE
FEDERAL BUREAU OF INVESTIGATION
WASHINGTON 25, D. C.

2

The following is the record of FBI number 618 863

J. Edgar Hoover, *Director.*

CONTRIBUTOR OF FINGERPRINTS	NAME AND NUMBER	ARRESTED OR RECEIVED	CHARGE	DISPOSITION
USM, Chicago, Ill.	Louis Campagna #15763	7-23-48	Cond.Rel Vio	del. to USP Atlanta, Ga.
USP, Atlanta, Ga.	Louis Campagna #63773-A	7-24-48	P.V.- consp.to interfere with trade and comm. by violence, threats, and coercion	2398 days 12-20-48 disch. by order of Court

* Represents nota...

UNITED STATES DEPARTMENT OF JUSTICE
FEDERAL BUREAU OF INVESTIGATION
WASHINGTON 25, D. C.

3

The following is the record of FBI number 618 863

J. Edgar Hoover, *Director.*

CONTRIBUTOR OF FINGERPRINTS	NAME AND NUMBER	ARRESTED OR RECEIVED	CHARGE	DISPOSITION

Description:

Color: white
Sex: male
Date of birth: September 23, 1900
Birthplace: Brooklyn, N.Y.
Height: 5 feet 3½ inches
Weight: 165 pounds
Build: short Heavy
Complexion: dark
Eyes: greyish brown
Hair: dark- thin in front
Occupation: farming
Address: in 1948 - 2927 Maple Ave., Berwyn, Ill.
Scars and marks: Oblique scar of 2½" at 3" above left wrist rear, nail L thum dfmd rslt injury; Ft.obl. ½ -1½ mid L Ibrow; Pit scr ½ ab R wing nose,large nose.

* Represents notations unsupported by fingerprints in FBI files.

NOTICE.—*This Record is furnished for official use only*

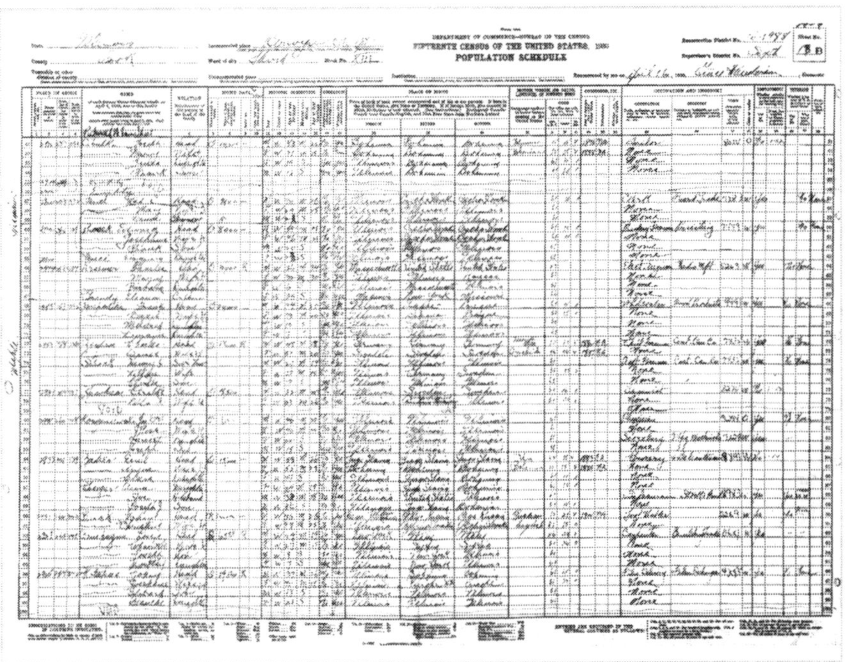

Louis Campagna 1930 Census

92	231	263	341	Campagna Louis	Head	R	65.00	R	M	W	29	M	19	No	Yes	New York
93				— Charlotte	Wife				F	W	27	M	17	No	Yes	Illinois
94				— Joseph	Son				M	W	9	S		Yes	Yes	Illinois
95				— Dorothy	Daughter				F	W	7	S		Yes	Yes	Illinois

New York	Italy	Italy		56	29	0	Carpenter	Building Trade	06X	W	Yes	-	-	92
Illinois	Sicily	Sicily		61	36	0	None							93
Illinois	New York	Illinois		61			None							94
Illinois	New York	Illinois		61			None							95

Charles Gioe

CHARLES GIOE

Charles "Cherry Nose" Gioe said he was born in Chicago on February 6, 1904 to Onofrio and Rosalie "Rose" Gioe. Both his parents were born in Italy and said to have entered the United States around 1900. His father Onofrio found employment in Chicago as a laborer and carpenter and died in 1934 at the age of 78. His mother Rosalie D'Amato died of a stroke in 1939 at the age of 63.

A young Charles Gioe had a steady childhood living at 2102 E. 70th Place in Chicago and attending Carpenter School on Racine Avenue in Chicago between 1911 and 1918. After he graduated from the 8th grade he took to the streets and began to hang out with local hoodlums as they employed him as an errand boy. His brother Anthony "Jackie" Gioe was 8-years younger than Charles and in the 1940's was working as a machine operator.

Gioe told prison authorities he spent most of his life working, managing fighters, being in show business, running exhibitions and running restaurants.

In 1950 he told U.S. Senators during senate hearings that he went to school with Tony Accardo as kids. The two grew up together and lived in the same neighborhood. According to Gioe, both attended The Washington School in Chicago.

In 1950 Gioe testified he was living in Iowa for a short time because he was involved in transporting illegal alcohol from Wisconsin to Iowa. He had been involved in bootlegging alcohol since 1928 but claimed he was never involved with any Capone Gang members.

Gioe claimed he was introduced to members of the Capone Gang in the early 1930's when he owned a printing company and he would go down to 22nd Street in Chicago where all the Capone boys would hang out and try to solicit some of these men to give him some business printing gambling cards. He even talked about how he went to the Midnight Frolics Café on 22nd Street and would see Al Capone there. However, Gioe claimed he NEVER met Al Capone or had ANYTHING to do with him.

However, in 1950 Phil D'Andrea testified that Charles Gioe was a messenger boy for Al Capone and his gang after 1930.

Many reports list different years as when Charles Gioe married his first wife. January 1930, 1932 & 1934 are the years listed on different official documents. What is known is that Charles Gioe married Marie Craig in Indianola, Iowa. However, Charles Gioe had two daughters born in 1925 and 1927 but there was no mention of who the mother was or if they were married. They were not Marie's children.

The marriage with Marie lasted for a few years until the union failed. Marie claimed the reason why she was leaving Gioe was that he was guilty of extreme and repeated cruelty towards her on numerous occasions, particularly on the night of November 25, 1940. Marie claimed that Charles slapped her severely in the face and pushed her rudely and violently across the room, using at the same time, vile and opprobrious epithets. On February 13, 1941 she claimed that Charles struck her a sharp blow to the mouth, knocking her down and severely injuring her. The last straw came on August 31, 1941 when she claimed that Charles struck and beat her without reason or provocation. When Charles went in front of the judge and was asked if these incidents happened, he said yes. The couple divorced in December 1941 with mobster Sidney Korshak as his lawyer.

Two years later in January 1943 Charles married Alberta Leach in Chicago. When Charles Gioe applied for a credit report to live in an apartment at 2211 East 70th Street in Chicago in the 1940's, the agency investigated Gioe in Iowa. They could find no evidence that Gioe lived at 3124 Ingersoll Street, Des Monies, Iowa. The owner of the house said that around 1935 a man by the name of Charles A. Vetre rented the property for $50-a-month. He said there were always two men, both Italian, hanging around the house. One went by the last name of Valentio and they were from Chicago, there to run a gambling racket. They did find a Charles A. Vetre in jail in Indianola, Iowa just one county over but they could not say for sure if that name was used by Charles Gioe.

Charles Gioe life in crime and connection to the Capone Gang were apparent. In June 1930 police pulled over an automobile at 22nd Street and Loomis in Chicago and arrested Jack "Machine Gun" McGurn and Charles Gioe. The two were brought in and questioned about a massacre killing of three hoodlums that occurred the night before on the Fox Lake in Illinois. Both were released.

In 1931 Gioe began a business in Chicago that he termed the "General Ticket Business." This business was operated solely for bookmakers. Gioe worked out a system whereby a safety ticket was prepared and printed for sale to bookmakers. The use of this ticket prevented employees of the bookmaker from fraudulently obtaining money through manipulation of bets. The business was so successful that he was selling these tickets all over the United States and British Columbia. With this business so profitable, a representative of Moe Annenberg approached Gioe with the intent to buy fifty percent of the business for Annenberg. Gioe turned down the offer which he himself later once said was a foolish thing to do. Annenberg, who had considerable "power" with all the bookmakers, notified all the bookies not to purchase Gioe's tickets and he soon was forced out of business. Then, according to Gioe, when Annenberg was being prosecuted by Federal authorities, another representative of Annenberg came to him and apologized to Gioe for being "pushed around" and offered Gioe the Omaha office of Annenberg's dispensing wire service. This representative told Gioe he would make an annual income of $15,000.

On February 16, 1931 Charles Gioe, under the name Charles Joye, was arrested with Tony Accardo for carrying a concealed weapon. Police had pulled the two over and found two revolvers under the cushions of the car.

While in Iowa Gioe said he went into wrestling promotion with a man named Pinkey George. The two would put on wrestling shows which cost him around

$300 to promote. After a year of shows there was very little profit so he gave it up.

In 1935 Gioe was indicted with John J. McLanghlin, a known gambler and politician of the time under the nickname of "Boss", for trying to dispose of stolen bonds obtained in a $237,000 mail robbery. The robbery occurred on December 6, 1932 taking place at Clark and Adams Streets in Chicago and it took three years for the indictment to be issued. On March 1, 1935 Gioe, along with 39 other individuals, was named in an indictment in federal court charging him with conspiracy to receive and conceal letters stolen from and out of the United States mail. The charges were later dropped on all 40 individuals issued by the Attorney General on February 14, 1936.

Between 1936 and 1939 Charles Gioe was in a handbook operation at 162 North State Street in Chicago with mobsters Ralph Pierce and the Russell brothers, David and Harry. Years later Gioe told investigators that this operation was a large betting commission house which took bets from other gambling joints. On one occasion they accepted a bet amount of $250,000 from one gambler on one football game. Friends of Gioe use to say that he always complained in the later years that if he had been permitted to remain with this gambling setup for two or three more years he would have been the youngest millionaire in Chicago.

In 1937 Gioe said he ran a handbook with gangster Rocco Fischetti. The handbook was located on Wabash Avenue in Chicago.

During World War II Charles Gioe had to register with the local Selective Service Board. He registered under the name of Charles James Joye. He gave his work history as being employed by the American Liquor Distributors in Chicago in 1941 and he said he was Vice-President of the Don the Beachcombers Restaurant located on Oak Street in Chicago in 1943. In actuality he was operating a baseball book on a commission basis out of the Seneca Hotel on Chestnut Street in Chicago.

In the early 1940's Charles Gioe was closely associated with gangster Ralph Pierce in the operation of a gambling club known then as the Carlton Hotel in Chicago. The two operated a commission horse gambling book. Through Pierce, who was higher up in the Capone Gang than Gioe, introduced George Browne and William Bioff to him which began a friendship between them. Gioe's tax attorney later said in early 1940 or 1941 that Gioe was in a partnership with Ralph Pierce, and the Russell brothers, David and Harry, then known as Harry "The Muscle" Russell. They called their partnership Russell, Russell, Pearce and Gioe. At the same time Tony Accardo was running a gambling house with the Russell brothers down the street from Gioe's and Pierce.

Gioe testified that this gambling operation took lay off bets from other bookies in the city such as Frank "Chew Tobacco" Ryan's operation and Joe Haas's gambling operation. They also took bets from other states. In Kansas City they took bets from Tony Gizzo, Gus Spozzateri and Charlie Carollo. In Omaha it was Eddie Berrick, the Hialeah race track in Florida and in New York it was Frank Erickson. They also took bets from Indiana, Cincinnati and Michigan.

Gioe said about this operation, *"Russell being in this business had what they called outlets. If you wanted to get rid of some money, you called up different places. If the bet was too much, and he wanted to move something, he moved it to these different bookmakers."*

In 1942 Gioe told FBI agents that he operated a commission baseball gambling book, which he described as being an operation wherein he received bets from various individuals and placed these bets against each other. The commission was two percent which was paid by the winner of any particular bet.

Gioe was convicted in the U.S. District Court for the Southern District of New York on December 31, 1943, for conspiracy to interfere with trade and commerce by violence, threats and coercion. He was sentenced to serve ten years imprisonment. He was originally committed to the U.S. Penitentiary at Atlanta, Georgia, on April 4, 1944. He was eligible for parole on July 13, 1947. The maximum expiration of his sentence was March 7, 1954, with the minimum expiration ending November 23, 1950. He was transferred to Leavenworth Prison on August 8, 1945 and maintained a clear conduct record while in prison.

While in Leavenworth Gioe worked in the hospital as a technician and took classes to learn how to speak Spanish and how to write, taking a journalism class. He had some difficulties since he was unable to urinate or move his bowels in the company of other men so he was awarded a single cell to live alone.

The prison listed him as lazy and evades work; unconcerned; just gets along; needs occasional checking up as to cleanliness; and emotional and moody.

Gioe was paroled from prison on August 13, 1947 and was given a job at the Consolidated Wire and Associated Corporation as a salesman by its owner, Paul Mann, who lived in the same building as Gioe on Marine Drive. Gioe's job was to sell plastic lamps to department stores. Years later Gioe's name was linked as the actual owner of this company with mobster Ned C. Bakes as a partner.

The FBI interviewed Gioe once out of prison and wanted to know how he got involved with William Bioff and George Browne. Gioe told the agents that back when Gioe was running shows and exhibits at the New York World's Fair, Browne did Gioe favors. Gioe said Browne was used mainly in connection with supplying labor when he needed certain electrical work and construction work done. He added that it was practically impossible to have this work done unless you knew someone who could secure the necessary labor and soften up the union heads. He added he also was operating five concessions at the fair and it was necessary to obtain labor in order to open these concessions and begin operation.

At the time Bioff was being held on a pandering charge, attempts were made to extradite Bioff from Los Angeles to Chicago, and that he, Gioe, and mob lawyer Sidney Korshak had intervened for Bioff in an attempt to forestall this extradition. Gioe claimed he did this because Browne was very close to Bioff and Browne had contacted him and asked for Gioe to do this as a favor. According to Gioe, it was in helping Bioff in the pandering case that he became involved in the extortion case, all as a favor to Browne.

Some time later Charles Gioe went into business with a Frank V. Pantaleo. They opened the Frank Pantaleo & Company Construction Company that had its offices at 1219 Blue Island Avenue in Chicago. Frank Pantaleo was a one-time combat engineer in the U.S. Marines who served in World War II. In 1946 he became a commercial building contractor and was given rent-free office space in a building owned by Chicago Taxi Cab Union Local 777, then controlled by mobster Joey Glimco. Pantaleo's client list mostly consisted of known gangsters and mobsters and had dealings with syndicate figure Joe Stein. In 1953 Joey Glimco used Local 777 funds to renovate the local's offices, paying Pantaleo $60,000 to $70,000 for the work. It was said that Glimco and Pantaleo "flamboozled" the union out of the funds and that there was no reason to remodel the offices since they had been remodeled five years earlier. In 1967 Frank Pantaleo was listed in the Chicago Crime Commission's list of syndicate business. Pantaleo had been associated with Eden Land and Building Company who listed Alphonse Cardamone, a self-admitted associate of Tony Accardo, Chuckie English, John Lardino and Joey Glimco, as its partner. Frank Pantaleo lived at 1141 Fair Oaks Avenue in Oak Park, Illinois in the 1960's and owned a concrete construction company called Marwood Construction Company at 8300 Center Avenue in River Grove, Illinois. Pantaleo was also president of the August H. Skoglund Company which was a contracting and engineering firm which he purchased in 1966.

In 1949 Gioe split from Pantaleo and opened the Calumet Construction Company. Gioe was always out to make a fast buck. It was also reported that year that Gioe was running a gambling wire room at the North Clark Street Club in Chicago. According to informants Gioe had a Melville Clark operating the wire room for him.

In 1950 government investigators learned Gioe was interested in a company that was marketing a toothbrush that contained tooth paste in the handle to be used in traveling kits. He was also traveling though the mid-west introducing a new pre-made pancake mix for fast use in the kitchen.

Once again the government tried to get rid of Gioe by notifying him that he was to appear before the Immigration and Naturalization Service in Chicago because of a new law requiring all aliens to register by January 31 of each year. Gioe, who always said he was born in America, was told the government found copies of his birth certificate showing that Gioe was born in Italy. Gioe protested the evidence. This went on the same time Gioe was fighting the government which wanted him to return to prison to finish his sentence in the extortion case.

In 1951 Charles Gioe was involved in an FBI investigation concerning Vito Dizonno and a theft from an interstate shipment. Also involved in the case was mobster Frank "One Ear" Fratto. It was reported during this investigation that Fratto and Gioe were close friends and that Fratto had been at one time a bodyguard for Gioe's daughter. Other reports state that in 1941 Fratto's brother, Iowa mob boss Louis Fratto, aka Lew Farrell, sent Gioe to Iowa to run gambling, phony liquor clubs and some labor racketeering. Years after Charles Gioe's death, his wife would still visit Lew Fratto in Des Moines.

By 1954 Charles Gioe was still upset about being involved in the movie scandal and the years in prison he had spent. Gioe felt he never should have been involved in the extortion case and that he should have been entitled to some concessions from Paul DeLucia and Louis Campagna. He was also very upset as to the way he was treated when he was released. Once out he was squeezed out of his concessions at the Beachcomber, the Seneca Bar and some interest in Iowa. Gioe always had some animosity towards Paul DeLucia because he, Gioe, was under the umbrella of the Accardo faction.

Frank Diamond also felt that he had been left behind when Paul DeLucia and Louis Campagna were released from prison and felt that the two owed him some concessions for his wasted time in prison like Gioe did.

Frank Diamond was said to be a stormy character who had gone a little screwy and made several attempts to talk to Louis Campagna about these concessions without success. In a few incidents, Frank Diamond went to the Hilltop gambling joint at 4819 West 65th Street in Chicago which was one of Campagna's gambling joints to see Campagna. One time when the manager told Diamond that Campagna was not there, Diamond accused the manager of covering for Campagna and began to punch him in the face. Once the manager was on the floor, Diamond began to smash and wreck everything he could get his hands on.

With both DeLucia and Campagna refusing to see either Gioe or Diamond, they decided they were going to give themselves payment for the extortion case and opened up pin ball and slot machine in the Cook County area without permission.

In retaliation for smashing the club and other open defiance's from Diamond and Gioe, mob bosses ordered that a couple of sticks of dynamite be thrown into a Howard Johnson Restaurant that both had an interest in, blowing a good portion of the building up. Then once more they bombed the restaurant after rebuilding began which caused Gioe and Diamond to reach out to Campagna to stop the bombings, but they were once again unsuccessful. Both Gioe and Diamond reached out to mobster Joey Glimco and when the three met, Glimco refused to go to DeLucia or Campagna on their behalf.

Even more upset, both Diamond and Gioe increased their slot machines in Cook County to take away profits that were going into DeLucia's and Campagna's pockets.

One FBI report states that in an attempt to get Gioe and Diamond to stop with the slot machines, Campagna sent north side mob boss Ross Prio to have a meeting with the two to convince them to stop at once. Prio met Gioe and his two operators at Ciro's Restaurant at 818 North Wabash Avenue in Chicago where Gioe refused to obey.

The other version of the story was that Paul DeLucia and Louis Campagna themselves requested that Charles Gioe meet them at Ciro's Restaurant. When Gioe arrived he was met by DeLucia, Campagna, Harry Dukatt, an ex-con, and Al Wainer, both of whom were operators for Gioe and Frank Diamond in slot and pinball operations out west of Chicago.

What is known is that on August 18, 1954 Gioe attended a meeting at Ciro's Restaurant, which was owned then by mob boss Jimmy "Monk" Allegretti, and became angered during the meeting causing him to leave in a hurry. He reached his car parked in front of 1148 West Erie and May streets in Chicago and was shot to death at 10:05 at night. He was shot 5 times as he entered a 1954 Buick sedan which belonged to his business partner Jack Weingarten.

After the killing, detectives interviewed Harry Dukatt and Al Wainer, both Dukatt and Wainer said they were there at the meeting that night to discuss the manufacturing of a doll that had been perfected since Prio and Gioe were in the plastics business.

Chicago police brought in many mobsters for questioning. Joseph "Ruffy" Liscaindrello was arrested and questioned about the murder before being released from Municipal Court. Later Ruffy would pass a lie detector test stating he knew nothing of the killing. The reason Lisciandrello was brought in was because he was a known killer for mob boss Jimmy "Monk" Allegretti. It was discovered that a few weeks before Gioe was killed he had marched into Allegretti's territory on the north side of Chicago and confronted Allegretti, Joey "Caesar" DiVarco and Anthony "Tony Mack" DeMonti demanding he be given a piece of the syndicate race wire racket. Back in the old days Charles Gioe had control of the handbook race information service in the old First Ward of Chicago. Gioe had lost that racket when he went away to prison and was not allowed to get it back once he was out. Back then it took almost 45 minutes after the horse race to get the information to the handbooks on who won the races. By 1954 it took only five minutes to get the information to the handbooks. When Gioe demanded he be given concessions by Allegretti, he was told to "get lost" resulting in Gioe threatening Allegretti, DiVarco and DeMonti. If those three wanted Gioe dead, Ruffy Lisciandrello was the one that would have made it happen.

Paul DeLucia, Louis Campagna, Claude Maddox, William Block, Sanford "The Gimp" Rosenbaum, Max Podolsky, Phil Mesi, Ralph Pierce and Louis and Frank Fratto were all brought in and questioned about the murder, all were released. Frank "Legs" Maritote (Diamond) was arrested and questioned about the murder. Diamond told police, *"I don't know anything about his business. I suppose if anyone else gets bumped off, I'll be questioned about that too."* Poor choice of words on Maritote part because he was killed soon after. However, after hours of interrogation, Legs Diamond gave up the name Joey Glimco. His statement to the police was, *"He (Gioe) was fronting for that Howard Johnson Restaurant that was bombed. Cherry Nose told me he had gone to see Little Joey in the Taxi Cab Drivers Union in regard to this deal. He wanted me to go back with him to see Little Joey, this guy who used to be with Witt Hanley, and intercede with him to take the heat off the restaurant. I'm an old man, and I cannot stand the drafts of prison cells any more. He wanted me to go in with him in muscling some of the building trade unions."* Later he added, *"This was a legitimate deal. We were going to build houses and stores in Cook County, around Wheeling, Wauconda, and Antioch. Of course I didn't have anything to do with Cherry Nose's death. He had it coming. He was trying to muscle in on unions. After all, the guy was away for years. You can't come out and break in right away."*

Joey Glimco was brought in but refused to answer any of Chief O'Malley's questions. O'Malley continued to have Glimco arrested a few times regarding the murder but he was never charged. Four days after Legs Diamond implicated Joey Glimco in the Gioe murder, he himself was killed.

Police questioned Hyman Weisman, a former bookie in Iowa and one time prize fighter who was associated with Gioe from years past when the two met in Des Monies where Gioe was running two theaters. Weisman's first story was that he last saw Gioe a few hours before the murder. Then the story changed and Weisman said that Gioe, himself and a one time deputy sheriff named Vincent Occhipinti had dinner at Ciro's Restaurant to discuss an idea for manufacturing a plastic doll that bore the signs of the Zodiac for the astrology trade. The doll was to be called the Zoty-Doll. Occhipinti left the dinner early while the two continued to talk about ideas.

Around 10 o'clock at night Gioe and Weisman walked to his car. Weisman's statement was, *"All of a sudden I saw flashes and heard shots and I dropped to the ground behind the car as the bullets were smashing into it. Then I heard the roar of a car speeding away. I got up and kept running until I got away. They were still shooting at me, and they'll be doing it again."*

Weisman, after hiding behind the car, ran to the intersection of Ogden and Milwaukee Road where he hailed a cab to take him to the Seneca Hotel where Gioe was living. When police asked him why he lied to them the first time he was interviewed he said he was "scared" and that he believed he was also a target that night and was afraid they would still come after him to finish the job.

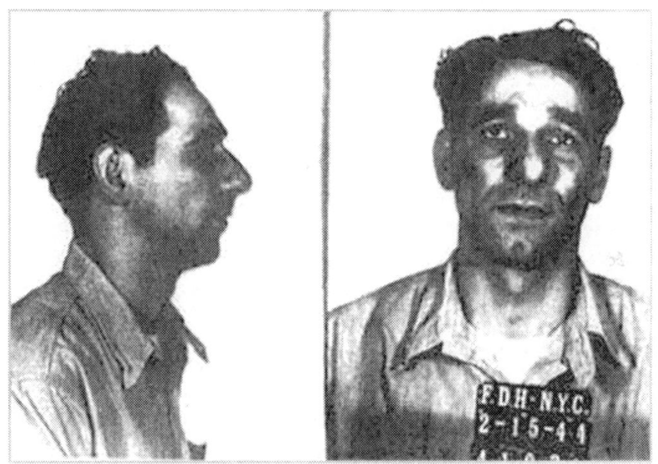

Charles Gioe 1944 arrest photo

Another witness did tell the police that the killer who shot Gioe pulled alongside Gioe's car, stood on the floor of the car to get himself looking over the roof of the car and began shooting at Weisman as he ran. When he realized he missed Weisman, he jumped down and sped away. Years later Hyman Weisman was back in Des Moines were he was operating the Run-Away Inn and working for Lou Fratto again.

One informant suggested the killing may have been related to the fact that Gioe had all the information on Paul DeLucia's phony naturalization papers since Gioe was the one who engineered the whole deal so DeLucia could gain naturalization.

Another confidential informant went to the Chicago Crime Commission and told them that Gioe had made arrangements for Sidney Korshak to make arrangements for the abolition of Paul DeLucia. The informant believed that Gioe had been talking too much which caused Paul DeLucia to give the order to have Gioe killed. While Gioe was in prison he openly complained that the reason he was in prison was because of Paul DeLucia who involved Gioe in the movie shakedowns without him asking to be involved. Some investigators believed that situation helped lead to Gioe's death.

Another informant said that Gioe was assassinated as a result of a dispute concerning the union's servicing the Howard Johnson Food Chain in the Chicago area.

One story at the time was that Gioe had approached Frank Diamond because Diamond was a giant man who was very formidable in appearance and because of his size, wanted to use him to shake down a building trade's labor union.

Throughout the following year's information on Gioe's murder surfaced through FBI informants but nothing that was considered a case-breaker. In 1954 an informant in Salt Lake City, Utah, told the FBI that mobster Marshall Caifano talked about Gioe being murdered shortly before the actual killing was committed because Gioe and Paul DeLucia were attempting to regain control of the Chicago Outfit from Tony Accardo. In the 1960's the FBI received information from an informant that Murray Humphreys was partially responsible for the death of Gioe.

Charles Gioe's wake was held at a mortuary at 1158 Grand Avenue in Chicago, just blocks from where he was killed. Like his gangster pals, he was laid out in an expensive bronze and copper casket surrounded by 28 expensive floral pieces. As police detectives watched the wake they didn't had trouble writing down the names of the people who attended, only 50 to 75 names made the list because "no one" came. When Cherry Nose Gioe was put in the ground the next day at Mount Carmel Cemetery in Hillside, Illinois, about 50 mourners turned out to say good-bye.

One FBI informant who said he became involved in organized crime in 1947 told the FBI in 1966 that had Charles Gioe lived into the 1960's that he, Gioe, would have been made boss after Sam Giancana's downfall. This informant said, *"At the time Gioe was handing union matters for the organization, was very wealthy, owned many business interests including a partnership in the Seneca Hotel with Louis Greenberg and Frank Diamond."*

However, it was reported that at the moment Gioe was killed the U.S. Immigration and Naturalization Department was building a case to have Gioe deported back to Palermo, Sicily. The Immigration Department had just found solid evidence that Gioe lied about being born in America. The department found a birth certificate in Palermo showing Gioe was born there and brought to America as a six-month-old infant in 1907.

Apparently months before his murder, Tony Accardo gave Gioe some advice that he did not take. Accardo told Gioe, "*Take the deportation and go over with Lucky.*" Lucky was Charles "Lucky" Luciano, mob boss from New York, who had been deported and sent back to Italy.

One report said that Gioe would have done anything to stay in America, even become a stool pigeon to the government in their labor rackets investigation which may have been another reason he had to go.

In the end, Chicago police said that the Gioe killing followed the same path as most of the other mob murders. No one knew anything; no one had any reason to kill good old Cherry Nose; he was a great guy and no one could figure out who would do this to their old pal. Even Gioe's wife said, "*Nobody had any reason to murder him that I know of.*" He just became another unsolved murder in Chicago which remains an open investigation to this day.

Authors Collection 2016 ©

Charles Gioe grave at Mt. Carmel Cemetery in Hillside, Illinois

Authors Collection 2016 ©

Authors Collection 2016 ©

Authors Collection 2016 ©

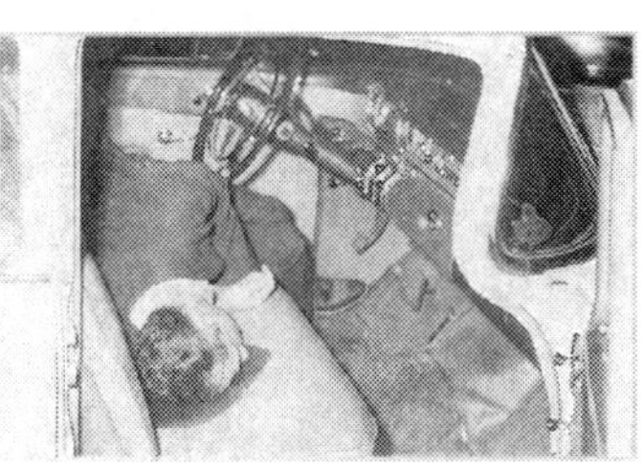

DEPARTMENT OF POLICE, CHICAGO

NON-TRAFFIC ACCIDENT REPORT

Died 8-18-54

№ 125997

29 Dist.

Date of Report 8-18 1954 Date of Accident 8-18 1954 Time 10:05 AM PM

Name of Injured GIOE (Last Name) CHARLES (First Name) Age 50

Address

Male [X] Female [ ] Single [ ] Married [X]

Occupation FACTORY OWNER

Nativity AMER. Phone No.

Place of Occurrence ON STREET ABOUT 11[redacted] W. ERIE St.

Injury or Sickness DEAD.

Description of Accident The above was sitting in his automobile, which was parked. When some unknown person or persons shot the above to death.

Refused Medical Aid [ ] First Aid by Police [ ]

Taken to C.C. Hosp. Hospital

By Sqd. roll #290 Officer Hartigan & Hoffing

Attended By Doctor Levitt Fatal [X] Non-Fatal [ ]

Removed to C.C. Morgue. Morgue

Address Phone No.

C. C. No. 56293 Stat. Comp. No. 933319

IN ANIMAL BITE CASES

Name of Owner Phone No.

Address Apt. Rm. Hse. Fl.

	Names of Witnesses	Addresses	Phone No.
1	[redacted]	[redacted]	[redacted]
2	[redacted]	[redacted]	[redacted]
3	[redacted]	[redacted]	[redacted]
4			
5			

Officer Thomas J. Kelly Star No. 6718 Dist. 29

H. O. Connell — COMMANDING OFFICER

C. Daniels Actg. — DESK SERGEANT

Charles Gioe's 1954 homicide report from the CPD

File Card

Charles James Gioe
AKA Cherry Nose
AKA Charles James Joye (Legally changed his last name to Joye)
AKA Chuck Joy
AKA Charles Veltre
AKA Charlie Valerie
AKA Cherry Nose Charlie
Born February 6, 1904 Chicago *(On Selective Service report he wrote 1905) (Said to be actually born in Palermo, Sicily in 1907)*
Died August 18, 1954 (Killed) Grave at Mt. Carmel Cemetery in Hillside, Illinois
FBI # 3339373
Height 5'10"
Weight 155 (1947)
Hair Black, wavy, streaked with gray
Build Slender
Characteristics Heavy beard, this face, neat dresser, dimple in chin (1947)
I.Q. 105 (Average Intelligence)
Armed Forces listing 3-A Classification
Wife Marie Craig, one report lists her as Opal Marie Joye *(One report states they married at Polk Country, Iowa on January 20, 1930, and another state on January 28, 1934. Filed for divorced on November 25, 1941 / granted December 12, 1941)*
Second wife Alberta Leach Joye (Born 1908) (Married January 2, 1943)
Daughter Maxie (Born 1925)
Daughter Katherine (Born around 1927)
Daughter Gloria Joye Fidler *(listed as step-daughter in one report and adopted in another. Listed as being born around 1910)*
Brother Anthony Ross Gioe, 633 North Central Park Avenue (1942) & 5510 Lowa Street Chicago (1947)

Known Arrest Record of Charles Gioe

Date	Charge	Agency	Result
2-24-1928	Rape	Chicago PD	Dismissed
10-18-1928	Rape	Chicago PD	Dismissed
6-2-1930	Investigation	Chicago PD	Released
2-16-1931	Concealed Weapon	Chicago PD	Released
3-2-1935	Conspiracy	Feds	Dismissed
11-9-1935	Investigation	Des Moines, Iowa	Dismissed
1940	Bookmaking	U/K	U/K
1943	Extortion	Feds	Guilty
6-8-1943	Mail Fraud	USM, New York	Guilty
9-1950	Drury Murder	Chicago PD	Released

Tony Dark

Known Addresses of Charles Gioe

2102 E. 70th Place, Chicago (1904-1937)
933 Grand Avenue, Chicago (1931)
3124 Ingersoll Street, Des Moines, Iowa (1930's)
4300 Marine Drive, Chicago (1937-1939) (One report list it as 4300 Lake Shore Drive)
North Lake Summer home, Illinois (1930's)
6826 Crandon Avenue, Chicago (1940's)
Lake Shore Drive, Chicago #75 (1940)
518 North Carpenter Street, Chicago
Seneca Hotel, Room 704 & 1204, 200 East Chestnut Street, Chicago (1939-1944)
House at Lake Voltz, Antioch, Michigan (1940's)
Summer home, Wilmot, Wisconsin (1949)

Known Occupations

Owner of Andrea's Restaurant, New York City (1930's)
General Ticket Company, Chicago, Illinois (Bookmaking tickets) (1931-1936)
Wrestling Promotion, Iowa (1930's)
General Manager, O.K. Motors, 620 May Street, Chicago (1933-1939)
Seneca Hotel Chicago (Had small investment in Hotel with Louis Greenberg and Frank Diamond) (1937-1939)
Russell, Russell, Pierce & Joye Promoters, Gambling joint, 162 North State Street, Chicago (1936-1939)
Owned several exhibits and shows, one of which was known as the "Strange as it Seems" show at the New York World's Fair (1938-1940)
Owner and operator of the Don the Beachcombers Restaurant, 101 East Walton & Oak Street, Chicago (1941-1943)
Rented an office at 145 North Clark Street, Chicago (1943)
Public Relations Man, American Liquor Distributors, 217 West Huron Street, Chicago (1941)
Gambling Joint, 2138 South Wabash Avenue, Chicago (1940) (Baseball hand book)
Cigar store, Clark and Lake Street, Chicago (1940-1943)
Nu-Way Beer Coil Company, 3118 West Touhy Avenue, Chicago (1940's)
Part Owner with Joe Rodgers in the "Rogers Corners" Restaurant in New York City (1947)
Leavenworth Hospital (1945-1947)
Consolidated Wire and Associated Corporations, Lamp Department, 1635 S. Clinton Chicago (1947 salesman)
O.K. Cartage Company, Chicago (1940's)
Consolidated Iron Association of Chicago (1949)
Gem Die and Tool Company of Chicago (1949)
North Clark Street Club, Chicago *(Wire room)* (1949)
Restaurant at Erie and Ogden Avenue, Chicago *(Owned by his wife)* (1949-1950's)
Restaurant on Damon and Lawrence Streets in Chicago *(Owned by his wife)* (1949-1950's)
Calumet Construction Company (1951-1952) *(Financial Interest in)*
Angelo's Restaurant, 600 North Ogden Avenue (1951) *(Financial Interest in)*
Consolidated Molding Company, 1148 West Erie Street, Chicago (1952)

Known Associates of Charles Gioe

Vito Dizonno
Frank Fratto (Bodyguard 1940's)
Dave Sbarbaro (Chauffeur)
Louis Greenberg
Frank Diamond

MONROE 6-3283
MONROE 6-7748

CALUMET CONSTRUCTION CO.
1331 W. GRAND AVENUE CHICAGO 22, ILLINOIS
Designers and Builders

September 20, 1950

NAME: CHARLES GIOE

AKA: CHERRY NOSE

RESIDENCES:

AREA OF OPERATIONS: Chicago

DATE AND PLACE OF BIRTH:

JUSTICE FILE NOS.: 123-51-18 (Sec. 2)

CITIZENSHIP STATUS: FBI NO.:

CRIMINAL RECORD:

Place	Name & Number	Date	Charge	Disposition
New York	Charles Gioe	1943	Violation Anti-racketeering Act	10 yrs. & $10,000 fine

ASSOCIATES:

ACTIVITIES AND GENERAL INFORMATION: Gioe was formerly a member of the old Capone mob and is reputed to be a member of the International Mafia Society. He was convicted with DeLucia, D'Andrea, and Compagna in 1943 in connection with the Hollywood Motion Picture shakedown and is presently out on bond pending appeal of revocation of parole. He is said to be operating restaurants and a general construction business at the present time, but is reported still to be connected with the present-day so-called syndicate. (23-5/11 N)

UNITED STATES PENITENTIARY
Leavenworth, Kansas
SPECIAL PROGRESS REPORT

Committed Name GIOE, Charles Reg No. 62121-L Date August 16,1945

RECEIVED IN TRANSFER FROM ATLANTA, GEORGIA.

OFFENSE : Conspiracy to Interfere w/trade & Commerce by Violence,threats & Coercion. ELIGIBLE FOR PAROLE: July 7,1947

SENTENCE : 10 years COMMITTED : Apr. 4, 1944-A

SENTENCED FR : New York, N.Y.:SD MINIMUM EXPIRATION : Nov. 23,1950

RACE: White DATE OF BIRTH: 2-6-04 MAXIMUM EXPIRATION : Mar. 7, 1954

ASSOCIATE WARDEN: Gioe was originally committed to the USP, Atlanta, Ga., 4-4-44 from New York, N.Y. to serve 10 years for Conspiracy to interfere with trade and commerce by violence, threats and coercion. He was received at this institution in transfer from Atlanta 8-8-45 to be nearer release destination. While at Atlanta he maintained a clear conduct record and will be eligible for conditional release 11-23-50.

Recommendations: Close Custody No transfer.

SOCIAL PAROLE:

This man was transferred here from the Atlanta Institution August 8, 1945.

Both parents were born in Italy, coming to this country prior to 1900. His father died in 1934 and his mother in 1939. Father's occupation was that of a laborer and carpenter, inmate being brought up in marginal economic circumstances. He is the oldest of two siblings, having one brother now living in Berwyn, Illinois.

Inmate has been married twice, the first marriage was to Marie Craig in 1932, obtained a divorce in December of 1941, there were no children although wife had two children by a previous marriage. He is at the present time married to Alberta Leach marrying this woman in January, 1942, she had one child by a former marriage. The wife not working at the present time and he claims that she is adequately able to support herself having sufficient funds available to do so.

He was born February 6, 1904 at Chicago, Illinois, completed his schooling in that locality, claiming an eighth grade education.

He registered for Selective Service in Chicago, Illinois, in 1939 and was classified 3-A according to his statement. He has had more or less steady employment in the city of Chicago.

Charles Gioe Prison Record

Record Form No. 1
(Revised Feb., 1936)

UNITED STATES DEPARTMENT OF JUSTICE
PENAL AND CORRECTIONAL INSTITUTIONS

Budget Bureau No. 43-R221
Approval Expires 7-31-47

copied 7-26-48--cfz

RECORD OF COURT COMMITMENT

U. S. PENITENTIARY,
(Institution)
LEAVENWORTH, KANSAS
(Location)

Inst. Name Charles Gioe — No. 62121 - L

Alias Charlie Joy; Charles Joye; Charles Veltre — Color White — Age 41 (2-6-04)

True Name Charles James Gioe — Name and number of prior commitments to Fed. Inst. 63774-A (current off)

Offense Consp. to Interfere with Trade & Commerce by Violence, Threats & Coercion

District SD-New York-New York

Sentence 10 years — Costs — Committed — Not Committed — Paid; Fine 10000.00 Committed x — Not Committed — Paid

Fine Paid 5-14-45

Sentence changed — New term — Reason therefor

Sentenced Dec. 31, 1943 — When arrested March 21, 1943

Committed to Fed. Inst. April 4, 1944-A — Where arrested Chicago, Illinois

Sentence begins Appealed-elected to serve Mar. 8, 1944 — Residence Chicago, Illinois

Eligible for Parole July 7, 1947 — Time in jail before trial None

Eligible for conditional release with good time Nov. 23, 1950 — Rate per mo. good time 10 — Total good time possible 1200

Eligible for con. rel. with extra good time

Forfeited good time — Amount forfeited

Restoration good time — Amount restored

Expires full term March 7, 1954

Former Com. on Sentence to Other Institutions

No.	Name of Institution	Location

Person to be notified in case of serious illness or death

Name Mrs. Charles Joye
Relation to prisoner wife
Address 200 E. Chestnut St
Chicago, Illinois
Telephone

ACTION OF BOARD

Date	No. app.	Parole Forth.	Parole Effect.	Parole Rel.	Parole Den.	Parole Cont.	War. is.	Rev.	Dis. from par.

Releases and recommitments on present sentence other than parole

Date	Method
8-8-45	Tr LK from A
8-13-47	Paroled

DETAINERS FILED

Date	Nature of Detainer	Notify Whom	Remarks

FPI—LK—4-4-47—80M—4729-5

Charles Gioe Prison Record

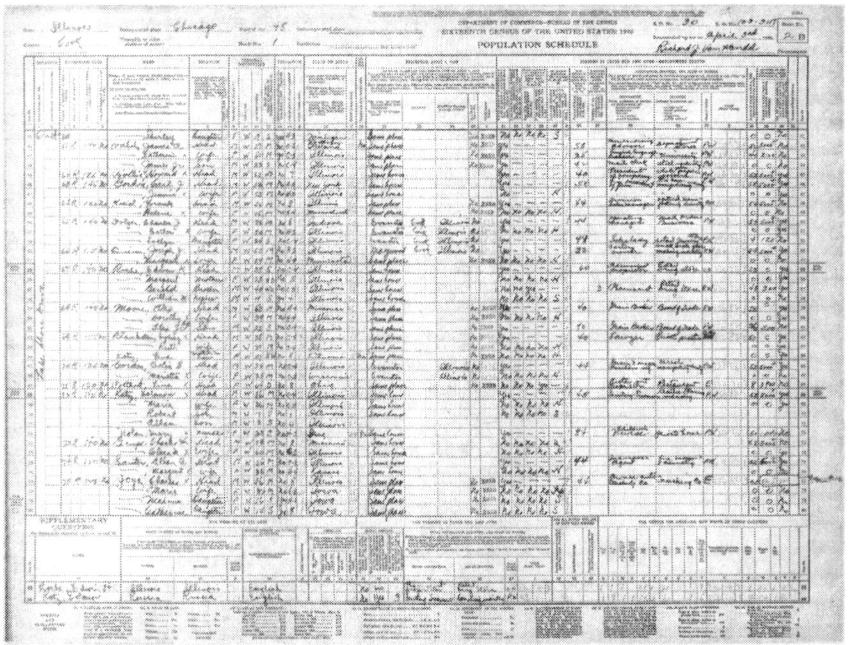

Charles Gioe 1940 Census under the last name of Joye

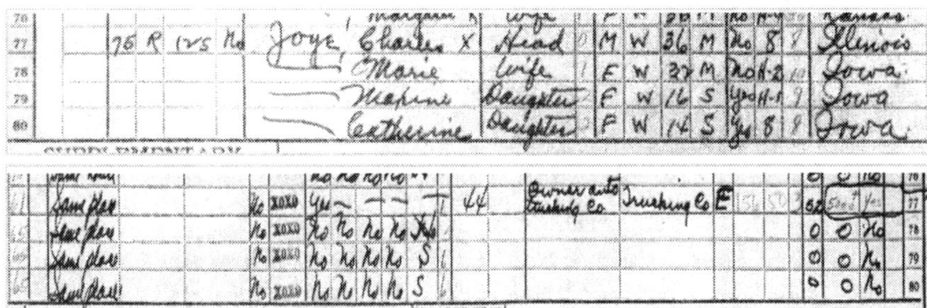

77	75	R	125	No	Joye	Charles	X	Head	0	M	W	36	M	No	8	Illinois
78						Marie		Wife	1	F	W	37	M	No	H-2	Iowa
79						Maxine		Daughter		F	W	16	S	Yes	H-1	Iowa
80						Catherine		Daughter		F	W	14	S	Yes	8	Iowa

Residence											Occupation	Industry						Row
Same place	No	XOXO	Yes						44		Owner auto trucking Co	Trucking Co	E				Yes	77
Same place	No	XOXO	No	No	No	No	H							0	0	No		78
Same place	No	XOXO	No	No	No	No	S							0	0	No		79
Same place	No	XOXO	No	No	No	No	S							0	0	No		80

Frank Diamond

Frank Maritote, aka Frank Diamond, was born on September 22, 1893. He arrived in Chicago in 1906 coming from New York City. He had entered the United States in 1897 coming from Brosiano, Italy which he once told a government agent was a former province of Caserta, Italy. His family's real last name was Maritato but Frankie had spelled it Maritote to sound more American.

In the early days he made money by becoming a prize fighter in the boxing ring. He was called "the big gorilla" by many who knew him because of his size and his ability to fly off the handle at any moment. He had big black bushy eyebrows that stood out as a main feature on his face.

He had a lengthy life in crime being arrested many times. He became one of Al Capone's top bodyguards under his boxing name of Frankie Diamond which brought him great power. He once admitted to IRS agents that he shared in profits totaling over $100,000-a-year from a Capone gambling house operating at the Lorraine Hotel at 411 South Wabash in Chicago.

Most of his time in Chicago he had managed to "beat the rap" on numerous arrest ranging from larceny to murder. Because he was able to always stay out of jail he was given the nickname "Frank the Immune."

In 1928 he decided to get into the construction trade with help from his pals Capone gangsters Mike "Dago Mike" Carrozzo and Sam Nanini and opened up the Erlanger Construction Company in Chicago. He was acting as a construction contractor getting many of Chicago's city contracts handed to him. It turned out to be bad timing for Frankie Diamond to enter the construction trade because the great depression would soon hit and all the contracts dried up.

During the 1930's Frank Diamond became close with Paul DeLucia and Frank Nitti. This association is what led to Frank Diamond being brought into the Hollywood extortion case in which he was arrested and sent to trial.

During the Hollywood extortion trial Frank Diamond would sit in the courtroom muttering imprecations in Sicilian and at times go berserk, punching newsmen and court deputies. On December 30, 1943 Frank Diamond was found guilty and sentenced to 10 years at Leavenworth Prison.

When he was found guilty he felt as though he had been robbed and wrongly convicted and from that day on he blamed the U.S. government for stealing years of his life. He refused to sign any government forms or do anything for the government from that point on.

He was one of the last Capone mobsters to be paroled on December 20, 1950. One of the stipulations for his releases was that he would NOT return to Chicago. As soon as he was released he returned to Chicago.

In the 1950's Frank Diamond claimed he returned to the contracting business. He was arrested many times and questioned for many hours in connection with almost every mob murder in the early 1950's.

On August 21, 1954 Frank Diamond was shot to death in front of a garage at 710 S. Keeler Avenue in Chicago. Diamond's son Rodger, then 4-years-old, crouched in his fathers Packard automobile in horror as Diamond was shot to death. Diamond was shot in the chest, arm and abdomen by shotguns and pistols. Frank Diamond was buried at Mount Carmel Cemetery where over 200 mourners attended.

Shortly after Frank Maritote's killing information was revealed that mobster Joey Glimco had tapped the phone lines from the Fulton Street merchants and learned that Maritote was giving the Internal Revenue Service (IRS) agents important information regarding hoodlum operations.

An informant came forward and told the FBI shortly after the murder that Ralph Capone had left his estate on Martha Lake at Mercer, Wisconsin right before Maritote was killed and headed to Chicago. Ralph Capone then returned to Mercer on the day before the killing and made it a point to have his presence known that he was back. On the day of the killing Ralph Capone made sure he was seen by many in and around the town of Mercer. It was not known if Ralph Capone had anything to do with the murder or if he was called back to Chicago in an attempt to save Maritote. He could have been called back to be told about the killing and warned not to retaliate. Frank Maritote's brother, John Maritote, was married to Ralph's and Al's sister Mafalda Capone. The murder of Frank Maritote is an unsolved murder and is still listed as active today.

File Card

Frank Maritote
Real name Frank Maritato
Aka Frank Diamond, The Immune, Legs, Frankie Legs, Frank Parmaratta, Frank Romano, Francis Tote, Francis Marotiti, Frank Permaritto, Francis Marititi, the Big Gorilla
Born September 22, 1893 in Brosiano, Italy
Died August 21, 1954 (Killed in Chicago) Grave at Mt. Carmel Cemetery in Hillside, Illinois
First Wife Unknown
Second Wife Rose (Born at Polk & Clark Streets in Chicago)
Third Wife Rena Candice, died June 10, 1970
Son Frank Jr. Maritote (Second marriage)
Son Rodger (Third marriage)
Daughters Frances, married Paul Cokinis, Marie McCaffer and Theresa Navarro (Daughters of second marriage)
Father Orazio Maritote "Maritato"
Mother Theresn Pescopo (Died September 1939)
Brother John Maritote
Sisters Theresa Sarvello, Sarah Canzolino, Jennie Senase, Rose Mattioli

Known Addresses

710 Miller Street, Chicago
1737 West Polk Street, Chicago (1932)
26 North Long Avenue, Chicago (1942)
Madison and Sangamon Streets, Chicago (1946)
4144 Fifth Avenue, Chicago (1952-1955)
60 West Madison Street, Chicago (1953) *(Gave this address when arrested)*

Known Arrest Record of Frank Diamond

Date	Charge	Agency	Result
April 1914	Receiving Stolen Prop.	New York	No Bill
2-27-1919	Indictment Robbery	Chicago	Not Guilty
4-29-1919	Robbery	Dixon Sheriff	Not Guilty
5-7-1919	Larceny	Chicago PD	Not Guilty
1-24-1920	Larceny, Frank Permoratto	New York	Not Guilty
4-23-1920	Threat to kill F. Bristol	Chicago PD	Released
5-3-1920	Sec. 22 MVL	Chicago PD	Discharged
6-10-1920	Disorderly Conduct	Chicago PD	$5 Fine
9-22-1920	Disorderly Conduct	Chicago PD	$5 Fine
10-31-1920	Murder	Chicago PD	Acquitted
3-9-1921	Ethel Tezel Complaint	Chicago PD	Discharged
6-18-1921	D.W.P	Chicago PD	Released
8-12-1921	Section 7-27	Chicago PD	Annulled
9-20-1921	Disorderly Conduct	Chicago PD	$1 Fine
9-20-1921	Not obeying a officer	Chicago PD	Guilty
10-24-1921	Section 2437A	Chicago PD	Discharged
3-27-1922	Disorderly Conduct	Chicago PD	Discharged
5-6-1922	Disorderly Conduct	Chicago PD	$1 Fine
1-20-1923	Possession Fire Arms	Chicago PD	Discharged
2-20-1923	14 MVL	Chicago PD	Discharged
4-19-1923	Section 1566	Chicago PD	Discharged
5-17-1923	Disorderly Conduct	Chicago PD	$10 Fine
6-20-1923	Section 1578	Chicago PD	$25 Fine
12-6-1923	Section 2655	Chicago PD	Discharged
9-4-1924	Gambling	Chicago PD	Discharged
2-20-1926	Concealed Weapon	Chicago PD	Not Guilty
7-27-1926	Burglary	Chicago PD	Nolle Process
1-4-1930	Burglary, Frank Romano	Chicago PD	Discharged
1-23-1930	Vagrant	Chicago PD	Released
3-17-1930	Concealed Weapon	Chicago PD	Quashed
9-16-1930	Vagrancy	Chicago PD	Not Guilty
3-2-1931	Concealed Weapon	Chicago PD	Stricken Off
3-11-1932	Vagrancy	Chicago PD	Discharged
8-9-1932	Concealed Weapon	Chicago PD	Reinstated
11-14-1932	Concealed Weapon	Chicago PD	Not Guilty
1-28-1933	Disorderly Conduct	Chicago PD	Not Guilty

Tony Dark

Date	Charge	Agency	Result
2-1933	Concealed Weapon	Chicago PD	Dismissed
2-22-1933	No 1933 license plate	Chicago PD	Dismissed
3-3-1933	U/K	Chicago PD	U/K
5-8-1933	Questioning	Chicago PD	Released
8-13-1933	Vagrancy	Chicago PD	Discharged
8-31-1933	Concealed Weapon	Chicago PD	Discharged
10-31-1933	Vagabond Warrant	Chicago PD	Warrant Arrest
8-5-1934	U/K	Chicago PD	U/K
3-16-1935	U/K	Chicago PD	U/K
8-26-1937	Assault of J. Costaldo	Chicago PD	Not Guilty
3-10-1938	Mistake	Chicago PD	Released
3-19-1939	Payment of Wages	Chicago PD	Nolle Prosequi
11-14-1941	Assault and Battery	Geneva PD	U/K
3-30-1943	Extortion	Fed	Guilty
3-30-1943	Mail Fraud	Fed	Guilty
3-20-1943	Conspiracy	Fed	Guilty
1952	Baldino Murder	Chicago PD	Released
1-6-1953	Disorderly Conduct	Chicago PD	Released
5-4-1963	Investigation	Chicago PD	Released
8-19-1954	Gioe Murder	Chicago PD	Released

Frankie Diamond's Mausoleum at Mt. Carmel Cemetery in Hillside, Illinois

NAME: FRANK DIAMOND
(real name: Francis Maritote)
AKA: Frank Romano; Franke Tote

RESIDENCES: 26 Long Ave., Chicago, Ill.
4144 W. 5th Ave., Chicago, Ill.

AREA OF OPERATIONS: Chicago

DATE AND PLACE OF BIRTH: 9/22/93 Italy

JUSTICE FILE NOS.: 123-51-18 (Sec. 2)

CITIZENSHIP STATUS: Naturalized U.S. FBI NO.:

CRIMINAL RECORD:

Place	Name & Number	Date	Charge	Disposition
Chicago	Frank Diamond	1920	Larceny	Not guilty.
"	" "	1921	Murder	Not guilty.
"	" "	1926	Burglary	Nol prossed.
"	" "	1931	Carrying concealed weapon.	Not guilty.
New York	Francis Maritote	1943	Conspiracy against trade - viol. of anti-racketeering act.	Sentenced to 10 years - Leavenworth.

(23-5/11-I)

ASSOCIATES:

ACTIVITIES AND GENERAL INFORMATION: Maritote was convicted with Compagna, Gioe, D'Andrea and others in connection with the Hollywood Motion Picture shakedown. He has a long criminal record with no convictions except the Bioff & Brown case. During the latter part of 1948 he made a fervent plea for executive clemency claiming that he was not guilty and was convicted by uncorroborated falsehoods of Bioff and Brown. His petition was presented by Atty. Wm. Scott Stewert who also represents Compagna and Gioe in their appeal. Sponsors follow:

Phil D'Andrea

Phil D'Andrea was born on September 7, 1891 in Buffalo, New York to Alosius D'Andrea (Louis) and Antonia Villo. Philip Louis D'Andrea was the brother of the powerful Antonio and Joseph D'Andrea. Both controlled portions of the Chicagoland area in the early 1900's through labor unions and political clout. Both men were killed at the peak of their power.

After coming to Chicago in 1899, D'Andrea claimed he completed three years of high school. However, an FBI report from 1949 states that he had attended 2 ½ years at the Hamilton Law School of Chicago. Phil D'Andrea went on to become the bodyguard and best friend of Al Capone. D'Andrea's power through Capone reached into the soul of almost every organized crime discussion concerning finances in Chicago between the early 1920's and the 1940's.

In his early business life D'Andrea was in the cartage business which would haul Torrio-Capone beer around Chicago. Later when mob lawyer Joseph Bulger stepped down as leader Phil D'Andrea became Supreme President of the powerful Italo-American National Union which was based in Chicago. The organization was said to be the successor to the Union Siciliano which housed most of Chicago Sicilian Mafia members. Al Capone and his associates witnessed internal fighting in this club for control of the power it wheeled. Many were murdered for control. Capone recruited the ones that were on the winning side of these fights for membership in his organization.

In the early 1920's D'Andrea's job was to be Capone's man at City Hall in Chicago. D'Andrea would hang out in the office of Daniel Serritella when he held the position of City Sealer. D'Andrea often had the ear of the Mayor of Chicago.

While acting as Capone's body guard, he always made sure Capone was safe no matter where they went. When Capone was locked away in jail, D'Andrea got himself arrested and put in the cell next to Capone to act as a bodyguard in jail. When the St. Valentines Day Massacre went down, D'Andrea made sure the two were out of the state and there was outside proof that they had left Chicago days before the killing. They boarded a ship together on February 2, 1929 and make sure they were seen by many people.

After Capone went away to prison in the early 1930's, D'Andrea was sentenced to 6 months for contempt of court for carrying a loaded gun and additional ammunition into the court room during Capone's trial. Once back in Chicago D'Andrea stayed in power, being a top adviser to Frank Nitti, Louis Campagna and Paul DeLucia. So when it came time to extort one million dollars from the movie industry Phil D'Andrea was included as one of the beneficiaries.

In 1936 gangster William Bryan Bolton, who was convicted in a kidnapping case and was on the payroll of the Capone syndicate, told the FBI that Phil D'Andrea was one of the top men in the Capone syndicate. When FBI agents interviewed D'Andrea in 1936 he did admit he was a member of the Capone Gang only because he said he was Al Capone's best friend and body guard.

Phil D'Andrea was arrested on March 26, 1943 in Chicago and found guilty and sentenced to 10 years on December 31, 1943. He was fined $10,000 with his eligibility for parole on July 13, 1947 and his conditional release from prison on November 23, 1950 and his full term to expire March 7, 1954. He entered Atlanta Prison in Georgia on April 4, 1944 staying until he transferred to Leavenworth on August 8, 1945. On January 13, 1947 he was transferred to the Medical Center for Federal Prisoners in Springfield, Missouri for mild chronic hypertrophic arthritis and angina syndrome.

The FBI investigated the steps and people involved in getting Phil D'Andrea out of prison. Handling D'Andrea's bid for parole was someone listed under the name of Anthony T. D'Andrea, their cousin mob labor union boss Anthony C. D'Andrea, then president of the Chicago District Council of Labor for the Hod Carriers Union, and mob lawyer Sam Shapiro.

FBI agents went to see a John "Jack" Robinson of the Public Relations Council on LaSalle Street in Chicago who had known D'Andrea since 1930 through the Italian-American Society in Chicago. D'Andrea had written Robinson a letter while in prison. When FBI agents interviewed Robinson he turned the letter over to the FBI. The letter showed what D'Andrea actually though of himself.

Dear Jack,

Accept my most grateful thanks for your interest and untiring efforts in my behalf. The knowledge of your friendship is my greatest forte. I have been imbued with new hopes and anticipation that all is not lost and that I maybe yet, to spend the last few years of my life, with my family and friends, as a reminder I just passed my 55th year mark while in here in spite of my failing health, due to ulcers, arthritis, and several spinal conditions—however the 'ticker' is in perfect shape.

Jack, at the very outset let me take a negative approach--sounds ridiculous, but people believe the ridiculous more readily, than sound sensible facts. You know that I was in the trucking business, trucking for municipalities and not bootlegger. You also know of my efforts toward publishing a worthy Italian newspaper, and not a gambler. For years you know of my very altruistic efforts in behalf of the Italo-American National Union, for the good of 'my people' not a swindler or an extortionist. In my capacity as president, the assets of the society increased for roughly $150,000 to close to half million--surely not a larcenist--for years I bore the responsibilities of pay-rolls, employer's welfare and striving to build a legitimate business. For 30 years, I paid taxes, Federal, State, County, City--surely not a racketeer. My faith in my God, my Church, my responsibilities to my family have made me guard my religious beliefs and for my family, not a muscle man or a Capone boy-guard. Jack, all these vicious accusations were bandied around in the courtroom during my en-masse trial. These seeds were planted and where their fruit fell, heaven only knows. You already have experienced some of their results. All the attorneys said then, was, those accusations have no bearing on the case. It may be possible that they may not have meant anything to the defendants collectively, but I have and am suffering the tortes of hell in not being allowed to *positively refute them. There were 15 witnesses ready to testify in my behalf at the trial, who could have shown very clearly by their unimpeachable testimony as to my innocence, but they or I did not testify, because of the peculiar legal logic used by the lawyers which pre-supposed that any testimony by them or I in my behalf would be detrimental to the others. This has never made good sense to me, but it is the story. This peculiar legal logic is the father & mother of all aftermaths, all the paradoxes which hurt me at the trial hurt me now, and will continue to do so, and act as barriers, until the truth comes to light. Surely after 2 years of imprisonment and individual defendant should be permitted to isolate himself from this en-masse logic. The 10-year maximum that was given to all without individual examination or qualification might now be adjusted as you know the term of court was left open for 3 years. This in itself should be helpful in designing a plan for a reduction of sentence. If my sentence could be cut to 5 years, I would automatically be placed in the parole bracket. Surely the government has had its pound of flesh, the cutting of a long sentence is not unusual and I would not be compelled to languish here for almost 2 more years before parole time. A visit would enable me to give you many details, which I find impossible to incorporate in this letter.*

'Thanks again and much good health and good luck to you.'

Sincerely,
Philip

At the parole hearing the officers asked Phil D'Andrea why should parole be granted? His reply was, *"The significant change that had occurred within me. The awakening as to the true values in life. The unfortunate death of my wife during my incarceration, virtually leaving my children parentless. The poor state of my health."* He was released.

In the 1950's it was reported that D'Andrea was living in Helmet, California and had half-interest in a Shell Service Station in Riverside, California. In 1950 D'Andrea said this about his day with Al Capone, *"Question, what was your association with him?"* Answer, *"Nothing, just purely foolish association. I thought it was smart to be identified with him. That was my only association. I never made a quarter from that source. I have always been on my own. I was in the cartage business at that time. I will say that he helped me put on a few trucks. I was doing cartage work for the city at the time."*

He went on to say that Capone helped him in First Ward politics in getting votes for the Democrat party.

Phil D'Andrea said, in his own words, the reason he was "dragged" into the extortion case was because of his dealing with the Rialto Theater in the Chicago Loop located at Van Buren and State Streets. He said in the early 1940's he was running his cartage business when he befriended the owner of the Rialto Theater named Mr. Barger. Barger came to D'Andrea and asked if he could assist in securing a license to re-open his theater which had been closed for running improper shows. At the time D'Andrea said the only one who could re-issue a license was an alderman of the old First Ward. So D'Andrea went to his good friends Mike Kenna and John Coughlin, two of the most corrupt political figures in Illinois history, and made a deal to have the theater open again. The agreement was that Barger would pay D'Andrea $10,000 a year in "protection money" for seven years. D'Andrea said he was allowed to keep all the money for himself which is why he was "dragged" into the extortion case with George Browne and William Bioff.

Phil D'Andrea died in a motel room in Riverside, California in September 1952. His body was flown back to Chicago and his wake was held at a funeral home located at 2600 Wentworth Avenue. Only a handful of people attended the 10 minute ceremony before his coffin was taken and buried at Holy Sepulchre Cemetery in Chicago.

File Card

Phil Louis D'Andrea
AKA Philip LaVerne, Philip Martin, Phil D. Andrea, Phil Verne
Born September 7, 1891, in Buffalo, New York.
Died September 1952
Height: 5'6"
Weight: 165
FBI # 602720
Chicago PD# C43653
Wife Margaret
Son Philip Jr.
Raised a young girl named Anna Macey

Relatives

Anthony D'Andrea (Brother) *(19th Ward Alderman and president of the Unione Siciliano. Murdered on May 11, 1921)*
Horsce D'Andrea (Brother) *(Catholic Priest)*
Louis D'Andrea (Brother)
Joseph D'Andrea (Brother) *(President of Chicago Hod Carriers Union Local 1, the Excavators Union, Local 4, which later became the Tunnel and Sewer workers union local 2. Murdered on September 16, 1914)*
Frances D'Andrea (Sister)
Mary D'Andrea (Sister)
Anne D'Andrea (Sister)
Anthony C. D'Andrea (Cousin) *(President of the Chicago District Council of Labor 1940-1955)*

Tony Dark

Known Addresses

732 Twenty-Sixth Street Chicago (1915)
3542 Lowe Avenue, Chicago (1923)
92 Palm Island, Miami Beach, Florida (1929)
Route 2, St. Joseph, Michigan (1928-1943) *(Official listing North West corner of section 35, St. Joseph Township, Berrien County, Michigan)*
Lexington Hotel Chicago (1931)
50100 Cornell Avenue, Chicago (1935) *(Beach View Apartments)*
Office at 30 West Washington Street Chicago (1937)
167 Park Avenue, Glencoe, Illinois (1930's)
531 Beckwith Lane, Lincolnshire, Crete, Illinois (1942)
511 Beckwith Lane, Crete, Illinois (1942)
Stevens, Piccadilly Hotel, 8100 Paxton Avenue, Chicago (1940's)
515 Blackwood, Lincolnshire, Illinois (1947)
9696 Magnolia Street, Arlington, California (1950)
House in Hemet, California (1950)
House in Palm Springs, California (1940's-1950's)
3441 Sixth Street, Riverside, California (1950)

Known Arrest Record of Phil D'Andrea

Date	Charge	Agency	Result
1916	Suspicion	Chicago PD	Discharged
12-14-1923	Assault to Murder	Chicago PD	Discharged
1-6-1924	Charge 137	Chicago PD	Discharged
10-10-1931	Contempt Court	Feds	6 Months Jail
11-2-1932	General Principles	Chicago PD	Released
9-2-1933	Vagrancy	Chicago PD	Warrant
10-31-1933	Vagabond Warrant	Chicago PD	Warrant
1-26-1934	Receiving stolen property	Chicago PD	Discharged
11-3-1938	Disorderly Conduct	Chicago PD	Discharged
3- 26-1943	Extortion	Feds	10 Years Jail

Mob Boss

Phil D'Andrea's Chicago Police Photo

NAME: PHILIF D'ANDREA

AKA: Philip Lavern

RESIDENCES:

AREA OF OPERATIONS: Chicago

DATE AND PLACE OF BIRTH:

JUSTICE FILE NOS.: 123-51-18 (Sec. 2)

CITIZENSHIP STATUS:

FBI NO.:

CRIMINAL RECORD:

Place	Name & Number	Date	Charge	Disposition
Chicago	Philip D'Andrea	1931	Contempt of Court	6 mos. sentence.
New York	" "	1943	Viol. Anti-racketeering Act.	10 yr. sentence & $10,000 fine.

ASSOCIATES: Louis Compagna, Tony Accardo, Charles Gioe, Paul DeLucia

ACTIVITIES AND GENERAL INFORMATION: Philip D'Andrea was formerly a member of the old Capone mob; he was convicted with DeLucia, Compagna, and Gioe in the Bioff and Brown investigation and is presently on parole (23-5/11-N). D'Andrea was sentenced to 6 months in 1931 for contempt of court. He had been serving as a body guard for Al Capone and the charge of contempt was based on the fact that he had been carrying a loaded gun and additional ammunition in the court room during the Capone trial; he sat with the defendant, only a few feet away from Judge Wilkerson (23-5/12-I). D'Andrea is now under supervision of the US Probation Office at Los Angeles and he is operating a Shell Service station at Riverside, Calif. (11-5/12-I).

U.S. Senate Telegram sent to Phil D'Andrea in 1950

WESTERN UNION

W. P. MARSHALL, PRESIDENT

DOMESTIC SERVICE — Check the class of service desired; otherwise this message will be sent as a full rate telegram. FULL RATE TELEGRAM X | SERIAL | DAY LETTER | NIGHT LETTER

INTERNATIONAL SERVICE — Check the class of service desired; otherwise the message will be sent at the full rate. FULL RATE | DEFERRED | CODE | NIGHT LETTER

NO. WDS.-CL. OF SVC.	PD. OR COLL.	CASH NO.	CHARGE TO THE ACCOUNT OF	TIME FILED
			WABASH 2-3997	

Send the following message, subject to the terms on back hereof, which are hereby agreed to.

OCTOBER 3, 1950

PHILLIP D'ANDREA
9696 MAGNOLIA
ARLINGTON, CALIFORNIA

IN ACCORDANCE WITH THE TERMS OF THE SUBPOENA SERVED UPON YOU BY U.S. MARSHALL BOYLE ON SEPTEMBER 26 AND FURTHER IN ACCORDANCE WITH INSTRUCTIONS RECEIVED BY YOU FROM MARSHALL BOYLE ON SEPTEMBER 30 YOU ARE COMMANDED TO APPEAR HERE WITH YOUR RECORDS AT 10:00 A.M. OCTOBER 5, 1950, IN ROOM 260 U.S. COURT HOUSE, OLD POST OFFICE BUILDING, CHICAGO 4, ILLINOIS.

ESTES KEFAUVER, CHAIRMAN SPECIAL
COMMITTEE TO INVESTIGATE ORGANIZED
CRIME IN INTERSTATE COMMERCE

Riverside, Calif
Oct. 14th 1950

Mr. George S. Robinson –
Committee Counsel –

Dear Sir –

Was informed by the marshall the evening after I testified before your committee, that it would be necessary for you to Ok a voucher for my traveling expenses to Chicago and return. As I left early the following morning I was unable to contact you. Will you kindly at your convenience take care of same.

Thanking you again for the cordial treatment granted me at the hearing.

I remain,
Yours very truly
Philip L. D'Andrea

3441 Sixth St.
Riverside, Calif.

JOHN EDGAR HOOVER

Federal Bureau of Investiga[illegible]
United States Department of Justice
Washington, D. C.

1-4

1891.M.W.

Aug 18 19[illegible] [illegible]108 hrs

The following is the record of FBI number 602 720

J. E. Hoover
Director.

CONTRIBUTOR OF FINGERPRINTS	NAME AND NUMBER	ARRESTED OR RECEIVED	CHARGE	DISPOSITION
U.S. Marshal Chicago, Ill.	Philip D. Andrea #--	10-10-31	contempt	6 mos. Cook Co. Jail
PD, Chicago, Ill.	Phillip LaVerne #C-43653	11-2-32	G.P.	
U.S. Marshal Chicago, Ill.	Philip D'Andrea #6839	4-1-43	extortion	
U.S. Marshal New York City, N.Y.	Philip L. D'Andrea #--	6-8-43	mail fraud	12-22-43, sent. 10 yrs. - $10,000 fine on chg. of anti-racketeering, nolle prosequi
FDH, New York, N.Y.	Phil D'Andrea #41919	2-15-44	anti-racketeering-consp.	10 years, 3-25-44 disch. to USP, Atlanta
USP, Atlanta, Ga.	Phil D'Andrea #63777	4-4-44	consp. to interfere with trade & comm. by coercion, threats & violence	10 years
USP, Leavenworth, Kans.	Phil D'Andrea #62120	8-8-45 in trans. fr. USP, Atlanta, Ga.	consp. to interfere with trade & comm. by coercion, threats & violence	10 years
Med. Center for Fed. Prisoners, Springfield, Mo.	Phil D'Andrea #5980-H	1-13-47 in trans. from USP, Leavenworth Kans.	consp. to interfere with trade & comm. by threats & viol.	10 years, 8-13-47 disch.; reg. par.

* Represents notations unsupported by fingerprints in FBI files.

NOTICE: THIS RECORD IS FURNISHED FOR OF

USPLK-62120-8-8-45

D'Andrea's Prison Photo from the 1940's

Louis Kaufman

Louis Kaufman was a mob associate and business manager of Local 244 of the Motion Picture Operators Union in Newark, New Jersey. With Kaufman's help $150,000 was collected from exhibitors in New York. He was found guilty and sentenced to 7 years in prison and a $10,000 fine.

Ralph Pierce

Ralph Pierce was an old-time Capone gang member who was first a bodyguard to Al Capone and then a bodyguard to Capone's lieutenant Murray Humphreys. His life in the Capone Gang centered around gambling and becoming a powerful south side mob gambling boss.

From the Collection of T.M.

In one report it suggests that Ralph Pierce's involvement with Louis Campagna and Johnny Roselli in the Hollywood extortion plot came from an informant in 1937. This informant told the Government that Pierce was in partnership with Campagna in regards to whatever allegations were made against Campagna as an extortioner.

Pierce once told FBI agents that when he, Pierce, was indicted by the United States Attorney in New York, the Government did not have sufficient information to prosecute him. The District Attorney attempted and failed to show through income tax returns that Pierce was associated with Campagna. So Pierce was convinced that the FBI was attempting to "frame" him and link him to the extortion.

The official reason he was not convicted was because Pierce was only the driver of a car that drove various people to and from meetings concerning the extortion plot.

Ralph Pierce remained a top gambling boss until 1965 when Murray Humphreys died and Pierce was given complete control of all gambling on Chicago's south side. Over time he lost control to the African American street gangs of Chicago which forced Pierce into semi-retirement.

Ralph Pierce died in July 1976 at South Shore Hospital of a heart attack after five weeks in intensive care. He is buried at Oak Woods Cemetery.

Mob Boss

File Card

Ralph Pierce
AKA P.R. Symmons
Born June 12, 1903, New Comerstown, Tuscaros County, Ohio
Also used Birthdates 6-12-1894 / 6-12-1904 Chicago/ 6-12-1904 Cleveland and Columbus, Ohio
Died July 7, 1976 Chicago
SS# 361-12-0891 *(Number he gave on his Select Service File May 1942)*
FBI # 768056
Chicago PD# C-33507
U.S.M. # 6899
Height 5'9"
Weight 180 pounds
Hair Light Brown
Eyes Blue
Wife Dorthy Lind, aka Dottie, Born 1-23-1902 Chicago *(Married Crownpoint, Indiana on February 23, 1940)*

Family Members

Father William Pierce
Mother Amanda Johnson (One report stated her name as Amanda Stewart) She was born around 1866, lived at 903 Vine Street, Koschocton, Ohio (1941)
Sister Jesse Dunn, born around 1892, lived at 5220 Harper Street, Chicago (1941)
Brother William Pierce Jr. Born April 12, 1903 in Newcomerstown, Ohio. Lived at 716 South 18th Street, Koschocton, Ohio (1942)
Brother Frank Peirce, died around 1957
Brother Fred Peirce, died around 1957

Known Addresses

1603 Paxton Avenue, Chicago (1930)
7630 Paxton Avenue, Chicago (1931)
Carlton Hotel, 2138 South Wabash Avenue, Chicago (1940)
7749 Kingston Avenue, Chicago (1941)
7727 Kingston Avenue, Chicago (1942)
7635 West Jackson Boulevard, Chicago *(Some reports say 7636 Jackson)* (1943)
7743 Merrill Avenue, Chicago (1952)
5020 Marine Drive, Chicago (1957) *(Police found just a parking lot at this address)*

Known Places of Employment

Chicago Radio Sales Company, Chicago (Salesman) (1931)
Rodger's Corners Restaurant, 50th and 8th Avenue, New York City (1942)
Proprietor of the Independent Worker, Manager (1940)
Commercial Broker (1942)

Tony Dark

Russell's Silver Bar and Restaurant, 400 South State Street, Chicago (Half Owner) (1946)
Brevort Hotel, 120 West Madison, Chicago (Alleged Owner) (1946)
Oil Broker, Capper, Wyoming (Alleged by himself) (1952)

Known Arrest Record of Ralph Pierce

(Original arrest record ordered destroyed by Chicago Police Commissioner Allan on December 2, 1943)

Date	Charge	Agency	Result
6-15-1926	VS 93 038	Chicago PD	Released
July 1926	Rape	Chicago PD	U/K
10-27-1927	Crime Against Nature	Chicago PD	Discharged
2-29-1928	Larceny	Chicago PD	Acquitted
4-4-1928	Concealed Weapon	Chicago PD	Discharged
5-10-1928	Kidnapping	Chicago PD	Released
10-16-1928	Kidnapping	Chicago PD	Bond Forfeited
10-19-1928	Robbery	Chicago PD	Nolle Processed
10-19-1928	Comeford Kidnapping	Chicago PD	Nolle Processed
10-19-1928	Assault & Murder	Chicago PD	Nolle Processed
12-11-1929	Robbery	Chicago PD	Dismissed
12-11-1929	Kidnapping	Chicago PD	Dismissed
12-11-1929	Assault to Kill	Chicago PD	Dismissed
2-11-1930	Vagrancy	Chicago PD	Discharged
6-12-1930	Disorderly Conduct	Chicago PD	Released
6-26-1930	Lingle Murder	Chicago PD	Released
11-6-1930	Weapon Charge	Chicago PD	Released
11-11-1930	General Principles	Chicago PD	Released
12-5-1930	Disorderly Conduct	Chicago PD	Released
11-15-1931	Questioning	Chicago PD	Released
6-29-1932	Larceny of License Plates	Chicago PD	$25 fine
6-29-1932	Disorderly Conduct	Chicago PD	Released
1-11-1933	Disorderly Conduct	Chicago PD	Discharged
1-11-1933	Concealed Weapon	Chicago PD	Discharged
4-21-1934	Disorderly Conduct	Chicago PD	Released
12-12-1934	Disorderly Conduct	Chicago PD	Released
3-8-1935	Disorderly Conduct	Chicago PD	Released
3-18-1942	Carey Murder Invest.	Chicago PD	Released
4-7-1942	Disorderly Conduct	Chicago PD	Released
3-25-1943	Extortion Postal Fraud	Feds	Dismissed 1943
June 1943	Mail Fraud	Feds	Dismissed
3-17-1945	General Principles	Chicago PD	Released
5-26-1945	James Fawcett Murder	Chicago PD	Released
10-1-1952	General Principles	Chicago PD	Released
Sept. 1955	Gioe Murder	Chicago PD	Released
12-12-1955	Greenberg Murder	Chicago PD	Released
1-26-1960	Investigation	Chicago PD	Released

UNITED STATES DEPARTMENT OF JUSTICE
FEDERAL BUREAU OF INVESTIGATION
WASHINGTON 25, D. C.

7-20-61H

J. Edgar Hoover
Director.

The following FBI record, NUMBER 768 056 is furnished FOR OFFICIAL USE ONLY.

CONTRIBUTOR OF FINGERPRINTS	NAME AND NUMBER	ARRESTED OR RECEIVED	CHARGE	DISPOSITION
Police Department Chicago Illinois	Ralph Pierce #C-33507	November 11, 1931	General principles	
United States Marshal Chicago, Illinois	Ralph Pierce #6899	March 25, 1943	extortion-postal fraud	
United States Marshal New York, New York	Ralph Pierce #--	June 8, 1943	Mail fraud	May 6, 1947 Nolle Prossequi
Police Department Chicago, Illinois	Ralph Pierce #--	January 26, 1960	Investigation	

disposition is not
possibly identical

NAME: RALPH PIERCE

AKA:

RESIDENCES:

AREA OF OPERATIONS: Chicago

DATE AND PLACE OF BIRTH:

JUSTICE FILE NOS.:

CITIZENSHIP STATUS:

FBI NO.: 768056

CRIMINAL RECORD:

Place	Name & Number	Date	Charge	Disposition
New York City	Ralph Pierce	1943	Violation of Anti-racketeering Act	Dismissed

ASSOCIATES: Louis Compagna, Charles Gioe, Capone Gang

ACTIVITIES AND GENERAL INFORMATION: Ralph Pierce is a former bodyguard in the old Capone syndicate. He was indicted with Compagna, Gioe, et al., but was acquitted. At present he is reported to be a gambling boss in the Loop District and near north side of Chicago (23-5/11-N).

Nick Circella

Nick Circella had a somewhat damaging childhood. He entered the United States on January 26, 1902 at the age of three-and-a-half and never was naturalized. In July 1909 at the age of 11 years old Circella was arrested for going onto a railroad track and breaking the seal on a freight car and damaging automobiles therein. He was given parole and sent to the Chicago Parental School in October 1909 by the Juvenile Court.

On November 28, 1911, Circella was sent to the Working Boys Home. Months later in February 1912 he was found sleeping outside in an outhouse covered in stolen coats from the home. Once again he was given probation until he was arrested in December 1914 and charged with malicious mischief. His life in crime moved to robbery with a gun in September 1915 and while on probation from that arrest he struck up an argument with a man and beat him with his fist. The man died a few days later from the punches but Circella was exonerated by a coroner's jury.

On July 20, 1916 Circella was sentenced to 14 years in Illinois Pontiac Prison for assault with intent to kill and robbery. He served only two years and was released on December 20, 1918. In May 1919 he was arrested with future Capone Gang members Frank Rio, John Gordana and Frank Diamond for stealing an automobile from the garage at 601 Independence Boulevard. He violated parole in May 1921 and was returned to prison until September 1, 1921.

After a few more arrest for robbery and larceny, he was arrested in January 1922 and questioned as an associate of Eddie Ginsberg. Ginsberg had shot and killed a Chicago Police Detective. In 1924 he was arrested in connection with a $759,000 mail robbery in Harvey, Illinois. The police had evidence Circella was involved but it was not good enough to make it stick. He was never charged for that crime.

In May 1930 Nick Circella was arrested with his boss Al Capone and his associates Albert Prignano, a former alderman of the old 20th Ward, and Sylvester Agogila, then an undertaker. The four were arrested in Miami, Florida while attending a prize boxing match. The arrest was to harass Al Capone and his pals; they were charged with vagrancy and released. Al Capone's wife Mae, and Nick Circella's wife Ernestine, were very close friends. When the Capone's were back in Chicago, Circella had full use of Capone's Miami residence whenever he pleased.

In March 1933 Nick Circella was dating Estelle Carey, his "sweetheart," which was well known by everyone in the Capone Gang. To send a warning to Circella for some unknown reason, it's believed that Tony Accardo killed Estelle. Police Captain William Drury arrested Accardo, Ralph Pierce and Lester "Killer Kane" Kruse for questioning. While Accardo was in the police station the police started receiving telephone calls threatening them to release the three gangsters "or else."

In the late 1930's Nick Circella needed a source of legitimate income. Informants had told the FBI in 1937 that Circella was a manager of the Yacht Club on Oak Street in Chicago. He had been seen associating with Jack Kirsch, then a power in the projectionist unions in Chicago. Kirsch had acted as a middleman and delivery boy for Circella in loans with other movie theater owners.

Circella had asked for an operator job in Local 110 but one problem stood in the way, there were no positions available. What to do? No problem, the Capone Gang killed a man named Hank Schneider so Circella could have his job at the Esquire Theater in Chicago.

It was around this time that Circella became a personal representative of George Browne in the International Alliance of Theatrical & Stage Employees Union. Once William Bioff moved to California between 1937 and 1940, Circella was given the job of going around collecting tributes from motion picture exhibitors in the Chicago area. He would threaten to call strikes if they did not pay up, which they did, totaling over $95,600.

When Circella was arrested for extortion he told investigators he did not have the money to fight the charge so he opted to work out a plea deal for a shorter prison sentence. He told investigators that Browne hired him solely to accompany him on business trips or as Circella called it, "a flunkey in plain English." According to Circella, once he discovered what Browne was up to, he quit in 1939 (he continued to work for Browne in 1940).

Ralph Capone told investigators that Circella and William Bioff were very good friends. Circella, on a few occasions, brought William Bioff and his wife over to Al Capone's Miami home for dinner.

Circella's prison record said, *"Subject's explanation is inadequate and is rebutted at every turn by the facts in the case. His is the attitude of a wise criminal whose silence probably is founded on reasons of self-protection. He apparently feels that he will be punished in any event, and hence his illogical explanation."*

Nick Circella entered Leavenworth on February 28, 1948. His time in Leavenworth was occupied by working as the switchboard operator in the power plant. He had only one mention of discipline when a dictionary from the library was found in his cell. He was released from Leavenworth Prison on February 9, 1948 and was employed as a manager of a movie theater on Chicago's South State Street.

In 1953 the Chicago Crime Commission was investigating rumors that Tony Accardo and Sam Giancana were attempting to "take over the shrimp boat industry." The CCC was never able to verify the rumors but they did uncover information that Nick Circella had some interest in shrimpboats down in Acapulco, Mexico which may have been the financed by Accardo and Giancana.

In April 1955 Circella and his wife Ernestine boarded the S.S. Delnorte at the port of New Orleans and sailed away to Argentina under a U.S. deportation order. Nick still had ties in Chicago and money coming his way in the form of his brother August "Augie" Circella. August was partners with Jerry DiGiacomo and Vincent Giuliano in the Follies Theater at 450 S. State Street in Chicago's Loop. The theater was a movie and burlesque show theater.

In 1963 an FBI informant said that a person of high standing within the Chicago Outfit had sent a lot of money to Nick Circella who was running gambling in Mexico for the Chicago Outfit. Investigators discovered that both Tony Accardo and Paul DeLucia were the two spearheading organized gambling in Mexico without Sam Giancana. At the same time Sam Giancana was spearheading organized gambling in the Dominican Republic, meeting with Porfirio Rubirosa, a former Ambassador to the United States from the Dominican Republic, in France.

Even with Circella in another country, the U.S. Government filed a suit in federal district court to attach two life insurance policies totaling $5,000 issued to Nick Circella in 1965. The States Attorney at that time, Edward V. Hanrahan, said the policies would have been applied to the $17,706 in income taxes Circella owed from the years 1936 thru 1941. The attorney handling the American side of this suit was Joseph Bulger.

File Card

Nick Circella
AKA Nick Dean
AKA Nicholas Deani Circella
AKA Nick Ledeem
AKA Nickolas, Nickolodean, Nicholodean, N.J. Dean, Sovello, Nick Ciriello, Mike Circella,
Born August 24, 1898 in Italy (Entered the United States on January 26, 1902)
FBI # 281962

Family

Father Joseph Circella (Came to America 1898)
Mother Marie Circella
Wife Ernestine Circella
Anthony Circella (Brother)
August "Augie" Circella (Brother)

Known Businesses

Movie Projectionist (1930's)
The Yacht Club, Oak Street, Chicago (Manager) (1937)
The Colony Club Restaurant and Casino, North Rush Street (1940's) *(Owner with mobster Lawrence "Dago" Mangano)*
Field Representative Theatrical and Stage Employees Union 1936-1941
Shrimp boats in Acapulco, Mexico (1953)

Known Addresses

426 South Humphrey, Oak Park, Illinois (1940's-1955)
410 South Austin Blvd. Oak Park, Illinois (1940's)
429 South Taylor Street, Chicago (1948)
Argentina (1955)
Mexico (1960's)

Known Arrest Record of Nick Circella

Date	Charge	Agency	Result
7-12-1909	Vandalism	Chicago PD	Juvenile Court
11-28-1911	Running away	W. Boys Home	U/K
12-28-1914	Malicious Mischief	Chicago PD	Juvenile Court
1-28-1915	U/K	Chicago PD	Discharged
12-15-1915	Robbery	Chicago PD	1 Year Probation
4-16-1916	Battery / Murder	Chicago PD	Coroner's Jury
9-14-1916	Robbery	Chicago PD	14 Years Prison
9-21-1916	Assault to Murder	Chicago PD	14 Years Prison
9-24-1916	Probation Violation	Chicago PD	Disposed
5-7-1919	Larceny	Chicago PD	Not Guilty
7-9-1919	Burglary	Chicago PD	Not Guilty
7-9-1919	Larceny	Chicago PD	Stricken
5-21-1920	Parole Revoked	U.S. Marshall	Pontiac Prison
1-10-1922	Murder Investigation	Chicago PD	Released
1-24-1922	Robbery	Chicago PD	Nolle Processed
1-28-1924	Mail Robbery	Harvey, IL	Not Guilty
4-8-1924	Robbing Mail	Chicago PD	U/K
5-6-1930	Vagrancy	Miami PD	Released
July – 1941	Fugitive Grand Jury	U/K	U/K
9-17-1941	Inquiry	Chucago PD	U/K
12-1-1941	Anti-Racketeering	New York	Guilty
4-7-1942	Extortion	New York	8 Years Prison
2-9-1944	Anti-Racketeering Act	Levenworth	8 Years Prison
10-2-1952	INS Laws	INS	U/K

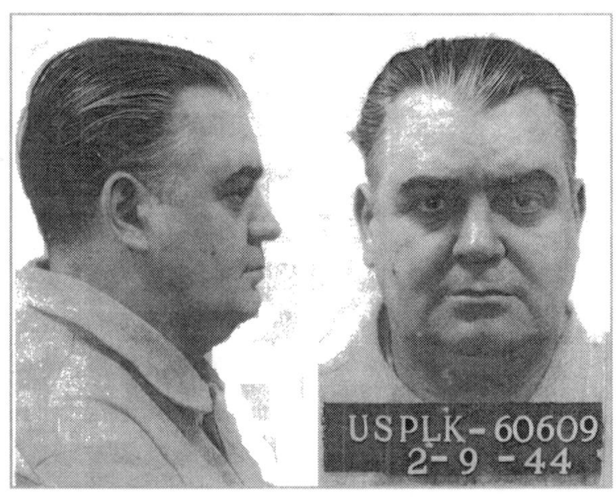

U[illegible]TED STATES DEPARTMENT OF [illegible]USTICE
FEDERAL BUREAU OF INVESTIGATION
WASHINGTON 25, D. C.

For.1898,M.W.

Aug 25 1950 4156 de

J. Edgar Hoover
Director.

The following is the record of FBI number 281962

CONTRIBUTOR OF FINGERPRINTS	NAME AND NUMBER	ARRESTED OR RECEIVED	CHARGE	DISPOSITION
Illinois State Reformatory,	Mike Circella, A-519	9/21/16	aslt. to murder	1-14 yrs.
PD Miami, Fla.	Nick Circelle, #3566	5/8/30	inv. vag.	rel. on writ 5/8/30
Fed. Det. Hdqts., NYC, NY.	Nicholas Circella #33738	12-1-41	anti-racketeering	disch. 12-4-41, bail
USM, NYC, NY.	Nick Circella #011-219	12-2-41	not given	
FIH, N. Y., N. Y.	Nick Circella #34717	4-7-42	viol. Anti-racketeering Act	8 yrs. 4-7-42, U.S.D.C. S.D.N.Y. sent. to U.S.P. and fined $10,000 and to stand committed until fine paid or otherwise disch. according to law. Disch. to Tombs Prison, N.Y.C. 4-29-42.
USP, Leavenworth, Kansas	Nick Circella #60609	2-9-44	Anti-racketeering Act	8 yrs. 2-9-48, cond. rel.
PD, Chicago, Ill.	Nick Circella #65937	inquiry 9-17-41		

* Represents notations unsupported by fingerprints in FBI files.

U. S. GOVERNMENT PRINTING OFFICE : 1950—O—[illegible]

NOTICE.—*This Record is furnished for official use only*

Nick Circella's FBI Rap Sheet of Arrest

U[NI]TED STATES DEPARTMENT OF [JU]STICE
FEDERAL BUREAU OF INVESTIGATION
WASHINGTON 25, D. C.

The following is the record of FBI number 281 962

J. Edgar Hoover
Director.

CONTRIBUTOR OF FINGERPRINTS	NAME AND NUMBER	ARRESTED OR RECEIVED	CHARGE	DISPOSITION

Description:

Color: white
Sex: male
Date of birth: 8-24-98
Occupation: Labor Union Represent.
Birthplace; Italy
Comp.: dk.
Height: 5 ft. 9½ in.
Eyes: dk. br.
Weight: 245 lbs.
Hair: dk. ch. mxgy
Build: st.
Scars and marks: Ft. vert 2" ba. R. thumb frt.; curv. 1" 1st jt. L. ind. rear & out.; Y-shaped ba. L. thumb. frt.; vert. 1" & obl. ½" L. forehead; sm. pit scar L. cheek; gunshot wound-groin.

NAME: Nick Circella

AKA:

RESIDENCES: 429 S. Taylor St., Oak Park, Ill. (1948)
426 S. Humphrey Ave., Oak Park, Ill. (1950)

AREA OF OPERATIONS: Chicago

DATE AND PLACE OF BIRTH: 1899 Italy

JUSTICE FILE NOS.:

CITIZENSHIP STATUS: Alien FBI NO.:

CRIMINAL RECORD:

Place	Name & Number	Date	Charge	Disposition
Chicago	Nick Circella	1915	Robbery	1-yr. probation on plea of guilty
Chicago	Nick Circella	1916	Assault to murder	1 to 10 years Paroled 1921
New York	Nick Circella	1943	Violation: Anti racketeering statute	8-yrs. sentence

ASSOCIATES:

ACTIVITIES AND GENERAL INFORMATION: Circella was associated with George E. Brown, William Bioff and others in the shakedown racket involving motion picture theatre owners and producers (23-5/11-I). Circella was conditionally released from Leavenworth on Feb. 9, 1948, and is now employed as manager of a movie theatre on Chicago's South State Street.

Record Form No. 1 (Revised Feb. 1936)

RECORD OF COURT COMMITMENT

Original
Central

Department of Justice
PENAL AND CORRECTIONAL INSTITUTION

8-24-1898-Italy-Italy-Married-labor union representative-Cafe Opr-6th gr-Catholic-No mil

(Institution)

(Location)

Inst. Name	Nick Circella	No.	60609-L
Alias	Nick Dean	Color	White Age 48
True Name	Nickolas Circella	Name and number of prior commitments to Fed. Inst.	33738-FDHNY-Curr. Case. None
Offense	Anti-Racketeering Act: Conspiracy to Interfere with Trade and Commerce by Violence, Threats, Coercion.		
District	SD-NY-New York		
Sentence	8 Years	Costs / Fine $10,000	Committed / Committed yes / Not Committed / Not Committed / Paid / Paid
Sentence changed	Fine paid to Clerk of Court 4-18-42	New term	Reason therefor
Sentenced	April 7, 1942	When arrested	Dec. 1, 1941
Committed to Fed. Inst.	Feb. 9, 1944	Where arrested	Chicago, Ills.
Sentence begins	April 7, 1942	Residence	Oak Park, Illinois
Eligible for parole	Dec. 6, 1944	Time in jail before trial	5 days & made bond
Eligible for conditional release with good time	Feb. 28, 1948	Rate per mo good time 8	Total good time possible 768 Days
Eligible for con. rel. with extra good time			
Forfeited good time		Amount forfeited	
Restoration good time		Amount restored	
Expires full term	April 6, 1950		

Former Com. on Sentence to Other Institutions

No.	Name of Institution	Location
~~A-319~~	~~Reformatory~~	~~Pontiac, Illinois.~~

Person to be notified in case of serious illness or death

Name Mrs. Ernestine Circella,
Relation to prisoner Wife
Address 429 So. Taylor Ave., Oak Park, Ills.
Telephone

Release and recommitments on present sentence other than Parole

Rev. | Dis. From par | To | Method

U. S. PENITENTIARY
LEAVENWORTH
CONDITIONAL RELEASE
FEB 9 1948

Whom | Remarks

District Court of the United States
Southern District of New York

UNITED STATES OF AMERICA

vs.

NICK CIRCELLA,
alias Nick Dean.

C.110-368.

Violation of U.S.C. Title 18, Secs. 420a (a), (b), (d); Anti-racketeering Act of June 18, 1934. Conspiracy to interfere with trade and commerce by violence, threats and coercion.

JUDGMENT AND COMMITMENT

On this 7th day of April 1942, upon the proceedings heretofore had herein and on motion of the United States Attorney, IT IS BY THE COURT

ORDERED AND ADJUDGED that the defendant be hereby committed to the custody of the Attorney General or his authorized representative for imprisonment in an institution to be designated by the Attorney General or his authorized representative for the period of **EIGHT (8) YEARS and Fined $10,000.**

White
8 yrs
Anti-Racketeering Act, Conspiracy interfere with trade & commerce by violence threats & coercion
$10,000 fine Comm. Begins 4-7-42

RECEIVE

IT IS FURTHER ORDERED that **defendant is to stand committed until fine shall be paid or until he shall otherwise be discharged according to law.**

IT IS FURTHER ORDERED that the Clerk deliver a certified copy of this judgment and commitment to the United States Marshal or other qualified officer and that the same shall serve as the commitment herein.

HENRY W. GODDARD
United States District Judge.

TRUE COPY. Certified this 7th day of April 1942.

Clerk.

Johnny Roselli

Giovanni Roselli was born on June 4, 1905 in Chicago to Vincenzo Roselli and Maria Russo, Italian immigrant parents who died while Johnny was an infant. He was raised by his uncle, Anthony D'Acunta. Johnny completed the 6th grade in education and worked around the city until he reached the age of 15. His uncle Anthony had sent Roselli to live with other family members. It was a short period after that when he decided to headed out west to Hollywood, California, when he was 16 years old. Roselli went to meet up with uncle who had established himself on the west coast.

Around 1930 his uncle Anthony died and Johnny became a "roomer" just roaming around the west coast. Between 1924 and 1927 the young Roselli found work as a movie extra. After 5 years of being an extra he was considered pretty much a "bum." From 1931 to 1932 he worked as the public relations officer for the Club New Yorker and in 1933 he went to work for Pat Casey Entertainment. At one point it was said that Johnny Roselli got a break when he became a bodyguard for the powerful Harry Cohen who was the President of Columbia Pictures.

When Roselli was interviewed in connection with an extortion case, he claimed he was in the general insurance business and was licensed as a solicitor. He said he was formerly engaged in public relations work for Pat Casey Entertainment in New York City and Los Angeles. He also had interest in the Nation Wide News Service in Los Angeles. He also had interest in the Agua Caliente Race Track in Mexico.

One informant to the FBI said that Johnny Roselli was in charge of bodyguards and was responsible for taking old members of the Capone Gang in Chicago to Los Angeles to act as gunmen for the International Alliance of Theatrical and Stage Employees. Another informant said Roselli was a gunman for Los Angeles gangster Joe Shaw, whose brother was Frank Shaw, mayor of the city. Joe Shaw was secretary and a political boss who employed Roselli as his personal goon.

Roselli at one point owned and operated a Los Angeles night club and was considered a "hanger on" in the fight game, doing some amateur boxing. Between 1940 and 1942 Roselli worked for Herman Spitzel and Company which was located at 215 West 5th Street, Los Angeles.

On April 1, 1940, Roselli married a Hollywood actress named Winifred June Vlasek, commonly known as June Lang, in Yuma, Arizona. The marriage lasted only a few years because in December 1942 Roselli was inducted into the U.S. Army, 5th Armored Division. There he would serve as a private until he was arrested on March 18, 1943 for extortion.

With the arrest came a fast divorce from June Lang. He was sentenced on December 28, 1943 to 10 years in prison and a $10,000 fine for conspiracy to interfere with trade and commerce by coercion, threats and violence and elected to start serving his sentence on March 8, 1944. He arrived at Atlanta Penitentiary on April 4, 1944.

Classification Form 1a
Rev. January 1939

UNITED STATES PENITENTIARY
ATLANTA, GA.
ADMISSION SUMMARY

Committed Name ROSELLI, John Reg. No. 63775-A Classified 4-27-44

True Name	John Rosselli	Judicial District	S-NY-New York
Date of Birth	6-4-05	Offense	Consp.to Inter.with Trade & Commerce by Coercion,Threats, & Violence
Age	38	Sentence	10 Years Comm. Fine $10,000
Race	White	Sentence begins	3 - 8-44
Country of Birth	U.S.A.	Committed	4 - 4-44
Citizenship	American	Eligible for Parole	7 - 7-47
Marital Status	Divorced	Conditional Release Date	11-23-50
Legal Residence	Los Angeles,Calif.	Expires Full Term	3 - 7-54
		Detainers	

REPORTS REC'D FROM: F. B. I. Yes U. S. ATTY. No PROSECUTING AGENCY No

1. PREVIOUS CRIMINAL RECORD:

Date	Place	Offense	Disposition	Source	Admi
1924	PD-Los Angeles,Cal.	Carrying Conceal-ed Weapon	Dismissed	Inmate	Ye
1926	PD-Los Angeles,Cal	Susp.	Dismissed	Inmate	Ye
5-11-26	PD-San Francisco, Cal.	$1,000.00 Vag.& Fug. Susp.	Dismissed	FBI	Ye
1931	PD-San Francisco, Cal.	Susp.	Dismissed	Inmate	Ye
6-8-43	USM-New York,N.Y.	Mail Fraud	Pending Under Bond	FBI	Ye

Johnny Roselli's Prison Record and Signature

John Rosell

Form T-2

Federal Bureau of Investigation
United States Department of Justice
Washington, D. C.

April 15 1944 824 mjb

The following is the record of FBI number 3339986

J. E. Hoover
Director.

CONTRIBUTOR OF FINGERPRINTS	NAME AND NUMBER	ARRESTED OR RECEIVED	CHARGE	DISPOSITION
PD, San Francisco, Calif.	John F. Stewart #38190	5-11-26	$1000 vag. and fug. susp.	
USM, New York, N.Y.	John Rosselli #023-462	3-19-43	unlawfully conspired to interfere with trade and commerce	
USM, New York, N.Y.	John Roselli #023-462	3-19-43	mail fraud	[illegible] anti-rack[illegible] [illegible], 10-28-43, sent. 10 yrs. $10,000 10 yrs. (fine)
FDH, New York, N.Y.	John Roselli, #41923	2-15-44	Anti-Racketeering Act-Consp.	
USP, Atlanta, Ga.	John [illegible] #63775	4-6-44	consp. to interfere with trade and comm. by coercion threats and violence	10 yrs.

COPY FOR BUREAU OF PRISONS

* Represents notations unsupported by fingerprints in FBI files.

NOTICE: THIS RECORD IS FURNISHED FO[R]

JOHN ROSELLI, was,

John Russelli, John Rasselli,
John F. Stewart

Age: 48 (1953)
Weight: 160 lbs.
Height: 5' 9"
Hair: Black-greying
Eyes: Brown

FBI #3339986

There was some speculation that Roselli's transfer from Leavenworth to Atlanta came from efforts by Samuel Roy Beard, a Washington D.C. gambler and political fixer. Sam Beard was also a representative of the Trams-American News outlet from Maryland. While in prison Roselli worked as a storeroom clerk and was then assigned to the culinary department for awhile. He was listed as exceptionally obedient, cooperative, excellent self-control, consistently pleasant, courteous, never argumentative or quarrelsome. Officers listed him as having above average leadership ability which he used constructively. He scored an I. Q. of 112. On the other hand the prison was aware that Roselli was a smooth individual who was "biding his time" until he was released from incarceration and was very well schooled in organized crime activities which would make him a very bad influence on the younger unstable type prisoner. He did have some health problems while in prison, he was listed as being very susceptible to upper respiratory infections and had been hospitalized numerous times with influenza and pneumonia.

In 1946 Roselli was permitted to see his fiancée, Miss Beatrice Ann Frank, which puzzled the prison since he had been married to another woman when he entered prison.

He was eligible for parole on July 7, 1947, with his conditional release on November 30, 1950 and his full-term sentence to end on March 7, 1954. There was even a report that in 1947 Johnny Roselli was working for Eagle-Lion Studios from prison as a writer and wrote a crime story script based on racketeering which the studio was going to make into a movie.

However, by 1948 Roselli was out of prison and was acting as an Associate Producer for Robert Kane Productions reading and producing screen plays or re-selling screenplays. FBI agents had received word that a gambling operation and handbooks were across the street from Roselli's office. However they could not connect Roselli to the gambling operations.

Two Los Angeles reporters were going to write a follow up story about Roselli for the local newspaper. Like he did before, one of the writers went to City Hall to view Roselli's arrest record. This writer was amazed that when Roselli was first arrested in 1943 this writer had gone to City Hall to view Roselli's records and found a rap sheet with over 16 arrests. In 1947 when he went back to view the records, they were gone and a smaller arrest sheet with just 5 arrests was available. No one in the police department would say what happened to Roselli's original arrest record and it never was seen again.

By 1954 Roselli was engaged in a race wire service with a Russell Brophy in Los Angeles, California. He was working with Monogram Studios as a motion picture producer. He lived at 1251 N. Crescent Heights Boulevard which happened to be the same apartment building that California Governor Goodwin J. Knight lived in. The building was owned by Cal Eaton, then Los Angeles's top boxing promoter. Knight spent time between the governor's executive mansion in Sacramento and the apartment building where his daughter spent most of her time. Roselli had used the apartment as a place that hopefully showed he was a respectable businessman. However, the L.A.P.D did not care where he lived and still watched him and questioned residents about suspicious activities.

In the summer of 1954 police officers stopped Roselli as he was pulling his car into the garage and "shook" him down to embarrass him. Roselli was so angry he could be heard screaming that he was legitimately employed and that he was living in the same building as the governor.

One report said that in 1955 Johnny Roselli was a member of the Los Angeles crime family controlled by Jack Dragna, with close ties to the Outfit. Once mob boss Sam Giancana was about to be made top boss of the Chicago family, Roselli transferred his membership into the Chicago Outfit. An informant once told the FBI that this transfer was arranged by either Sam Giancana or Paul DeLucia.

In June 1957 Roselli was brokering deals involving Las Vegas casinos. For instance, he was observed racing back and forth between Las Vegas and Los Angeles with an attorney named James Cantillon and was involved in representing certain eastern groups who were investing large sums of cash in casino operations in Vegas.

He was often observed hanging around the Charley Foy's Supper Club on Ventura Boulevard west of Hollywood, California. Charley Foy was the brother of Bryan Fox and they were the sons of Eddie Foy, a one-time famous vaudeville actor.

WESTERN UNION

W. P. MARSHALL, PRESIDENT

Send the following message, subject to the terms on back hereof, which are hereby agreed to

SEPTEMBER 29, 1950

UNITED STATES MARSHALL
LOS ANGELES
CALIFORNIA

PLEASE NOTIFY D'ANDREA AND ROSELLI TO APPEAR WITH RECORDS BEFORE COMMITTEE AT ROOM 280 OLD POST OFFICE BUILDING CHICAGO ILLINOIS 9:30 A.M. OCTOBER 5, 1950 PURSUANT TO SUBPOENA. WIRE WHEN NOTIFIED AND FURNISH ADDRESSES COLLECT SO THAT REGISTERED LETTERS MAY BE SENT THEM.

ESTES KEFAUVER, CHAIRMAN
SPECIAL COMMITTEE TO
INVESTIGATE ORGANIZED CRIME
IN INTERSTATE COMMERCE

CLASS OF SERVICE

This is a full-rate Telegram or Cablegram unless its deferred character is indicated by a suitable symbol above or preceding the address.

WESTERN UNION

W. P. MARSHALL, PRESIDENT

1201

(02)..

SYMBOLS

DL=Day Letter

NL=Night Letter

LT=Int'l Letter Telegram

VLT=Int'l Victory Ltr.

The filing time shown in the date line on telegrams and day letters is STANDARD TIME at point of origin. Time of receipt is STANDARD TIME at point of destination

LB207

1950 OCT 4 PM 3 06

L.AYA556 PD=ALBUQUERQUE NMEX 4 146P=

RUDOLPH HOLLEY=

280 US COURT HOUSE OLD POST OFFICE BLDG CHGO=

MR ROSSELLI AND I ARE EN ROUTE ON SANTA FE SUPER CHIEF ARRIVING THURSDAY THURSDAY 1:45 PM. WHICH WAS EARLIEST TRANSPORTATION STOP SHOULD YOUR COMMITTEE PLANS REQUIRE MR ROSSELLIS PRESENCE IN THE MORNING PLEASE WIRE ME ON TRACER COMPARTMENT I CAR 186 AND I SHALL WIRE AHEAD AND ENDEAVOR TO OBTAIN A FLIGHT OUT OF KANSAS CITY. WE SHALL REPORT TO YOUR COMMITTEE FORTHWITH UPON ARRIVAL=

OTTO CHRISTENSEN=

THE COMPANY WILL APPRECIATE SUGGESTIONS FROM ITS PATRONS CONCERNING ITS SERVICE

Parole Form No. 17
January 1937

The United States Board of Parole
Washington, D. C.

Certificate of Parole

Know all Men by these Presents:

It having been made to appear to the United States Board of Parole that John Roselli, Register No. 4305-TH, a prisoner in the United States Penitentiary, Terre Haute, Indiana, is eligible to be PAROLED, and that there is a reasonable probability that said prisoner WILL REMAIN AT LIBERTY WITHOUT VIOLATING THE LAWS, and it being the opinion of the said United States Board of Parole that the release of this prisoner is not incompatible with the welfare of society, it is ORDERED by the said United States Board of Parole that the prisoner be PAROLED from the said Penitentiary on August 13, 19 47, and that said prisoner remain within the limits of Southern District California until March 7 [handwritten] 19 54; or in the event of a committed fine or a committed fine and costs, until the same have been paid or he has been discharged under the provisions of Section 641, Chapter 19, Title 18, U. S. Code, or until other action may be taken by the said United States Board of Parole.

Given under the hands and the seal of the United States Board of Parole this 8th day of August, nineteen hundred and forty-seven.

UNITED STATES BOARD OF PAROLE,
T. WEBBER WILSON, *Chairman.*
FRED S. ROGERS, *Member.*
B. J. Monkievics, Member

[SEAL]

By Walter K. Urich
Parole Executive.

UNITED STATES BOARD OF PAROLE:

The above-named prisoner was released on the 13th day of August, 19 47

[signature]
Warden or Superintendent.

NAME: JOHN ROSELLI

AKA:

RESIDENCES: 1701 South Jefferson St., Chic., Ill. (1934)
1259 N. Crescent Heights, Los Angeles, Cal.

AREA OF OPERATIONS: Chicago & Los Angeles

DATE AND PLACE OF BIRTH: 8/13/07 Lithuania

JUSTICE FILE NOS.: 93-1-1713
93-1-1360

CITIZENSHIP STATUS: FBI NO.:

CRIMINAL RECORD:

Place	Name & Number	Date	Charge	Disposition
Chicago	John Roselli	1928	Grand larceny	Guilty plea 6 years.
"	" "	1934	Petty larceny	6 months. (23-5/11-A)
New York	" "	1943	Anti-racketeering statute viol.	10 years.

ASSOCIATES: Louis Compagna, Charles Gioe, Philip D'Andrea, Paul DeLucia

ACTIVITIES AND GENERAL INFORMATION: John Roselli was convicted with Compagna, Gioe, D'Andrea, and others in connection with the Bioff & Brown shakedown. Roselli at the present time is under the supervision of the United States Probation Officer and is the personal employee of producer Bryan Foy of Eagle-Lion Studios (11-5/12-I).

John Roselli's 1950 Senate Information Sheet

In January 1960 Chicago Mob boss Sam Giancana and Frank Ferraro had a conversation about Roselli:

Giancana	Did Roselli, did Johnny leave?
Ferraro	Yeah.
Giancana	He's nutty. He's a crazy son-of-a-bitch. He thinks he's a banker.
Ferraro	Yeah, he's talking about somebody out in Vegas, always talks himself out of the jackpot. I says, you're no Barber John. You got a silver tongue, too. Hump (Murray Humphreys) told me John got mad at him. Hump says his eyes popped. You know how his eyes pop.
Giancana	Johnny gets hot, though.
Ferraro	He says, listen, I live like a millionaire.
Giancana	He ain't got a dime.
Later Murray Humphreys and Charles "Babe" Baron talked about Roselli:	
Baron	Is John living in Los Angeles?
Humphreys	L.A., but he goes to Vegas to play golf. He's running into a bad spot.
Baron	I assumed that he represented you people out there. At least he had me to understand that when I was out there.
Humphreys	Sure, he does.
Baron	Johnny does more fucking crazy things. He wanted me one day to make a luncheon date with Katelman at the country club, pick a fight with Katelman.... I'm not afraid of anybody, Hump, like I told you, if you do nothing wrong, you have nothing to be afraid of. I can fight.
Humphreys	Why didn't you use your hands?
Baron	I don't believe in that. I believe in what you just said. You don't go around hitting people. So, furthermore, Katelman is a pretty good fighter himself. I couldn't see why I should go and pick a fight with Katelman. He never did nothing to me. He's liable to get me thrown out of town. Johnny (Roselli) got real fucking hot. And said, I ordered you to do that, why the fuck did you not hit him? I said, because I didn't think it was right, Johnny, it was against my principles. He said, since when do you have principles, I said, Johnny, I always have principles, whether you like it or not.

Baron	So he says, you do what I tell you, I says, I'll fucking do what you tell me, I says, if I think it's wrong, I won't do it. I says, I have an obligation to the people in Chicago, I says if you feel that way, I'm packing up right now, and I'm gonna go home, and I'm gonna tell the people just the way I feel, and I'm gonna tell them about you, so when I said that he turned white, he said, Jesus Christ Babe, don't feel that way, and then he changed, and he says, after all, you're my friend, he says, we been friends for years, don't go back and beef to them. He says, aren't you my friend, and I says, yes, you're my friend, but when you hit me with that kind of shit, I'm gonna go back and tell them that they can have my piece and I want out. I says, you can have my piece, if that's the way you feel, but there are other people, and you're gonna make me do those kinda things, I won't do anything that I don't think is right, and I'm sure the people in Chicago won't approve of that. So he changed it entirely, he dropped it. (Baron ended with) I told Mooney (Sam Giancana) about it, Mooney said the S.O.B is crazy.

On September 14, 1960 Robert A. Maheu, a former FBI agent with questionable contacts, was sent to see Johnny Roselli by the Central Intelligence Agency (CIA) to ask Roselli if there was anything that could be done about Fidel Castro, who had recently taken over the country of Cuba and made himself dictator. Maheu's cover story to tell Roselli was that he was representing several international business firms which were suffering heavy financial losses in Cuba as a result of Castro's action. These business firms believed the answer was the removal of Castro and wanted to know if Roselli could make it happen. The meeting took place at the Hilton Plaza Hotel in New York City. At first Roselli's reaction was to not get involved but Maheu persuaded Roselli to agree to arrange a meeting with an associate of his named Sam Gold. Roselli made it clear that he, himself, did not want any money for his part nor would this Sam Gold want any for his part.

Weeks later Maheu met with Sam Gold and a man named Joe at the Fontainebleau Hotel in Miami Beach, Florida. However, Sam Gold turned out to be Sam "Momo" Giancana, then Chicago mob boss and the Joe turned out to be Santo Trafficante, then mob boss of Tampa, Florida. At the meeting, ways of killing Castro were discussed. Giancana did not want to resort to using a gun, but tossed out the idea of using a man named Juan Orta, then a Cuban official who had been receiving kickback payments from gambling in Cuba and was in a financial bind. Giancana explained to Maheu that Orta still had access to Castro and he had access to Orta. Giancana explained that if they, "the CIA," could furnish some kind of poison pill that could be placed into Castro's drink or food, he could have Orta sneak it into Castro's compound and kill Castro.

According to the CIA report, the poison pills, six in all, were delivered to this Joe,

"Trafficante" and attempts were made to get Castro to take the pills. However, all the attempts failed. Orta apparently got cold feet and backed out. A Dr. Anthony Verona, who was a principal officer in the Cuban Exile Junta, also attempted to slip the pill to Castro but failed. There were reports that five attempts were made including an attempt with the use of a gun. The last attempt failed when the assassin was captured and tortured by Castro until he gave up the plan that the CIA was attempting to assassinate him. One report mentioned that after the initial attempt failed, Maheu was removed as the "case agent" to assassinate Castro and replaced by CIA agent William Harvey. There was even a report stating that Castro was so upset about the assassination plot he told his men that if this is the way John F. Kennedy wanted to play it he could play the same way.

The CIA wrote that during the negotiations about this plot with Giancana, Sam expressed concern about his girlfriend, Phyllis McGuire, who had been receiving too much attention from entertainer Dan Rowan. Giancana wanted Maheu to place a bug in Rowan's room to determine if McGuire and Rowan were having sexual relations. Maheu had a man acutely go and bug Rowan's room but the man was caught in the process and arrested by the Sheriff's office. FBI agents believed that Giancana never had anyone try to kill Castro and that he pretended to see how far he could get the government to do his bidding.

As the 1960's went on, CIA documents state that Roselli was said to be a very high ranking member of the syndicate and controlled every ice machine on the Las Vegas strip. But, he was also making some powerful people not so happy. One informant said that when the Detroit mob took over a large ownership investment of the New Frontier Hotel and Casino in Las Vegas, Johnny Roselli was "cut in" on a few points of the deal. But after the deal was complete, the New Frontier was doing poorly losing $250,000 on gambling tables in the first week they opened.

In August 1967 the Detroit mob sent St. Louis mob boss Tony Giardano to the Beverly Hilton Hotel in Los Angeles to have a sit-down with Roselli. The Detroit mob decided they needed some top entertainment to get people into the casino. Giardano asked Roselli to help secure the entertainment since Roselli was receiving money from the casino. They wanted Roselli to use his influence with top theatrical agents to get "talent." Roselli refused to help, causing problems that went up the ladder between Chicago and Detroit. Chicago wanted to purchase 15 points of the Frontier casino from the Detroit family. However, since Roselli was a member of the Chicago Outfit, and had refused to help get entertainment, Detroit refused to sell to Chicago. This was another black mark on Roselli in mob circles.

At the end of the 1960's Roselli was back on trial in Los Angeles, California. He had ambitions to become the top mob boss in Los Angeles. To do this Roselle contacted Florida mob boss Santo Trafficante and up-and-coming Chicago mob boss Felix "Milwaukee Phil" Alderisio who was running the day-to-day operations of the Outfit for mob boss Sam Battaglia. The three set a meeting with New York mob boss Tom Eboli to hear Roselli's case. However, the Detroit family had not forgotten about the New Frontier Hotel and Casino situation and was against Roselli becoming boss. The Detroit family put up Nick Licata, a Roselli's rival, for the top spot.

Mob Boss

While Roselli was making a bid for the top Los Angeles mob boss position he was indicted on six counts of illegal entry into the United States. In 1968 Roselli, along with four other individuals, was also indicted on charges of conspiracy to cheat members of the Friars Club out of $400,000 in rigged gin rummy games.

A Los Angeles informant close to Roselli said that he, Roselli, was getting telephone calls from Chicago Outfit Capo Frank LaPorte inquiring about the prosecution. In turn, LaPorte was reporting all developments concerning Roselli to Tony Accardo and Paul DeLucia who were concerned about the case. Roselli then turned to LaPorte to convince DeLucia, Battaglia and Accardo to help him. Roselli expressed an interest in obtaining influence with political figures and attorneys to obtain favorable treatment in his court cases.

When both DeLucia and Accardo agreed, they sent their three top political mobsters to Palm Springs, California to meet with Roselli to hear his case at the Canyon Club Hotel. They sent Outfit mobsters Pat Marcy, Charles "Doc" Nicosia and Anthony "Tony X" Esposito Sr. to Palm Springs for the meeting. Marcy, Nicosia and Esposito set the meeting to be held at the resort's exclusive spa and both Marcy and Esposito brought their wives, Kathrin and Marilyn, to use as decoys in case investigators were watching.

Roselli was eventually convicted on both conspiracy charges and illegal entry into the United States. The conviction crushed his attempts to be mob boss in Los Angeles.

Both Accardo and DeLucia were concerned about an incident in April 1970 concerning Johnny Roselli. He was extorting money from top Jewish hoodlum Morris "Moe" Dalitz. Dalitz was the owner of many Las Vegas hotels and was in "league" with organized crime to skim money from his casinos.

A month later word reached Chicago that Roselli had made several appearances before a Federal Grand Jury under immunity of prosecution. It was obvious to Chicago that Roselli was naming names and "talking" or he would have been sent to jail under contempt of court. To find out information, DeLucia and Accardo sent mob Capo Frank LaPorte out to California to question Roselli.

Both DeLucia and Accardo were worried because Roselli knew who was involved in the skimming of money in Las Vegas; who carried the money to Sam Giancana; which casinos had hidden Outfit interest; points; ownership money; the skim going through Chicago from Moe Dalitz after the sale of the casinos to Howard Hughes; who was getting what and how much each was getting; skimming operation in the Stardust, Desert Inn and Sands Hotels. If Roselli "flipped" sides and became a government witness, he could lay it all out on a nice chart placing most of America's top syndicate leaders in prison.

First LaPorte made arrangements with Roselli to meet him at Roselli's lawyer's office. LaPorte and Roselli's lawyer, James Cantillon, sat waiting for Roselli but after two hours Roselli never showed up. When LaPorte attempted to question Cantillon about what Roselli was saying at the Federal Grand Jury appearances, Cantillon told LaPorte he could not comment on Roselli's testimony without Roselli's approval, in view of his client-attorney relationship. However LaPorte got the impression that it was not Cantillon's idea for Roselli to testify but rather the decision was Roselli's.

Angered with Roselli not showing up, Frank LaPorte insisted Cantillon set up another meeting and this time he had better be there. The next day Frank LaPorte arrived at Cantillon's office for the Roselli meeting and found neither Roselli nor Cantillon there, but Roselli had left a two-page letter addressed to LaPorte. In the letter were 12 paragraphs of Roselli attempting to explain to LaPorte what testimony he had given to the Grand Jury involving the Chicago Outfit.

Among the things listed in the letter that Roselli answered questions to were about his relationship with Frank LaPorte and Frank Bompensiero and why was he, Roselli, having lunch at Paul's Steak House in Beverly Hills with the two of them? What was LaPorte's interest in Lake Tahoe? How many times had he met with Paul DeLucia, Tony Accardo and Sam Giancana and why? And questions about the Detroit mob family including people like mob boss Anthony Zerilli. Roselli said he knew Paul DeLucia since he, Roselli, was 18 years old and that DeLucia was in the restaurant business. He added that DeLucia had attended his wedding to June Lang. He said he had met Accardo many times and had been to his house a few times but was not close to him and that Giancana was an associate he met here and there in Las Vegas and Chicago.

Frank LaPorte was stunned and furious by this letter and decided he was not going to waste anymore time with Roselli. Just writing a letter like that and leaving it for him proved to LaPorte that Roselli had gone "crazy" and it was up to DeLucia or Accardo as to what was to be done about him.

A few weeks later after DeLucia and Accardo decided what to do with Roselli, Frank LaPorte was sent back to California to have one last meeting with him. FBI agents watched as Frank LaPorte met with Johnny Roselli at the Continental Cuisine Restaurant at 9045 Burton Way in Beverly Hills, California. At the meeting LaPorte told Roselli that he was there on orders from Tony Accardo and Paul DeLucia to instruct Roselli not to make any further attempts to extort money under any conditions from Dalitz. Roselli became very angry and kept repeating over and over that he was being made to look like a fool. Roselli was heard saying that he was instrumental along with a man named "Ruben" in making it possible for Dalitz to sell his Las Vegas Desert Inn and Stardust Hotels to Howard Hughes while keeping Dalitz on the management so that the skimming operation could continue after the sale. Roselli said that when this "Ruben" died he, Roselli, never received any of the money out of Dalitz that was owed to him. Dalitz brought in his own people and set up a new percentage cut out of his skimming operations. Roselli explained to LaPorte that he was financially pressed after his legal expenses and being cut off from Las Vegas and needed the money that he believed was owed to him.

Roselli wanted LaPorte to take a message back to Chicago to give to Accardo and DeLucia with all the facts as to why he was extorting Dalitz. Roselli explained that he owed $100,000 to attorneys and investors and complained that his own people were turning their backs on him. LaPorte refused to do what Roselli asked. He told him that he was not going to be placed in a position of having to run back and forth from Chicago to Los Angeles with messages. He told Roselli if he wanted to make his position clear and to ask for permission to demand money from Dalitz he should go back to Chicago himself and have a sit-down with Accardo or DeLucia. Roselli told LaPorte that he had just returned from Miami, Florida and while he was there Tony Accardo was also in town. Roselli said he tried to contact Accardo through Joe Fischetti knowing that if Accardo was in Miami, Fischetti would be the only one in a place to contact Accardo but when he got in touch with Fischetti, Fischetti acted as if nothing was going on and made no mention of Accardo. Roselli said that was an indication that Accardo would not see Roselli or talk to him.

When Frank LaPorte headed back to Chicago he traveled with someone who in turn was a "rat" giving information to the FBI. The informant told the FBI that on the way back LaPorte told him that Tony Accardo had no further use for Johnny Roselli and that Roselli had lost all his power with the Chicago Outfit when his former boss Sam Giancana left the country. Accardo and DeLucia refused to use Outfit money to pay for Roselli's legal expenses.

Johnnie Roselli was extremely angry at the Chicago Outfit because they denied him the right to shake down Moe Dalitz. Because of it, Roselli continued to testify under immunity trying not to say anything that would have anyone from the Chicago Outfit arrested or indicted but at the same time trying to avoid being in contempt of court.

When all of Roselli's avenues of appeals failed in the courts, Roselli was going to be deported from the country. On November 17, 1970, Roselli's new lawyer, Thomas Wadden, contacted Robert Maheu, the one time CIA operative and informed him that if someone did not intercede on Roselli's behalf, Roselli was going to expose the details of the Castro meeting to the public. Maheu called Roselli's bluff and said no one from the government would intervene. Roselli went to the press and the story was printed in all the newspapers.

At the same time another problem developed for the Chicago Outfit. A majority of the Jewish hoodlum element had their own "Jewish Mafia" and was making waves concerning Roselli and his continuous "shaking down" of wealthy Jewish hoodlums. Some in the Outfit were worried that if Roselli continued to shake down Jews like Moe Dalitz the "Jewish Mafia" would have to kill Roselli themselves which in turn would be a great insult to the Chicago Outfit because it would show a lack of control by Chicago bosses over one of their members. One informant added that if you looked at almost every organized crime group, whether it be in Chicago, Kansas City or New York, they all had "Jewish" members controlling their money. It was said that the Jewish Mafia would rather take $2 of $5 working with the Outfit and take orders from the Outfit than only make $1 out of $5 operating on their own.

The decision to have Johnny Roselli killed made it all the way to a contract being issued but as it turned out Roselli was on his way to prison.

One report came from an FBI informant stating that Chicago mob boss Joey Aiuppa was overheard complaining that mob boss Santo Trafficante Jr. had "botched the job." That FBI informant very close to mobster Frank LaPorte told the FBI that he had met with LaPorte and was told that Johnny Roselli was going to be murdered by the Chicago Outfit. However, no date had been set as LaPorte indicated that there was no hurry in accomplishing this murder at that time because of all the FBI investigations going on concerning the Chicago Outfit but said eventually they would kill Roselli. This informant said that it was his opinion that the Outfit would use someone close to Roselli such as Florida mob boss Santo Trafficante. Five years later Joey Aiuppa was complaining that Santo screwed up the murder job.

On February 25, 1971 Johnny Roselli was sent to McNeil Island Federal Penitentiary on the Pacific coast. There the constant moist sea air and cold winds had an effect on Roselli's health, he developed pneumonia. After almost 3 years he was paroled on October 5, 1973 and he headed right back to Los Angeles getting a room at the Beverly Hilton Hotel and ate dinner at the old La Dolce Vita. By then the winds of fortune had changed for Roselli, Paul DeLucia was dead and Tony Accardo did not see Roselli as much a problem as he once did. FBI reports state that Roselli even helped Tony Accardo in getting mob killer Tony "The Ant" Spilotro set up in Las Vegas.

He moved to Plantation, Florida were he lived off his Social Security check and some profits from a gift shop he owned with a Joe Breen in the Frontier Hotel in Las Vegas. Most of his mob money was pissed away on good times and lawyers.

Through most of the early 1970's Johnny Roselli made appearances before government hearings on Watergate, CIA hearings, and his name was brought up in JFK Assassination plots. When Sam Giancana was murdered in 1975 Johnny Roselli was not worried, even though he was being called to testify before the Select Senate Committee on Intelligence, the same hearings as Giancana was called to appear in front of and he knew the Outfit wanted him to keep his mouth shut.

On July 28, 1976 Johnny Roselli was visiting his sister and brother-in-law Joe Daigle. Roselli left borrowing her car to go and play a few holes of golf, or so it was speculated.

One report stated that Johnny Roselli met an old friend whom he knew very well and another unidentified man from Chicago and the three took a boat ride out into the ocean. There Roselli was suffocated and chopped up.

Roselli's brother-in-law found his wife's car parked on the third level of the Miami International Airport parking garage. A few days later Roselli's body was found stuffed in a 55-gallon steel drum floating in Biscayne Bay near Miami. The barrel was not supposed to be found since it had chains around the outside which failed to weight it down enough to sink the barrel to the bottom of the ocean.

Some believed that Roselli was killed because he testified in front of a Senate Intelligence Committee about his involvement in the Castro plot in June 1975. Roselli gave his testimony a week after Sam Giancana was killed by an unknown assassin. Others said that Roselli was killed by the Cubans for trying to kill Castro.

What was known was that many people wanted Roselli dead. Maybe it was payback from some other powerful people not in organized crime. Maybe it was payback for the "shake downs" on the rich Jewish people in the Los Angeles and Las Vegas areas. Maybe one of them hired a hit man to get rid of Roselli.

Most of the people who knew him said he was not worried about anything right before his death. The only thing Roselli was concerned about was the decision to file a Freedom of Information Act request against the FBI to see if they had broken into his residence while he was incarcerated.

One informant told the FBI that people in the Mafia usually did not kill its members who were in their old age, past the age of 70. To punish those members they would "cut off" their relations and flow of money and put them out to pasture. This same informant also added that Roselli was the type of person who could not be scared by a gun. If you put a gun to Roselli his reaction would be "shoot".

It was the opinion of this informant that Roselli was lured somewhere to be killed by someone he knew and trusted and it was to be a silent hit the same way the Jimmy Hoffa disappearance turned out. He theorized that prior to Roselli being placed in a steel drum rigor mortis had set in and this is why his body was chopped up. No one was ever arrested for the murder. John Roselli was cremated in Miami, Florida.

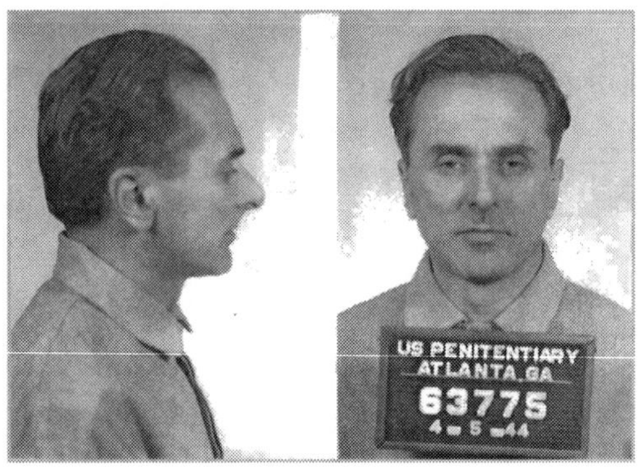

51247

John Rosselli, aka
Roselli, John F. Stewart,
Jack Russell
Male
Caucasian
Age ? 47 (1953) ?
Ht 5'8"
Wt 171
Hair Gray-brown
Eyes blue
LAPD #23903 M 1
LASO #51247, B-70091
FBI # 3339986

John Roselli

284-1019

Tony Dark

File Card

John Roselli
Real name Giovanni Roselli
AKA Johnny Rosselli, Johnny Russelli, John Rasselli, John F. Stewart,
FBI # 3339986
Born June 4, 1905, Chicago, Illinois (One report suggest he was born in Lithuania on 8-13-07)
Died July 1976, Florida
First Wife Winifred June Vlasek, aka June Lang (Divorced 1943)
Engaged to Ann Corcoran aka Beatrice Ann Frank (1946)
Sister, Edith Daigle, husband Joseph.
Peter Cardillo, Listed as a brother in law, New Jersey

Known Addresses

Colonial House, Los Angeles, California (1934-1935)
Garden of Allah Apartments, Los Angeles, California (1935-1936)
1220 Sunset Plaza, Los Angeles, California (1936-1938)
10333 Wilshire Boulevard, Los Angeles, California (1938-1942)
215 West 5th Street, Los Angeles, California (1947)
1259 "A" North Crescent Heights Boulevard. Los Angeles, California (1950's)
1333 South Beverly Glenn Blvd., Los Angeles, California (1960's)
5220 Southwest 10th Court, Plantation, Florida (1976)

Known Businesses

Assistant Purchasing Agent for Eagle-Lion Studios, 7324 Santa Monica Boulevard, Los Angeles California (1947)
Gifts Galore, Frontier Hotel, Las Vegas, Nevada (1970's) (Partner Joe Breen)

Known Arrest Record of John Roselli

Date	Charge	Agency
1924	Carrying Concealed Weapon	Los Angeles PD
1-28-1925	Grand Larceny	Los Angeles PD
3-26-1925	Violation Gun Law	Los Angeles Sheriff
5-4-1926	Robbery	Los Angeles PD
5-11-1926	Vagrant & Fugitive	San Francisco PD
1-31-1929	Disturbing the Peace	Los Angeles PD
6-18-1930	Robbery	Los Angeles PD
7-29-1930	Robbery	Los Angeles PD
1931	Suspicion	San Francisco PD
6-3-1932	Robbery	Los Angeles PD
11-14-1941	Gun Permit	Los Angeles PD
3-19-1943	Extortion	Chicago
6-8-1943	Mail Fraud	New York, N.Y.

2-15-1944	Conspiracy	New York, N.Y.
4-4-1944	Conspiracy Threats & Violence	New York, N.Y.
10-7-1946	Interfere with Trade & Commerce	Terre Haute, Indiana
7-27-1948	Parole Violation	U.S. Marshal Los Angeles

Johnny Roselli's arrest record contained an arrest at the age of 19 on January 28, 1925 by the Los Angeles Police Department on suspicion of grand larceny. He was released on January 29, 1925. On March 26, 1925 he was arrested by the Los Angeles County Sheriff's office and charged with violation of the "gun law" and claimed to be a native of New York. This charge was dismissed on June 8, 1925. On May 4, 1926 he was again arrested by the Los Angeles County Sheriff's Office on suspicion of robbery, and this charge was dismissed. On May 11, 1926 he was arrested as a vagrant and a fugitive, suspicion, by the San Francisco Police Department. No disposition was given for this arrest. On January 31, 1929 he was arrested at Los Angeles for disturbing the peace, for which he paid a $100 fine on March 29, 1930. He was arrested at Los Angeles on suspicion of robbery on June 18, 1930 and was released on June 19, 1930. On July 29, 1930 he was arrested at Los Angeles on suspicion of robbery and was released on July 30, 1930 when he was found not guilty. There was an undated arrest from the Los Angeles P.D. that reflected on an arrest while riding in a car with three other hoodlums who were armed with guns. However, one of the other hoodlums had a gun permit. On June 3, 1932 he was arrested on suspicion of robbery at Los Angeles and was released on June 6, 1932. Years later Johnny Roselli was said to be a small independent dealer in narcotics.

Joseph I. Bulger

Joseph I. Bulger was known as one of the top mob lawyers in the world. His ranking in the syndicate was very high. He had the ability to get any top mobster in the country on the phone in seconds. When a syndicate member needed a lawyer it was Joseph Bulger who would give the "ok" for which mob lawyers to be used.

Joseph Imburgio was born in New Orleans, Louisiana to poor Italian parents in 1899. By the age of 11 his father Giuseppe died leaving his mother Caterina with five children to raise. Joseph went to work on the Bayou docks as a water boy to help put food on the table for his family. He still managed to attend school which he excelled at. In 1918 his family moved to the small town of Melrose Park, Illinois where a large population of German immigrants had settled but a growing Italian population was being established. There Joseph went to work for the American Can Company while he went to night school. A year later he was working as a clerk

Form 54 A

886286

State of Illinois, Cook County. } ss.

Marriage License

To any Person Legally Authorized to Solemnize Marriage,

GREETING:

Marriage may be Celebrated in the County of Cook and State of Illinois,
between Mr. Joseph Imburgia of Melrose Park
in the County of Cook and State of Ill of the age of 22 years,
and Miss Elsie Tomm of Melrose Park
in the County of Cook and State of Ill of the age of 20 years.

Witness, Robert M. Sweitzer, County Clerk of the County of Cook, and the Seal thereof,
at my office in Chicago, this 7 day of Oct A.D. 1920

Robert M. Sweitzer County Clerk.

The Person who Solemnizes Marriage is cautioned against making any changes in this License.

STATE OF ILLINOIS, COUNTY OF COOK. } ss. I, William C. [illegible] a Clergyman
hereby certify that Mr. Joseph Imburgia and Miss Elsie Tomm
were united in Marriage by me at Melrose Park, in the County of Cook and State of Illinois,
on the 10th day of October, 1920

Rev. William C. [illegible]

(The Names in this certificate must be identical with Names in above License) Address 141 Broadway - Melrose Park

N. B.— This License, with certificate of marriage properly made, must (within 30 days) be returned to the COUNTY CLERK, by the person who performed the marriage ceremony.

at the Citizens State Bank in Melrose Park.

In October 1920 Joseph Imburgio married Elsie Tomm at the age of 22-years old. The two went on to have three children- Joseph Jr., Robert and Patricia. One report on the family life of Joseph Bulger reported that Joseph Jr. was killed during World War II and his other son Robert was allegedly injured during the same war and was a paraplegic. His daughter known as Pat was alleged to be adopted. However, this report conflicted with others. Another report stated that Joseph Bulger was the first cousin to Zena Rosa, the wife of Melrose Park mobster Sam "Slicker Sam" Rosa. Joseph's mother and Zena's mother were sisters.

After his marriage, Bulger moved into the real estate and insurance business and was associated with Sol Bloch, a builder. He then opened a delicatessen in Maywood, Illinois for a period of time before becoming more associated with Melrose Park's politics and Chicago's top gangsters. By 1928 Joe Bulger, then using his real last name Imburgio, was listed as a trustee in Melrose Park when he was involved in the Village of Melrose Park's illegal bootlegging still problem. Over 100 homes in the small town were producing alcohol during Prohibition. The incident involved a Prohibition agent named William Koejan who got drunk in the Melrose Park tavern run by Capone mobster Nick DeGrazio. The agent spilled the beans that a raid was coming which lead DeGrazio to inform the village attorney Guy Guerine so he could have Imburgio take care of the stills. Nick DeGrazio was the brother of Rocco DeGrazio who was a top member in the Capone Gang.

With the help of the Capone Gang in 1928, Joseph Bulger organized the Veterans Park District in Melrose Park. He ruled the park district as a tax-supported private country for decades steering millions of tax dollars earmarked for the village into the arms of the Chicago mob. Bulger also had a hand in the operations of the Clyde Park District of Cicero, Illinois where he was listed as the park district's main attorney for controlling all legal operations and more importantly, helping to steal the money. By the 1960's the Veteran's Park District controlled more than five thousand acres of land in parts of Melrose Park, River Grove, Northlake, Franklin Park and Berkeley, Illinois.

In 1932 he provided $45,000 so the Italian Village at the Century of Progress Exposition Worlds Fair in Chicago could open which solidified his connections with the Capone Gang. However, in 1934 he was closed down when two of the shows in the Italian Village were labeled obscene. One show called the La Nymph featured women in loin cloths with their breasts covered in a mermaid-like effect and disported in water was shut down for indecency. The other show called Venus had artist's models in a frame with a back stage light behind them to show the image of a naked woman. The complaint was that the shows looked like underwear ads.

In 1933 Joseph Bulger became Mayor of Melrose Park, Illinois. Among things Bulger did as mayor was sign his name to the restoration of the Chicago Grand Opera Company with Dr. Eugene Chesrow. From time to time he had to do things that went against organized crime like dealing with the very corrupt Melrose Park Police Department. In 1930 he had demanded one of the town's officers, Rocco Passarella, resign from the police force when he was under investigation connected to bootlegging rings in the town. In 1933 he suspended Melrose Park Police lieutenant Paul Maggio when he was shot in the arm during a quarrel with a young woman in a beer tavern at 3119 Lake Street. Maggio refused to answer any questions about th shooting to investigators.

One report stated Bulger held the mayor position until 1935 when he was defeated by a landslide against Andy Frenzel, a German. Another report says Bulger retired in April 1935 and was succeeded by Michael Sorvillo. According to one report, Frenzel thought he was going to lose the election because Bulger was backed by the Capone mob so he called in Illinois state police to assure an accurate count of the votes. Frenzel's approach to Melrose Park, which was already in the hands of the Capone Gang, was to let the Outfit have what they already had acquired in the way of legitimate business and to curtail them from expanding further. Frenzel served as village president until his death in 1958. After his death the Corporation Counsel leader of Melrose Park, Guy Guerine, appointed Chester Carson, an attorney, to fill out Frenzel's unexpired term.

Joseph Bulger still maintained his power through his position as president of the Democratic Veterans Park District and the Melrose Park Democratic Party and through his control of the Melrose Park Police Department. Once Carson was acting mayor of Melrose Park, Joe Bulger met with Carson and the two formed an alliance for the next election. Even though Carson was a Republican, Bulger promised the backing of the Democratic Veterans Park District. In the deal, all village decisions would "go" the Outfit's way. Carson was elected in a landslide and the first thing he was ordered to do by the Outfit was to close his eyes to the gambling at the Casa Madrid gambling house and ignore the large horse betting parlor then known as J.C.'s at the corner of 25th and Lake Street.

During his time as Mayor in Melrose Park and with the help of prohibition, Joseph Bulger had become a millionaire at the age of 32. It was said that Joe Bulger received a small percentage from every gambling joint in Melrose Park between the 1930's thru the 1960's.

In August 1934 Joseph's brother Sam Imburgio, was wanted for questioning by police about the shooting of Joseph Griffin, a Bellwood, Illinois constable. Sam Imburgio had been in a Melrose Park tavern when Griffin was shot and fled immediately after. His pals Joseph Priaino, Mike Russo and Charles Kunowski were arrested for questioning. Russo was holding the pistol that shot Griffin and refused to give up his pals.

After Joe Bulger's defeat as Mayor of Melrose Park he attended the John Marshall Law School and in 1938 he received his degree to become a lawyer. From that point on he was a "mob" lawyer for the Chicago mob.

In 1942 the Ninth Naval District made a file on Joseph Bulger for war purposes. The file listed Joe Bulger, aka Joe Imburgio, as:

"Subject, an Italian presently employed in the Buick Plant in Melrose Park, is reportedly a Fascist and has been heard to say that he would rather live in Italy under Mussolini than in the U.S. under Roosevelt."

In 1948 Joseph Bulger was called before a Congressional Committee in Washington D.C. and questioned about the Italo-American Union of America. He told the committee that the organization had been given a bad rap because it was formerly owned by the Unione Siciliano in Chicago which may have contained some old Italian Black Hand members. Bulger said he became a member around 1928 and was called upon to save this organization because it was changing from a fraternal mutual society to a legal reserve basis. Bulger added that when he was finished with all the work he quit and Phil D'Andrea was elected Supreme President. When D'Andrea died a man named Marino took over, who was later replaced once again by Bulger. By 1958 ninety percent of the membership was once again Sicilian.

In February 1954 the Illinois States Attorney was attempting to bring charges against Joseph Bulger and his fellow attorney Michael A. Serritella for harboring a fugitive. Bulger produced Joseph Adduci as a witness before the Disciplining Committee of the Bar Association even though he was a fugitive in a conspiracy to defraud the county in placing ghost pay rollers on the city payroll when no services were performed.

That same year it was reported that Joseph Bulger controlled almost everything that happened in Melrose Park including the Melrose Park Police Department which was said to be Bulger's personal enforcement squad.

In 1958 Joe Bulger opened The Bulger Company at 1806 Lake Street, Melrose Park, Illinois. The company's purpose was to buy, sell, trade, exchange, construct, deal in mortgage, improve real estate, and to carry on a general real estate and brokerage business and a general insurance brokerage business.

Officers of this company were:

Joseph Bulger President
Robert T. Bulger Secretary
William Ireland

He also was in business calling it the 16th and Lake Melrose Park Illinois Building Corporation, 1806 West Lake Street, Melrose Park. This business purchased materials for construction of buildings, to erect buildings and sell buildings. They also repaired, altered, and did whatever it took to improve a building.

Officers of this company were:

Rocco Culotta President
Robert T, Bulger Secretary
Joseph Bulger Registered Agent
G.J. Devanna
Francis Fanelli

In 1961 a FBI informant told the feds that Joseph Bulger had the most elaborate finished paneled basement recreation room he had ever seen at his modest looking house at 1103 Broadway in Melrose Park. It contained a poker room, full bar, the most expensive TV of the times and the most expensive furniture money could buy. On the north wall of the basement about midway in the room there was a safe located behind a sliding panel in the wall. The panel was activated by a button located on the left side of the panel. It was said that is where he kept all his cash.

Still controlling the Veteran's Park District, Bulger made sure the money coming in for the district went right to Outfit members and of course, Bulger himself. For a while the money became a lucrative source of income for the Outfit. There was no accounting of the money what-so-ever and there was no one around who had the nerve to question it. Bulger also decided which other mobsters would benefit from the money. For example, all the maintenance and repairs for the park district went to mobster Nick Palermo. One time the park district's pool needed a tile job and the contract was given to Palermo. The district paid close to $9,000 for this job when the real cost to the district was only $3,000.

In 1967 it was determined that the Veteran's Park District collected $111,000 in special playground taxes but only $17,000 of that amount actually went to the playgrounds. They still kept no financial records or printed material of any kind but did have staggering bonded indebtedness around four million dollars. Because of this the FBI opened an investigation into the Veteran's Park District. What Joe Bulger pulled on taxpayers was:

1)Sold park district bonds to build a warehouse and shelter for the town but instead pocked the money.

2)Appropriated district money for water and electrical service at the parks along with money for nonexistent custodians. Both were lies and he pocketed the money.

3)Issued bonds to renovate the parks, install fencing, new playground equipment and new blacktop which never happened. He pocked the money. On top of that, Bulger claimed that he received a two percent commission for his part in arranging the sale of the bonds, on top of stealing all the bond money.

4)The plans that showed how $1,090,000 of district money was spent after selling three bonds disappeared, thanks to Joseph Bulger.

5)No parks were maintained or equipment fixed year after year, yet the money to have it done was spent year after year and one no could remember how or what the money was spent on.

6)Holdings found in the name of Joseph Bulger with park district money were a $50,000 plane; 100-acre, $60,000 ranch home in Florida; a tourist cave in the Missouri Ozarks and a hacienda in Cuba that was confiscated by Fidel Castro.

In all they found 29 missing major projects which were suppose to be built and the money set aside for these projects could not be found.

By 1964 Joseph Bulger was said to be the "brains" for the Chicago Outfit concerning financial transactions. Because of this ability it was believed for awhile that Bulger was the liaison man between Las Vegas and Chicago representing the Outfit. Another job that fell into Bulger's hands was to use his influence in Cook County, DuPage County and Kankakee County in Illinois to get liquor licenses for Outfit-controlled establishments. One informant told the FBI that if anyone told Joe Bulger anything in confidence regarding hoodlum operations or gave him any indication they were cooperating with the authorities, he, Bulger, would go to mob bosses and have the man hit. This informant did say Joe Bulger was responsible for several individuals being killed by the Outfit.

One informant named John Romano told the FBI that Joe Bulger was still the real power in Melrose Park. He said that when problems arise in Melrose Park pertaining to administration matters, police matters, or matters involving other hoodlums, everyone goes to Joe Bulger to have them straightened out. For this reason Joe Bulger placed his brother Charles Imburgio on the park board of Melrose Park and his lieutenant Joseph Lelivelt, then a State Representative for Melrose Park, in positions of power so they could assist in sorting out these problems.

For instance, since Melrose Park was a strong Democratic town back then, the Democrats kept a close eye on the Republicans in the town when it was time to vote. When there was a question as to how they would vote the loyal Democrat precinct workers would put a tiny pencil notation or mark in the upper right hand corner on the back side of the ballot and when the ballets were counted the workers would look for his mark to identify that person to see which way they voted for future election purposes.

When there came time for a city council meeting all the members would go elsewhere and rehearse what was going to be said and be approved before the public town meeting. What ever was approved at the meeting was cleared by Joe Bulger and mob boss Sam "Teets" Battaglia so a "show" could be put on in front of the public.

When Melrose Park began building their new upper-scale subdivision known as Winston Park they noticed many of the Republican votes were coming from these new homeowners. Whenever a good candidate was proposed for office in Melrose Park, the Outfit would step in and "buy him off" so he would not run. This system worked for a long time in Melrose Park and the Outfit always stopped any chance of reform candidates from entering Melrose Park elections.

Joseph Bulger also had a very strong friendship with Chicago Mayor Richard J. Daley. Bulger and Daley became close friends in the days when Daley was the Director of Revenue and Bulger had helped with Daley's campaigns for mayor.

Being one of the Outfit's top attorneys meant getting "inside" men to give information from inside the government. When FBI agents investigated a former Assistant United States Attorney named John Powers Crowley, who had left the government to go into private practice and began representing known hoodlums connected to the mob, they learned that Crowley had at one time before his government job worked for Joseph Bulger as a part-time law clerk which Crowley "forgot" to put down on his job application before he was hired. His uncle, Wilbert F. Crowley, was a Judge for the Cook County Circuit Court who was known to be very close to mob attorneys Mike Brodkin and George Bieber. It was alleged that Crowley was a pipeline of information to the syndicate. After Joe Bulger died, it was alleged that John Crowley took over many of Bulger's criminal cases and it was alleged at the time that he was the "up and coming" syndicate defense attorney.

When Joe Bulger was unable to make trips concerning Outfit business, he would send his leg-man named Joseph DiVannah to places like Las Vegas where agents would watch him hold meetings with owners of the Stardust and New Frontier casinos. It was also alleged that Bulger would use attorney Paul Brust to find new investments for Outfit money.

In 1965 FBI agents were told that Joseph Bulger had put the word out that if anyone had run against Chester "Ted" Carson in the election for Mayor of Melrose Park they were either "scared off" or "bought off". Carson won unopposed. They were also told that both Carson and Melrose Park police chief Anthony Iosco had made a deal with Joe Bulger that in the spring of 1966 both would resign their positions so Francis Fanelli could be pushed in as Mayor and Paul Martino would fill Finelli's Village Clerk position. However, Iosco died in November 1967 and Carson was still mayor in 1968.

One informant from Melrose Park told the FBI that Joe Bulger and mob boss Sam "Teets" Battaglia were the "rulers" of Melrose Park in 1965 and had allegedly forced Carson to falsify records in order to prevent liquor license revocations of Outfit bars.

In June 1966 Joe Bulger was having some difficulties with mob boss Tony Accardo. Bulger had been an administrator for Northlake Community Hospital in Northlake, Illinois. Apparently the hospital had borrowed $1,200,000 from Tony Accardo's Apollo Loan Company but had not paid any of it back to Accardo. Tony Accardo telephoned Bulger and pressed him for the money. Information developed was that Bulger was diverting funds through various financial maneuvers for his own personal use. It was alleged that Bulger used Charles Pallardy, one of the founders of the hospital, to pull this off. The allegation said that Pallardy had obtained a controlling interest in the corporation by the conversion of Class A stocks granting one vote for each share of class A stock. Those stocks were sold at $1 a share which gave the person owning it a holding of 100 shares and 100 votes in the company. Contrast this with class B stock issued at $100 a share which meant that person holding $100 of class B stock or one share was entitled to only one vote. Through this maneuver Pallardy and Bulger were the controlling stockholders. This gave both Pallardy and Bulger large amounts of cash which Pallardy would allegedly fly to Nassau, Bahamas and deposit the money in one of the foreign banks on the island.

On December 2, 1966 Joseph Bulger boarded his $100,000 twin-engine Aero Commander private airplane alone and took off from Chicago Midway Airport. One report stated he made a stop in Joliet, Illinois to pick up another passenger. Allegedly he landed one more time in Springfield, Missouri to pick up another passenger all en-route to Miami, Florida. However, when all planes land at airports and they put fuel in their tanks, it is registered in logs no matter what. No listing of this plane or Joseph Bulger could be found in the books in Joliet or Springfield, Missouri.

He was flying at night in a sleet storm so it is not certain what happened but the plane crashed into a mountainside at Spring City, Tennessee, about sixty miles southwest of Knoxville, Tennessee. Reports said that Bulger radioed an Atlanta, Georgia traffic control center stating that his wings were taking on ice and he was flying in an inverted position (upside down) and was crashing. One report stated he was flying by plane instruments only.

When authorities arrived at the crash site they found only the plane which was buried 6 feet into the rocky hillside and the mangled body of Joseph Bulger. The fuselage was smashed downward into the cockpit. Police could not find the two other bodies, which one officer said must have been an erroneous report. It was later learned that the first officer on the scene found so many body parts he believed it had to be three different bodies. A witness saw the plane spiraling nose down when it hit the hillside.

Back in Chicago the local FBI office had been contacted by one of the city's newspapers asking for information on the plane crash and if they could confirm that it was Joseph Bulger's plane that had crashed. At one point the Chicago American newspaper was speculating that one of the other dead bodes on the plane was that of Paul DeLucia which was not true.

Bulger would be waked at Ed Prignano Funeral Home in Melrose Park for two nights, December 5 and 6. Law enforcement agents said every hoodlum with any stature showed up, from Chicago, New York, Las Vegas, Miami and St. Louis. Detectives tried to write down every license plate number they could find but most of the well-known hoodlums used limo's or parked blocks away and walked to the building. Agents noticed after the wake a large group of mobsters walked to Tom's Steak House in Melrose Park, which was right next door to the funeral parlor, to have a farewell drink in Bulger's name.

People observed by law enforcement at the wake

Tony Accardo
Joey Aiuppa
Sam Aiuppa
Joe Aukel
Ned C. Bakes
Donna Bagnule
Joseph Barracca
Lawrence Bongi
Nick Bruno
Huge E. Burns
Michael Bugiel
Larry "The Hood" Buonagudi
Georgia Buuak
James Cacamesi
Tony Campo
Chester Carson
Castriota
Frank Catizone
Frank "Skippy" Cerone
Jackie Cerone
Jack Cerone Jr.
Joseph Colletta
Ross & Marisue Cortion
John Powers Crowley
Paul DeLucia
Mario DeStefano
Vito DeStefano
Francis Fanelli
Joseph Fanelli
Ben Fillichio
Mike Fish
Joey Glimco
George Graziadei
Anthony Iosco
Joseph Iosco
William "Big Bill" Johnson
Stanley "Duke" Jonikas
James Larry
S. Lisuzzo
Leo Manfredi
Robert Mooney
Charles Nicoletti
Nick Palermo
Charles Pallardy
Sam "Slicker Sam" Rosa
Rocco Salvatore
Dominic Senese
Ben Stein
Kenneth Tank
Carl Unger
Joseph Urso
August Zamboni

Company Vehicles Observed

Advance Cartage Company
Allen Chevrolet Inc.
Allined Label Die-cutters
Assoc. Piping Company
Auto Spec. Mfg Company
B&B Service Station Melrose Park
Bank of Broadway
Bongi Cartage Company
Carpet Land USA
Commercial Credit Corp.
Consolidated Wire Assoc.
DeBello Catering
Division Medical Center
Eden Garden Investments
Expressways Terminals Inc.
Fulton Meat Co.
Gateway Chevy Sales
Gaucho Food Products Inc.
G. J. Construction Company
Journeymen's Barber Local 548
Lazarus Company
Lee Industries Inc.
Lipin Enterprises
Melrose Park Heating
Melrose Park Plumbing Company
Northlake Community Hospital
Republic Molding Company
Republic National Life Insurance Company
Sangamon Builders
United Maintenance Service Company
West Legg Corp.

However, the story did not end with Bulger's death. After Bulger's body had been removed from the accident site two men from Chicago arrived in Tennessee to take the body back to Illinois for his services. The men were Robert Mooney and Carl Unger. Just as they were about to take the body a young man from Miami, Florida arrived dressed in cowboy cloths and said he was there to pick up his father's body. Joseph Bulger had been living a double life with two wives and two sets of children with both wives.

His first wives Elsie Tomm, lived in Melrose Park while the second wife, Sallee M. Young, a one time Chicago model and fan dancer under the name of Sally, ran in mob hangouts, lived in Miami Florida, San Amrino Island, Cuba and on a farm in Northern Florida. Both families attempted to claim the body for the funeral a week after the crash.

When Sallee Young was interviewed she said she met Joe Bulger in 1938 at Arlington Racetrack just outside of Chicago. At the time she was a twenty-something, well-built model, believed the story told to her by Bulger that he had been married three times and his last wife, Elsie, was dead. She claimed the two married each other in Reno, Nevada in 1939.

Sallee Young said their life together meant living in apartments and hotel suites in Chicago and New York City for nine years while Bulger worked on the Hollywood extortion case with Paul DeLucia. Finally at the end of the 1940's Bulger bought her a stylish townhome in Chicago at 111 East Bellevue Place. Then Salle gave birth to Lawrence Joseph Bulger and the happy couple moved south to San Marino Island in Miami, Florida due to Salle's health, (her doctor said she was as fragile as an orchid.). Once in Miami Salle said the two would enjoy life sipping martinis and enjoying the sun while a governess looked after there son.

In 1955 Sallee sold the Miami home and moved to Cuba where Joseph bought her a big house with a swimming pool. They had plenty of land with horses and Joseph would fly to Cuba on most weekends in his private plane where he would have business meetings for his mob bosses in Havana. This was perfect for Joseph since he told his wife Elsie he had business in Cuba and he could hide his second wife and son in another country. One neighbor in Miami told the press Joe Bulger was a happy guy who would never let anyone pay for anything and always was seen with his wife. Back in Melrose Park, Joseph was always having meetings at the Bismarck Hotel in the Chicago Loop and could always be found working at his offices in Melrose Park. He was almost never seen in the company of Elsie and was never known to drink any alcohol. In Chicago he was a mob lawyer in fine Italian tailored suits while in Miami he dressed in cowboy clothes and wore a brimmed straw had.

In 1961 Joseph and Sallee were forced out of Cuba and returned to Miami where they rented an apartment and later purchased two homes at 611 S.W. 29th Road and a horse farm at 6400 S.W. 120th Avenue.

As the FBI investigated, they were receiving information that Bulger was not really dead but faked his death and planted a body at the crash site. The body found was beyond recognition or identification but the authorities said it was Bulger's body based on papers found near the body saying the name Joseph Bulger and had his home phone number on them. No inquest was ever held to determine if the body was Joseph. The family was told that the body was identified through fingerprints but the coroner in Spring City insisted that this was not true and no attempts in any way were conducted to identify the body.

At his wake there were whisperings that the body that was waked was way too big to be the body of Joseph Bulger. His wife Sallee looked at pictures of the plane crash months later and was convinced that the body in the photos was not her husband. She told the press, "*Those aren't his shoes. And that can't be his wallet, he never carried one. As far as I know, nobody saw the body who knew him. I can't believe he's dead.*"

One informant said Bulger was a mob courier who had been observed in places like South America, a month in Rome and one time in a London, England bathroom where Bulger was observed being given a mysterious box by an unknown person who he passed off to another unidentified person. On all these trips were his wife Sallee and his son.

After the crash, both families said they were left penniless since no legal accounting of his assets was ever made. Found in Bulger's safe in his Melrose Park home was an envelope with $60,000 cash in it marked Veteran's Park District on it. That money was said to be turned over to the district. A little black book of Bulger's was found that contained codes, safe combinations and a few listings of unidentified deposit boxes along with private telephone numbers of political fixers, a Wisconsin congressman and top mobsters in America from coast to coast including Chicago mobsters Tony Accardo, Paul DeLucia and Dominic Senese.

One report stated that found on the mountain where the plane crashed were eight large briefcases that had been ripped open with everything inside gone. No one could really investigate what was in the plane wreckage because when the plane crashed a search party of local hill people found the plane and many of the searchers took papers and items for souvenirs. Months after the crash the wreckage was still on the hillside. The owner of the land, Arlie Jenkins, put up a no trespassing sign to keep people from getting to the plane because it became a tourist spot of onlookers who wanted to see the mobster's plane. There were also reports about how Bulger had business meetings in Havana, Cuba and some sort of influence he exerted on its president and dictator Fidel Castro. Joseph Bulger's sister Rose Larry of Melrose Park began a quest to find $5,000 that she said her brother was carrying when the plane crashed. After multiple letters to law-enforcement and the FBI she discovered that the briefcase that had the money in it which was supposed to be on the plane was left behind in Chicago. The coroner in Tennessee said that only $61 was found on the body and not the $10,000 he always had on him held in a gold horse head money clip.

Over time rumors that Bulger was living as a millionaire on some beach island was common knowledge on the streets of Melrose Park. One rumor said that Bulger knew that his bigamy would be discovered and he may have had tremendous legal problems because of it so he took his millions and faked his death.

Some believed that he was escaping from a Cook County grand jury investigation in which Bulger was linked to the Melrose Park Veterans Park District involving millions of dollars missing from the village. All the parks records disappeared detailing how taxpayer money was spent.

After years of searching for all his alleged millions, only one hundred thousand dollars was found and both families attempted to claim the money. Sallee told a reporter from the Chicago Daily News named Don Barlett that she truly believed that Joe Bulger was still alive and deliberately staged this accident and planted another body in his private plane.

One thing was for sure, Joseph Bulger was the one man in the mob who knew where most of the Outfit's money was hidden and how to get at it. To remember what a great man Joseph Bulger was, a sign with his name on it still stands as of 2015 at 17th and Hirsch in Melrose Park dedicating a park to him. The man who embezzled money from every person living in Melrose Park between 1928 and 1966 can look at his name everyday to celebrate.

Bulgur Park at 17th and Hirsch Streets in Melrose Park, Illinois

Mob Boss

File Card

Joseph I. Bulger
Real Name Giuseppe Imburgio Jr.
Once said his middle name was "Israel"
AKA Joe Bolger, "Mayor of Melrose Park"
Had his name changed to Joseph Imburgio Bulger by court decree #35C16242 on November 5, 1935 for the purpose of Americanizing his name for business.
Born April 28, 1899 in New Orleans, Louisiana (Also used Birth Date 4-28-1900 and 4-28-1902)
Died December 2, 1966 (plane crash Spring City, Tennessee) (Or did he?)
Height 6'2"
Weight 195
Hair Black
Eyes Brown
Democrat
Pilot's license # 1154759 (10-4-1950)

Family

Father Giuseppe "Joseph" Imburgio Sr. (Born Italy around 1870 / Died 12-4-1910 in New Orleans, Louisiana) (One report says he died in 1908)
Mother Caterina Scanio (Catherine) (Katherine) *(Born in Provinica Di Rochella, Italy around 1881)*
Brother Lawrence Imburgio, gangster in the Capone Gang 1920's to 1940's. Known as "The Hindu". *(He was the Capone Gang's respective at a gambling joint located at 186 North Clark Street in Chicago during 1943. The gambling house was run by the notorious brothers David and Harry Russell. Lawrence was born in 1904.)*
Brother Sam Imburgio, born in 1901 in Louisiana *(was employed by the York Theater in Elmhurst, Illinois in the 1940's) (Wife Mary born around 1913 and one daughter Joan born around 1933)*
Brother Charles Imburgio, born in 1905 in Louisiana *(Listed as Calsie on 1910 censes) (Democratic precinct committeeman and head of the Democratic organization in Melrose Park in the 1960's and was employed as a superintendent for the Sanitary District of Chicago under Frank Chesrow)*
Brother (Alleged) Dominic Imburgio *(Lived at 624 W. Washington Street in Chicago, the Page Building Company)*
Sister Rosie Larry *(Married Richard "Dick" Larry, other reports say name was James, the post master of the Melrose Park Post Office)*
Wife # 1 Elsie Ann Tomm (One report says married in October 1920, another says October 15, 1922) *(Daughter of a well known Melrose Park Jeweler being born on August 15, 1902 in Bellwood, Illinois. Died July 1975)*
Wife # 2 Sallee M. Young (Married in Reno, Nevada 1939) *(Miami, Florida wife and one time Chicago model)*
Salvatore Scanio *(Godfather to Joseph, lived at 120 N. 21st Street in Melrose Park, died November 1933)*

Tony Dark

Children

Sons and Daughter with Elsie Tomm
Joseph I. Bulger Jr., Born around 1922 *(Killed in action while serving in the U.S. Armed forces during World War II)*
Robert Bulger, Born around 1924 and married to Bruna D. Bulger *(Real estate broker in Melrose Park) (One report names him as Charles)*
Daughter Patricia Bulger Jones *(Moved to Pennsylvania after marrying William Jones and was employed as a teacher) (One report named her as Elsie Smith)*
Son with Sallee Young
Lawrence Joseph Bulger (One reports says Joseph P. Bulger) (Born November 15, 1949)

Education

University of Illinois High School Exam March 1932
Central YMCA College, Chicago Illinois June 1932 to March 1933 (Pre-Law) (Received BA)
John Marshal Law School February 1935 to February 1938 (Received his LLD)
Chicago Bar Association June 16, 1938
Admitted to the Chicago Bar Association on May 11, 1938
Certified Pilot's License October 4, 1950

Known Addresses

1103 Broadway, Melrose Park, Illinois (1930's) (Two story, 12 room home at the corner of Broadway and Augusta Streets) *(With Elsie Tomm)*
612 North 16th Street, Melrose Park (1940's) *(Mothers house)*
333 North Euclid Avenue, Oak Park, Illinois (1940's) *(Alleged)*
3000 North Sheridan Road, Chicago (1946) *(Alleged)*
111 East Bellevue Place, Chicago (1940's) *(With Sallee)*
San Marino Island, Miami, Florida (1940's-1955) *(With Sallee)*
House in Cuba (1955-1961) *(With Sallee)*
611 S.W. 29th Road, Miami, Florida (1961)
6400 S.W. 120th Avenue, Miami, Florida (1960's)

Known Occupations

Water Boy on the docks of New Orleans (1911)
Merchant Maries (1914) *(Listed in Melrose Park Diamond Jubilee)*
American Can Company, Melrose Park, Illinois (1918)
Delicatessen, Maywood, Illinois (1920's)
Citizens State Bank, Melrose Park, Illinois (1920's)
Mayor of Melrose Park, Illinois (1930's) (Offices at 1806 Lake Street)
Veterans Park District President, Melrose Park, Illinois (1930's)
Buick Plant, Melrose Park, Illinois (1942)
Lawyer, Offices at 160 North LaSalle Street Chicago (1939-1945)
Lawyer, Offices at 139 North Clark Street, Chicago (1943-1954) *(Shared office with lawyers D.H Andernacht, Paul W. Brist, Paul D. Newey, Francis A. Fanelli*

and George Finerman)
Offices at 188 Randolph Street, Chicago Room 1203 (1954-1960's)
Offices at 161 Broadway, Melrose Park, Illinois (1950's)
Offices at 1804 Lake Street, Melrose Park, Illinois (1960's)
President of the Italian Village at the Century of Progress exposition Chicago Worlds Fair (1933)
Attorney for Northlake Community Hospital, Northlake, Illinois (1960's)
Vice President of the Northlake Reality Corporation, Northlake, Illinois (1960's)
Attorney for the Master Barber's Association (1960's)
Law Officer at Fifth and Lake Street in Maywood, Illinois (1965)

Known Businesses of Joseph Bulger

The Italian Village at the Worlds Fair Chicago (President) (1934)
Dale Motors, 6949 Ogden Avenue, Berwyn (1950's)
Northlake Realty Corporation (1960's)
The Bulger Company, Inc. 1806 Lake Street, Melrose Park, Illinois (1958) *(In the name of Joseph I. Bulger, Robert T. Bulger and William Ireland)*
Melrose Park Illinois Building Corporation, 1806 West Lake Street, Melrose Park, Illinois (16th and Lake Street) (1958) *(Listed in the names of G.J. Devanna, Francis Fanelli, Joseph I. Bulger with Rocco J. Culotta as President, Robert T. Bulger as secretary and Joseph Bulger as registered agent)*
Nationwide Motorists Association, 188 West Randolph Street, Chicago (1962)
Mitchell Aviation Company Incorporated *(Listed as secretary treasure and registered agent)* (1960)
Palwaukewee Air Port, Wheeling, Illinois (1960) *(Suspect as having an ownership in this airport)*

Best Quote

Humphreys says about Bulger *"Here's what Bulger's like, he reminds me of a kid lawyer, and puts a lot of law in there."*

Known Melrose Park Positions

Board of Trustees (Member) 1928-1933
President Board of Trustees 1933-1935
Secretary of Veterans Park District 1928-1966
Mayor of Melrose Park 1933-1935
Chamber of Commerce

Some Honors

President of the Unione Siciliano (1928-1930's)
Supreme President of the Italo-American Union, 20 West Washington Street, Chicago (1930's and 50's)
Italian American Victory Council Executive Committee member (1944)
Melrose Park Tanagers' Tom Naples Memorial Citizenship Award 1962
Kiwanis Club
Loyal Order of Moose

Most well known clients of Joseph Bulger

Paul DeLucia *(Top mob boss)*
Tony Accardo *(Top mob boss)*
Joey Glimco *(President of Chicago Local 777)*
Louis Campagna *(Top mob boss)*
Joseph Bronge *(Melrose Park Beer distributor killed in 1959)*
James Adduci *(Illinois State Representative)*
Charles Fischetti *(Al Capone's cousin)*
Ralph Pierce
Murray "Curley" Humphreys
Lester "Killer Kane" Kruse

Known Auto's

1961 Ford Galaxie, two-door (License plate number 828-072)
1964 Ford Thunderbird, two-door hardtop (License plate number 838-335)
1965 Lincoln, four-door, sedan (License plate number 838-336)

Known Arrest Record of Joseph Bulger

Date	Charge	Agency	Result
3-5-1957	False Income Tax Return	USM, Chicago	Not Guilty

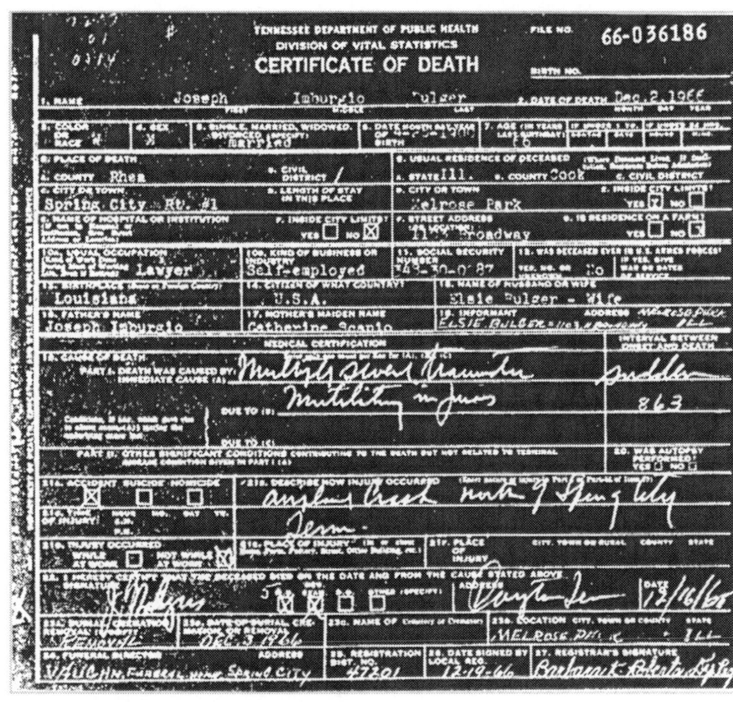

TENNESSEE DEPARTMENT OF PUBLIC HEALTH
DIVISION OF VITAL STATISTICS
CERTIFICATE OF DEATH

FILE NO. 66-036186

BIRTH NO.

1. NAME Joseph Imburgio Bulger
2. DATE OF DEATH Dec. 2, 1966

3. COLOR OR RACE W
4. SEX M
5. SINGLE, MARRIED, WIDOWED, DIVORCED (SPECIFY) Married

8. PLACE OF DEATH
a. COUNTY Rhea
b. CIVIL DISTRICT /
c. CITY OR TOWN Spring City Rt. #1
d. LENGTH OF STAY IN THIS PLACE
e. NAME OF HOSPITAL OR INSTITUTION
f. INSIDE CITY LIMITS? YES ☐ NO ☒

9. USUAL RESIDENCE OF DECEASED
a. STATE Ill.
b. COUNTY Cook
c. CIVIL DISTRICT
d. CITY OR TOWN Melrose Park
e. INSIDE CITY LIMITS? YES ☒ NO ☐
f. STREET ADDRESS Broadway
g. IS RESIDENCE ON A FARM? YES ☐ NO ☒

10a. USUAL OCCUPATION Lawyer
10b. KIND OF BUSINESS OR INDUSTRY Self-employed
11. SOCIAL SECURITY NUMBER
12. WAS DECEASED EVER IN U.S. ARMED FORCES? No

13. BIRTHPLACE Louisiana
14. CITIZEN OF WHAT COUNTRY? U.S.A.
15. NAME OF HUSBAND OR WIFE Elsie Bulger - Wife
16. FATHER'S NAME Joseph Imburgio
17. MOTHER'S MAIDEN NAME Catherine Scanio
18. INFORMANT Elsie Bulger
ADDRESS Melrose Park, Ill.

MEDICAL CERTIFICATION

19. CAUSE OF DEATH
PART I. DEATH WAS CAUSED BY: IMMEDIATE CAUSE (A) Multiple Severe Trauma
DUE TO (B) Mutilating Injuries
DUE TO (C)
PART II. OTHER SIGNIFICANT CONDITIONS
INTERVAL BETWEEN ONSET AND DEATH Sudden
20. WAS AUTOPSY PERFORMED? YES ☐ NO ☐

21a. ACCIDENT ☒ SUICIDE ☐ HOMICIDE ☐
21b. DESCRIBE HOW INJURY OCCURRED Airplane Crash North of Spring City Tenn.
21c. TIME OF INJURY
21d. INJURY OCCURRED WHILE AT WORK ☐ NOT WHILE AT WORK ☒
21e. PLACE OF INJURY
21f. PLACE OF INJURY

22. I HEREBY CERTIFY THAT THE DECEASED DIED ON THE DATE AND FROM THE CAUSES STATED ABOVE.
SIGNATURE
ADDRESS Dayton Tenn
DATE 12/16/66

23a. BURIAL, CREMATION, REMOVAL Removal
23b. DATE OF BURIAL Dec. 3 1966
23d. LOCATION Melrose Pk. Ill.
24. FUNERAL DIRECTOR Vaughn Funeral Home Spring City
25. REGISTRATION DIST. NO. 47201
26. DATE SIGNED BY LOCAL REG. 12-19-66
27. REGISTRAR'S SIGNATURE

1-4 (Rev. 9-30-63)

UNITED STATES DEPARTMENT OF JUSTICE
FEDERAL BUREAU OF INVESTIGATION
WASHINGTON, D.C. 20537

10-7-66

J. Edgar Hoover
Director.

The following FBI record, NUMBER none assigned, is furnished FOR OFFICIAL USE ONLY.

CONTRIBUTOR OF FINGERPRINTS	NAME AND NUMBER	ARRESTED OR RECEIVED	CHARGE	DISPOSITION
USM Chgo Ill	Joseph Imburgio Bulger #57761	3-5-57	making false income tax return	not guilty

Since neither fingerprints nor an identifying number which is indexed in our files accompanied your request, FBI cannot guarantee in any manner that this material concerns the individual in whom you are interested.

Information shown on this Identification Record represents data furnished FBI by fingerprint contributors. Where final disposition is not shown or further explanation of charge is desired, communicate with agency contributing those fingerprints.

Notations indicated by * are NOT based on fingerprints in FBI files but are listed only as investigative leads as being possibly identical with subject of this record.

1940's photo of Joseph Bulger

Authors Collection 2016 ©

Authors Collection 2016 ©

Joseph Bulger's house at 1103 Broadway, Melrose Park, Illinois (Photo's taken 2014)

Authors Collection 2016 ©

Joseph Bulger's 1940 Census

46	1103	0	12000	No	Bulger	Joseph	Head	M	W	40	M	No	C4	Louisiana			House
47						Clair D	Wife	F	W	37	M	No	H1	Illinois	61		Same House
48						Joseph J	Son	M	W	18	S	Yes	C1	Illinois	61		Same House
49						Robert	Son	M	W	16	S	Yes	H2	Illinois	61		Same House
50						Patricia	Daughter	F	W	5	S	No	0	Illinois	61		Same House

No	No	No	Yes	—		40	Lawyer	Attorney at Law	Oa	52		Yes	46
No	No	No	No	H						0	0	No	47
No	No	No	No	S						0	0	No	48
No	No	No	No	S						0	0	No	49
													50

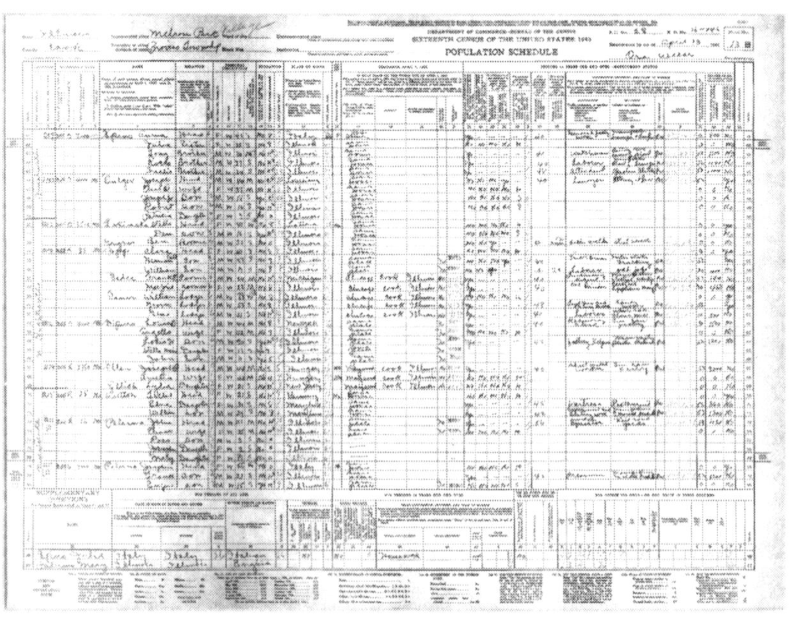

SIXTEENTH CENSUS OF THE UNITED STATES: 1940

POPULATION SCHEDULE

Chapter 6

Back as They Were

On August 13, 1947, Paul DeLucia, Louis Campagna, and Charles Gioe were released from Leavenworth Prison. They boarded a prison bus that took them to the Kansas bus terminal in the town of Leavenworth. There mob lawyer Eugene Bernstein was waiting in a black Cadillac convertible Sedan car with a driver. They drove to the Kansas City Airport where they all boarded a plan heading back to Chicago and freedom.

Phil D'Andrea was released the same day from the medical center for federal prisoners in Springfield, Missouri. When D'Andrea was released he was met by mob lawyer Sam Shapiro where the two flew back to Chicago together. Shapiro was married to D'Andrea's cousin.

Johnny Roselli was released from Terre Haute Prison on August 13, 1947. He was met by Jack Kearns and driven to Chicago where he spent the night in a first class hotel. The next day he took a flight to Los Angels where he was reunited with his fiancée Beatrice Ann Frank, aka Ann Corcoran. Terms of his parole meant he was to be employed as an assistant purchasing agent for Eagle Lion Films in Los Angeles for $65-a-week.

The terms of DeLucia's parole was that he was to reside with his family at 812 North Lathrop Avenue in River Forest, Illinois and his employment would be the operation of an 1100 acre farm at Big Grove, Illinois, which he owned. His parole advisor was Reverend C. Marzano, then Assistant Provincial Director of the Victorian Fathers at 6219 Sheridan Road in Chicago. However, one report list phone calls being made from Brooklyn, New York some time after DeLucia's release from a Mr. and Mrs. Paul Ricca at 125 Ocean Parkway, Brooklyn, New York. The calls were to Francis Curry, who was running DeLucia's farm and calls to Chicago mobster Joey Glimco in Riverside, Illinois. It was later discovered that these calls were placed by Paul DeLucia.

The FBI began its investigation to see whether any violation of the federal bribery statute or other criminal statutes within the investigative jurisdiction of the FBI were violated or used and if there were any irregularities in connection with the granting of the paroles of the Capone hoodlums. In September 1947 the FBI received word that Congressman Fred Busbey in Chicago wanted to speak to the FBI about information concerning the recent parole of Paul DeLucia and his fellow Capone gangsters.

When FBI agents went to the Congressman's office at 10 South LaSalle Street in Chicago, Busbey told the agents that there were many rumors flying around Chicago to the effect that a quarter of a million dollars was paid to have the Capone mobsters released from prison. He added he believed the money to have these men released might have passed through the hands of an attorney in St. Louis, Missouri named Paul Dillon. Dillon was allegedly given $250,000 for a successful parole. Busbey said his information came from a Chicago newspaper reporter named James Dohery who worked for the Chicago Daily Tribune Newspaper. Paul Dillon was mixed up in the affairs of the International Union of Movie Picture Operators and close to it president and vice president John Nick and Clyde Weston. An informant told the FBI that Dillon had an unsavory reputation as an attorney and was very active in the Democratic Party. In 1934 it was said that Dillon was campaign manager for President Truman in his successful race for U.S. Senate.

Leading up to DeLucia parole political pressure was being used in anticipation of all the hoodlums' paroles during the 1946 fall elections in Chicago. The Italian Republicans on the west side of Chicago were terrorized in order to force them to vote Democratic. The purpose was to lay down ground work for a DeLucia-Campagna-D'Andrea parole.

When FBI agents sat down to talk to DeLucia, they asked if they could place him under oath since agents had the power in matters of bribery of government officials to administer oaths. And if DeLucia had lied to the agents while under this oath, DeLucia could be charged with perjury. DeLucia agreed to be placed under oath stating he had nothing to hide. DeLucia was then asked questions with regard to any influence of bribery ascertained to affect his parole from prison. DeLucia told the agents at that time he did not know of any money that had passed hands to effect his transfer from Atlanta to Leavenworth nor did he know of any money which had passed hands between anyone to effect his parole. He added he knew of no political pressure or promises of any kind which had been made by anyone.

For the most part he was telling the truth. When the four mobsters were released they all were summed to a meeting with Tony Accardo once back in Chicago. Accardo told the men to tell the truth so they would not get caught and have to be sent back to prison. He also told them not to worry about involving anyone else as he would see to it that all the politicians would be paid for whatever they did on there behalf. Accardo also added that if their testimony hurt any of the gang they should not worry since he, Accardo, had issued orders that there was to be no "rough stuff" until after the parole period had ended and the four men were free. The only one who really knew what money was being paid and to whom was Tony Accardo. Then the FBI wanted to know why alleged mobster Sam Nanini, then owner of Rock Road Construction Company in Chicago, had written a letter to the parole board for the release of mob boss Louis Campagna. Nanini denied he was a mobster or connected with them in any way other than on a social basis. Nanini told the FBI he had known Campagna for many years and because of their friend ship, he wrote the letter on the request of Charlotte Campagna.

It was later learned that mob lawyer Sidney Korshak played a role in the 1947 paroles. Harry A. Ash, then Superintendent of Crime Prevention for Illinois Governor Green, said he received a communication from Leavenworth Prison asking him to become a Parole Supervisor for Charles Gioe. He said at the same time he received a phone call from Sidney Korshak making the same request. Ash said he subsequently wrote a letter to the Federal Parole Board in Gioe's behalf at the behest of Korshak. Some time after Gioe was released from prison he was given a job as a manager of the Gem Die & Mold Company at 2411 Clybourn Avenue in Chicago. Owner of 50% interest in this company was mobster Nick DeJohn, a Capone gangster who was killed in San Francisco in 1948.

Ash's intercession for Gioe may be explained by what happen in 1940. At that time Chicago police received information that the old Seneca Hotel on Chestnut Street was being used as a site for sex orgies by prominent business men and attorneys of Chicago. Gioe and Ash had both been living there. The information stated that business men would hold a dinner at the hotel with nude teenage girls. The hotel was also where Sidney Korshak lived. The hotel was owned by Chicago mobster Louis Alexander Greenberg, a former associate of mobster Bugsy Siegal in the ownership of the Flamingo Hotel in Las Vegas, Nevada.

On December 16, 1940, Sidney Korshak, Harry Ash, Gibby Kaplan, a owner of a restaurant, Joseph Goldblatt, then owner of Goldblatt Department Store in Chicago and Lou Pelton, a Capone Gang associate who held a post in the mob controlled Chicago Bartender's Union, were arrested at the Seneca Hotel for contributing to the delinquency of a minor in connection with these parties. Another source said that Chicagoans Bishop Shell, a high Catholic Church figure and construction mobile Steve A. Healy were involved in securing the paroles through mob attorney Joseph Bulger who handled the money transfer. When attorney Harry Ash was asked by Sidney Korshak to be Charles Gioe's parole sponsor he was told by Korshak that Bishop Shell was also acting as Gioe's parole supervisor. When Ash called Bishop Shell to confirm this, Shell secretary said it was not true and they would sue for libel if Shell's name was mentioned in connection with the parolees. As for Steven A. Healy, he admitted he knew Charles Gioe from back in 1937 when the two were in Hot Spring's Arkansas playing golf with common friends. Healy denied knowing any of the other hoodlums and had nothing to do with securing the parole of Gioe. Healy was well known back then in Chicago as the man who purchased the famous Chicago Stevens Hotel on Michigan Avenue. He eventually sold it to the Hilton chain of hotels for a large profit.

An inmate serving time with Charles Gioe reported that three months before the Capone hoodlums were paroled Gioe told him that they were going to be paroled and it was going to cost them $300,000. According to this inmate $100,000 was going to Charles Fisher, a probation Officer in Chicago and Chairman of the Parole Board Mr. Wilson was to get the remainder of the money. The money was to come from each of the families of the hoodlums and half from the Capone Gang. The money was collected by mobster Jake Guzik, who took the Capone Gangs portion from the mobs $500,000-a-week gambling profit intake. The payment to Fisher and Wilson was to be made by mob lawyer George Bieber. When asked why the inmate would "rat" on Gioe he answer that Gioe was a bragger and he was mad that only inmates with big money behind them could be released from jail sooner than the majority of inmates that had to do their time. Gioe was interviewed by FBI agents after his parole and denied he said anything to anyone.

Campagna Parole Contributors

Sam Nanini
Rock Road Construction Company
5915 North Rodgers Avenue Chicago

Reverend M. A. Canning
Pastore, St. Ferdinand's Rectory
3116 North Marmora Avenue Chicago

Guy F. Heim
Berrien Springs, Michigan

Michael J. Romano
Morand Brothers Beverage Company
818 South May Street Chicago

John Svitak
2931 Maple Avenue Chicago

Marin Hans
Burton Auto Springs Corporation
2433-41 West 48th Street Chicago

L.E. Lucas
The Journal-Era
Berrien Springs Michigan

Walter Lawrence, M.D.
6400 West Cermak Road
Berwyn, Illinois

Dominick J. Sibilano
Sibilano Furniture Company
5541-43 West Belmont Avenue Chicago

Campagna's Lawyers

Eugene Bernstein
William Scott Stewart

DeLucia Parole Contributors

Francis Curry
516 Western Avenue Joliet, Illinois

Reverend C. Marzano
6219 Sheridan Road Chicago

Curtis N. Vilas
Sarasota Florida

James Lupori
Bell Oil Company
5915 Rodgers Avenue Chicago

Morris W. Lev, M.D.
104 South Michigan Avenue Chicago

Timothy Dineen
5419 Van Buren Street Chicago

Gioe Parole Contributors

David Fisook
100 West Monroe Street, Chicago

Albert V. Turner
Turner Brothers Clothing Company
Roosevelt Road and Walstead Street, Chicago

Harry A. Ash
Attorney-at-law
222 East Chestnut Street, Chicago

Lloyd J. Butler
Diamond Broker
133 North Clark Street Chicago.

Paul Lessing Mann
Consolidated Wire and Associated Companies, 1635 South Clinton Street, Chicago
(Paul Mann, aka Paul Mankowitz was part owner of his company who offered to give Gioe a steady job. Mann had underworld connections and also financed Capone gangster James Weinberg in Chicago.)

The FBI investigated the path the paroles took. Right before DeLucia and his cronies were paroled they all still had indictments against them pending in the Southern District of New York. Maury Hughes, an attorney in Dallas Texas, was engaged by a mysterious "Mike Ryan" to obtain dismissal of these indictments pending in New York in order that the indictments would not be a road-block to their paroles. An extensive investigation was conducted by the FBI all over the country in an attempt to identify this "Mike Ryan" but his identify was never discovered.

What was discovered that Maury Huges came to Chicago with other individuals from Dallas who were involved in obtaining the paroles and met with Murray Humphreys in the old Stevens Hotel and the old Edgewater Beach Hotel in 1947.

The FBI speculated that this "Mike Ryan" was actually Murray Humphreys and that Humphreys went to then Attorney General Thomas Clark to help with the case. Clark formerly practiced law in Dallas with a attorney named Nash who was close to Humphreys and was able to obtain favorable treatment in having the other indictments against the hoodlum leaders removed by Clark after Clark was contacted by Nash in this regard. FBI Agents overheard Murray Humphreys discussing the situation involving Nash and Clark in 1964. Humphreys complained that after Thomas Clark helped out with the indictments Humphreys tried on another occasion to contact Clark for help but was refused by Clark to assist in anything else. Thomas Clark went on to become a Justice of the U.S. Supreme Court in the 1960's.

The FBI also concluded that an old time Capone member named Ned Bakes, who was known as "Little" Ned Bakes. In the 1940's Little Ned Bakes was a "fixer" in Chicago who was feared by many. He had a son named Ned Bakes Jr. who went by the name of "Big" Ned Bakes. Ned Bakes Junior was reported to be a deputy sheriff of Cook County until May 1, 1946 at which time he turned the job over to his brother. Both men were sponsored by Peter Fosco who at the time was Cook County Commissioner and Democratic boss of the old 20th Ward in Chicago. Either Ned Bakes Sr. or Jr. was said to be the right hand man of Peter Fosco.

In 1948 Little Ned Bakes was running a hand book operation on Chicago's west side out of a building he owned in the old 26th Police District. One report listed Ned Bakes as, *"Ned Bakes is 43 to 45 years old, Italian decent, paunchy and large, born in Chicago, and a bachelor living with his mother at 1118 South Ashland Avenue."* One report list an incident in Los Angeles involving Little Ned Bakes and the LAPD where he claimed his real name was Ignatius Spacchesi. In April 1954 Little Ned Bakes, Illinois State Reprehensive James J. Adduci, bootlegger Dominic Volpe and future First Ward Republican committeeman Peter Granata were sought by Milwaukee Police for questing in the murder of a liquor store owner in Wisconsin. All claimed no knowledge of the murder.

Investigator over heard talk at Sportsman Park Race Track in Chicago that Little Ned Bakes was instrumental in obtaining the parole for DeLucia as the pay-off man. Also over heard discussing Little Ned Bakes was Outfit attorney's George Callaghan and Maury Hughes at the criminal courts building.

When Paul DeLucia was called to answer questions about "Mike Ryan" and his parole before the congressional committee all he had to say was he did not know who Mike Ryan was. United State's Marshal's attempted to serve Ned Bakes and labor union czar Peter Fosco subpoenas to appear and be questioned as to who was Mike Ryan.

During the hearing DeLucia was asked if he knew a man by the name of Tony Gobels? DeLucia admitted knowing Gobles (his real name was Anthony Ricci) but when the representative asked, *"Isn't he recognized as the syndicate boss in the United States?"* DeLucia made a sharp retort answering with a question, *"Is he?"* which the representative replied. *"I'm asking you?"*

DeLucia was then shown a photo of Chicago mobster Mike Spranze who used the alias of Mike Kelly. The representative believed that Spranze could have been the mysterious Mike Ryan. DeLucia replied to the photo, *"Look's like I might know the guy, but I can't give you his name."* However later he did admit knowing Spranze. Questing when on:

Question	Whom did you authorize to go to Dallas, Texas, to hire Maury Hughes?
DeLucia	I never authorized nobody.
Question	Who paid the $15,000 in your behalf?
DeLucia	I don't know.
Question	Do you know Ned Bakes?
DeLucia	No. I know there are lots of fellows named Bakes, but I don't know them.
Question	Do you know the man who has the handbook concessions on the near southwest side?
DeLucia	I don't know about handbooks.
Question	You testified here some time ago, didn't you, that you did quite a bit if gambling?
DeLucia	Yes, but I never run no handbook. I was more of a free lance. Those places, they change.
Question	You sure do have a poor memory. Do you want this committee to believe you don't know about the operations of the syndicate?
DeLucia	I don't know what you mean by the gambling syndicate and I must say no.
Question	What was your share of the parole expense?
DeLucia	What expense?
Question	How much did it cost you to get out?
DeLucia	I paid $5,000 to Dillon. (Attorney Paul Dillon of St. Louis.)
Question	What did you pay Maury Hughes?

DeLucia	Nothing.
Question	Which of your pals paid him?
DeLucia	I don't know.
Question	Did you authorize anyone to collect money to pay Hughes or to give to Attorney Eugene Bernstein for you income tax settlement?
DeLucia	No.
Question	Have you been asked to refund any of the money paid in the settlement of your income tax case?
DeLucia	No.
Question	Did you have any money accrue to your account while you were in prison that was given to your release?
DeLucia	No.
Question	Do you have any income aside from your farm interest?
DeLucia	No.

During further questioning Paul DeLucia admitted he had a long time friendship with Peter Fosco for over 30-years and stated that their wives were very close friends and constant companions. DeLucia denied he had any dealings with any labor union, with Peter Fosco or Jacob Arvey, then the Chicago Democratic county chairman. He even added that he did not know mob labor union boss Anthony C. D'Andrea was related to Phil D'Andrea.

In the end mob lawyer George Bieber made a convincing case that the Capone hoodlums should have never been convicted in the extortion case. The stories told by Browne and Bioff were falsehoods. The judge him self in the case stated that the stories told by both Bioff and Browne could not be believed. Bieber pointed out that the fact that these parolees were incarcerated based primarily on the information furnished by Browne and Bioff was wrong and the hoodlums deserved their parole.

When it was learned Nick Circella was going to be released with the other Capone hoodlums, an anonymous citizen wrote and letter to the FBI. It read:

"Nick Circella, Dean, a Capone mobster in Fort Leavenworth who is not even a citizen is supposed to be paroled in December. According to his brother, Augie, who is bragging, he is going to be a big shot upon his return. Don't let him get out, please. Deport him, he is a killer."

Chapter 7

Getting the Power Back

As 1947 began the Chicago Outfit was said to be *"More potent financially and politically than ever before."*

Gambling in Chicago consisted principally of horse race betting and policy. The policy racket in 1947 was mostly in the African-American areas of Chicago. Only two white men, Petey Tremont and Pat Manno, were able to control most of the policy games. The big stake in the policy racket for DeLucia and Accardo was that they controlled the sale of paper and numbering machines for the policy business. There were only a few slot machines within the city limits so they could send their clients out into the suburbs where they had considerable amount of slot machines.

Chicago was under the control of the crime syndicate but it was still loosely broken up into gangs. One of the gangs, the James Weinberg Gang, was frustrated with most of its endeavors during 1946 and 1947 which caused the gang to basically disintegrate. Weinberg and Paul "Needle Nose" LaBriola were in charge of the gang. They spent most of 1947 trying to reestablish themselves in the Town Hall District of Chicago.

Another gang operating was the Red Hawk Gang whose leader, who was called Red Hawk, was considered a "Booster" gang that specialized in safe-cracking burglaries. They made their headquarters out of a liquor store in the 1200 block on West 79th Street in Chicago. Later this gang would be taken over by the Panczko family and become known as the Panczko Gang. In 1947 members of the Red Hawk Gang housed some of the Outfit's up and coming mobsters. Some of the members were James "Cowboy" Mirro, Stanley Jasinski, Sam Ferrara, Adolph Starzyk, James Lubiak and John Quinn.

Then there was the Red Barnes Gang who found themselves being mostly inactive that year. They specialized in cartage thefts. The Christiano Bookie Gang was holding up mob handbooks all over Chicago. It was said at the time that they had the best automatic revolvers and machine guns in the city. The Friday Night Gang was given its name by the Chicago Police Department since they were holding up taverns on the South Side of Chicago every Friday night in the summer of 1947. They were known by the U.S. Army carbine rifles they used. One of the men arrested in this gang was Walter Janiak. The last was the Hebda Safe Gang who met at a tavern at 4811 North Broadway known as "The Dock" tavern to plan their safe burglaries. This gang was credited with many of that year's safe robberies.

That year also saw the killing of Vincent Bozik on August 2, 1947, a Chicago South Side gambler and racketeer who received a shot gun blast while sitting on his front steps. Gus "Slim" Alex was said to be the shooter. William "Big Irish" Quinn, a gambler and pinball operator who was connected to Italian mobsters was killed at the door of his residence at 3315 West Madison Street on July 17. Police arrested Albert Spagnola and John DeBartolo for the murder. Spagnola told police that he shot Quinn in an attempted holdup.

For Paul DeLucia and Tony Accardo, 1947 saw a new boss in control of Chicago.

Mayor Martin Kennelley assumed office on April 15, 1947. With a new mayor, DeLucia and Accardo ordered practically all handbooks in the city of Chicago to close down. During this period which was known as the "tight" period, a number of raids on gambling joints were conducted by the Chicago PD. Many police captains were shifted from one district to another and several police captains were suspended from duty for failure to suppress gambling in their districts. After a few months or a "grace period" DeLucia and Accardo resumed their gambling operations.

In the suburbs the mob had focused on the village of Skokie, Illinois. DeLucia and Accardo had given money to the Mayor, Chief of Police and trustees in Skokie to allow slot machines to be run freely without any interruption. The Illinois State's Attorney's office charged the village officials and a trial got underway. However, the cases against these officials were nolle processed when the state could not line up the necessary number of witnesses.

The FBI stopped by to see Jake Guzik on October 6, 1947, to find out how life was since he was the syndicate's top boss of all gambling operations within the city limits. Guzik told the agents that he would give $20,000 cash to anyone who could prove that he was connected with any handbook. So then the agents went to Tough Tony Capezio two days later for an interview. Capezio admitted to the agents that he was operating several handbooks in Chicago but denied the existence of a so-called "syndicate" claiming that it was all a newspaper fairy tale.

In the late 1940's Accardo and DeLucia had what was called at the time an off-shoot of the Chicago syndicate. This group was headed by Rocco Fischetti who at the time was operating the Vernon Country Club which housed a large and lucrative gambling establishment one mile north of the Cook County line in Lake County Illinois.

Fischetti was safe there because the State's Attorney of Lake County and the Sheriff's office for many years tolerated the operation of gambling by the Chicago mob in their area because of the lucrative pay-offs each official was receiving. The officials felt that the Chicago mob was the "top dogs" in gambling in Lake County and because of their power they would keep the other gambling elements in line so that there would be no public disturbances.

In the Illinois town of Waukegan in the 1940's the gambling was controlled by the mob with the consent of the Police Department. The handbooks in Waukegan were fined every two weeks and the fines collected were used by the City of Waukegan to support an increase in the number of policemen in the police department.

Tony Accardo had Frank LaPorte controlling the Joliet area working out of Chicago Heights, Illinois. There he controlled slot machines, pinball machines and prostitution activities. LaPorte had a small gang of hoodlums in his section that were involved in safe burglaries and white slave operations.

While DeLucia was away, Accardo had attempted in the spring of 1946 to make Joliet one of his key spots for the dissemination of the mobs racing news service then known as the Trans American Racing News Service. The Joliet Police chief Ernest Overbey raided the offices of the news service and confiscated all the equipment so the mob could not operate. That angered Joliet mobster Francis

Curry which caused Curry to make threats against Overbey.

William E. Meade, then Commissioner of the Police in Joliet, filed charges of malfeasance against Overbey on the basis that there was dissension in the Police Department due to Overbey's management. On October 11, 1947, Overbey was discharged by action of the police board and Meade took over the Joliet Police Department. Overbay was said to be one of the most efficient police captains the Joliet Police Department had seen to that date. One informant speculated that Overbey had fallen under the spell of Ted Blair, alias Charles Henry Boyle, formerly a radio announcer in Joliet who was discharged and left the city to work at Chicago's WBBM radio station. Blair had spent time in prison for impersonation of a federal officer. This informant labeled him as a "psychopath" who was a dominating influence in the Law Enforcement League in Will County.

While Paul DeLucia was in prison he had mobsters Ben and Anthony Fillichio looking after his handbooks for him and had mobster Francis Curry personally oversee and run DeLucia's farm in Kendall County located in the northwestern section of Joliet, Illinois. Francis had run the farm from 1944 to 1947. Once DeLucia was released from prison they moved into the 1200 acre farm.

When interviewed by FBI agents about DeLucia's farm, Francis Curry was asked if he gave money to DeLucia or any of the Capone gangsters that was used for their parole. Curry told the FBI, *"Now really, if I knew of monies being paid you wouldn't expect me to tell you, but honestly I think the idea of monies being paid in connection with these paroles is foolish. In my opinion, the whole thing is a fairy tale."*

One of the things Paul DeLucia liked the most about Francis Curry was that he was a smart Irish organized crime figure when it came down to business involving the syndicate. For example when it came time for Curry to pay his income taxes he always had his auditor add $15,000 to the final total he owed so if the Government ever came back and said you made all this money gambling and never paid taxes on it he could say *"Yes I did, take a look at the filings."*

When the FBI interviewed Curry in 1947 he told them that the income from the farm in 1946 grossed $50,000. He admitted he was a close friend of DeLucia's, Phil D'Andrea, Charles Gioe and Louis Campagna. He also admitted that he operated slot machines and handbooks but never placed a bet or used a slot machine for in his life.

The FBI wrote about Curry in 1947, *"Chief of Police Ernest E. Overbey claims that Francis Curry is extremely influential in behind-the-scene politics in Joliet. He had further stated that Curry is solidly entrenched with A.F. Schupp, Chairman of the Will County Republican Committee, and Commissioner of Police and Fire William E. Meade. According to Overbay, Curry had demanded of Meade that Overbey be removed as Chief of Police in order that gambling will be permitted in the city of Joliet. Overbay further stated that Francis Curry is reputed to have contributed $8,000 to Commissioner Meade's campaign fund and, therefore, is in a position to make such a demand. Overbay believes also that Meade wants to get rid of him because Meade also would like to have Joliet run wide open in order that he can make as much money as possible during his four-year term."*

Tony Dark

File Card

Francis Jerome Curry
AKA Slim
AKA The Thin Man
AKA Fran
AKA Frank Curry
Born December 11, 1902 in Joliet, Illinois
Died May 6, 1970 (One report says May 4)
Height 6'
Weight 140 Pounds
Build Slender with a slightly stoop
Eyes Blue
Hair Brown, Thin Balding
Peculiarities Small Head; Long Face; Squinty Eyes; Large Protruding Ears; Large Adams Apple
Characteristics Nervous Type; Chews Gum; Takes Large Steps
SS# 361-32-1451Driver's License # C600-2500-2352

Family

Father, Robert E. Curry *(Born around 1870 and died May 5, 1941)*
Mother, Alice McCraney
Brothers, Harold, Robert Jr. and Hubert *(All dead by 1970)*
Wife, Marian Zalar, born 1910 *(Belonged to Catholic Woman's League and was an artist conducting classes on ceramics and china painting)*
Daughter, Mary Alice, Born 1938 *(Was employed as a teacher by 1969 in the Joliet Board of Education. Husband, Dr. Joseph B. Carney)*
Son, Robert J. Curry, born June 1, 1940 in Joliet, Illinois *(Robert attended Lewis College at Lockport, Illinois; Joliet Junior College; the University of Miami and St. Mary's University in San Antonio, Texas in 1963. Married Marlene Chovan)*
One report listed a Son-in-law of Francis Curry as an Illinois Sheriff named Mike Breen

Known Addresses

Seelbach Hotel, Suite 730-732, Louisville, Kentucky (1946)
Brown Hotel, Louisville, Kentucky (1946)
736 North East 74th Street, Miami, Florida (1946)
Stevens Hotel, Room 1918A, Chicago (1947)
516 South Western Avenue, Joliet, Illinois (1940's-1950's) *(Large 10-room house, 3,888 square feet. Worth $289,000 as of 2014)*
5801 La Gorce Drive, Miami Beach, Florida (1950's) *(Built in 1936 with 2,980 square feet. Worth around $1.4 million as of 2014)*
Cabana at the Hotel Martinique, Miami Beach, Florida (1954)
115 St. Jude Street, Joliet, Illinois (1964) *(Could be a relative's address)*

Known Businesses of Francis Curry

Saloon Keeper in Joliet, Illinois (1924)
Curry's Cigar Store, 416 Cass Street, Joliet, Illinois (1927)
Elks Bar, Joliet, Illinois (1935)
Royal Bodago Tavern, Joliet, Illinois (1935)
Scale and Vending Machine Company, Joliet, Illinois (1942)
Farmer of grain and dairy, owned 3,000 acres of farmland in Kendall County located 18 miles west of Joliet (1940's)
Illinois Distribution Company, Joliet, Illinois (1940's-1950's) *(Distributor of slot machines)*
Clinton Publishing Company, Joliet, Illinois *(Bookie supply company)* (1946)
Commonwealth News and Publishing Company, 314 South 5th Street, Louisville (1946)
Wilco Company (1940's)
Publishing Company, Kentucky (1950's)
Midwest News Service (1950's)
Cooperative Music Company, 1728 Halsted Street, Chicago Heights (1950's-1960's)
Reputed syndicate chief of Joliet, Illinois in the 1940's and 1950's
Wurlitzer Coin Operated Machine Distributor, Louisville, Kentucky (1950's)
Shepley Trucking Company of Joliet, 2 North Des Plains Street, Joliet, Illinois *(Also known as Shepley's Garage) (His headquarters and stored slot machines here 1950's)*
LaSalle Country Court House, LaSalle Illinois (1950) *(Gambling house)*
J & J Picnic Grove, 159th Street and Wolf Road, Will County, Illinois (November 9, 1959 -1960's)
Little Jack's Restaurant, Joliet, Illinois (1960's) *(Burned down for insurance money)*
Automatic Coin Machine Company of Joliet, 2 North Des Plaines Avenue, Joliet, Illinois (1950's & 60's)
D'Amico's Restaurant, Route 52 W. Jefferson Street, Joliet, Illinois (1960's) *(Used as meeting place)*
Large housing development in Texas (1960's)
Shopping Center in Joliet, Illinois (1965)
Brozmans Tavern, 510 Moen Avenue, Rockdale, Illinois (1966) *(Handbook)*
Stellas, Rockdale, Illinois (1966) *(Handbook)*
Joliet Athletic Club, 2nd floor, North side of Cass Street, East of Chicago (1966) *(Handbook)*
Angelo's Restaurant (1966) *(Alleged handbook connected to Curry)*
Town House Tavern (1966) *(Alleged handbook connected to Curry)*
Co-op Trucking Company, Joliet (1970) *(Partners Frank LaPorte, Frank Bompensiero and Frank Franze)*
Valley Music Company, Aurora, Illinois (1960's-1970's)

Known Arrest Record of Francis Curry

(Official criminal recorded destroyed by police order)

Date	Charge	Agency	Result
7-24-1920	Disorderly Conduct	Joliet PD	Released
2- 8-1925	Liquor Violation	Feds	Acquitted
4-1-1927	Liquor Violation	Joliet PD	Acquitted
6-6-1967	Improper Lane Usage	U/K	Fine
10-24-1968	Speeding (76 in a 60)	Joliet PD	$15 Fine

Known Organizations he belonged to

St. Joseph Baptist KSKJ Lodge 143
Holy Name Society of the Cathedral of St. Raymond

Known Auto's of Curry

1962 Cadillac white Convertible (Florida license plates)
1962 Buick, brown in color
1963 Chevrolet, four-door (License plate number DW-9832)
1964 Buick
1969 Buick two-door sport coupe *(Registered under Co-Operative Music Company number CF2077)*

Blurry FBI photo of Francis Curry

Known Associates of Curry

Webster Armstrong
Joseph Barrett
William Biech
Frank Bompensiero (San Diego)
Clinton Brayton
James Burns
Andrew J. Burns
Russell Carney
Frank Carreio
Charles Costello
Joseph Costello
John Costello
Sam Costello
Nick Cuda
Sam DeGiovanni
Frank Desimone
Ralph Emery
Anthony Falzone
George Faucett
Frank Franze
Moroni Freehauf
Virgil Floyd (Teamster Agent)
Nose Gallagher
Joseph Gallagher
Kenneth Greffin
Marolc Greffin
Joseph "Big Joe" Guzzino, aka Joe Guzzini,
Sam Guzzino
Matthew Hartford (Police Officer)
Max Hester
Frank J. Jones (Attorney)
Leann Kelly
Dr. Raymond J. Kennedy
John Kirincich (Sheriff)
Frank LaPorte
Al Lawrence
John Maley (Lawyer)
Paul Metzger (Police Captain)
Joseph Neroni
Sam Perry
John Prendergast
Al Pilotto
Art Pilotto
Dom Roberts
Al Rosetti
Frank Sanello
A.F. Schupp
Wesley Shay
Charles Spears
William Tighe
Glen Truett
Tom Tuite
Ralph Verrecchia
Anthony Wagner
Ed Walsh
Pete Wood

Louisville Hoodlum Associates

Earl Vincent Burton (Leader of the Louisville Burton Gang)
Sam Campo
John Fitzgerald
Earl Gaar Sr.
James Wilford Humphreys (Louisville top hoodlum)
George Jack Hutchison
Bernard Wolfred Jacobs
Red Jacobs
Ellis "Gyp" Joseph (Former police officer)
David Jarrett
Busty O'Brien

Tony Dark

Francis Curry was a bootlegger from the early days in Chicago. He was known as a slugger and gunman who was not afraid to do what was needed. He was educated having completed grade school and four years of high school. One of his first known arrests was on July 24, 1920 when he was arrested for disorderly conduct. Francis Curry's father, Robert E. Curry, was a small-time gambler who worked in the Joliet steel mines as a mill worker. He went on to own a tavern before dying of natural causes. His brother, Robert Curry Jr., became very prominent in hoodlum circles in the bootlegging days being known as one of the best rum runners in Illinois. He was also active in gambling in Will County and used his strong connections with the Will County Sheriff's office to stay out of jail even though he had a lengthy arrest record. Robert Jr. was said to be killed in an automobile accident in 1944. One report stated that in that accident two men were found in the auto and the coroner later discovered two bullet holes in one of the men. His other brother, Hubert Curry, was killed in an automobile accident just outside the city limits of Joliet a year later.

Francis Curry was arrested by Alcohol and Tobacco Tax agents for violation of the Prohibition Act for running a wild-oat brewery in Lemont, Illinois. He was also listed as being associated with the Shelton Gang, an old time gang dating back to the Al Capone days.

In 1924 he was investigated by the FBI for his involvement in what was titled "attempt to intimidate a government witness." On March 7, 1924 a P.J. Burgess, then a chauffeur for the president of the First National Bank of Joliet, was driving his vehicle to pick up his boss when a car of five hoodlums ran his car off the road to a stop. One of the hoodlums named Wesley Shay, then a saloonkeeper in Joliet, jumped out of the hoodlum car into Burgess's car and began to punch him. As Burgess tried to fight Shay off he noticed the other four hoodlums jump out of the car and heading towards him so he shifted his car into gear and stepped on the gas to make his escape. As Burgess attempted to drive, with Shay still punching him, he noticed Shay was attempting to draw a gun from his hip pocket. Burgess slammed on the brakes and got out of the car, running away leaving his car and Shay behind. One of the hoodlums, Francis Curry, was chasing him down the street attempting to pull out a gun he had tucked away in his pocket while hollering, *"Stop, darn you, or I'll shoot you"*. However, Burgess was too fast for Curry and made his escape. It turned out that P. J. Burgess had worked as an investigator for the Will County Law & Order League of Joliet and had gathered evidence of sales of intoxicating liquor against four Joliet saloonkeepers, including Curry and Shay. The other two hoodlums were said to be Charles Spears and William Biech.

In 1927 Francis Curry was arrested for possession of beer and warehousing barrels of beer. The beer was found at his business, named Curry's Cigar Store, located at 416 Cass Street in Joliet. He was later acquitted of these charges.

In August 1935 the U.S, Treasury Department was investigating him on charges of conspiracy to violate internal revenue laws. It was around this time that Francis Curry was called a protégé of mob boss Eddie Vogel. At that time Vogel was the juke box king of Will County, Illinois.

Francis Curry had gained power when he married Marian Zalar. They had two children together. Marian's father, Joseph Zalar, was a powerful political figure in Will County, Illinois. Joseph Zalar was highly respected in Joliet since he held the positions of Supreme Secretary of the Capital KSKJ and in the Slovenian Catholic organization. Curry's political connection to Zalar placed Curry on the Joliet Police and Fire Board as a personal representative. However, when Zalar retired in the 1940's Curry lost most of his contacts in influential places.

In the early 1940's Francis Curry and "Nose" Gallagher went down to Alabama to kidnap a gambler with the intention of killing him. However, when they arrived and made their move, the gambler was able to grab a side arm he had. He pointed and shot at Curry and Gallagher. Curry escaped the bullets but Nose Gallagher was shot six times. Gallagher survived and was hospitalized for almost a year before he recovered. However, his luck was intact; about a year after his recovery he was shot again with five bullets and lived. Gallagher's luck came to an end while he and several of his fellow hoodlums were preparing a hijacking job when one of his own men accidently fired a round from a shotgun and hit Gallagher in the chest. The hoodlums took Gallagher's body and dropped it at the front door of a hospital where Nose Gallagher finally died.

In 1944 despite his mob image, a local newspaper in Joliet called Francis Curry *"one of the local boys who did good in life"* referring to Curry's farms and all the produce he was providing.

In 1946 Joliet police raided and arrested a handbook in the Louis Joliet Hotel owned by Curry. They discovered that Curry owned the Trans-American at 58 North Chicago Avenue in Joliet. The Trans-American was Curry's bookmaking operation. Curry then went to the local radio station in Joliet, then called WJOL, and paid-off the manager to do Curry's bidding. For instance, when the police were shutting down his handbooks, he had the radio announcer broadcast *" While two murders in Joliet, Illinois, remain unsolved, the police department is devoting its time to war on bookmakers"* to gain public support to solve the murders and lay off the gambling.

Francis Curry even had one of his men named Abe Aronin purchase a Joliet newspaper called the Farmer's Weekly Review at Joliet to print what stories Curry felt were necessary to help his business.

Another one of Curry's men was Ed Walsh, then a paving contractor, who for some reason was awarded every paving job in the Joliet area even though he charged several thousand dollars more than other bids that were submitted. Curry even had Walsh approach the wife of the then police chief Ernest Overbey who was the one man leading the fight against Curry and the mob, and flash a roll of money saying that all this could be hers if they would "go along with the boys."

Among other duties Francis Curry had to perform for his mob bosses, in 1946 Curry was contacted by Clarice Accardo and asked to find a collie dog for the Accardo's to purchase.

On orders from Paul DeLucia, Francis Curry had Joseph "Big Joe" Guzzino and Joseph Barrett set up gambling operations in Louisville, Kentucky and run the operation for DeLucia. Curry also attempted to take over the wire service for bookmakers in Louisville but found that to be a challenge. The bookmakers in

Louisville were so organized that they had the local police department run Curry and his men out of the state. He set up a Morse code wire at 314 South 5th Street in Louisville to use in his operation. He had paid off the telephone company inspectors to overlook all of his 50 phone lines running into the building. Curry was ordered to tell everyone in Louisville that he was there representing Chicago mobster Murray "Curley" Humphreys.

In 1947 after being run out of the state, Francis Curry was back in Louisville acting as a financial backer in a trotting race track that was being built on the County-Shelby County line on Shelbyville Road, 18 miles from Louisville. Curry's plan was to use the track for dog races on days the track was not being used for trotting races.

By 1948 Curry had managed to get control of the Continental Press wire service in Louisville and was acting as the district manager of the company. He was also known to be in business in Louisville with James Wilford Humphreys, then a Kentucky top hoodlum and Ellis Joseph, the one-time Assistant Chief of Police in the Louisville Police Department. Curry and Joseph had become partners in gambling establishments and night clubs around the city.

One report said information developed showed that Francis Curry had approximately sixty million dollars which he could draw from, if needed, to establish the race wire service in Louisville. Eventually, after constant interruptions, Francis Curry was run out of Louisville once again.

At the end of the 1940's, after being labeled "the missing witness" due to the fact that he had been sought for a long time to appear in Paul DeLucia's parole scandal, Curry was in control of handbooks in Lockport, Illinois. Informants told investigators that Curry's "take" during 1949 from the racing information business was $500,000. However, the informant could not verify that amount and it was not known if that was the gross figure of his net profit.

At the end of the 1940's Francis Curry had to re-establish himself with the new political powers that were in Joliet. His link to political figures and politics in the Joliet area were made through his contact, a Mrs. Ford June. Mrs. June was an old friend of Curry's since the two went to school together.

As the 1950's arrived Curry was boss of all syndicate operations in Will County, Illinois and all of the territory between Joliet and the far south of Illinois down to East St. Louis, Illinois where mobster Frank "Buster" Wortman was boss. What Curry would do in Joliet politics is finance political candidates running on both sides so he would win either way.

Over in New York City, police noticed Francis Curry was making many trips to their city and every time the first thing he did was to make contact and meet with mobster Anthony Ricci, aka Tony Gobels. Curry always registered under a different name but always stayed at the swank Waldorf Astoria Hotel.

In the early 1950's a rival of Francis Curry's named Lee Kelly, also known as Leahm, was shot to death. Lee Kelly and his brother Dennis, aka Denny, then bookshop owners who were active in politics and the rackets for most of their life, had a string of slot machines and juke boxes in the Joliet area. The Kelly brothers had their hands all the way out to Willowbrook, Kentucky where they owned a coin machine distributor company. Dennis "Denny" Kelly was also the business agent for the Bartenders and Waiters Union in Joliet. Curry wanted Kelly's rackets and used syndicate hoodlums to get it.

•What Curry would do was if he or his boys found a strange juke box or pinball machine in his town that he did not own he would send one of his trucks filled with syndicate men and a new machine in the back. The hoodlums would jump out, turn the strange machine around so it faced the wall and could not be used, place the new machine which was owned by Curry and would inform the owner of the establishment that he was only allowed to use Curry's machine. If Curry found a pinball machine that was not his he would send his boys to the establishment; take sledge hammers and destroy the pinball machine in front of the proprietor and replace it with one of his. The proprietor was helpless because Curry's boys would hold a gun to his back to make sure the proprietor "didn't have a problem with what was going on." When someone asked the sheriff why they never attempted to stop this action they replied by saying no one ever made a complaint and there was nothing they could do. The Curry-Kelly war started when a machine of Kelly's was taken away and replaced with Curry's. Kelly would then immediately call a strike of the waitresses and bartenders who worked at Curry's places and would not call off the strike until Kelly's machines were put back.

For a while the Kelly brothers were left alone and had no trouble running their jukebox business. Once the Italian mob discovered the amount of money the Kelly brothers were making they attempted to run the brothers out of town until they discovered that getting controlled of Kelly's union was difficult.

The "difficulty" the Outfit had with the Kelly's came to an end when Lee Kelly was killed. Rumored around the time was that Kelly was killed by the personal bodyguard of Chicago Heights's mobster Jim Emery, at the time was Frank LaPorte. It was later learned that Frank LaPorte had ordered the death of Lee Kelly. Francis Curry took over Kelly's juke boxes and coin machines. One report said it was generally believed that Lee Kelly was killed because he was involved in a hijacking of slot machines in which he caused the slot machines hijacked to be located and returned to the owner.

After Lee Kelly's death his brother, Denny, operated a tavern and gambling joint on route 4A just north of Lockport. One night on his way home back to Joliet he was shot by a syndicate hoodlum. Curry became angry when he learned Denny had survived the shooting. However, soon after Denny was released from the hospital another attempt was made and Denny was successfully killed in Hammond, Indiana. Francis Curry was a main suspect in both killings. Investigators noted that the description of the killer fit Francis Curry perfectly. However, no one was ever charged with the murders. There was one report at the time that focused on Denny Kelly and his love life. He would often pursue married women as conquests and it was speculated that he may have been killed by a jealous husband whose wife Kelly was courting.

With the Kelly boys dead, Curry took their business and their union. Curry was now in control of the Teamsters, the laborers, the electricians, the retail clerks, the food handlers and the bartender and waitress unions in Joliet.

By 1955 Curry was running Joliet. It was reported that Francis Curry, Frank LaPorte, Emery Roberts and his brother John Roberts had taken control of all mob interest from the south section of the state of Illinois along the line drawn from Rockford to Blue Island to Michigan City and south to the state line.

Curry made his headquarters at a place known as the Shepley Garage under the company name of the Wilco Company. It was reported that this company was once called the Wilco Music and Tobacco Company when it was allegedly owned by the Kelly brothers. However, that was not verified and there are reports that the Wilco Company was started by Curry and Frank LaPorte in the 1940's. Running the company in the 1950's for Curry was his number one lieutenant, Frank "Snuffy" Sanello, then a business agent for the Teamsters Union Local 179 of Joliet.

1955 also saw Francis Curry attempt to get back into Louisville unmolested by police by putting "pressure" on the chief of police at that time to make it so. The chief of police told Curry if he took one step into Louisville he would be arrested and "thrown in jail." When Curry's attorney told the chief that just arresting Curry for no reason was a violation of his civil rights the chief's response to the lawyer was, *"Curry can take any legal action he saw fit, but he would regret the day he attempted it."* The chief added he would arrest Curry on vagrancy charges and if that charge did not "stick" in court he would harass Curry through the newspapers by furnishing them with photographs of Curry and all the information about his alleged Capone Gang connections.

One informant in 1955 told the FBI that Curry had ignored the threats and went ahead attempting to re-establish his gambling in Louisville. He added that Curry had "been in town" setting operations up for a while.

Curry had other problems such as difficulty handling his girlfriends. One incident occurred in April 1955. His former girlfriend Molly Zelko tossed a piece of iron with firecrackers tied to it into Curry's backyard to scare him into thinking someone was shooting at him. It was common knowledge that Zelko had tried on two occasions to run Curry over with her car. Curry was seriously worried that Zelko was going to kill him.

In 1956 the Chief of Police in Joliet informed investigators that Curry was still very close to many of Joliet's police officers and one of them, Sergeant Harry Thomas, acting as a body guard, was still driving Curry to Calumet City so Curry could attend meetings on gambling operations. Apparently at the time Curry was fighting with a rival hoodlum named Julius Shlensky who was running his own gambling operations in Joliet. Curry was tipping off the police to Shlensky's gambling house so they could be raided and put out of business.

Months later FBI agents investigated Francis Curry in a different anti-racketeering case involving organized labor. The investigation turned up very little as the FBI had a hard time finding proof that Curry controlled the labor unions. Agents tried to link Curry to the business manager of Teamster Local 179 in Joliet named Virgil S. Floyd. Floyd had a questionable past since he had been indicted by a federal grand jury in 1954, charging him with violation of labor laws.

FBI agents received word that Curry was involved with alleged "payoffs" to certain sewer and water contractors in the city of Joliet such as the McCarthy

Construction Company and the Walsh Oil Company. FBI agents received word that Virgil S. Floyd was "sore" at Francis Curry because Curry and the Outfit did not give much support during Floyd's trial before he was convicted and sentenced to two years in prison. Agents enjoyed the fact that Floyd was mad at Curry so he would get even and tell the FBI about the "payoffs" Curry was receiving from the construction companies. However, that did not happen.

The investigation did reveal several payoffs to the Joliet Hod Carriers Union Local 75 union boss Tony D'Augustino. D'Augustino was one of Frank "Frankie X" Esposito's men who was considered "mobbed up" controlling all the street laborers in Joliet. There were reports in 1940, right after Esposito became top union boss in Chicago, that Curry had moved in on D'Augustino and the labor union taking 1/3 to ½ of all the money taken in as initiation fees. Another Joliet union boss close to Curry receiving payoffs was Bill Downey, a business agent for the Joliet Plumbers local.

Unfortunately, agents could not get enough proof that Curry or Floyd were receiving "payoffs" and the investigation was closed.

At the end of the 1950's Francis Curry was working with mobster Rocco Fischetti acting as a manager in Fischetti's J & J Picnic Grove gambling house in Will County. At the time it was said to be one of the biggest gambling houses in the world.

In the 1960's some reports listed Francis Curry as Frank LaPorte's lieutenant, but it was commonly known that Curry's position was what it was because of his friendship with Paul DeLucia. It was said Curry held all the political connections while LaPorte held the position in the Outfit and answered to Sam Giancana. Both Curry and LaPorte had a stormy relationship. They were close enough where LaPorte gave Curry's family expensive gifts such as giving Curry's son Robert a $1,000 bill on his 21st birthday and another $1,000 bill on his 22nd.

That was not always the case. In the 1940's it was said that Curry and LaPorte were partners in the Wilco Music and Tobacco Company together. On September 20, 1957 an informant said that Curry frantically ordered his wife and children to leave Joliet and head to their Miami home because Curry had lost control of the Joliet slot machines to Frank LaPorte. Apparently the situation was taken care of since both became good friends again in the 1960's. When FBI agents attempted to verify this information they received countless stories, all different.

Francis Curry never considered himself a "gangster" or "mobster" and was always attempting to give the impression that he was someone of importance such as a respectable businessman. In the 1960's he would tell other respectable people that he was an attorney from Florida. However, Curry, not a "made" member of the Outfit, was an extremely powerful political figure who always protected the Outfit's interests in that area and shared the privileges of a top mob boss, being able to speak to Paul DeLucia and Sam Giancana any time he deemed necessary.

In November 1960 investigators watched as Francis Curry held a fashionable ball benefiting the Children's Guild at his home in Joliet. Investigators discovered that Curry sent out 100 invitations to the richest and most powerful families in the area around Joliet.

In the early 1960's Francis Curry was a staple on hidden microphone conversations from the offices of Cooperative Music Company at 1728 Halsted Street in Chicago Heights. There he would talk to Frank LaPorte about real estate purchases, business in California and his limousine and car leasing service which he and his brother, Charles Curry, were working on starting at the Joliet Airport.

In September 1960 FBI agents listened in on a conversation between mob boss Gus Alex, Ralph Pierce and mob tailor Jimmy Celano. Celano said this about Francis Curry, *"Curry is getting awful sloppy. He had a suit on that must be four or five years old. He owes me about $1,200 and he only paid me a thousand."*

Curry was also back in Louisville in the 1960's attempting to set up another wire service but was having trouble finding someone with proper contacts to pull it off.

There was an arrest of Francis Curry around 1962 when he was pulled over for speeding in Chicago Heights. When Curry refused to hand over his driver's license or give his name, the police officer arrested him and took him to the police station. Once inside Curry was loud and uncooperative and created such confusion that the police chief, a Phil Howard, had to come out of his office to see what the commotion was. Chief Howard then invited Curry into his office for a private meeting and after ten minutes and possibly a phone call or two, they walked out and Curry gave a fake name to the arresting officer, paid a $10 fine and was released. That year Curry was controlling the gambling at the Tally Ho Lounge in Burnham with Ralph Pierce and Frank Palermo.

In June 1964 Francis Curry's son, Robert, married Marlene Chovan at St. Raymond Nonnatus Church in Joliet. After the nuptials most of the 500 friends were not invited to the reception. Only those with invitations gathered at D'Amico's Restaurant located at 214 Ottawa Street. Standing outside to make sure only those invited could get in were two Joliet police officers and a few Andy Frain ushers. Marlene was a former model bureau instructor. FBI agents sat across the street and took photos of Paul DeLucia and his wife arriving with mob attorney Tony Gobels. Tony Accardo was spotted at the reception sitting alone because his wife did not attend. Others observed were Frank LaPorte, Murray Humphreys, Felix "Milwaukee Phil" Alderisio, Lester "Killer Kane" Kruse, Al Pilotto, Sam D'Giovanni and Frank Franze.

Four months later in October 1964 Francis Curry's daughter married Dr. Joseph B. Carney from Kankakee, Illinois. The ceremony was held at St. Joseph's Church in Joliet and the reception was once again held at D'Amico's "214" Restaurant. Once again the 700 guest included many of Chicago's top mobsters and many of Joliet's "respectable people" including bank presidents and public officials. It was said that time that Francis Curry was attempting to create a respectable reputation because of his feeling that since his daughter was now married to a doctor he should gain a reputation as a respectable citizen.

In 1965 Francis Curry was listed as attempting to take over the vending machine racket in Kane County, Illinois with mobster Charles English as his partner. A year later it was reported that Curry had stepped aside and let English take control of Joliet using English's own people. Chuckie English also purchased Curry's interest in the Wilco Music Company in Joliet. English also brought in mobster Dominic

"Butch" Blasi to take over sections owned by Curry, including the purchase of a golf driving range and shopping center near Joliet.

In August 1966 Francis Curry, Frank LaPorte, Frank Franze and Ralph Emery were all subpoenaed in an investigation by the Illinois Crime Commission for several loans made to business firms by the Mercantile National Bank of Chicago. These firms were all under investigation as having hoodlum influence.

Francis Curry was also watched that year as he would often visit the Crossroads Restaurant in Oak Forest, Illinois to meet with mobster Red Larner. Informants told the FBI that Curry, among other mobsters such as Frank LaPorte, William Palermo, James "The Bomber" Catuara, William "Willie Potatoes" Daddono, James "Muggsy" Tortoriello, and Sailor Allen, would visit the Crossroads to pick up or drop off envelopes filled with cash. The restaurant was a payment center for area bookmakers giving their "cut" to the Outfit.

Curry still had many handbooks operating in the Joliet area. One of them was at the Joliet Athletic Club on Cass Street. There he ran a layoff and collection joint that had police protection and was also alleged to be connected with a judge named Donald F. Delaney from the U.S. Court of Claims.

In 1968 Francis Curry and Charles English established a beachhead for the Outfit in a bid for the riches of a payroll totaling millions of dollars in a new steelmaking complex in the river valley area near Hennepin and Putnam Counties. The steel complex was to employ 15,000 people which meant those 15,000 people had to do something with their paychecks so if the Outfit could gain control of all the small taverns, restaurants, tobacco shops and liquor stores in the area, all that money could go to the Outfit. The other plan was for English and Curry to control all the gambling and lotto tickets in that area to help insure the paychecks wound up in the hands of the Outfit. It was not determined if those plans ever worked out.

By the end of 1969 FBI documents list Francis Curry as having serious health problems such as latent syphilis, gout, heart disease, and hypo chromic anemia. He was also believed to have cancer and was no longer able to conduct organized crime business personally. There was also a report that his house in Miami, Florida was falling apart, in need of serious repairs.

On May 5, 1970 Francis Curry died at 2:55 PM from cardiac arrest at St. Joseph Hospital in Joliet. He had been rushed to the hospital on May 2 with a history of heart trouble and cancer. He was waked at Tezak Funeral Home on May 6th and buried in St. Olivet Cemetery in Joliet.

Detectives looking on at the funeral could only make out one mobster in the crowd, Frank LaPorte.

By 1971, with Francis Curry gone, his family was still in control of various sections in Joliet. An FBI informant told the government that Francis Curry's son, Robert Curry, purchased Frank LaPorte's Cooperative Music vending machine business in the Chicago Heights area in 1974 from the widow of LaPorte. The informant said Robert Curry was actually buying it for the Outfit and allegedly made the paperwork look so that it appeared like he owned it. One informant alleged that a situation arose by a mobster's wife or wives who believed that Robert Curry was cheating them out of their money and because of this Robert attempted to sell the business but the wives refused. In 1975 the business was allegedly taken over by Dino Valente but it was unclear if he owned the company or if he was acting as a front for the wives. Cooperative Music was moved to 1015 East 162nd Street in South Holland, Illinois. Al Pilotto replaced Frank LaPorte as Capo in the Chicago Heights area and ordered all gambling to stop in 1974 since his brother was the chief of police.

Authors Collection

Photo of Francis "Slim" Curry

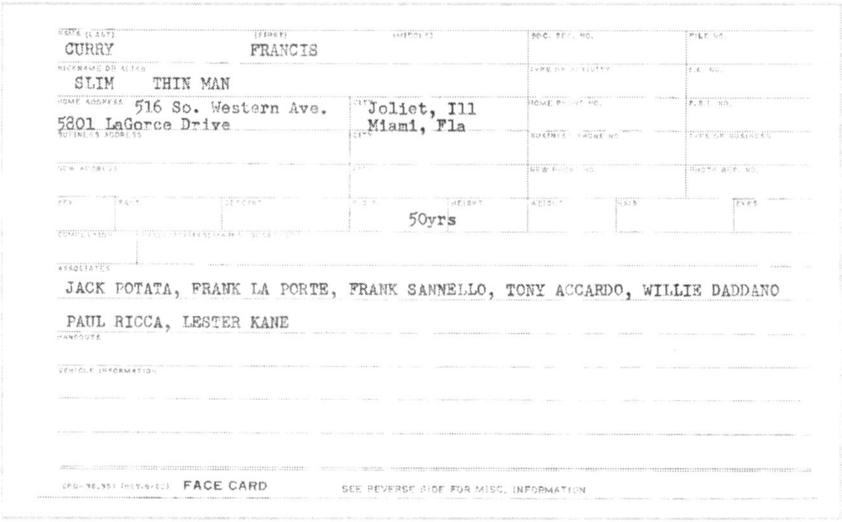

NAME (LAST) CURRY (FIRST) FRANCIS

NICKNAME OR ALIAS SLIM THIN MAN

HOME ADDRESS 516 So. Western Ave. CITY Joliet, Ill

5801 LaGorce Drive Miami, Fla

AGE 50yrs

ASSOCIATES

JACK POTATA, FRANK LA PORTE, FRANK SANNELLO, TONY ACCARDO, WILLIE DADDANO

PAUL RICCA, LESTER KANE

HANGOUTS

VEHICLE INFORMATION

FACE CARD SEE REVERSE SIDE FOR MISC. INFORMATION

Photo's of Paul and Nancy DeLucia arriving at Francis Curry's daughters wedding accompanied by an unidentified person, possiably Tony Gobels.

From the Collection of T.M.

More photos of the outside of Francis Curry's daughters wedding

From the Collection of T.M.

From the Collection of T.M.

From the Collection of T.M.

From the Collection of T.M.

From the Collection of T.M.

From the Collection of T.M.

By the end of the 1940's Paul DeLucia decreed that no member of the Chicago Outfit would have anything to do with narcotics. When DeLucia issued this law can be debated, however the reason as to why the law was issued was a sad point in his life. It was reported that DeLucia's son had allegedly become addicted to drugs and he witnessed first hand how drugs could destroy a life and what effect it had on society. The "no drugs" rule became written in stone though almost every mobster had a hand in drugs at one point, or at least they did not turn away money they generated.

In 1983 Senate hearings on the mob said this about DeLucia and his take on drugs, *"The influence of the mob would wane, according to the Ricca theory, if the heinous crime of narcotics was associated with them. According to his thought, as long as 'victim-less' crimes such as gambling were the sole support of the mob, their contacts outside the organization could be maintained."*

Commissioner of Police John Prendergast and State's Attorney William Tuohy decided that they were going to go after the Chicago Outfit. In September 1947 they made a list available classifying the top fifteen men to be investigated by the Chicago Police. The list released was:

1. Tony Accardo, aka Joe Batters
2. Murray "The Camel" Humphreys
3. Sam "Golf Bag" Hunt
4. Sam and Gus Alex
5. Charles and Rocco Fischetti
6. Paul Ricca (DeLucia)
7. Louis "Little New York" Campagna
8. Dom Bello
9. James "Mooney" Cancani
10. Claude Maddox "Johnny Moore"
11. James Redden
12. Jake Guzik
13. Eddie Vogel

Commissioner Prendergast transferred 50 men out of the Detective Bureau saying it was designed to *"cut the dead wood out of the Detective Bureau."* However, Prendergast had a questionable past himself. Chicago Police Captain Thomas Connelly and Lieutenant William Drury told the FBI that John Prendergast was formerly police captain in the old 1st District of Chicago during the time Al Capone was operating in the city and that Prendergast was more or less controlled by the remnants of the Capone Gang. Both officers believed in 1947 that Prendergast was still closely associated with the leading hoodlums and racketeers in Chicago.

In 1948 Paul DeLucia and mob attorney Joseph Bulger were indicted on making false statements concerning DeLucia's income. In June 1948 DeLucia placed his 4-1/2 acre Long Beach Indiana mansion estate in trust to Joseph Bulger just in case the government took steps to seize the property. In 1951 after DeLucia and Bulger were found not guilty, Bulger released the property back to DeLucia.

Chapter 8

Wedding Bells

On January 24, 1948 Paul DeLucia's daughter Marie married Alex B. Ponzio in what was labeled the "Extravaganza" or more commonly known as the "coming out" party to celebrate both a wedding and a DeLucia release party from prison. The wedding cost $25,657 which DeLucia paid in cash. The liquor bill was around $15,000 with $2,500 of that for 396 bottles of top shelf champagne. The bride and groom received $35,000 in cash as gifts which was placed in a large punch bowl when guests arrived to the reception.

When FBI agents went to Paul DeLucia to ask about the wedding, DeLucia told them that when he was released from prison he contacted Thomas Kelly, a friend who was the manager of the St. Hubert's Grill on Playmouth Court in Chicago, a well-known hang out for Chicago mobsters. He asked this manager to make the arrangements for his daughters wedding.

The large wedding was held in the Art Room and Ball Room at the Blackstone Hotel in Chicago which was located on Balbo Drive. First the wedding breakfast at 1:00 PM with only 22 guests and then the reception with the Buddy Moreno Band performing at 7:30. The orchestra cost $1,000 which had one of the Dorsey brothers brought in from New York City just for the occasion. The walls were lined with camellias and palms.

Around 700 to 800 guests were invited and the reception ran from 7:00 to 2:00. (Years later Alex Ponzio told investigators he believed there were 3,000 guests.) The owner of the St. Hubert's Grill would only admit to investigators that he saw a few syndicate figures he knew such as the Fischetti brothers Charles, Joe and Rocco, Frank Garnett, Frank "Chew Tobacco" Ryan, Harry Russell and Joe Fusco.

Surveillance photo of Paul DeLucia

The bride and groom spent a day or two at the Blackstone before leaving for their honeymoon at the Waldorf-Astoria hotel in New York City and then three weeks in Florida at the Saxony hotel.

One investigator wrote about the affair, *"The gathering has been unexcelled for gayety, splendor and lavishness by few, if any, of the parties staged by the first families of Chicago."*

The federal parole board had something to say about the wedding. Afterward they hit DeLucia with five charges showing how DeLucia violated his parole agreements. The five violations were:

1. Failure to report the $13,325.58 wedding breakfast and reception cost, for which DeLucia paid from a roll of $100 bills taken out of his pocket.
2. Failure to reveal documents to a federal grand jury in 1947 and the Kefauver Senate crime investigating committee in September 1950 in Chicago.
3. The source of the money used to settle his income taxes.
4. Failure to identify two of six companions who flew with him to Chicago from Leavenworth prison when he was paroled on August 13, 1947.
5. A general charge of failing to conduct himself honorably.

When investigators were done going through the copies of the records for the wedding (somehow originals of all the bills and paperwork disappeared, what luck), they determined that most of the people they interviewed had "bad" memories, stories that did not line up, and the actual amount of money spent and collected was a mystery.

From the Collection of T.M.

Paul DeLucia

TELEPHONE
HARRISON 7-4300

The Blackstone

MICHIGAN AVE. AT BALBO DRIVE

CHICAGO 5, ILLINOIS

COPY OF LUCHEON AND WEDDING
January 24 1948

Mrs. Alex Ponzio

$

KINDLY WRITE HEREON THE AMOUNT OF YOUR PAYMENT. DETACH AND MAIL THIS COUPON WITH CHECK.
A RECEIPTED BILL WILL NOT BE RETURNED UNLESS REQUESTED.

DATE	DESCRIPTION	CHARGES	CREDITS	BALANCE
	COPY from City Ledger Back Sheet AS PER STATEMENT RENDERED		1/26	$13824.58
1-24-48	22 lunceons @ $7.50	165.00	Paid cash	
	tax	3.30	Mrs. Alex	
	fee	20.00	Ponzio on	
	captains fee	5.00	wedding	12324.58
	1 check room girl	12.50	ALLOWANCE	1500.00
			on food	
	600 covers @ $15.00	9000.00	dated Jan 27th	
	wedding cake	200.00		
	beverage	2151.10		
	tax	227.02		
	396 bottle service	594.00		
	6 bartenders	69.00		
	6 check room girls & 2 wash room attendants	95.00		
	waiters fees	1200.00		
	local phones	.48		
	micraphone	10.00		
	room service	10.68		
	rooms; de Lucia	13.50		
	ponzio	21.00		
	kelly	27.00		

THE BLACKSTONE, MICHIGAN AVE AT BALBO DRIVE
TELEPHONE HARRISON 7-4300

LAST BALANCE IS AMOUNT DUE UNLESS OTHERWISE INDICATED. BILLS ARE PAYABLE WHEN PRESENTED.

A copy of bill from the Ponzio wedding

THE BLACKSTONE

SATURDAY, JANUARY 24th, 1948

ENGLISH ROOM

Mr. Tom Kelly,
St. Hubert's Old English Grill
316 So. Federal St.,
Chicago, Ill.

Wedding Breadfast at 1:00 P.M.
Persons @ T. X. E.

M E N U

FRENCH SERVICE

FRESH FRUIT SUPREME

Serve Champagne only

ONE SINGLE THICK LAMB CHOP
BROILED HAM ON BACON
SCRAMBLED EGGS

ONE CHECKROOM FIRL.

Ideal Potatoes
Frozen Asparagus, Hollandaise

ROLLS, SPLIT & TOASTED - Buttered.

Assorted coffee Cake and Sweet Rolls

Orange Marmalade & Jam

Plenty of Coffee

SATURDAY, JANUARY 24, 1948

ART HALL & BALLROOM

....

MR. TOM KELLY,
St. Hubert's Old English Grill
316 South Federal St.,
Chicago, Ill.

Buffet Dinner at 7:30 P.M.
500 Persons @ B.K.X.E. per person

HOT AND COLD HORS D' OEUVRES
SHRIMPS ON ICE
Celery - Olives - Stuffed Celery - Stuffed Olives

MEMO:

2 Bars set up
One for Champagne only
One for Liquor
6 Bartenders

Wedding Cake
Good Rm Filling $200.00
as large as you can make it.

Own music
Own flowers

Bell Boys (Paid)

1 Chef
2 or 3 Cooks

Cordials & Brandy must be imported

5 Checkroom Girls

Brid's table on platform
on Outside in Ballroom for 16.

Platform for
14 Men on Northside

Own Cigars
Own Cigarettes

ROAST PRIME RIBS OF BEEF
BAKED SUGAR CURED HAM
ASSORTED COLD MEATS
HOT AND COLD POTATO SALAD
SHRIMPS A LA NEWBERG
LOBSTER NEWBERG
CHICKEN A LA KING (WHITE MEAT ONLY)

Cole Slaw
Chef's Salad
Chicken Salad
Cold Salmon in Jelly on ice
Cold Lake Trout in Jelly

Candied Sweet Potatoes
Parisienne Potatoes

Petits Fours - Heart Shaped
Assorted French Pastry

Coffee

Ice Blocks

Chapter 9

New Decade, New Charges

The end of 1948 was not kind to Paul DeLucia. He suffered from an infected kidney and had it removed at Michael Reese Hospital in Chicago.

In 1949 the Chicago syndicate was out to purchase an unusual thing. Word was out that Paul DeLucia, Rocco Fischetti and Tony Accardo were interested in buying any and all Protestant Cemeteries they could get their hands on. One report suggests that they were able to purchase a Protestant cemetery in Boston, Massachusetts. The reason for this was never made known or why they were looking into just Protestants.

Other reports around that time stated that Paul DeLucia had developed an interest in blooded cattle and was spending most of his time on his 110-acre farm near Newark in Kendall County, Illinois.

To show how well organized crime paid off, the Chicago FBI field office laid out how many people either in the mob or connected with the mob were living in the exclusive residential area of River Forest. The 1949 map is listed below:

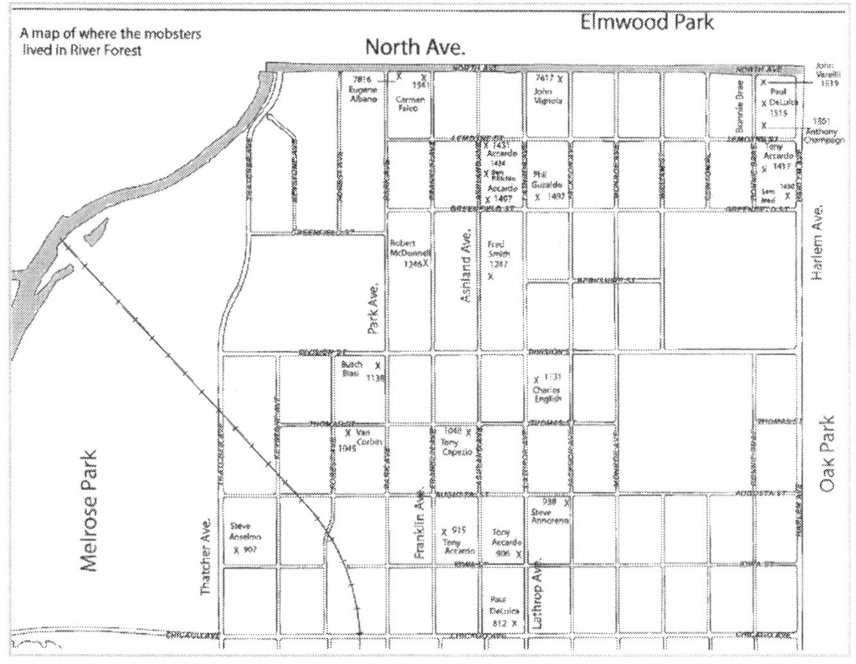

During the winter season of 1949, the Broward County Florida sheriff went to see Florida Governor Fuller Warren about a situation developing in his area. He reported that Chicago mobster Murray Humphreys, Jake Guzik and Paul Ricca "DeLucia" were in the middle of a bitter struggle with New York mobsters Meyer Lansky, Jack Lansky, Joe Adonis and Abner "Longie" Zwillman for control of gambling in South Florida. The problem was FBI agents discovered that the Chicago mob had contributed $40,000 to Warren's campaign which helped him win the office. In return Warren arranged "open gambling" in certain Florida counties. Nothing was done about the situation.

It had been a miserable decade for DeLucia who had spent several years of it behind bars; he was looking forward to a comfortable decade in the 1950's. DeLucia and Jake Guzik were doing very well in their control and operation of a nationwide racing wire and betting tip sheet service.

The 1950's started off with good publicity for Paul DeLucia when a newspaper article appeared stating that the City Council in Ottawa, Illinois expressed their appreciation to one of its citizens, Paul Ricca. Ricca had furnished 20-tons of fire wood to use during the coal storage for free from his farm located near Ottawa.

On October 3, 1950 Paul DeLucia and Louis Campagna were arrested and questioned about the murder of former Chicago Police Lieutenant William J. Drury who was shot to death in his garage in Chicago.

DeLucia admitted he was acquainted with Drury but denied having anything to do with the murder. Detectives were acting on a confession from a Trenton, New Jersey ex-convict who claimed he was paid $9,000 to murder Drury and that Paul DeLucia had a part in arranging the killing. DeLucia said he was at his home at 812 Lathrop Avenue at the time of the killing and his wife, father-in-law, Minni Gigante and their horseman, Tony Giacondi, could confirm his alibi.

Drury was killed shortly before he was to appear as a witness against Paul DeLucia in the Kefauver Committee hearings in Washington D.C. The New Jersey hoodlum claimed he was hired by crazy Chicago killer Samuel "Mad Sam" DeStefano to kill Drury and since DeStefano was considered "one of DeLucia's men" DeStefano was the go-between. Detectives for the Chicago Police believed Drury was killed as the result of extorting money from local handbook operators by threatening to expose their operations. Drury may have "attempted to shake down the wrong man" and was killed for it.

In October 1950 Paul DeLucia was relieved that the U.S. Supreme Court upheld the New Orleans Circuit Court of Appeals ruling that DeLucia and Charles Gioe did not have to go back to prison to finish their sentence for extortion. The Supreme Court votes went 4 votes for them to return and 4 votes for them not to return, a split. However, weeks later on November 25, 1950, Paul DeLucia was arrested on a parole warrant for failure to make proper reports. He was released on $5,000 bail.

In 1950 Tennessee U.S. Senator Kefauver headed a Senate committee investigating organized crime in America officially called the Senate Special Committee to Investigate Crime in Interstate Commerce. No high ranking mobster in America was exempt from the target of Kefauver. Hearings were held in fourteen U.S. cites, questioning over 600 witnesses "most of them hiding behind the 5th Amendment" testifying about organized crime. Kefauver sent out many investigators to gain as much information on top hoodlums they could find. Paul DeLucia and Tony Accardo were at the top of their list.

Senate investigators got the impression that Paul DeLucia's vagueness was due to his poor knowledge of the English language. But after they examined the transcripts of DeLucia's testimony, they found instances which indicated that his replies were evasive and not even truthful. For example, on one occasion when being questioned, DeLucia was asked how many different names he used. His reply was, *"I don't know, any place I go I mention any name that comes to mind."* A Committee Senator asked him why he did that, he replied, *"Oh, just a habit."*

Another example was when DeLucia was asked about his attorney in his parole case, he professed ignorance, and answered, *"What do you mean?"* Shortly thereafter in the testimony he was asked the same identical question and replied, *"That story is well known."*

When the committee questioned him about how he made his money he told them he was a gambler, *"I used to go out to the race track. Somebody wants to put out a lot of money and somebody wants to bet $10,000 on a horse, and if he put it in the totalizer, naturally the price goes down, so I used to hold the bet. If I thought it was all right, I hold it."* DeLucia was asked, *"Were you a betting commissioner?"* DeLucia replied, *"No; I was betting for myself." "Did you handle bets for anyone else?"* asked the Committee, *"Why, sure. No; what do you mean by anyone else? You mean they bet with me? Yes."* answered DeLucia. The committee asked, *"Who bet with you?"* DeLucia replied, *"A lot of people bet with me. I don't recall. That is a long time ago." "Can you recall anyone of the larger bettors with you?"* asked the committee, DeLucia replied, *"Yes, Al Capone was one."*

DeLucia told the committee that he never worked as a waiter anywhere and that when he lived at the Lexington Hotel in Chicago, which is where Al Capone lived and his headquarters was, that he would often meet up with Capone and Frank Nitti but did not know what line of business they were in except *"business with them was to try and make some money."*

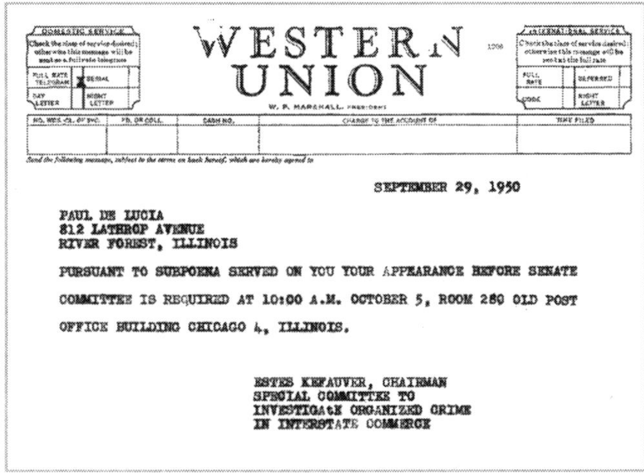

WESTERN UNION

SEPTEMBER 29, 1950

PAUL DE LUCIA
812 LATHROP AVENUE
RIVER FOREST, ILLINOIS

PURSUANT TO SUBPOENA SERVED ON YOU YOUR APPEARANCE BEFORE SENATE COMMITTEE IS REQUIRED AT 10:00 A.M. OCTOBER 5, ROOM 280 OLD POST OFFICE BUILDING CHICAGO 4, ILLINOIS.

ESTES KEFAUVER, CHAIRMAN
SPECIAL COMMITTEE TO
INVESTIGATE ORGANIZED CRIME
IN INTERSTATE COMMERCE

Mob Boss

Paul DeLucia was asked about his life during the hearings, the transcripts are as follows:

2 ORGANIZED CRIME IN INTERSTATE COMMERCE

Mr. ROBINSON. Do you have these records with you?
Mr. DELUCIA. Yes, sir.
Mr. ROBINSON. Would you produce them?
Mr. Chairman, may I offer in evidence the subpena?
The CHAIRMAN. Yes; the subpena will be received in evidence. It describes upon the face of it the records that the witness has been required to bring. It will be put in the record at this point as exhibit No. 1.
(Exhibit No. 1 appears in the appendix on p. 1379.)
Mr. DELUCIA. May I explain something? The subpena was to bring the records for 10 years. I only got the records from 1947. That is the day I came out from the penitentiary. Before that I was 3 years and 8 months in the penitentiary, and during that time there was a tax settlement, so all the records I don't have any more. I can only give you the records since I came out.
Mr. ROBINSON. When did you go to the penitentiary?
Mr. DELUCIA. 1944—the last day of 1943.
Mr. ROBINSON. When did you come out?
Mr. DELUCIA. 1947.
Mr. ROBINSON. I understand these records which you are producing are only from the time that you came out of the penitentiary.
Mr. DELUCIA. Yes; that is all I have.
Mr. ROBINSON. You have no records from 1940 until the time that you went into the penitentiary?
Mr. DELUCIA. No; I filed my income tax regularly but I haven't got them.
Mr. ROBINSON. You have no canceled checks for that period?
Mr. DELUCIA. No; that is all gone.
Mr. ROBINSON. Did you have any canceled checks?
Mr. DELUCIA. Oh, sure.
Mr. ROBINSON. Where are they?
Mr. DELUCIA. I don't know. When I come out, I was told by my lawyer that the old records were no good any more and they were all settled and I could do what I want.
Senator WILEY. Who told you that?
Mr. DELUCIA. My lawyer.
Senator WILEY. Who is your lawyer?
Mr. DELUCIA. Bernstein. The tax man told me the records were no good any more so I just got rid of them.
Senator WILEY. Give me the name of that lawyer.
Mr. DELUCIA. Bernstein, Eugene Bernstein. He is a tax man. He is the fellow who took my income-tax case with the Government!
Senator WILEY. Was he a Government man?
Mr. DELUCIA. No; he was my lawyer.
Senator WILEY. Chicago?
Mr. DELUCIA. Yes. I got these records from him when I came out.
Senator WILEY. Did you have any Kansas City lawyer?
Mr. DELUCIA. No.
Senator WILEY. No?
Mr. DELUCIA. No.
Mr. ROBINSON. Did you destroy the records or did Mr. Bernstein?
Mr. DELUCIA. I did. I got a room and got rid of them.
Mr. ROBINSON. When did you destroy them?

ORGANIZED CRIME IN INTERSTATE COMMERCE 3

Mr. DELUCIA. Shortly after I come out. Shortly after he gave them to me.
Mr. ROBINSON. Shortly after you came out?
Mr. DELUCIA. Shortly after he give them to me.
Mr. ROBINSON. Can you fix the approximate time when you did destroy them, what year?
Mr. DELUCIA. I think 1947, the latter part of 1947.
Mr. ROBINSON. You destroyed the records that you had from 1940 up until the time that you went into the penitentiary in 1947; is that right?
Mr. DELUCIA. No. Let me explain this. Mr. Bernstein told me that my income-tax case was cleared up to 1943. All my tax with the Government was settled up to 1943. That was the year I went to jail. After that I was 3 years and 8 months in jail, and of course I had nothing to show, so when he gave me the records, he said, "You can do as you want with the records, the records are worthless, the tax is settled," and that is all.
Mr. ROBINSON. Did Mr. Bernstein tell you to destroy them?
Mr. DELUCIA. No; he told me they are useless and do what you want.
Mr. ROBINSON. Let us get it clear. During the time from 1940 to the time you went to the penitentiary, was Mr. Bernstein preparing your income-tax returns?
Mr. DELUCIA. No; not from 1940.
Mr. ROBINSON. I am saying from 1940 until the time you went into the penitentiary.
Mr. DELUCIA. No. He got my case when I was in jail.
Mr. ROBINSON. Who prepared your tax returns from 1940 to the time you went to jail?
Mr. DELUCIA. Myself.
Mr. ROBINSON. You prepared them yourself?
Mr. DELUCIA. Yes, sir.
Mr. ROBINSON. And you have no cancelled checks, no books showing receipts and expenditures for the period from 1940 until the time you went into the penitentiary?
Mr. DELUCIA. Yes; that is right.
Mr. ROBINSON. You destroyed all of them?
Mr. DELUCIA. Yes, sir.
Mr. ROBINSON. Did you keep such books?
Mr. DELUCIA. Oh, yes; I had a checkbook with Northern Trust. You know those records. After all, them days there was nothing for me to keep.
Mr. ROBINSON. Did you have a bank account at that time?
Mr. DELUCIA. Yes; with the Northern Trust.
Mr. ROBINSON. Did you have bank statements?
Mr. DELUCIA. Yes.
Mr. ROBINSON. Did you destroy all the bank statements?
Mr. DELUCIA. Yes. The Northern Trust.
Mr. ROBINSON. Did you destroy all check stubs?
Mr. DELUCIA. Yes.
Mr. ROBINSON. Did you destroy all the copies of your tax returns for that period?
Mr. DELUCIA. Whatever I got from him, I destroyed. It was all that he had. He had all the stuff to prepare my case with the Tax

4 ORGANIZED CRIME IN INTERSTATE COMMERCE

Court. So I got those records back, and he said, "Do what you want," and I destroyed them.
Mr. ROBINSON. During that time that you were in the penitentiary, did somebody operate your business for you?
Mr. DELUCIA. Yes.
Mr. ROBINSON. Who?
Mr. DELUCIA. They did not operate it. I rent my farm to Frances Corri, and I got $7 an acre rent. That was filed.
Mr. ROBINSON. Who kept the books for you while you were in the penitentiary?
Mr. DELUCIA. Bernstein.
Mr. ROBINSON. Where are the books that were kept at the time you were in the penitentiary?
Mr. DELUCIA. Them 3 years went together with all the stuff he gave me. Naturally I got rid of all that.
Mr. ROBINSON. You destroyed all that at the time you came out of the penitentiary?
Mr. DELUCIA. Yes; from the time I come out, there it is [indicating].
Mr. ROBINSON. Now, when Mr. Bernstein was preparing your tax returns, what information did you submit to him as a basis for preparing the returns?
Mr. DELUCIA. It was very easy. The rent I was getting from the farm was so much. I think it was about 6 or 7 thousand dollars a year.
The CHAIRMAN. How did you destroy the records? Did you throw them away or burn them?
Mr. DELUCIA. I burned them. They were useless. I didn't know this was going to come up.
The CHAIRMAN. Did you burn them?
Mr. DELUCIA. Yes; I burned them.
Mr. ROBINSON. Would you take these records and describe what each one is?
Mr. DELUCIA. This is the book where all the people work, their security number and all that.
The CHAIRMAN. Will you identify them as we go along for the record, so we can put them in as exhibits?
Mr. ROBINSON. Yes.
Mr. DELUCIA. These are my income tax.
The CHAIRMAN. Let this be marked as "Exhibit No. 2."
(Exhibit No. 2 was returned to witness after analysis by the committee.)
Mr. ROBINSON. Directing your attention to exhibit 2, would you describe what that book is?
Mr. DELUCIA. You know I am not familiar with the book because Bernstein kept it. That is supposed to be the agenda where the men work and how much they get a year. You know, you are supposed to report to the Government how much you pay them a year. If you pay over $500, you have to report that, and their security number.
Mr. ROBINSON. On exhibit 2, when did you start keeping that book?
Mr. DELUCIA. In 1947. What is there, I am not very much familiar. He has been taking care of all that.

Tony Dark

Mr. ROBINSON. Who keeps the book for you?

Mr. DELUCIA. Bernstein.

Mr. ROBINSON. All right.

The CHAIRMAN. All right, let us go on with the next exhibit. That will be made exhibit No. 2 to the testimony.

Mr. ROBINSON. What are these papers?

Mr. DELUCIA. These are the income-tax returns.

Mr. ROBINSON. For what period?

Mr. DELUCIA. 1947, 1948, 1949.

The CHAIRMAN. That will be exhibit No. 3.

Mr. ROBINSON. These two red books are marked "Exhibit No. 4."

The CHAIRMAN. These will be combined as exhibit No. 4.

(Exhibits Nos. 2 and 4 were later returned to witness.)

Mr. ROBINSON. What are those?

Mr. DELUCIA. That is all the expense.

Mr. ROBINSON. Exhibits 4 and 5 pertain to what?

Mr. DELUCIA. To the farm—my business.

Mr. ROBINSON. Do you have any books or records showing interest held in any property or any business other than the ones you have submitted?

Mr. DELUCIA. No. I own no interest. I only own about 170 shares or 180 shares of Bank of America. I think that is in there, too. Those shares turn dividends, and that is coming in, and I turn that in. Anyway I have about 170 or 180 shares of Bank of America stock. That book does not show my house at River Forest and my house at Long Beach.

Mr. ROBINSON. You receive income from those properties?

Mr. DELUCIA. No, sir.

Mr. ROBINSON. Do you have any correspondence relating to any of these documents?

Mr. DELUCIA. What?

Mr. ROBINSON. Do you have any correspondence relating to any of these documents?

The CHAIRMAN. Any letters.

Mr. DELUCIA. Anything that is there can be backed up with checks or bills.

Mr. ROBINSON. Do you have the canceled checks?

Mr. DELUCIA. Yes.

Mr. ROBINSON. Where are they?

Mr. DELUCIA. I did not bring them with me. If you want them, I will bring them. I didn't think it was necessary.

Mr. ROBINSON. Do you have those?

Mr. DELUCIA. Yes, sir.

Mr. ROBINSON. Do you have them in your possession?

Mr. DELUCIA. All the records from 1947, I got.

Mr. ROBINSON. Do you have them in your possession?

Mr. DELUCIA. No, sir.

Mr. ROBINSON. Does Mr. Bernstein?

Mr. DELUCIA. I have.

Mr. ROBINSON. Why were those not produced?

Mr. DELUCIA. I didn't know you needed it. That is all there. I didn't know you wanted that.

Mr. ROBINSON. They are called for by the subpena, that is, the canceled checks.

Mr. DELUCIA. I am sorry. I did not understand that.

The CHAIRMAN. Will you send or bring in the canceled checks as Mr. Robinson directs?

Mr. DELUCIA. Certainly.

Mr. ROBINSON. Do you have any other documents besides the canceled checks that you did not produce?

Mr. DELUCIA. What other documents are you talking about?

Mr. ROBINSON. Do you have any bank statements?

Mr. DELUCIA. Yes.

Mr. ROBINSON. Will you produce all of those statements?

Mr. DELUCIA. Certainly.

Mr. ROBINSON. What properties do you presently own, Mr. DeLucia?

Mr. DELUCIA. I own a house in Long Beach and a house at River Forest.

The CHAIRMAN. Where is that?

Mr. DELUCIA. Illinois. And the farm in Illinois.

The CHAIRMAN. Where is the farm?

Mr. DELUCIA. In Kendall County, Ill.

Mr. ROBINSON. How large is the farm?

Mr. DELUCIA. 1,100 acres.

Mr. ROBINSON. What is the value of it?

Mr. DELUCIA. Well, you mean right now?

Mr. ROBINSON. If you know?

Mr. DELUCIA. They just sold some land around there for $450 an acre, so you can figure it out.

Mr. ROBINSON. Did you buy that farm?

Mr. DELUCIA. Yes, sir.

Mr. ROBINSON. When did you buy it?

Mr. DELUCIA. I think in 1941 or 1942.

Mr. ROBINSON. How much did you pay for it?

Mr. DELUCIA. I paid $150 an acre from the Prudential Co. I paid down $35,000 and year by year I have been paying the mortgage. I think I still owe about $80,000.

Mr. ROBINSON. How much improvements have you put on it?

The CHAIRMAN. What was the total purchase price?

Mr. DELUCIA. $180,000, something around there.

Mr. ROBINSON. How much improvements have you put on it?

Mr. DELUCIA. Oh, I would say over $100,000.

Mr. ROBINSON. Since 1947?

Mr. DELUCIA. Yes, sir. I build something previous to that, but most of the building I did from 1947 on.

Mr. ROBINSON. You put $100,000 improvements on it since 1947?

Mr. DELUCIA. Maybe more than that. Don't keep me to it.

Mr. ROBINSON. Approximately.

Mr. DELUCIA. Yes.

Mr. ROBINSON. How much improvement did you put on it before 1947?

Mr. DELUCIA. Well, I suppose I build a corn crib there about $4,500. It is too far gone. I believe $10,000 or something like that. I wouldn't know for sure.

Senator WILEY. When you bought the farm, did you buy any cows, horses, or machinery?

Mr. DELUCIA. No; you see, the insurance company had that.

Senator WILEY. You just bought the land?

Mr. DELUCIA. They had it rented. I bought the land.

Senator WILEY. How much do you have on it now in horses, cows, machinery, and so forth?

Mr. DELUCIA. Oh, I got about 190 steers—not milk cows, but heifers, steers, you know; about 300 pigs; about two or three hundred chickens, horses.

Senator WILEY. Machinery?

Mr. DELUCIA. Huh?

Senator WILEY. Machinery?

Mr. DELUCIA. Yes.

Senator WILEY. How much did you spend for all that?

Mr. DELUCIA. It is all in there, Senator. I wouldn't know.

Mr. ROBINSON. Do you receive any revenue from the farm?

Mr. DELUCIA. Yes.

Mr. ROBINSON. Approximately how much do you receive annually in revenue from the farm?

Mr. DELUCIA. It is in the income tax. I had a little memorandum. I think the first year was $8,000, or something like that, the second year $25,000, the third year was $42,000, or something like that.

Mr. ROBINSON. What year did you receive $42,000?

Mr. DELUCIA. Last year. That is all in there on the income tax.

Mr. ROBINSON. What is the property that you have at River Forest?

Mr. DELUCIA. That is a house and a lot.

Mr. ROBINSON. Is that your residence?

Mr. DELUCIA. Yes.

Mr. ROBINSON. When did you acquire that?

Mr. DELUCIA. 1938.

Mr. ROBINSON. How much did you pay for it?

Mr. DELUCIA. $25,000. I paid $25,000 for the house and I paid about $4,000 for the lot. It was a good buy.

Mr. ROBINSON. How much improvements have you put on that?

Mr. DELUCIA. On the house I put around $30,000 improvement and on the lot, which cost me around $4,000 as close as I remember, that is to improve. It was all a mess. I leveled it off.

Senator WILEY. Did you build the house?

Mr. DELUCIA. No; I built an addition to the house.

Mr. ROBINSON. What was the value of the other property at Long Beach?

Mr. DELUCIA. I bought a house for $14,000. I bought that in 1934, I remember that. Since then I made some improvement and all that. Then I bought about four extra lots. Do you want to know the value now?

Mr. ROBINSON. If you know.

Mr. DELUCIA. The house burned down, and I only got a caretaker house there, so you can figure for yourself. I don't know. It probably went up a lot. I suppose I can get forty or fifty thousand dollars for that place if I wanted to sell it.

Mr. ROBINSON. What other property do you have?

Mr. DELUCIA. That is about all.

Mr. ROBINSON. "That is about all." Is there any other that you do have?

Mr. DELUCIA. No, sir.

8 ORGANIZED CRIME IN INTERSTATE COMMERCE

Senator Wiley. Stocks and bonds?
Mr. DeLucia. Yes, I have stocks. I have about $11,000 worth of stock.
Senator Wiley. What company?
Mr. DeLucia. Government stock, what you call it, war bonds.
Mr. Robinson. Government bonds.
Mr. DeLucia. Yes, sir.
Mr. Robinson. Do you have any other bonds?
Mr. DeLucia. No, sir.
Mr. Robinson. Do you have any stock?
Mr. DeLucia. Stock I told you.
Senator Wiley. Bank of America.
Mr. DeLucia. Yes, and I think I have two or three shares of the Farmer Grange company. That is a mutual affair there. You bring your stuff in and you get a dividend there every year. You buy from them. It is a Farmer Grange company.
Mr. Robinson. Approximately what is the total value of the stock you have?
Mr. DeLucia. The Bank of America today costs about $27 a share.
Mr. Robinson. How many shares did you say you have?
Mr. DeLucia. About 180.
Mr. Robinson. That is all the stock you own?
Mr. DeLucia. That is all I can recall.
Senator Wiley. How about cash? How much cash do you have?
Mr. DeLucia. How much cash I got. Do I have to tell you that, sir?
Mr. Halley. Yes.
Mr. DeLucia. I don't know. I think I got about close to $40,000.
Senator Wiley. In cash?
Mr. DeLucia. Yes.
Senator Wiley. Do you have any safety deposit boxes?
Mr. DeLucia. No; I got it in the room or some other place.
Senator Wiley. Where is it?
Mr. DeLucia. If I tell you, you can't get it out of there anyway.
The Chairman. This is an executive session.
Mr. DeLucia. Do I have to tell it?
The Chairman. You have to tell it.
Mr. DeLucia. I got it home.
Senator Wiley. Do you have any safety deposit boxes in any banks?
Mr. DeLucia. Yes.
Senator Wiley. What bank?
Mr. DeLucia. First National Bank.
Senator Wiley. Any other bank?
Mr. DeLucia. No, sir.
Senator Wiley. First National Bank of Chicago?
Mr. DeLucia. Yes.
Mr. Halley. What do you keep in your safety deposit box?
Mr. DeLucia. All the documents and stuff.
Mr. Halley. Any cash?
Mr. DeLucia. I keep money there, too.
Mr. Halley. Do you have cash there now, too?
Mr. DeLucia. Not now.
Mr. Halley. Do you own any diamonds?
Mr. DeLucia. My Mrs. has.

ORGANIZED CRIME IN INTERSTATE COMMERCE 9

Mr. Halley. Will you estimate the value of the diamonds?
Mr. DeLucia. Now, I don't know what she has. She has a ring——
Mr. Halley. Would you estimate the value of the diamond?
Mr. DeLucia. No. A bracelet or something like that.
Mr. Halley. What is your best estimate of the value? What did you pay for them altogether?
Mr. DeLucia. I don't know about the pricing of those things. It was kind of a small affair.
The Chairman. $5,000 or $10,000?
Mr. DeLucia. I would say around four or five thousand dollars, something like that.
Senator Wiley. That is your wife you are talking about?
Mr. DeLucia. Yes.
Senator Wiley. Did you make any gifts to anybody else during this period since you came out?
Mr. DeLucia. No.
Senator Wiley. Does your wife have any stock in her name?
Mr. DeLucia. No.
Senator Wiley. Any property?
Mr. DeLucia. The house at River Forest and the house at Long Beach is in her name and the farm is in my name and her name.
Senator Wiley. Does she have a safety deposit box?
Mr. DeLucia. No; we have a joint deposit box.
Senator Wiley. Have you given to her any other property except what you mentioned?
Mr. DeLucia. No, sir.
Senator Wiley. Have you any children?
Mr. DeLucia. Yes, sir.
Senator Wiley. How many?
Mr. DeLucia. Three.
Senator Wiley. What have you done for them?
Mr. DeLucia. Well, the one is married.
Senator Wiley. I understand. But what have you given to them, or conveyed to them? Have you given them any property?
Mr. DeLucia. No.
Senator Wiley. Any stock?
Mr. DeLucia. Oh, I had a trust fund for them.
Senator Wiley. How much did you set that up for?
Mr. DeLucia. $20,000.
Senator Wiley. When did you do that?
Mr. DeLucia. 1936.
Senator Wiley. Have you set up any other funds since?
Mr. DeLucia. For my boy, $20,000 at the same time.
Senator Wiley. One boy and one girl?
Mr. DeLucia. Yes.
Senator Wiley. That was in 1936?
Mr. DeLucia. Yes.
Senator Wiley. Have you put any money in it since then?
Mr. DeLucia. No, not since then.
Senator Wiley. Do you carry any insurance?
Mr. DeLucia. Yes.
Senator Wiley. Life insurance?
Mr. DeLucia. Yes.

62958—51—pt. 5——2

10 ORGANIZED CRIME IN INTERSTATE COMMERCE

Senator Wiley. How much are the premiums on your life insurance?
Mr. DeLucia. With the Northwest Wisconsin.
Senator Wiley. That is a good company.
Mr. DeLucia. I think I pay about seven or eight hundred dollars a year. It is a $20,000 policy. There are different ones, five, five, and ten.
Senator Wiley. That is all you carry?
Mr. DeLucia. Yes, as far as I recall.
The Chairman. Very well. Let us proceed.
Mr. DeLucia. My boy, the little one, I took a policy—I was going to take the same policy for the little boy, and I was paying $2,000 a year, but I dropped it since 1940 or 1936.
Senator Wiley. This book indicates your income since you came out of prison?
Mr. DeLucia. Yes.
Senator Wiley. You were paroled, were you not?
Mr. DeLucia. Yes.
Senator Wiley. And that is your only source of income, that which you have enumerated here?
Mr. DeLucia. Yes.
Senator Wiley. From your farm and from your stocks.
Mr. DeLucia. Yes, sir.
Senator Wiley. Any other sources?
Mr. DeLucia. No, sir.
Senator Wiley. And from the you have made all the improvements and investments since 1947?
Mr. DeLucia. No, I put my money in there.
Senator Wiley. You had some money when you went to the penitentiary?
Mr. DeLucia. Yes.
Senator Wiley. How much did you have when you went to the penitentiary?
Mr. DeLucia. Three hundred thousand dollars.
Senator Wiley. Who paid the fine?
Mr. DeLucia. I don't know.
Senator Wiley. There was $10,000 paid.
Mr. DeLucia. Yes, sir.
Senator Wiley. You never found out who paid it?
Mr. DeLucia. No, sir.
Senator Wiley. You have no suspicion?
Mr. DeLucia. No.
Senator Wiley. Who was your attorney in your parole case?
Mr. DeLucia. What do you mean?
Senator Wiley. When you came out of prison you were paroled.
Mr. DeLucia. Yes.
Senator Wiley. How big a sentence did you get?
Mr. DeLucia. Ten years.
Senator Wiley. You served 3 years?
Mr. DeLucia. Yes, sir.
Senator Wiley. You are out on parole now?
Mr. DeLucia. Yes.
Senator Wiley. You were not pardoned?
Mr. DeLucia. That is right.

The committee believed Paul DeLucia was lying when they were told that he had secured a loan of $80,000 in 1948 from Hugo Bennett. DeLucia's explanation for this was so he could purchase his home. The Committee also established that DeLucia had spent nearly $391,000 in almost four years. When DeLucia was asked by the committee as to what the money went for, he would not say. Speculation was that he spent a good amount of the money repaying the "so called" anonymous people who raised $128,000 for him to settle the government income tax claim against him.

Around 1951 Paul DeLucia and Tony Accardo had still been struggling for control of gambling in Florida. This time throughout Florida a gambling syndicate known as the S & L had taken control of all the bookmakers and gambling joints. S & L had all the Florida judges and politicians on their side and had refused to allow the Chicago Outfit to operate any gambling in Florida. To change this DeLucia and Accardo sent Capone gangster Harry Russell to Florida backed with a lot of Chicago muscle to take over gambling and plant the Chicago mob flag. But DeLucia knew this would not sit well with his mob brothers in other cities because of the history they had in trying to control gambling over each other so he did the right thing, he asked New York mob boss Meyer Lansky along with mob bosses in Philadelphia, Pittsburgh and Cleveland to back him and send representatives and muscle of their own so Florida could become open to all mob families and not just have one syndicate controlling all of the gambling. As history shows, they won and S & L was wiped out.

From the Collection of T.M.

Paul DeLucia

Chapter 10

Immigration and War

In May 1954 Paul DeLucia was subpoenaed to appear before the U.S. Immigration Department to answer questions about lying on his naturalization papers and to determine if his naturalization should be stripped because of his illegal activities. Flanked by his two attorneys William Scott Steward and Richard Gorman, Paul DeLucia took the 5th Amendment to every question placed to him during the hearings.

This battle between DeLucia and the Immigration Department would linger on for over two years until the U.S. Supreme Court ruled the immigration service did not have "private inquisitorial power in denaturalization cases." Immigration officers could not subpoena and question naturalized citizens in a search for evidence that might lead to taking away their citizenship. The government dropped the case against DeLucia, at least for that moment.

An important meeting was called in October 1953 at the Saxony Hotel in Miami Beach, Florida. Summoned were Paul DeLucia, Louis Campagna, Tony Accardo, Marshall Caifano, Sam Giancana, Sam Hunt, Jake Guzik and Eddie Vogel. The purpose of the meeting was to decide the pensioning of some of the older Chicago mobsters such as Murray Humphreys, Jake Guzik, Louis Campagna and Paul DeLucia.

In 1954 investigators of the Department of Justice made a report concerning the "Ricca-Accardo Syndicate" control of labor in Illinois. They listed two men as their number ones, Joey Glimco who controlled labor north of Kankakee, Illinois covering Chicago and northern Illinois with his lieutenant Claude Maddox. Just south of Kankakee all labor was controlled by mobster Frank "Buster" Wortman.

There were signs that not all was running so good between mobsters in Chicago during 1954. After a long a painful time of staying out of trouble, Paul DeLucia's federal parole expired on March 7, 1954. No longer on parole, DeLucia wanted his old job back as top boss of the Chicago mob. However, Tony Accardo was not going to back down so easily.

There were rumblings around Chicago that war would break out at any moment in the struggle for control of the Chicago syndicate. Paul DeLucia had been making plans for his takeover. While DeLucia was away in prison it was his opinion that Accardo had kept too much of the profits from the Outfit's ventures. Once DeLucia was out of prison he found out that many of the younger up-and-coming mobsters who owed much of their alliance to Accardo began to desert him because they believed he had bungled the cigarette tax fraud and horse meat racket in Chicago. As reports go, when DeLucia requested that Accardo step down and hand over control, Accardo refused.

Evidence that Accardo may have been losing the battle for control of the Outfit came in April 1954 when Tony Accardo applied for a passport with the U.S. Government and was planning on going to South America on what he said was a fishing trip. Investigators went to ask one of Accardo's long time associates and former Capone Gang member Sam "Golf Bag" Hunt what Accardo was up to. Sam Hunt told investigators, *"He just wants to go fishing. He loves to fish."*

However, the fishing trip was really a diamond buying expedition in the Chilean diamond area with $100,000 cash in hand. When Accardo applied for his new passport he listed as his two reasons for the trip as to go fishing and to invest a fortune in gems. Investigators became interested in the place they were going because they had a report from a year earlier that mobster Anthony "Tough Tony" Capezio and his wife had spent a considerable time "vacationing" in the same Chilean area.

Some reports said that Accardo and his family were going to move to South America and their house in River Forest was being groomed to be sold. However, Clarice Accardo set the story straight saying they only wanted to take a trip and the house was not for sale. In the end, Tony Accardo was not granted a passport because there was an $89,000 tax claim against him for his partnership in the Owl Club gambling spot in Calumet City.

What had led to the sudden trip came after Tony Accardo met with three representatives of Paul DeLucia for a meeting to further discuss Accardo handing over control of the mob. As Accardo walked away from this meeting disgruntled, allegedly Rocco Fischetti fired his gun over the head of Accardo as a warning. Other reports state that Accardo, Jackie Cerone, Sam Battaglia and Sam Giancana sat in a car while a representative demanded that Accardo turn over control of gambling and vice receipts from the southern sections of Cook County and from Kankakee County Illinois.

Some believed that this was the reason Accardo wanted to leave for Chile because he believed he was going to be assassinated. Further evidence he feared for his life came that same month when he gained permission to place a $20,000, 6-foot wrought-iron fence around his mansion on Franklyn Street for protection.

It was learned that Tony Accardo was actually going to South America to meet with Charles "Lucky" Luciano, then leader of the national crime syndicate in America to plead his case and gain his backing to remain in control of Chicago.

One FBI informant told the FBI about the fight for control of the Outfit where Tony Accardo was going to be killed. This informant said that a man known as "the Don" or the "Old Man," which was a nickname for Paul DeLucia, sent for mobster Nick DeJohn who was resided in San Francisco, California at the time. De John was to come back to Chicago for a job. DeJohn was to aid some other hired individuals from Chicago Heights and Kansas City to figure out a way to kill Accardo. He added that this man "the Don" was associated with mobster Ross Prio, Joseph DiVarco, Dom DiBella, Dom Nuccio, Dom Brancato, Anthony Pinelli and James DeGeorge and owned many legitimate businesses including a cheese business in upper Wisconsin.

This informant told the FBI that Nick DeJohn refused to carry out the assignment to kill Accardo and was killed in San Francisco on orders from "the Don." DeJohn's bodyguard, who had the last name of Neglia, was also killed during the course of the struggle in a barber chair. The informant said that Tony Accardo leaned about this revolt against him and the results produced approximately 12 murders. This man named "the Don", who was supposed to have lived at West Grand Avenue east of Noble Street in Chicago, was killed shortly after for his failed attempt. It was possible the informant had his stories mixed up or maybe there was another mobster named "the Don." The FBI made a check to see if Paul DeLucia was still alive, which he was. The story was placed aside because too many of the facts given in this story were either not true or could not be verified.

To settle things down between the bosses they all agreed to a meeting and to an arbitrator they all could trust and all had great respect for. On September 3, 1954 Tony Accardo, Paul DeLucia, Louis Campagna, Murray Humphreys, Joey Glimco and Sam Giancana met at the Croyden Hotel in Chicago to hammer out their differences. The arbitrator brought in was none other than their old time boss that started it all, Johnny "The Fox" Torrio, who had been in retirement in New York City for almost 30 years and Anthony Ricci, who was known as Tony Gobels and was close to both Accardo and DeLucia. Ricci also acted as a representative of Charles "Lucky" Luciano.

Up to that point there had been many murders in Chicago linked to the Accardo-DeLucia fight. One investigator said it was basically Tony Accardo versus Paul DeLucia for control and most of the murders favored DeLucia since the men murdered were traced back to the Accardo faction.

Among those murders were mobsters Paul "Needle Nose" LaBriola and James Weinberg, both lieutenants of Accardo. It was believed that LaBriola and Weinberg had attempted to shake down Louis Campagna for profits from a west side gambling spot in Chicago. DeLucia had ordered them killed. It was also believed that DeLucia had Anthony Papa and his brother James killed on March 16th, 1954. Anthony Papa was leader of a million dollar narcotics ring in Chicago who had been arrested by federal agents and was in the Accardo group.

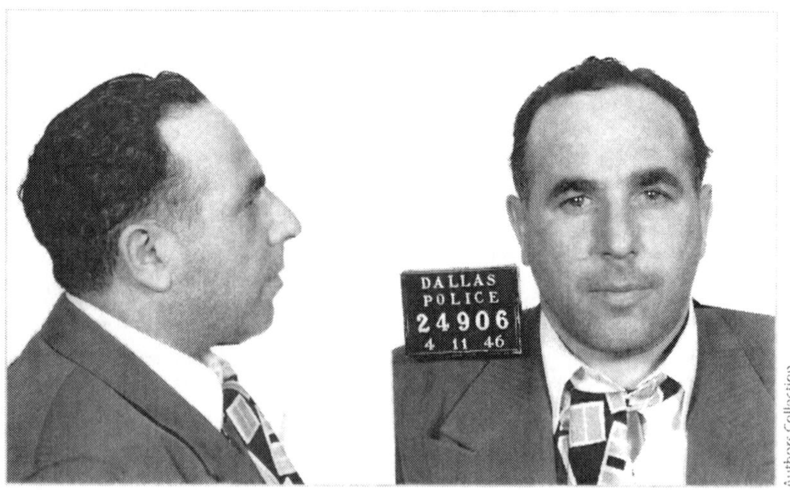

Authors Collection

1946 Photo of James Weinberg

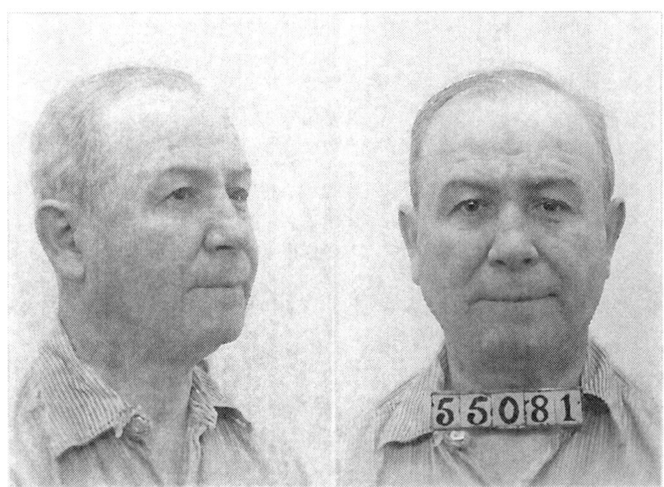

Photo of Johhny Torrio

Johnny Torrio tried to get Accardo to accept the authority of DeLucia but Accardo refused and showed indications he would go to war. However, a deal was worked out and everyone left the meeting in agreement. One investigator said he believed the DeLucia faction received the better deal since DeLucia was in a stronger position with the Mafia.

Investigators learned while watching Harry Hochstein, a syndicate private-detective, that Paul DeLucia and Jake Guzik where using a Chicago office building in the Loop to make phone calls to other hoodlums across the country. Phone records showed that DeLucia personally phoned United States Congressman William A. Dawson in Washington D.C. on many occasions.

Then the FBI discovered a connection between the Chicago Syndicate and the hoodlums who were collecting from labor rackets in the Minneapolis and St. Paul areas in Minnesota. Running the labor rackets in Minnesota was a man by the name of Keating. This Keating did prison time with Virgil Litsinger on a 1929 mail robbery conviction. Both Litsinger and Keating did twenty-five-year prison sentences in Leavenworth Prison and were incarcerated while Paul DeLucia and Louis Campagna where serving time there. Virgil Litsinger was a one-time clerk for the Chicago Sanitary District until he became a fugitive on a false murder charge which he was later acquitted of. His uncle E. R. Litsinger once ran for Mayor of Chicago.

While Keating was in prison he made a connection with DeLucia and Campagna who in return granted Keating the mob connection in the Minneapolis and St. Paul area when Keating was released. Keating began taking money from Teamsters and other labor racketeers from that area and when Virgil Litsinger was released from prison, he headed back to Chicago to work at Litsinger Motors where he would receive the money from Keating and give it to Joey Glimco, who passed the money on to DeLucia.

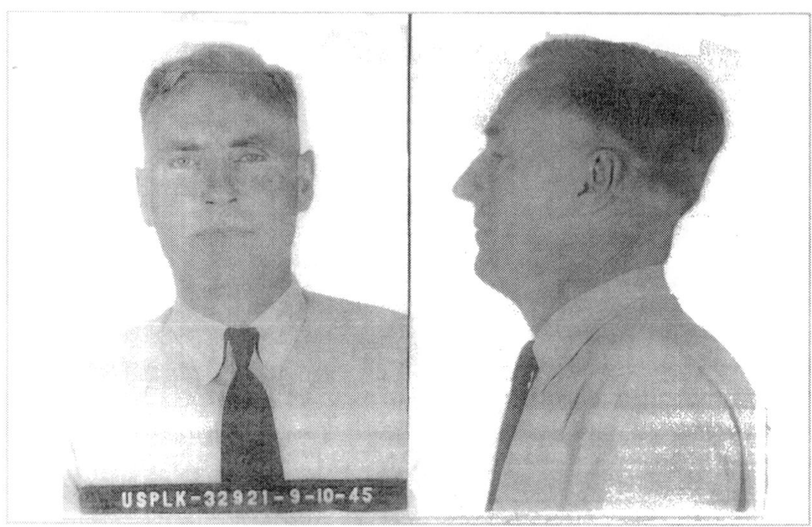

Virgil Litsinger mug shot photo

Once Paul DeLucia was released from Leavenworth Prison, he had to live on legitimate income while on parole. He claimed he had no money to live on and could not live beyond his means. When the government tried to convict him for lying on his immigration papers, he sold his River Forest home and moved to Miami, Florida.

Paul DeLucia and his wife Nancy were now spending as much time in Miami Beach, Florida as possible. There Nancy DeLucia would often be observed in the company of the wife of Jack Lansky, brother of New York mobster Meyer Lansky. Jack Lansky lived across the street from the house the DeLucia's were renting at 1145 Harrison Street in Hollywood, Florida. Jake Lansky was running the International Casino at the Hotel Nacional in Havana, Cuba.

At the time DeLucia was being watched in Miami by the Narcotic Unit in Washington D.C. because he was listed as an associate of Phillip Magano who was later murdered in New York in April 1955.

Part of the deal he struck with Tony Accardo was that Paul DeLucia would spend more time in Florida and stay out of Chicago but get the amount of money paid to him as if he was the top boss. On May 11, 1954, DeLucia bought the home of New York mobster Anthony Solerno and his wife Bernice for $25,000. The house was at 4385 Pine Tree Drive, Miami Beach, Florida.

Agents often observed Paul DeLucia spending a good portion of his time at the Hialeah Race Track in Hialeah, Florida. At the track he was known to everyone as "Pete" and would always wear brown pants with a light brown jacket and a porkpie type yellow hat. He was known as a heavy better on the horses and a big tipper to the waitresses.

One informant in Miami told the FBI that as of 1957 DeLucia was not involved in any organized crime but was receiving money from the rackets in Chicago as his "pension" for a life in the mob.

Law Enforcement Spot Surveillance 1949-1955

January 1949 – Paul DeLucia is observed at the 25th wedding anniversary of mobster Ben Fillichio.

July 29, 1954 – Paul DeLucia is observed at the wake of Sam Giancana's father.

September 1-3, 1954 – Paul DeLucia, Johnny Torrio, Tony Accardo, Louis Campagna, Murray Humphreys, Joey Glimco and Sam Giancana held meetings at the Croyden Hotel in Chicago.

January 23, 1955 - Paul DeLucia, Joey Aiuppa and Tony Accardo are guests at the wedding of mobster Claude Maddox's daughter. Patricia Katherine Moore married Robert E. Rickey at the Club Hollywood in Franklin Park, Illinois with 500 guests in attendance.

March 6, 1955 - Paul DeLucia was in Miami Beach, Florida playing golf. On his team was mobster Jimmy "Monk" Allegretti and John Capone. They were playing against a group headed by mobster Dom Nuccio.

April 4, 1955 – Paul DeLucia, John Capone and Jimmy Allegretti were observed at the Miami Beach Golf Tournament together.

June 7, 1955- Paul DeLucia, Tony Accardo, Sam Hunt, Lester Kruse, Sam Giancana, Jake Guzik, Tony Ricci, Joseph Fischetti and Gus Alex left Chicago to attend the funeral of Louis Campagna in Florida. DeLucia, Ricci and Joe Fischetti are picked up at Miami airport by Fischetti's gril friend Lee Pollock.

December 1955 – Tony Accardo, Murray Humphreys, Sam Giancana, Gus Alex and Paul DeLucia arrive in Miami Beach, Florida, to attend organized crime meetings at the Thunderbird Motel.

Chapter 11

Vengeance

It was alleged that around 1955-1956 Paul DeLucia was behind a plot to extort $200,000 from the owner of the Saxony Hotel in Miami, Florida. According to reports, mob labor lawyer Abraham Teitelbaum was in Miami during a hotel and restaurant strike when he was in the company of Chicago mobster John Lardino and James Blakely. Blakely was then Vice President of the Hotel and Restaurant Employees, and Bartenders Union and Secretary Treasurer of Chicago Local 593. Lardino, a Capone gangster, was employed by Local 593 as Supervisor of Business Agents. Teitelbaum was approached by the Chicago mob through Lardino and Blakely and asked to act as a go-between in a plot to extort $200,000 from a Mr. Sachs of the Saxony Hotel. With the money paid, his hotel would not be closed down by pickets during the strike.

Teitelbaum admitted he met with Sachs to help settle the strike but denied that he tried to extort any money. Paul DeLucia was on hand in Miami during the strike and was seen meeting with Teitelbaum during the time period of the alleged shakedown.

In 1955 Paul DeLucia's name surfaced in the killings of Chicago money man Alex Greenberg and mob rat Willie Bioff. Both men had been killed on orders from Paul DeLucia for refusing further shakedowns. Greenberg owed DeLucia more than $300,000 and when he refused to pay he was killed by two triggermen. The informant giving the information gave the names of the gunmen as M. Calfam and Sam Giancorra which police believed were Marshall Caifano and Sam Giancana.

In November 1955 William Bioff was living in Phoenix, Arizona under his new legal name William Nelson. He had purchased an upscale home in a fashionable part of Arizona which was an old orange grove. Next door to Bioff was the home of Charles Guzik, son of Chicago mobster Jake "Grease Thumb" Guzik.

Around noon Bioff said goodbye to his wife Lauria at the door step and walked to his truck parked in the driveway. Bioff got into his truck, stepped down on the starter pedal and was blown up by a bomb connected to the ignition pedal. The blast shook the town and could be felt a mile away. Police said it was done by a professional because the killers used TNT, not dynamite. The TNT was so powerful that it turned the medal into tiny shreds of shrapnel ripping both legs from his body and tossing his torso twenty-five feet away. They found Bioff's severed right hand a few hundred feet from the explosion site.

A year before Bioff was killed he had been seen meeting with Tony Accardo. Bioff clamed the two ran into each other while both were in Phoenix. After the two met many of Bioff's friends said he was living in fear of being killed. Police in Arizona said they believed Bioff may have been trying to muscle in on minor rackets under control of the Chicago syndicate in Arizona; selling protection to shady Phoenix businessmen; buying diamonds and other precious jewels from refugees fleeing Europe; or his killing was revenge for "squealing" in 1943 sending the mobsters to prison but if that was the case, why did they wait 12 years to kill him?

On the eve of the killing of Bioff, Paul DeLucia left Chicago. Some speculated at the time that he went into hiding because he knew he was going to be pulled in by the Chicago PD for questioning in the murder. The murder still remains unsolved.

Photo of William Bioff blown apart body in Phoenix, Arizona

After the death of Louis "Little New York" Campagna in May 1955 a decision had to be made as to who would be the successor to Campagna's position in the mob. The meeting to elect the mobster was held in Florida. Law enforcement was tipped to the meeting which led United States Attorney Robert Tieken to make an attempt to try to catch the mobsters as they boarded their plane in Chicago, to serve them with subpoenas to appear before a Federal Grand Jury investigating Chicago's policy racket. When Deputy Marshals appeared at Midway Airport in Chicago on June 7, they discovered that DeLucia, Tony Gobels (Ricci) and Joe Fischetti had been tipped off to the subpoenas and had taken an earlier flight. Tony Accardo, Sam Giancana, Gus Alex, Sam Hunt, Lester Kruse and Jake Guzik also managed to avoid the subpoenas as they made their way to Florida for the meeting. It was said that mob boss Frank LaPorte was picked over Sam Giancana and William "Potatoes" Daddono as the person to replace Campagna.

Before Campagna died, the list of succession for the board of directors was rumored to be:

1. Tony Accardo / Paul DeLucia
2. Either Accardo or DeLucia (who ever did not win the top spot)
3. Jake Guzik
4. Murray Humphreys
5. Louis Campagna
6. Sam Giancana
7. William Daddono
8. Frank LaPorte
9. Joey Aiuppa

The year 1956 included an investigation by the Internal Revenue Service into the finances of DeLucia. The investigation revealed that mobster Charles English, who DeLucia referred to as "his boy Red," was a principal aid of DeLucia. When the Kefauver Committee looked into a loan of $80,000 given to DeLucia for racing interest, they noticed a second mortgage on his farm as security on the loan. The IRS learned that in 1951 when DeLucia sold his farm he was asked how he was going to get the money to pay off this $80,000 second mortgage so that a purchaser could obtain a clear title to the property. DeLucia replied, *"Oh that, I'll just burn that, it wasn't actually borrowed money, that was for letting the boys operate at the tracks in Florida. My boy 'Red' takes care of that for me. We just record it as a mortgage to make it look good."*

The Fed's were also investigating why Paul DeLucia was making many telephone calls to mob labor union boss Frank "Frankie X" Esposito and Chicago First Ward Alderman John D'Arco Sr. at their homes in Hollywood, Florida. Agents believed DeLucia was meeting with both Esposito and D'Arco in Miami often but they could never determine if these visits were related to organized crime or social visits. They tried to link the meetings to show DeLucia was controlling the political scene in Chicago.

At the same time, Paul DeLucia was also mentioned in the disappearance of Nicholas Avolio. Avolio was once Frank Nitti's chauffeur and became DeLucia's chauffeur when Nitti killed himself. Avolio was in trouble with immigration stemming from a 1951 incident when he was picked up by Chicago police in the murder of Chicago police officer William Drury. Avolio admitted that he had entered America illegally through Boston on a ship from Italy in 1922. Avolio settled in New York City where he was arrested a few times under the name Luigi Silvestra. He went to jail in 1927 for carrying a concealed weapon and once out, he headed to Detroit to work in the rackets before ending up in Chicago. In 1943 Avolio had been subpoenaed in the Hollywood extortion case but could never be found by authorities. In 1954 Avolio was very worried that he was going to be killed just before his disappearance. His family came forward in 1956 to say Avolio had disappeared and they wanted help from the authorities in finding him. Some believed Nick Avolio was killed because of his connection to DeLucia and the extortion case in 1943.

Tony Dark

By the end of 1956 DeLucia felt he was cleared of any charges and began to have a new home built for himself back in River Forest, Illinois. His relationship with Tony Accardo had also changed and the two were on better terms with each other. Residents in River Forest who had found relief at not having DeLucia in the neighborhood turned to outrage when they learned the hoodlum had returned to build what was then a $150,000 home. The new home was at 1515 Bonnie Brae Road.

Paul DeLucia's home at 1515 Bonnie Brae Road taken in 2014

Authors Collection 2014 ©

Authors Collection 2014 ©

The house was being built by the William Cohan Associated Company. The house was a three-story white stone building in an ultra-modern style. It had 17 rooms, with the first floor used for servants' quarters, game room and storage. The second floor was for his daughter and her family and the third floor housed DeLucia and his wife. The walls were 12-inches thick reinforced concrete with reinforced concrete floors. If a bomb was to go off on the first floor of the house, the third floor, where DeLucia lived, would be safe and intact. He was building a bomb shelter out of his 17-room house. The front door of the house led into an imported marble vestibule. It would then lead to the elevator to take you up to the other floors.

The bathrooms, 8 in all, were said to contain poolroom proportions with imported marble and square bathtubs. He had a tiled kitchen, an office quarters, sun deck, and a 4-car garage. In 1963 Paul DeLucia filed an official complaint with the county assessor stating that his assessment was too high. They had it at $11-a-square-foot. Being a mob boss, he won his complaint and the assessor lowered his assessment to $5.80-a-square foot.

Spot Surveillance 1956

January 13, 1956 – Paul DeLucia, Murray Humphreys, Tony Accardo, Sam Giancana and Gus Alex attended an organized crime meeting at the Thunderbird Motel in Miami Beach, Florida.

Summer 1956 – DeLucia's son-in-law, Alex Ponzio, lived at the Nancete estate in Long Beach, Indiana year round before moving to Florida when the house was sold to the Teamsters in 1957. Surveillance discovered that Ponzio employed a male cook, a governess and an African-American laundry woman.

From the Collection of T.M.

Surveillance photo of Paul DeLucia

Chapter 12

Not an American!

The deportation case against Paul DeLucia, which had gained steam again, came to a head in April 1957. The U.S. Government was going to prove that DeLucia lied on his immigration papers to become a U.S. Citizen by using the stolen identity of another man. They were also going to prove that DeLucia lied that he was never convicted of any crimes in Italy.

The first witness was the sister of Raffaele Perillo, the man who Paul DeLucia killed in 1917 in Italy. Margaret Parrillo Terribile was then living in New York City but spoke freely to government officials about the killing of her brother. Mrs. Terribile had no problem testifying but became scared when two men appeared at her home in New York before the trial and told her that they *"came a long way across the sea to see how her health was and the health of her husband."* Meaning if she opened her mouth her "health" situation would change. She gave the deposition and fled the country back to Italy as fast as she could.

The real Paul Maglio was a surprise witness at DeLucia's trial. He told the court how he was born on July 10, 1898 in Apricena, Italy, a town of 6,000 people at the time almost 200 miles from Naples. In Apricena, Paul Maglio worked in the town's city hall handing all the birth and death records. He assured the court that no one else in his town was named Paul Maglio. He had at one time studied to become a priest in Italy, another thing DeLucia was known to have used as his own.

His father was Enrico and his mother, Nunza Maria Clotilde Terelli Maglio. He had five sisters and no brothers. All this information Paul DeLucia used in 1928 as his own. Maglio said Paul DeLucia lifted his information from his passport since the passport was in the hands of a travel agency in Naples until the day before he left Italy on July 23, 1920, arriving in America on August 3, 1920. He was heading to Chicago to work as a factory worker. On the 1930 census Paul Maglio is listed as living in the rear building of 11926 Calumet Avenue in Chicago with his wife Marie and his daughters Cladys and Anne. He was listed as working as a machinist helper.

The real Paul Maglio's 1930 Census Report

45	57	90	Maglio	Paul	Head	R	20.00	No	M	W	30	M	25	No	Yes	Il
46			—	Marie	Wife-H			V	F	W	21	M	16	No	Yes	Il
47			—	Gladys	Daughter			V	F	W	3 4/12	S		No		Il
48			—	Anne	Daughter			V	F	W	1 1/12	S		No		Il

Italy	Italy	Italy	Italian	Yes	Machinist Helper	Paint Works	77X6	W	Yes	No	45
Illinois	Italy	Italy		Yes	None						46
Illinois	Italy	Illinois			None						47
Illinois	Italy	Illinois			None						48

It was said that after testifying against DeLucia in court the real Paul Maglio lived in fear and was under FBI guard for protection. Every time the front doorbell would ring, Maglio would send his wife to answer the door with their huge German shepherd dog.

During the trial, newspapers in Italy reacted to the idea that they were about to get Paul DeLucia sent back to their country. One paper in Milan, Italy wrote, *"Another of the Italian-Americans whom we soon will see stepping down the gangplank at Naples, with a flashy tie and his fingers loaded with rings."* Other papers in Rome, Italy called DeLucia "malavita American" meaning the major exponent of America gangsterism.

The news articles in Italy worked to DeLucia's benefit because the U.S. Government had secured two witnesses in Italy who were to come to America and testify against DeLucia. When these two witnesses found out that if they were successful and DeLucia was found guilty and was going to be forced back to Italy for life, they realized they would be killed by the Camorra for their role in the trial. The witnesses quickly backed out and even denied knowing DeLucia.

On June 8, 1957 Paul DeLucia was found guilty of fraud for entering the United States in 1920 under the name of Paul Maglio, an identity stolen from another individual. His citizenship was ruled invalid.

During this same period, DeLucia was indicted in a federal income tax case. The IRS claimed DeLucia failed to report income of more than $300,000 between the years of 1948 to 1950. The IRS claimed DeLucia owed $128,346 in back taxes. He was facing 20 years in prison and a $40,000 fine if convicted.

At his income tax trial in May 1958 a long parade of witnesses testified how much money DeLucia made which added up to well over millions of dollars. Even his old cellmate Harry Winkelblack testified how DeLucia asked him to get his hands on DeLucia's Leavenworth file to sneak a peek. Winkelblack worked as the prisons secretary and had access to all the files. Winkelblack also told how DeLucia complained to him every time Anthony Accardo would show up at the prison using the name Joseph Bulger. Each time Accardo showed up DeLucia said it was embarrassing and he wished Accardo would leave him alone. When Winkelblack asked DeLucia what Accardo wanted he told him that Tony Accardo and Francis Curry were having differences over running slot machine and coin machine rackets and how DeLucia's business interest were being handled.

After 16 hours of deliberation, the jury found Paul DeLucia guilty on three counts of income tax evasion for the years 1948 to 1950. His co-defendant mob attorney Joseph Bulger was found not guilty on charges of conspiracy to make false income tax returns. DeLucia was freed on a $10,000 bond to wait for his appeal to be heard.

Other problems on DeLucia's plate concerned his son-in-law Alex Ponzio. Word reached DeLucia that he and Ponzio were being investigated by the Senate labor committee because they uncovered information that Ponzio once owned Northwestern Electric Company in Chicago whose employees were organized by Chicago Local 134 of the International Brotherhood of Electrical Workers Union. When labor difficulties arose, Paul DeLucia could straighten them out with the union. Senate investigators were looking into reports that Tony Accardo, Joey Glimco, Fred "Juke Box" Smith and Mike Spagnola were holding many meetings discussing control of Local 134.

The FBI was starting its "Top Hoodlum Program" where they were opening investigations into every top hoodlum in America. When they began in 1957 they had files on DeLucia dating back to the 1940's. In the first few sections, an informant who had always given the FBI reliable information said that when Paul DeLucia returned to Chicago he was going to resume his leadership role as top boss. Tony Accardo refused to relinquish his power and a rift developed between the two juggernauts. This reliable informant added that as of 1957 Accardo's replacement,

Sam Giancana, had ordered Accardo to stay within six blocks of his home except to answer court subpoenas. Giancana had had enough of the publicity the rift between Accardo and DeLucia had created and both were out of favor with the younger mobsters.

This was music to the FBI's ears as they explored the possibility of making Accardo an informant. However, that would never happen since Accardo was one of organized crimes most loyal observant of omerta. To even think Accardo could be turned into an informant was just crazy.

Another informant from those days remembered that when the so-called "young bloods" such as Sam Giancana, Chuckie English and Sam Battaglia were challenging Accardo and DeLucia for operational control, an agreement was entered into whereby Accardo and DeLucia agreed to relinquish their control and enter into a retirement state as long as they continued to receive their "cut" of the "take." That agreement continued for many years. For years Sam "Teets" Battaglia had been an intimate acquaintance of Paul DeLucia, acting in the capacity as DeLucia's main enforcer.

Sensing a bad storm on the horizon from the U. S. Government, Paul DeLucia sold his Miami Beach home at 4385 Pine Tree Drive for $183,500 to a Ralph Herbert. One story ringing through the air among law enforcement at that time was that Paul DeLucia had most of his money hidden in his home in the form of bundles or bails, in cash, which he stored on wooden pellets to allow the air to circulate so as not to allow the money to rot.

Unfortunately DeLucia's name was pulled into the U.S. Senate hearings on improper labor practices headed by Robert F. Kennedy in Washington DC.

Tony Accardo had already been through the mill concerning the Senate hearings when he was called to appear in April 1958. He had his lawyers Richard Gorman and Louis Karton ask for a temporary and permanent injunction against the ABC TV network which was showing the hearings live. A judge denied the request, stating Accardo could not expect the same privacy in the Senate hearings room as he enjoys in his River Forest mansion. Accardo stood behind the Fifth Amendment 172 times.

The Senate committee named Paul DeLucia and Tony Accardo as the "supreme bosses" in Chicago stating that they were the "Sicily-spawned" Mafia which runs a criminal enterprise.

Investigators found information linking DeLucia to the Teamsters. They listed that Joey Glimco, head of Chicago Taxi Cab Union Local 777 of the International Teamsters, was operating the union in connivance with DeLucia.

When it was DeLucia's time to appear, the committee began with the 1934 purchase of his 4-1/2 acre estate in Long Beach, Indiana for $14,000. This English Tudor-style mansion consisted of 20 rooms, an oval stone swimming pool, tennis courts and a 12-room servants building. It suffered a major fire when the main house burned down just before World War II, then was rebuilt and restored. The mansion was located on Moore Road. The property was said to be one block from Lake Michigan.

From the Collection of T.M.

Paul DeLucia

The Senate hearings were investigating Teamsters president Jimmy Hoffa when then ran across documents about the purchase of this estate in Long Beach by Detroit Teamsters Locals 299 and 337 of the International Union. In 1956 the Teamsters locals purchased the mansion from Paul DeLucia for $150,000 to use the property as a Teamsters training school.

Then in March 1958 a confidential informant told the committee that the sale of DeLucia's property was engineered by Paul Dorfman after many meetings with DeLucia at the Bismarck Hotel in Chicago. Dorfman was a mob associate close to Jimmy Hoffa.

After the sale of the property it was once again transferred to a title and loan company because it was found that an unincorporated labor union could not hold title or land in Indiana. Long Beach authorities ruled that zoning regulations forbid the use of the grounds and building as a training school for business agents of the Detroit locals.

As it turned out, not all of the property was sold to the Teamsters. The caretaker's house and roughly one-half of the land and one-half of the swimming pool apparently were retained by DeLucia.

In September 1957 investigators went to mob attorney Joseph Bulger's office which used to be at room 1203 at the building at 188 West Randolph Street in Chicago to ask him questions about the Nancette estate but were told he could not answer any questions since he was indicted for conspiring with DeLucia in connection with DeLucia's income tax payments.

When Jimmy Hoffa was asked by the Senate Committee about the purchase of DeLucia's home for $150,000, he denied knowing the property belonged to DeLucia. Investigators then went to interview Owen Bert Brennan, the person who arranged for the purchase of the property. Brennan denied that he knew anyone by the name of Paul DeLucia. He said the availability of the property was brought to his attention by Chicago Teamster boss Sandy O'Brien, who showed him news clipping of an estate for sale. Brennan then gave the clipping to Joe Prebenda who made an investigation and returned with Joseph Bulger, who handled the sale of the estate for the seller. However, it was learned that Brennan lied about knowing DeLucia. Chicago police reports and investigation records showed that Brennan had been arrested many times for using explosives with intent to cause damage to property. One report showed that one of his "closest" friends in Chicago was Paul DeLucia.

In regards to Hoffa, he stated that an "oversight" at the Teamsters Joint Council meeting failed to mention the purchase of this estate. Joseph Prebenda motioned at a Joint Council #43 meeting after this "oversight" that this estate be purchased by the Joint Council from the other Teamster locals for the purpose of *"establishing a training center for health and welfare pensions, to be used for contract negotiations and for general welfare of the local unions affiliated with Joint Council 43."* It was later learned that Hoffa was an associate of Paul DeLucia's.

One occasion was when New York mob boss Frank Costello was released from a Milan, Michigan prison in October 1953, he and Paul DeLucia immediately went to the Teamster hall in Detroit to see Hoffa for a meeting.

Years later there were reports that the house was used by the nuns from the Michigan City-Notre Dame Catholic School as a nunnery and reports that Outfit Teamster boss Sandy O'Brien was living at the estate in the summer months from 1961 to 1963.

THE WESTERN UNION TELEGRAPH COMPANY

NOTICE REGARDING TELEGRAM

W. P. MARSHALL, PRESIDENT

BEA062 SN WASHINGTON, D. C. AUG 4 19

DELIVERY NO. (STREET ADDRESS, CITY, AND DATE)

ROBERT F KENNEDY CHIEF COUNSEL SENATE
NAME

RM 101
ADDRESS

Your telegram of JULY 30 19 to PAUL DI LUCIA OR PAUL RICCA
DATE ADDRESSEE

at 812 LATHROP AVE BERWYN ILL is undelivered for the following reason:
ADDRESS AND CITY

HAS NOW BEEN DELIVERED

AUG 4 1958

If you have occasion to correct the address originally supplied, please call

and ask for

Form 101 (Rev. 2-49)

THE WESTERN UNION TELEGRAPH COMPANY

DOMESTIC SERVICE — Check the class of service desired; otherwise this message will be sent as a fast telegram: TELEGRAM X / DAY LETTER / NIGHT LETTER

WESTERN UNION
TELEGRAM
W. P. MARSHALL, PRESIDENT

1211 (4-55)

INTERNATIONAL SERVICE — Check the class of service desired; otherwise the message will be sent at the full rate: FULL RATE / LETTER TELEGRAM / SHORE SHIP

NO. WDS. CL. OF SVC.	PD. OR COLL.	CASH NO.	CHARGE TO THE ACCOUNT OF	TIME FILED
			Senate Select Committee on Improper Activities in Labor or Management Field	

Send the following message, subject to the terms on back hereof, which are hereby agreed to

31 July 1958

Mr. L. G Morgan, Clerk-Treasurer
Town Clerk's Office
Long Beach, Indiana

THE FOLLOWING TELEGRAM WAS SENT TO MR. ROBERT L. BAIL

AT MICHIGAN CITY, INDIANA, QUOTE:

IN MATTER UNDER INVESTIGATION BY SENATE SELECT COMMITTEE

ON IMPROPER ACTIVITIES IN LABOR OR MANAGEMENT FIELD, PLEASE

ADVISE SPECIFICALLY:

(ONE) PRESENT ZONING REGULATIONS AND RESTRICTIONS ON FORMER

RICCA (DE LUCIA) PROPERTY MAYFIELD AND MOUNT CLAIRE WAYS,

LONG BEACH, WHICH WAS TRANSFERRED TO A TRUSTEE FOR INTERNATIONAL

BROTHERHOOD OF TEAMSTERS;

(TWO) WHETHER SUCH PROPERTY COULD BE USED AS A TRAINING OR OTHER

SCHOOL FOR BUSINESS AGENTS;

(THREE) WHETHER SUCH PROPERTY COULD BE USED AS A REST HOME OR

RECREATION CENTER FOR TEAMSTER OFFICIALS AND EMPLOYEES.

TIME IS OF THE ESSENCE. URGENT WE RECEIVE PROMPT REPLY

ROOM 101, SENATE OFFICE BUILDING, WASHINGTON, D. C.

Robert F. Kennedy, Chief Counsel
Senate Select Committee on Improper
Activities in Labor or Management Field

OFFICIAL BUSINESS

Servants' Quarters

Tennis Court

Swimming Pool

Mansion

AERIAL VIEW OF PAUL RICCA'S MANSION NEAR MICHIGAN CITY

Trace Union Mansion Deal

WASHINGTON, Aug. 8—Senate rackets probers today were to question Paul (The Waiter) Ricca, Chicago mobster, in their investigation of James R. Hoffa's alleged ties with the underworld.

The investigators want details about the sale of Ricca's palatial summer home to the Teamsters Union for about $150,000.

It was reported that two Detroit Teamster locals bought the Ricca mansion at Long Beach, Ind., several years ago.

ever, refused to give their permission. The big house, with a dining room seating 50, stands vacant.

Ricca was brought in on a subpena as the probers dug further into Teamster President Hoffa's alleged underworld ties.

Newspaper article showing Paul DeLucia's house from above

When DeLucia was questioned by a congressional committee in July 1958, he was asked many questions concerning his parole back in the 1940's and his association with Maury Hughes, then a pal of Attorney General Clark whose office agreed to the dismissal of the indictment which made the paroles possible, and his knowledge of organized crime in Chicago.

FBI agents decided to go after Paul DeLucia's brother-in-law, Mario Gigante, then known in Outfit circles as Mack. Mack Gigante lived at 6269 North Knox Street in Chicago. FBI agents discovered that Mack was a bookmaker who operated out of the Picture Lounge at 199 North LaSalle Street on the corner of Lake Street in Chicago in 1948. When FBI agents went to interview him in 1958 he admitted to them that he was once a bookmaker but said he gave it up in 1951 and got a job working for the Anichini Brothers Company at 549 North Wells Street in Chicago, which was a wholesaler of meats and groceries to hotels and restaurants. FBI agents tried to get information out of Mack about his brother-in-law but would not budge. Before ending the interview, Mack told the agents that there was nothing wrong with making a living gambling since it was a means to earn a livelihood and that there was nothing wrong with his brother-in-law being a professional gambler. FBI agents did say Mack was very friendly during the interview but that getting information through him was a dead-end street.

On August 8, 1958 Paul DeLucia appeared once again before the Rackets Committee and took the 5th Amendment to every one of the 47 questions. Some of the questions were about his alleged "retirement" as mob boss, his aliases, home purchases, associates, activities, checks he wrote, his income and about members of the Teamsters Union.

Murray Humphreys was the mob's man when it came time for the upper members to go to court. He had a legal mind and gave his advice to all the top bosses about what should be done. In preparation for Paul DeLucia's trial, Murray Humphreys hired a detective agency in New York City and had detectives follow and dig up any and all information on the jurors that were to be in the trial. Humphreys' idea was if he could uncover anything that could be used to blackmail a juror; he would use it in exchange for a vote of not guilty. The detective agency did uncover information on one of the jurors and Humphreys went in front of the Board of Governors of organized crime in Chicago with his findings and asked for permission to use it. The idea was voted down and it was decided that no approach would be made to a juror in DeLucia's case.

The year 1959 started off with Paul DeLucia appearing before the Special Inquiry Officer before the second phase of DeLucia's deportation hearings. Paul DeLucia had been denaturalized and had been forced to register as an alien back in November 20, 1958.

On January 26, 1959 Paul DeLucia was ordered deported on grounds he entered the country illegally from Italy. DeLucia and his attorney, William Scott Stewart, had to show the INS (Immigration and Naturalization Service) cause why he should be allowed to stay in America. During this question, DeLucia invoked the Fifth Amendment to all questions placed to him.

Around this time DeLucia learned that a man named Tom Karrigan, a Chicago FBI agent living in Long Beach, was living down the street from him. He was so worried this agent would do something to his house that he had a neighbor watch his house and report anything out of the ordinary. Lucky for DeLucia, Karrigan reported to the FBI that their was "absolutely no activity at the Ricca estate and does not think it is being used for any purpose."

Paul DeLucia and Tony Accardo had other problems on their minds. One informant told the FBI that he had gone to see mob lawyer Joseph Bulger at his offices in Chicago. According to this informant, Bulger complained that the "Young Turks" in the Chicago mob, consisting of William Daddono, Marshall Caifano, Phil Alderisio, Jackie Cerone, Sam Battaglia, Obbie Frabotta and Joseph Gagliano were attempting to take control of the Outfit away from Giancana, Accardo and DeLucia. Bulger said that at that moment Sam Giancana was unable to control those individuals who were wild and unreasoning.

On top of that, government agents did not let up on the DeLucia family even though Paul DeLucia was out of commission. They watched DeLucia's son-in-law, Alex Ponzio, and noticed he frequented the Vignola Furniture Company in River Forest. The place was owned by Adam and John Vignola, both of whom had mob connections with Tony Accardo and Joey Glimco. The furniture store also employed the daughter of mobster Sam Battaglia. The thinking was that if the FBI could not get to DeLucia the way they wanted to, maybe they could get to his son-in-law. That too failed.

In May 1958 Paul DeLucia had been convicted in his income tax case. He was being sent once again to a federal prison. This was the second time DeLucia was going away to federal prison. Even though Joseph Bulger was unsuccessful in keeping his mob boss out of prison he did manage to win an appeal, getting 6 years of DeLucia's sentence "chopped off." Bulger had taken the appeal to the U.S. Circuit Court and had two of the three counts reversed. Had he not won the appeal, DeLucia would have had to serve three convictions consecutively. In July 1959 Paul DeLucia surrendered himself to the U.S. Marshal's office in Chicago to begin serving his prison sentence at Terre Haute Prison in Indiana. Once he surrendered to authorities he was put into a government van with 10 other criminals and taken to Cook County Jail before going to Terre Haute. He signed his name at the jail as Paul DeLucia and his occupation as "retired."

FBI hidden microphones caught Murray Humphreys talking about Paul DeLucia being convicted and income tax situations and how the I.R.S. comes after you. He said, *"If you show them your books and records they find out how they can get you anyhow just like they did Paul. Paul didn't owe them nothing and he had records of every expenditure he ever had, but they found out about an Italian Insurance Company that was formed just for buying purposes, for the poor people, that Paul and a few guys went into. No profit, just like welfare. They found that out and they were convinced that this was Black Hand stuff and they made it look terrible. So what's the use of being in these things if they're gonna dirty you up."*

As DeLucia sat in a Federal Penitentiary, 1959 ended with an informant going to the FBI with information that an associate of DeLucia's named Cameron H. Pulley, who was known as a "promoter" and "fast operator" and was living in a boarding house in Washington, told him that Paul DeLucia had a great deal of information regarding communism. Pulley also enjoyed shooting his mouth off that he had considerable knowledge of former communist dictator Batista. The FBI decided that no further action was required with this information.

Word came that the U.S. Circuit Courts of Appeals had reduced DeLucia's maximum prison term by reversing two counts of the income tax conviction and upholding a third. That meant instead of receiving a sentence of nine years and a $15,000 fine, he was to get three years and a $5,000 fine. He finally settled with the IRS when he handed over a check for $104,000 on the $181,000 owed. He actually had mobster Lou Brady sell his Miami Beach home for him to get the money.

Spot Surveillance 1958-1959

January 1958 - A complaint was made by Paul DeLucia to the telephone company that the phone at his mansion at 1515 Bonnie Brae in River Forest, Illinois had too many "false busy" signals. DeLucia believed his phone was tapped and someone was listening in on his conversations.

June 25, 1958 - Tony Accardo is spotted driving a 1957 Oldsmobile registered to Joe Matia of 4201 Albany Street in Chicago. Matia was a "clean" guy with no police record. Observed in the passenger side is Paul DeLucia. The two are driving to the wake of mobster Claude Maddox.

November 25, 1958 – FBI Agents observed Paul DeLucia, Tony Accardo, Frank Ferraro, Gus Alex, Murray Humphreys, Hy Godfrey and James "The Bomber" Catuara at a lunch meeting at Mike Fish's Restaurant on Ontario Street in Chicago.

December 1, 1958 - 11:15 a.m. - Paul DeLucia was seen leaving Celano's Custom Tailors Shop at 620 Michigan Avenue in Chicago. He was there for a meeting.

January 22, 1959 - Paul DeLucia and two unknown individuals were wagering freely at the Hialeah Race Track in Hialeah, Florida.

May 4, 1959 – Paul DeLucia, Frank Ferraro, Gus Alex, Ross Prio and Lennie Patrick held a meeting on the entire top floor of Mike Fish's Restaurant on Ontario Street in Chicago.

July 1959 - Paul DeLucia begin serving his prison sentence at Terre Haute Prison in Indiana.

December 24, 1959 – Mob associate Jimmy Celano sends Paul DeLucia an artificial floral plant for Christmas.

Chapter 13

The 1960's Come; Paul Stays

With Paul DeLucia in prison, the FBI overheard lots of conversations asking how DeLucia's wife Nancy was doing. On January 20, 1960 one of those conversations took place when Murray Humphreys asked mobster Joey Glimco if he had been over to see Nancy. Glimco said he had not because she always had her family there but said that she always plays cards with the wives of Tony Accardo and Sam Battaglia.

While Paul DeLucia sat in prison his associates devised ways to visit him. In August 1960 Congressman Roland Libonati, the Chicago mob's man in the Washington D.C., got the "ok" from the Bureau of Prisons to do an inspection of federal prisons. He toured Chillicothe prison in Ohio, Ashland prison in Kentucky and finally Terre Haute prison in Indiana. While there Libonati toured the facility inspecting its operation and just before he was to leave he made one request to the warden, to visit Paul DeLucia and another inmate Frank Keenan who was also in Federal prison on income tax violations. When Libonati was escorted to DeLucia's cell, they both displayed great affection to one another as they hugged and kissed.

One good thing for Paul DeLucia happened while in prison. For some time Paul DeLucia and Tony Accardo had been laying down negotiations for financial and controlling shares which they called "points" in Las Vegas, Nevada casinos. The three-way deal involved the Stardust, Desert Inn and Riviera Hotels and Casino's. Involved in these deals were DeLucia, Tony Accardo, Sam Giancana, John Drew, Morris "Moe" Dalitz, Murray Humphreys, Morris Kleinman, Eugene "Jimmy" James, Gus Alex and Frank Ferraro. It was reported that the contribution given by the Chicago group amounted to $36,000 a month.

On October 21, 1961 Paul DeLucia was released from prison after serving two years and four months of his three-year sentence. He was picked up at the prison by his son.

A champagne party was held in honor of Paul DeLucia to celebrate his freedom. The party was held at the Plan-it Travel Company in Oak Park, the new business owned by Nick Nitti and Anthony Ross Accardo, Tony Accardo's son. The celebration was both for the freedom of DeLucia and the opening of the business. However, this party may have not been a "who's who" of the Chicago mob. In January 1962 FBI agents listened in on a conversation with Sam Giancana and heard him say that days before was the first time he had seen Paul since he had been released meaning DeLucia was out for almost 3 months until Giancana saw him.

Weeks before DeLucia's release IRS agents received word that one million dollars in cash was placed in a safety deposit box at the County Federal Savings and Loan Association located at 2720 West Devon Avenue in Chicago. The information said that the money inside was Paul DeLucia's in case he was deported and needed money fast. IRS agents watched the box and noticed one day that a car with three hoodlums arrived. One of the men who was an associate of mob labor boss Joey Glimco went into the bank and entered the box. The vehicle the men arrived in was registered to mob lawyer Joseph Bulger. After the men left, FBI, IRS and ATTD agents went in and opened the box. Inside the box was a canvas bag which seemed to be filled with money. When the agents opened the bag inside were 14 packs of plain white paper which had been cut to the size of money. Each pack was wrapped in a money wrapper saying $100 on them. Also found was a no protest cash order drawn on an account from a Swiss bank in Zurich, Switzerland. The receipt was for $2,750,000.

One of the other men who arrived at the bank was a known con-man connected with the Chicago mob. Agents speculated that the transaction receipt could have had something to do with the purchase of the New Fortier Hotel and Casino in Las Vegas which was reported to be purchased by the Outfit. Another theory was the transaction was the result of a confidence-type game where the money could have been removed from the safety deposit box by a bank official and this dummy package substituted.

DeLucia received word in December of that year that the U.S. Court of Appeals in Chicago upheld the order of deportation against him.

Police detectives began seeing Paul DeLucia and Tony Accardo driving around in cars that were from the Chateau Leasing Company located at 600 North Parkside in Chicago. Accardo was the one observed driving most often with DeLucia in the passenger seat.

It was around this time that FBI agents were told that the son of Paul DeLucia was dating one of the daughters of mobster Lennie Patrick. That drew more attention to Patrick.

DeLucia's daily routine was to do nothing. In January 1962 FBI agents listened in at Celano's Tailor Shop day after day of DeLucia doing almost nothing. One day Tony Accardo, Paul DeLucia and Jimmy Celano were heard saying:

Accardo :	Get the cards out, I'll play you a couple hands.
DeLucia :	Got your money out?
Celano :	I don't need to, Paul, I don't need to.
Accardo :	A guy retired like you, Paul, nobody should have a chance with you at cards. You should know every one of them. (Laughs)

Another conversation disclosed how fed up both Paul DeLucia and Tony Accardo were with law enforcement following them everywhere they went.

Accardo:	We got to go to Florida Sunday Paul. We got to go and see...... (Unintelligible) Do you want to drive or fly?
DeLucia:	I don't give a damn how you go. ......(Unintelligible) ....by jet.
Accardo:	I don't blame you, I'd just as soon go by jet myself and I don't give a shit who knows I'm down there. No matter how you get there two or three hours afterwards they're gonna know we're there. I got to go and get set up for my fishing.

Though DeLucia had resumed his friendships with his close friends, the rest of the mob was a different story. FBI agents listened in on Sam Giancana as he held his daily conferences. At one meeting an un-named individual asked Giancana *"how is Paul getting along?"* Giancana's answer was, *"Nobody has seen him."* Paul DeLucia was not holding any meetings with anyone concerning mob business.

In April 1962 Paul DeLucia was certain he was going to be deported back to Italy. The FBI listened in as DeLucia, Frank Ferraro, Tony Accardo, Jackie Cerone, Jimmy Celano, Butch Landon and Hy Godfrey discussed the neck ties Celano sold at his tailor shop. The group noticed that DeLucia was looking at ties while wearing dark sunglasses indoors. Accardo and Ferraro began a few moments of making fun of DeLucia asking him if he could even see what color they were. DeLucia replied back to Celano that when he is deported back to Italy he is going to send for some ties. Accardo then tells Celano that his ties are *"like a whore house, all the same price."*

In April 1962 the Supreme Court denied a hearing to DeLucia concerning his deportation. Paul DeLucia was ordered to be deported from the United States at once. However, three months later the Immigration Department was having trouble deporting him. The problem was not Paul DeLucia; it was that no country would take him.

Then an ingenious plan came to DeLucia. He had written letters to over sixty countries asking them if he could be deported there. To make sure they all said no, DeLucia attached newspaper articles outlining his criminal past with every letter, making sure they read that he was once with Al Capone, assuring each country would take one look at who he was and say "NO". The INS had no choice but to release DeLucia on a supervised parole and made him report to an INS officer on a regular basis until a country could be found.

The courts had ruled that DeLucia was to be deported by October 1962. When October arrived and DeLucia was still here, the district director of immigration, John Lehmann, said he was convinced DeLucia had shown good faith in trying to leave America. Then came news that one country would accept DeLucia. That country was the tiny principality billionaire playland of Monaco. The only problem, Monaco would only allow him on the island in a visitor status and only if he could obtain a French visa. France said no to the visa.

For DeLucia it was back to work and back to his position as top mob boss. When it was time to end the life of someone who went against the Chicago Outfit you would think it would be a big thing. Not so, as FBI agents were amazed at how little Tony Accardo, Paul DeLucia and Gus Alex cared about having someone murdered. On December 5, 1962 the three held a meeting, with the FBI listening in, talking about handing out contracts after Accardo takes his vacation with his daughter. The conversation was as follows:

Alex	I'll see you Saturday, huh?
DeLucia	No, No, Saturday. I'm busy. What do you want from me? I'm gonna be busy. What do you want from me? Aaaah, tomorrow I got a date at 12:30 at the Imperial House. Want to come?
Alex	NO, you can't. That's when the show is on. (Fashion Show)
Accardo	On Thursday? I thought it was on Friday?
DeLucia	No, that's right. It was the Palmer House.
Accardo	Now, you say one joint, and then you wind up at another. Do you know where the hell you are going?
DeLucia	Empire Room.
Accardo	Oh, that's in the Palmer House. (Laughs) We got our own show out in the country. We don't need no models. We got Buddy Arvey's old lady out there. Modeling. Skinny ass blond. We haven't gone to press yet. I'm glad you got a date tomorrow. That gives me a chance to vacuum out my swimming pool.
Alex	I didn't get a chance to tell you. I got the contract, and on Sunday, the thing was consummated. We get to find the little guy. The guy that counts. (Laughs)
Accardo	I was figuring on Marie (Pyle) coming back. She's gonna go to New Orleans for the Sugar Bowl game. Then they want to go to Mexico and Acapulco, and I want to go with them.
Alex	When do you figure on giving these contracts?
Accardo	Right after I come back. We'll start planning something.
Alex	Paul, how many relatives do you have over there? (Referring to Naples Italy)
DeLucia	Four or five, maybe, why?
Alex	I'm going over there.
Accardo	Don't bother to go to Naples. You won't miss anything there.
DeLucia	They watch you there. If you want to go to Naples, I'll send word.
Alex	My purpose is to go skinning, Paul.
A few days before this conversation on December 12, 1962 mob burglar Virgil "Doc" Summers was killed in East St. Louis, Illinois and it was believed that he is who the "contract" was on.	

Spot Surveillance 1962

January 1, 1962 – Paul DeLucia and Tony Accardo are overheard by the FBI discussing Tony Accardo's income tax trial.

January 8, 1962 – Paul DeLucia, Tony Accardo, Jimmy Celano and Jackie Cerone discuss plans to go to Florida on January 14, 1962. Later they met with Hy Godfrey and Las Vegas mobster Moe Dalitz at the St. Clair Hotel in Chicago.

January 23, 1962 – Paul DeLucia, Jackie Cerone, Jimmy Celano and Tony Accardo are playing gin rummy, discussing coats.

January 26, 1962 – Paul DeLucia meets with mobsters Ross Prio and Chuckie English at the Sherman Hotel in Chicago. Both Prio and English leave the meeting and board a plane to Miami, Florida where a gathering of mobsters is taking place.

February 16, 1962 – Paul DeLucia plays cards with Tony Accardo, Jimmy Celano, and Morris Norman. He then is picked up by someone named "Louie" (possibly Louis Briatta) and had a meeting before meeting back up with Tony Accardo at Pete Fish's Restaurant.

February 17, 1962 – Paul DeLucia, Tony Accardo, Gus Alex, Sam Alex and Hy Godfrey met at Celano's Tailor Shop. The group discussed the possibility that Mike Fish's Restaurant had a hidden microphone planted by the FBI.

February 20, 1962 – Paul DeLucia, Jackie Cerone, Rocco Fischetti, Ed Vogel, Joe Lanza, Anthony Pinelli and Dominic "Butch" Blasi are observed together at Puccini's Restaurant at 10th Avenue and 79th Street Causeway in Miami, Florida.

April 1, 1962 – FBI informant tells the feds Paul DeLucia has been in constant contact with Tony Accardo and Frank Ferraro due to his status in the Chicago Outfit. DeLucia is the senior advisor with Tony Accardo.

April 10, 1962 – Paul DeLucia, Tony Accardo, Hy Godfrey and Jackie Cerone hang out at Celano's Tailor Shop.

August 30, 1962 – Paul DeLucia and Tony Accardo board a plane for New York to meet with New York Mob bosses.

September 12, 1962 – Paul DeLucia, Murray Humphreys, Ralph Pierce, Gus Alex, Les Kruse, Hy Godfrey, and Frank Ferraro are seen holding a meeting at the King Arthur's Pub on Wells Street, between Adams and Monroe Streets in Chicago. Moments after they all leave, Jackie Cerone is seen entering the pub looking for them, then hurries out the back of the club.

October 25, 1962 – Agents observed Paul DeLucia at the King Arthur's Pub at 126 South Wells Street in Chicago with Murray Humphreys, Frank Ferraro and Ralph Pierce.

October 30, 1962 – Paul DeLucia, Tony Accardo and Sam Giancana discuss matters in the First Ward. The three try and decide if there is a "rat" in the First Ward talking to the FBI.

November 30, 1962 – Paul DeLucia, Tony Accardo and Sam Giancana met to discuss New York mobster Meyer Lansky. Accardo is heard saying, *"I see they made the Jew an avagaud and he's really reaching out."* They then discussed a newspaper article about mobster Frank Ferraro that appeared in the Chicago American newspaper. Tony Accardo believed that Ferraro created his own trouble because of his abusive conduct during an interview by FBI agents. Accardo suggested that Ferraro and the others in the mob should at least be courteous when approached by FBI agents for an interview.

December 1, 1962 – Paul DeLucia and Tony Accardo are called to the Armory Lounge by Sam Giancana in an emergency meeting. The day before, Giancana and mob First Ward Alderman John D'Arco Sr. had their meeting broken up by FBI agents. Accardo wanted to know how much the government knew. He was heard saying, *"We don't know how much they know."*

December 5, 1962 – Paul DeLucia, Tony Accardo and Gus Alex meet about giving a contract to kill Virgil Summers. Summers and his brother, Neal "Little Monk" Summers, had robbed syndicate gambling spots in Chicago in the past.

December 6, 1962 - DeLucia met with two unknown individuals at the Palmer House Hotel in Chicago. There he held a three-hour luncheon conference. One of the men believed to be in attendance at the meeting was Arnie Bauer who was an acquaintance of Chicago Heights mob boss Frank LaPorte.

Paul DeLucia's Miami House around 1960

An aerial view of Paul DeLucia's Miami House in the middle

Paul DeLucia's Miami House in the middle

Chapter 14

The Beginning of the Fall

By summer 1963 the Outfit's situation was open to interpretation. Mob boss Sam Giancana was in control, traveling throughout the world, dating show girls and movie actresses and hanging out with the Rat Pack in Las Vegas.

Back in Chicago, two men sat and watched in dislike of what was becoming of the Chicago mob. The two men were Paul DeLucia and Tony Accardo. A meeting was called between Accardo, DeLucia, Murray Humphreys and Frank Ferraro to make some changes.

On the fourth of July Ferraro and Humphreys had a meeting where Ferraro told Humphreys how upset he was over Sam Giancana's decision to allow mobster Chuckie English to be interviewed by FBI agents. A few days earlier FBI agents had met English at the Armory Lounge, Giancana's headquarters, and Ferraro said that they talked for over four hours. Ferraro was also under the opinion that Chuckie English brought up the name of Frank Sinatra as being the person who could act as an intermediary between Giancana and President John F. Kennedy or Robert Kennedy. Ferraro was furious at the belief that English bragged to the FBI agents that Giancana was in a position to assist in the re-election bid of John F. Kennedy for the presidency and for the election of Democratic Senators. The truth was that the meeting was only two hours and English never did say to the fed that Giancana could help Kennedy but did mention that Sinatra could be the branch between the Kennedy's and Giancana. It is known because the FBI listened in on the entire conversation over a hidden microphone.

Ferraro, who was acting as second-in-command of the Outfit in 1963, called a meeting with Accardo and DeLucia to inform them that Giancana made a "terrible blunder" in allowing English to meet with the FBI. Before the meeting Ferraro told Humphreys that he had informed Giancana that he was going to Accardo and DeLucia about this blunder which Giancana did not show much concern over. Humphreys was pleased with Ferraro that he had told Giancana because Humphreys warned Ferraro that had he not done it, he would have been in violation of the rules and viewed as Ferraro going behind Giancana's back which could have been bad for Ferraro.

The meeting was held on July 29, 1963 at the old Staley's Restaurant in Chicago. Called to this meeting by DeLucia and Accardo were mob bosses Frank Ferraro, Jackie Cerone and Joey Glimco; highest ranking non-Italian bosses Gus Alex, Ralph Pierce and Murray Humphreys; underlings Hy Godfrey and Fred "Juke Box" Smith; and mob lawyers Eugene Bernstein and Mike Brodkin.

DeLucia addressed the group by saying he was concerned by the actions of Sam Giancana because Giancana was constantly traveling outside of Chicago and was leaving many decisions which were required to be made only by Giancana, unmade, and as a result, the underlings in the Outfit were receiving no direction as to their activities rendering a somewhat chaotic state within the organization.

Ferraro asked that Chuckie English be isolated from Giancana due to English's extreme bad judgment.

Both DeLucia and Accardo had to take over these decisions in an attempt to keep the organization from breaking into several disgruntled factions which would make the entire organization extremely vulnerable to investigations by government agencies, not to mention the possibility of these factions going to war with each other over rackets and territory.

By 1963 an urgent memo was sent from the Chicago FBI to their headquarters in Washington D.C. concerning the increased activities of Paul DeLucia in the affairs of organized crime. DeLucia was holding meetings with top mob bosses in the game room of the first floor of his mansion in River Forest. It was pointed out that Chicago had already wanted to place a hidden microphone in the house of Paul DeLucia in his private study but they had four reasons why they could not. One was because DeLucia's house had a fortress-like construction to it. Two, the house had a single entry doorway. Three was the fact that two of DeLucia's neighbors were close acquaintances and always on the lookout for things out of the normal. Four, DeLucia always made sure he had someone in his house at all times no matter what so there was no way the FBI could get into the house to plant the bug.

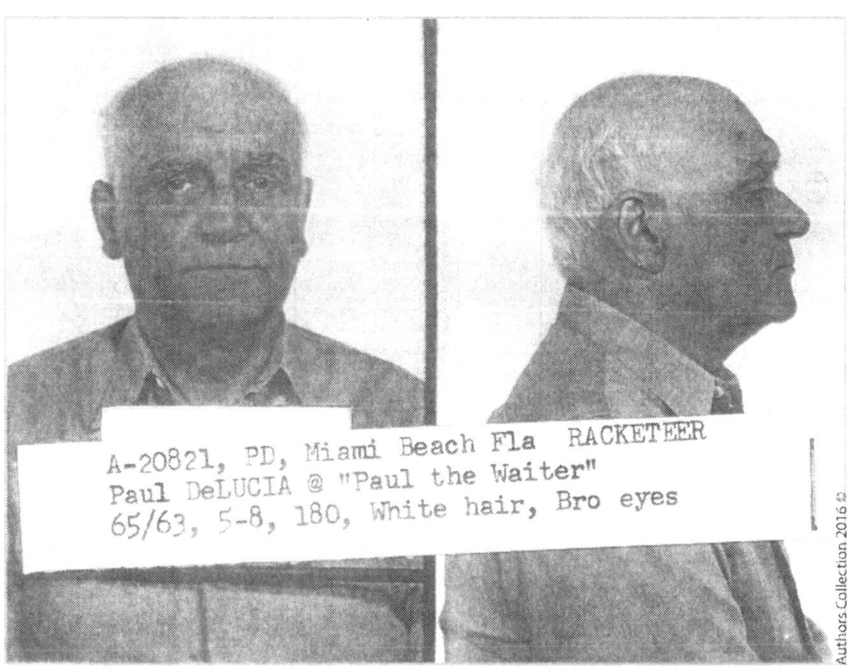

Dade County Sheriff's Office mug photo taken on November 16, 1963

NAME (LAST)	(FIRST)	(MIDDLE)	SOC. SEC. NO.	FILE NO.
DE LUCIA	PAUL			

NICKNAME OR ALIAS: Paul Ri ca, "The Waiter", Paul Viela, Paul Villa, Paul Salui, Paul Maglio, "The Porter"

HOME ADDRESS: 1515 Bonnie Brae — CITY: River Forest — F.B.I. NO.: 832514

SEX	RACE	DESCENT	D.O.B.	HEIGHT	WEIGHT	HAIR	EYES
Male	White		64yrs.	5'8"	180	White	Brown

ASSOCIATES: RALPH PIERCE, TONY GOEBELS AND CHARLES FISCHETTI.

VEHICLE INFORMATION: 1963 Chev. Ill 1963 DS-1133 Registered to Chateau Livery Service

FACE CARD — SEE REVERSE SIDE FOR MISC. INFORMATION

Paul DeLucia's Chicago Police file cards from 1963

Subject is considered an elder statesman of the local outfit. Presently he is resisting deportation proceedings by the Federal Government. He entered this country on a false passport. His rise within the Capone organization was extremely rapid and rewarding. He is an ex-convict, his last sentence was the result of evading the payment of income tax. Subject's record of arrest with the Chicago Police dates back to 1927 No Military Service.

CONFIDENTIAL

NAME : RICCA, PAUL
1515 Bonnie Brae
River Forest, Illinois

ALIASES : (True Name - Paul De Lucia)
The Waiter; Paul Viela; Paul Villa; Paul Salue;
Paul Maglie; Paul Barstow; "The Porter"; & "Mops".

DESCRIPTION : M/W, Italian, 5'-8", 180 lbs, white hair; brown eyes;
D.O.B. 10 July 1898.

LOCALITIES FREQUENTED : West Side.

FAMILY BACKGROUND :

CRIMINAL ASSOCIATES : Anthony Accardo; Ralph Pierce; Charles Fischetti.

CRIMINAL HISTORY : F.B.I. No. 832514 - I.R. No. 78267
Subject's arrest record dates back to 1927. Subject is an ex-convict and has done time for Evasion of Income taxes. He entered this country on a false passport and is presently resisting deportation proceedings by the Government. He was twice charged with Murder in his native Italy.

BUSINESS :

MODUS OPERANDI : Subject is considered an elder statesman of the local outfit.

Mob Boss

In August 1963 the FBI discovered that the reason for Paul DeLucia's and Tony Accardo's increased activity with the Chicago Outfit was that the Outfit was opening gambling operations in Mexico. Tony Accardo had been seen by agents flying to Mexico with Jackie Cerone to meet with mobster Nick Dean (Circella) who was overseeing the operation. Then information was developed concerning the Outfit's gambling operation in the Dominican Republic. Both Sam Giancana and Leslie Kruse had been making trips to Santo Domingo concerning this gambling but word reached the FBI that DeLucia and Accardo had sent their men, mobsters Carmen Bastone and Albert Meo, to organize the operation.

Alarming news was reported that Paul DeLucia was attempting to place his nephew, Anthony Spina, in the Chicago office of the Immigration and Naturalization Services in an attempt to get some clout in the office to help get his deportation troubles settled. When the FBI found out about this plot, FBI agent William F. Roemer Jr. went to see Anthony Girolami, then the Probate Court Clerk of Cook County who had been ordered by DeLucia to sponsor Spina for the immigration position. Later the FBI listened in as Pat Marcy, John D'Arco, Tony Tisci and Girolami talked about Roemer investigating Spina. Tony Tisci was recorded as saying, *"I don't like to hear that name"* referring to Roemer.

In December 1963 Chicago Police received word that an organized crime meeting was being held in the suburbs of Chicago. Though the detectives never found the meeting place they were informed that Tony Accardo, Paul DeLucia, Sam Battaglia, William Daddono, Rudy Fratto, Albert Travolta and Albert Frabotta attended this meeting and the topic was how DeLucia and Accardo were unhappy with the personal conduct and running of the Outfit by Sam Giancana.

Spot Surveillance 1963

January 8, 1963 - Paul DeLucia, Tony Accardo, Sam "Teetz" Battaglia, William "Willie Potatoes" Daddono, Felix "Milwaukee Phil" Alderisio, Albert "Obbie" Frabotta, Frank "One Ear" Fratto and his brother Rudy Fratto met to discuss the future of mob boss Sam Giancana in Chicago.

January 23, 1963 - Paul DeLucia, Tony Accardo and Sam Giancana hold a meeting at the Flamingo Motel in Rosemont, Illinois. Most of the conversation was about a recent trip to Mexico.

February 26, 1963 – Paul DeLucia and Tony Accardo depart from Accardo's house for an unknown location to hold a hoodlum meeting.

March 1963 - DeLucia is often seen by FBI agents at the home of Tony Accardo.

April 5, 1963 – Paul DeLucia, Tony Accardo and Sam Giancana hold a meeting at the Armory Lounge.

June 21, 1963 – Paul DeLucia and Tony Accardo meet with the owner of the Atlas Wrecking Company at Meo's Norwood House regarding financial difficulties.

July 1963 - Paul DeLucia, Tony Accardo, Jackie Cerone, Sam Giancana and Manny Skar hold a conference at the Sahara Motel.

July 5, 1963 – Paul DeLucia, Tony Accardo, Frank Ferraro and Murray Humphreys hold a secret meeting concerning a "terrible blunder" that Sam Giancana committed. Giancana allowed mobster Chuckie English to be interviewed by the FBI while Giancana sat a few feet from the table listening in on the conversation.

July 8, 1963 – Paul DeLucia, Tony Accardo and Jackie Cerone meet an attorney from the Standard Securities Company at the Sahara Motel.

July 29, 1963 - Paul DeLucia, Ralph Pierce, Frank Ferraro, Hy Godfrey, Tony Accardo, Jack Cerone, Murray Humphreys, Joey Glimco, Mike Brodkin, Fred Smith and Gus Alex meet at Staley's Restaurant at 501 South Wells, the corner of Congress Parkway and Wells Street in Chicago. It was believed the meeting was to discuss the actions of Sam Giancana always being "absent" from Chicago.

August 21, 1963 - FBI agents approach Paul DeLucia at 1:30 PM near his residence in River Forest for an interview. DeLucia tells the agents that he is in good health but would like to spend more time in Florida because of his arthritis. He also added that he does not go to Florida that much any more because the FBI always follows him and it distresses him greatly. He said he was aware that other government agencies besides the FBI were interested in his activities but wished that all of the government agencies would just leave him alone. He ended the interview by telling the FBI that if he decided he had something to tell the FBI he would notify them.

September 14, 1963 – Paul DeLucia was observed at the wedding of mobster Ben Fillichio at the Conrad Hilton Hotel in Chicago. DeLucia, Tony Accardo, Sam Giancana, Frank Ferraro, Jimmy Allegretti, Frank LaPorte and Murray Humphreys paid for a separate room next to the wedding to use that night as a secret place to hold an Outfit meeting, knowing the FBI would not be able to listen in on them.

October 10, 1963 – FBI agents listen in as Buddy Jacobson gave a "pep" talk to Pat Marcy. Jacobson told Marcy that he had just spoken to Sam Giancana and Paul DeLucia and they informed him that they were extremely satisfied with Marcy's handling of various matters. Jacobson assured Marcy that that they felt that there was nothing any person could do at that time since they had never seen conditions as bad as they were in Chicago at that time. DeLucia told Jacobson that the organization had to be patient and wait for the pressure of law enforcement to lift.

October 22, 1963 – Paul DeLucia met with Tony Accardo at the Roosevelt Coffee Shop on Roosevelt Road.

Mob Boss

October 23, 1963 - Paul DeLucia left his residence at 1515 Bonnie Brae in River Forest and was observed driving a 1963 Light Blue Bonneville Pontiac Convertible. He drove around the block and back into his garage checking to see if he was being followed. After 25 minutes he left his garage once more heading to an unknown meeting.

November 9, 1963 – Paul DeLucia and Tony Accardo arrive together at the wake of Angelina Sortino, mother of mob boss Frank "Strongy" Ferraro.

November 16, 1963 - Paul DeLucia and Guido DeChiaro board a plane to Miami and were met at the airport by Miami mobster Anthony Ricci, aka Tony Gobels. All three were arrested by the Dade County Sheriff's Office and questioned. DeLucia was photographed and released. DeLucia told the sheriff he was staying at the Thunderbird Motel in Miami Beach.

November 22, 1963 - Paul DeLucia and Tony Accardo met at the Roosevelt Coffee Shop at 716 Roosevelt Road to discuss the fact that while DeLucia was in Miami, authorities tried to serve DeLucia with a subpoena to appear before a Federal Grand Jury on organized crime in that area.

December 3, 1963 – FBI agents followed Jackie Cerone and watched as he picked up Paul DeLucia at his house and then headed to pick up Tony Accardo at his house. The three drove to the Chicago Loop area where Accardo and DeLucia were dropped off and disappeared into the crowd on the street.

December 15, 1963 – Paul DeLucia, Tony Accardo and Willie Daddono attend the wake of the sister of mob boss Jimmy "Monk" Allegretti.

December 16, 1963 – Paul DeLucia, Tony Accardo and Frank Ferraro have lunch at Jacques Restaurant.

December 31, 1963 – Paul DeLucia, Tony Accardo, Sam Battaglia and Phil Alderisio observed sitting together at a table celebrating New Year's Eve at Riverwoods Country club that was managed by mobster Lou Rosanova.

In January 1964 one of Paul DeLucia's long time lawyers, William Scott Stewart, had settled his own income tax case for $29,674. The IRS claimed that Stewart never mentioned six bank drafts totaling $45,000 that were sent to him right after Paul DeLucia was released from prison.

By that time Paul DeLucia and Tony Accardo were said to be almost equal in power as the actual acting boss Sam Giancana. One incident involving mobsters Joey Glimco and Joe "Crackers" Mendino occurred when Glimco found out Mendino was muscling in on juke box locations of his. He contacted Mendino and told him he had to stop at once. Being unsuccessful, Glimco went to DeLucia and Accardo concerning this problem and not Giancana. Mendino was told by Accardo to sell his juke box routes to Eddie Vogel which he did. That enraged Giancana because apparently Giancana was in secret partnership with Mendino in the juke box business. For some time Joey Glimco was not in good favor with Giancana for going to DeLucia and Accardo instead of him. Mendino was later killed.

In March 1964 the Immigration and Naturalization Service in Miami, Florida reported that a group of Chicago hoodlums called the Oak Park Fellowship Club members had traveled to Freeport, Bahamas and stayed at the Lucayan Beach Hotel and Casino. Names listed were Paul R. DeLucia, Anthony Ponzio, Mario Gigante and Frank "Skippy" Cerone. It was believed this meeting involved money owed to the Chicago Outfit.

Months later Paul DeLucia was served with a subpoena to appear before the Illinois Crime Commission concerning the McHenry County rackets probe. Charles "Chuckie" English and Jackie Cerone were also subpoenaed. Nothing became of the hearings concerning DeLucia.

In July 1964 expert attorney Jack Wasserman was brought into Chicago to handle Paul DeLucia's deportation proceedings. When Wasserman arrived he was met by mob boss Gus Alex and entertained at a party Alex hosted with his German model wife Suzanne Fueger. DeLucia's appeal was based on the claim that Italy was an unfriendly country and would cause DeLucia's failing health to progress further. The night of the party at Alex's luxurious apartment, FBI agents listened in on a hidden microphone they had installed. Wasserman told Alex that night how they had to go to two courts that day or DeLucia would have been deported by 5:00 in the afternoon. They accomplished their goal by 3 o'clock.

Gus Alex was later heard talking to his brother mobster Sam Alex, aka Sam Taylor about the position Paul DeLucia was in. In Alex's opinion, DeLucia's only worry was if he was deported back to Italy, he, DeLucia, would be fine if he was to go to a large town or city where he would have no headaches because there would be good food, clubs, restaurants and theaters. However, if DeLucia was confined to his village he came from, then he felt sorry for him.

With deportation hanging over his head, Paul DeLucia found the time to enjoy his son's wedding.

On September 19, 1964 Paul DeLucia's son, Paul R. DeLucia, married Mary Meatte, a model, at St. Vincent Ferrer Catholic Church in River Forest, Illinois. Around 100 guests attended the wedding with only Tony Accardo and Jackie Cerone noticed by investigators as representing the Outfit. While the wedding was taking place, for some strange reason, crazy organized crime figure Sam "Mad Sam" DeStefano drove around and around the block of the church staring down policemen and investigators. The onlookers enjoyed the display of craziness from DeStefano, celebrating and clapping every time he passed the front of the church.

The reception was held at Sam Giancana's Villa Venice with around 400 guests. One by one, Outfit members showed up wearing black tuxedos and enjoying champagne served from a fountain and the music of a 24-piece band. The only excitement outside was when mobster Chuckie English arrived. He screamed to police writing down the license plates of the auto parked in the parking lot, *"You guys are wasting the taxpayers' money."*

Mobsters observed by police attending the reception were:

Phil Alderisio	Gus Alex	Jimmy Allegretti	Sam Battaglia
Marshall Caifano	Jackie Cerone	Sam DeStefano	Charles English
Sam English	Albert Frabotta	Joe Gagliano	Joey Glimco
Ralph Pierce	Murray Humphreys		

Spot Surveillance 1964

January 3, 1964 – Paul DeLucia, Jackie Cerone and Tony Accardo were seen driving at a high rate of speed away from DeLucia's home.

January 9, 1964 – Paul DeLucia, Tony Accardo, Frank Ferraro, Murray Humphreys and mob lawyer Mike Brodkin had lunch at the old Jacques Restaurant. After the lunch Brodkin was heard saying to Pat Marcy that the lunch was, *"Just like old times."*

March 19, 1964 – Paul DeLucia is observed at the funeral of mobster James Roti.

May 5, 1964 – Paul DeLucia and Gus Alex were on their way to meet with Frank Ferraro when DeLucia got "spooked" that he was under surveillance. The meeting was postponed.

June 6, 1964 – Paul DeLucia is observed at the wedding of Francis Curry's son at the Cathedral of St. Raymond Nantus in Joliet, Illinois. The wedding reception was held at D'Ameco's Restaurant in Joliet. There DeLucia was seated with Tony Accardo, Murray Humphreys, Gus Alex, Eddie Vogel, Hy Godfrey and Frank LaPorte. He was observed socializing with Chicago Heights hoodlums Frank Franze, Peter Zaranti, Sam Geraci, Sam D'Giovanni and Nick Costello.

June 10, 1964 – Paul DeLucia attends the wedding of Anthony Ross Accardo, son of Tony Accardo, at St. Vincent Ferrer Church in River Forest and then at the mob's

Villa Venice. The bride and groom received over $240,000 in cash and gifts.
June 17, 1964 – Paul DeLucia is served a subpoena to appear before the Illinois Crime Commission investigating mob rackets in McHenry, Illinois.

July 4, 1964 – The government attempted to surprise Paul DeLucia and deport him that day. His lawyer, Jack Wasserman, was able to stop the deportation.

August 17, 1964 – Paul DeLucia, Tony Accardo, Murray Humphreys, Jackie Cerone, Lester Kruse, Ralph Pierce, Hy Godfrey and Frank Ferraro gather at the Cart Restaurant, 601 South Wabash Street in Chicago as a sort of going away party for Ferraro who would die weeks later. Chicago Police detectives sat outside watching and were discovered by the group. A telephone call was placed to mob lawyer George Bieber by Hy Godfrey wanting to know if warrants were issued for any of their arrests. Murray Humphreys uses himself as a guinea pig to see what the officers would do when he attempted to leave the restaurant. A half hour later mobster Ralph Pierce called Bieber to let him know nothing happened and the group left without incident.

August 25, 1964 – Paul DeLucia and Tony Accardo attend the wake of Frank Ferraro held at Montclair Funeral Home. This action was in defiance of Sam Giancana's orders that no mobster was to attend even though Giancana himself attended. Others observed with Accardo and DeLucia were Sam DeStefano, Joey Glimco, Joey Aiuppa, Joseph LaBarbara, Dominic "Butch" Blasi, Jackie Cerone, Clarice Accardo and her son, Anthony Ross.

September 1, 1964 – Paul DeLucia, Tony Accardo and Jackie Cerone had dinner at the Air Host Motel.

September 14, 1964 – Paul DeLucia, Tony Accardo and Jackie Cerone hold a three-hour meeting at the Air Host Motel in Schiller Park, Illinois.

Chapter 15
Paul Witnesses the Down Fall

In 1965 the FBI sat and watched as Tony Accardo, Sam Battaglia and Sam Giancana made many trips to Paul DeLucia's house to "up date" policy and decisions concerning organized crime in Chicago. One informant said that it was every Sunday afternoon that the four meet to discuss business.

In July 1965 Paul DeLucia and Tony Accardo were faced with a big problem. Acting day-to-day mob boss Sam "Momo" Giancana was sent to Cook County Jail on a contempt of court citation. With Giancana behind bars for a year, who was running the day-to-day operations? One report stated that a mob meeting was held on December 15, 1965 with Tony Accardo, Paul DeLucia, Jackie Cerone, Sam Battaglia, Phil Alderisio, Marshall Caifano and Fiore "Fifi" Buccieri to determine who would fill that roll. First Accardo and DeLucia offered the position to mobster Sam Battaglia, who declined. Then John "Jackie the Lackie" Cerone was chosen to assume the position as boss. But Tony Accardo was actually running the Outfit through Cerone. However, in later reports it stated that Sam Battaglia was defiantly running the day-to-day operations of the Chicago mob with Cerone.

In their attempts to find out who was running what, FBI agents went to one of its informants who was a top mob boss in another area other than Chicago to see what he had been told. He told the agents that there was a group in Chicago referred to as the "Big Five" who were running the Outfit at that moment. This informant named the "Big Five" as Paul DeLucia, Tony Accardo, Sam Giancana, Sam Battaglia and the unexpected name of Sam Lewis, an old-time Outfit "juice" loan man. Lewis' true name was Salvatore Carmen Lusi, who was known to be one of Paul DeLucia's oldest friends which may have been a reason Lewis was included in this group. However, the FBI did not concur with the informant as to the ranking given to Lewis in this situation.

Paul DeLucia faced other problems that year. The Immigration Department of Appeals re-opened his deportation case. His wife Nancy testified during the hearing that while Paul DeLucia was in prison, she was financially taken care of by "close friends" and admitted that Tony Accardo, Jackie Cerone and Murray Humphreys were regular visitors to her home. When Paul DeLucia was called to testify, he admitted that his son-in-law, Alex Ponzio, owned two parking facilities near Van Buren Street and Wabash Avenue in the city and that he rented two other parking lots on the south side of Van Buren. He also admitted he gave Ponzio $110,000 to purchase the parking company which he said he received stock in the company as security for the loan. He added that his son Paul Richard DeLucia was also associated with the company, Town Parking Stations Incorporated at 332 South Michigan Avenue.

The Immigration officials asking the questions asked DeLucia who he was associated with. He admitted to the following people; Tony Accardo, said he knew him but had no idea what he did for a living; Gus Alex, said he knew Alex owned a juke box company; Murray Humphreys who he said he knew for a very long time and was connected with the laundry business; Guy DiChiaro, who was in the juke box business; Lester Kruse, who he had known for twenty years and was in the plumbing business; Ralph Pierce whom he knew for twenty-five years but did not know what he did for a living; Dominic "Butch" Blasi whom he knew for fifteen years; Marshall Caifano whom he knew for thirty years; William Daddono whom he knew for twenty years and was in the liquor store business *"or something like that"*; Sam Battaglia whom he had known for thirty years who trained horses; Jimmy Allegretti, Sam DeStefano and Eddie Vogel, all of whom he knew for thirty years; Jackie Cerone who was in the meat business; Frank Ferraro, Phil Alderisio and Albert Frabotta, all he had known for many years.

Still looking to deliver DeLucia that knock-out punch, the FBI launched a new investigation into Paul DeLucia to see if he perjured himself in connection with his testimony at the U.S. INS Deportation hearing held in Chicago regarding his winning wagers at Chicago area race tracks. DeLucia claimed he won $85,000 in 1964 by going to the window at the race tracks and placing bets himself. When investigators went to all the tracks he claimed to have won at, everyone they could find that worked at these tracks told investigators that they had never seen DeLucia there, ever. DeLucia even gave investigators a list of when and what time he was at race tracks. For example, he, DeLucia, said he was at Arlington Park Race Track at 4:14 pm on August 8, 1964. FBI agents produced observation logs stating that an FBI agent observed Paul DeLucia at his River Forest home at 3:30 pm on August 8, 1964. There was no way DeLucia could have left his home between 3:30 and 4:14 and made it to the race track in time to place a bet. The distance was too far between his house and the track.

On top of this perjury charge, the Illinois State's Attorney wanted to do to Paul DeLucia what they did to Sam Giancana-bring him before a Grand Jury. Since the

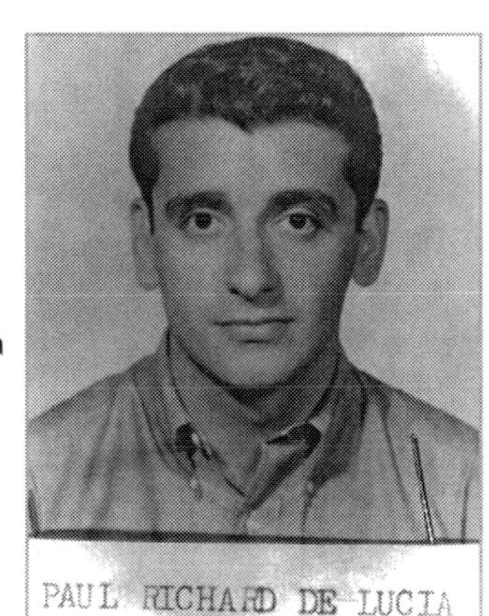

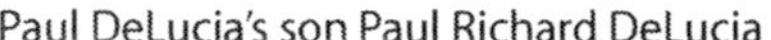
Paul DeLucia's son Paul Richard DeLucia

immigration department was proceeding very slowly in their attempts to deport DeLucia, questions were raised if Italy would still accept DeLucia. So the thinking was, place DeLucia in the same position as they did Giancana by granting him immunity during questioning. If DeLucia refused to answer, he would be found in contempt of court and sent to jail for one year and if he did speak and answered questions, the agency was confident they had enough sufficient evidence in their files to convict DeLucia of perjury. The chance of DeLucia telling the complete truth was never considered as an option. It was later decided that if they were to bring DeLucia in front of a Grand Jury it would be a "slap in the face" to immigration authorities. Not to mention that if there were any open cases against DeLucia such as a perjury case, he could not be deported by law until that case was resolved. It would be another way for DeLucia to remain in the country for years.

Spot Surveillance 1965

January 18, 1965 – FBI agents observed Paul DeLucia, Jackie Cerone, Murray Humphreys, Ralph Pierce, and Anthony Pinelli having lunch at the Palmer House Grill at 114 S. Wabash in Chicago.

February 5, 1965 – Paul DeLucia and Gus Alex have dinner at Fritzels Fashionable Loop Restaurant in Chicago to discuss DeLucia's deportation hearings.

March 22, 1965 – Paul DeLucia, Tony Accardo, Frank LaPorte and mob lawyer Mike Brodkin hold a meeting at Pete Fish's Restaurant in Chicago.

June 21, 1965 – Paul DeLucia, Tony Accardo and Jackie Cerone meet at Meo's Norwood House Restaurant to discuss syndicate business.

June 28, 1965 – Paul DeLucia, Jackie Cerone, Gus Alex and Ralph Pierce are observed by FBI agents gathering at the Rockery Restaurant in the Chicago Loop.

July 28, 1965 – Paul DeLucia and Tony Accardo are seen at Meo's Norwood House discussing replacement for mob boss Sam Giancana.

September 22, 1965 – FBI Agents observe Paul DeLucia, Tony Accardo, Jackie Cerone, Ross Prio, Joseph DiVarco, Joseph Arnold and Dominic Nuccio holding a meeting to discuss Outfit policy.

November 12, 1965 – Paul DeLucia and Tony Accardo meet at Meo's Norwood House to inform Accardo the status of organized crime while he was away on a safari in Africa.

November 16, 1965 – Paul DeLucia and Tony Accardo are observed sitting in a parked car discussing something.

December 13, 1965 – FBI agents watched as Tony Accardo, Dominic "Butch" Blasi, Jackie Cerone and Paul DeLucia arrived at the Armory Lounge. Moments later mob lawyer Anthony Champagne arrived for a meeting.

In April 1966 the FBI was still going after DeLucia in a perjury case. The government had watched Paul DeLucia and his lawyers use every legal "loophole" in DeLucia's favor and decided that it was time to try and force DeLucia to maybe voluntarily depart the U.S. if he was facing prison time again.

The FBI would watch DeLucia's attorney, Jack Wasserman, meet with mobsters Gus Alex and mob lawyer Joseph Bulger at O'Hare Airport before Wasserman and Bulger would stand before the judge hearing the case. They also observed as Dominic "Butch" Blasi would act as a courier between the group and mob boss Tony Accardo.

On April 28, 1966 the FBI received the indictment and went out to arrest DeLucia. At 11:50 a.m. FBI agents had been following Jackie Cerone's car and watched as he picked up Tony Accardo and Paul DeLucia at their houses. The FBI followed the car and decided to pull them over to arrest DeLucia once they reached Norridge, Illinois. Once the FBI had DeLucia in handcuffs, DeLucia instructed Tony Accardo to, *"Contact Joseph Bulger at once and arrange for the necessary bond."*

With DeLucia out on bond, the FBI received information that DeLucia, Tony Accardo, Sam Giancana and Fifi Buccieri were trying their hardest to get their money out of the country as a result of the "heat" generated by a federal investigation into Las Vegas night clubs. These men were also trying to sell their interest in Las Vegas establishments.

That's when DeLucia received the news he had exhausted all his appeals in the U.S. Courts, and had been ordered to be deported, without delay, by the government. DeLucia had told the government that he chose England as the place to be deported to but when U.S. officials contacted England, they once again said no. The only country that said yes to accepting Paul DeLucia this time was Italy and the U.S. Government told him that's where he was heading. However, in Rome, Italy, DeLucia had filed a civil suit with the Italian government declaring he, DeLucia, was not an Italian citizen. A tribunal was launched by the Italian government to decide if DeLucia was an Italian citizen or not. DeLucia would not be allowed into the country until this situation was finally resolved. Once again Paul DeLucia's lawyers bought him more time in the states.

Another blow to the DeLucia family came in June 1966 when his son-in-law Alex Ponzio withdrew plans to build a Loop parking garage when he received opposition from local financial and civic groups. Ponzio had started the Monroe-Dearborn Stations Incorporated Company with himself as president and director and with Anthony F. Spina, a DeLucia relative and lawyer, as secretary-treasurer. The two had planned to build a five-story garage at 55-67 West Monroe Street where the old Monroe Theater and Toffenetti Restaurant stood.

That year saw a clear and evident path that Paul DeLucia and Tony Accardo were clearly in charge of the Chicago Outfit with Sam Battaglia being forced to act as day-to-day boss because of the Giancana jailing. One of the signs was around Christmas when the FBI followed Phil Alderisio around delivering very expensive Christmas gifts from the five Mafia families in New York. The only three mobsters in Chicago who received these gifts were DeLucia, Accardo and Battaglia.

Word in mob circles in 1966 also showed that many members, who all called DeLucia "Papa Paul," were afraid of him because he controlled certain people in the mob that caused the most fear. Many informants reminded the FBI that the "DeLucia Group" still had the most violent killings attached to them.

The FBI received information that DeLucia, Tony Accardo and Jackie Cerone gathered every Friday night on a regular basis at a private residence in Oak Park, Illinois. The residence was owned by an unknown individual who was believed to be an employee in the Illinois Secretary of State's Office and a close friend of then Secretary of State Paul Powell. Apparently DeLucia and Accardo used this man as a "fixer" when dealing with Powell.

In November 1966 the FBI was confused by the activities of DeLucia. For months between the hours of 1:15 pm and 2:30 pm Paul DeLucia would drive to O'Hare International Airport and hang out at the Mexicana Airlines terminal for no apparent reason. As the FBI watched DeLucia, he never met or contacted anyone and he merely wandered around for no apparent reason. One time they noticed DeLucia speaking to a pilot from the Al Italia Airlines but nothing became of it. Another day DeLucia hovered around the crew of the Italian airlines scanning each of the crew members very closely. He never spoke to any of them and after some time left the airport and drove home.

It was not known if his appearing at the airport had anything to do with his brother-in-law. In September 1966 an anonymous letter was received at the FBI stating that the brother-in-law of Paul DeLucia, named Michelangelo Chiacchio, was a guest in New York City, Newark and Trenton, New Jersey for a month. Chiacchio, who was married to Lisia DeLucia, Paul's sister, was the mayor in the town of Grumo Nevano, just outside of Naples, Italy. The letter stated that Chiacchio managed to slip a suit case past Italian customs agents in Italy but the letter did not say what was inside. It did mention Chiacchio was handing out many cigarette lighters and various other items from Italy while in Newark, New Jersey. Later investigation determined that Michelangelo was visiting a Gaetano Chiacchio who operated the Hudson Garden Restaurant at 419 Hudson Street, Trenton, New Jersey.

One report suggested that Paul DeLucia simply liked airplanes and airports but was to afraid to fly because he feared a plane being hijacked and taken to Cuba were he would be released and not be allowed to re-enter the United States.

Spot Surveillance 1966

January 23, 1966 – Paul DeLucia is arrested at O'Hare Airport on a traffic violation of speeding. DeLucia said he was there to "pick someone up" from an international flight but refused to name who it was he was picking up.

February 1966 – Paul DeLucia and Tony Accardo are seen at Passavant Hospital visiting mobster John Matassa who was recovering from a second heart-attack.

February 14, 1966 – Paul DeLucia, Ben Fillichio and Tony Accardo observed at Meo's Norwood House. The discussion was about the anniversary of the St. Valentine's Day Massacre. All are heard laughing.

February 17, 1966 – Paul DeLucia, Tony Accardo and Dominic "Butch" Blasi sat in a court room watching a Federal Grand Jury hearing involving Fifi Buccieri and Charles "Chuckie" English.

May 3, 1966 – Paul DeLucia, Gus Alex, Hy Godfrey and Ralph Pierce meet to discuss Outfit business. It was believed that since the deaths of Murray Humphreys and Frank Ferraro, Ralph Pierce had taken over some of the responsibility of Humphreys for strategy to be used in legal situations involving heads of organized crime.

July 21, 1966 – DeLucia and Tony Accardo are at Meo's Norwood House and meet with a man who looks like a small jockey weighing about 130 pounds. This little man is always present at Meo's when DeLucia and Accardo are present and is always included in most of their conversations.

December 5 & 6, 1966 – Paul DeLucia, Tony Accardo, Nick Palermo and Jackie Cerone arrive together at Prignano Funeral Home at 1815 North Avenue in Melrose Park for the wake of mob lawyer Joseph Bulger who was killed in a plain crash in Tennessee.

By 1967 Sam Giancana was hiding out of the country in his mansion in Mexico and Sam Battaglia, who had no choice in taking over running the day-to-day operations of the Outfit, was locked up in jail. It was reported at the time that Tony Accardo and Paul DeLucia wanted either Jackie Cerone or Fifi Buccieri to take over as day-to-day boss but both Accardo and DeLucia saw a disturbing pattern arising. One informant told the FBI that Paul DeLucia was handling the affairs of organized crime until a solution could be found. The solution was Tony Accardo would once again become day-to-day boss of the Chicago mob.

Once again like before, both DeLucia and Accardo were attempting to keep the organization from breaking into disgruntled factions which would make the entire organization extremely vulnerable to investigations. Both Accardo and DeLucia wanted the factions inside the Outfit to get along. Had Tony Accardo and Paul

DeLucia not joined together and assumed their old roles again faction wars were certain.

Even older FBI informants had nothing good to say about the Chicago Outfit in 1967. One long-time Outfit member who was ratting on his friends told the FBI that the "Outfit" as he knew it was so different than the Outfit he knew under Al Capone, Paul DeLucia and Tony Accardo, that he did not believe there was a future for the mob. He said that under Capone, DeLucia and Accardo their loyalty and honor were the prerequisites, where, as of 1967, the younger members were comprised of a "bunch of animals" that had no morals or scruples.

On January 9, 1967 an FBI informant attended the wake of Chicago Police Captain Ralph Cantonese at the Montclair Funeral home at 6901 West Belmont Avenue in Chicago. This informant said that Paul DeLucia had shown up and looked in bad shape. He did not recognize his friends anymore and the talk going around the funeral home was that DeLucia was having a nervous breakdown and was going "berserk" from the pressure against him by the FBI and other agencies. The informant watched as DeLucia sat in a chair in a "trance-like" state.

It was also learned that Paul DeLucia was seeing a psychiatrist to try and help with the pressure on him. In March 1967 Paul DeLucia filed a lawsuit for derogatory judgment against the Attorney General in Washington D.C., alleging that the U.S. Government falsely represented to England and Italy that he, DeLucia, was an Italian citizen when in fact he was stateless. To advance his deportation even further, DeLucia's lawyers filed an injunction against additional deportation proceedings until this civil suit was resolved. However, the suit was dismissed by a Federal Judge.

On the other hand, the Italian tribunal had ruled in favor of DeLucia and he was declared a non-citizen of Italy. DeLucia's lawyer, Jack Wasserman, filed a petition in Rome asking the Italian government to declare that DeLucia was not a citizen of Italy. U.S. officials argued back to Italy that since DeLucia's naturalization in America was fraudulent that meant he was never a U.S. citizen and should have not lost his Italian citizenship. The Italians disagreed. The Italian government had nullified DeLucia's 45 year outstanding murder conviction.

The bad news is it would not stop the Italian government from accepting DeLucia when the U.S. deported him.

The next trick by DeLucia was to file a case in the U.S. Courts to declare himself a man who is stateless. He had lost his Italian citizenship in 1928 when he was granted citizenship in the U.S.

Since his U.S. citizenship was revoked he was now a man who belonged to no country, therefore he could not be deported from any country. With that came a refusal by the Italian Embassy to issue a travel authorization sending DeLucia back to Italy.

In May 1967 DeLucia was juggling court cases. His five-day perjury trial was underway because the government said DeLucia was lying when DeLucia told the immigration board that he won $80,159 while betting at the $10 windows at local race tracks. DeLucia had reported the income as miscellaneous on his 1963 income taxes.

The first trial was declared a mistrial because the jury was affected by prejudicial publicity. The second trial in November of that year produced a verdict of not guilty. After the not guilty verdict, then State's Attorney Edward V. Hanrahan charged the four witnesses in the trial, Marion Pacelli, James Picardi, Joe Krampat and mobster Eugene Albano with perjury. Pacelli, Picardi and Krampat were ticket sellers at the $10 windows who testified that they witnessed Paul DeLucia purchasing tickets on the day in question. Eugene Albano testified that he and mobster Guido DeChiaro accompanied DeLucia to the track that day and witnessed DeLucia win on the races.

Hanrahan had received a letter in the mail stating that the four men were paid $2,500 a piece by the Outfit for their testimonies. Even DeLucia's lawyer, Maurice J. Walsh, was placed under investigation from this trial when the government said Walsh claimed he obtained information from a man who had been dead 11 months before Walsh claimed to have met him.

In July 1967 Tony Accardo and William Daddono went to Miami Beach Florida to attend a meeting. An FBI informant said that Accardo left that meeting officially replacing Sam Giancana as the day-to-day boss of the Chicago Outfit. This informant who was a close friend of Tony Ricci's said that Ricci told him after this meeting that there had not been an interim boss in Chicago after Giancana was sentenced to jail and fled the country. This informant was also told by Ricci that Accardo was to share the responsibility for the Chicago family of the La Cosa Nostra with Paul DeLucia acting as the "Commission" representative. Accardo was "boss" and answerable only to DeLucia.

Another informant in Chicago who was close to mobster Joseph Ferriola told the FBI that a big "Outfit" meeting was held out in the western suburbs of Chicago on Memorial Day. Attending this meeting were Tony Accardo, Paul DeLucia, Jackie Cerone, Fifi Buccieri, Ross Prio and a few others who were representing Sam Giancana. It was at this meeting, according to the informant, that it was decided that Accardo and DeLucia would handle everything in the mob until the status of Sam Battaglia and William Daddono, who were both either in or on their way to prison, could be definitely determined.

Months later an informant told the FBI that the Outfit was being run by Tony Accardo through Jackie Cerone. Accardo, DeLucia and Cerone met daily where orders would be passed on to Cerone, who passed them on to Fifi Buccieri, who in turn passed them on to Gus Alex, Ross Prio and Phil Alderisio and they passed them on to all the little solders, to be executed. The informant also added that Phil Alderisio was present every day at Accardo's residence and that Alderisio could have been acting in the role as underboss along with Jackie Cerone.

Paul DeLucia would hold a meeting at least once a week with mobster Dominic "Butch" Blasi at the Golden Bear Pancake House on North Avenue. With Sam Giancana gone, Butch Blasi was handling both Giancana's and DeLucia's affairs in Chicago.

On September 30, 1967 Paul DeLucia's granddaughter Nancy Marie Ponzio was a debutante at the First Annual Columbus Day Cotillion held in the International

Ballroom of the Conrad Hilton Hotel in Chicago. Among those in attendance were Jackie Cerone and his family, John D'Arco and his family, Louis Briatta and his family, Alex Ponzio and his family, Frank "Frankie X" Esposito and his brother Anthony "Tony X" Esposito Sr. and his family. Honored guests of the night were:

His Excellency Most Reverend Aloysius A. Wycislo, D.D.
Very Reverend Salvatore DeVita, C.S.
The Honorable Frank Annunzio and Mrs. Annunzio
The Honorable Victor A. Arrigo and Mrs. Arrigo
Very Reverend Paul Asciolla, C.S.
The Honorable Louis Capuzi and Mrs. Capuzi
Dr. August Daro and Mrs. Daro
Deputy Consul General, Dr. Italo DiMarco and Mrs. DiMarco
Mr. and Mrs. Frank Esposito
Sister Mary Eugenia
Mrs. Serafina Ferrara
The Honorable Peter Granata and Mrs. Granata
Mr. and Mrs. John Hohenadle
The Honorable Roland Libonati and Mrs. Libonati
Sister Mary Marjorie
Mrs. Mary Meyer Muscato
The Honorable Parillo and Mrs. Parillo
Mr. and Mrs. Anthony Paterno
Mr. and Mrs. Charles Restano
Dean Philip Romiti and Mrs. Romiti
Dr. Mario O. Rubinelli and Mrs. Rubinelli
The Honorable Pasquale Sorrentino and Mrs. Sorrentino

The First Annual Columbus Day Cotillion

Organizations

25th WARD REGULAR DEMOCRATIC ORGANIZATION
LE PRIME DONNE
OUR LADY OF POMPEII CHURCH MOTHERS' GUILD
OUR LADY OF POMPEII CHURCH FATHERS' CLUB
OUR LADY OF POMPEII CHURCH HOLY NAME SOCIETY
OUR LADY OF POMPEII CHURCH SACRED HEART GUILD
OUR LADY OF POMPEII CHURCH CHRISTIAN MOTHERS
SANTA FE SADDLE AND GUN CLUB

Friends

REV. VALERIO BAGGIO, C. S.
TONY COZZI
MR. AND MRS. PAUL DE LUCIA, JR.
MR. FRANK ESPOSITO
PHIL AND ELEANOR GUZALDO
MR. AND MRS. ANTHONY F. MORELLI
MR. AND MRS. CARL MOSTACCI
MR. AND MRS. MIKE PALASTINE
MR. AND MRS. SAM SIGNORE
MR. AND MRS. SAVINO TIRITILLI
A FRIEND

Banks

BELLWOOD SAVINGS AND LOAN ASSOCIATION
NATIONAL BANK OF AUSTIN

Certified Public Accountants

D. B. BOOKKEEPING SERVICE
KWICK RECORDS
ANTHONY P. NUZZO AND COMPANY
MR. AND MRS. WILLIAM S. STRATTON
UNION REALTY AND MORTGAGE

Automobile Dealers

BUTTITTA BROTHERS
GRAND CENTRAL MERCURY

Parking Garages

DOWNTOWN PARKING
RENEE ASSOCIATES, INCORPORATED
TOWN PARKING STATIONS, INCORPORATED
WELLS-LAKE GARAGE CORPORATION
PISCOPO BROTHERS AUTO REPAIR

Debutante Cotillion

INTERNATIONAL BALLROOM
CONRAD HILTON HOTEL
SEPTEMBER 30, 1967

Nancy Marie Fonzio
Daughter of
Mr. and Mrs. Alex Ben Fonzio

The Debutantes	*and their Escorts*
PATRICIA ALBANO	JOHN TIRITILLI
MARIA AMBROSIA	ALEERT PETER BARTUCCI, JR.
MARY LOU BRIATTA	JOSEPH DAVID GIGANTE
LOIS ANN COSTABILE	NICHOLAS JOHN DI VITO
ANNA MARIE D'ARCO	PASQUALE F. DE LEO
THERESA DELAURENTIS	ALBERT L. DE BARTOLO, JR.
YVONNE DEL PRINCIPE	JOHN GENNARO
DEBRA JOYCE DEMMA	CLEM FIANDALO
CARMELINE TERESE DE VITO	BRYANT MINCY
SANDRA GRACE FORMUSA	JIM CERONE, JR.
LINDA LOU GRECO	PETER ANTHONY MAGNINE
DENISE MARIA GUARDINO	ROBERT A. DAVINO
JAN HOWARD	JOSEPH ANTHONY LANZITO
ROSE LOTORIA	MICHAEL J. ACCETTURA
MARIE ELENA MAGNINE	TED C. MAZOLA
VERA LYNN NUCCIO	LOUIS C. RUSSO
LUCILLE MARION NUZZO	CHRIS JOSEPH MESSINO
ANGELA ANTOINETTE PIRAGINE	GREGORY RICCIO
NANCY MARIE FONZIO	JOHN A. D'ARCO
SUSAN LYNN TARDI	DENNIS J. FORD
SANDRA VALENTINO	MICHAEL MARASCO
JOANNE ANGELA VIGILANTE	ROBERT W. ROWLEY

Spot Surveillance 1967

March 25, 1967 – Paul DeLucia's son's car is observed at the Edgewater Beach Hotel at 5349 North Sheridan Road in Chicago. Over 1,000 persons attended a $25-a-plate dance sponsored by the Santa Fe Saddle and Gun Club which was said to be controlled by mob boss Fifi Buccieri.

April 1967 – Paul DeLucia and Jackie Cerone head to New York to meet with East Coast mob bosses.

July 3, 1967 – Paul DeLucia, Tony Accardo and Jackie Cerone are seen together, Accardo and DeLucia drive to a medical clinic where DeLucia is seen entering the building for five minutes and then leaving.

August 29, 1967 – Paul DeLucia, Tony Accardo and Jackie Cerone drive out to Elgin, Illinois and have lunch at the Milk Pail Restaurant.

November 14, 1967 – Paul DeLucia's trial for perjury began. The incitement charged him with lying in his 1965 deportation hearings about the source of $80,159 he reported as "miscellaneous income" on his 1963 tax returns.

November 18, 1967 - Paul DeLucia is acquitted of his perjury indictment by a jury.

December 4, 1967 – Paul DeLucia was observed meeting with mobster Rocco Salvatore at the Golden Bear Pancake House at 7300 North Avenue in River Forest, Illinois. One informant said that DeLucia owned the land the restaurant was on and paid him $465-a-month rent when the land should have gone for over $2000-a-month rent based on the other property in the area.

December 5, 1967 – Paul DeLucia and Guido DeChiaro are subpoenaed to appear before a federal grand jury for testimony they gave in DeLucia's perjury trial.

December 6, 1967 – Paul DeLucia, Tony Accardo, Phil Alderisio, Ross Prio, and Leonard Gianola hold a meeting at Meo's Norwood House Restaurant.

In May 1968 Paul DeLucia's name was mentioned in the killing of Valerie Percy who had been killed in Kenilworth, Illinois on September 18, 1966. An unnamed person went to the FBI clamming Paul DeLucia had issued orders to have Percy kidnapped and unharmed so he could demand $4 million ransom for her release. No known action was taken with this information.

By August 1968 Paul DeLucia was watched almost daily as he had lunch at Armand's Restaurant on West Grand Avenue in Elmwood Park, Illinois. He was also a target to see if government agents could link DeLucia and the Outfit to known positions in Chicago. They did manage to get some evidence in May 1969 when Chicago detectives watched as mobsters Rocco Salvatore and Joe Rocco, who was the manager of mob boss Sam "Teetz" Battaglia's farm in Kane County Illinois, walked out of Paul DeLucia's house and drove to a vacant store front at 701 North Humphrey Avenue in Oak Park where they met with city politicians, delivering orders from Paul DeLucia. Also caught in the investigation was Anthony Fosco, an old 25th Ward Republican committeeman and one time Illinois State tax revenue investigator, meeting with Paul DeLucia at his pancake house in River Forest. Fosco was later arrested and charged with gambling.

At the end of 1968 and the beginning of 1969 Paul DeLucia was being mentioned in many investigations. He was being watched as he showed up almost nightly at 10:00pm at the Golden Bear Pancake House on North Avenue, just blocks from his home, to meet with various mobsters such as Rocco Salvatore and Guido DeChiaro. To make sure DeLucia had his booth available two men, both Italians, would show up to the restaurant hours before 10 o'clock and sit in the booth holding it until DeLucia showed up. Once DeLucia was there, the two men would leave.

There was speculation that DeLucia was meeting with Guido DeChiaro about new "juice" operations. FBI agents had been watching as up-and-coming mobster Frank "Frankie C" Calabrese would visit with DeChiaro at his house located at 1725 Thatcher Avenue in Elmwood Park, Illinois. At that time Frank Calabrese was becoming a power in the mob's "juice" loan operations. Calabrese would later become one of the Outfit's top killers.

Another situation on January 29, 1969 was when word was sent that an inmate in prison called for FBI agents because he had information on Paul DeLucia. This inmate told FBI agents that when he was confined to Terre Haute prison between 1960 and 1962 he became acquainted with Paul DeLucia in the prison common area. When DeLucia was being released he told this inmate to look him up when he gets out and he would put him to work. Months later when this inmate was released he called DeLucia asking for employment and DeLucia told him to meet at a bar on Mannheim Road in Stone Park. At this meeting DeLucia told him to drive to Mountain, Michigan and pick up a briefcase for him. The inmate did and when he returned to the same bar, DeLucia was sitting with Tony Accardo. After being introduced to Accardo and handing over the briefcase Accardo gave the man $200. Then DeLucia told the inmate he had another job for him. He was to meet with another man and kill two relatives at the same time. Once the hit was performed he would be paid $8,000. The inmate refused and said he was leaving town. After another short stint in prison, the inmate once again called DeLucia looking for work which DeLucia agreed to and sent him to a person in Cokomo, Indiana. The inmate said that he was making narcotic pick-ups for this man and believed Paul DeLucia was getting a cut of this operation. Later the inmate said that the two men DeLucia asked him to kill were found murdered in the trunk of a car because DeLucia and Accardo were suspicious of them stealing a shipment of narcotics from them. FBI agents were not sure what to make of this information since the inmate could not remember anyone's name other than DeLucia's and Tony Accardo's or where any of the locations he supposedly went to for these jobs. This inmate was sent back to prison until he asked to speak to agents once again. He said he was now giving up this information so his wife could get some money so she could come and visit him in prison. This information went no where.

Then in March 1969 Paul DeLucia's name came up in an investigation with criminal influence in the gasoline retailer's association of metropolitan Chicago. The gasoline retailer's association was a trade association consisting of twelve hundred gasoline service station owners representing some five thousand service stations in the Chicagoland area.

Paul DeLucia was a close personal friend of Eugene Albano and used Albano's bakery on the west side of Chicago as a prime meeting place for mobsters. This was the same Albano who testified in DeLucia's trial and was charged with perjury. Albano was a first cousin of mobster Joseph "Joe Shine" Amabile, and Paul DeLucia was Albano's Godfather. Albano's mother Millie was at one time Paul DeLucia's lover and after the relationship ended both stayed close friends. Eugene Albano, who was an executive director of the Gasoline Retailers Association of Metropolitan Chicago, would often pitch promotional ideas and contracts to members that would be favorable to Chicago hoodlums. For example, mob members who owned sign companies would be given all contracts for service station signs through the association. The wiring of these signs would be given to Louis Celano, brother of mob associate Jimmy Celano who owned Celano's Tailor Shop in Chicago where Tony Accardo and Paul DeLucia would hold Outfit meetings. Louis Celano was a union official of Chicago's Electrician Union Local 134. Albano once proposed that all asphalt paving work that had to be done involving service stations and the association's members properties was to be given to mobster Frank "Frankie X" Esposito who owned a private asphalt company. Another involved business was being steered to mobsters David Yaras and Nick Bravos who owned A1 Uniform Company which supplied lines and uniforms to all gas stations in the Chicagoland area. There was an oil additive marketed by Andy Granatelli, then a race car driver who won the Indianapolis five hundred car race, that was being pushed on members. Granatelli was not a member of organized crime but had mob connections. Albano and DeLucia would take a "cut" from the kick-backs on all these deals.

Back in February 1968 Paul DeLucia and Eugene Albano were observed almost every Saturday night at the Albano Bake Shop located at 7816 North Avenue in Elmwood Park, Illinois. There a large-scale card game would be held.

Another bad thing for DeLucia in 1969 started in October 1968 when the United States Attorney was given permission to grant immunity to Paul DeLucia in a Federal Grand jury that would wind up being the launching point of the government's interstate transportation and gambling conspiracy trial against Jackie Cerone.

DeLucia was summoned to answer questions before a Federal Grand Jury headed by Chief Justice William Campbell. The plan was that when DeLucia hid behind the Fifth Amendment to all questions placed to him, like all good mobsters do, he would be granted immunity which meant he could never be charged with any crime he talked about or he could never be criminally charged for being involved in any crime he discussed with the exception of perjury. If DeLucia refused to answer under granted immunity, he would be charged in contempt of court and taken to jail where he would have to sit until he answered the questions placed to him. DeLucia's attorney fired back, stating that the government was using the "immunity" situation as a means not to gather information but rather to create a situation where DeLucia would be imprisoned without a trial before a jury or without being formally charged with a crime which would not interfere with DeLucia's other cases.

After six appearances before the Grand Jury throughout December 1969, DeLucia talked, he talked so much that other witnesses such as mobsters Fiore "Fifi" Buccieri and Gus Alex, who were there to testify on subpoenas, had to be moved since DeLucia was talking hours a day. But what was he saying? He was attempting to talk enough to stay out of jail but not enough to be killed by his mob pals. After the six appearances Jackie Cerone, Donald "Don Angle" Angelini and Frank Aureli were indicted on interstate gambling charges. Many said after the indictments were issued that DeLucia may have said too much by the way of DeLucia giving what seemed to be innocent answers to innocent questions which gave basic facts the government needed for the indictments. This did not make the up-and-comers in the Outfit very happy.

The feared subpoena hung over DeLucia's head about the up and coming interstate trial of his mob pals until April 1970 when he was scheduled to appear.

Jackie Cerone had been arrested in the driveway of Paul DeLucia's home in River Forest by FBI agents in February 1969. DeLucia was walking to Cerone's car when Cerone was there to pick DeLucia up for a meeting. When agents told DeLucia they were there just for Cerone, DeLucia was beyond happy that he was not the target and walked back into his house.

DeLucia was served with the subpoena while he was in Oak Park hospital being treated for a fractured pelvis from a fall he took on April 8th. DeLucia's attorney, Maurice Walsh, attempted to quash the subpoena, calling for DeLucia's appearance as a government witness on the grounds that DeLucia was in Oak Park Hospital with a fractured pelvis but was denied by Judge Abraham Marovitz. Then Walsh had DeLucia's orthopedic surgeon testify that because DeLucia was a diabetic, clearance was needed first from DeLucia's doctor in order to get permission for DeLucia to testify due to his health problem. The judge did not buy that excuse and ordered DeLucia to testify.

On April 28th, 1970 DeLucia appeared in court being brought there by an ambulance, wheeled into court on an ambulance bed, and then placed into a wheelchair wearing a tan robe over blue striped pajamas. First DeLucia tried to take the Fifth Amendment to every question placed to him. Then the judge granted DeLucia immunity and it was either answer the questions or jail. DeLucia furnished his name, address and record of felony conviction before being asked questions about Jackie Cerone. After being labeled as a hostile witness he answered questions about his association with Cerone. When asked if he had ever seen Cerone in a red turtleneck sweater DeLucia replied, *"He wears a lot of things. He's a snappy dresser. He can wear anything."*

The government's main witness in the case against Cerone was Louis Bombacino. Most of the questions placed to DeLucia were about Bombacino's testimony.

DeLucia admitted he dined regularly with Cerone at Meo's Norwood House in 1966 and that the two had been friends for over twenty-five years. Louis Bombacino had told the authorities that he had dinner with Jackie Cerone and Paul Ricca at Meo's Restaurant that year. When DeLucia was shown a photo of Bombacino, he refused to identify or admit he knew who Bombacino was. Then the prosecution brought in Bombacino and had him stand three feet from DeLucia. He told the court he did not think he knew Bombacino but later admitted that Bombacino's face was familiar and that he may have known him. In the end the government felt DeLucia's testimony strongly substantiated Bombacino's testimony and was a very important part of the trial presentation as to Jackie Cerone's involvement in organized crime.

Spot Surveillance 1968-1969

July 25, 1968 – Tony Accardo and Paul DeLucia were observed at the wake of Anthony Colianni at Montclair Funeral Home. Anthony, the son of Carlo Colianni, was muscle man for the Master Barbers Association. The wake was a star-studded affair and both DeLucia and Accardo met with mobsters Jackie Cerone, Charles Nicoletti, Joseph Gagliano, Guido DeChiaro, Louis Briatta, Sam Cesario, Joey Aiuppa, William Messino, Joseph Ferriola, James Catuara, Bernard Morgano, Anthony Gruttadauro, James Caporale, Sam DiGiovanni, Joe Verriola, Angelo Froio, Dom "Lee" Laino, Frank Traficanti, Biagio "Blessie" Messino, Dan Miroballi, George Dicks, Max Inserro, James Marcello, Anthony Pinelli, Ernie Sansone, Rocco Potenzo and mob lawyer Mike Brodkin.

September 10, 1968 – Paul DeLucia was observed meeting individuals at the Golden Bear Pancake House at 7300 North Avenue in River Forest, Illinois.

November 4, 1968 – Paul DeLucia, Tony Accardo, Jack Cerone, Phil Alderisio, Northern Indiana mob boss Anthony Pinelli and New York and Miami mob boss Anthony Ricci were all observed meeting at Meo's Norwood House Restaurant in Harwood Heights, Illinois. After the meeting police followed Alderisio driving Pinelli to a rundown hotel on Cicero Avenue.

November 19, 1968 – Tony Accardo, Nick Nitti and Anthony Ricci arrive at O'Hare Airport in Chicago returning from Italy. With them is Emilia DeLucia, Paul's sister, who came to visit her brother.

November 20, 1968 – Tony Accardo, Jackie Cerone, Tony Ricci and Paul DeLucia hold a meeting at Meo's Norwood House Restaurant.

December 9, 1968 – Emilia DeLucia, while staying at her brothers home in River Forest, is summoned to appear before an Immigration hearing to show cause why her visitor's visa shouldn't be revoked. The government claimed she falsely stated on her application for the visa if she had ever been convicted of a felony. Since she was found guilty in Italy for murder and served time in prison, she was going to be arrested in the U.S. Instead of answering the summons, she boarded a plane and fled America back to Italy.

April 3, 1969 – Paul DeLucia is picked up by Guido DeChiaro and driven to the Chicago Loop area. There DeLucia meets with mob lawyers Eugene Bernstein and Maurice Walsh.

April 4, 1969 - Paul DeLucia was driven by his son to Meo's Norwood House Restaurant in Harwood Heights, Illinois. There he met mobster "Milwaukee Phil" Alderisio for a four hour meeting and was later driven home by Alderisio. DeLucia wore a blue and white checkered sports coat with a tan coat and Alpine hat.

May 2, 1969 – Tony Accardo, Paul DeLucia, Phil Alderisio and Jackie Cerone hold a meeting at Meo's Norwood House Restaurant. With Tony Accardo doing most of the talking, a Chicago Tribune report overheard Accardo saying, *"You can't go anywhere these days without there being a lot of cops."* At the end of the meeting fashion show models came to sit with the boys and DeLucia attempted to make a pass at one of the brunette models but he was turned down and she just held his hand.

May 7, 1969 – Paul DeLucia, Vince Solano, Ross Prio and Jackie Cerone held a meeting at Meo's Norwood House Restaurant. Solano was Prio's bodyguard and driver who held a no-show day job as the president of Chicago's International Hod Carriers Union Local 1.

May 8, 1969 – Paul DeLucia, Ross Prio and Vince Solano held a meeting at Meo's Norwood House Restaurant. DeLucia was overheard saying, *"No, he was a good Jew"* and *"If he tries that, he's dead."*

May 9, 1969 – Jackie Cerone, Paul DeLucia and Phil Alderisio held a day time meeting at Meo's Norwood House Restaurant.

May 13, 1969 – Paul DeLucia meets with mob boss Ross Prio and Vince Solano at Meo's Norwood House Restaurant.

May 14, 1969 – Just Paul DeLucia and Jackie Cerone eat lunch together at Meo's Norwood House Restaurant.

May 15, 1969 – Vince Solano, Ross Prio and Paul DeLucia hold a meeting at Meo's.

May 16, 1969 – Jackie Cerone and Paul DeLucia meet at Meo's for a meeting. DeLucia was wearing baggy pants and a checkered shirt. Cerone called some of the fashion models over to his table to inspect the clothes and the women wearing

them. However, DeLucia was not in the mood for models that day.
July 3, 1969 – Paul DeLucia is observed at the wake of Dominic Alderisio, father of mob boss Felix "Milwaukee Phil" Alderisio.

July 14, 1969 – Paul DeLucia is observed at the wake of mobster Nick Bravos held at Marzullo Funeral Home.

July 16, 1969 – Paul DeLucia, Jackie Cerone and Tony Accardo are observed at the wake of mob labor leader Anthony "Tony X" Esposito Sr. at Galewood Funeral Home on Harlem Avenue.

August 5, 1969 – Miami mobster Anthony Ricci spent the night at Paul DeLucia's home at 1515 North Bonnie Brae in River Forest.

November 12, 1969 – Paul DeLucia, Jackie Cerone, Frank LaPorte and Tony Accardo meet at Meo's Norwood House for a meeting.

Chapter 16

The New Outfit

There were many problems for the Outfit in the 1970's. Paul DeLucia and Tony Accardo experienced troubles maintaining control of the lower echelon mobsters.

DeLucia was mostly concerned with the situation with the diminution of income from one of the mob's longest and most reliable sources of easy income, its income from labor unions.

From 1940 to 1969 Paul DeLucia had one of his men in control of Chicago's largest work force. Frank "Frankie X" Esposito and his brother Anthony "Tony X" Esposito Sr. had controlled the Chicago District Council of Labor and the street labors union Local 1001 consisting of thousands of men paying labor dues that made its way into the pocket of Paul DeLucia. Both Esposito's were under the DeLucia faction and both died in 1969. One of Tony Accardo's men, Joseph Spingola, had taken over the unions until Frankie X's nephew, Anthony "Sonny" Esposito Jr., could gain some time and regain the presidency of the unions that would put it back into the hands of the DeLucia faction. However, this did not work when Sonny Esposito was set up by mob turncoat Charles "Chuckie" Crimaldi in a drug sting ending the Esposito's chance of control for both Local 1001 and the Chicago District Council of labor. Joseph Spingola remained in control of the union until the 1980's.

For the first time in thirty five-years the DeLucia faction was no longer in control of Local 1001. Besides the Esposito brothers, most of the other officers in the local were in the DeLucia faction. Those members consisted of Anthony Gianfrancesco, the union's vice president, and Thomas Crivellone, the union's sergeant-at-arms and later vice president when Gianfrancesco died in 1968.

For many years DeLucia relied on the practice of organized crime controlling labor unions in Chicago. Periodically these labor unions would strike a major manufacturer and then have one of their lawyers, like mob lawyer Sidney Korshak, make a contact with the plant owners discreetly and bid for an under-the-table payoff of money, which when paid, would end the striking labor men. Chicagoans now call it "pay-to-play" which has become the common daily routine of Illinois politics. The money would then wind up in the hands of DeLucia and other mob bosses and the corrupt labor union bosses.

By the summer of 1971 many of the Chicago labor unions who in the past had been under the control of the Chicago mob had resisted the leaders of organized crime, feeling that the climate was not right to continue with such practices listed above. With the reluctance of its own members in the unions to create this income, the money stopped flowing in and the leaders of organized crime lost some of their influence.

One informant for the FBI said that in Chicago during 1970 there were two organized crime groups, the DeLucia group and the Accardo group. According to this informant, the go-between between the two groups was Alex "Bennie" Ponzio, DeLucia's son-in-law. This informant said that Bennie Ponzio had become very powerful and held a position high in mob circles. Ponzio was also a business partner with Tony Accardo. This informant said of the three, Ponzio, Accardo or DeLucia owned a huge warehouse building 40-miles west of Chicago where all the stolen or "hot" merchandise was stored.

Another informant said that by 1970 Bennie Ponzio was operating a pizza place at 4224 West Chicago Avenue in Chicago, owned eight parking lots in the Loop of Chicago and was in control of mob "hit men" who the informant believed were some Chicago policemen. Ponzio's close associates were listed as Tony Accardo, Charles "Chuckie" English and William "Wee Willie" Messino. The informant added that Ponzio was running a "juice" loan racket with the monies obtained from the operation of the parking lots with Paul DeLucia.

Ponzio's Town Parking Stations company was exposed in November 1970 when it was learned that he received a real estate property assessment reduction of almost $70,000 in 1969 when four of their neighbors' assessments were increased. This was not something new in Cook County, both the mansions of Tony Accardo and Jackie Cerone paid lower assessments than their neighbors. It seemed the Cook County assessor's office gave breaks to millionaire mobsters.

In July 1970 both Paul DeLucia and Tony Accardo were summoned to appear before a secret federal grand jury in Los Angeles, California which was investigating skimming and mob control of the Silver Slipper Casino in Las Vegas. Both appeared before the committee for 10 minutes each while being questioned about "skimming" the total profits of Las Vegas casinos under the direction of the Chicago Outfit before the totals of money taken in was reported to the government. Both men refused to answer any questions.

Two months earlier both DeLucia and Accardo were listening to a pitch by a Los Angeles attorney to have both men become hidden investors in the Deauville Hotel and Casino in Las Vegas.

In April 1971 both Paul DeLucia and Tony Accardo called a meeting and summoned mob boss Ross Prio. The message to the Capone-era gangster with 45 years of syndicate experience--straighten up your rackets or else. No one was being spared scrutiny from the top guys.

In September 1971 a meeting was called at the Caravelle Motel in Rosemont, Illinois to discuss the future leadership of the Chicago Outfit. In attendance were Paul DeLucia, Tony Accardo, Ross Prio and Joey Aiuppa. Accardo and DeLucia had been grooming Felix "Milwaukee Phil" Alderisio but he died. Both Accardo and DeLucia had held a previous meeting at Meo's Restaurant with Frank "The Horse" Buccieri, James "Turk" Torello and mob boss Fifi Buccieri to discuss the possible succession of Fifi who was in very bad health and not expected to live very long. Since Sam Giancana had left Chicago in 1966 the spot of day-to-day boss was up for grabs. Sam Battaglia, Jackie Cerone and William Daddono all went to prison while Fifi Buccieri and Phil Alderisio either died or was about to die. Their decision was to form a leadership board with four men with the sole purpose of exploring and considering investments of Outfit money in legitimate areas and businesses. The four picked to head this board were Paul DeLucia, Tony Accardo, Joey Aiuppa and Charles Nicoletti. Also agreed on was to put in a good effort and stand on a non-violence attitude, refuse to "lose their cool" and refrain from unnecessary "hits" in an attempt to "keep the ship afloat."

In November 1971 Paul DeLucia, his son Paul Jr., Tony Accardo and his son Anthony Ross Accardo, went down to Miami, Florida to watch the Chicago Bears play against the Miami Dolphins. Law enforcement watched as an old-time Chicago bookmaker by the name of Joseph Sonken took care of the DeLucia's and Accardo's every need. They were treated like gods at Sonken's place known as the Gold Coast Restaurant in Hollywood, Florida. Sonken once ran the Devonshire Lounge on Chicago's North Side where he ran his gambling operation along with mobsters Ross Prio and Jimmy "Monk" Allegretti. He was also involved in the Chicago scene being close to mob union boss Gus Zappas.

In August 1972 Paul DeLucia had to tell mob boss Gus Alex that he was not allowed to leave Chicago. Alex wanted "out" of the mob and asked for permission to move to Florida to "retire" from the rackets. Paul DeLucia told him "no" because Alex was one of the top "brains" in the Outfit and he had too many connections in Chicago's Loop area and had control over the "Greek Mafia."

By this time Paul DeLucia was very sick due to complications from diabetes and other ailments. For months leading up to the death of Paul DeLucia, he was observed many times attending several meetings at Tony Accardo's house in River Forest. He spent most of his days waiting for Tony Accardo to pick him up as the two would go and have lunch and discuss who would live, who would die and how much more money could they steal by just giving the word without actually doing anything.

DeLucia's personality could change in a heartbeat. Looking at DeLucia, he looked like your nice old grandfather who had little to say and would occasionally smile as a sweet old man. But the real DeLucia was a killer at heart. DeLucia was once best described by a reporter who witnessed an incident at Meo's Restaurant one day. DeLucia arrived, walked up to the bar and waited for the bartender to serve him his drink. However there was a new bartender working the bar who was peeling lemons while DeLucia waited. Finally after a while the bartender walked over to DeLucia to ask him what kind of drink he wanted, DeLucia just stared at the bartender with fire in his eyes. He told the bartender with the wrath of god in his voice, *"Ok you son-of-a-bitch, I'm going to tell you this only one time. When I come up to this bar, you drop everything. You get here right away. You drop it all. You get here right away! Do you understand me?"* The frightened bartender scared out of his mind in fear said, "*Yes Sir Mr. Ricca, Yes Sir.*"

Spot Surveillance 1970-1972

May 13, 1970 – Ross Prio, Tony Accardo, Paul DeLucia and Jackie Cerone held a meeting at Meo's Norwood Home Restaurant.

November 2, 1970 – Paul DeLucia was observed in attendance at a wedding reception at the Sheraton Blackstone Hotel in Chicago. DeLucia was observed in the company of Tony Accardo, Rocco Potenzo, Sam Cesario, Dominic "Butch" Blasi, Sam Samarco and Frank Buccieri.

January 22, 1971 – Paul DeLucia, Tony Accardo and Ross Prio meet at Meo's Restaurant for a meeting.

April 8, 1971 – Paul DeLucia, Tony Accardo and Ross Prio have lunch at the La Chimenee Restaurant at 1157 North Dearborn Avenue in Chicago.

May 20, 1971 – Agents observed Paul DeLucia, Tony Accardo, Ross Prio and Dom DiBella having a meeting at Meo's Norwood House Restaurant. After the meeting Prio and DiBella drove to the Cosmopolitan National Bank at 801 North Clark Street in Chicago and entered a private office inside the bank.

July 24 to August 3, 1971 – Paul DeLucia enters Michael Reese Hospital in Chicago for an illness.

September 27, 1971 – A sick Paul DeLucia attended the wake of mobster Phil Alderisio at Montclair Funeral home.

December 14, 1971 – Paul DeLucia attended the wake of Joseph "Joe Gags" Gagliano.

January 5, 1972 – Paul DeLucia and Tony Accardo attended the wake of Joseph Priolo at Montclair Funeral Home.

Chapter 17

Death

In 1972 Paul DeLucia's health was beginning to fail and he spent a good portion of the year not being able to do very much. On October 11, 1972 Paul DeLucia died at 12:25 in the afternoon at Presbyterian St. Luke's Hospital in Chicago. The cause of death was from a heart ailment. The last person said to see Paul DeLucia alive was mobster Joey Glimco.

Within one hour of his death, Chicago Police went by DeLucia's house and parked down the street to see what activity was going to occur within the first few hours of his death. Three mobsters showed up and went into the house. The first was Leslie "Killer Kane" Kruse, an upper echelon leader in the Outfit who controlled organized crime in Lake County, Illinois. Then mobster John "Big John" Cimitile showed up, Cimitile was a made man in the DeLucia faction who had been close to DeLucia for a few decades. The last to show up was Clarence Jalas, then president of Local 110 of the Moving Picture Operators Union in Chicago. Police did not know what their function at DeLucia's house was, but at the time when someone would die, burglars and thieves would rob a house because they knew no one would be there when everyone was at the wake or funeral. With the amount of cash and jewels DeLucia had in his home, it was believed the three men were armed and at the

From the Collection of T.M.

house to protect it. But it was just speculation.

The wake was held at Galewood Funeral Chapel at 1835 North Harlem Avenue in Chicago, Illinois on October 12 and 13, 1972. Galewood Funeral Home was owned by Frank Granata who was a member of the DeLucia faction in the Chicago mob and was related to Paul DeLucia by marriage. His son, Frank Granata Jr., was a member of the Outfit's Elmwood Park Crew and another son, Joseph Granata, was a member of the Outfit's Cicero Crew under mob boss Joseph Ferriola. In the early 1990's Joseph Granata became a government rat and was used as a witness in many mob and mob-related court cases. He had been in and out of prison and was even allegedly kicked out of the FBI's witness protection program.

Before the wake, Tony Accardo and his wife Clarice had dinner with members of the DeLucia family at Horwath's Good Food Restaurant at 1850 North Harlem Avenue in Elmwood Park.

DeLucia was laid-out in a dark blue suit with a checkered tie, in a coffin covered in baby red roses. DeLucia's body was in parlor B of the funeral home while Tony Accardo occupied the parlor across the hall from him so when his mob subjects walked in they would kneel and say their good-bye's to DeLucia and then walk across the hall to pay homage to Accardo, now the top and only king of his empire.

The FBI received a report of the wake from one of their informants who attended the services. The informant said when he arrived he noticed that the two entrances to the funeral home were covered by the media and plain-clothe detectives from the Chicago PD. This informant then had to park many blocks away from the funeral home so his license plate would not be written down by detectives. He noticed many of the hoodlums attending the wake took rented cars and taxi cabs. As the informant reached the funeral home, he was greeted outside by Louis "Lou the Barber" Briatta. As he shook the hand of Briatta, a newspaper reporter snapped their photo but none of mobsters were bothered by that action and continued to talk briefly outside before entering.

Once inside Tony Accardo was acting as the official "greeter" shaking the hands of everyone who entered. This informant told the FBI that almost every mobster he knew in the city of Chicago and its surrounding areas either was there or was said to be there.

The informant said while he was inside he was greeted by the nephew of Joey Aiuppa, who at the time was a lawyer and a magistrate in Melrose Park, Illinois. As the two talked, Aiuppa's nephew told the informant that Joey Aiuppa was now an important leader in the organization and that since DeLucia's death was not unexpected that over the previous six months DeLucia, Accardo and Aiuppa had held many meetings to make sure the transition was a smooth one. The only top Chicago mobster that was not seen or believed to be there was Sam Giancana.

The general observation was that not one person at the wake or funeral shed one tear. No one cried or felt they lost someone special, and one unidentified person standing against the wall as a Catholic priest gave a eulogy mumbled, *"Let's bury him, already."* Another mourner, a woman, mumbled, *"For Christ's sake, what's he gonna do, keep talking about Jesus for the whole hour? He ain't mentioned Paul's name once."*

According to the Chicago Police Department, here is a list of some of the mobsters and associates who attended Paul DeLucia's wake.

INTELLIGENCE DIVISION

CHICAGO POLICE DEPARTMENT

OBSERVATION OR SURVEILLANCE REPORT

CASE

DATE OF SURVEILLANCE: 12-13-14 October 1972

DATE OF REPORT 13 Nov, 1972

SUBJECT MATTER OF INVESTIGATION
WAKE OF PAUL DeLUCIA (RICCA)
Galewood Funeral Chapel
1857 North Harlem Ave.
Chicago, Illinois

TYPE OF SURVEILLANCE
Fixed

INVESTIGATORS

PURPOSE OF SURVEILLANCE OR OBSERVATION

TIME OR LICENSE NO.	OBSERVATION OR IDENTIFICATION OR DESCRIPTION

The following is a list of visual personal identifications of persons attending the wake and/or funeral of the deceased SUBJECT at the Galewood Funeral Chapel, 1857 North Harlem Avenue, on 12-13-14 October 1972.

Tony & Clarice Accardo
Joseph Accardo
Joey Aiuppa
Eugene Albano
Gus Alex
Sam Alex
Joseph Allegretti
Joe "Black Joe" Amato
Anthony Amendo
Richard Bernas
Dominic "Butch" Blasi
Anthony Bova
Lawrence "Lou" Brady
Dom Brancato
Joseph Briatta
Louis "Lou the Barber" Briatta
Mike Briatta
Thomas Briatta
Rocco Caifano
Andrew Carsello
Frank "Skids" Caruso
Joseph "Shoes" Caruso
James 'The Bomber" Catuara
Jackie Cerone
Jack Cerone Jr.
Michelangelo & Lisia Chiacchio (Sister and Brother-in-law)
John "Big John" Cimitile
Thomas Crivellone
John D'Arco Sr.
Guido DeChiaro
Anthony Paul DeLucia (Son)
Paul DeLucia Jr. (Son)
Nancy DeLucia (Wife)
John DiBiase
Dom DiBella
Charles "Spec" DiCaro
George Dicks
Joseph "Caesar" DiVarco
Ralph Emery
Charles English
Anthony "Sonny" Esposito Jr.
Joseph "Puddy" Esposito
Albert "Obie" Frabotta
Sam Faruggia
Leonard "Needles" Gianola
Edward Gigante
Mario Gigante
Mary Gigante (Sister-in-law)
Richard Gigante
Salvatore Gagliano
Gus Giovenco
Joey GlimcoEnrico & Clementina Iervolino (Brother-in-law and Sister)

Mob Boss

Max Inserro
Vincent "Saint" Inserro
Clarence Jalas
Leslie "Killer Kane" Kruse
Louis Lombardo
Joseph Lucania
Vincent Lucania
Leo Manfredi
Pat Marcy
Paul Marcy
Ralph Marterie
Joseph Masse
John Matassa Sr.
Albert Meo
William "Wee Willie" Messino
Vito Moretti
Frank Mulea
Dominic Nuccio
Charles Nicosia
Joe Nicosia
Frank Orlando
Frank Pantaleo
Ralph Pierce
Anthony Pinelli
Alex Ponzio (Son-in-law)
Maria Ponzio (Daughter)
Ross Prio
Larry Rassano
Anthony "Gobels" Ricci
Fred Roti
Frank Roti
Ernest Sansone
Ralph Scaccia
Dominic Senese
Vince Solano
Vince Solano Jr.
Joseph Spingola
Lawrence Taormina
James "Turk" Torello
Frank Trumfio
Ray Vogel
Maurice Walsh

Some of the company cars used to hide the occupants

Able Construction
A-1 Industrial Wall Frame
Anco Insurance Company
Baciagalupo Funeral Home
John R. Boyle Associates
Central Glass Company
Co-Op Music Company
DiNicolo Funeral Home
D.L Peterson Trust Company
Dominos Pastry Incorporated
Granata Funeral Home
Great Atlantic / Pacific Tea Company
Gregg Motor Sales
Growers Fruit Distributors
Harmon Electric Company
House Doctor Company
Kenosha Motors Company
Lipin Enterprise Company
Chicago District Council
Leco Manufacturing CompanyJohn C. Long Incorporated
A J Lowe / Son Company
Mayo Plumbing Company
McHenry County Tobacco & Candy Company
National Republic Bank
Norwood House Corporation
Park Avenue Realty Company
Pearl Brewing Company
Professional Tape Company
John Rago Sons Funeral Home
Stroll-O-Chair Company
Susco Systems Company
Chicago Taxi Cab Union Local 777
Chicago Truck Drivers Union Local 705
Town Parking Stations
Sewer and Tunnel Miners Union
Warehouse Mail Order Employees Union
West Suburban Florist
20 different auto leasing companies

The next day, October 14, 1972, the family wanted a Catholic funeral mass to be held but was turned down by the Catholic Church because DeLucia was a mobster.

The procession from Galewood Funeral home consisted of 125 cars as they drove by DeLucia's mansion one last time at 1515 N. Bonnie Brae Avenue in River Forest. The procession headed to Queen of Heaven Cemetery in Hillside, Illinois where DeLucia was interned at the Sacred Heart Mausoleum. Once they arrived at the mausoleum, mobsters Tony Accardo, Leo Manfredi, Frank "Skids" Caruso and Joey Aiuppa stood up front as DeLucia's coffin was carried into the chapel for his final send-off by a Catholic priest who gave the words of "forgiveness" in God's eyes for a life of killing and greed and not playing by the rules of society. Paul DeLucia was buried in a luxurious $23,000 Italian marble covered vault in the mausoleum. It was somewhat of a private room being right next to the main stairwell on the bottom floor.

On the way out of the mausoleum, Tony Accardo noticed a newspaper reporter who he knew. The reporter asked Accardo for a comment about the funeral, Accardo put his arm around the reporter and said, *"Just say I lost the greatest and finest friend that a man could ever have."*

Many of the Outfit members left the funeral and headed to the Red Fox Restaurant at 6400 W. North Avenue in Oak Park for the funeral lunch which was a tradition among mob members.

In January 1975 Paul's wife, Nancy DeLucia, entered St. Luke's Presbyterian Hospital and died on the 17th of that month. Like her husband, she was waked at Galewood Funeral Home on Harlem Avenue and buried next to her husband in the mausoleum.

Paul DeLucia's Sacred Heart Mausoleum vault, they are on the right of this photo

Mob Boss

White and black Italian marble hides the DeLucia name

Tony Dark

File Card

Paul DeLucia
Real Name Pablo DeLucia
AKA Felice DeLucia *(Felice means "happiness of spirit" in Italian)*
AKA Paul Ricca
AKA Paul Richard De Lucia
AKA Felice Maglio
AKA Paolo Maglio
AKA Paul Maglio
AKA The Waiter
AKA Paul Salvy and Salvi
AKA Paul Villa
AKA Paul Viela
AKA Paul DeLucca
AKA Paul Ricci
AKA Papa Paul
AKA The Old Man
AKA The Barber
AKA The War Department
AKA Paul Barstow
AKA Pete
AKA Paul Serte
AKA Paul Reach
AKA Poopsie *(DeLucia called this by Sam Battaglia in 1960, recorded on a hidden mic)*

From the Collection of T.M.

Birth

Claimed to be born on July 10, 1898 in Apricena, Italy. He used this birth date on all his documents in America including his 1942 Selective Service Records. Some documents state he was born on January 14, 1897 in Apricena, Italy. Italian court records from his murder conviction and Italian records say his real birth date was November 14, 1897 being born in Naples, Italy.

The U.S. Government finally decided the following facts about Paul DeLucia:

Real name Felice DeLucia
Born November 14, 1897 in Naples, Italy
Entered U.S. illegally on August 12, 1920 using name Paul Maglio
Naturalized U.S. Citizen on September 27, 1928 in Chicago. Revoked June 1957

Died - October 11, 1972 *(Buried in Queen of Heaven Mausoleum in Hillside, Illinois. In a private room with his wife Nancy and son Anthony next to him. Below him are the Russo family, Vincent (1921-1991) Anna (1899-1973) Sandra*

(1928-2009). (Below the Russo's is mobster Pasty DiConstanzo)

Height - 5' 7"
Weight - 158 (1947)
Eyes - Brown
Hair - Brown then turned white then bald
Scars and Marks - 6" vertical scar on left thigh and crushed heel on right foot
Complexion - Dark, Shallow
Peculiarities - Spoke with a soft Italian accent
Religion - Roman Catholic
Occupation - Gambler
IQ Test - Scored a 101 (average intelligence)
FBI # 832514
Chicago PD Number - 4365
U.S. Penitentiary Atlanta, GA # 63776
Naturalized U.S. District Court, Chicago Docket # 55072
Certificate of Naturalization #2827322
Prison Record #63776-A

Education

Claimed 3 years of high school in Italy

Family

Father Antonio DeLucia (Said to have died in Italy in 1924)
Mother Maria Annunziata (Said to have died in Italy in 1917)

Sisters

Emilia Beatrice "Amelia", born 12-8-1898 *(Lived in Ottaviona, Italy in 1965)*
Anna, born 3-13-1901 *(Lived in Ottaviona, Italy in 1965)*
Clementina, born 5-23-1905 *(Lived in Genoa, Italy in 1965) (Married Enrico Iervolino)*
Luisa or Louisa, born 3-4-1907 *(Married Michelangelo Chiacchio, born 11-22-1906) (Lived at Corso Garibaldi Gruno Nivanio, Naples, Italy, in 1966)*

Wife

Nancy Emily Gigante, born October 2, 1905 in Naples, Italy. Father Ciro Gigante born in 1873 and her mother Anna Porzio born in 1876. She had seven brothers and one sister, named Mary A. Gigante, born around 1917 and lived with the DeLucia's in River Forest. She was an employee of the City of Chicago. Married January 3, 1927, she died in 2009. (Other spelling of last name Gigiante)

Known Brothers –in-laws

Dr, Leonard Gigante and Marie Gigante, 256 Washington Boulevard, Oak Park Illinois (1955)

Angelo Gigante, born around 1904 *(Owned and ran a boarding house in the 4300 block on North Sheridan Road)*

Patsy Gigante *(A motion picture projectionist in Local 110 who lived at 1928 North Oak Park Avenue. It was reported that Pasty attempted to obtain a job in the local in 1935 from Frank Clifford. When Clifford gave Pasty "the stall" he mentioned it to his brother-in-law Paul DeLucia. Soon after, DeLucia had a sit-down with Clifford Pasty and Patsy was ushered into the union)*

Mateo "Mack" Gigante, aka Mario *(One-time bookmaker, operator of a cocktail lounge known as the Picture Lounge at the corner of LaSalle Street and Lake Street in the Chicago Loop. He lived around the 5400 block of Jackson Boulevard in the 1940's; 6269 North Knox Street in Chicago in the 1950's; and 7522 W. Bryn Mawr in Chicago in the 1960's. He was a known associate of Sam "Sambo" Cesario and Michael Fillichio)*

Joseph Paul Gigante *(A movie projectionist at a movie theater in Local 110 since 1937 through his sponsor Frank Clifford. He was known to have worked at the York Theaters in Elmhurst, Illinois. He lived at 824 North Mozart Avenue, Chicago in the 1960's)*

Leonard Gigante *(A dentist who had offices at Angelo Gigiante's apartment building at 4300 N. Sheridan. It is possiable he went by the name of Jerry)*

John "Shorty" Curtis *(A 1951 FBI report listed a John Curtis as the brother-in-law of Paul DeLucia. Curtis was employed as a teletype operator by the Illinois Sports News wire service. No information was listed if this was true)*

Children

Anthony Paul (1929-1993)
Paul Richard, alleged to be born around April 27, 1938 and was in the U.S. Armed Forces. *(Married Mary Catherine Meatte in September 1964) (One report alleges he was born in Miami Beach, Florida)*
Marianna "Marie Anna" born around 1928 (Attended St. Lukes Resurrection High School and the University of Illinois. Married Alex "Bennie" Ponzio in 1948 held at the Blackstone Hotel in Chicago) (One known child, daughter Nancy Marie Ponzio)

Paul DeLucia's Alleged Military Service and Groups

Royal Italian Army, Honorable discharge January 2, 1920
Beneficial membership in Italo American National Union 11-25-1932

Known Addresses

917 Blue Island Avenue, Chicago (1927) *(Now an intersection of a road)*
4920 West Monroe Street, Chicago (1928)
901 South Halsted Street Chicago (1932) *(Now part of the University of Chicago)*
5300 West Jackson Boulevard, Chicago (1932-1939)
Long Beach, Indiana Mayfield (1935-1957)
3351 Lexington Street, Chicago (1938) *(Under name Paul Richard DeLucia)*
Stop 29, Long Beach, Michigan City, Indiana (1945)
Hog Farm, 1,100 acre farm in Kendall County, Illinois (1942-1951)
2940 Mount Claire Ways, Long Beach, Indiana (1950's)
812 North Lathrop Avenue, River Forest (1938-1957)
125 Ocean Parkway, Brooklyn, New York (1947)
1145 Harrison Street, Hollywood, Florida *(House rented by DeLucia 1953-1954)*
4385 Pine Tree Drive, Flamingo Bay Subdivision, Miami Beach, Florida (1954-1958)
420 Lincoln Road, Miami, Florida *(Used by DeLucia in 1955 as a business address)*
1515 Bonnie Brae, River Forest, Illinois (1956) *(First floor alleged to be occupied by Alex Ponzio, son-in-law. Second and third floors occupied by Paul and Nancy DeLucia) (1969 real estate taxes $4,680. 3-story brick and stone residence, reinforced concrete, elevator to third floor, 8 baths, all with marble walls, tiled kitchen, sun deck, office quarters, 4-car garage, air-conditioned "which was only for the wealth back then")*

Known Businesses

Blue Grotto Restaurant (1930's)
Vesuvia Restaurant, Chicago (1930's)
World Playhouse Sound Picture House, 410 South Michigan Avenue, Chicago (1933)
World Amusement Corporation, Chicago (1933-1940) *(Listed as Vice President)*
Old Falstaff Café, 543 South Wabash, Chicago (1930's)
Austin Liquors, Chicago (1960's) (Alleged partners with James Nuzzo & Louis Briatta)
Hollywood Kennel Club, Hollywood, Florida (1963-1964)
West Flagler Kennel Club, Miami, Florida (1964)
Ram Tool Company, 2110 Walton Street, Chicago (1966)
Harlem-Irving Plaza Shopping Center (1966)
Building at 7410 West North Avenue, Elmwood Park, Illinois (1967) (Partner with Guido DeChiaro)

Tony Dark

Golden Bear Pancake House, North Avenue, River Forest (1967)
Cameo Towers, North Avenue, Elmwood Park (1960's)
Des Plaines shopping center (1971)
Un-known Resort Complex in Illinois (1970's)

Known Favorite Restaurant

Henricis in New York City

Known Auto's

1947 Oldsmobile
1947 Cadillac
1948 Oldsmobile, four-door, Black with White sidewall tired (License plate number 1365 869)
1954 Cadillac, Blue in color (Florida License plate number 1WW-819)
1955 Cadillac Convertible Pale Green in color (License plate number 1WW1245)
1955 Cadillac, White over Blue, 2-door Hard Top (Florida License number WW2583) (Stolen on July 20, 1957 from a parking lot at 1121 S. Boulevard, Oak Park, Illinois. It was found with all its tires stolen)
1956 Studebaker Hardtop (License plate number 1-12671)
1957 Ford Custom 300, grey, four door (Florida License plate number 1-117263)
1963 Light Blue Bonneville Pontiac Convertible
1960's Jaguar
1960's Cadillac (White)
1964 Buick Riviera (Red) (License plate number 780-524)

Known Servants of DeLucia's

Jim Amorino (Italian immigrant groundskeeper for the Long Beach estate)
Herman Ulrich (DeLucia servant at his Indiana mansion)

People Describing Ricca

Murray Humphreys 1960 – *"You know Paul, when he puts his eyes on you, he makes you realize that it's serious."*

Son-in-law

Alex Ben Ponzio
Aka Bennie
Born - January 24, 1916 (Chicago)
Died - August 1979 (Los Angeles, California)
U.S. Army as a T-4 Sergeant in the Infantry (3 years)
Attended Loyola University Chicago

Father was a Sergeant of the Pennsylvania Railroad Police Force

Ponzio's Known Addresses of Owned Property

7800 Courtland Street, Elmwood Park, Illinois (1940's)
812 Lathrop, River Forest, Illinois (1950)
2940 Montclair Way, Long Beach, Indiana (1953)
Property in Yorkville, Illinois, (1943)
1138 North Oak Park Avenue, Oak Park, Illinois (1958)
1515 Bonnie Brae, River Forest, Illinois (1959)

Known Businesses of Ponzio

Northwestern Electric Contracting Company, 3835 West Augusta Boulevard, Chicago (1947-1952)
President and alleged owner of Town Parking, 59 East Van Buren Street, Chicago in early 1952-1960's
Renne & Associates Inc. Chicago (1965)
Town Parking Stations Incorporated, 328 & 339 South Wabash Avenue, Chicago (Leased to Airport Parking Company of America) (1960's)
Monroe-Dearborn Stations Inc., 332 S. Michigan Avenue Chicago (Incorporated 5-13-1965)
Des Plaines Shopping Center (1960's)
Parking Garage at 410-16 South Wabash Avenue, Chicago (1966)
Parking Garage 55-57 West Monroe Street, Chicago (1966)
Owned the building at 7410 West North Avenue, Chicago with Guido DeChiaro (1967)
Golden Bear Pancake House at 7300 North Avenue in River Forest, Illinois (Alleged ownership) (1967)
Pizza Restaurant at 4224 West Chicago Avenue, Chicago (1970) (Alleged)
Cameo Towers, North Avenue and Harlem, Chicago (1971)

DeLucia's Known Lawyers

Maurice Walsh
Joseph Bulger
Eugene Bernstein
George Callaghan (1950)
William Scott Stewart (1950's)
Ben Cohen (Florida Attorney) (1950's)
Bradley Eben
T.E. Rein
Jack Wasserman (1966)

In 1947 when the FBI asked Paul DeLucia about his criminal record, he told them he had been arrested by the Chicago Police Department from five to ten times on the charge of general principles; that in such arrests he was always held for one or two days and then released without any charges having been placed against him.

Paul DeLucia's Known Arrest Record

Chicago PD # 4365

Date	Charge	Agency	Result
7-17-1915	Murder	S. Eframo Naples, Italy	Guilty
1917	Murder	Naples, Italy	Guilty
1-23-1927	General Princ.	Chicago PD	Under Paul Viella
6-11-1930	Suspect	New York PD	Under Paul DeLucia
6-1930	Lingle Murder	Chicago PD	Released
11-5-1930	Disorderly Con.	Chicago PD	Under Paul Ricca
4-19-1932	Disorderly Con.	Chicago PD	Under Paul Ricca
11-2-1932	Disorderly Con.	Chicago PD	Released
12-2-1940	Conspiracy	Sheriff Office	Nolle Processed
6-23-1941	Conspiracy	Reinstalled	Nolle Processed
3-24-1943	Postal Fraud	U.S. Marshal	Guilty
4-27-1943	Extortion	U.S. Marshal	Guilty
6-8-1943	Mail Fraud	U.S. Marshal	Guilty
2-15-1944	Anti-Racketeering	Federal Detention	10 Year's Prison
4-4-1944	Conspiracy	U.S. Trade & Commerce	10 Year's Prison
6-16-1948	Parole Violation	U.S. Marshal	$10,000 Bond
9-7-1948	Inquiry	Chicago PD	Under Paul Viela
10-3-1950	Drury Murder	Chicago PD	Released
11-25-1950	Parole Violator	U.S. Marshal	$5,000 Bond
4-27-1954	Criminal Reg.	Miami PD	Released
3-6-1957	Income Tax	IRS	Prison
11-16-1963	Investigation	Dade County SO	Released
1-23-1966	Traffic Speeding	Chicago PD	Fined $14
4-28-1966	Perjury	U.S. Marshal	U/K

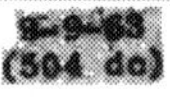

UNITED STATES DEPARTMENT OF JUSTICE
FEDERAL BUREAU OF INVESTIGATION
WASHINGTON 25, D. C.

J. Edgar Hoover, Director.

The following FBI record, NUMBER 832 514, is furnished FOR OFFICIAL USE ONLY.

CONTRIBUTOR OF FINGERPRINTS	NAME AND NUMBER	ARRESTED OR RECEIVED	CHARGE	DISPOSITION
United States Marshal Chicago Illinois	Paul De Lucia #6880	March 24	Extortion and Postal Fraud	
United States Marshal Chicago Illinois	Paul DeLucia #6988		Extortion	pending
United States Marshal New York City New York	Paul DeLucia #---	June 8, 1943	Mail Fraud	pending, May 6, 1947, nolle prosequi
Federal Detention Headquarters New York City New York	Paul DeLucia #41920	February 15, 1944	Anti-Racketeering Act	10 years, March 25, 1944 discharged to United States Penitentiary Atlanta
United States Penitentiary Atlanta Georgia	Paul DeLucia #63776	April 4, 1944	Conspiracy to Interfere with Trade and Commerce by coercion, threats and Violence	10 years
United States Penitentiary Leavenworth Kansas	Paul DeLucia #62118	August 8 1945 in transfer from United States Penitentiary Atlanta Georgia	Conspiracy to Interfere with Trade &and Commerce by violence, coercion and threats	10 years, August 13, 1947 paroled Violation date-divers occasions since release Warrant Issued November 22, 1950
United States Marshal Chicago Illinois	Paul DeLucia #156k9	June 16, 1948	not given	pending
Police Department Chicago Illinois	Paul Viela #C-4383	inquiry September 7, 1948		
Police Department Chicago Illinois	Paul DeLucia #D-78267	October 3, 1950	General Principles	

Notations indicated by * ARE NOT BASED ON FINGERPRINTS IN FBI files. The notations are based on data formerly furnished this Bureau concerning individuals of the same or similar names or aliases and ARE LISTED ONLY AS INVESTIGATIVE LEADS.

Paul DeLucia's FBI Rap Sheet of Arrest

12-9-68 674 KEH

UNITED STATES DEPARTMENT OF JUSTICE
FEDERAL BUREAU OF INVESTIGATION
WASHINGTON 25, D. C.

J. Edgar Hoover, Director.

2 The following FBI record, NUMBER 832 514, is furnished FOR OFFICIAL USE ONLY

CONTRIBUTOR OF FINGERPRINTS	NAME AND NUMBER	ARRESTED OR RECEIVED	CHARGE	DISPOSITION
United States Marshal Chicago Illinois	Paul DeLucia #18278	November 24, 1950	Parole Violation	pending
Police Department Miami Beach Florida	Paul DeLucia #A 20821	April 27, 1954 voluntary Criminal Registration		
United States Marshal Chicago Illinois	Paul DeLucia #57766	March 6, 1957	Internal Revenue Violation, making false statement Income Tax	3 years and $500 fine June 1959 committed July 2 1959-on charge of false statement incom tax
United States Immigration Naturalization Service Chicago Illinois	Paul De Lucia #--	December 10, 1958	Immigration Violation	
Cook County Jail Chicago Illinois	Paul DeLucia #236440	July 1 1959	Safe Keeping United States Marshal	July 2 1959 delivered to United States Marshal
United States Penitentiary Terre Haute Indiana	Paul DeLucia #16855	July 2 1959	income tax evasion	three yrs October 21 1961 mandatory release
Metropolitan Public Safety Department Miami Florida	Paul DeLucia #CR ID 67861	November 16, 1963	criminal registration	released instantly
USINS Chgo Ill	Felice (Paul) DeLucia #A 11 129 289	appl FP 2-4-65		

Notations indicated by * ARE NOT BASED ON FINGERPRINTS IN FBI files. The notations are based on data formerly furnished this Bureau concerning individuals of the same or similar names or aliases and ARE LISTED ONLY AS INVESTIGATIVE LEADS.

Paul DeLucia's FBI Rap Sheet of Arrest Page 2

12-9-68 674 KEB

UNITED STATES DEPARTMENT OF JUSTICE
FEDERAL BUREAU OF INVESTIGATION
WASHINGTON, D.C. 20537

3

J. Edgar Hoover
Director.

The following FBI record, NUMBER 832 514, is furnished FOR OFFICIAL USE ONLY.

CONTRIBUTOR OF FINGERPRINTS	NAME AND NUMBER	ARRESTED OR RECEIVED	CHARGE	DISPOSITION
FBI Chicago Ill	Paul DeLucia	4-28-66	Perjury T18 USC 1621	TOT USM
USM Chicago Ill	Paul DeLucia #65480	4-28-66	perjury	

Information shown on this Identification Record represents data furnished FBI by fingerprint contributors. Where final disposition is not shown or further explanation of charge is desired, communicate with agency contributing those fingerprints.
Notations indicated by * are NOT based on fingerprints in FBI files but are listed only as investigative leads as being possibly identical with subject of this record.

Paul DeLucia's FBI Rap Sheet of Arrest Page 3

UNITED STATES DEPARTMENT OF JUSTICE
FEDERAL BUREAU OF INVESTIGATION
WASHINGTON 25, D. C.

J. Edgar Hoover
Director.

3 The following FBI record, NUMBER 832 514, is furnished FOR OFFICIAL USE ONLY.

CONTRIBUTOR OF FINGERPRINTS	NAME AND NUMBER	ARRESTED OR RECEIVED	CHARGE	DISPOSITION
	WANTED: Paul DeLucia for failing to Register Criminal Record. Notify Sheriff's Office Miami Florida per information received therefrom dated July 23 1954. NO LONGER WANTED: Paul DeLucia per information received Sheriff's Office Miami Florida on wire dated July 29 1954			

Notations indic... formerly furnis... ONLY AS IN...

JOHN EDGAR HOOVER

Federal Bureau of Investigat
United States Department of Justice
Washington, D. C.

1-4

2 The following is the record of FBI number 832 514

J. E. Hoover
Director.

CONTRIBUTOR OF FINGERPRINTS	NAME AND NUMBER	ARRESTED OR RECEIVED	CHARGE	DISPOSITION
	Description; Color, white Sex, male Residence, 812 Latrobe, River Forest, Ill., in 1948 Birthplace, Italy Date of birth, July 10, 1898 Height, 5 feet-8 inches Weight, 170 pounds Complexion, light Eyes, brown Hair, gray Build, medium Scars and marks: light tan birthmark 1/2 below right elbow rear, operation scar outer & operation scar inner right foot and operation Scar lower left leg, operation scar 7 upper left leg outer, limps when walking.			

* Represents notations unsupported by fingerprints in FBI files.

U. S. GOVERNMENT PRINTING OFFICE 16—15190-1

NOTICE: THIS RECORD IS FURNISHED FOR OFFICIAL USE ONLY

FBI's list of Paul DeLucia's other criminal associates he was in contact with

Guido DeChiaro

Guido DeChiaro was known as a distant relative of Paul DeLucia's. DeChiaro had gained the respect of the Outfit not by running rackets or killing people but rather by handling investments for the Chicago group and acquiring a number of real estate holdings at a good price. During Prohibition he was in charge of illegal stills in Melrose Park, Illinois. Later he was involved in the Juke Box rackets while running his company, B&M Appliance Company at 9762 Franklin Avenue in Franklin Park, Illinois. On October 14, 1960 DeChiaro's son-in-law, Michael Urgo, then an attorney from Melrose Park, was shot and killed when he, Urgo, attempted to stop a kidnapper or robber who was attacking DeChiaro. Michael Urgo was said to be related to mobster Rocco DeGrazio. In 1971 it was said that no other guy on the streets of Chicago had access to Paul DeLucia or Tony Accardo as did Guido DeChiaro.

Peter Fosco

In 1940 Peter Fosco was Democratic Committeeman of the old 20th Ward in Chicago. He was president of Chicago Local 2 of the Sewer and Tunnel Workers Union. Later he would become president of the International Hod Carriers Union.

In the 1940's Peter Fosco was a close friend to Paul DeLucia. Fosco was a "pay-off" man for DeLucia between the Capone Gang and the Mayors Office. Fosco also had Washington D.C. connections and was utilized by DeLucia in various ways.

Joseph Esposito

As of 1965 Paul DeLucia was in the constant company of Joseph "Puddy" Esposito. Puddy Esposito was said to be the "right arm" of Paul DeLucia since the two were very close. Puddy Esposito was born around 1897 and was said to be an extremely wealthy man and held a position as a foreman of the asphalt crew of the City of Chicago. Puddy Esposito was not related to Frank "Frankie X" Esposito but the two were close friends and Puddy was often seen delivering messages from DeLucia to Frankie X.

Joseph Fischetti

Brother of mobsters Rocco and Charles Fischetti. Joseph lived at 7601 Miami View Drive, North Bay Village, Florida. He was observed at DeLucia's home on many occasions in January 1958. He was DeLucia's "right-hand-man" when DeLucia was in Florida.

Tony Dark

Anthony Ricci

Anthony Ricci was known by the name of Tony Gobels in mob circles. He lived at 5980 Indian Creek Drive, Miami Beach, Florida, and was observed many times at DeLucia's home in Miami. Ricci was known to be very close to DeLucia.

SUBJECT: Anthony Ricci

ALIASES: Anthony Gobel, Gaetano Ricci, Tony Goebels.

DATE OF BIRTH: Jan. 1, 1893 - Italy

NATIONALITY: Italian

RESIDENCE: 125 Ocean Parkway, Bklyn, - Apt. 6-B, (residence of girl- friend and employer Anna Friedman). See Below.

OCCUPATION: Tracer

NUMBER IN OUR FILES: B#4591 PHOTO ON FILE? Yes (Chicago

NUMBER OF ARRESTS: 5 Previous arrests:

(2) Felonious Assault
(2) Grand Larceny, Vagrancy (Chicago)

Convictions: (1)

7/30/15 - S.S. final - Assault 3rd.

ASSOCIATES: Joe Adonis, Tony Schoemaker, Owney Madden.

ACTIVITIES: Alleged to be a lieutenant of Adonis.

Alleged to be connected with the following:

1. Steel Window Service Corp., 1 DeKalb Ave., Bklyn.
2. Nathan Outfitters, 1135 Broadway, Bklyn., (Owned by girl-friend Anna Friedman) Employed as a tracer at $2,500. per year.

Frequents vicinity of Court Square, Bklyn.

JOHN EDGAR HOOVER

Federal Bureau of Investigation
United States Department of Justice
Washington, D. C.

Aug 25 1930

The following is the record of FBI number 51 338

J. E. Hoover
Director.

CONTRIBUTOR OF FINGERPRINTS	NAME AND NUMBER	ARRESTED OR RECEIVED	CHARGE	DISPOSITION
PD Oakland Calif	Gaetano Ricci #8800	7-29-22	ADW	dism 8-28-22

JOHN EDGAR HOOVER

Federal Bureau of Investigation
United States Department of Justice
Washington, D. C.

2

The following is the record of FBI number 51 338

J. E. Hoover
Director.

CONTRIBUTOR OF FINGERPRINTS	NAME AND NUMBER	ARRESTED OR RECEIVED	CHARGE	DISPOSITION
	Description: Sex: male Height: 5 ft. 1 in. Age: in year 1922, 41 yrs. Weight: 118 lbs. Comp.: ruddy Hair: d. brown Eyes: brown Build: small Occupacion: laborer Birthplace: Italy			

Anthony Ricci, aka Tony Gobels

* Represents notations unsupported by fingerprints in FBI files.

NOTICE: THIS RECORD IS FURNISHED FOR OFFICIAL USE ONLY

Mike Spranze

Mike Spranze was born on March 3, 1905 in Chicago. He was known as Mike Kelly and Mike Raymond when he was a bodyguard, terrorist, strong arm man and handbook operator for the Al Capone Gang. In the 1940's he was in charge of gambling for the syndicate on the south side of Chicago. In the late 1950's Paul DeLucia was observed meeting with and socializing with Mike Spranze weekly.

Hugo Bennett

Real name Hugo Benvenuti
Wife Josephine
9517 Carlyle Avenue, Surfside, Florida (1950)

Hugo Bennett, an Italian who changed his name to sound American, was the individual who gave Paul DeLucia a loan of $80,000 for the purchase of DeLucia's Long Beach, Indiana home.

On April 1, 1950 Hugo Bennett was arrested in Miami Beach, Florida for drunk driving, disorderly conduct and resisting arrest.

Hugo Bennett was a personal accountant for Johnny Patton who was a member of the Capone Gang in Chicago and was connected with mob treasurer Jake Guzik. Patton went by the nickname of "boy Mayor of Burnham, Illinois."

Bennett was also the auditor of the Miami Beach Kennel Club which both he and his wife Josephine were stockholders. He was also auditor of the National Jockey Club in Cicero, Illinois, The Hawthorne Kennel Club, The Jacksonville Kennel Club, the Tropical Park Race Track, The Orange Park Kennel Club, The Associated Outdoor Club of Tampa Florida and the Sportsman's Park Race Track in Chicago.

In 1948 Bennett was carried as director of Sportsman's Park in Chicago. He had been connected to Eddie O'Hare in the 1930's. O'Hare was the power behind the dog racing at Sportsman's Park until he was murdered on November 29, 1939.

When Paul DeLucia was released from Leavenworth Prison in the 1940's Hugo Bennett visited DeLucia at his summer home in Michigan City, Indiana and gave DeLucia $30,000 in cash for DeLucia to place as a down payment on his summer home in LaPorte, Indiana.

Anthony Solerno

A New York City mobster who sold his Miami Beach home at 4385 Pine tree Drive to Paul DeLucia in 1954.

Michael Pietro

Listed as an associate of Paul DeLucia, Mike Pietro lived at 3342 Polk Street in Chicago and was arrested once for speeding on 1-19-1956. He was born 10-22-1900 and in 1957 he lived at 270 N, W. 96th Street, Miami, Florida. His relationship with Paul DeLucia was not mentioned but both were said to be very close friends.

Salvatore Falcone

In the late 1950's Sal Falcone was known as a Miami Beach, Florida hoodlum. On many occasions he was observed by FBI agents at the home of Paul DeLucia. However, it was not known why he was there.

Robert Larry McCullough

Robert Larry McCullough was known as Peter J. Walsh, born on February 6, 1892 in Chicago. McCullough's life as a criminal started in 1909 when he was arrested for burglary in Chicago. He spent four months in the Chicago House of Corrections. In 1912 he was arrested for robbery but was later released.

When Johnny Torrio killed his uncle James "Big Jim" Colosimo, McCullough went to work for the Torrio Gang as a gunman. In 1923 he was known to be working with a rising star in the Torrio Gang named Al Capone.

By 1926 he was one of Al Capone's drivers and bodyguards when he was arrested and charged with general principles. After Capone went away to prison, McCullough went to Miami, Florida in the 1930's to operate rackets for the Capone Gang. In 1944 he was arrested by the FBI as a missing witness in New York for the movie extortion case involving Paul DeLucia. In 1950 McCullough was made Chief of Police at the Miami Beach Kennel Club during the winter season and during the summer season in Chicago he was Chief of Police at Sportsman's Park Race Track.

While in Chicago McCullough was a suspect in the murder of Chicago Police Captain William Drury, which Paul DeLucia was said to have ordered. McCullough had been observed at the home of Paul DeLucia in Miami in the late 1950's and would often hold meetings with McCullough to discuss mob business.

John Vignola

John Vignola lived down the street from Paul DeLucia and was observed many times in the company of DeLucia, Tony Accardo and Tony Capezio. Vignola was the owner of Vignola Furniture Company at 7617 West North Avenue in River Forest, Illinois.

Charles Cresa

In 1958 FBI agents kept observing the auto of Charles Cresa in the driveway of DeLucia's Chicago residence. Charles Cresa was an electrician with a criminal past.

Cresa Known Arrest Record

Date	Charge	Agency	Result
10-8-1934	Larceny	Chicago PD	8 Months Jail
3-19-1949	General Principles	Chicago PD	Released
5-18-1953	General Principles	Chicago PD	Released
6-3-1953	Assault Deadly Weapon	Chicago PD	U/K

Known Addresses

1515 Bonnie Brea, River Forest, Illinois (1958)
1622 West Jackson Boulevard, Chicago (1955)
1912 Taylor Street, Chicago (1940's)

Christ Scialo

In the 1950's Christ Scialo was listed as a courier for Paul DeLucia.

John Catrone

In 1966 John Catrone was alleged to be a front man for Paul DeLucia. Catrone operated the Ram Tool Company at 2110 Walton Street in Chicago. This company was alleged to be owned by Paul DeLucia. Catrone was seen at many social events in the company of Paul DeLucia.

Chapter 18

They Called Him Joe Batters

With Paul DeLucia dead, Tony Accardo was now the czar of the Chicago Outfit. There was no one left with the knowledge and power that Accardo possessed. For the first time in his life, he controlled EVERY aspect of the Chicago Outfit as he saw fit.

Shortly after DeLucia's funeral Tony Accardo called a meeting between himself, Joey Aiuppa, Gus Alex, Ralph Pierce and Lester Kruse. At the meeting Accardo announced he would remain top leader of organized crime in Chicago and no one would be replacing DeLucia. However, he informed Gus Alex that he would be relying on Gus more and more concerning policy matters. He then turned to Joey Aiuppa and told Aiuppa that he was going to be relied on more heavily concerning the operation of the Outfit. Accardo finished the meeting by saying that if any change were to be made in structure he would consult with Gus Alex and Joey Aiuppa before the decision was finalized. He ended the meeting by telling everyone that Fifi Buccieri would be more involved if he was not so sick; he was expected to die soon.

The Tony Accardo story starts back in the early days of the 20th century. Someone once said about Tony Accardo, *"Tony's got more brains before breakfast than Al Capone had all day."* He would pride himself on never talking to police officers, no matter what. He wasn't impolite to law enforcement, but would never give them the time of day. He enjoyed hunting and fishing and traveled all over the world in pursuit of that love. He almost never permitted his wife, Clarice, or the wives of his traveling companions to take the same airplane flight, they would always fly separately.

Anthony Joseph Accardo told everyone that he was born in Chicago on April 28, 1906 to Francesco "Frank" Accardo and Mary Tilotta. Both parents were born in Italy.

According to Francesco Accardo himself, he came from the Italian village of Casarnzo, born there in either January 30, 1975 or May 1, 1876. When he applied for U.S. citizenship in 1904 he said that he had entered America on March 13, 1892 at the port entry of New York City under the name of Francisco Accardto, with a "T" in the name. He filed for U.S Citizenship on June 9, 1904 in Cook County, Illinois and was awarded citizenship in 1909. He signed his name under the last name of Accarto with a "T" in stead of a "D". Francesco's other son Martin Leonard Accardo believed his father could not read or write and the witness, Francesco's friend Frank Thomas, signed Francesco's name incorrectly.

Frank Accardo made his occupation as a laborer between 1892 and 1906 before becoming a shoemaker in 1906.

Francesco had said that he had been in America for 12 years when he applied for U.S. citizenship but investigators discovered that his wife, Maria "Mary" Accardo nee Tilotta, Tillotto or DeLotta, was born in Italy around 1884, entered the United States on July 4, 1905 at Port of New Orleans, with 2-year old son Leonard Accardo.

Questions were raised as how Maria could have a 2-year-old son if her husband had been residing continuously in the U.S. for 12 years. Investigators did discover that the discrepancy in the stories may be because the Clerk of Court, John A. Cooke, who had signed Francesco's naturalization record, was subsequently convicted for fraudulent naturalization certificates.

Later, over the years, Francesco was questioned as to whether Tony Accardo had actually been born in America or Italy. When Martin Accardo went to prison in 1932 he said he was born in Italy in 1900 and came to America in 1905. On the 1920 census Martin is listed as being immigrated to the U.S. in 1906 under the name Leanardi with Tony being listed as being born in America.

Line	Street	House number	Dwelling	Family	Name	Relation	Home owned or rented	Mortgaged	Sex	Color or race	Age	Marital condition	Year of immigration	Naturalized or alien	Year of naturalization	Attended school	Able to read	Able to write	Place of birth	Mother tongue
1		1351			Stroh Helen	daughter			F	W	13	S				yes	yes	yes	Illinois	
2		1353	78	43	Accardo Frank	Head	O	M	M	W	44	M	1905	Pa	1908		no	no	Italy	Italian
3					— Maria	Wife			F	W	37	M	1904	Al			yes	yes	Italy	Italian
4					— Leonardi	Son			M	W	19	S	1904	Al			yes	yes	Italy	Italian
5					— Tony	Son			M	W	14	S					yes	yes	Illinois	Italian
6					— Bessie	daughter			F	W	9	S				yes	yes	yes	Illinois	
7					— Martha	daughter			F	W	7	S				yes	yes	yes	Illinois	
8					— Mary	daughter			F	W	4	S							Illinois	
9					— Johnslie	son			M	W	1	S							Illinois	

NATIVITY AND MOTHER TONGUE.

Line	Father: Place of birth	Father: Mother tongue	Mother: Place of birth	Mother: Mother tongue	Able to speak English	Occupation	Industry	Employer, salary or wage worker
1	Canada	English	Canada	English	yes			
2	Italy	Italian	Italy	Italian	yes		shoemaker	
3	Italy	Italian	Italy	Italian	yes	none		
4	Italy	Italian	Italy	Italian	yes	driver		
5	Italy	Italian	Italy	Italian	yes		shoemaker	W
6	Italy	Italian	Italy	Italian	yes	none		
7	Italy	Italian	Italy	Italian	yes	none		
8	Italy	Italian	Italy	Italian	yes	none		

DEPARTMENT OF COMMERCE—BUREAU OF THE CENSUS

FOURTEENTH CENSUS OF THE UNITED STATES: 1920—POPULATION

State: Illinois. County: Cook. Name of incorporated place: Chicago. Supervisor's District No. 4. Enumeration District No. 998. Sheet No. 3 A. Enumerated by me on the 3rd day of January, 1920.

1920 Census above and 1930 Census below and other page

Name	Relation	Sex	Color	Age	Marital condition	Place of birth	Father's birthplace	Mother's birthplace	Language	Occupation	Industry
Accardo Frank	Head	M	W	54	M	Italy	Italy	Italy	Italian	Proprietor	Shoe Repair
— Mary	Wife	F	W	47	M	Italy	Italy	Italy	Italian	none	
— Bessie	Daughter	F	W	19	S	Illinois	Italy	Italy		none	
— Martha	Daughter	F	W	17	S	Illinois	Italy	Italy		none	
— Mary	Daughter	F	W	14	S	Illinois	Italy	Italy		none	

DEPARTMENT OF COMMERCE—BUREAU OF THE CENSUS
FIFTEENTH CENSUS OF THE UNITED STATES: 1930
POPULATION SCHEDULE

A young Tony Accardo attended kindergarten at the Otis Elementary School in September 1911, while living at 1000 Grand Avenue in Chicago. He later attended Washington public school in Chicago. Tony Accardo's file with the Chicago Board of Education gave the flowing information, *"The record states pupil as Tony Accardo, Washington School, date of birth 4-28-1905 for school year 1916-1917 and April 8, 1905 for school year 1917-1918. Parent or Guardian, Frank – Mother's name not shown. Address 1353 Grand Avenue, Chicago, Illinois, 1916-1917."*

By 1920 Tony Accardo was a young and rough kid who dropped out of school to work as a shoemaker for his father. It was believed that his parents were not satisfied with the young Accardo attending school and filed a delayed birth certificate stating Tony Accardo was born in 1904 so he could drop out of school and go to work. Some reports suggest that the young Accardo also worked as a delivery boy for a florist and as a grocery store clerk. These three jobs may have shown Accardo that you can work a full day of honest work and be paid almost nothing in return. He quickly learned that's not the way he was going to live, not like every other shmuck slaving away for no pay.

Tony Accardo's first known conflict with the law occurred on March 22, 1922 at the age of 16 when he was arrested for violation of the Motor Vehicle Code in Chicago. He was a member of the Circus Gang with gangsters Tony "Caps" Capezio, Vincenzo DeMora, aka Machine Gun Jack McGurn, and John Moore, aka Claude "Screwy" Maddox. The gang was based on the near west side of Chicago and made their headquarters at the restaurant called the Circus Café, located at

1857 North Avenue in Chicago. This place is the reason they called their gang the Circus Gang. It was said that the gang was actually set up by Al Capone himself originally to muscle in on the beer trade on the North side of Chicago which was controlled then by the Aiello brothers.

Others mentioned as possible Circus Gang members were:

Lawrence Cozzi
Mike Farvia
Edward Konowski, aka Casey
Sam Leverde
Edward Piranio, aka Frank "Fat" Estes
Fred Burke (Alleged in a 1949 FBI report)
John Scalise (Alleged in a 1949 FBI report)
Albert Alselmi (Alleged in a 1949 FBI report)
Murray Humphreys (Alleged in a 1949 FBI report)
Sam "Golf Bag" Hunt (Alleged in a 1949 FBI report)

Accardo rose quickly as a leader in the gang which made Maddox notice his potential leadership skills. Accardo had been out mugging people, committing robberies, assaulting people on the streets and driving a truck delivering moonshine to speakeasies around the west side of Chicago. One story has Maddox, who was already in with the Capone Gang, bringing Accardo to Al Capone to use as a bodyguard. Another version is Capone turned to Jack McGurn for a bodyguard who in turn brought in Accardo for the position. Either way, Tony Accardo was now working for Al Capone.

In 1961 FBI agents interviewed Joseph Bagnola, who changed his name to Joseph Logan which he used as his boxing name in the 1920's. Bagnola told FBI agents that back when Al Capone was running things, Tony Accardo was nothing more than a driver for leading members of the Capone Gang. Other stories have Accardo being summoned to Al Capone's office at the Metropole Hotel in 1926 and was ordered to take Jack McGurn's hand and swear to Omerta. By doing so he became a "made" man in the Capone organization. McGurn was his sponsor and therefore responsible for Accardo's actions.

Some informants told the FBI that Accardo was nothing more than a truck driver in the Al Capone days who got lucky. One informant remembered that in the late 1920's he contacted Al Capone at one of his headquarters and set up a meeting. When this informant arrived to see Capone, Accardo, known then only as JB, was acting in the capacity of doorman and called up top to Capone's room to announce that the informant was on his way up to see him.

There is the report from September 20, 1926 when Al Capone and Tony Accardo were in the lobby of Capone's headquarters at the Hawthorn Inn in Cicero. Eleven carloads of gangsters from the Hymie Weiss Gang (Capone's enemy) drove by spraying the hotel with bullets in an attempt to kill Capone. As the story goes, Tony Accardo, who often was seen sitting in the lobby of the hotel with a Thompson machine gun on his lap, grabbed Capone and pulled him to the ground to shield him from all the bullets. No one was killed but that incident spelled the end of Hymie Weiss as Capone had him killed sometime after.

Accardo was also mentioned as one of the killers of Frankie Yale, a one-time close friend of Capone's who fell out of favor. The story goes that Capone sent Albert Anselmi, Jack McGurn, John Scalise and Tony Accardo to New York to kill Yale. As Yale drove by in his Lincoln automobile in Brooklyn, Thompson machine guns opened fire and killed Yale. One report mentioned that this was the first machine gun murder in New York having to do with the mob.

1920's Chicago Police line up photo of Sam Hunt, Tony Accardo, Danny Covico and Rocco DeGrazio

Early mug shot photo's of Tony Accardo taken by the Chicago Police Department

Between 1922 and 1959, Tony Accardo was arrested over 18 times on charges ranging from disorderly conduct to investigations in connection with murders. Accardo was never convicted of a felony and the highest fine he ever paid in that time period was $200 for disorderly conduct. Many of his arrests were with Murray Humphreys. Every time Accardo was arrested with Humphreys, he listed his occupation as "betting commissioner."

On the next few pages are transcripts of Tony Accardo being questioned by Senators in 1950.

The CHAIRMAN. Your objection is overruled.

Mr. HALLEY. Will you show the witness a list of arrests and ask him to look it over and state whether or not they are his, the list beginning in 1923 and going to 1945 [handing document to counsel].

Mr. CALLAGHAN. Same objection to that question.

The CHAIRMAN. Well, the objection is overruled.

Will you show the witness what purports to be his criminal record, or at least a part of it.

Senator TOBEY. I might point out, Mr. Chairman, that that list, as shown to me, shows an average of one a year in the 23 years that have been cited.

Mr. ACCARDO (looking at the document). I don't know whether that is my list or not, sir. I don't know if I have been arrested that many times.

Mr. HALLEY. It shows 23 arrests, does it not?

Mr. ACCARDO. I don't know.

The CHAIRMAN. Well, the question is, Were you charged with the matters stated in that record, and does it show the outcome of those various charges?

Mr. ACCARDO. I don't remember, sir.

The CHAIRMAN. Rather than going over them specifically.

Mr. HALLEY. Do you remember being convicted of disorderly conduct in 1923, and fined $200?

Mr. ACCARDO. No; I don't remember.

Mr. HALLEY. Is it possible that you could have been convicted in 1923?

Mr. ACCARDO. I don't remember.

Mr. HALLEY. Were you ever convicted of disorderly conduct?

Mr. ACCARDO. Once or twice, I think.

Mr. HALLEY. Once or twice.

Could it be three? The record just shows three.

Mr. ACCARDO. I don't know.

Mr. HALLEY. But at least once or twice.

Mr. Accardo, after 1923, in any event, you were never convicted of anything, isn't that right?

Mr. ACCARDO. According to this list, I have not.

Mr. HALLEY. Is that right?

Mr. ACCARDO. All I remember is a fine.

Mr. HALLEY. In 1923, and again twice in 1924, isn't that the fact?

Mr. ACCARDO. I don't know what year; I don't know of what year.

Mr. HALLEY. A long time ago?

Mr. ACCARDO. Yes, sir.

Mr. HALLEY. And after that you managed to avoid conviction at all times, is that not right?

Mr. ACCARDO. I don't know what you mean by "managed."

Mr. HALLEY. Well, you were never convicted since.

Mr. CALLAGHAN. You mean the evidence was not sufficient.

Mr. HALLEY. You were never convicted since 1924, were you?

Mr. ACCARDO. If that is the last day of the fine; no, sir.

Mr. HALLEY. But since 1924 you have been arrested on 18 occasions, is that not right?

Mr. ACCARDO. That is right.

Mr. HALLEY. Including, is it right to say, disorderly conduct on several occasions?

Mr. ACCARDO. Yes.

Mr. HALLEY. And carrying a concealed weapon on one occasion; isn't that right?

The CHAIRMAN. Well, Mr. Accardo, looking over that list, do you think that is substantially representative of the charges that have been made against you, and what happened to them, without going into each one of them?

Mr. ACCARDO. Some of them may be and some I don't know anything about, sir.

The CHAIRMAN. All right, go ahead, Mr. Halley.

Mr. HALLEY. Well, in any event, you were arrested on many occasions; were you not?

Mr. ACCARDO. That is right, sir.

Mr. HALLEY. Did they include kidnaping on one occasion?

Mr. ACCARDO. No, sir.

Mr. HALLEY. Weren't you arrested in connection with the kidnaping of Guzik——

Mr. ACCARDO. Sir?

Mr. HALLEY. Weren't you arrested in connection with the kidnaping of Guzik and the slaying of one Jens Larrison at Matt Capone's tavern?

Mr. ACCARDO. You must have everything all wrong there.

Mr. HALLEY. Well, isn't that the fact?

Mr. ACCARDO. No; it is not the facts.

Mr. HALLEY. Not that you have been arrested?

Mr. ACCARDO. I have been arrested, but not for what charges you are talking about.

Mr. HALLEY. Well, were you arrested in 1945?

Mr. ACCARDO. Let's see; I don't remember, sir.

Mr. HALLEY. Did you know Matt Capone?

Mr. ACCARO. I refuse to answer, sir.

Mr. HALLEY. Do you know Jens Larrison?

Mr. ACCARDO. Sir?

Mr. HALLEY. Do you know Jens Larrison, L-a-r-r-i-s-o-n?

Mr. ACCARDO. Who?

Mr. HALLEY. His first name is Jens, J-e-n-s.

Mr. ACCARD. Who?

Mr. HALLEY. Larrison.

Mr. ACCARDO. Larrison? I don't know anybody by the name of Larrison.

Mr. HALLEY. Well, you certainly knew Guzik?

Mr. ACCARDO. I refuse to answer, sir.

Mr. HALLEY. Could you tell the committee how you were able on so many occasions to beat the rap since 1924?

Mr. ACCARDO. I don't know what you mean by "beat the rap."

Mr. HALLEY. Did you have any political influence which would help you avoid successful prosecution?

Mr. ACCARDO. No, sir.

Mr. HALLEY. Did you know any members of the State assembly?

Mr. ACCARDO. I refuse to answer.

Mr. HALLEY. Did you know James Adducci?

Mr. ACCARDO. I refuse to answer.

Mr. HALLEY. Did you ever have any business relationships with Adducci?

Mr. ACCARDO. I refuse to answer.
Mr. HALLEY. Did you ever have a bodyguard or chauffeur?
Mr. ACCARDO. I refuse to answer.
Mr. HALLEY. Well, do you know Sam Gintana?
Mr. ACCARDO. I refuse to answer.
Mr. HALLEY. Doesn't he drive your car?
Mr. ACCARDO. I refuse to answer.
Mr. HALLEY. You have a car, do you not?
Mr. ACCARDO. My wife has a car.
Mr. HALLEY. What kind of car?
Mr. ACCARDO. Cadillac.
Mr. HALLEY. What year?
Mr. ACCARDO. 1947.
Mr. HALLEY. What model?
Mr. ACCARDO. Convertible.
Mr. HALLEY. Do you have any other automobiles?
Mr. ACCARDO. No, sir.
Mr. HALLEY. You or your family?
Mr. ACCARDO. No, sir.
Mr. HALLEY. Where do you have a home?
Mr. ACCARDO. 1431 Ash, River Forest, Ill.
Mr. HALLEY. Do you have any in Miami Beach? Do you rent a home in Miami Beach?
Mr. ACCARDO. I refuse to answer.
Mr. HALLEY. You did rent a home in Miami Beach for many years, did you not?
Mr. ACCARDO. I refuse to answer.
Mr. HALLEY. Was Sam Gintana ever in your home?
Mr. ACCARDO. I refuse to answer.
Mr. HALLEY. Did you ever employ him to act as your bodyguard?
Mr. ACCARDO. I refuse to answer.
Mr. HALLEY. Do you know whether or not he was in jail in 1940?
Mr. ACCARDO. I refuse to answer.
Mr. HALLEY. Is it not a fact that Gintana is a brother-in-law of a man who owns a company called the Central Envelope & Lithographing Co.?
Mr. ACCARDO. I refuse to answer.
Mr. HALLEY. You have heard of the Central Envelope & Lithographing Co., have you not?
Mr. ACCARDO. I refuse to answer.
Mr. HALLEY. Gintana worked for it at one time when he also was working for you, did he not?
Mr. ACCARDO. I refuse to answer.
Mr. HALLEY. Is that not the company that pays James Adducci, the State legislator, for getting——
Mr. ACCARDO. I refuse to answer.
Mr. HALLEY (continuing). Contracts in the State legislature?
Mr. ACCARDO. I refuse to answer.
Mr. HALLEY. Do you have any friends in the city of Chicago?
Mr. ACCARDO. I refuse to answer.
Mr. HALLEY. Well, a man must have a friend. [Laughter.] Don't you have any friends?
Mr. ACCARDO. I still refuse to answer.
Mr. HALLEY. I am sorry.

Mr. ACCARDO. I still refuse to answer.
Mr. HALLEY. How well do you know Pat Manno?
Mr. ACCARDO. I refuse to answer.
Mr. HALLEY. Is it not a fact that he was once a partner of Harry Russell?
Mr. ACCARDO. I refuse to answer.
Mr. HALLEY. How well do you know Tremont—Pete Tremont?
Mr. ACCARDO. I refuse to answer.
Mr. HALLEY. Do you know them at all?
Mr. ACCARDO. I refuse to answer.
Mr. HALLEY. Weren't they also associated with Harry Russell?
Mr. ACCARDO. I refuse to answer.
Mr. HALLEY. When did you last see Manno?
Mr. ACCARDO. I refuse to answer.
Mr. HALLEY. When did you last see Tremont?
Mr. ACCARDO. I refuse to answer.
Mr. HALLEY. Don't they also own homes in Florida?
Mr. ACCARDO. That I don't know.
Mr. HALLEY. Well, did you ever have them out on your yacht in Florida?
Mr. ACCARDO. I refuse to answer.
Mr. HALLEY. Did you ever go into the numbers racket with Manno or Tremont?
Mr. ACCARDO. I refuse to answer.
Mr. HALLEY. Do you know a man named Pardy?
Mr. ACCARDO. Who?
Mr. HALLEY. Sam Pardy?
Mr. ACCARDO. I refuse to answer.
Mr. HALLEY. Isn't he your partner in the numbers racket?
Mr. ACCARDO. I refuse to answer.
Mr. HALLEY. Did you ever hear of the Erie & Buffalo Co.?
Mr. ACCARDO. I refuse to answer.
Mr. HALLEY. Where did you derive your income in 1949?
Mr. ACCARDO. I refuse to answer.
Mr. HALLEY. You have a home in River Forest; is that right?
Mr. ACCARDO. Yes, sir.
Mr. HALLEY. And you at least rode on a yacht named the *Clara Jo* in Florida?
Mr. ACCARDO. Sir?
Mr. HALLEY. You rode on a yacht named the *Clara Jo* in Florida?
Mr. ACCARDO. I refuse to answer.
Mr. HALLEY. And you have rented homes in Florida, have you not?
Mr. ACCARDO. Yes, sir.
Mr. HALLEY. Did you buy that Cadillac convertible new?
Mr. ACCARDO. I don't remember whether it was new or second-hand.
Mr. HALLEY. When did you buy it, in what year?
Mr. ACCARDO. In 1947.
Mr. HALLEY. A 1947 car.
And your children go to camp?
Mr. ACCARDO. Sir?
Mr. HALLEY. Your children attend camp.
Mr. ACCARDO. Camp or mass?
Mr. HALLEY. Camp.
Mr. ACCARDO. I did not hear you.

Many have asked why Tony Accardo's nicknamed was Joe Batters or JB for short. One of the stories as to why involved a tale of how Jack McGurn went to see Al Capone one day and told this story how Tony Accardo took a baseball bat and smashed the skulls of two men, killing them both. Capone smiled and said, *"This guy is a real Joe Batters"* and history was made. From that point on, all his pals referred to him as Joe Batters or JB.

In February 1929 Tony Accardo's name was linked to one of the most well known stories ever in American history. Many believed Tony Accardo was one of the plotters in the St. Valentine's Day Massacre which occurred on the North Side of Chicago. Four men, two dressed as Chicago police officers and two plain clothes men went to the SMC Cartage garage of Al Capone's e enemy Bugs Moran on North Clark Street. There the phony policemen raided the garage where Moran and seven of his men were awaiting a shipment of booze. Moran was running late that day and noticed the fake policemen raiding his garage before making a getaway. The seven men of the Moran Gang were lined up against the wall and shot to death by two Thompson machine guns and two shotguns.

So many names have been linked as to who the four men who held the guns were. There is Tony Accardo, John Lardino, who was said to be one of the shooters dressed as a policeman, Fred Burke, Jack McGurn, Tony Capezio, Albert Anselmi, John Scalise, out of town killers from New York, Michigan, Ohio--the names keep going on and on. Many believe the killers were real Chicago police officers who were about to be exposed by Moran over police corruption which would have been the end for many Chicago police officers' careers. Al's brother Ralph Capone's granddaughter said in her book that Ralph and Al were very mad about the killing of Moran's men and wanted to know who was behind it. Meaning they had nothing to do with the killing of the seven gangsters.

The truth is, those who did know never spoke and the truth may remain a mystery for the rest of time as the incident fades into history forever.

In the 1930's Accardo made his way as a Capone "muscle man" and specialized in taking over handbooks for the Capone Gang.

Just the Facts

One incident in February 1930, Tony Accardo and Jack McGurn were arrested in a taxi cab by Chicago Police Officers William Drury and John Howe. Chicago police had been out rounding up hoodlums suspected in the murder of syndicate stool pigeon Julius Rosenheim. Once the two were pulled over, Drury found a revolver in the back seat of the cab. Both Accardo and McGurn denied the gun was theirs. The two were arrested and each went in front of the judge separately for carrying a concealed weapon. On March 31, 1930 the case was stricken from the docket with leave to reinstate because Accardo had not been apprehended and had jumped his $10,000 bond.

In April Accardo turned himself in to the police after two months of dodging the law. However, the assistant state's attorney entered a motion of nolle prosequi in favor of an indictment for the same charge which carried a higher bond. The end of this case came when Accardo appeared in court with his lawyer Roland V. Libonati, a future U.S. Senator, and the case was nolle processed because the case against Accardo was not as strong as the case against Jack McGurn and the Supreme Court of Illinois had reversed McGurn's conviction on this charge. Accardo walked free.

In November 1930 Tony Accardo surrendered to Chicago police when he found out he was wanted for questioning in the killing of Chicago north side gang leader Joseph Aiello. After being questioned and viewed by witnesses, Accardo was booked on a disorderly conduct charge and released on a $25 cash bond.

On February 17, 1931 Tony Accardo was arrested with Charles Gioe and charged with carrying a concealed weapon. Three months later in May 1931 Tony Accardo, Lawrence Mangano and four other Capone mobsters were arrested and questioned in the murder of top gangster Mike "de Pike" Heitler. Accardo was also charged with disorderly conduct but those charges were dropped.

Accardo became listed as a "public enemy number 2" by the Chicago Crime Commission on July 31, 1931. His poster read *"member of the Circus Café Gang, suspected of the St. Valentine's Day Massacre, alcohol dealer and bodyguard of Machine Gun Jack McGurn."*

When Chicago police investigated the "Public Enemy List" they were concerned because 18 of the 28 hoodlums listed on the list did not have police records with the Chicago Police Department. Accardo did have an index card that read, *"Pal of Jack McGurn and Capone killer, suspect in the slaying of Joe Aiello, Jack Zuta and Mike de Pike Heitler, freed on appeal after being convicted of gun-toting."*

That year it was reported that Tony Accardo was a suspect in the killing of gangster Ted Newberry whose body was dumped in a ditch in Porter County, Indiana. It was said that Frank Nitti had given the order for Accardo to kill Newberry.

Accardo was charged with vagrancy on May 3, 1932 and a court date was set for May 23. This was to be a special court hearing because every Chicago police officer who had ever arrested him in the past two years was going to attend and testify against him. Eight officers testified but it still was not good enough to get Accardo a conviction. He was found not guilty and walked once again.

On March 4, 1933 Tony Accardo was arrested by the Chicago Police to be questioned in the murder of Estelle Carey, the girl friend lover of Capone mobster Nick Circella, aka Nick Dean. Accardo was released without being charged.

On May 17, 1933 Accardo was arrested on suspicion while standing at the corner of Canal and Jackson Streets in Chicago's Loop area. Police slapped a disorderly conduct charge on him and labeled him as "a member of the Murray Humphreys Gang." Once in front of the judge Accardo admitted he had not had a job for six months but had $500 cash in his pocket. The judge wanted to know why he had so much money while the rest of the country is in a depression and why Accardo gave the address of a vacant lot as his home address. Accardo just answered, *"If I gave my right address to the police they would be all over my place all of the time."* He was found guilty of disorderly conduct and fined $25.

In August 1933 Tony Accardo was arrested and released by the Chicago police department. Two days later he was arrested again while standing in front of a building at 1511 Taylor Street in Chicago's Little Italy and held on an investigation charge. This time Accardo had Illinois State Representative Robert Petrone from the old 21st District call the chief of detectives to have him released. The phone call failed and Accardo was held on an investigation. He was later released and not charged.

Some time after, Al Capone went away to prison and Louis Campagna, Frank Nitti and Paul DeLucia were considered the top bosses of the Capone Gang. It was said that when the Capone Gang was "reinventing" themselves and re-organizing, it was Tony Accardo who stepped forward with a plan proposal whereby mob activities were departmentalized and placed in charge of an expert hoodlum. It's believed that this proposal was the final step in Accardo's progression when Frank Nitti rewarded Accardo by making him one of his Lieutenants otherwise known as being made a Capo.

Now that Accardo was a Capo and the money situation had change substantially he decided that was a good time to get married. Tony Accardo married Clarice Porter at Crown Point, Indiana by Howard H. Kemp, then Justice of the Peace. One report states it was on June 11, 1934 when the two married. At the time of the marriage, Tony Accardo wrote down chauffeur as his occupation. They would go on to have two daughters Marie Judith and Linda Lee, and adopt two sons, Anthony Ross and Joseph Frank Accardo.

CERTIFICATE OF MARRIAGE

THE STATE OF INDIANA, LAKE COUNTY, S.S.

THIS CERTIFIES, that I joined in marriage as husband and wife Tony Accardo and Clarice Porter on the 11th day of June 1934

Howard H. Kemp J.P.

A 30654

THE PERSON SOLEMNIZING THE MARRIAGE WILL DETACH AND RETURN THIS CERTIFICATE TO COUNTY CLERK AT ONCE

LICENSE

APPLICATION FOR MARRIAGE LICENSE—MALE

Application is hereby made for a license for marriage

Upon the following statement of fact relative to said parties:

1. *The full christian and surname of the man is* Tony Accardo
2. *Color* White 3. *Where born* Chicago Ill (Town, County, State or Country)
4. *When born* April 28-1906 (Day, month and year)
5. *Present residence* 2724 N. Meade Ave Chicago Ill
6. *Present occupation* Chauffeur
7. *If no occupation, what means has the male contracting party to support a family?* —
8. *Is the male contracting party of nearer blood kin to the female contracting party than second cousin?* no
9. *Full christian and surname of father* Frank Accardo
10. *His color* White 11. *His birthplace* Italy
12. *His occupation* Shoemaker 13. *His residence* Chicago Ill
14. *Full christian and maiden name of mother* Mary DeLotta
15. *Her color* White 16. *Her birthplace* Italy
17. *Her occupation* housewife 18. *Her residence* Chicago Ill
19. *Has the male contracting party been an inmate of any county asylum or home for indigent persons within the last five years?*
20. *If so, is he now able to support a family and likely to so continue?*
21. *Is this his first marriage?* yes
22. *If not, how often has he been married?*
23. *Has such prior marriage, or marriages, been dissolved?*
24. *If so, how and when?*
25. *Is the male contracting party afflicted with epilepsy, tuberculosis, venereal, or any other contagious or transmissible disease?*
26. *Is he an imbecile, feeble-minded, idiotic or insane, or is he under guardianship as a person of unsound mind?*

Signature of Applicant Tony Accardo

State of Indiana, Lake County, ss:

The applicant, being duly sworn, deposes and says that he has personal knowledge of the facts above stated and that they and each of them are true.

Tony Accardo

JUN 11 1934

Subscribed and sworn to before me, this 11 *day of* ______, 193__

[signature]

Clerk Lake Circuit Court

315

No. A.

APPLICATION FOR MARRIAGE LICENSE—FEMALE

Application is hereby made for a license for marriage

Upon the following statement of fact relative to said parties:

1. The full christian and surname of the woman is Clarice Porter
2. Color White 3. Where born Chicago Ill (Town, County, State or Country)
4. When born Dec 10-1910 (Day, month and year)
5. Present residence 428 St James Chicago Ill
6. Present occupation none
7. Full christian and surname of father Ross Porter
8. His color White 9. His birthplace McComb Ill
10. His occupation 11. His residence dead
12. Full christian and maiden name of mother Nettie McCloud
13. Her color White 14. Her birthplace McComb Ill
15. Her occupation housewife 16. Her residence Avon Ill
17. Has the female contracting party been an inmate of any county asylum or home for indigent persons within the last five years?
18. Is this her first marriage? Yes
19. If not, how often has she been married?
20. Has such prior marriage, or marriages, been dissolved?
21. If so, how and when?
22. Is the female contracting party afflicted with epilepsy, tuberculosis, venereal, or any other contagious or transmissible disease?
23. Is she an imbecile, feeble-minded, idiotic or insane, or is she under guardianship as a person of unsound mind?

Signature of Applicant Clarice Porter

State of Indiana, Lake County, ss:

The applicant, being duly sworn, deposes and says that she has personal knowledge of the facts above stated and that they and each of them are true.

Clarice Porter

Subscribed and sworn to before me, this JUN 1 1934 day of 193

George [illegible]

Clerk Lake Circuit Court

Tony Dark

In 1941 Tony Accardo and mobster Lawrence Imburgio were partners in running a handbook on the first floor at 186-92 North Clark Street in Chicago under the ruse of a cigar store. The two were partners until the end of 1942.

After a few raids by law enforcement at the mob handbook charges were brought against Tony Accardo in December 1943. He was indicted for conspiracy to operate a gambling house forcing him to make a few court appearances. Others charged as partners in this gambling operation with Tony Accardo were David Russell, Abe Cohen, Gerald McCann, Joseph Mausby, Charles Johnson, Milton Waldman, Harry Strauss, Sam Miller and Sam "Sal" Goodman. The owner of the building, E. M. Bareuther was also charged with conducting illegal acts injurious to the public morals. Accardo's lawyer filed a motion to suppress the evidence since the Chicago police did not have search warrants for their raids.

One report says that the charges were nolle processed on a motion from the state since there was an understanding that Accardo was going to be inducted into the U.S. Army go fight overseas in World War II. In 1944 he was rejected for military service by his local draft board which ruled him "morally unfit" and classified as a 4F.

By 1949 the building which housed the cigar store was torn down and the site became a parking lot.

One of Tony "JB" Accardo's Chicago Police Arrest Photos

IN THE CRIMINAL COURT OF COOK COUNTY

THE PEOPLE OF THE STATE OF ILLINOIS	)	
vs.	)	No. 43 - 1664
TONY ACCARDO, alias, etc., et al.	)	

BILL OF PARTICULARS

Now comes the People of the State of Illinois, by Thomas J. Courtney, State's Attorney of Cook County, their attorney, and files the following Bill of Particulars.

1. That on May 2, 1942, and on May 25, 1942, and on July 21, 1942, and on November 5, 1942, and on December 9, 1942, and on February 20, 1943, and on June 2, 1943, and on June 21, 1943 and on July 31, 1943, and on August 26, 1943, and on September 18, 1943, the defendant, E. W. Bareuther, being then and there the agent and person in charge for the owner of the premises commonly known and described as the first floor number 186 North Clark Street in the City of Chicago, County of Cook and State of Illinois, unlawfully, wilfully and deceitfully conspired, combined, confederated and agreed with the defendants Dave Russell, Abe Cohen, Joseph Mausby, Charles Johnson, Milton Waldman, Harry Strauss, Sam Miller, and Sol Goodman, to do divers illegal acts injurious to the public morals; that is to say, that the said defendant, E. W. Bareuther, then and there being the agent and the person in charge for the owner of the premises commonly known and described as the first floor Number 186 North Clark Street, in the City of Chicago, County of Cook, and State of Illinois, rented, leased and knowingly permitted the said premises to be used by the said defendants Dave Russell, Abe Cohen, Joseph Mausby, Charles Johnson, Milton Waldman, Harry Strauss, Sam Miller, and Sol Goodman, to keep said premises, stores, rooms, and parts thereof with certain books, instruments and devices known as "bet tickets," "hard cards," "wall sheets," and other writings therein, for the purpose of recording and registering bets and wagers upon the result of trials and contests

Tony Dark

Tony Accardo's power was growing and it helped that he had three powerful Chicago politicians in his pocket. The three were State Senator James Adduci, State Representative Robert Petrone and Chicago Alderman George Kells. He also had four of Chicago's top lawyers on his side George Callaghan, George Beiber, his brother Harold Callaghan and Roland V. Libonati.

Around 1943 is when the decision was made that Tony Accardo would be acting boss of the Outfit while Paul DeLucia and Louis Campagna served their time in prison. As acting boss, Accardo took it upon himself to further re-work the system that Al Capone had set up and later that Frank Nitti, Louis Campagna and Paul DeLucia refined.

Tony Accardo built up the Outfit and gave it something it had been missing, harmony. The first thing Accardo did was focus on making the Italians happy with all his fellow Italians. He gave each member of the Italian extraction his own territory and area of control.

Accardo was also very close with political powers Michael Kenna, who was the former Alderman Al Capone had placed in the old First Ward, and Joe Clark, who was the former committeeman of the First Ward. Both still held considerable political influence in Chicago which Accardo used to his advantage.

He had his hands in a gambling joint at 217 North Clark Street in Chicago with Mel Clark. Subsequently Bernie Korshak, brother of mob lawyer Sidney Korshak, took over Clark's gambling interest. It was said Korshak was fronting for Charles Gioe. This place had phone wires running all over Chicago from the 9,000 taverns, cigar stores, newsstands and candy shops that took in bets. These places would call the bets in to the room on Clark Street. The net profit, after payment of all the expenses, overhead and "ice" was in excess of $25,000-a-day which net $7,500,000 a year in "clear" profit.

On September 27, 1943 Tony Accardo surrendered himself to the FBI who were looking for him for some unknown reason. He was fingerprinted and photographed. He refused to answer any questions and was turned over to the U.S. Marshal where he was later released.

In 1944 Accardo's name surfaced in an investigation on Anthony Pope who was under investigation for theft from interstate shipments. Accardo was said to be "brought in" on the ownership of the Pulaski Radio Store at 1180 Milwaukee Avenue by mobster William "Smokes" Aloisio. The store used to be owned by William Wytrykus who was murdered on December 2, 1943. Pulaski Radio Store was the scene of illegal liquor negotiations.

On February 14, 1944 Tony Accardo was arrested by the County Highway Police on a charge of "Investigation". They had information that Accardo was muscling in on gambling operations and they tried to charge him with conspiracy to violate gambling laws. Accardo's lawyer George Bieber filed a writ to habeas corpus and Accardo was released.

Weeks later a confidential informant told investigators that Tony Accardo, Sam Rinella and a bookkeeper by the name of "Bloom" were convicted in Federal Court for violation of the NPA and sentenced to 5 years in prison. Both Rinella and Accardo were partners in a liquor business. When investigator searched the U.S.

Courts for these records, they failed to find a conviction on Accardo. Sam Rinella was shot to death in front of his home on November 1, 1951.

On February 12, 1945 Tony Accardo was arrested in the 500 block of W. Worthington Street in Chicago with Sam Giancana and Daniel Beneduce. All three were questioned in the kidnapping of gangster Jake "Greasy Thumb" Guzik. Accardo was released on a writ of habeas corpus but Giancana and Beneduce were charged with disorderly conduct. Allegedly Guzik was held for two days until his "pals" paid $25,000 to $100,000 for his release. Accardo was arrested by the Chicago police on April 13, 1945 to answer further questions concerning the kidnapping.

They also wanted to know what role Accardo played in the murder of J. D. Larrison in April 1944. Larrison, aka Larkin, was shot to death in Matt Capone's tavern at 4839 Ogden Avenue in Cicero. Accardo denied knowing anything about the murder. Two days later Tony Accardo was subpoenaed to appear before a Cook County Grand Jury to answer questions regarding the alleged kidnapping of Guzik. Jake Guzik later denied he had been kidnapped.

Also that year, reports that mobsters Rocco "Gramps" DeGrazio, Paul LaBriola and James Weinberg were operating the A&L Sales Company in Kansas City, Missouri. From there they would transport bootleg whiskey to the dry states all over America. This operation was owned by Tony Accardo and Jake Guzik.

Accardo's power reached ultimate heights by 1945. One example was when the Illinois State Legislature attempted to enact legislation removing the personal responsibility of policeman for damage to personal property when engaged in official duty. One of the state senators at the time named James Adduci told his fellow senators, *"It would be necessary to get the approval of Tony Accardo for this."*

Adduci even made his wife, Lillian Costello, give their license plate number on her car to Tony Accardo because it was a low number, number 928. The number was transferred to Clarice Accardo as a gift to the new and powerful boss.

CRIMINAL COURT
OF
COOK COUNTY, ILLINOIS
26th and California Ave.

TELEPHONE CRAWFORD 7300

THOMAS J. BOWLER, *Clerk*
HARRY BELL, *Chief Deputy.*

Chicago, JAN 10 1944 194

THE PEOPLE OF THE STATE OF ILLINOIS
vs
Tony Accardo

No. 43-1664

To: 1431 Ashland Ave

You are hereby notified that the above entitled cause will be called for trial on the 13th day of Jan A. D. 1944

before Judge RUDOLPH F. DESORT

And on the failure of said defendant to appear the bond will be forfeited and a capias issued for the arrest of such defendant.

Please be present at opening of Court in forenoon.

Thomas J. Bowler
Clerk of the Criminal Court of Cook County.

Chapter 19

The Next Step

One fellow mobster once described Tony Accardo as the most intelligent mobster that ever lived. In the past when men like Al Capone made a decision they would just make it, not Tony Accardo. When it was time to make a decision, he consulted his lawyers, fellow mobsters and politicians to cover every angle that might arise from the decision.

By the late 1940's Accardo had Jake Guzik as his expert on handbook gambling, Harry Russell as his wire service expert, Charles Fischetti as his night club expert, and Murray Humphreys as his labor union expert.

In the basement of his home was a long directors table which he controlled the empire from. The room had indirect lighting with oak panel walls with an antique gun collection adoring them, worth tens of thousands of dollars. Neighbors would talk to each other about the many cars that would gather on board meeting nights when the gangsters met to discuss business and play cards. Often the streets around his house were lined in the finest cars money could buy and many had license plates from all over the United States. Cars that carried such important mobsters as New York's Frank Costello, Kansas City's Tony Gizzo, and Miami's many mob bosses.

Accardo and his family lived as kings, his children wore the finest clothes money could buy, and they spent their summers at an expensive camp near Eagle River, Wisconsin. For Christmas 1949 Tony Accardo had the finest Christmas decorations in all of Chicago out on his front lawn. A 40-foot lighted tree dominated the scene with wooden colorful figures representing Santa and his reindeer and sled. There were moving figures made of wood on tracks representing people ice skating around and around the yard from one side to the other with a loud speaker playing Christmas songs. However, the constant line of cars that slowed down to take a look caused traffic jams and did not please Tony Accardo. ALL the decorations were taken down and hauled away on December 26, the day after Christmas. Next Christmas, 1950, there were no decorations at all.

Tony Accardo had a reputation of never having to spend a night in jail after being arrested. However, on Lincoln's Birthday in 1945 Accardo was driving through Chicago when he was pulled over and arrested for questioning in a gambling case. Since it was a federal holiday, the courts were closed and Tony Accardo had to spend the night in jail awaiting the courts to open back up.

Tony Accardo's relationship with his father may have been not so good. Evidence of this came on August 3, 1946 when the phones at Tony Accardo's house were tapped by law enforcement. As they listened in to Clarice talking to Bessie Accardo Meris, Tony's sister, she referred to Tony's father as the "old man" and how he was over the previous night for dinner. She mentioned that Tony could not even talk nice to him. Clarice said she told the "old man" that Tony cannot be bothered with all of his little arguments since he had real problems on his mind. Clarice had mentioned that they were attempting to find his parents Frank and Mary a new place to live. They had been living with Tony's sister Mary Simonelli.

The day before that phone call, Tony Accardo had spoken to George King, who operated the Lumber Gardens gambling spot in Melrose Park for Rocco DeGrazio, and King had suggested they go and look at the house located at 1549 North 32nd Avenue in Melrose Park for his parents to live. Tony Accardo decided the house was too small for his parents. Two days later a phone call was made by mobster Rocco Fanelli from Accardo's home to Peter DeFrancesca, who lived at 2112 Lake Street in Melrose Park and was known then as a bookie, and offered him $1,500 for 2 empty lots at 1319 Broadway in Melrose Park. DeFrancesca wanted $4,500 for the two lots but quickly agreed to the $1,500 when he found out it was for Accardo.

The problem was at the end of World War II all of the soldiers coming home had government loans to purchase a new homes. Because they were veterans, there was a veteran's priority clause enabled that gave veterans priority in having new homes built for them. So what did Accardo do? He found a veteran, had the new home built in his name, and then when the home was finished, the veteran would transfer the title of the home to Accardo's parents.

The veteran he found just happened to be his brother. John P. Accardo, who had just been released from the service on April 17, 1946, was asked by Tony Accardo to do this for him as a favor. Apparently Tony Accardo did not know that much about Johnnie Accardo because he called Clarice and asked her if Johnnie was married and what his wife's name was, which was Ann Accardo. Both Johnnie and Ann had been either living or staying at 3536 Harlem Avenue in Chicago which was the home of John Moore, aka Claude Maddox, who was very close to Tony Accardo.

Once Johnnie Accardo and another veteran named Louis Mack agreed to have their names used as veterans for the two lots, Tony Accardo's lawyer Joseph Bulger filed the application with the Federal Housing Administration. It was approved two weeks later, and had the two "veterans" sign over the house to Frank and Mary Accardo once it was completed in November, 1946. Louis Mack was given an envelope of money for his help.

The house was completed in just two months by the Louis S. Macro Company, which used to be located at 1206 5th Avenue in Melrose Park. The house turned out to be a five-room unit, 52 x 125 feet in size.

When law enforcement officials discovered this situation, they looked into developing charges against Accardo for fraud. However, they decided it would have been too hard to convict him on that charge. Two plots of land that should have gone to veterans who put their lives on the line for their country so they could have a home once they arrived back in America were stolen by a multi-millionaire gangster. God Bless America.

However, it is not known if Frank and Mary Accardo actually lived in the house. One report stated that the parents of Tony Accardo went to live with their son Martin Accardo in Miami in 1947. It was there that Frank Accardo died on December 29, 1949. His body was shipped back to Chicago for the funeral. Many of America's top mobsters attended the wake. The street which the funeral home was located on was blocked off so only invited mourners were allowed in. Mob bosses from New York, New Jersey, California, Kansas City, St. Louis, Detroit, Florida and Cleveland attended. They all ate and drank heavily while gambling together the entire time. There was over $50,000 worth of floral designs sent to the wake and the line to pay final respects took hours. All of the funeral arrangements were actually handled by mobster Joseph Fischetti.

The home Accardo had built for his parents at 1319 North 19th Avenue, Melrose Park. Photo was taken in 2014

On the next few pages are law enforcement reports when they listened in on the Accardo home in 1946.

ANTHONY ACCARDO, with alias, JOE BATTERS
TECHNICAL SURVEILLANCE

The following is a summary of the results obtained from the technical surveillance conducted on the ACCARDO home, 1431 North Ashland Avenue, River Forest, Illinois, from Friday, July 19 through Thursday, July 25, 1946.

In a conversation had by Mrs. ACCARDO with an unknown woman on Friday, July 19, Mrs. ACCARDO indicated that her husband, TONY ACCARDO, alias, JOE BATTERS, was home as of that date; however, in another conversation had with the plumber on the same date, Mrs. ACCARDO told him that her husband was out of town.

Director, FBI 7/26/46

On Saturday, July 20 an unknown man talked to Mrs. ACCARDO and told her he might leave Monday. It is possible that this man was ANTHONY ACCARDO and the leaving referred to may have been in connection with the alleged meeting of big-shot hoodlums throughout the country in New York City

A woman, believed to be Mrs. TONY CAPEZIO, asked CLARISE ACCARDO for the telephone number of NICK, the gardener. From this conversation it is believed that reference was made to N. R. ROTH who occupies quarters over the ACCARDO garage and who has been previously referred to.

In a conversation between CLARISE ACCARDO, TONY ACCARDO's wife, and a man referred to as WILLIE, it was indicated that TONY ACCARDO would be at home on Sunday, July 21 and it was suggested that WILLIE bring "that stuff" out to him on Sunday before noon.

On Sunday, July 21, the ACCARDOS entertained CHARLIE and CORA, whose last names are not known, and also the KELLYS for dinner. It is believed that the KELLYS are identical with Mr. and Mrs. MIKE SPRANZE. MIKE SPRANZE is a former AL CAPONE bodyguard and is referred to by Syndicate members as "KELLY".

On the morning of Thursday July 25, TONY ACCARDO, JR. talked to DANNY O'NEIL, the son of Mr. and Mrs. DANIEL J. O'NEIL, 1730 North 78th Court, Elmwood Park, Illinois. It is believed that DANIEL J. O'NEIL is identical with DANIEL BENEDUCE, a well known hoodlum.

DANIEL O'NEIL asked TONY, JR. if his father was home and when TONY replied that he was DANIEL said he thought he had gone to New York. TONY, JR. advised DANNY his father came back the same day he left, arriving in the evening.

This conversation indicates that TONY ACCARDO was in New York perhaps sometime between Sunday, July 21 and Thursday, July 25, 1946.

ANTHONY ACCARDO, wa JOE BATTERS
TECHNICAL SURVEILLANCE
1431 North Ashland

The following information has been obtained from the technical surveillance of the residence of ANTHONY ACCARDO, 1431 North Ashland, River Forest, Illinois, for the period July 26 to August 2, 1946.

On July 26, 1946, CLARISF ACCARDO, the wife of TONY ACCARDO, alias JOE BATTERS, made a date with MARIE CAPEZIO to meet at 6:30 PM. MARIE CAPEZIO is the wife of TOUGH TONY CAPEZIO, who resides at 1408 North Ashland Avenue, River Forest.

Mr. EUGENE BERNSTEIN called and asked for Mr. ACCARDO, but ACCARDO's wife advised he was out of town. BERNSTEIN, it is to be noted, is the attorney for JACK GUZIK.

A general conversation was also had between Mrs. ACCARDO and MARIAN CURRY, who is the wife of FRANCIS CURRY, 517 Western Avenue, Joliet, Illinois. FRANCIS CURRY at one time was reported to have been the slot machine king in Will County, Illinois, and is the son-in-law of former Sheriff MIKE BREEN.

In a conversation held on July 27, 1946 between CLARISE ACCARDO and her sister, IRENE STAGGS, 1407 North Kellogg, Galesburg, Illinois, Mrs. ACCARDO indicated that her husband, JOE BATTERS, is home, and that they would probably be down to Galesburg, Illinois, on or about August 10, 1946 for a visit.

On Sunday, July 28, 1946, the ACCARDOS entertained numerous guests at their home for dinner, and it is believed that among the guests was JOHN E. MOORE, alias CLAUDE MADDOX. It was indicated that TONY ACCARDO invited many people over that day, especially those who lived in his neighborhood. Such individuals would probably include SAM GIANCANA and TONY CAPEZIO.

On Monday, July 29, 1946, numerous unknown individuals phoned the ACCARDO home and were advised by Mrs. ACCARDO that her husband was out of town; however, in a conversation had between TONY CCARDO, Jr. and DANNY O'NEILL, it was indicated that both his mother and father were home that day.

An individual believed to be JOHN CERONE talked with his wife from the ACCARDO home on July 29.

The case entitled "Anthony Pape, et al, Theft of 603 Cases Old Grandad Whiskey-Theft From Interstate Shipment", indicates that JOHN CERONE is

a gambler and hoodlum of the North Side of Chicago, and with WILLIAM ALOISIO. FRANKA BALLETINO and JACK REDISO, CERONE was known to have participated in the purchase of an unknown quantity of liquor stolen in September, 1943. ALOISIO, BALLETINO and CERONE operate the Show Tap Lounge, 2024 Milwaukee Avenue.

On July 30, 1946 an unknown man called the Delta Air Lines and asked what time the next plane was leaving for Los Angeles, California. This man was advised that Delta Air Lines did not have any planes going to California and it was suggested that the best route would be via United Air Lines, T.W.A. or the American Air Lines.

On July 31, Mrs. ACCARDO talked to a real estate man concerning the purchase of a cottage, location unknown, and mentioned that the prospective buyers are an elderly couple.

ANTHONY ACCARDO, wa, Joe Batters, Technical Surveillance
1431 North Ashland, River Forest, Illinois

The following information has been obtained from the technical surveillance from August 1 through August 38, 1946:

8/1/46: GENE BERNSTEIN, who is believed to be identical with EUGENE BERNSTEIN, an attorney who has represented JACK GUZIK and other hoodlums of Chicago, called CLARISE ACCARDO and told her to tell TONY ACCARDO that he, BERNSTEIN, would be out at 5 o'clock tonight.

8/2/46: A man named GUIDO (phonetic) called CLARISE ACCARDO and asked to speak with JOE BATTERS). GUIDO stated that JOE had called him up. Mrs. ACCARDO left the phone for a minute and then

advised GUIDO that "they want you to come out here. It's nothing special."

GEORGE KING asked CLARISE ACCARDO if JOE (BATTERS) was home and was advised that he is away. Evidently JOE had asked GEORGE KING to find him a house for his, ACCARDO's, parents, for GEORGE KING advised that he found something that JOE had asked him about and mentioned that houses go like hotcakes. (It is possible that GEORGE KING is identical with the GEORGE KING who manages and operates the Lumber Gardens at Melrose Park for the DeGRAZIOS.) (The DeGRAZIOS are alleged to have Syndicate connections.) GEORGE KING again called and said that he would not be able to get out to the ACCARDO home that afternoon but suggested that she look at a five room house at 1549 North 32nd Avenue in Melrose Park.

In a call by Mrs. CLARISE ACCARDO to Bayport 1513, which is listed to ALBERT W. NICKSON, 9606 South Avenue L, she conversed with MAE (who is possibly Mrs. ALBERT NICKSON). MAE advised that MARY and DANNY were over for dinner the last night and that DANNY is working at the steel mill. (This reference is, no doubt, to Mr. and Mrs. DANIEL J. O'NEILL of 1700 North 78th Court, Elmwood Park, Illinois. It is believed that DANIEL J. O'NEILL is actually DANIEI BENEDUCE, for DANNY O'NEILL is an oft'time used alias of BENEDUCE.

8/3/46: CLARISE ACCARDO phoned her sister IRENE (Mrs. HARVEY S. STAGGS, 1407 North Kellog, Galesburg, Illinois) and mentioned that she would see her next Sunday. Mrs. ACCARDO is bringing her children down to her sister's in Galesburg to spend a week. Mrs. ACCARDO mentioned that she would like to go to California next week but did not know whether she could get reservations.

In a conversation with an unknown woman concerning the old folks (TONY ACCARDO's parents), Mrs. ACCARDO mentioned that the old man was over last night and he mentioned that his son can' even talk nice to him. Mrs. ACCARDO told the old man that he (TONY ACCARDO) can't be bothered with all of the old man's little arguments since he has real things on his mind. In this conversation mention was made to the ACCARDOS trying to find a house for the old folks to live in.

8/4/46: A man named FANELLI (who is possibly identical with ROCCO M.

8/7/46: In a conversation between an unknown man and CLARISE ACCARDO concerning joists for the house which is being built for the ACCARDO parents, the man mentioned that JOHNNIE ROCCO understands what was wanted. The man told Mrs. ACCARDO to have MOONEY (MOONEY is an alias often used by SAM GIANCANA) call him at Monroe 6143, which is the Wreckers Union, Local 225, 804 West Polk Street.

At 2:00 p.m., an unknown man called and asked for JOE (BATTERS). CLARISE ACCARDO said that he was out and she was asked to have JOE call HYMIE LEVIN at the hospital.

8/8/46: CLARISE ACCARDO called Mrs. PATRICK MANNING, 1439 North Franklin Avenue, River Forest. (It is to be noted that PATRICK MANNING is Vice President of the Tremont Auto Sales Company associated with PETER G. TREMONT, and MANNING may be identical with PAT MANO. MANNING is also Director of the Joliet Citizens Brewing Company.) CLARISE ACCARDO told Mrs. MANNING that the KELLYS were over to her home last night. (KELLY is a known alias of MIKE SPRANZE, former AL CAPONE bodyguard.) Mrs. MANNING advised Mrs. ACCARDO that the lumber for the house was ready and suggested that she get in touch with the O'Brien Lumber Company (WALTER W. O'BRIEN, 1105 Lathrope Avenue, River Forest.)

ANTHONY ACCARDO, with alias, JOE BATTERS
1431 North Ashland, River Forest, Illinois
Technical Surveillance

The following information has been obtained from this surveillance for the period August 10 to August 16, 1946:

JAKE, probably JACK GUZIK talked to CLARISE ACCARDO, wife of TONY ACCARDO, and asked what time the family was going to eat, indicating that he would like to come to dinner.

JOE BULGER has been in communication with CLARISE ACCARDO and indicated that they would need a contract, possibly for the house being built for the parents of TONY ACCARDO. The Chicago files reflect that one JOSEPH I. BULGER is an attorney at 139 North Clark Street, and is also the brother of LAWRENCE IMBURGIO. LAWRENCE was once mayor of Melrose Park, Illinois, and attorney for CHARLES FISCHETTI. Chicago telephone directory lists J. IMBURGIO BULGER, attorney at law with offices at 139 North Clark Street, residence at 3000 North Sheridan Road, Chicago, Illinois.

MARIE CAPEZIO, wife of "TOUGH TONY" CAPEZIO, a lieutenant in the Syndicate, has been in communication with CLARISE ACCARDO, and indicated that she, Mrs. CAPEZIO was not going to Galesburg with Mrs. ACCARDO.

Mrs. ACCARDO has also been in communication with DOROTHY MANNING at Forest 6028. This number was listed to PATRICA MANNING, 1439 Franklin Avenue, River Forest. PATRICK MANNING is associated with the Tremont Motor Sales Company of Chicago and has dealt with various members of the Syndicate, obtaining automobiles for them.

Mr. EUGENE BERNSTEIN, attorney for JACK GUZIK, has also been in contact with CLARISE ACCARDO and made inquiry as to the whereabouts of her husband. This contact was made on August 12, 1946 and Mrs. ACCARDO indicated that she thought BERNSTEIN could see her husband there (at the ACCARDO residence) in an hour.

On August 13, 1946 WILLIE BELMONTE contacted CLARISE ACCARDO and asked if TONY (CAPEZIO) was there. Mrs. ACCARDO advised that CAPEZIO was not at the ACCARDO residence but gave BELMONTE the CAPEZIO phone number. Subsequently Mrs. ACCARDO contacted BELMONTE telephonically and asked if he had been successful in contacting CAPEZIO. BELMONTE's telephone number is Forest 4024 and he is listed as WILLIAM M. BELMONTE, 7620 Washington Boulevard, River Forest, Illinois.

ANTHONY ACCARDO, with alias, JOE BATTERS
1431 North Ashland
River Forest, Illinois
TECHNICAL SURVEILLANCE

The following information has been obtained from this surveillance for the period August 16 through August 22, 1946:

On August 16 CLARISE ACCARDO and her son, [redacted], left for an unidentified place in Indiana to spend the day with the intention of returning to their home on Saturday, August 17. It is not known where they were actually going to visit and it is believed that TONY ACCARDO, SR. was to be met by Mrs. ACCARDO and her son. On August 17 in a conversation with MARIE CAPEZIO, wife of TONY CAPEZIO, Mrs. ACCARDO mentioned that she was home and had a very nice time and indicated that LOU NEUSAL's house was beautiful. The identity of LOU NEUSAL is unknown and the Chicago Field Office indices are negative. Mrs. ACCARDO further advised Mrs. CAPEZIO that they played cards and that NANCY and CLARE came over and that MOLLIE was up there. MOLLIE is a friend of the NEUSALS from Detroit whom CLARISE ACCARDO met in Florida. Mention was also made that ROSE FLANDO, undoubtedly the wife of ANDREW J. FLANDO, the Republican Ward Committeeman for the 25th Ward of Chicago, was the big winner in the card game, having won $80.

On Sunday, August 18, there were no outgoing calls and one incoming call was unanswered, indicating that no one was home at all that day.

On August 19 an individual named TONY LANCE (phonetic) called and told CLARISE ACCARDO that he wanted to see "that fellow", referring undoubtedly to TONY ACCARDO, alias, JOE BATTERS. Mrs. ACCARDO told LANCE to take a ride by if he wanted to. The Chicago Field Office indices are negative on LANCE.

On the same day an individual named BOB, last name unknown, called Mrs. ACCARDO and said that he was going to take a run over and she indicated that he had better make it a little later because "he is kind of busy right now". Mrs. ACCARDO was undoubtedly referring to her husband, JOE BATTERS. BOB said that he would be over between 4 and 5. BOB's identity is unknown.

Also on the same date, August 19, MIKE, who is probably MIKE SPRANZE, alias MIKE KELLY, called Mrs. ACCARDO to say "hello" and she suggested that he take a ride out when he had time. MIKE said that he just wanted to deliver his love and to tell her that he was around whenever she wanted him. This reference is undoubtedly double talk and is meant to let Mrs. ACCARDO know that MIKE is home in case her husband, TONY ACCARDO, wants him.

On August 20 Mrs. ACCARDO called JOSEPH IMBURGIO BULGER who is a hoodlum attorney with offices at 139 North Clark Street, and she asked if he could stop by at her house on his way home. BULGER said that he would. BULGER is the brother of LAWRENCE IMBURGIO and as previously mentioned he is handling the legal arrangements regarding a house which the ACCARDOS are building for TONY ACCARDO's parents, said house being placed in the name of JOHN ACCARDO, TONY ACCARDO's brother, because JOHN is a G.I.

On August 20 ANDREW, probably ANDREW FLANDO, Republican Ward Committeeman for the 25th Ward, called and asked Mrs. ACCARDO if [redacted] is going to be in town Friday, August 23. Mrs. ACCARDO said that he was and asked ANDREW if he got tickets (probably for the All-Star Football Game). Mrs. ACCARDO advised ANDREW that [redacted] will be home Friday; that he is planning on going, and ANDREW indicated that he would pick him up and take him and bring him back.

In a call to the Fair Store, a Chicago Department Store, on August 20, Mrs. ACCARDO talked to Mr. OILER (phonetic) in the furniture department and stated that Mr. VIGNOLA told her to come down and see Mr. OILER about a maple dining room set. Mention was made later in the day to an unidentified woman by Mrs. ACCARDO that JOHN VIGNOLA went down to the Fair Store for her to see about her getting a dining room set.

JOHN VIGNOLA resides at 930 Lathrop Avenue, River Forest, Illinois, and according to [redacted] assigned

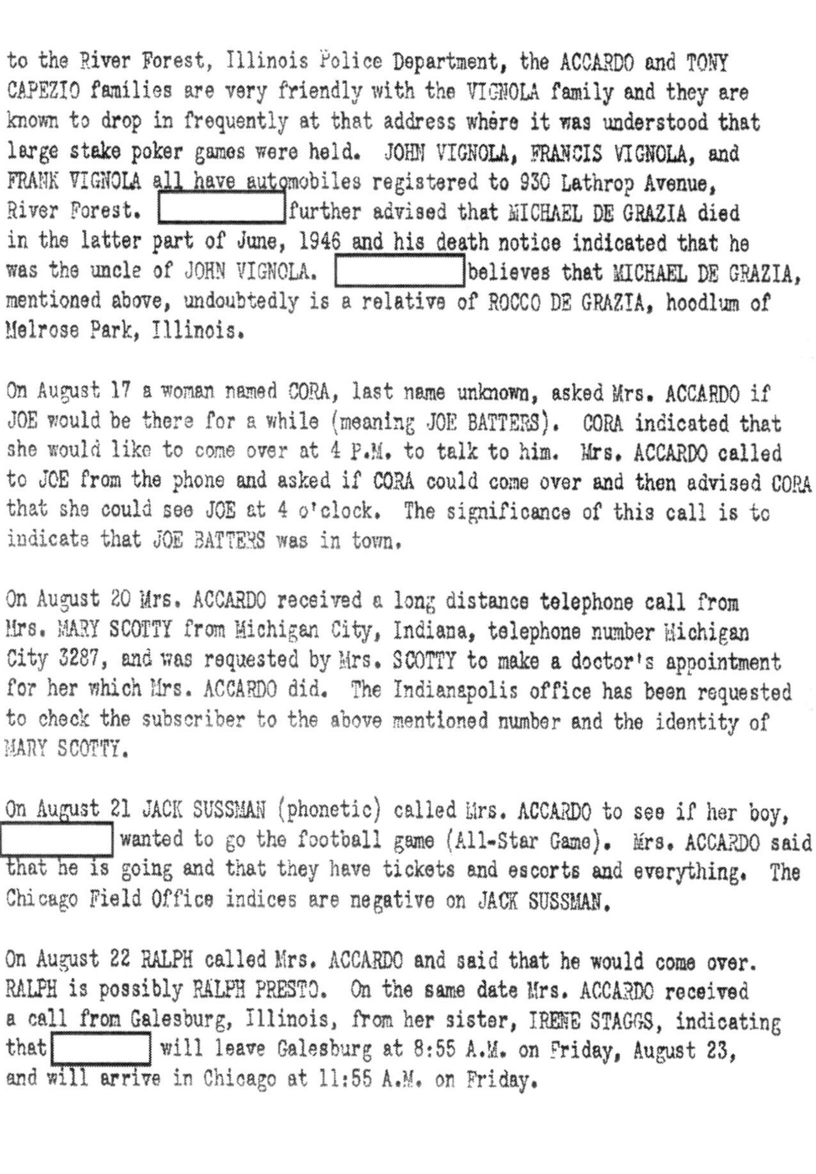

to the River Forest, Illinois Police Department, the ACCARDO and TONY CAPEZIO families are very friendly with the VIGNOLA family and they are known to drop in frequently at that address where it was understood that large stake poker games were held. JOHN VIGNOLA, FRANCIS VIGNOLA, and FRANK VIGNOLA all have automobiles registered to 930 Lathrop Avenue, River Forest. [redacted] further advised that MICHAEL DE GRAZIA died in the latter part of June, 1946 and his death notice indicated that he was the uncle of JOHN VIGNOLA. [redacted] believes that MICHAEL DE GRAZIA, mentioned above, undoubtedly is a relative of ROCCO DE GRAZIA, hoodlum of Melrose Park, Illinois.

On August 17 a woman named CORA, last name unknown, asked Mrs. ACCARDO if JOE would be there for a while (meaning JOE BATTERS). CORA indicated that she would like to come over at 4 P.M. to talk to him. Mrs. ACCARDO called to JOE from the phone and asked if CORA could come over and then advised CORA that she could see JOE at 4 o'clock. The significance of this call is to indicate that JOE BATTERS was in town.

On August 20 Mrs. ACCARDO received a long distance telephone call from Mrs. MARY SCOTTY from Michigan City, Indiana, telephone number Michigan City 3287, and was requested by Mrs. SCOTTY to make a doctor's appointment for her which Mrs. ACCARDO did. The Indianapolis office has been requested to check the subscriber to the above mentioned number and the identity of MARY SCOTTY.

On August 21 JACK SUSSMAN (phonetic) called Mrs. ACCARDO to see if her boy, [redacted] wanted to go the football game (All-Star Game). Mrs. ACCARDO said that he is going and that they have tickets and escorts and everything. The Chicago Field Office indices are negative on JACK SUSSMAN.

On August 22 RALPH called Mrs. ACCARDO and said that he would come over. RALPH is possibly RALPH PRESTO. On the same date Mrs. ACCARDO received a call from Galesburg, Illinois, from her sister, IRENE STAGGS, indicating that [redacted] will leave Galesburg at 8:55 A.M. on Friday, August 23, and will arrive in Chicago at 11:55 A.M. on Friday.

ANTHONY ACCARDO, wa: Joe Batters
1431 North Ashland Avenue
TECHNICAL SURVEILLANCE:

The following information has been obtained from this surveillance for the period from September 6 through September 12, 1946:

On Friday morning, September 6, 1946, at approximately 8:00 o'clock A.M., TONY ACCARDO left his home for a vacation in Wisconsin, but it is not known who accompanied him. Further information from this technical surveillance leads us to believe that ACCARDO is visiting at the home of JOHN E. MOORE, alias: Claude Maddox, at Winter, Wisconsin. Originally it was believed that ACCARDO would be gone for approximately one week, but additional information now indicates that he may be gone for a longer period of time. The Milwaukee Field Office has been advised of ACCARDO's presence in Winter, Wisconsin and that office was instructed to discreetly ascertain his activities and associates there.

On Saturday night, September 7th, Mrs. CLARISE ACCARDO attended a wedding at the Blackstone Hotel, and it is believed that MARIE CAPEZIO drove Mrs. ACCARDO to the hotel. The following individuals were present at the wedding:

ALICE MOORE - the wife of JOHN E. MOORE.

MARIE CAPEZIO - the wife of Tough Tony Capezio.

Mr. and Mrs. JAMES NUZZO. NUZZO is reported to be the gambling boss for the River Wards (20th, 25th, 27th and 28th).

Mrs. NANCY DE LUCIA - the wife of PAUL DE LUCIA, with aliases: Paul "The Waiter" Ricca, Paul Salvi.

Mr. and Mrs. MIKE SPRANZE.

CHARLOTTE (believed to be CHARLOTTE CAMPAGNA).

Mr. and Mrs. SAM GIANCANA.

DOROTHY MANNING - wife of PATRICK MANNING.

Mrs. ROBERT ANSANI - wife of ROBERT ANSANI, who has an interest in the Havana Beverage Company and at one time was a partner of JOHN E. MOORE, alias: Claude Maddox, in the Paddock Lounge.

JANET CARREY, alias: Johnnie, the ACCARDOS' Negro maid, stated that TONY ACCARDO doesn't work at all and spends all of his time at home. JOHNNIE further indicated that he is retired at the age of 38. It is to be noted that ACCARDO is 40 years of age, having been born April 28, 1906.

ANTHONY ACCARDO, with alias,
Joe Batters
1431 North Ashland Avenue
Technical Surveillance

The following information has been obtained from this surveillance for the period from August 23 through August 29, 1946:

A man named MORRIE called and asked CLARISE ACCARDO if JOE (BATTERS) were home and she advised him that he was out of town. When questioned as to who he was, MORRIE advised that he was a friend that took them out for a boatride in Florida. MORRIE was asked if he was in town and he said "No" but he wanted to know if JOE would be in in the evening. Mrs. ACCARDO suggested that he come out between 4:30 and 5 o'clock.

An unknown woman asked CLARISE ACCARDO what the address of the project is and Mrs. ACCARDO stated it was 1319 Broadway. The project no doubt refers to the home which is being built for the ACCARDO parents and it is believed the location is in Melrose Park or West Melrose Park, Illinois.

A man named ANDREW, believed to be ANDREW J. FLANDO, Republican Ward Committeeman for the 25th Ward, told Mrs. ACCARDO that he would be out at 6:30 to go to the All Star football game. ANDREW said that his two boys were going and JAMES NUZZO's [redacted] was also going. The office files reflect that JAMES NUZZO is the gambling boss for the River Wards (20, 25, 27, and 28) and has a book and gambling place over the Roosevelt Coffee Shop at 12th Street and Halsted. He also has a summer home at Longbeach, Indiana, valued at $80,000 and a home in Chicago and one in Florida. The telephone number at Longbeach is Michigan City 3287.

Reference is made to a conversation on August 17, 1946, wherein CLARISE ACCARDO advised MARIE CAPEZIO that they had a good time over the weekend at LOU NEUSAL's. It is now believed that LOU NEUSAL is actually LOU NUZZO and it was at the NUZZO home where the ACCARDOS visited at that time.

An unknown man telephoned the Orchid Florist Shop, 2408 West Chicago Avenue, Humboldt 5600, from the ACCARDO home and spoke to a woman named LILL. The Orchid Florist Shop is owned by MARIE CAPEZIO, the wife of Tough TONY CAPEZIO, and by CHARLOTTE CAMPAGNA, who is possibly related to LOUIS CAMPAGNA. LILL recognized the man's voice and said man ordered a $30 bouquet for SAM ORLANDO and told LILL to indicate it was from JOE, ROCKY, and CHARLES FISCHETTI. The indices are being checked on SAM ORLANDO but information regarding him is not available at this time.

Tough TONY CAPEZIO called his wife, MARIE, from the ACCARDO residence and told her that he was going to have "that little guy up the river" named DANDY (phonetic) for dinner.

The above conversations occurred on August 23, 1946.

August 24, 1946:

No pertinent telephone calls were made or received.

August 25, 1946:

No pertinent telephone calls were made or received.

August 26, 1946:

Mrs. ACCARDO called DOROTHY MANNING, the wife of PATRICK MANNING, and DOROTHY advised Mrs. ACCARDO that PAT had made an appointment for CLARISE ACCARDO for Wednesday at 1 P.M. at the Thomas E. Maddox Company (carpets), 207 West Monroe Street. Mrs. ACCARDO was to pretend she was MANNING's sister.

<u>August 27, 1946:</u>

Mr. GALLAGHER, a real estate man, advised CLARISE ACCARDO that he had some report that the DE LUCIA home on Lathorp Avenue was going to be put on the market for sale. According to [redacted] of the River Forest Police Department and National Academy Graduate, PAUL DE LUCIA, with aliases Paul "The Waiter" Ricca and Paul Salvi, is presently serving time in the Browne-Bioff case and is the owner of the nine-room house at 812 North Lathrop Avenue, River Forest, Illinois. DE LUCIA's wife, NANCY, presently resides at the above address and there are two Cadillac automobiles at the premises, one registered in the name of NANCY DE LUCIA and the other in the name of MARY DE LUCIA.

<u>August 28, 1946:</u>

CLARISE ACCARDO telephoned Stanley 1221 which is an unpublished telephone listed to JOHN E. MOORE (probably CLAUDE E. MADDOX), 3536 Harlem Avenue, Riverside, Illinois, and spoke to ANN. Mrs. ACCARDO stated that some fellow showed up at their home this morning with a paper for JOHN to sign and ANN said that he would come by and pick it up. From this conversation it is believed that ANN is ANN ACCARDO, the wife of JOHN ACCARDO (brother of TONY ACCARDO).

Mrs. ACCARDO telephoned Joliet 24481 and left a message for Mr. FRANCIS CURRY that she had called to see if he had heard anything about the dog they were supposed to have shipped on Monday from New York and which had not been received as yet.

<u>August 29, 1946:</u>

No pertinent telephone calls were made or received.

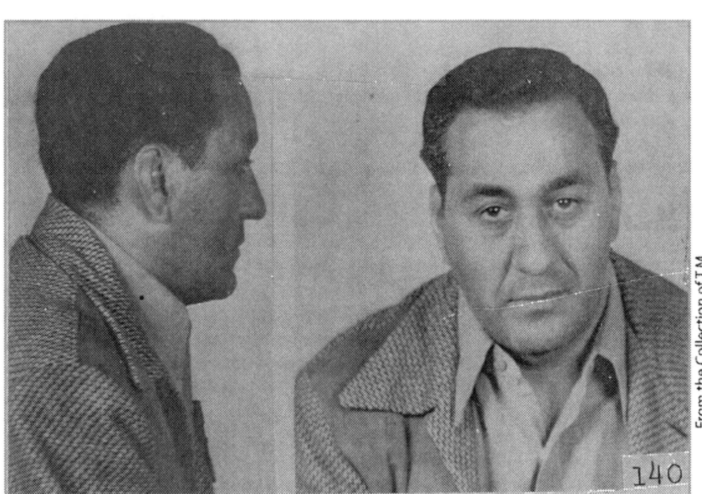

Chicago Police mug shot of Tony Accardo taken September 27, 1943

ANTHONY ACCARDO, with alias Joe Batters
1431 North Ashland Avenue
TECHNICAL SURVEILLANCE

The following information has been obtained from this surveillance from the period September 13 through September 19 inclusive:

September 13, 1946

Regarding the home that is being build for the ACCARDO parents, information indicates that the house will be completed in approximately two weeks and ACCARDO's parents will probably move in either on Friday, September 27, or Saturday, September 28.

In a conversation between CLARISE ACCARDO and MARIE CAPEZIO, Mrs. ACCARDO indicated that she thought her husband would be home this evening. It is to be noted that TONY ACCARDO left on Friday morning, September 6, for Wisconsin, where he sojourned at the home of JOHN E. MOORE, with alias CLAUDE MADDOX. at Winter, Wisconsin. Mrs. ACCARDO said that MOONEY (the alias used by SAM GIANCANA) was supposed to have put a call through to MOORE's home in Wisconsin, but she had not heard from MOONEY.

MOONEY advised CLARISE ACCARDO in double talk that her husband, TONY ACCARDO, was on his way home from Wisconsin.

September 14, 1946

In a conversation between Mrs. ACCARDO and an unknown woman, Mrs. ACCARDO indicated that she was not going out tomorrow night (Sunday, September 15) because her husband would be home.

September 15, 16 and 17, 1946

No pertinent calls.

September 18, 1946

JIM BETTINUS called Mrs. ACCARDO and said that he was out hunting and had a couple of birds he would like to bring over. It is not known whether this is double talk indicating that he had some friends to bring over to the ACCARDO home. JIM BETTINUS was arrested with ROCCO FISCHETTI in 1943 on a gambling indictment issued by a Cook County Grand Jury for operating a gambling establishment at the Rock Garden in Cicero. This indictment was dismissed because of lack of witnesses.

September 19, 1946

SPENCER MICELLI (phonetic) talked to Mrs. ACCARDO and wished to speak with JOE BATTERS, who was not in. Mrs. ACCARDO suggested that SPENCER drive out late tonight or early the following morning, and TONY ACCARDO would be there. The indices of the Chicago Field Division were checked with regard to SPENCER MICELLI with negative results.

ANTHONY ACCARDO, with alias
Joe Batters
1431 North Ashland Avenue
Technical Surveillance

The following information has been obtained from this surveillance for the

period of August 30 through September 5, 1946:

On August 30, 1946 FRANCIS-CURRY of Joliet called and wished to speak with Mrs. ACCARDO, who was out. JOHNNIE CARREY, the colored maid, advised Mr. CURRY that the collie dog arrived yesterday. It is to be noted that through Mr. CURRY arrangements were made with MARY B. BROWNING of Kingston, New York to provide a collie dog for [redacted] Mr. CURRY later talked to Mrs. CLARISE ACCARDO concerning the dog, and he stated that he would send Mrs. BROWNING a wire indicating that the dog had arrived in view of the fact that Mrs. BROWNING was concerned about it.

On August 31, 1946 Mrs. ALICE MOORE, the wife of JOHN E. MOORE, alias CLAUDE MADDOX, called CLARISE ACCARDO, and said that she had gotten in last night but the traffic was terrible. Mrs. MOORE drove the Cadillac home and BOBBY drove the Ford. Mrs. MOORE said that JOHN and ANN ACCARDO, who were staying in her home while she was away, left right away. (JOHN ACCARDO is a brother of TONY ACCARDO). Mrs. MOORE said she heard CLARISE ACCARDO's husband (JOE BATTERS) is going up to Wisconsin. Mrs. ACCARDO said that she did not know, and Mrs. MOORE said that if he does, be sure that he takes warm clothes. This conversation possibly means that TONY ACCARDO is planning a trip to Hayward, Wisconsin, where JOHN E. MOORE has a home.

No pertinent calls were made or received on September 1 and 2, 1946.

On September 3, 1946 a man named ROCKY (possibly ROCCO FISCHETTI or JOHNNY ROCCO) asked CLARISE ACCARDO if JOE (BATTERS) was there, and she replied that he is out of town, and inquired who was calling. When ROCKY said he wanted to see JOE, Mrs. ACCARDO said that she would be there and to stop by. ROCKY said that he would. CLARISE ACCARDO called MIKE SPRANZE and suggested that the SPRANZE's take a ride out some night this week. MIKE said they would.

On September 4, 1946 JOE FANELLI advised Mrs. ACCARDO that he was sending a man over there for some money this morning, and asked CLARISE ACCARDO to tell her husband that they have to get some nails (evidently to be used in the new house which is being built for ACCARDO's parents at 1321 North Broadway Avenue, Melrose Park).

On the above date NANCY DeLUCIA, the wife of PAUL DeLUCIA, aliases PAUL RICCA and PAUL SALVI, called CLARISE ACCARDO and told her that she got back Friday because they had to get PAUL back to school. NANCY asked if her husband (TONY ACCARDO) was there because she wants to ask him about something but won't be able to see him until probably next week, because she is going away tomorrow. NANCY DeLUCIA lives at 812 North Melrose Avenue, River Forest, Illinois, and her husband, PAUL DeLUCIA, with aliases, is serving time in the BROWNE-BIOFF case.

On September 5, 1946, Mrs. ACCARDO endeavored to call NANCY DeLUCIA at Forest 2105 (unpublished) but the line was busy. She also endeavored to call Forest 783, but the line was also busy. This number is listed to WILLIAM A. REMUS, 7453 Madison Street, River Forest, and also is listed to ROY H. MOHR, the township assessor.

On the same date JANET CARREY, the colored maid at the ACCARDO residence, called Drexel 4559 and asked for MONROE, a boy friend of hers, who was not in. This number is listed to EUGENE CURTIS, 523 East 50th Street, Chicago. MONROE then called JANET and said that he went up to the policy place a few minutes ago and that they told him that JANET called while he was gone. From this conversation, it is quite possible that 523 East 50th Street is the location of a policy wheel.

ANTHONY ACCARDO, wa., Joe Batters
1431 North Ashland Avenue
TECHNICAL SURVEILLANCE

The following information was obtained from this surveillance for the period from Friday, September 20, through Thursday, September 26, 1946:

9/20/46 - No pertinent calls not previously reported.

9/21/46 - An unknown woman, believed to be MARIE CAPEZIO, the wife of TONY CAPEZIO, advised Mrs. ACCARDO that she had not heard from her boy friend. Mrs. ACCARDO said that she thought it was all right. It is possible this unknown woman's husband (possibly TONY CAPEZIO) accompanied ACCARDO to Florida. The Bi-Weekly Summary of September 20, 1946 indicated that ACCARDO had gone to Miami.

9/22/46 - In a conversation between JANET (JOHNNIE) CARNEY, the ACCARDOS' colored maid, and her boy friend or possibly her husband, MONROE, last name unknown, it was indicated that JOHNNIE is contemplating leaving the employment of the ACCARDOS. In the event the ACCARDO maid does leave, consideration will be given to interviewing her regarding all information in her possession as to the activities in the ACCARDO home while she was employed there.

Mrs. ACCARDO called SAM GIANCANA, alias "Mooney" at his home, but GIANCANA was not in.

9/23/46 and 9/24/46 - No pertinent calls.

9/25/46 - WILLIE MOORE (phonetic) called Mrs. ACCARDO and asked for JOE (BATTERS). CLARISE ACCARDO stated that she did not expect him back for a couple of days; that he was out of town. MOORE then asked if CHARLIE FISCHETTI is home. Mrs. ACCARDO replied that she wouldn't have any idea, but stated that she imagined that he is in town. WILLIE MOORE's identity is unknown.

9/25/46 - CLARISE ACCARDO called Mrs. KELLY, an alias used by HELEN SPRANZE, the wife of MIKE SPRANZE, and made arrangements to take a ride out there tonight because it rs MICHAEL's birthday. MICHAEL is the son of HELEN SPRANZE.

CLARISE ACCARDO then called MARIE CAPEZIO and mentioned that she was going to the KELLYS' tonight, but Mrs. CAPEZIO did not care to join her.

9/26/46 - No pertinent calls.

Mob Boss

When Paul DeLucia was sent to Federal Prison, Tony Accardo was the acting boss with Jake "Greasy Thumb" Guzik as his top adviser. It was Accardo and Guzik who went into Florida and took over half of the gambling from the "S & G syndicate" bringing millions of new money into Chicago's crime family.

Accardo and Guzik also instigated a gang war resulting in the various killings of individuals involved in the policy racket on the South Side of Chicago. Accardo hand picked mobster Pat Manno as a "front" to run the then quarter-of-a-million-dollar-per-year racket. Accardo partnered up with mobster Frank LaPorte in strip joints in Calumet City Illinois. Evidence to that came when the Chicago Police Department seized some papers from Jake Guzik showing that Accardo was a partner with LaPorte in the Owl Club in Calumet City.

Jake Guzik opened the Owl Club in 1936 with Jim Emery and Butsy Perri as his partners. Accardo was bought into the club in 1936 for $1,000 when it was not doing very well, along with Frank LaPorte and Lester "Killer Kane" Kruse. Accardo and LaPorte cleaned the place up and decorated it, installing roulette wheels, dice tables and poker games. They charged fifty-cents a bet in the hand book and called it the Owl Club because it never closed.

Ten years later the club was taking in two million dollars a year from illegal gambling. In 1955 the U.S. government would go after Accardo for back taxes on this gambling amount claiming he owed $89,425 based on his cut of the gambling profits from the Owl Club. The government charged that Accardo evaded tax payment by having one of the sheet writers make out fictitious losses from bookie operations in the place. Other bet takers in that same place at the same time all showed huge profits.

It was believed at the time that Frank LaPorte's wife, a Marguerite "Mickey" LaPorte, who was from Rockford, Illinois, was a close relative of Tony Accardo. However, there are other reports stating that LaPorte's wife was born in Hungary. Neither claim was investigated further.

Tony Accardo's Top Men in 1946

Jake Guzik - Controlled gambling for Accardo
Murray Humphreys – Controlled labor unions, laundries and policy for Accardo
Eddie Vogel – Controlled slot machines and juke boxes for Accardo
Charles and Rocco Fischetti – Controlled night clubs and booking establishments
Tony Capezio – Controlled bookmakers and Accardo's enforcement squad
Louis Greenberg – Controlled breweries
Joe Fusco – Controlled liquor and its distribution for Accardo
Fred Morelli – Controlled First Ward politics and juke box racket for Accardo
Sam Giancana – Acted as bodyguard and underboss for Accardo

Tony Dark

Tony Accardo wasted little time building his empire. He had Benny Fillichio head his Rush Liquor Store chain in the Chicago area with Louis Briatta. He sent mobster Marshall Caifano to head gambling operations in Nevada and partnered with Bernie Korshak in a gambling joint and wire service grossing $25,000 a day. To legitimize the new cash flow he legally attached himself to various enterprises in the juke box distribution for the state of Illinois.

Accardo commanded and helped Southern Illinois mob boss Frank "Buster" Wortman get rid of the leaders of the Shelton Gang while Paul DeLucia was in prison. From that point on Wortman was a frequent visitor to Accardo's home and gave his loyalty to Accardo and the Accardo faction.

In 1947 news made its way around Chicago through circles that Tony Accardo, who was the number one boss of Chicago, was dying from cancer of the stomach. Because of this, rumor had it at the time that Tony Capezio was to take over Accardo's position and be the number one boss of Chicago. This was never the case.

Accardo's name surfaced in the murder of James Regan on June 24, 1946. Regan was then the owner of the Continental Press, a racing wire service that supplied horse racing results to bookies. Regan made a claim that the old Capone Gang, then made up of Tony Accardo as the ruling head, Tony Capezio as his number two, Jake Guzik, Murray Humphreys and Sam Hunt making up the rest of his crew, were attempting to muscle into the racing new service. Regan received an offer from this group for 40 percent of the Midwest News Service, which he refused. According to informants, that is when Tony Accardo gave the order to "do away" with Regan. An assassination attempt on Regan was made on June 23, 1946. Regan was shot by shotguns but survived and did not die until August 14. After his body was entombed at Mount Olive Cemetery, a judge order that his body be exhumed and his organs be tested for mercury poisoning. Many of the nurses that attended to Regan at the hospital were all brought in to the Chicago Police Station and questioned. It was rumored the nurses finished off Regan for the Outfit with poison.

Right after the death, Chicago detectives received word that Accardo had ordered the killing and gave the contract to his two best killers at the time. They were Sam and Gus Alex, Accardo's executioners who always liked to use shotguns to kill their victims. Another theory was that mobster William Heeney, then a high-ranking lieutenant in syndicate gambling, got permission from Accardo to have Regan killed since Heeney was at war with him. Heeney wanted to take over Regan's business to furnish race track news to different sources and dealers. The case was never solved.

An FBI agent wrote in a 1946 file, *"Accardo is at times reputed to be head of the syndicate at Chicago and has been publicized as such. He has considerable money and is more or less a man of leisure. He is believed, however, to be the strong man who takes care of difficult situations. He is probably assisted in this by his assistant or bodyguard, Sam Giancana and Tony Capezio."*

At the end of 1946 investigators noticed that when Tony Accardo would go out of town, his wife Clarice would spend numerous evenings night-clubbing with

Sam Giancana and his wife, Angela, in Chicago.

In October 1946 investigators determined that Tony Accardo rented a house in Miami, Florida to stay there for six months and avoid the Chicago winter. Accardo's kids were said to be enrolled in a school in Miami. Accardo's brother John Accardo and his wife Ann were said to be living in Accardo's Chicago home while Tony was in Florida.

Spot Surveillance 1946

June and July 1946 – Tony Accardo spent a considerable amount of time in Florida staying at the Versailles Hotel.

July 26, 1946 – Tony Accardo is called to New York City by Crime Commission bosses to discuss national gambling matters.

August 14, 1946 – Clarice Accardo and her son Anthony Ross Accardo spent the day in Long Beach, Indiana at the home of James Nuzzo. Clarise played cards with James wife Lou Nuzzo, Nancy DeLucia, Paul's wife and Rose Flando, wife of Andrew J. Flando, then Republican Ward Committeeman of the old 25th Ward in Chicago. Rose Flando was the big winner that night winning $80.

August 23, 1946 – Tony Accardo and his wife Clarise were observed at an all-star game being held at Soldier Field in Chicago.

September 16, 1946 – Tony Accardo is observed at Claude Maddox's private home on Goose Lake between the towns of Hayward and Winter, Wisconsin.

September 20, 1946 – Tony Accardo leaves Chicago for Florida where it was rumored he was going to either rent or purchase a winter home for his family.

October 11, 1946 – Tony Accardo and Sam Giancana leave Chicago to represent the Outfit at a Syndicate meeting in Miami Florida at the Wofford Hotel. Accardo was observed leaving for the airport with his wife. When investigators searched the list of people aboard, Accardo was under the name of Mr. Joe Salerno.

October 12, 1946 – With her husband away, Clarice Accardo spent the evening with mobster Mike Spranze at the Cameo Room in Chicago.

October 13, 1946 – Clarice Accardo spent the night at a party held at the Chez Paree.

In 1947 with Paul DeLucia back in Chicago and out of prison, Tony Accardo was still in control because part of DeLucia's parole was that he was not to communicate with other criminal associates. It was also confirmed in 1947 that Tony Accardo, Sam Giancana, and Tony Capezio made barrel loads of money from the Illinois Simplex Distributing Company which was the largest distributor of juke boxes in Illinois during that year.

Law enforcement learned that Accardo was now the real power of the Chicago family came in February 10, 1947 when Frank Sinatra made his way to Miami, Florida and stayed at the Chicago mobster Charles Fischetti's mansion. The next day Sinatra left for Havana, Cuba with Charles brother Rocco Fischetti for the purpose of meeting deported mob boss Charles "Lucky" Luciano and to attend a Mafia convention. While there Sinatra attended parties and gambled with other mobster such as Albert Anastasia, Carlo Marcello, Santo Trafficante, Joe Adonis, Tommy Lucchese, Joe Profaci, Meyer Lansky, Joseph Bonanno, Augie Pisano, Vito Genovese, Frank Costello, Willie Morretti, Joe Magliocco, Phil Kastel and Joe Stacher. Also there was Tony Accardo representing Chicago.

In 1948 Tony Accardo went to court on a conspiracy charge and was charged with fraud and concealing material facts. However, on November 21, he was acquitted of the charges.

At the end of 1948 Tony Accardo was working on strengthening his position. He was observed meeting other mob bosses in other cities. In November of that year Accardo, Charles Fischetti and many other top mob bosses held a conference at the Tic Toc night club in Milwaukee. Many of the other mob bosses from other cities developed a strong affection for Tony Accardo and considered him a real power in organized crime.

The end of the 1940's was a time when Accardo and Paul DeLucia had to find a way to work together. Accardo was still running the day-to-day operations of the Outfit and Chicago was entering a very profitable time.

There was even talk that mobster Ben "Foggie" Fillichio was going to take over the day-to-day operations of the Outfit from Tony Accardo for a short period of time. One reason given which was un-proven was that Accardo was still in trouble with the government on forging government records when he went to visit Paul DeLucia in Leavenworth Prison. One report did say that for a while Foggie Fillichio was running daily operations but he was really just implicating the orders of Accardo. Another report stated that Fillichio was being chosen over Sam Giancana in 1949 for this position because Giancana was caught trying to line up the west side of Chicago without consulting the organization first. Giancana did not follow instructions to keep the "heat" off his activities. Giancana decided he would set up a protection racket in Chicago where he ordered his men to smash large numbers of windows around town. It was reported that when Accardo and Paul DeLucia found out they demoted Giancana.

Chapter 20

Compromise

A new decade, the 1950's, started off with health problems for Tony Accardo. He was suffering bleeding ulcers, no doubt a side effect from the up-and-coming storm known as the Senator Kefauver hearings.

In 1949 came the news that law enforcement agents would be using a new tool in the fight against organized crime. The government released a statement saying they would now pay money to informants for information leading to an arrest and conviction. The news hit home when it was announced that by 1950 the government had almost $500,000 waiting to be paid out to informants for secret information they obtained. Actually law enforcement always had informants snitching on the other guy to help his own butt out, but now, if the information given lead to a conviction, thousands and thousands could be paid to the snitch.

One of those paid snitches was asked by Tony Accardo to come over to his house and fix a television set. The snitch told investigators that Tony Accardo showed him a gun collection containing over 200 guns of all types, ranging from Civil War relics to modern firearms. Tony Accardo was so nice to this snitch that he and his wife invited the snitch to visit their home in Florida so they could go out onto the ocean in Accardo's luxurious cruiser. Accardo even told the snitch that even if Accardo was not in Florida the snitch could use his cruiser and he, Accardo, would contact the captain telling him that he would take the snitch anywhere he wanted to go. Accardo trusted this snitch and went out of his way to be nice to him and he, in turn went to the government trying to get paid.

Other informants in 1950 said that Tony Accardo spent a good amount of time in Florida and had taken at least 3 to 4 vacations in Honolulu, Hawaii.

In September 1950 Senator Kefauver from the U.S. Senate was launching his Organized Crime hearings and subpoenaed Tony Accardo and his underboss Tony Capezio. The subpoenas were given to the River Forest Police Department to serve since both Accardo and Capezio lived in River Forest. They had a hard time locating the two but they received information that Capezio was going to be at the Blue Moon Tavern in Melrose Park on a certain date. When River Forest police officers asked the Melrose Park police department to help with serving the subpoena they refused and basically told the officers to "go to hell." Days later both Accardo and Capezio were at the Blue Moon together for a short while before a party was to occur with many Outfit members attending. When River Forest police arrived to serve the subpoenas both Accardo and Capezio were gone having been tipped off about the subpoenas. The only ones who knew River Forest police were coming were the Melrose Park police and passed the information onto Capezio.

Later Accardo appeared before the Kefauver Crime Committee where he refused to answer any questions, hiding behind the Fifth Amendment. Accardo was cited for contempt of Congress and it took almost a year for him to be freed of this charge. Lucky for Accardo he did not have to spend that time in jail.

Tony Accardo arrest records and documents

IV. CRIMINAL RECORD

It should be noted that in addition to the arrests listed here, there are several referred to in the second section of this summary.

DATE	CHARGE	DISPOSITION
3/22/22	Sec. 7 CC Sec. 27 MVL	Fined #2 Dismissed,3/24/22
5/26/23	2655 (D.C.)	Fined $200. & Costs 5/31/23
12/10/23	2655 (D.C.)	DWP, 1/8/24
1/18/24	2655 (D.C.)	Fined $10.& Costs 1/19/24
4/5/24	2655 (D.C.)	Fined $25.& Costs 4/7/24
10/12/24	2655 (D.C.)	Dismissed, 10/13/24
11/16/25	Sec. 22 MVL	Dismissed, 11/17/25
1/5/26	2655 (D.C.)	Dismissed, 1/6/26
3/3/27	2655 (D.C.)	Dismissed, 3/3/27
5/30/27	2655 (D.C.)	Dismissed, 6/6/27
10/13/27	2655 (D.C.)	Dismissed, 10/14/27
1/28/28	2655 (D.C.) Par. 155 Sec. 4, Ch. 38 (CCW)	Dismissed, 1/30/28
1/1/30	C. C. W.	S. O. L., 3/31/30
7/29/30	C. C. W. Re-instated	N. P., 3/13/31
9/30/30	2656 (D. C.)	Dismissed, 10/2/30
11/12/30	VS 2655 CC (D. C.)	Dismissed,11/13/30

Bureau of Identification number C-25251.

- 9 -

Accardo's record is as follows:

May 31, 1923, disorderly conduct - fined $200 and costs.

January 3, 1924, disorderly conduct - discharged.

January 19, 1924, disorderly conduct - fined $10 and costs.

April 7, 1924, disorderly conduct - fined $25 and costs.

October 13, 1924, disorderly conduct - discharged.

January 6, 1926, disorderly conduct - discharged.

March 3, 1927, disorderly conduct - discharged.

June 6, 1927, disorderly conduct - discharged.

October 14, 1927, disorderly conduct - discharged.

January 30, 1928, disorderly conduct and carrying concealed weapon - discharged.

February, 1930, arrested with "Machine Gun" Jack McGurn charged with carrying a concealed weapon. Indicted in the Criminal Court on this charge and was discharged on March 13, 1931 upon a nolle prosse order.

October 2, 1930 disorderly conduct - discharged.

November 13, 1930 disorderly conduct - discharged.

February 17, 1931 arrested with Charles Gioe on charge of carrying concealed weapon.

May 10, 1931 arrested with Dago Lawrence Mangano and four other Capone gangsters in a raid following the torch slaying of "Mike de Pike" Heitler, vice overlord.

May 3, 1932 arrested as a vagrant. Discharged on May 24, 1932.

May 17, 1933 $25 and costs for disorderly conduct.

August 1933 arrested for the second time within a week and held for investigation.

Arrested March 4, 1943 with Ralph Pierce and Lester Cain in connection with murder of Estelle Carey, sweetheart of Nick Circella alias Nick Dean. Dean was convicted in the movie extortion trial and sentenced to the penitentiary with other members of the Capone mob.

September 27, 1943 picked up by the FBI as a material witness in the New York movie trial of Capone mobsters.

January 3, 1944 Accardo and other persons indicted in criminal court for conspiracy to operate a handbook at 186-92 Clark Street. Nolle prossed on March 20, 1944 to enable Accardo to be inducted into the Army. He was subsequently rejected.

February 15, 1944 arrested for investigation in connectiān with gambling - discharged.

February 12, 1945 arrested in connection with the alleged kidnapping of Jack Guzik and the slaying of one Jens Larrison in the tavern of Matt Capone. Released on habeas corpus.

NAME: TONY ACCARDO

AKA: Joe Batters

RESIDENCES: 1117 S. California Ave., Chicago, Ill.

AREA OF OPERATIONS: Chicago

DATE AND PLACE OF BIRTH: 11/8/99 Italy

JUSTICE FILE NOS.: 46-23-56

CITIZENSHIP STATUS: U.S. FBI NO.:

CRIMINAL RECORD:

Place	Name & Number	Date	Charge	Disposition
Chicago	Tony Accardo	1948	Conspiracy to defraud US by arranging to visit DeLucia & Compagna at Leavenworth (registering under false name.)	Acquitted.

ASSOCIATES: Paul DeLucia; Jack Guzik; Joe Fischetti; Charles Fischetti; Murray Humphreys (23-5/11-N); Louis Campagna.

ACTIVITIES AND GENERAL INFORMATION: It is reported that Tony Accardo is a member of the Mafia Society. He is a former member of the old Capone organization and is presently associated with the so-called Chicago Syndicate. At the present time he confines his activities almost exclusively to gambling enterprises (23-5/11-N). The Chicago Police records show a great many arrests from 1933 to 1944, all of which resulted in small fines and dismissals (23-5/11-A).

Tony Accardo's 1950 Senate Information Sheet

UNITED STATES OF AMERICA

Congress of the United States

To ANTHONY "TONY" ACCARDO aka MARTIN, 1431 Ashland Avenue, River Forest, Illinois

, Greeting:

Pursuant to lawful authority, YOU ARE HEREBY COMMANDED to appear before the Special Committee on Senate Committee to Investigate Organized Crime in Interstate Commerce of the Senate of the United States, forthwith, 1950, at 2:00 o'clock P. m., at their committee room #900 - 101 Indiana Avenue, N. W., Washington, D. C., then and there to testify what you may know relative to the subject matters under consideration by said Committee.

and bring with you:

1. All ledgers, vouchers, cancelled checks, check stubs, bank deposit slips, bank statements, financial statements, notes, copies of tax returns, records of accounts receivable and payable and records of cash receipts and disbursements, for the period from January 1, 1940 to date;

2. All books, records or other documents showing ownership of, or other holding or interest in any business company or enterprise, or in any property, real, personal or intangible, for the period from January 1, 1940 to date;

3. All correspondence relating to the subject matter referred to in paragraph 2 hereof, for the period from January 1, 1940 to date.

to serve and return.

Given under my hand, by order of the Committee, this 26th day of August, in the year of our Lord one thousand nine hundred and Fifty

SGD ESTES KEFAUVER

Chairman, Committee on Senate Commiteee to Investigate Organized Crime in Interstate Commerce

WESTERN UNION

W. P. MARSHALL, PRESIDENT

AMERICAN EMBASSY
REPUBLIC OF PANAMA

ANTHONY "TONY" ACCARDO ALSO KNOWN AS MARTIN, CHARLES AND ROCCO FISCHETTI, ALSO KNOWN AS CHARLES FIELDS AND RALPH FISHER, REPORTED TO BE IN PANAMA. IF POSSIBLE TO CONTACT, PLEASE NOTIFY THEM THAT THEY ARE EVADING FORTHWITH SUBPOENAS TO APPEAR BEFORE THIS COMMITTEE WHICH WERE ISSUED ON AUGUST 26th. WOULD APPRECIATE IF POSSIBLE AIR MAIL REPORT ON METHOD OF THEIR ENTRY INTO PANAMA, PROBABLE DURATION OF STAY, AND DATE OF RETURN TO UNITED STATES. PLEASE NOTIFY U. S. IMMIGRATION AUTHORITIES AND BORDER PATROL.

ESTES KEFAUVER, Chairman
Special Committee to Investigate
Organized Crime in Interstate
Commerce.
280 U. S. Court House
Chicago 4, Illinois

Western Union Telegram to the American Embassy in Panama looking for Tony Accardo and the Fischetti's

Authors Collection

Charles Fischetti mugshot (left)

Authors Collection

Rocco Fischetti mugshot (right)

1950 Senate Hearings

Tony Accardo (Right) sitting with his lawyer while being questioned

Spot Surveillance 1950

January 1950 – Tony Accardo, Sam Giancana and Murray Humphreys take a trip together to Florida.

May 24, 1950 – Tony Accardo, Sam Giancana, Charles Fischetti and Murray Humphreys leave for a Bimini fishing trip.

October 1950 – Tony Accardo, Rocco and Charles Fischetti were hiding out in Mexico City, Mexico while the Kefauver Crime Committee investigation issued a subpoena.

October 5, 1950 – Tony Accardo, along with the Fischetti's, land in Brownsville, Texas together. Accardo quickly boards a plan to Houston, Texas to avoid being served a subpoena while the Fischetti's board a plan for Brooklyn, New York.

December 1950 – Accardo accepts a senate committee subpoena after Christmas because he missed his family.

The year 1951 began with Tony Accardo making three appearances in three weeks before a Cook County Grand Jury investigating a policy wheel operation in Chicago. Accardo refused to answer any questions when questioned about evidence that Accardo and Jake Guzik obtained $271,000 from this operation.

Accardo was behind forming new organizations in Chicago under his control. In 1951 evidence of this came from Lt. Morris of the Chicago Police Department. Morris received information that syndicate labor lawyer Abraham Teitelbaum was going to be murdered by Chicago mobsters James Weinberg and Paul "Needle Nose" LaBriola. In an effort to verify this information, Lt. Morris placed a wire recording device in the offices of Weinberg and LaBriola. As Morris listened to phone conversations, he heard LaBriola confirm the murder plot. LaBriola was heard saying, *"We'll have to kill him, but we don't want a big uproar in the papers. We'll push him out of his window. He's in income tax troubles and everyone will think it was suicide."* Lt. Morris stepped in and saved Teitelbaum's life by thwarting the plan.

Lt. Morris continued to listen in and discovered that Tony Accardo was the man behind the two mobsters organizing various taverns in Chicago. They often spoke about returning from Accardo's home. Both Weinberg and LaBriola were murdered in 1954.

In February 1951 a confidential informant told the FBI that Tony Accardo and Murray Humphreys had agreed and decided to groom a younger mobster by the name of John Cerone, aka Jackie Cerone. At the time Jackie Cerone owned a tavern on North Crawford Avenue in Chicago and the Rite-Light Neon Company at 482 Milwaukee Avenue. Jackie Cerone had told this informant that Accardo and Humphreys desired to stay in the "back ground" and Cerone was to take over the operation of the Outfit's "big wheel" game in Chicago. He also added that the policy wheel generated enough money to fund the Outfit's investments in legitimate businesses.

In March 1951 Tony Accardo moved into the mansion at 915 Franklin Avenue in River Forest. It was said he paid $125,000 for the 22-room masterpiece. Built in the 1930's by William C. Grunow, a wealthy radio manufacturer, it had six master bedrooms, an indoor pool, two bowling alleys, a pipe organ, six bathrooms with gold plat fixtures, an open-air garden on its roof, a two story reception hall, a 40-by-24 feet social room and a $10,000 bathtub carved out of a solid block of Mexican onyx stone. The brass fireplace screen was handmade with the initials AA, for Anthony Accardo, marked at the bottom which still remains in the home as of the 2000's. The lavish lawns surrounding the mansion hosted many lawn parties with organized crime's "Who's Who" in attendance. The back yard had a silver fountain bubbling with champagne, it was said.

On June 23, 1951 Tony Accardo was arrested by the Chicago Police and questioned in the murder of Leonard "Fat Lenny" Caifano, who, at the time was one of Accardo's men. To keep Accardo out of jail for the night, Chicago Municipal Court Judge George Lancelot Quilici made a special trip to the central police building and personally made sure Accardo was released. When Quilici was leaving the police station he was asked by a reporter how much he knew about Accardo. His response was, *"I don't know much about Accardo, but I am told he is a substantial man with a large home in a good suburb. He has a wife and children."* Then he was asked if he heard Accardo was a hoodlum, he replied, *"I read the papers, but I don't believe everything I read in them."* Quilici then admitted he had never done this, released a prisoner in this manner since 1944.

On October 22, 1951 the Emergency Crime Committee of the City of Chicago released its official report stating that Tony Accardo, Jake Guzik, Peter Tremont and the Manno brothers solely and exclusively controlled the policy wheels in the entire Chicagoland area.

Photos of the Tony Accardo's home at 915 Franklin Avenue in River Forest. Photo's taken December 13, 1957

This photo was taken from Franklin Street facing East showing the North end of the property housing the garage and servants quarters

This photo was taken from Franklin Street showing the North side and part of the West side

This photo was taken from Franklin Street facing East showing the carriage entrance

This photo was taken from Augusta Street facing South

This photo was taken from Iowa Street facing North

Tony Accardo's home in the late 1990's early 2000's

Photo of the home at 915 Franklin Avenue in River Forest in 2014

Spot Surveillances 1951-1952

January 5, 1951 - Tony Accardo appears before the Kefauver Crime Committee and refuses to answer any questions.

January 24, 1951- Tony Accardo is cited for contempt of Congress.

March 28, 1951 – Tony Accardo, George Ciancola, aka George King, Frank Ferraro, Charles Fischetti and Sam Giancana take Accardo's yacht, named the Clarijo, to Bimini Island to fish.

February 1952 – Accardo is said to be in Reno, Nevada with Sam Giancana playing cards in a private room at a hotel. Accardo wins $103,000 and asks for the winnings to be made out in two checks since he did not want to carry it all back to Chicago in cash. He is given a check which makes him very mad.

November 20, 1952 – The January 1951 charge of contempt of Congress against Accardo is dropped.

In 1952 authorities tried to go back and see if Tony Accardo was actually born in the United States and not Italy, in hopes they could deport him. None of the official documents the U.S. government had on Accardo matched up with dates or places. INS agents investigated the matter and came to the conclusion that his parents entered America through the Port of New Orleans in 1905 with one child, that being Martin Accardo. After a few weeks in New Orleans the family moved to Chicago. Once again INS agents could not determine if Tony Accardo was born in America or Italy.

In December 1953 it was learned that Tony Accardo and Rocco Fischetti were attempting to seize control of the Downtown Civic and Social Club at 126 ½ North First Street in Las Vegas, Nevada. This club was going to be the nucleus for a "dealer's" labor union for employees of the casinos. Accardo and the Fischetti gained interest once the membership reached 700 members and were collecting a $10 initiation fees from every new member.

On January 15, 1953 Tony Accardo, Michael Mancuso, Sam Giancana and Dr. Eugene Chesrow land in Los Angeles, California and were met by mobster Frank "Strongy" Ferraro and Anthony Pinelli. All were arrested and questioned by L.A. police officers. Accardo, Giancana, Mancuso and Chesrow were told to leave Los Angeles. It was later learned that the men were there to attend a meeting to discuss taking over control of the Golden Hotel and Casino in Reno, Nevada. The group left and went to the Desert Inn Hotel which was located in Clark County, just outside the city limits.

Los Angeles Police Department
OFFICER'S MEMORANDUM

D. R. No.

ANTHONY J. ACCARDO AND PARTY
SUBJECT

Division Reporting Intelligence Clerk n/a Division of Occurrence
Date and Time Occurred 1-2-3-53 Location of Occurrence
DETAILS:

Capt. Hamilton:

Above subject arrived International Airport on TWA Flight #93 at 8:13 PM. Subject was accompanied by a Dr. E. J. Chesrow, MD, and a Micheal Mancuso. These 2 subjects are described as follows:

Anthony J. Accardo, born 4-28-06, 5-11, 185 lbs, swarthy appearance. Grey felt hat, blue overcoat. Tatoo of a swallow smudged between the thumb and the forefinger of the right hand, Italian.

E. W. Chesrow, MD, Italian, 59 yrs, 5'4", 140 lbs, wears glasses, brown hair, grey eyes. Surgeon Cook County General Hospital. Retired Colonel United States Army.

Michael Mancuso, Italian, 44 yrs. 5'9½", 170 lbs, Cook County Hospital.

Subjects were met on arriving at the airport by Anthony Pinelli, Italian, 53 yrs, 5'4", 180 lbs, 500 W. Monticito, Sierra Madre. Frank Ferraro, Italian, 48 yrs, 5'11", 180 lbs, brown hair, hazel eyes. Identified himself as being a tailor, business address 53 W. Jackson St., Chicago, Illinois. Local residence is 15208 Starbuck, Whittier, Calif. Subject works at Celano Tailoring Company, Chicago, Illinois, Operator.

Ferraro was driving a Cadillac rent car 1791456, and Pinelli was driving a 1953 black Buick sedan. Accardo, Chesrow and Mancuso were taken by Ferraro and Pinelli in Pinelli's Buick, leaving the airport at approximately 8:45 PM and were taken to Perinos Cafe on Wilshire Blvd. Subjects returned to the International Airport at 11:50 PM, at which time the 5 subjects were taken into custody and were brought into our airport office.

Subjects were interrogated singly, and Accardo stated that he lived at 9115 River Forrest, Cook County, Chicago, Illinois, and that he had come out here on the plane by himself. He later changed his story when we brought in the various pieces of luggage and stated that he had come out with Dr. Chesrow and Micheal Mancuso. He further stated that Dr. Chesrow was his personal physician and he had known him for 20 to 25 years. Accardo was carrying a large amount of money in 2 rolls, and when I asked him to count the money he counted $5,000 in one roll and had reached $1,700 in the other roll. He stated that he was on his way to Las Vegas with Chesrow and Mancuso and was going to be there approximately a week and that he had reservations at the Desert Inn. He stated that he wanted no part of Los Angeles and was just passing through and had no interest out here. When questioned as to his acquaintanship with subjects Ferraro and Pinelli he stated that he knew them slightly as former Chicago people.

18-244

Date and Time of This Report Officer Serial
Officer Serial
Approved Signature

Los Angeles Police Department
OFFICER'S MEMORANDUM

D. R. No.

ANTHONY J. ACCARDO AND PARTY
SUBJECT

Division Reporting Clerk Division of Occurrence
Date and Time Occurred Location of Occurrence
DETAILS:

Page 2

It was noted that Pinelli paid Accardo a great deal of respect. Accardo stated that his reason for going to Las Vegas was solely a vacation and he planned to do a little gambling there and that was all.

Micheal Mancuso stated that he lived at 1164 So. Maple Avenue, Chicago, Illinois, and was the owner of a used car business at 5707 Madison Avenue and that he had known Accardo for 2 or 3 years. He further stated that he had been in Reno, Nevada, six months ago. He was carrying approximately $5,000 on his person and stated that he hoped to win considerable more gambling. He tells substantially the same story as Accardo and Dr. Chesrow as to their leaving Chicago, arriving here, being met by Pinelli and Ferraro here and being taken to Perino's Cafe.

E. J. Chesrow who identified himself as a MD attached to the Cook County hospital, Chicago, Illinois, stated his residence was in Oakforrest, Illinois. Stated that he was personal physician to Tony Accardo from 15 to 20 years and that he had been invited by Tony Accardo to make this trip to Las Vegas 3 or 4 days ago and that it was his understanding that they would only be in Las Vegas 2 or 3 days as he had to return to Chicago. Dr. Chesrow stated that his offices are at 375 West Jackson Blvd., Harrison 70819, Chicago. His story as to leaving Chicago with subjects Accardo and Mancuso was identical with the subjects. He further stated that he was a retired army surgeon having the rank of colonel. The doctor was carrying $250.00 in cash.

Anthony Pinelli, who is the father of Salvatore Pinelli, owner of the Moristown Motel, who figured in the Mosari investigation. Pinelli identified himself as a friend of Accardo and Mancuso and was very antagonistic under interrogation. Refused to answer questions as to how long he had known them, where he had met them this evening, where they had gone, and all other pertinent data. Was uncooperative from the very start and left no other course of action open other than to take him down to the City Hall for further investigation.

Frank Ferrar who identified himself as an owner of a tailoring establishment at 53 W. Jackson St., Chicago, Illinois, currently living in Whittier, Calif., stated that he had rented a Cadillac sedan and had driven out to the airport to meet Accardo and his party and whom he knew to be here on a stopover flight to Las Vegas. He stated that the party was out here just for kicks.

Accardo, Mancuso and Chesrow were using the names: J. Man, S. Star, S. White. The subjects baggage was gone through and contained only expensive clothing.

8 308

Date and Time of This Report Officer Serial
Officer Serial
Approved Signature

The actual 1953 reports from the LAPD

Mob Boss

Spot Surveillance 1953-1954

February 16, 1953 – Tony Accardo was observed by agents at the wake of Joseph Sortino, father of mob boss Frank Ferraro, at the funeral home at 2500 North Cicero Avenue in Chicago.

May 14, 1953 – Tony Accardo and Michael Volpe return from a Bimini fishing trip.

May 15, 1953 – Tony Accardo, Jake Guzik, Eddie Vogel and Gus Alex meet with Bill Graham; a gambling czar from Reno, Nevada, about Chicago's gambling interest in Reno.

August 1953 – Tony Accardo cashes a check at a River Forest Bank for the amount of $103,000. When the bank asked Accardo for his endorsement of the check, he refused. After arguing, Accardo agrees to sign his name and demands all the money in big bills. This is the check from the Reno, Nevada casino. This launched a long investigation into Reno casinos and Tony Accardo's interest in them.

October 1953 – Tony Accardo, Sam Giancana and Jake Guzik hold a meeting in Miami Beach, Florida to decide that Eddie Sturch would be replaced on the North Side of Chicago. Sturch was an ex-convict gambler and a self-styled important politician in the old 42nd Ward of Chicago. Also discussed was that Capone gangster Sam "Golf Bag" Hunt would be permitted to operate in his own area in Chicago.

October 23, 1954 – Tony Accardo, Sam Giancana, Eddie Vogel and Sam Hunt are in New York City meeting with New York mob bosses. Tony Accardo registers his name at the hotel as M. Brown.

July 29, 1954 – Accardo was observed by Chicago Police at the wake of Antonio Giancana, father of Sam "Momo" Giancana, at the Cermak Funeral Home in Cicero, Illinois.

As Accardo went to war for control of the Chicago Outfit in 1954, he was focusing on a new racket that came from the theft of a federal tax stamp machine which was used to place federal tax stickers on cigarette sales. Accardo was trying to get control of legitimate tobacco houses of good reputation so they could purchase millions of cartons of unstamped cigarettes from manufacturers. By counterfeiting the three cent state tax, they would make a profit of 10 millions dollars a year.

On July 4, 1954 Tony Accardo hosted a lawn party to celebrate the holiday at his mansion at 915 Franklin Avenue in River Forest, Illinois. The event was well published in the media and only a who's who of organized crime and politics was invited. The party had the notorious silver fountain flowing with champagne. There were four taps of beer and the guests were given silver steins to drink from.

Tony Dark

Every table had red, green or blue umbrellas over them. Known Guess seen were:

Martin Accardo
Joseph Aiello
Gus Alex
Phil Alderisio
William Aloisio
Joey Aiuppa
Joe Amato
Tony Amato
Robert Ansani
George Bieber
A. M. Cannella
Ralph Cantonese
Tony Capezio
Jackie Cerone
Joe Colucci
Van Corbin (Sam Panveno)
John D'Arco Sr.
Rocco DeGrazio
Anthony DeLuca
Anthony DeRosa
Chuckie English
Sam English
Frank Eulo
Rocco Eulo
Rocco Fischetti
Albert Frabotta
Sam Giancana
A. Giovenco
Bernard Glickman
Joey Glimco
Frank Granata
Jake Guzik
Buddy Jacobson
Leslie Kruse
Frank LaPorte
John Lardino
Pat Manno
Bessie Meirs
Alfred Meo
Nick Palermo
P. Palermo
Morris "Potsy" Pearl
Anthony Pinelli
Ralph Pierce
Rocco Potenzo
Ross Prio
Dominic Sibilano
Tarquin Simonelli
Joe Siracusa
Thomas Siracusa
Mike Spranze
Henry Susk
Tony Tisci
Marion White

<u>Cars whose license plates were registered to:</u>

American Offset Corporation
Automatic Coin Machine Company (Joey Glimco partner in this company with Francis Curry)
Charden Farms Grey Lakes
Chicago Specialty Equipment Company
Courtesy Lease Save Plan (Car leased by Chicago Barbers Union, 320 West Ashland)
Cool Vent Metal Company "Bernard Glickman Company"
Eli Bridge Company
Amco Corporation
Illinois Cartage Company
Illinois Department of Revenue Springfield, Illinois
McHenry County Tobacco Company
Rago Brothers Funeral Home
Nu-Way Beer Coil Service (Eddie Vogel, Lester Kruse or Charles Gioe's car)
Meadowmoor Dairies

Tony Accardo and Sam Giancana arrested by the CPD late 1950's

That same month another report stated that Tony Accardo was being paid $75,000 a year from the profits of the gambling place known as "The Fort." This place was managed by Rocco Fischetti.

Not even close personal friends were safe knowing Accardo. In 1954 Tony Accardo was the directing power of the Chicago Restaurant Association which he controlled through his mob lawyer, Anthony Champagne, who was given the job as the local's labor council on Accardo's orders.

In July of that year Champagne resigned from the Chicago Restaurant Association because he said he was neglecting his regular law practice. The real reason was that Champagne got into serious trouble with Accardo. Difficulty developed between Accardo and Champagne in reference to tax payments on the fee the Chicago Restaurant Association was paying Champagne. Due to this argument between the two, Champagne wanted Accardo to order James Blakely, then International Vice President and Secretary-Treasurer of Chicago Local 593, and mobster John Lardino, then Blakely's assistant who was really the boss of the local, to cooperate with Champagne to the damage of the union and to the benefit of the Chicago Restaurant Association. Accardo quickly ordered the murder of Anthony Champagne. However, his brother, Dr. Carl Champagne, an old-time mobster dating back to Johnny Torrio and Al Capone, had great influence, intervened to save his brothers life. Accardo agreed not to kill him but forced Anthony Champagne to resign and refused to pay Champagne his last month's salary from the union.

December 1954 confirmed that the Accardo group had gained control of casinos in Reno, Lake Tahoe and Las Vegas, Nevada. Accardo was receiving payouts of $100,000 alone from the Reno casino.

From the Collection of T.M.

Our marriage { has not been terminated. / was terminated by (death) (divorce) } on .... (Date of death or divorce)

CONFIDENTIAL

A WOMAN APPLICANT WHO IS OR HAS BEEN MARRIED MUST FILL IN THIS PORTION

My maiden name was ...., and

I { was not previously married. / was previously married to } ....

on .... (Date), at .... (City and State), who was born

at ...., and the marriage was terminated by { death / divorce } on .... (Date)

(If married more than twice, set forth facts in a supplemental statement)

THE FOLLOWING INFORMATION IS REQUIRED ONLY IF HUSBAND OR FORMER HUSBAND WAS NOT BORN IN THE UNITED STATES

My { husband / former husband } emigrated to the United States on ....

and { his father / he } .... (Name of father) } was naturalized as a citizen of the United States before the

.... Court of .... at .... (City and State)

on .... (Month, day, and year) as shown by the Certificate of Naturalization { submitted herewith. / previously submitted.

MY TRAVEL PLANS ARE AS FOLLOWS:

Port of departure Miami Fla

Approximate date of departure June 1 ST

Proposed length of stay abroad 3 Weeks

Means of transportation Pan Am air lines (Name of ship or air line)

Countries to be visited South Am. Chile

Purpose of trip Fishing

I solemnly swear that the statements on both sides of this application are true and that the photograph attached hereto is a likeness of me.

I { have / have not } been naturalized as a citizen of a foreign state; taken an oath or made an affirmation or other formal declaration of allegiance to a foreign state; entered or served in the armed forces of a foreign state; accepted or performed the duties of any office, post or employment under the government of a foreign state or political subdivision thereof; voted in a political election in a foreign state or participated in an election or plebiscite to determine the sovereignty over foreign territory; made a formal renunciation of nationality before a diplomatic or consular officer of the United States in a foreign state; been convicted by court martial of deserting the military or naval service of the United States in time of war; been convicted by court martial, or by a court of competent jurisdiction, of committing any act of treason against, or of attempting by force to overthrow, or of bearing arms against the United States.

OATH OF ALLEGIANCE

Further, I do solemnly swear that I will support and defend the Constitution of the United States against all enemies, foreign and domestic; that I will bear true faith and allegiance to the same; and that I take this obligation freely, without any mental reservation, or purpose of evasion: So help me God.

Anthony J. Accardo (Signature of applicant)

Subscribed and sworn to before me this FEB 23 1954 day of ...., 19....

[SEAL OF COURT] Lucile L. ....

Clerk of the AGENT, DEPARTMENT OF STATE CHICAGO *Court at* ....

AFFIDAVIT OF IDENTIFYING WITNESS

I, the undersigned, solemnly swear that I am a citizen of the United States; that I reside at the address written below my signature hereto affixed; that I know the applicant who executed the affidavit hereinbefore set forth to be a citizen of the United States; that the statements made in the applicant's affidavit are true to the best of my knowledge and belief; further, I solemnly swear that I have known the applicant personally for 20 years.

Nicholas .... (Signature of witness)

If witness has been issued a passport, give number if known and date or approximate date of issue.

No. None Date of issue ....

not related (Relationship to applicant; if not related, so state)

No lawyer or other person will be accepted as witness to a passport application if he has received or expects to receive a fee for his services in connection with the execution of the application or obtaining the passport.

1124 .... Blvd Oak Park, Ill (Residence address of witness)

Subscribed and sworn to before me this FEB 23 1954 day of ....

[SEAL OF COURT] ....

Clerk of the AGENT, DEPARTMENT OF STATE CHICAGO *Court at* ....

Tony Accardo's Pass Port Application

Tony Dark

It was rumored that the 1955 Fourth of July lawn party held at Tony Accardo's mansion in River Forest was to be a celebration that Paul DeLucia was officially stepping down as top mob boss and Accardo was claiming the position. Accardo wore blue Bermuda shorts with a blue sports shirt, high blue socks and black moccasins. The party was watch by law enforcement officials from the house directly behind Tony Accardo's home. The neighbor, Richard Schultz, then an owner of a Chicago tool and die plant, allowed law enforcement into his home to watch. One FBI agent was able to watch Accardo, Tony Capezio, Paul DeLucia, Jake Guzik, Joey Glimco and Claude Maddox discussing business away from other guests while standing in the garden. Unfortunately, Tony Accardo found out about Schultz allowing his house to be used and Schultz's tool plant was bombed, causing five people to be seriously hurt. Then a few weeks later Schultz received an anonymous phone call saying *"You'll get another bomb if Accardo gets in trouble."* The Illinois State's Attorney's Office launched an investigation into the bombing but the investigation went nowhere.

<u>Known 1955 July 4th party guests:</u>

John Accardo
Joey Aiuppa
Phil Alderisio
William Aloisio
Gus Alex
Joe Amato
Robert Ansani
Sam Battaglia
Domonic "Butch" Blasi
Ralph Cantonese
Tony Capezio
Jackie Cerone
William Daddono
Anthony DeBendo
James DeGeorge
Rocco DeGrazio
Paul DeLucia (Wearing blue and brown checked sports shirt with grey pants)
Joseph DiVarco (Wearing a pink sports shirt with black trim)
Rocco Fanelli
Albert Frabotta
Rocco Fischetti
Sam Giancana
Bernard Glickman
Joey Glimco
Frank Granata
Jake Guzik
James Hoffa
Sam Hunt
Angelo Inciso
Leslie Kruse
Frank LaPorte
John Lardino
Claude Maddox
Pat Manno
Joe Mendino
James Mesi
Charles Nicoletti
Ralph Pierce
Ross Prio
Anthony Ricci
Harry Russell
Tarquin Simonelli
J. Spoto
Mike Spranze
Pasquale Stella
Sam Venturi
Abner "Longie" Zwillman

Known 1955 July 4th party guests cont.:

Cars registered to:

Beck Theaters Elmwood Park
Dale Motors
Economy Freight Lines Incorporated
Kool-Vent Metal Awning Manufacturing Company "Bernard Glickman Compnay"
Melrose Park Plumbing Company
Panama Banana Distributing Company
West Suburban Motor Sales
K Dealer Oldsmobile

In 1955 mobster Dominic "Butch" Blasi became Tony Accardo's bodyguard and chauffer, or, as the FBI called him the "general functionary of Tony Accardo." Blasi remained with Accardo for two years until Sam Giancana took over for Accardo and Blasi aligned himself with Giancana. Blasi and Giancana had been boyhood friends.

Spot Surveillance 1955-1956

1955 - Tony Accardo, Mike Spagnola, Joey Glimco and Fred "Juke Box" Smith were observed on many occasions meeting about syndicate "Juke Box" meetings.

June 3, 1955 – Tony Accardo, Rocco Fischetti, Sam Hunt and Claude Maddox arrive together at the funeral of mobster Louis "Little New York" Campagna.

January 13, 1956 – Tony Accardo, Sam Giancana, Paul DeLucia, Rocco Fischetti and Murray Humphreys attend an organized crime meeting at the Thunderbird Hotel in Miami Beach, Florida.

Dominick "Butch Blasi

Chapter 21

Accardo's Local 110

CONSTITUTION
and
BY-LAWS

of the
CHICAGO MOVING PICTURE
MACHINE OPERATORS' UNION,
LOCAL No. 110
of the
I. A. T. S. E. and M. P. M. O. of the
UNITED STATES and CANADA

EFFECTIVE JUNE 4, 1954

Affiliated with
CHICAGO TRADES UNION LABEL LEAGUE
CHICAGO FEDERATION OF LABOR
ILLINOIS STATE FEDERATION OF LABOR
AMERICAN FEDERATION OF LABOR

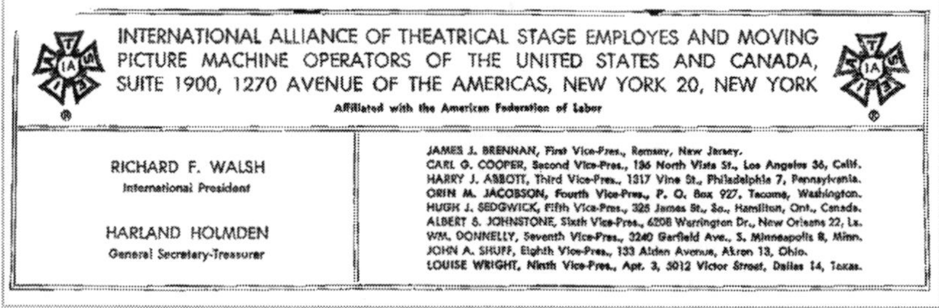

INTERNATIONAL ALLIANCE OF THEATRICAL STAGE EMPLOYES AND MOVING PICTURE MACHINE OPERATORS OF THE UNITED STATES AND CANADA, SUITE 1900, 1270 AVENUE OF THE AMERICAS, NEW YORK 20, NEW YORK

Affiliated with the American Federation of Labor

RICHARD F. WALSH
International President

HARLAND HOLMDEN
General Secretary-Treasurer

JAMES J. BRENNAN, First Vice-Pres., Romsey, New Jersey.
CARL G. COOPER, Second Vice-Pres., 136 North Vista St., Los Angeles 36, Calif.
HARRY J. ABBOTT, Third Vice-Pres., 1317 Vine St., Philadelphia 7, Pennsylvania.
ORIN M. JACOBSON, Fourth Vice-Pres., P. O. Box 927, Tacoma, Washington.
HUGH J. SEDGWICK, Fifth Vice-Pres., 325 James St., So., Hamilton, Ont., Canada.
ALBERT S. JOHNSTONE, Sixth Vice-Pres., 6208 Warrington Dr., New Orleans 22, La.
WM. DONNELLY, Seventh Vice-Pres., 3240 Garfield Ave., S. Minneapolis 8, Minn.
JOHN A. SHUFF, Eighth Vice-Pres., 133 Alden Avenue, Akron 13, Ohio.
LOUISE WRIGHT, Ninth Vice-Pres., Apt. 3, 3012 Victor Street, Dallas 14, Texas.

In March 1956 Tony Accardo invoked the Fifth Amendment in refusing to testify before a Federal Grand Jury investigating possible misuse of the welfare fund of the Chicago Moving Machine Operators Union, Local 110.

The union was officially called the Chicago Moving Picture Machine Operators Union, Local 110 of the International Alliance of Theatrical Stage Employees and Moving Picture Machine Operators of the United States and Canada. Chartered in 1915, Local 110 represented operators of motion picture equipment used commercially in the Chicago area.

Mob Boss

How did the Chicago mob gain control of Local 110? The answer came from Herman Posner who was Vice President of the local in the 1920's. In 1928 Chicago was in the middle of the Capone-Bugs Moran war for control of the city. Posner told the story that one day he was working at a theater and two of Bugs Moran's gangsters named Pete and Frank Guzzenberg showed up and forced Posner to go with them to the old Belmont Hotel where their brother Henry Guzzenberg lived. They told Posner that Bugs Moran wanted to put Henry Guzzenberg in the local as a business agent. The business agent at that time was Thomas Malloy. Posner sat and watched as one of the Guzzenberg's called Al Capone on the telephone and told him that they were going to kill Tom Malloy in order to put Henry Guzzenberg on as business agent. Guzzenberg wanted to know if Capone had any objections which he did not, Capone simply said, *"I don't care."*

Guzzenberg then told Posner that since he, Posner, was considered the leader of the operators that he was now considered to be on Moran's side. Posner said he agreed and then convinced the Guzzenberg's not to kill Malloy at the time since the next day was the election for the union's business agent.

The next day at the Union Hall there were four squads of policemen and members of the Guzzenberg Gang. Pete Guzzenberg told Posner that he was going to start a fight with Malloy and then throw him out a seventh-story window. Once again Posner had to talk Guzzenberg out of killing Malloy.

Shortly after, the president of the union named Reynolds approached Posner and informed him that Bugs Moran had sent for him and he did not know what to do. Posner told Reynolds that he should go see Moran but tell Malloy all about it. The purpose for the meeting was so Moran could get Reynolds in his pocket and control him. A frightened Reynolds became very scared because he did not want to be controlled by Bugs Moran, so he went to see Al Capone for help. This meeting between Al Capone and Reynolds was the actual beginning of the takeover by the Capone Gang of Local 110.

Al Capone and the Guzzenberg brothers sat down and worked out a compromise whereby Henry Guzzenberg was to replace the current assistant business agent and Malloy was to remain the business agent. However, it did not matter; maybe Al Capone knew his compromise did not mean anything. Before any change could be made in the union, the St. Valentine's Day Massacre happened and Peter and Frank Guzzenberg were killed in a hailstorm of bullets from Thompson machine guns. After the killings, the Moran Gang was no more and Henry Guzzenberg lost all his support in his bid to take over Local 110. That's when Capone put the iron lock on Local 110 where it remained for almost 70 years.

But Capone's interest in the union was mostly to get his cut of the money from union's treasury. In 1931 when Al Capone went away to prison for income tax evasion, the remaining Capone Gang members started putting their men into the operator positions which caused a problem. Most of the men were inexperienced which lead to many problems for the theaters. Losing money employing these men who did not know what they were doing, theater mangers complained and the situation resulted in a lock-out by the theaters. To counter the lock-out, the Capone Gang began setting bombs and blowing up the theaters. Posner said that he went to see a man by the name of Arron Saperstein about the situation and both agreed to let the International President, William Cannavan, arbitrate the situation. Herman Posner and 21 of the local union men went to New York to see Cannavan but when they arrived someone had gotten to Cannavan and he refused to arbitrate the situation.

On the way back to Chicago, Posner, with his group, received a telegram warning him to be careful when he returned to Chicago. When his train arrived, a group of Capone mobsters was waiting to "talk" to Posner and his union pals. However, someone was smart enough to call for help and the police showed up to stop any violence.

The mighty hand of Local 110 came crashing down on Posner when they pressed charges against him and his 21 union escorts for taking matters to the International Union which caused seven of the men to be expelled from the union because they would not accept the suspension and fines which were levied by the union. However, Sapperstein saw that he could not settle the matter peacefully so he decided to use the same methods as the union had used. He went to William Pacelli, then the Alderman for Chicago's Bloody 20th Ward and a Capone Gang representative. With Al Capone sitting in County jail, Pacelli contacted Capone and pleaded with him to end the lock-out. One of the principal difficulties in the dispute was the fact that the theater managers objected to using two to three men in each booth to run a film. This was un-necessary once sound was introduced to movies.

A settlement was reached between the mob, Thomas Malloy and the theater owners. The mob agreed to take out one man per booth for a payment of $1,150 per man. That meant that $350,000 went to Al Capone.

By 1935 Thomas Malloy's time had come to an end. Shortly after a convention held in Louisville in 1934, George E. Browne was backed by most of the key delegates. These delegates were from Chicago, New York and St. Louis and at the convention many of the U.S. top mobsters were in attendance to make sure George Browne was elected president, which he was.

In February 1935 Aaron Sapperstein approached Posner to inform him that Malloy was going to be killed. Posner noticed that members from the Executive Board of the International Union came to Chicago on a Wednesday and two days later Malloy was murdered.

According to Posner, Ralph O'Hare and Dr. Emmett Quinn, both of whom were Malloy's right-hand men, were involved in the murder. Quinn was usually Malloy's day-to-day driver, except the moment Malloy was killed, Malloy was driving. An informant said that Malloy was killed because he had been called in by a Grand Jury investigating his income tax returns and the mob became scared that Malloy was going to talk, so they killed him.

Ralph O'Hare was president of the Trans-American News Service and the White Way Electric Sign and Maintenance Company. He was at one time a member of Local 110 but remained on the union books just to receive union benefits without paying into the union. He was not listed as a member of the union or as one of its officers but controlled all the activities of contacting theater owners for shake downs with threats of union strikes.

With Malloy dead, George E. Browne grabbed Local 110 as trustee and placed Harland Holden, who at the time was Vice President of the International Union, as Malloy's replacement. He also placed Frank Clifford as the business agent.

Once Browne was boss of the local, he started bringing in members of Local 2 of the Stage Hands Union to work as motion picture operators. That's when Browne also brought in William Bioff and Nick Circella as his representatives and that's when Bioff and Circella began shaking down the movie picture companies.

He used gangster Joe Montana Jr. as his number one muscle for the local. Montana was employed by the Armitage Theater at 3553 West Armitage Avenue in Chicago as a movie operator but his real job was to keep members of the union in line.

Joe Montana Jr. was born on June 26, 1906 in Italy under his real name of Mauro J. Montana and entered the United States as an alien. His father, Joseph Montana Sr., had a grocery business at 914 West Polk Street in Chicago. There he operated a moonshine establishment in the back of the store. On October 28, 1923 Chicago police raided the store and a 17-year-old Montana shot and killed one of the policemen and wounded the other. Both Montana's were freed by a jury for the killing.

On July 27, 1941 Joe Jr. shot and killed hoodlum Frank Zito. He was convicted of murder and sentenced to Joliet Prison on a 10-to-14-year sentence which was later reduced through political connections to 1-to-14-years in prison.

The Montana family was known for losing their temper at any second. Many times Joe Jr. had assaulted his co-workers but nothing was ever done about it by the union. At one meeting in 1943, Joe Jr.'s brother, John Montana, made a dash towards Herman Posner with the intent to beat the crap out of him but was held back by his cronies because Posner was a cripple. The officer presiding over the meeting showed no inclination to reprimand Montana for his disorderly conduct.

In the early 1940's Peter Shayne, then president of Local 110, started to administer its affairs in a democratic order. A new constitution was being considered, one that would allow members in the local to consider it article by article. When "certain" members in the local got wind of this new constitution they went to Richard Walsh, then President of the International Union, declaring the union's business was being taken over by its members. Walsh hurried to Chicago and forced Shayne to resign, along with his business agent John Smith. Both Shayne and Smith would go on to testify in the Hollywood extortion trial against Paul DeLucia, Louis Campagna, Phil D'Andrea, Charles Gioe, Johnny Roselli and Frank Diamond.

After Browne, Circella and Bioff went to prison for extorting 1 million dollars from the movie industry, Richard Walsh came to Chicago and opened up the membership to Local 110. Over 400 applications were considered and committees were set up to screen the applicants. Posner was one of the men chosen to be on the committee. According to Posner, he eliminated 55 men, such as the brother of Willy Bioff and the cousin of Al Capone, and other relatives of hoodlums. That did not sit well with Walsh who discharged the committee and named a second committee to interview. When that second committee did the same thing, Walsh ruled that all of the applicants should be admitted to membership including the 55 hoodlum connected men.

A rigged election followed and the administration of union affairs was shifted from members to three of the union officers. The president then ordered the members to be disciplined and said that they were no longer allowed to exercise freedom of speech in the union. The business manager now controlled the employers, not only as to whom to hire but also whom not to hire. The Secretary-Treasurer was now in control of the millions in the welfare fund and was the one who determined who was to be paid and who was not to be paid.

George Hall claimed that he and Clyde Osterberg tried to start a new independent union to resist the infiltration of the mob in 1935. They opposed Thomas Malloy and wanted to rid him from the union. On May 18, 1935, Hall and Clyde and his wife, Mona Osterberg, were standing at the corner of 18th and Laflin Streets in Chicago making plans for this new union when a car pulled up, a man got out, knocked Osterberg to the ground, stood over him and fired two bullets into his head killing him. Hall, acting as Osterberg's bodyguard, was able to escape the bullets by running down the street with Mona. During the coroner's hearing on the killing, Hall testified that he and Osterberg had gone to see George E. Browne to ask if there was anything they could do to get them work. When they arrived at Browne's office, he was not there, but William Bioff was sitting in his chair. Osterberg asked Bioff what were the chances of them finding work, with Bioff informing them that there were no more permit men going to work. Osterberg then informed Bioff that he had a charter to start another union to rival his. Bioff then told Osterberg, *"You go ahead and start one and we will make an example of you."* Three weeks later Osterberg was attacked and beaten on the street by union thugs. Five weeks later he was murdered.

Later Hall was asked by Local 110 business agent Eugene Atkinson to go and pick up some dynamite so they could bomb the operators school. As Hall went to get the dynamite, he was caught in the act by the authorities and sentenced to five years in prison. There were rumors it was a set-up for Hall for trying to go against Local 110. However, year's later Hall said he took the rap for Atkinson and he was not set up. Hall was released from prison in 1939 and rejoined the union.

Posner said that the business agent at the time named John Smith was going to run against a Frank Galluzzo for Secretary-Treasurer of Local 110. However, at the last minute Clarence Jalas became the candidate for that position. Posner learned that Paul DeLucia and Claude Maddox had stepped in and demanded that Jalas be given the position as the Outfit's man.

Clarence Jalas was an associate of hoodlum Arthur "Fish" Johnston. In 1945 Johnston was released from Joliet Prison after a prison term for receiving stolen property. Once Johnston was released he went to work for Jalas at Jalas's business. Throughout the years, Jalas and Johnston had been involved in many dealings.

George Laris, a projectionist since 1917 explained that when Jalas was nominated for the position of Secretary-Treasurer it was at a union meeting and it was announced that the election was to be held at the next meeting. That was in violation of the unions constitution which said the election should have been at that meeting. But Jalas didn't care much about the union constitution. Days before the election, Laris said he was called to a work meeting at the old Morrison Hotel in Chicago. When he arrived he found an elaborate dinner of steaks and lobsters being served in honor of Jalas' candidacy. Around 500 "who's who" in Chicago attended and Jalas was on a platform with Eugene Atkinson. Later Laris was told the dinner was financed by the Chicago mob for Jalas. Jalas, Atkinson and James Gorman were all elected by secret ballots.

Another party was thrown when Eugene Atkinson was elected business agent of the union. A party was given by Jack Kirsch of the Allied Theater Company in hopes the company could have Atkinson in their pocket. When Atkinson sat down he found a $1,000 bill under his plate. Atkinson laughed and gave the money back to Kirsch telling him to *"come up with some real money."*

With Jalas in, he used George Hall to solicit gifts in return for operators to receive preferential treatment. One incident Jalas accepted $2,000 cash from a George Travils to get into the union.

The operators had to be licensed and a complicated learning program had been set up. In order for an operator to get his license he had to first serve a year's apprenticeship with an apprentice's license. Then he had to submit monthly appraisals of his work by the theater manager and submit to an examination. However, when Jalas took over all that was necessary was to mail a letter from out of town stating that the person had experience as an operator. George Hall told Posner that he personally had written a letter for someone to get his license.

Under the control of Jalas and Atkinson, when it was time to get their way with movie theater owners they would not send their men out on the streets to strike with signs, they would order the men to disrupt the movie theater. One example on Halloween night in 1946, Jalas order his projectionist to either show the Halloween film programs in reverse, out of focus, or kill the sound track so there was no sound.

Clarence Jalas's childhood was spent in Milwaukee, Wisconsin where he was raised by his grandparents. The rest of his family, his parents, his brother Henry and sister Alma lived in Chicago. His brother Henry told the FBI in 1963 that he was never close to his brother Clarence and had very little contact with him.

By the 1950's Local 110 had around 550 members but was considered a "closed union" meaning you had to know someone to get in. The reason given by Ralph Mooney was that there were not enough projectionist jobs to go around so the union was closed. But everyone knew the jobs were handed out by Tony Accardo and Paul DeLucia to family members of mobsters. The Moving Picture Machine Operators of Chicago were licensed under the Chicago Department of Streets and Electricity which was under the complete control of the Outfit.

Clarence Jalas was a co-owner, with his sister, of the Essenary Electric Manufacturing Company, located at 1438 North Clark Street in Chicago, which he said he started before the great depression in Chicago. The company manufactured accessories which he would rent out for special shows in Chicago, and would furnish and lease moving picture machines for exhibition pornographic movies in hotels. Jalas had the only 16MM projectors in the United States, fifteen in all, and used that advantage to get many conventions to come to Chicago, like cooking schools that needed to use 16MM projectors to show their training films.

Most of the projectors were World War II surplus. Jalas used the union offices and the union "cash" to conduct his business dealings so he did not have to pay any expenses. FBI agents once called the union offices and asked about leasing some projectors. Jalas's secretary had said she could handle the order because she worked for both the union and Essenary Electrical Manufacturing Company at the same time. She also unwittingly told the FBI that Jalas could be found at the union offices between 11:30 am and 2:30 pm, working 3 hours per day. There were reports that William Bioff had an interest in this company with Jalas.

Jalas was also Secretary Treasurer of Chicago Local B-46 of the IATSE. This local organized cashiers and ushers in theaters but went defunct after six months in 1958. Some of the members of this union wondered why there were never any meetings or any information from the union. It had taken 25 cents from each member and when the union went defunct, no one knew where all that money had gone. Jalas knew--in his pocket.

One time Clarence Jalas refused to let his operators show a movie called Salt of the Earth because Jalas believed the movie was a communist movie. The company that produced the movie sued Jalas and Eugene Atkinson, personally, and the union. However, Jalas and Atkinson took out $30,000 of union money and the suit suddenly disappeared.

By 1957 both Jalas and Atkinson were enjoying envelopes of money being delivered to both of them by the members who had the better operator jobs in the city. Most of the envelopes contained $1,000 up to $2,000 each. When business agent Eugene Atkinson died in March 1958, he left an estate close to one million dollars.

Around this time members were also complaining that the union's officers were floating the idea of outing the charter membership in the local and selling their jobs for $5,000 each.

There were men working in the union known as "permit men" which had been set up at the end of the 1940's. Ten percent of a moving picture operator income was taken by the union. The lowest paid member in the 1950's made $5,000 a year. By the middle of the 1950's, these permit men generated over $300,000 and when investigators looked into where this money went they could find no indication that the money ever made its way into the union's treasury for union business.

In 1958 Ralph Mooney tried to pass off Local 110 as any normal union that gives eight weeks a year vacation. He had increased the vacation from two to eight weeks on the basis that there was a shortage of work. Two months after doing so, he contradicted himself by announcing that 60 younger members, mostly the sons of connected mobsters, were doubling up their jobs on the grounds that there was too much work. The younger members were working five-hour shifts. Projectionists were being paid $2.82 to $3.93 an hour depending on the size of the theater and the number of seats inside which came to $120 a week. With the doubling, they now made $240 a week. During this announcement, many of the older union members who were not connected to the mob could find no work and found themselves unemployed. While this was going on the older unconnected projectionists were living on a pension payout of $35 a week.

Ralph Mooney said he was paid only $2,500 a year and had to work a regular job as a film projector operator at the North Avenue Outdoor Theater. Mooney also said he was a Trustee for the Welfare Fund which hovered around 3 million dollars in 1958.

At Christmas time they would set up a Christmas tree in the lobby of the union headquarters and place a paper dollar bill at the very top of the tree. Then union representatives would go out and visit all the members "suggesting" they had better put a Christmas card with some money in it and place it under the Christmas tree as a thank-you to their union leaders. They would tell the members that it would be in their best interest to do so. One older member said for Christmas his union representatives gave its union members corruption for splitting salaries, selling jobs and receiving forced Christmas gifts.

Mooney answered to Clarence Jalas who was so cocky he boasted that he could write a check from the union for a million dollars to use on personal stuff and put it back when he had the time. He made a motion into union law where every couple of years Local 110 records could be destroyed to help cover the money trail. He voted himself a $5,000 personal expense fund while acting as business agent. When the McClellan Senate Committee subpoenaed him about corruption in his union and its ties to organized crime, he laughed it off, stating he was not afraid of the government, or anyone.

Another incident showing how Jalas used people concerned the case of Jack Sweeney. Jack Sweeney was the son of Glenn Sweeney, who had been a long time member of Local 110. Glenn Sweeney wanted his son to take his place in the union when he retired. Jalas agreed but told Jack that he would be placed with the Altec Company and after a few years he would obtain membership in Local 110. However, during those few years Jack had to contribute 10% of his salary as a Christmas gift to Jalas. As years went by, Jalas never had any intention of letting Jack become a member, which he did not, but still demanded that 10% Christmas gift each year. Jalas also used union money to pay for his personal attorney, who happened to be mob lawyer Sidney Korshak.

In the 1950's Tony Accardo's brother John Accardo had been a projectionist at the old Mercury Theater and later a projectionist at one of Chicago's race tracks. There he would take the photo finishes at the finish line and would make up to $30,000-a-year. He was also employed at the old Cinerama at the Place Theater which at the time was the highest paid job available as a projectionist. He even worked a double shift on Sundays that was all double-time pay.

In 1958 Herman Posner approached John Accardo to tell him he was going to run for president of the union against Jalas but did not want to be killed by the mob. He wanted John Accardo to find out if the mob would care if he ran for president. Allegedly John Accardo came back to Posner and told him he did not care what Posner did because the mob was not making any money off of controlling the union since Paul DeLucia and the others went to prison in the extortion case. John Accardo allegedly admitted to Posner that he and the others had gotten into the union illegally and said they were in now and only wanted to be left alone. As long as Posner did not hurt him and the other mob guys in the local, they did not care what Posner did.

Posner was the backbone of the resistant movement for the "un-privileged" in the union. Posner even approached George Hall to see if he would stand behind him if he challenged Jalas. Hall himself had been contemplating running against Jalas, stating he had a great deal of information to use against Jalas. Posner had gotten a signed petition with enough signatures to challenge Jalas.

Posner lost the election by a landslide. He knew the fix was in and even threatened to go to the press about it. Almost a year later in February 9, 1960, Herman Posner was found stabbed to death at the rear of his home at 125 North Pine Street in Chicago. His son, Maurice, told police his father was into buying diamonds and old gold at auctions and believed he was killed in a failed robbery attempt. However, homicide detectives discounted that theory because Posner still had a diamond ring on his finger and his wallet with $46 in cash was still on him.

Jalas's comment about Posner's murder was that Posner was a grumpy old man and was hard to get along with but he didn't know anyone who would want to kill him.

The petition Posner had put together with all the names that were against Jalas disappeared and George Hall became too afraid to come forth with all the information he had gathered fearing he would be killed next.

Clarence Jalas, Howard Blackwood, Ralph Mooney, Frank Galluzzo, Charles Battaglia, Robert Clark, Leonard Meyers, Zadig Paloian and Glenn Kalkhoff were brought in and questioned in the murder but all were released without being charged. Two days after the killing his other son, Leo Posner, received a letter in the mail advising him and his brothers to "cool down or else" about their father's murder.

It was later learned that Herman Posner had a briefcase with documents showing how Jalas and his associates accepted kickbacks and shakedowns. Posner was going to turn the briefcase over to the U.S. Department of Labor; the day before he was going to give it he was stabbed to death and the briefcase was taken by the killers with all the evidence.

DEPARTMENT OF POLICE, CHICAGO
NON-TRAFFIC ACCIDENT REPORT — № 536266

28 Dist.
Date of Report 2-9 1960 Date of Accident 2-9 1960 Time 1:53 AM
Name of Injured POSNER HERMAN Age 73
Address 1[redacted] No PINE AVE — Male ✓
Occupation MOVIE OPERATOR — Married ✓
Nativity RUSSIA Phone No. Es 8-9786
Place of Occurrence REAR OF 1[redacted] No PINE
Injury or Sickness STAB WOUNDS IN ABDOMEN
Description of Accident INFLICTED BY UNKNOWN ASSAILANT

Refused Medical Aid ☐ First Aid by Police ☐
Taken to LORETTO Hospital
By AMB-SQUAD #15 C.F.D.
Attended By Doctor G. ECONOMON — Fatal ✓ Non-Fatal ☐
Removed to ... Morgue
Whom Notified [redacted] (WIFE)
Address SAME Phone No. SAME
C.C. No. 12137 Stat. Comp. No. 351175

IN ANIMAL BITE CASES
Name of Owner ... Phone No. ...
Address ... Apt. ... Rm. ... Hse. ... Fl. ...

Names of Witnesses	Addresses	Phone No.
1.		
2.		
3.		
4.		

Officer J. BOHAN, R. CORCORAN Star No. 4366 Dist 28
Commanding Officer — H. NEBERGALL, Desk Sergeant

Herman Posner

Herman Posner's homicide report

DEPARTMENT OF POLICE—CITY OF CHICAGO
OFFENSE REPORT
(TO INCLUDE ATTEMPTS) — 9431

DATE OF THIS REPORT February 9th, 1960 Central Complaint Room No. 12137
OFFENSE Murder - by stabbing ORIGINALLY REPORTED AS Stabbing possible murder
NAME OF COMPLAINANT State of Illinois ADDRESS
DATE AND TIME OF OCCURRENCE 2-9-60 12:40 A.M. and 1:48 A.M.
PLACE OF OCCURRENCE 1[redacted] N. Pine rear Parking lot
BETWEEN WHAT STREETS Washington and West End
REPORTED BY Leo Posner (son) — HOW REPORTED: BY TELEPHONE X
ADDRESS 30 N. Central
DATE AND TIME 2-9-60 2:10am
REPORTED TO CCR
COLOR AND NO. OF OFFENDERS Unknown
VEHICLE USED IF ANY Unknown
WITNESSES None
ANY OTHER OFFENSE: NATURE OF LOCATION Rear parking lot; HOW INJURED Stabbed; MEANS OR METHOD Apparently a knife; MOTIVE Murder

DESCRIPTION OF PROPERTY LOST AND DETAILS OF OFFENSE

Investigation disclosed that deceased, Herman R. Posner, age 73, of 1[redacted] N. Pine who is employed as a movie operator at the State Theatre at 5814 W. Madison St. had left the theatre at about 12:30 A.M. and entered his car presumably to go directly home.
At about 1:30 A.M. wife of the deceased, expecting him home looked out of window and saw his car parked in customary place in parking lot at rear of building.
After about ten minutes when deceased did not enter house, Mrs [redacted] (wife) called her son [redacted] age 47 at 3[redacted] N. Central Ave to tell him about the car being parked, but no sign of his father. Upon his arrival at the scene of the car he saw the deceased lying on the ground alongside his car, unconscious, but apparently breathing, and suffering from what appeared to be knife wounds. He ran into his parent's home and told [redacted] to call the Fire Dept. Amb #15 CFD with G. Graham and Barrett removed injured to Loretto Hospital where he was pronounced dead at about 2:10 A.M. by Dr. Economon. Body was taken to County Morgue. Stabbed by persons unknown.

STATION COMPLAINT NO. 351175 TELETYPE MESSAGE NO. 9478
INVESTIGATING OFFICERS Detective J. Bohan #4366
IF NOT BONA-FIDE GIVE REASONS WHY
COMMANDING OFFICER

Support the Administration Ticket - Local 110

SAMPLE BALLOT

Special Election of Officers

To unexpired terms in accordance with the minutes of meeting of February 5, 1959

Tuesday, March 3, 1959

CHICAGO MOVING PICTURE MACHINE OPERATORS' UNION

Local Number 110 of the I. A. T. S. E. and M. P. M. O.
OF THE UNITED STATES AND CANADA

POLLS OPEN — 9:30 A.M TO 5:00 P.M.
12th Floor — 32 W. Randolph St.

PRESIDENT
(One to be Elected)

[X] **HOWARD C. BLACKWOOD**
[ ] HERMAN POSNER

SECRETARY-TREASURER
(One to be Elected)

[ ] PHILLIP J. KORE
[X] **RALPH R. MOONEY**

BUSINESS MANAGER
(One to be Elected)

[X] **CLARENCE A. JALAS**
[ ] HARVEY W. SCHRAUT

BOARD OF TRUSTEES
(One to be Elected)

[ ] EDWIN J. JOSEPH
[X] **ARNOLD C. SWANSON**

423

A 1959 election ballot from local 110

CAMPAIGN COMMITTEE FOR
THE ADMINISTRATION TICKET
1959

ARTHUR TUCHMAN
CHARLES FUNK
SAM KLUGMAN

JACK STRAHL
GEORGE KAR

GEORGE GEMEINHARDT
JULIUS DICKSTEIN
FRANK HYLAND

ADMINISTRATION CANDIDATES
★ ★ ★ ★
JALAS
MOONEY
BLACKWOOD
SWANSON

Dear Brother:

It is usually customary for candidates to barrage their constituents with literature extolling their qualifications and accomplishments, however this hardly seems necessary in our coming election.

Everyone knows CLARENCE JALAS and his outstanding record. We know that he has consistently devoted long hours and much thoughtful planning to minimize the effects of any adverse conditions in our industry. We know, too, that he is a co-originator of our Welfare Plan and how he has worked during the past ten years (which saved our Union not less than $200,000 by eliminating the office of Assistant Business Manager and by assuming the work of the Business Manager this past year.) He provided the highly stable and excellent management of our affairs unstintingly, reserving no time for personal vacations for the past eight years. In short, his record speaks for itself.

RALPH MOONEY, we know, has the necessary experience in our business affairs to be well qualified to assume the office of Secretary-Treasurer.

HOWARD BLACKWOOD has the ability, as well as the integrity, to be an excellent President.

ARNOLD SWANSON'S long and equally as loyal membership assure that he will be a perfect Trustee.

All of these candidates have always been unselfishly dedicated to the collective progress of all the members of Local 110.

THEY SHOULD BE ELECTED!

THE CAMPAIGN COMMITTEE FOR THE ADMINISTRATION

Arthur Tuchman
Charles Funk
Sam Klugman
Jack Strahl
George Karg
George Gemeinhardt
Julius Dickstein
Frank Hyland

THE VANGUARD

A MODERN PLATFORM FOR A MODERN UNION

Dear Brother:

For most of us in Local No. 110 our Pension and Welfare Fund is the closest we'll ever come to high finance. The agreement between our Union and the Employer is clouded in legal talk that is difficult to understand. But its meaning in terms of security and welfare should be a different story. There is so much at stake in the Welfare Fund that unfounded rumors are possible. Put all the rumors aside, however. There is a large enough problem in reality to merit some serious consideration.

As we said in the last letter, policies overshadow personalities, and here is a perfect example. When the "Trust" was born on November 26, 1948 and for the first few years thereafter, it had great potential. Times (in our Craft) were better.

With the change in the economic picture the tail has come to wag the dog. The Welfare Fund has been turned into a crutch to prop us up. The administration, trying to find an answer to closing theatres and loss of jobs, looks no further than the end of its nose. They rely solely on the Fund to create jobs. As the job situation has become tighter, the administration factions answer has been to have more frequent vacations. This makes more jobs to take up the slack as more theatres close. Thus, many men, some with years of seniority, have had only swing or vacation jobs. (Meanwhile some of the administration faction, in no great financial trouble, have two and in some cases three jobs. Some of these men have no Union Card.) This is a matter of record.

But this policy is a viscious circle. In time, if the practice continues, we come to have all vacation and no work, but we'll also have no money in the Pension Fund. Let's face facts. There are better ways to improve the job situation than to overspend the "Trust" money. WE NEED A CHANGE IN LEADERSHIP!

Our answer is this. In spite of the fact that they say it can't be done, consider: If we raise the retirement benefit to $150 or $175/month, plus other benefits, part of which could be in the form of dues reduction, many men who are eligible would be encouraged to retire. This would open many new jobs, and would give a DRAMATIC OPPORTUNITY FOR ADVANCEMENT TO YOUNGER MEMBERS SEEKING BETTER JOBS. Add to these the ones where men are doubling or tripling and we have, at a bare minimum, somewhere between 50 and 75 jobs in surplus. Then vacations would become a matter of sheer leisure for you as a person instead of a question of the necessity for us to maintain our strength as a Union.

If our policy were followed we would probably even need some new members to cover a part of these new jobs. Therefore, A VOTE FOR US IS A VOTE TO:

1) INCREASE PENSION BENEFITS. THEREBY WE WOULD
2) CREATE NEW JOBS
3) PLACE SWING MEN PERMANENTLY
4) BRING IN SONS AND BROTHERS

With Point 4 (above) in mind, we further propose the return of the election of new members to you. We pledge revocation of Article 43 of the By-Laws, which leaves sole choice of who shall become a member of this Union to the discretion of the Business Manager. This is in complete violation of the International Constitution and By-Laws.

Perhaps you say to yourself, "This isn't what we're voting for at the election. We vote for men." Ordinarily this would be true. But too many years of "DO-NOTHING" have passed. We need planned action on new policies. We appeal to you on the issues. Your vote for us next Tuesday will guarantee fulfillment of our pledge. You demand certain things in return for your confidence, in secret ballot, that we must deliver.

Fraternally yours,

Herman Posner	Edwin Joseph	Harvey Schraut	Phillip Kore
for	*for*	*for*	*for*
President	*Trustee*	*Business Manager*	*Secretary-Treasurer*

P.S. The man who seeks the office of Secretary-Treasurer for the opposition, made one demonstration of his ability as an officer at the November meeting of this Union. His rulings at that meeting came under such fire that many members were forced to appeal to a higher authority for redress. The result was the intervention of the International, throwing out our whole November meeting as illegal. What kind of Secretary-Treasurer can he make? The record speaks for itself.

In 1960 a long time Local 110 member named Zadig M. Poloian filed charges against Clarence Jalas for accepting payoffs which angered Jalas. Poloian was "forced" to take an extended vacation and upon returning was informed he had lost his projection job to another member. Poloian laid out that everyone in Local 110 had to pay Jalas at least $800 a year to get a decent assignment, except for the relatives of hoodlums. They had to pay nothing, just their name was sufficient to qualify for the top assignments. The problem was that everyone who was not a relative or knew the hoodlums was afraid to stand up to Jalas so no one would talk and the charges went nowhere.

Another member with the last name of Cull had to move to Cincinnati to find work because of Jalas. FBI agents tracked this member down to interview him. He told the agents that when he was leaving Chicago after losing his projectionist job he was paid two checks for services rendered. When he went to cash the checks they turned out to be worthless. He attempted to contact officers in Local 110 for help but was ignored. They refused to see him, answer his letters or take his phone calls.

He did tell the FBI that it was his belief that Clarence Jalas had something to do with Herman Posner's murder. He added that because of Jalas, Local 110 had lavish offices and its officers drove very expensive cars but were never around or willing to help its members.

In many ways the Chicago Outfit perfected the corruption of this union. FBI agents were having a difficult time getting information about corruption in the local because most of its members were either connected to the hoodlums or scared of the hoodlums. FBI agents wrote that there were no assurances that the projectionists, if interviewed, would not contact news reporters or inform the hoodlums, which would have disclosed the FBI interest in the activities of Local 110.

Jalas also kept a secret pool of about 20 to 30 non-union men working for the union who did not receive any union benefits. The reason for this was when Jalas had to lay men off for whatever reason, he would always have the non-union men to lay off and keep the hoodlum union men always working.

One time a newspaper reporter approached Paul DeLucia and asked him how he was able to get his brothers-in-law and nephews jobs in Local 110. He actually gave an answer to this reporter making it look like any old friend did a favor by saying it was a result of his acquaintanceship with Thomas Malloy, who at different times was able to secure jobs for a few of his friends and relatives. The truth was DeLucia controlled Malloy.

In 1962 Local 110 was investigated in connection with corruption at Chicago's McCormick Place Convention Center. Most of the union men who worked at the trade shows were members of Chicago Local 136, another local under the control of the Chicago mob. The contract for all projector equipment went to Essenary Electrical Manufacturing Company, Clarence Jalas's company.

In April 1965 Clarence Jalas, his sister Alma Long, his nephew Donald Racine, and Ralph Mooney were indicted by a Federal Grand Jury for violation of the Taft-Hartley law for embezzlement. The government claimed Jalas accepted gifts of money and other gratuities and used union funds to finance certain operations of his own company, Essenary Electric Manufacturing Company, which his sister and nephew ran.

Clarence A. Jalas

File Card

Clarence A. Jalas
Born October 2, 1894 Milwaukee, Wisconsin (Illinois State Drivers license list birth date 10-2-1896)
Driver License # J420-1019-6281
Height 5' 9 1/2"
Weight 225 pounds
Eyes Brown
Hair White, mostly bald
Build Heavy
Rank of Private in the U.S. Army 1916-1917
Brother Henry V. Jalas (Spelled his name as Jalass) (Lived in Detroit, Michigan and then Pompano Beach, Florida)
Sister Alma Long
Listed as being paid $32,494 by the union in 1973

Known Addresses

1419 Winona Street, Chicago (1940's–1950's)
188 West Randolph Street, Chicago Apartment 2105 (1950's-1960's)
8911 North Lamon Avenue, Skokie, Illinois (1956)
8465 Skokie Blvd, Skokie, Illinois (1960's)

Known Companies Owned

Owner of Essenary Electric Manufacturing Company, 1438 North Clark Street Chicago (1940's to 1960's) 454 North Halstead Street Chicago (1960's) (Some reports spelled Essannay)
Essannay Film Rental Company (1960's)
Perkins Lease Oil, Wichita County, Texas (1950's)
Oil wells in Washington & Nevada Counties, Oklahoma (1950's)
Lorraine Fulton, Inc.

Known Jobs

Secretary Treasurer & Business Agent Local 110 (1942-1970's)
Board of Examiners (1948)
Trustee of Welfare Fund (1950's-1970's)
Secretary Treasurer of Chicago Local B-46 (1950's)

Known Auto's

1963 Cadillac Fleetwood Sedan, License plate # DS 8465 (Listed under Local 110)

Known Arrest Record

Date	Charge	Agency	Verdict
10-29-1956	Disorderly conduct	CPD	Discharged
10-29-1956	Resisting Arrest	CPD	Discharged
10-29-1956	D.U.I.	CPD	Discharged

In January 1968 Jalas plead guilty to violating the Taft-Hartley Act and was fined $1,000. He also plead guilty to accepting $8,500 from Essenary Electric Manufacturing Company and 500 shares of stock to an interior decorating firm. It did not matter. There was no jail time and Jalas had been elected president of the union once again. However, the U.S. Attorney went after Jalas to try and oust him from the union under the provisions of the Landrum-Griffin Act which prohibited union officials from holding office for five years after a conviction. Jalas' lawyer struck back stating that Jalas plead guilty to misdemeanors, not felonies, so he was not barred from holding his union job.

In October 1969 a Federal Grand Jury returned an indictment charging Clarence Jalas of another violation. However, it was dismissed on January 1970.

Jalas still had the Outfit on his side. In February 1971 Jalas was once again elected president of Local 110. He had managed to keep Local 110 quiet and make its members the wealthiest with a union contract and some of the highest paid workers in America at that time. Projectionists took home more money than their counterparts in 16 other top U.S. cities.

In 1974, Clarence Jalas and his millions retired, leaving Joey Johnston as the new commander and boss of Local 110. Rumor was sometime after retiring Clarence Jalas suffered a stroke and was going senile.

During his tender, Clarence Jalas survived countless labor racketeering investigations while making the Chicago Outfit very happy and rich. Joey Johnston's father, Arthur "Fish" Johnston, was an outfit thief and fencer in the 1940's, 50's, & 60's. "Fish" Johnston once claimed he ran with John Dillinger and Al Capone. Fish Johnston was very close to Clarence Jalas and at one time had a portion of Jalas's film supply company. He was considered one of Chicago's top thieves who went to prison in the 1950's for dealing in stolen goods across state lines. After his release in 1959 he "officially" went to work as a manager at the Duneland Village Trailer Park in Indiana. At least that's what he claimed and wrote on paper.

Fish Johnston was once questioned in the murder of his brother-in-law Elmer "White" Madsen. Both Fish and Madsen were partners in the operation of a clothing store located on Armitage Avenue. When people discovered White Madsen was also a fence with Fish they speculated there could have been a disagreement between the two leading to the murder. However, police could find no evidence that Fish was responsible for Madsen's murder.

Joseph Johnston moved the union offices to the famous John Hancock Building on Chicago's Michigan Avenue. At the time it was one of Chicago's most expensive buildings to rent office space in.

During Johnston's watch, a string of mob bombs were hitting Chicago porno theaters in an attempt to organize small local theaters. The theaters were using non-union projectionists paying them under the union scale pay of $11.75 an hour.

Among theaters bombed were the Bijou Theater at 1394 N. Wells; the Follies Theater at 540 S. State Street; the Rialto Theater at 546 S. State Street; and the Newberry Theater at 854 N. Clark Street all in Chicago.

Bijou Theater

Follies Theater

Newberry Theater

Rialto Theater

Mob Boss

In 1975 FBI agents re-opened their investigation into Local 110 when a cinema in Meadowbrook, located at 2119 W. 63rd Street, was bombed. The theater had no union men working there and FBI agents received word that fellow theater owners with ties to Local 110 officers had allegedly said they were going to *"get Meadowbrook cinema in line."* One informant told the story that allegedly when the Meadowbrook Theater was getting ready to open a year or so before the bombing, an Edward DiDominico was preparing the cinema for opening day when two new projectors arrived costing $10,000 each. DiDominico then hired a union man to install the projectors in the theater. While the union man worked installing them, a black limousine pulled up in front of the cinema and two men in business suits got out. One of the men was a "big thug-type guy". As they approached DiDominico, allegedly the big guy said to DiDominico *"You're gonna put a union man in here, or you're not opening. I don't want no if's, and's or but's about it."*

Then the big man turned to the union man installing the projector and said, *"You, out!"* The installer, looking not a bit surprised, got up and left.

Allegedly fearing trouble, DiDominico hired a union projectionist. However, he employed this union man for only a few months until he could not afford to keep paying him union wages then let him go and hired a non-union man for half the salary. DiDominico was approached a few times and asked why he had to let the union man go, his response was he could not afford the union scale. Union officers informed DiDominico that they had the ability to go to film distributors and candy companies and reconstruct a theater's cash flow and if they felt there was enough money to support a union man then one would be sent.

DiDominio became so scared that he would be killed by the mob he sold the theater. The new owner was approached by a Local 110 field representative and was told he needed to have union men working in his theater. The new owner informed the union rep that he would be running the projectors himself and did not need any help. The field rep smiled and left the theater. The next morning the theater was bombed, blowing up the lobby. No one from Local 110 came around after the bombing and the new owner decided he was not going to be scared away by anyone. He had the damage fixed and on the morning of his grand opening another bomb exploded causing even more damage. After the bombing, the new owner was told by Local 110 *"now that we got your attention, we want to talk to you."*

The new owner was summoned to the John Hancock building and was told that the union was willing to cut him a deal. They would leave him alone for six months and after the six months they would review his financial situation and if he was able to afford a union projectionist he would have to hire one, even if it was for two days a week. As long as a union man was working and money was coming into the union treasury, everything would be fine. It was not known if the new owner ever complied.

Another theater owner who was using non-union projectionists was summoned to Local 110 offices in the Hancock building for a meeting. Allegedly at this meeting an oral "under the table" agreement was offered whereby the owners would be required to have one union projectionist at a yearly cost of $33,000. Allegedly one of the union officers said, *"The agreement reads harsh and we won't enforce it. It would be less expensive for you to take the projectionist who is already a union member and carry him as your projectionist and merely pay $2,500 a year into the union health, welfare and benefit fund and his dues of $75 a quarter. What we don't know about who is in your booth won't hurt us."*

Another theater owner complained that his front windows were shot out by a shotgun when he refused to hire a non-union projectionist.

The FBI focused on the fact that Tony Accardo had many of his relatives still in Local 110; Joey Aiuppa had four relatives; Sam Giancana had three relatives and Sam "Teets" Battaglia had at least one working in local theaters.

Between 1992 and 1997, Joey Johnston allegedly made millions while controlling prostitution rackets inside a Hammond, Indiana tavern and a bar known as "Fanny's" in Gary. In September of 2001, Johnston plead guilty to federal conspiracy charges and was sentenced to four years in prison. Joey's son, Jeffrey, also plead guilty in the case.

In March 2004 Albin Brenkus, then second in command of Local 110, was charged with conspiring to commit arson and to interstate travel to commit arson. His conviction came from the years 1998 and 1999 when Local 110 was locked out by two Chicagoland theater chains that later merged into Lowes Cineplex Entertainment Group and another theater chain known as AMC Entertainment. Negotiations were not going well so Brenkus sent two union members named Kent Dickinson and Joseph Marjan to 20 theaters in 10 states to set off chemical smoke bombs. The bombs were made of an incendiary combination of chlorine and brake fluid. The tactic of vandalism was used as a bargaining tool; Dickinson would later testify that members of Local 110 were expected to take part in the vandalism before they were allowed to join the projectionists union. Union members Peter C. Lipa and Gregory Tortorello were also charged.

Lipa and Tortorello were acquitted on all charges and Albin Brenkus was convicted of one count of obstructing justice for instructing union members not to help in the federal investigation.

Chicago Local 110 had always been the comfort home of Chicago Outfit members. A place to make sure their family members and friends received lots of money with very little work.

Known Local 110 Union Offices

188 West Randolph Street, Chicago (1958-1970's)
John Hancock Building, 41st floor Michigan Avenue, Chicago (1970's)
Motion Picture Operators Union, Local 110 in Chicago covered all of the movie theaters in Cook County Illinois.

Known Officers of Local 110

Presidents

Reynolds (President 1928)
Thomas Malloy (1929-1935)
George E. Browne (1935-1940's)
Peter Shayne (1940's)
James Gorman (1951)
Ralph Mooney (1955-1958)
Howard C. Blackwell (1958-1965)
Ira F. Jacobsen (2-14-1965)
Clarence Jalas (1960's-1973)
Donald MacKinnon (1973)
Richard F. Walsh (International President 1950's)

Vice Presidents

Herman Posner (Vice President 1920's)
Frank Galluzzo (1951-1960's) (Born 12-17-1890 in Italy, Lived at 6201 N. Legett, Chicago)
LeRoy "Ray" McCracken (1960's-1970's)
Secretary Treasure
Neal Bishop (1935)
Ora Bebb (1944)
Ralph R. Mooney (1958–1965)
508 South Austin Boulevard, Oak Park, IL. Winter home in Hot Springs, Arkansas.
Clarence A. Jalas
Alvin V. Wrobel (1973)

Business Agents

George Hall (1935)
Frank Clifford (1930's)
John Smith (1940's)
Eugene Atkinson (1943-1957) Died March 1958
Clarence Jalas (1957-1973)
Joseph Johnson (1970's)
Albin Brenkus (2003-2004)

Others

Neal C, Bishop, Union Officer (1943)
Howard Blackwood, Union Officer (1951)
Robert P. Burns, Union Officer (1942)
George Carg, Chairman of the Trustees (1958)
Arthur Devent, Exertive Board (1970's)
Carl D. Giacomo, Trustee (1970's)
George Hall (Right hand man to Clarence Jalas 1950's)
Harold Huchberger, Chairman and Trustee (1970's)
837 South Dunton Street, Arlington Heights, Illinois
Jack Kirsch, Executive Board Member (1950's)
William Meissner, Executive Board (1970's)
Eugene Mosley, Trustee (1970's)
John Overbeck, Unions Attorney (1950"s)
Andrew Reinholz, Sergeant-at-Arms (1970's)
Russell W. Schlecht, Executive Board (1970's)
Neal C. Shayne, Union Officer (1940)
James Sisco, Union Officer (1943)
Clara Skorup (Clarence Jalas Secretary 1950's)
John P. Smith, Business Agent (1940's)
Glenn Sweeney, Union Officer (1943)
Thomas M. Thomas, Unions Attorney (1950's)
David Wallerstein, Executive Board Member (1950's)
George B. Williams, Executive Board (1970's)

1944 FBI List of Local 110 Members

Eugene J. Atkinson	4736 Magnolia St.	Chicago, Ill.
O. D. Bebb	Box 85	Palos Park, Ill.
John E. Behlke	121 Gillick St.	Park Ridge, Ill.
Sam Biller	7931 Vernon Ave.	Chicago, Ill.
Allen Bioff	1036 Washington Blvd.	Oak Park, Ill.
Hyman Bioff	6440 N. Claremond Ave.	Chicago, Ill.
Robert Bird	4130 N. Harding Ave.	" "
Oscar Bland	4837 N. Avers Ave.	" "
Angelo Brescia	4712 W. 21st St.	Cicero, Ill.
Joseph Britsk	4945 N. Wolcott St.	Chicago, Ill.
Joseph Coscioni	721 S. Carpenter St.	" "
Anthony T. D'Andrea	511 Beckwith Lane-Lincolnshire	Crete, Ill.
Julius Dickstein	6041 Fletcher Ave.	Chicago, Ill.
Carl Digiacomo	254 W. 24th Pl.	" "
Jerry Digiacomo	2814 Cambridge Ave.	" "
William Dokupil	1846 S. 57th St.	Cicero, Ill.
Henry N. Feigenbaum	6751 Jeffery Ave.	Chicago, Ill.
Charles Forberg	10636 S. Seeley Ave.	" "
Frank Galluzzo	6210 N. Leggett Ave.	" "
Pasquale Gigante	1928 N. Oak Park Ave.	" "
Anthony Gioe	2107½ S. Oak Park Ave.	" "
Frank Gordon	3623 N. Harding Ave.	" "
Jerry Greenspon	5465 Ingleside Ave.	" "
Harry J. Grosse	1140 Argyle St.	" "
Harry Guthrie	12107 Longwood Dr.	Blue Island, Ill.
Edward Halliday	6918 Olcott Ave.	Chicago, Ill.
Samuel Imburgio	612 N. 16th Ave.	Melrose Park, Ill.
Clarence A. Jalas	1419 Winona St.	Chicago, Ill.
John Karatinos	819 E. 63rd St.	" "
Sig Kaufman	134th St. and Klane	Orland Park, Ill.
Phillip Kore	5516 N. Kimball Ave.	Chicago, Ill.
Frank Korte	1217 Woodbine Ave.	Oak Park, Ill.
James Kostakis	1928 S. 60th Ct.	Chicago, Ill.
Joseph P. Kramer	850 Washington St.	Evanston, Ill.
Hugo Krause	2237 Lincolnwood Dr.	" "
Jack Krulewitch	5522 W. Monroe St.	Chicago, Ill.
George LaRoi	2440 Catalpa Ave.	" "
Joseph Mace	4034 S. Grove Ave.	Brookfield, Ill.
Sam Mansfield	7852 Langley Ave.	Chicago, Ill.
John Maritote	7244 S. Prairie Ave.	" "
John Montana	5240 W. Harrison St.	" "
E. H. Moore	Belair Hotel 420 Diversey Pkwy.	" "
LeRoy McCracken	7947 S. Morgan St.	" "
Elmer Olson	5304 Woodlawn Ave.	" "
John Pabich	5037 W. Newport Ave.	" "
Robert Pacelli	1120 N. Lawler Ave.	" "
Barney Posner	1637 W. Pratt Ave.	" "
Maurice J. Posner	3951 W. Van Buren St.	" "
Morris Price	12132 S. Wallace Ave.	" "
Dave Raff	30 N. Central Ave.	" "
Harry Ragan	162 E. Ohio St.	" "
Richard J. Ray	4842 Fulton St.	" "
Joseph Romano	4616 W. Jackson Blvd.	" "
John Sbarbaro	4733 W. Chicago Ave.	" "
Harvey Wm. Schraut	7427 S. Union Ave.	" "
Peter Shayne	6327 N. California Ave.	" "
James Sisco	1309 S. Ridgeland Ave.	Berwyn, Ill.
Edward P. Smith	5820 N. Kilbourn Ave.	Chicago, Ill.
P. W. Smith	5649 Grace St.	" "
Stanley J. Smith	3533 Newcastle Ave.	" "
Sam Spiros	1438 E. 72nd Pl.	" "
Glen Sweeney	3535 N. Lakewood Ave.	" "
Dominick Toste	1421 S. 61st Ave.	Cicero, Ill.
Arthur Tuchman	7548 Eastlake Terrace	Chicago, Ill.
Otto F. Vonesh	3300 East Ave.	Berwyn, Ill.

Known Member of Local 110 list as of 1959

John Accardo *(Brother of Tony Accardo)*
Anthony Ross Accardo *(Son of Tony Accardo)*
Joseph Accardo *(Adopted son of Tony Accardo)*
Thomas Addison
Sam Aiuppa *(Brother of mob boss Joey Aiuppa)*
P.I. Akins
David J. Allman
Gus Anders
Edward Anderson
V.H. Anderson
George Armstrong
Willie Arndt AKA Bill Nevins *(Spent years in prison for murder) (1975)*
Eugene Atkinson *(Lived at 4736 Magnolia Street, Chicago 1940's)*
Louis Atkinson
R.N. Atkinson *(Lived at 618 N. 11th Street, Melrose Park 1944)*
James Badenius
Charles Bambera, aka Fidela *(1920's)*
E. M. Bannister
George Barkes
Frank Bartkus
Benjamin Bassoff
Ora Bebb Jr.
Frank Bee
George Bee
Charles Behounek
Oscar Beitz
Barnie Bendersky
Michael Benedetto
Dan Beres *(In 1975 demanded FBI agents help him because he was being harassed by "the Mafia". FBI listed him in the front office "nut box")*
Gust Beres
Fred Berg
E. G. Berger
Arno Bergh
Joe Berinstein
M. Bernstein
Al Besser
James Best
Fred Biddle
George Biltgen
John T. Biltgen
Allen Binafield
Allen Bioff *(Brother of William Bioff) (Lived at 1460 Sandburg Terrace, Chicago Apartment 210A in 1975)*
Herman "Hymie" Bioff, AKA Bill Nelson (Brother of William Bioff)
Frank Bishop
Neil Bishop *(1930's) (Possiable brother-in-law of Louis Campagna)*
Howard Blackwood
Roy Blanchard
W. Blanchard
Herman Bland
Lee Bland
Phillip Bland
Frank Bloore
Roland Boening
Phil Bohmann
Nick Bonomo
Oreste Bosicia
Frank Bosco
Carl Brenner
Peter Bridges
Thomas BrightonO.H. Bronson
Ted Brooks
Joey Bucey
J.T. Bunce
T. John Burns
F.G. Burtscher
Herman Busch
Lester Busch
Charles Butwill
Jas. Cahill
Thad Calloway
Joe Campbell
William Campbell *(One time stable operator of Claude Maddox)*
Joseph Canick
Sid Caplan
Joe Capone *(Said to be a relative of Al Capone)*
John Casagrande
W. Channell
John Chestnut
Thomas Christos
Nick Chronis
Ross Cicero
Anthony Circella *(Brother of Nick*

Circella)
August Circella *(Brother of Nick Circella)*
Nick Circella *(Mobster)*
John "Jack" Clark *(Trustee for Local 110 and President of National Association of Theater Owners of Illinois)*
John J. Clarkson
Frank Clifford
Harry Cohen
Arthur Colby
R.J. Coleman
Jas. Coles
F.R. Connelly
John Connelly
Joseph Coscione *(Frank Nitti's Chauffer)*
James Albert Costo *(Associate of Nick Circella, one time operator of barber shop at 810 South Loomis Street in Chicago)*
W. Covey
Dan Crededio
Dom Cristallo
Frank Cuphaver
Fred Currier
Stanley Dakoski
Jerry Daly
Charles Demory, aka Gebhardt *(Brother of "Machine Gun Jack McGurn)*
Anthony T. D'Andrea *(Nephew of Phil D'Andrea) (511 Beckwith Land, Lincolnshire)*
Stanley D'Andrea *(Relative of Phil D'Andrea)*
Carl Danielson
Hernam David
Porter Davis
Dave Day
Edward Decker
Nick DeFabio
Lee DelMargro
Louis Deobler
Sheldon Deobler
Ward Deobler
Frank DeLandi *(One spelling DoLendi) (Nephew of* Frank *Nitti)*
Frank Desermeaux
Vladimir Desort
L.L. Deutisch
Arthur Devent
William Devine
John P. Dial
F.C. Dietarle
William Dietz
Walter Dietze
Adolph Diez
Gerlando DiGiacomo
Carl Dinwiddle
O.J. Dinwiddle
Frank Dobes
John Doetsch
Frank Dolendi
John Dombroski
Joe Domino
George Dravillas
Joe Dunn
Earl Eatinger
Joe Edelen
A. Edwards
Arthur Ehmann
John Ehrmeyer
Harry Elman
Elmer Enke
Rocco Eulo *(Brother of Frank "Sharkey" Eulo)*
George Evens
Alex Farber
Patrick Feltman
E.J. Ferney
Anthony Ficaro *(Associate of Louis Campagna and Willie Bioff)*
Charles Fine
Rudolph Fisher
H.W. Flack
Tim Flanagan
Earl Flood
Joe Florian
Thomas Foley
Edward Fontana
Harry Forberg
Henry Fox
Frank Frandsen
F. Freiwald
Ralph French
Joe Friend
Cecil Fry
Charles Funk
John Funk
Ed Gabriel
Henry Gaddes
Arthur Gagnon
Lewis Gallagher
Frank Galluzzo
Fred Galluzzo
William Galluzzo
Paul Gardner
Al Garlick
Frank Gaynor
Charles Gebhardt
D. Gebring
Elmer Geis
Joseph Geiser
Geo. Gemeinhardt
Fred George
Harry Geselter

Charles Giancana *(Brother of Sam "Momo" Giancana)*
Nick Giancana *(Relative of Sam Giancana)*
Joseph Paul Gigante *(Brother-in-law of Paul DeLucia)*
Pasquale "Pat" Gigante *(Brother-in-law to Paul DeLucia)*
Gus Gilard
Anthony Gioe *(Brother of Charles "Cherry Nose" Gioe, Lived at 2107 ½ S. Oak Street, Chicago)*
Louis Glickman
Nate Glicksberg
Sol Glicksberg
B. Gloss
Monte Gloss
Al Gnady
Harry Goldberg
Herman Goldberg
M. Goldberg
Irving Goldman
Kal Goldman
Sol Goldman
Frank Golinda *(Nephew of Frank Nitti)*
Ben Goltz
Ed Golub
Sam Golub
Ed Gordon
Joseph C. Gordon
Francis Gorey
James Gorman
John Gormn
W. Gramer
Ernest Graudin
Roy Gray
H. Graudin
David Grear
Morris Green
Joe Greenberg
Fred Grieco
Carl Guercio
Edwin Guenther
Joseph Guercio
Sam Guercio
Walter Gury
Henry Gusenburg
Harry Guthrie
John Haas
Charles Hall
Edward Hall
George R. Hall *(Spent 5 years in prison for conspiracy)*
Edward Halliday
George Halliday
Joe Hamp
Ward Hanagin *(Chairmen of the Board of Examiners) (1948-1950's)*
William Hanely
Milton Hannsberg
William Hart
W. Hassett
Charles Havill
Percy Havill
Edward Haydock
Christ Heinen
W. Heintz
David Heiss
Geo. Heiss
John Gerington
Louis Herman
Walt Hesterman
Gus Hetzel
Frank Heuser
Geo. High
Charles Hill
Albert Hillertz
Ed Hillertz
DeKoven Holland
Arthur Hillins
Claude Holmes
Fred Holmes
W. Holtzman
A. Hopkins
Ray Horrall
Joseph Hovorka
Dudley Howell
W. Hoyer
John Hubacek
Matt Hughes
John Hulka
Hobart Hudson
Matt Hughes
John Hulka
George Humphreys *(Brother of Murray Humphreys)*
Jack Humphreys, AKA Jack Wright *(Brother of Murray Humphreys)*
Frank Hyland
Harry Igel
Sam Imburgio *(Brother of Joseph Bulger)*
Abe Issacson
Sam Issacson
Clarence Jalas
Ira Jacobsen
Joseph Johnson *(1979)*
LeRoy Johnson
Edwin Joseph
Arthur Jung
Ed Kappel
John Kara
Joseph Karmazin
Sol Katz
Ben Kaufman
Chester Keller
Warren Kennedy
Dallas Kephart
Walter Kerr

Nick Khronis
F. King
James King
Joe King
Smith King
R. Kirkbride
Jack Kirsch *(Trustee of Welfare Fund, Allied Theaters Owners union, deceased by 1961)*
John Kirwin
Herbert Kleinbeck
Leo Kline
Sam Klugman
W. Koenen
Tom Kolar
Fred Konsack
Harry Koonts
Phil Kore
Harry Kosberg
James Kostakis
Eail Kounovsky
Hugo Krause
Morton Krugman
Fred Krumphois
Fred Kude
Ed Kuhn
Frank LaBrun *(Associate of Louis Campagna and Nick Circella)*
Joe Lack
Joe Langen
Herbert Langenbacher
Arthur Lapin
Romeo LaPoint
George Laris
George LaRoi Jr.
Carl Lasker
George Lawson
Frank LeBrun
Felix Lenard
Charles Leverence
Phillip Levy
Walter Leyku
Sal Lictra
Rudolph Lightfoot
Leslie Linick
Howard Lorenz
Chauncey Lossong
Ralph Lowry
W. Lubin
J.P. Lucas
Stanley Lukes
Arthur Lyons
Charles Mack
Don MacKinnon
Peter Makar
Louis Malisoff
Louis Malloy
George Mandel
Ed Mansfield
Joe Mansfield
Peter Marazzo
Sam Marazzo
Arthur Marbach
E. Marbach
O.L. March
Frank Maritote *(Hoodlum)*
John Maritote *(Husband of Mafalda Capone, sister of Al Capone. Brother of Frank Maritote, aka Frank Diamond)*
Ben Marshall
Joe S. Martin
Tony Martin *(Listed as Tony Accardo brother-in-law)*
Robert Matin
Fred Mason
L.E. Mason
Arthur Matheny
Ben Matthews
Frank McBrien
LeRoy C. McCracken *(Local 110 Vice President) (Retired around 1975)*
George McCree
H. McCullough
Ellis McDorman
Roy McEwen
Clifford McGee
Charles McNeill
Les Meilinger
George Meissner
William Meissner
Felix Melnick
Ed Merkle
Carl Merollo
W. Meyers
Sam Mitchell
Arthur Miller
Charles Miller
Harold Miller
Jack Miller
Sam Miller
W. Millington
Sam Mitchell
George Mitchel
Scott Mitchell
George Mock
Ted Mohr
James Montford, AKA Mudroff
Burt Montgomery
John Montana *(Brother of Mauro)*
Mauro John Montana Jr. *(Prohibition hoodlum and ex-convict who shot and killed a police officer at age 16. Brother James S. Montana was a probate court assistant judge)*
Ed Mooney
Ralph Mooney
Dean Moore

Frank Morris
Louis Morris
Richard Morris
William Morris
Eugene Mosley
Herbert Mrock
Joseph Mucek
August Mueller
Charles Mueller
W. Muhlig
Harry Mulvaney
John Mulvaney
Louis Neukon
Sam Newburger
Joseph Newton
Seth Nobel
Frank Nordmeyer Jr.
Raymond Nukom
John Oakes
John O'Connor
Joseph O'Connor
David Okanoff
Harry Olsen
Oscar Olsen
Joseph Omerzo
Harry Ongman
W. Orsinger
Walter Ostrowski
Jack Oswald
Lee Owens
Frank Pagen Perlman
Elmer Pahlke
Zadig Paloian
Joe Palumbo
John "Gasser" Pane
Ray Parker
Fred Patsold
Herman Paul
Ed Pearl
Max Pearl
Tom Pechousek
Nello Pellicci
Millton Perlman
John Perren
A. Perry
Herbert Personne
Mike Perum
Jacob Peska
Otta Peska
George Petsold
George Pickrell
Casimir Piotrowski
John Piotrowski
Ross Pohlo
Fiore Pope
Alex Posner
Herman Posner *(Killed)*
Leo Posner
Maurice Posner
Ed Priban
Julius Price
Al Purcell
Eugene Purcell
W. Purple
Dan Quinto
Albert Raff
David Raff
Don Racine
Roy Randegger
Serge Randle
George Raparowitz
Fred Ray
Tom Rayman
Ivan Rayner
Everett Ranfroe
Ora Rebb
Harry Regan
E. Reilly
Walter Reiter
John Repasi
M. Rest
George Raynolds
Harry Richardson
George Rinehart
Walter Ristor
William Roach
Sam Robbin
Seymour Robbin
Charles Robinson
Alvine Robel
Bill Roach
Joseph Romano
Albert Ropinske
Conrad Ropinske
Joseph Rossberger
Robert Rountree
Ellis Rubin
Clarence Rush
Ralph Rush
Joseph Russell
Jake Russo
Frank Ruth
Everett Ryan
Timothy J. Ryan *(1929-1960's) (Board of Examiners 1952-1960's)*
Henry Slkin
Robert Sanderson
Peter Sarelli
Arron Saperstein *(Died around 1938, President of the Allied Theaters Owners Union)*
Sam Savitt
John Sbarbaro *(Relative of Chicago Judge Sbarbaro)*
Louis Sbarbaro *(Relative of Chicago Judge Sbarboro)*
John Schaefer
Leo Schaffer
Charles Schapiro
John Scheu
Fred Schmidt
J. Schaits
Russell Schlecht
Morris Schoenwald
Harry Scholl
Harvey Schraut
Al Schubert
Jack Schults

Ed Schulse
Albert Schwind
George Shikany
Christ Scialo
Charles Scolaro
Ed Seltser
Isadore Seltzer
Howard Shayne
Sam Sherman
George Shikany *(Louis Campagna Brother-in-law)*
Steve Sidkany
Rich Siechen
Harry Siff
Eddie Silverman
Leslie Silvermank
Frank Simas
Sam Singer
Mike Skeffington
Robert Skeffington
John Sloane
James Small
James Smiley
E. Smith
Henry Smith
John Smith
Alvin Solar
Harry Sommer
John Sortino *(Frank "Strongy" Ferraro's Brother)*
Robert Souter *(A member of Local 110 and a dentist)*
Al Stange
Pat Stege
Nate Stein
Christ Stevens
Charles Stolerow
Alex Stonis
John Strahl
Larry Strong
Everett Struck
Charles Svinning
A. Swanson
Oscar Swanson
Edward Sweeney
Glenn Sweeney
Tom Sweeney
Byron Sylvester
Standly Szczepanisk
Harry Tannhauser
Joseph Taylor
Lawson Taylor
Pat Tervin
Morris Thacker
Bert Thomas
Walter Thoss
Alphonse Tomaso *(Relative of Al Tomaso, street department boss)*
Salvadore Tomaso *(Relative of street department boss)*
Olaf Torkelson
Roscoe Trainor
George Trakas
W. Tross
George Tucker
K. A. Ukso
A. Ungretti
Phil Upp
William Urban
Louis John Vacca
Ed Valha
George Van Ness
Alfred Vernon
Joe Volpe *(Son of Tony "Mops" Volpe)*
Joseph P. Volt
Otto Vonesh Jr.
Eugene Vuillaume
Cliff Wales
Steward Wall
A. S. Waller
David Wallerstein
Francis Walters
Charles Warmbold
Herbert Waschke
Walter Weigand
August Weigand
Art Weigman
Louis Weinberg
Al Wienstein
Harry Weisberg
Benjamin Weiss *(Relative of gangster Hymie Weiss)*
Steve Welsh
John Wesley
John Wesley Jr.
J.J. Whalen
Charles Wiedder
Arthur Wiegman
Harry Wilkinson
George Williams
Jack Wolfberg
Louis Wolfberg
Harry Woolf
E.C. Wright
Jack Wright *(Murray Humphreys brother)*
Alvin Wrobel *(1979)*
Victor Wrobel
Charles Yario
Charles Young
Sylvester Zalewski
Leo Zalewski
Dom Zelan
Frank Zeien *(Hoodlum)*
Joe Zid
Joseph Zid Jr.

Chapter 22

Not Going Down Like Capone

1956 saw Tony Accardo in tax court as the government claimed he underpaid his taxes in his partnership with the Owl Club in Calumet City. The IRS said that Accardo and Frank LaPorte cheated on income taxes by faking gambling losses. The government wanted Accardo to pay an additional $89,525 in taxes and LaPorte to pay an additional $60,539. The IRS listed his partners as Frank LaPorte, Lawrence Imburgio with the owner being listed as John "Buttsy" Perry. Perry took the stand stating that the club made close to 2 million a year in gambling.

In June 1956, once again Accardo was upset about being called before a Federal Grand Jury in Chicago. The grand jury was investigating possible racketeering of the Upholsterers and Furniture Workers Union and in Local 18B of the Affiliated Picture Frame Workers Union. Accardo was questioned about a transaction which he allegedly witnessed. Accardo, as usual, took refuge behind the Fifth Amendment.

Tony Accardo's appearance came from a complaint made by Adam Vignola, then owner of Alonzi Furniture Company at 1840 West Hubbard Street in Chicago. Vignola said he was contacted by Michael Gaglione, who was president of the Picture Frame Union at that time, and his secretary, Charles Rizzo. Both Gaglione and Rizzo demanded that Vignola grant them recognition for the purpose of organizing employees of Vignola's company. Vignola, who had mob connections because he once was president of the Outfit-controlled Italian Welfare Council of Chicago, hired mob union lawyer Abraham Teitelbaum to represent the company. Teitelbaum tried to arrange an election by the employees so they might choose the union they desired. This allegedly enraged Gaglione and he refused to agree to an election and demanded unqualified recognition for his union and proceeded to set up picket lines around Vignola's company. To back Giglione up, Teamsters power house Ray Schoessling ordered the truck drivers to not cross the picket line. When Vignola complained to the National Labor Relations Board, Vignola was visited by mobster Joey Glimco who threatened him which scared Vignola into signing an agreement recognizing the Picture Frame Union. The reason Tony Accardo was called to testify was because investigators learned that Vignola was told by another person to contact Joey Glimco at the residence of Tony Accardo, which he did. When Vignola was called to testify, he stayed strong to his Italian promises of not saying anything incriminating and he denied he was ever threatened in any way by the mob or Accardo.

Accardo's 1956 Lawn Party

Most of the names were taken from identification of the cars parked at the party; many of the mobsters had their cars under their wives names or under business names.

James Adduci
C. Affinito
Gus Alex
Phil Alderisio
Joey Aiuppa
Joe Amato
Anthony Balsamo
P. Bartolo
Sam Battaglia
G. Belmonte
C. Bergren
R. Biase
George Bieber
Dom "Butch" Blasi
Joseph Bulger
Eugene Bernstein
C. Buzanis
Ralph Cantonese
N. Casciato
John Cimitile
Jimmy Celano
Jackie Cerone
Joseph Costello
Francis Curry
Anthony DeBendo
James DeGeorge
Rocco DeGrazio
Sam "Sal" DiGiovanni
John Drew
Joseph DiVarco
M. Domuccio
G. Duro
Charles English
Lee Escoff
Rocco Fischetti
I. Flando (Relative of Tony Capezio)
Albert Frabotta
Ray Fritz
J.R. Gargano
Bernard Glickman
Joey Glimco
Hy Godfrey
Frank Granata
Frank Greco
Harry Gregar
T. Grotto
F. Guenther
P. Hagney
R. Hamilton
Angelo Inciso
James "Jimmy the Swede" Johnson
G. Kasper
W. Koukola
W. Krueger
Leslie Kruse
H. Labinger
Robert Lake
Frank LaPorte
Anthony Lemke
Pat Manno
Claude Maddox
Lou Madia
J. Marshall
M. Matalone
W. Montet
H. Olivieri
S. Pappas
John Perri
Anthony Pinelli
Ralph Pierce
Larry Rassano
Tarquin Simonelli
Mike Spranze
O. Thorsen
M. Turco
Dr. M. Turek
Nick Valkan
John Varlos
Dominic Volpe
Ann Weber (Capezio Relative)
Marion Weston
Jack Wilkins
Frank Zimmerma

Business Cars Observed

Beck Theaters Elmwood Park
Dale Motors Inc. (Joseph Bulger Firm)
General Kar Incorporated
Meadowmoor Dairies
D Federal Auto
Spinelli Plastering Company

Mob Boss

Spot Surveillance 1956

July 1956 – Tony Accardo, Jackie Cerone, Sam Battaglia, Joe "Black Joe" Amato and John Drew hold a meeting at Meo's Norwood House.

In 1957 it was reported that Tony Accardo was receiving payoffs from union leaders of the Restaurant Owners Association. Accardo and Abe Teitlebaum both had the big "say so" and were pulling the strings with respect to the activities of the Hotel and Restaurant Workers Union.

Another labor union leader under the control of Accardo was Angelo Inciso, then head of a 4000-man local once affiliated with the Allied Industrial Workers. It was reported in July 1957 that Accardo's daughter, Marie Accardo, was fired from her job, along with Inciso daughter Kay Inciso, as the two were given summer jobs as clerks in the Chicago Sanitary District. Both had been sponsored for their jobs by Joseph Porcaro, then a Republican Committeeman of the old 28th Ward and a member of the old "West Side Bloc." When the newspapers picked up on the story and investigated why the two mob daughters were fired, they found out that the call came from Anthony Olis, then District President, who advised his workers to *"get rid of them immediately!"*

Tony Accardo also had a man by the name of Leon Bell working for him at a collection agency called Tax Control Incorporated located at 330 South Wells Street in Chicago. Bell was a former collector for the Chicago district of the IRS office. He had been fired from the IRS when his name surfaced in a scandal in Chicago known as the "Deep Freeze Scandal" years back. This collection agency was the headquarters for another collection agencies in Los Angeles, California that preyed on losing gamblers at the Desert Inn Casino in Las Vegas, Nevada. There, these collection agencies had a waitress who would get the names of big-time losers who would get in debt from gambling and they would go after them, threatening bodily harm if they did not pay up. It was discovered that the Tax Control Company was owned by Tony Accardo and John D'Arco Sr. who used this Leon Bell as their front man.

On March 18, 1957, for some reason, a Chicago newspaper printed a story that Tony Accardo had been shot. River Forest Police began receiving phone calls to see if this was true. At the same time Chicago Police were receiving phone calls asking if it was true Accardo had been killed. It was all set straight when a short time later Tony Accardo himself called the police to say, *"For your information, I am very much alive. I am downtown having dinner with my family."*

Months later in July 1957 a news reporter showed up at Accardo's home to get information on Accardo's annual July 4th lawn party but found no one there. When the reporter noticed Tony Accardo standing all alone on his lawn, he asked him, *"Why no party this year?"* An annoyed Accardo replied, *"I don't want to talk about it. Get off my property."*

It's believed that the change of power from Tony Accardo to Sam Giancana came at the same time the two were in Appalachian, New York for a national crime meeting. That meeting was raided by the police and Accardo and Giancana got away running into the woods surrounding the area. One informant said that he believed that Felix "Milwaukee Phil" Alderisio may have been with Accardo and Giancana as their bodyguard and driver that night in Appalachian.

In Philadelphia years later, FBI agents were listening to mob boss Angelo Bruno from a hidden microphone when they heard him talking about a meeting in 1957. He said that the meeting was to be held at a beautiful farm owned by Joe "The Beast" Ricci and Tony Accardo, Sam Giancana, Antonio Pollina, Albert Anastasia and Dominic Oliveto were to attend. Bruno then said the meeting had been moved to a restaurant, for some reason, and Albert Anastasia was afraid to attend the meeting for an unknown reason. Anastasia was murdered in October 1957.

Bruno had went on to talked about how Accardo and Giancana were both Sicilians. However, from Giancana's perspective Giancana could care less if a person was Sicilian or Calabrese, he treated people as he found them.

As Tony Accardo stepped aside to let Sam Giancana take over as day-to-day boss of the Chicago mob, an informant close to Accardo told the FBI, "*Because his (Accardo) family was now reaching adulthood and he was desirous of establishing himself in some type of legitimate enterprise which would give a cloak of respectability to him for the sake of his children. Accardo is reportedly first and foremost a family man and his family is uppermost in his mind at all times. Accardo was well liked and respected as a leader and much of his success in establishing this illegal organization was based upon this fact.*"

However, other FBI reports claimed that Accardo had no choice but to step aside because Sam Giancana took over control.

When the time came for Tony Accardo to step down he held a meeting at the Armory Lounge in Forest Park with Paul DeLucia, Frank Ferraro and Murray Humphreys to vote if Sam Giancana would take over as top boss with Sam "Teets" Battaglia as his underboss. To make it official, Tony Accardo then summoned Sam Giancana, Gus Alex, Ralph Pierce, Leslie Kruse and Edward Vogel to announce it to them. Sam Giancana was now top mob boss of the Chicago mob.

Sam Giancana

Chicago PD Arrest Photo of Tony Accardo (Left) and Sam Giancana (Right)

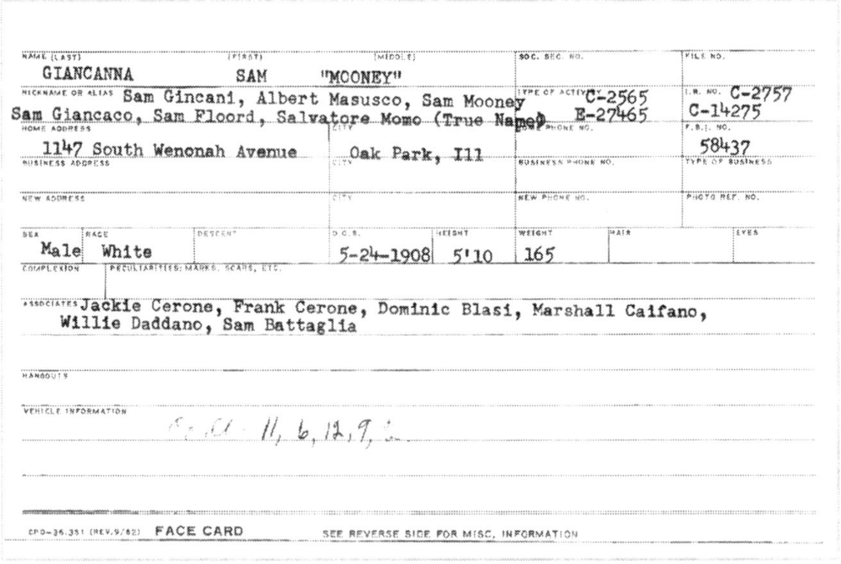

NAME (LAST) GIANCANNA (FIRST) SAM (MIDDLE) "MOONEY" SOC. SEC. NO. FILE NO.

NICKNAME OR ALIAS Sam Gincani, Albert Masusco, Sam Mooney Sam Giancaco, Sam Floord, Salvatore Momo (True Name)

TYPE OF ACTIVITY C-2565 E-27465

I.R. NO. C-2757 C-14275

HOME ADDRESS 1147 South Wenonah Avenue CITY Oak Park, Ill HOME PHONE NO. F.B.I. NO. 58437

BUSINESS ADDRESS CITY BUSINESS PHONE NO. TYPE OF BUSINESS

NEW ADDRESS CITY NEW PHONE NO. PHOTO REF. NO.

SEX	RACE	DESCENT	D.O.B.	HEIGHT	WEIGHT	HAIR	EYES
Male	White		5-24-1908	5'10	165		

COMPLEXION PECULIARITIES; MARKS, SCARS, ETC.

ASSOCIATES Jackie Cerone, Frank Cerone, Dominic Blasi, Marshall Caifano, Willie Daddano, Sam Battaglia

HANGOUTS

VEHICLE INFORMATION E.A. 11, 6, 12, 9, 2

CPD-36.351 (REV.9/62) FACE CARD SEE REVERSE SIDE FOR MISC. INFORMATION

Sam Giancana's 1950's CPD file

RICHARD J. DALEY
MAYOR

TIMOTHY J. O'CONNOR
COMMISSIONER

CHICAGO POLICE DEPARTMENT
Office of the
BUREAU OF IDENTIFICATION
1121 S. STATE STREET
CHICAGO 5, ILL.

May 13, 1958

Record of SAM GIANCANA (N.B.B.)

F.B.I. # 58437

N.G.	Sam Gincana	- Sept.25,1925. 30 days H.of C. Larc.Auto.Judge Allegretti.
As	" "	- Jan.18,1926.$10.00 & costs. V.S.22,M.V.L.Judge Gentzel.
		- May 17,1926.In v.Rel.
		- July 23,1926.Arr. Louisville,Ky.Vag.
C-2757		- Indicted Sept.Term1926.G.J.Murder.
		- Apr.28,1927.S.O.L.Murder.Judge Brothers.
C-5755		- June 27,1927.Not Guilty.Larc.Judge Gemmil.Offs. Mikes & Sq.17-A.,D.B.
		- Jan.3,1928.$50.00 & costs. Dis.Cond.Judge Gentzel. Offs.O'Neil & Co.,26th.Dist.
		- Mar.13,1928. $200. & costs. Dis.Cond.Judge Finnegan.Lt.Ronan & Co.,23rd.Dist.
C-14275	Sam Gincanni	- Feb.15,1929.Bonds Forf. Burg. & Larc.Judge J.J. Sullivan.
		- Mar.12,1929.Joliet Pen #2807.Att.Burg.Plea Guilty Judge J.J.Sullivan.
		- Mar.12,1929.Nolle Prossed.Larc.Judge J.J.Sullivan Dec.24,1932.Disch.Offs.Sloey & Sq.20 A-D.B.
		- Feb.11,1939.G.G.J.Chgo,Ill.Int.Rev.
		- Feb.12,1945.Inv.Offs.McGuire & Weir & Sims.,D.B.
		- May 14,1946.Inv.Offs.Colander & McKeon,5th.Dist.
As	" Ginncana (Giancana)	- Oct.30,1940.Rec'd.U.S.Inst.Terre Haute,Ind.#104. Int.Rev.Law.(Liq.)Sent.4 yrs.
		- Dec.14,1942.PAROLED.- Oct.15,1943.Disch.
C-62565	" "	- Nov.2,1934.G.P.Off.Gapinski,7-B.,D.B.
As	Sam Giancana	-Mar.20,1952.S.O.L.-N.A.Permitting Bldg. to be used for Hand Book.Judge Kluczynski.
E-27465	" "	- Apr.15,1957.G.P.Offs.Carroll & Noonan,D.B.
		- Apr.15,1957.Re-Instated Permitting.Bldg. to be used for Handbook. Judge Crowley.

SLK

James C. Devery
DIRECTOR OF IDENTIFICATION

Sam Giancana's 1958 Chicago Police Rap Sheet

UNITED STATES DEPARTMENT OF JUSTICE
FEDERAL BUREAU OF INVESTIGATION
WASHINGTON 25, D. C.

SEP 10 1963 427

J. Edgar Hoover
Director.

The following FBI record, NUMBER 58 437, is furnished FOR OFFICIAL USE ONLY.

CONTRIBUTOR OF FINGERPRINTS	NAME AND NUMBER	ARRESTED OR RECEIVED	CHARGE	DISPOSITION
PD Evanston Ill	Sam Giancana #14-P	5-17-26	inv	rel
PD Louisville Ky	Sam Giancana #15037	7-23-26	vag	7-24-26 case dism
PD Chgo Ill	Sam Giancana #C-2757	9-17-26	murder	indicted Sept Term GJ
SP Joliet Ill	Sam Gincana #2807	3-26-29	att burg	1-5 yrs
PD Oak Park Ill	Sam Giancana #2535	11-13-33	GP	TOT Cicero Ill PD fined $5 ancomt on chg of dis cond
ATU Chicago Ill	Sam Giancana #5484-M	2-11-39	consp to vio Int Rev Laws	10-16-39 4 yrs Pen fines tot $2700 penalties tot $1000
USM Chicago Ill	Sam Giancana #263	2-11-39	IR	sent to Leavenworth Kans 4 yrs del to said Inst 10-28-39
Co Jail Chicago Ill	Sam Giancana #8229	2-11-39	IR	2-15-39 del to USM
USM Lena Ill	Sam Giancana #--	not given (prt rec 10-19-39)	liq vio Int Rev Laws	4 yrs
USP Leavenworth Kans	Sam Ginncana #55966	10-28-39	Int Rev still mfg conc poss consp	4 yrs
USP Terre Haute Ind	Sam Ginncana #104	10-30-40 in trans from USP Leavenworth Kans	Int Rev Laws	4 yrs disch 12-14-42 cond rel *prob from 12-14-42 to 10-15-43 CR

Notations indicated by * ARE NOT BASED ON FINGERPRINTS IN FBI files. The notations are based on data furnished this Bureau concerning individuals of the same or similar names or aliases and ARE LISTED ONLY AS INVESTIGATIVE LEADS.

Sam Giancana's 1950's FBI Rap Sheet of Arrest

UNITED STATES DEPARTMENT OF JUSTICE
FEDERAL BUREAU OF INVESTIGATION
WASHINGTON 25, D. C.

2

J. Edgar Hoover
Director.

The following FBI record, NUMBER 58 437, is furnished FOR OFFICIAL USE ONLY.

CONTRIBUTOR OF FINGERPRINTS	NAME AND NUMBER	ARRESTED OR RECEIVED	CHARGE	DISPOSITION
PD Chgo Ill	Sam Gincana #C-2757	inquiry 4-5-57		
PD Chgo Ill	Sam Giancana #E-27465	4-15-57	GP	released

Notations in
furnished th

UNITED STATES DEPARTMENT OF JUSTICE 6 1 6 '58 H
FEDERAL BUREAU OF INVESTIGATION
WASHINGTON 25, D. C.

J. Edgar Hoover
Director.

The following FBI record, NUMBER 58 437, is furnished FOR OFFICIAL USE ONLY.

CONTRIBUTOR OF FINGERPRINTS	NAME AND NUMBER	ARRESTED OR RECEIVED	CHARGE	DISPOSITION

Aliases: Albert Masusco - Sam Giansana - Albert Manusco - "Mooney"

DESCRIPTION:
Race: White
Sex: Male
Height: 5-9
Weight: 174
Hair: D chest
Eyes: Hazel
Complexion: Fair
Build: Medium
Scars and marks: Ob sc 2 c rt frt of nose
Birth: 7-18-08 Chgo Ill

Residences: Chgo Ill in 1926
910 So Hermitage Ave Chgo in 1933
(as on prt #2535)
2822 W Lexington St Chgo in 1939
(as on prt #5484-M)
1147 S Winona Oak Park Ill in 1957
Occupations: Chauffeur - Steam fitter & electrician

Notations indicated by * ARE NOT BASED ON FINGERPRINTS IN FBI files. The notations are based on data furnished this Bureau concerning individuals of the same or similar names or aliases and ARE LISTED ONLY AS INVESTIGATIVE LEADS.

Mob Boss

Spot Surveillance 1957

June 29, 1957– Mobster Dominic "Butch" Blasi purchased a fully loaded new convertible car in cash at Allen Chevrolet Company at 6225 West Roosevelt Road and put the car under the name of Clarice Accardo. The car was then driven by Blasi to Tony Accardo's house and dropped off.

August 3, 1957 - Mobster Dominic "Butch" Blasi purchased a new four-door Belvedere, eight cylinder, sports suburban station wagon from Manhattan Motors at 4660 West Washington and placed it under the name of Clarice Accardo.

August 17, 1957 – Tony Accardo lands in Mexico City Mexico. He then goes to Acapulco for vacation before flying out of Mexico City on September 1, 1957.

October 28, 1957 – Tony Accardo, his wife Clarice, Jackie Cerone and his wife Clara, boarded the U.S.S. Matsonia and sail to Honolulu, Hawaii and stay at the Royal Hawaiian Hotel. There they were chauffeured by a person named Jesse Kalima who took them on shopping tours and several dinners. A private Hawaiian luau was arranged just for the Accardo's and Cerone's.

November 12, 1957 – Accardo and Jackie Cerone leave Hawaii together and head back to Chicago. Clarice and Clara take a separate flight a half hour after their husbands leave. Jesse Kalima told the FBI he thought it was strange but was told that in the event of an accident; at least one member of the family would be spared to inherit their money and care for the children.

November 1957 – Tony Accardo sends Paul DeLucia a telegram on Thanksgiving Day from Chicago to Miami saying, *"Thanksgiving Day and far away, but not too far for us to say Happy Thanksgiving to all."*

Information coming in to law enforcement around this time centered on some of the perks Tony Accardo received for being a mob boss. FBI agents learned from an informant from the Philadelphia mob that in August 1958 Chicago mobsters John Matassa Sr. and Joe Fischetti chauffeured Frank Sinatra, Dean Martin, Leo Durocher and mob Chicago police captain Ralph Cantonese to the house of Tony Accardo for a private command performance. Dean Martin, Frank Sinatra and Leo Durocher were filming the movie "Some Came Running" in Indiana.

A report was made detailing what it was like to communicate with Tony Accardo either at his home in person or over the phone. On the phone Tony Accardo would answer but would never say anything, not even hello until the person calling identified themselves. If you were someone he knew or knew of, he may say hello or simply hang up, and he never made the first move of saying anything. If you struck up a conversation with him on the phone, his only words spoken were "Yes" "No" "Come out" or "Meet me." Allegedly if you somehow made it into Accardo's house, it was said every room had a microphone hidden in it feeding into a tape recorder. He would only answer questions in phrases such as, *"I can't talk about that"* or *"You seem to be on the right track"*. One person who had been to see Accardo said that if you mentioned the name of Paul DeLucia he would make faces which lead to believe he hates DeLucia.

In 1958 Tony Accardo had the Federal Trade Commission investigating him for violation of the Clayton Act. Accardo was allegedly selling olive oil below cost. The commission was trying to link Accardo to New York mobster Joe Profaci because Profaci was also in the olive oil business selling Mama Mia Olive Oil. Accardo's name was also linked to New York mobster Frank Costello. Apparently Accardo was sending pay-off money to Costello for some unknown reason.

Accardo was also dealing with other investigations in which his name was being dragged into. On April 9, 1958 a subpoena was issued for Tony Accardo to appear before the Senate Committee in Washington DC concerning the Hotel and Restaurant Employees and Bartenders International Union. He refused to say anything.

Also around this time, Tony Accardo was listed as having an interest in the Balistrieri Boxing Promotions Company in Wisconsin which was owned and operated by Milwaukee mob boss Frank Balistrieri. Investigators were trying to link the company to Accardo.

In July 1958 FBI agents received information from one of their most reliable sources that Tony Accardo was selling his mansion at 915 Franklin Avenue in River Forest. First the informant said he had been talking to Paul DeLucia and DeLucia told him that all dealings regarding the sale of Accardo's house were to be arranged through him and the sale price was $300,000. Then this informant toured Accardo's house with Accardo and when the informant told Accardo how much the house was to be sold for, Accardo was shocked upon learning the price was $300,000. Accardo told the informant that he just wanted the best possible deal and was only interested in a cash transaction. He added that he and his wife were both in agreement that the house was too big for their needs and if the house did not sell before Christmas 1958, he would leave the main house and live in the garage apartment. This information was followed by another informant close to Accardo stating that Accardo was attempting to make a serious effort to decrease his activities in the syndicate in Chicago. The reason believed was Accardo was getting pressure from his wife and family who became increasingly disturbed over all the notoriety Accardo had received in the 1950's. The informant believed that the Accardo family was attempting to influence Tony Accardo to leave the Chicago area and, if possible, the United States in order to leave the past behind them and allow his family to live a more normal life.

Chapter 23

Fox Head Beer

In 1955 Fox Head Brewing Company in Waukesha, Wisconsin merged with the Peter Fox Brewing Company of Chicago. The name was changed to Fox De Luxe Beer Sales Incorporated. This company entered into a contract with Premium Beer Sales Incorporated in Chicago which just happened to be owned by the Chicago Outfit. Premium Beer Sales gained exclusive rights to distribution of the beer in Illinois, New York, New Jersey and Wisconsin.

Premium Beer Sales was actually the controlling and policy-making organization behind Fox Head Brewing Company controlled by Henry Morgan, then chairman of the board. He placed all his relatives on the Board of Directors so he could control the brewery. As time went on, the Chicago group slowly robbed control of the company away from Morgan.

Jackie Cerone was hired as a salesman for the company in 1956. It was through Cerone that Tony Accardo was given the title of "salesman" on the books so Accardo could get a legitimate cut of the business for his tax returns. In 1960 FBI agents listened as mobster Carmen Fanelli confirmed that the meeting to place Accardo on the books of the beer company was held at the mob's Armory Lounge at 7427 West Roosevelt Road. Accardo was on the books of the company making $65,000 a year selling Fox Head 400 Beer to taverns around Chicago.

Accardo and Cerone were not the only mobsters placed in the company for legitimate income. Fellow mobsters Dominic "Mops" Volpe and Joseph "Gags" Gagliano were placed in the company as salesmen. One of the members on the board of directors for Foxhead Brewing Company who had a major hand in Accardo being hired was Joseph Antonow, a lawyer and a third cousin of mob lawyer Sidney Korshak and his politically powerful brother Marshall Korshak.

In 1958 Morgan sent one of his relatives to Tony Accardo's house in an attempt to break the contract. Accardo informed this relative that he, Morgan, should handle this matter personally and not send "an errand boy" in his place. There was no way Tony Accardo was going to give up his or the Outfit's position in the company simply because the money was too good and too easy to make.

Allegations were received by the FBI in 1959 that illegal pressure was being brought to bear upon tavern owners and other retail liquor dealers, as well as certain sub-jobbers, to carry and promote the sale of Fox Head Products to the exclusion of other beers.

In one case, Accardo forced the old Cabana Club in Chicago to take 350 cases of his Foxhead beer. A strip join operator said he was forced to take 150 to 200 cases of beer a week if he sold it or not. The old Santa Fe Hotel was forced to purchase 200 cases or else.

Murray Humphreys was able to obtain the same list of Chicago customers that the FBI was going to interview to see if Tony Accardo, Dominick Volpe or Joseph Gagliano used force or threats so they would buy their beer. Humphreys plan was to contact these customers before the FBI got a hold of them to make sure they didn't say anything that would incriminate Accardo.

On April 26, 1960 Tony Accardo was taken into custody by U.S. Deputy Marshals and charged with a three-count indictment. He was charged with making fraudulent entries on his income tax returns for the years of 1956, 1957, and 1958, whereby he deducted the expense of his automobile for business ventures, namely Premium Beer Sales. In a nutshell, the IRS was going to put away a top mob boss for writing off expenses of his little red sports car as a business deduction on his tax returns.

The government was going to attempt to prove that Accardo did not use his automobile in connection with the business in that he did not actually perform real duties in connection with Premium Beer Sales. Accardo was bailed out of jail by Chicago bail bondsmen Irvin Weiner and Louis Volin on a $25,000 bond.

That day the Fed's listened in as Accardo met with mobsters Gus Alex, Irvin Weiner and former Assistant U.S. Attorney turned private Chicago criminal lawyer Richard Gorman. The conversation was as follows:

Accardo	I didn't want to fight it.
Alex	They didn't give you a judge yet, did they?
Accardo	Hoffman. The only guys I figured were too cute......the guy says that this is the first time they're trying something like that. You put down an expense, the guy checks your books, you understand, and disallow that and disallow this.
Alex	They didn't have to check your books, because that's the law, just booked you?
Accardo	That's right. I was jumping in too see why I made this mistake, now I see where I made the mistake. It's no mistake. The worse that could have happened, Gus, is disallow it, that's the worst. Instead, they indicted me. (*Accardo then tells how he found out*) I left the house about 20 minutes to seven. What am I gonna do? Nothing I can do. I don't think. So they called the house this morning, must have been about 6:15, Marie answered the phone, and she wakes up her mother, and she says, somebody wants to talk to daddy, the Justice Department, and I heard it. She comes back, and she said the Justice Department, I said, well I'm indicted, well, I didn't want to tell her anything last night. Then we looked out the fucking window, seven cars were out there, eight of them walking up and down. So I put my robe on, and I went down to open the door, and what could I do. Four of them came in, and one was the Marshal, must have been reading the indictment, and I said, will you give me time to get dressed?

Accardo	They said, sure, and I said do you want to sit in the library? You know, the other guys went back in the car, and the one guy, he says, it's custom, we got to be with you. So I says, come on. So the one guy comes up with me. I took a shower, and went.

One of the first things Tony Accardo's lawyer, Stanford Clinton, did was take steps to have a change of venue and that the case be assigned to another Federal Judge other than Judge Julius J. Hoffman. The reason being that Judge Hoffman sent Accardo's brother, Martin, to jail on a similar charge in 1954.

One person was going to do everything he could to make sure Tony Accardo did not go to jail. On January 28, 1960 FBI agents listened in as Murray Humphreys, John D'Arco and Frank Ferraro discussed Accardo's case. The conversation when as follows:

D'Arco	What the fuck, all they know is what I'm telling em, if I don't work out well then we say shit. They finally fucked Joe Batters (Accardo). Last week.
Humphreys	I doubt it.
D'Arco	Well for him to make a statement like that, lets be sensible and lets be practical, to be indicted today its almost a cinch that your gonna have to go to trial, I would say that its almost a cinch that they got the jury. It's almost a cinch that they are gonna get him convicted. It's gonna be a headache from now on.
Humphreys	I heard they're gonna come down with indictments.
Ferraro	Here's essentially the same thing he told these two guys, they finally got Joe Batters.
Humphreys	He's still OK.
Ferraro	Do you think he's gonna get indicted?
Humphreys	I don't know about Joe, but the other guy is.
Ferraro	Volpe?
Humphreys	Volpe.
Ferraro	How about you?
Humphreys	Me? I maybe in it too.
Ferraro	I don't think so, they would have said it, wouldn't they?
D'Arco	Anyway, they're gonna fuck us the way we used to fuck them. They have all the answers.

Humphreys	Let me give you the story, if they had nothin', the guy was in on the indictment. They have nothing but they're gonna indict anyway and that they're gonna jungle it until after the election then what they do to you, from my experience, they try to get you to plead guilty, they give ya so much time or they make a deal with ya or they go to bat, they don't want to lose it so they keep workin on ya and try to get ya to say well I'll take a plea for a year or eighteen months or something, see, but as far as them doing on the beer or anything, I'll tell this right now there isn't one fucking thing wrong with the beer that we know of and we got all those guys, we got a guy like, ahhh that lawyer, we got all high class guys were indicted which were not indicted with all hoods, it makes a little different question, do you under stand?
Ferraro	How can they indict Joe on conspiracy? For taking money under false pretenses?
Humphreys	No they can indict him.
Ferraro	I say this, I say the mistake was made when they went to these people, where the beer was sold and every one said that Joe B. and Jackie, that nobody approached them for the beer.
Humphreys	Now wait a minute. Joe B. approached a lotta people for the beer, mostly out of town, now wait a minute I did too, and everything was done very orderly. There was no force, an we know we didn't have the best beer in the world and you can't tell them to force them to sell the beer, the only one place that I know that there was anything put out that Morgan (*Henry Morgan, owned a Schlitz and Premium Beer distributorship in the Chicago Loop*) hollered about when you put the sign on Randolph Street, remember the saloon there, you put the sign on the corner, Morgan hollered like a bitch about that. That's when I got in a fight with him about selling Foxhead, were not selling Lowenbrau, if you want to give us a piece of Lowenbrau we will talk business to you, but other than that we're sellin' this beer, and that's when he went and bought the Coverbar, he owned it you know, and he put his sign there and I tried to get him to put the Foxhead and he wouldn't do it. That was all over the spot down there.

Murray Humphreys finished with this to say, *"I'm gonna tell you this, we're not like we used to be. There's not gonna be no more shit if they lose a case, cause I'm gonna fight everybody around, and I'm not going to lose any more of our guys. I don't give a fuck if we go to jail trying, gonna go to trial. We're not gonna lose another guy like we lost Paul.* (Paul DeLucia in prison) *We should have never blown Paul and we did, and listen, lemme tell you something, if a fucking general is out in the field with an army, and he's getting the fuck beat out of him, he has to throw caution to the wind and try and stuff, he can't just stand there and get shot down. That's what we have to do, if we think we're gonna get beat anyhow, we have to take a chance, we don't have to sit there and say, gee, don't do this and don't do that. Old guys do it, they're more conservative, when you're young you take a little more chances and you do those things. Sometimes you have to revert back to your young days. Anytime you become weak, you might as well."*

Humphreys was to make sure every person interviewed or called to testify said that Accardo drove to their location to sell them the beer in his own personal car, a red two door Mercedes-Benz sports car. Accardo had deducted the cost of the Mercedes as a work expense on his 1956-1958 tax returns and the government was not buying it.

Fearing mobsters Frank LaPorte and Ralph Pierce would be called to testify against Tony Accardo, Accardo ordered them to leave the country. They went to Mexico City and remained there until ordered back.

Days later FBI Agents listened in as Murray Humphreys told mobsters Ross Prio and Jimmy Allegretti how the Outfit was going to take care of Accardo. Humphreys was recorded as saying, *"There's only one thing we can do here, see? I've already questioned the lawyers. We're going to have good lawyers in this. We're not going to fuck around. We're going after these guys in a different way. We're not gonna go the same way each time."*

This time mobster Jimmy "The Monk" Allegretti was going to be a witness in Accardo's defense whereby it could be pointed out that Accardo actually met Allegretti on numerous occasions for the purpose of selling beer. Humphreys tactic for the trial was to stress general points rather than infinite details that the FBI could run out and check and things that could be easily traced.

When the case against Accardo went to court in Chicago, mistakes were made not in Accardo's favor. One mistake was when mob associate Bernie Glickman testified in Chicago that Accardo was in the beer business. When Glickman was called to testify in New York about Accardo, he said that he did not know what business Accardo was in. FBI overheard from undercover microphones that Accardo was steaming hot over this and had to be calmed down.

Mob boss Alfred Pilotto, then president of Chicago labor union Local 5 of the Hod Carriers Union, was called to testify about Accardo being a salesman. Pilotto testified that he owned two taverns called the Palace Tap and the Club Palace on State Line Road in Calumet City, Illinois. In 1956 Pilotto stated that he met Tony Accardo and Jackie Cerone at Campagna's Park Inn Lounge in Calumet City and told Accardo he would try to help him sell Fox Head 400 Beer. A month later he met Accardo at the Skyline Lounge in Chicago Heights, then owned by Mike Costabile who was with Accardo at the time, and once again agreed to help Accardo sell the beer. One last meeting with Accardo was at John's Pizza on State Street in Calumet City, then owned by John Baccino. He told Accardo of the places in Calumet City which would go along and sell Fox Head 400 Beer.

Dominic Volpe went to see Joseph Bronge in Melrose Park and wanted Bronge to put a beer salesman on his payroll. Joseph Bronge was an old time Melrose Park mobster who had held the exclusive distributorship rights of Fox 400 Beer and would drive up to the brewery in Wisconsin to pick up his orders. In January 1959 he lost the rights to distribute the beer and may have blamed Accardo. That year Joseph Bronge was shot as he ran from his warehouse on Division Street in Melrose Park and died months later from his wounds.

Tony Accardo was later found guilty of falsifying his federal income tax returns. In November 1960 Tony Accardo was sentenced to serve six years in prison and a five thousand dollar fine on each count of a three count indictment to run consecutively.

Accardo believed that he was finally going to prison, or the "can" as he called it, after almost 35 years of being in the rackets. On January 1, 1961 the FBI listened in as Accardo talked to Gus Alex and Frank Ferraro about going fishing without the courts permission:

Ferraro	Joe, you're going away without permission of the court, you know.
Accardo	I got the thing here, I don't even want to disturb it. I don't even want to go in and ask. I'm going fishing, and if I get out all right, and if I don't, to hell with it.
Alex	Think it over Joe.
Accardo	If you go and ask, you won't get anything. Shit, I may as well be in the can.
Ferraro	Joe, you have to wait this thing out.
Accardo	Ah, I'm goin' to the can anyhow.
Ferraro	No you're not. You're getting too jumpy.

However, the case was reversed and a new retrial was ordered by the Illinois Appellate Court because Accardo's' lawyers convinced the court that newspaper publicity prevented Accardo from getting a fair trial.

The FBI heard over a hidden microphone how Murray Humphreys and Frank Ferraro obtained the new list of jurors for Accardo's second trial. Humphreys, Ferraro, Gus Alex and Jackie Cerone were all going make "personal approaches" to some of the jurors to get them to vote not guilty. On October 3, 1962 Tony Accardo was found not guilty in his second trial. Accardo was a free man.

Casualties from the Accardo trial fall out included defense witnesses Joe Nicoletti and Thomas Letchos who were convicted in Federal Court on two counts of perjury during their testimony in the Accardo trial. Letchos was the owner of the infamous Tom's Steak House on North Avenue in Melrose Park. After Dominic Volpe's appearance before the Federal Grand Jury in the Accardo case, he was shot and subsequently died from his wounds.

This was the closest Tony Accardo came to going to jail but once again, either by luck or most likely connections, Accardo walked, AGAIN!

Tony Accardo makes bond in clerk's office of U.S. Courthouse.

'Just Another Pinch' On Accardo Record

Could Be Long Time Before He Spends First Night in Jail

Tony Accardo's latest troubles with the federal government is only "just another pinch" on the long arrest record of the reputed foreman of the Chicago crime syndicate.

[illegible]

Tony Accardo Before Jury 12 Minutes

Tony Accardo, said to be chief of the Chicago crime syndicate, apparently took the 5th Amendment today before the special federal grand jury probing the underworld.

Accardo, who appeared at the U. S. Courthouse alone, spent only 12 minutes closeted with the grand jury.

RUNS FROM NEWSMEN

Before he entered the fourth floor jury room and after he left, Accardo sullenly refused to answer reporters' questions. Departing, he dashed down the stairway without waiting for the elevator.

Five reporters followed Accardo as he walked from the courthouse to Washington street and Michigan avenue, where he hailed a cab. During the five-block sojourn, Accardo walked against a red light and crossed in the middle of Adams street, east of Clark street—both violations of city ordinances.

ANGER MOUNTS

Accardo's anger mounted with every block. Finally he snarled:

"Why don't you guys quit abusing people!"

Only other witness before the jury adjourned until next Monday was Dominic Volpe, president of Premium Beer Sales Inc., 2555 Armitage.

Volpe likewise refused to answer reporters' questions.

'LEARNED SOMETHING'

Volpe spent about five minutes with the grand jury, emerged to get some records from his attorney, A. Bradley Eben, who was waiting outside and reentered for about 10 minutes.

Richard B. Ogilvie, special assistant to the U. S. Attorney General, when asked if the jury had obtained anything useful, replied:

"We always learn something from every witness."

Scope to Trace A-Rays

KNOXVILLE, Tenn., Feb. 11 (UPI)—Two University of Tennessee physicists have designed a monster microscope capable of tracing tiny particles of nuclear explosions.

(Chicago American photo)

TONY ACCARDO
Did he talk?

Trailed by a squad of reporters and photographers, rackets boss Anthony J. (Tony) Accardo enters U.S. Courthouse for appearance before a special U.S. grand jury. While he waited to be called before the jury he tried to parry newsmen's questions. (Sun-Times Photos)

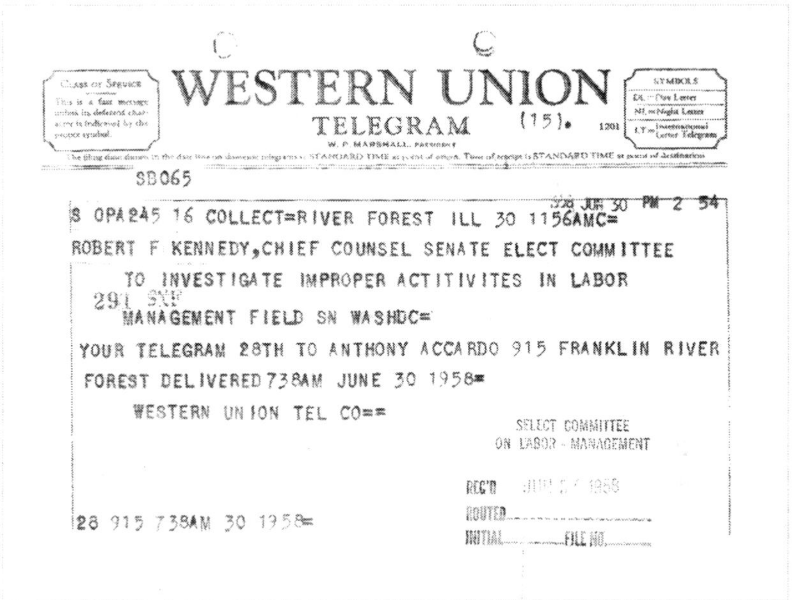

WESTERN UNION
TELEGRAM (15).

SB065

S OPA245 16 COLLECT=RIVER FOREST ILL 30 1156AMC=

ROBERT F KENNEDY,CHIEF COUNSEL SENATE ELECT COMMITTEE
TO INVESTIGATE IMPROPER ACTITIVITES IN LABOR
MANAGEMENT FIELD SN WASHDC=

YOUR TELEGRAM 28TH TO ANTHONY ACCARDO 915 FRANKLIN RIVER FOREST DELIVERED 738AM JUNE 30 1958=
WESTERN UNION TEL CO==

SELECT COMMITTEE ON LABOR - MANAGEMENT

REC'D
ROUTED
INITIAL FILE NO.

28 915 738AM 30 1958=

Spot Surveillance 1958

February 5, 1958 – Tony Accardo held a meeting with mobster William Messino at Rupcich's Restaurant at 106th and Indianapolis Boulevard.

January-June 1958 – Accardo and his group were seen meeting in a private dining room at Meo's Norwood House Restaurant on an almost daily basis.

March 24, 1958 – Accardo was in a meeting at Sam Giancana's Armory Lounge.

March 26, 1958 – Tony Accardo is seen at the wake of Michael Simonelli, the uncle of his brother-in-law, Tarquin Simonelli. The wake was held at Rago Funeral Home, 624 North Western Avenue in Chicago.

July 4, 1958 – Tony Accardo was spotted at 4th of July lawn party now held at Jackie Cerone's house located at 2000 77th Avenue in Elmwood Park, Illinois.

October 1958 – Tony Accardo, Jackie Cerone, Rocco DeStefano, Marshall Caifano and Sam Battaglia were observed in Waukesha, Wisconsin at the Mohr's Mud Baths.

September 1958 – Accardo is seen at the Chez Paree Restaurant in Chicago with comedian entertainer Jimmy Durante.

December 25, 1958 – A Christmas party at Accardo's home at 915 Franklin Avenue in River Forest. Mostly hoodlum cars were seen parked in front of the house

Many different reports were flooding into the intelligence division of the Chicago Police Department in 1959 concerning Tony Accardo. One was that Accardo had lost favor with the syndicate and his position as top leader was completely taken over by Sam Giancana. That was not true. Giancana was boss of the family but Accardo still was in charge of organization matters such as the allocation of districts. Giancana never refused that order from Accardo.

One FBI informant reported an interesting look at the Outfit's chain of positions. Though some of the "facts" are wrong, it was still an interesting explanation. An informant explained it like this, *"The Chicago syndicate hierarchy contained two top positions, the most prominent being that of 'The Man.' He is comparable to the chairman of the board of a large corporation. 'The Man' is the overseer and policymaker for the Outfit. 'The Boss' carries out his directives. Prior to 1955, 'The Man' was Louis Campagna. Upon his death, Paul Ricca (DeLucia) assumed this position. After Ricca went to prison, Sam Giancana moved in and took over both positions of 'The Man' and 'The Boss.' From 1952 to 1957 the position of 'The Boss' was held by Tony Capezio, and upon his death, by Tony Accardo. Giancana in 1957 forced Accardo into semi-retirement and assumed the reins of the syndicate. The informant said that, as a supposition, one can be 'The Man' only if one holds Mafia connections. Accardo was not a member of the Mafia, therefore was 'boss' and subservient to the directives of 'The Man.' Accardo, it was said, stepped down when Giancana moved in because 'when you have a man like Mooney Giancana at your back, you either get out or you die.' One reason for Accardo's forced retirement is that Accardo was not anxious to push into new fields of investment for the syndicate. After Accardo was forced out of his position, he indicated a desire to retire altogether, but this was not possible. He therefore is available for consultation purposes, and is more or less an elder statesman, as is Paul Ricca."*

The New York FBI field office received word from some of their informants concerning the situation in Chicago. In mob circles, Chicago was looked at as one of the most tightly controlled syndicates or organizations in the country, particularly in the illegal gambling area. Informants said that an independent operator in Cook County Illinois was unheard of as all bookmakers and number men gave a large share of their proceeds to the Outfit. One New York informant said that Chicago First Ward Alderman John D'Arco Sr. was the clearinghouse or "contact man" though which all request, for opening new gambling operations must have been cleared. Once D'Arco agreed, he, in turn, would see mob boss Gus Alex and Accardo to have the final "go ahead" given. As it turned out Pat Marcy was really the one who made the decision with D'Arco as his front man.

Murray Humphreys was overheard on a FBI hidden microphone talking to mobster Sam Battaglia about how the upper bosses would communicate in code.

He told Battaglia that Tony Accardo, Gus Alex, Sam Giancana, Frank Ferraro and himself would each be assigned a number instead of using their names in case someone was listening. Humphreys said, "*At one time we used to have 1, 2, and 3 and 4 and we'd change back and forth, but that was amongst ourselves. I defy them to find out where we was at, unless they follow, say, number 4. Then they would break it down, but then we'd change out numbers every month, and Mooney (Giancana) would come to me and say, 'now this month it's going to be such and such,' you know, so we'd change the numbers. Joe (Tony Accardo) used to say 'shit, I don't know where number 3 is.'*"

On February 11, 1959 Tony Accardo appeared alone before the special Federal Grand Jury in Chicago's U.S. Courthouse. As he waited outside in the hallway, awaiting his name to be called to appear, reporters watched as Accardo paced up and down the hall replying to ever question placed to him by a reporter *"no comment, no comment, no comment."* After a few no comments he snapped at one reporter, *"I have no comment regardless to anything. Now what does that cover? What does that mean?"*

Once called into the courtroom, he spent twelve minutes repeating his 5th Amendment rights to every question placed to him. Once out of the courtroom he darted for the stairs with five newspaper reporters chasing him out onto Washington Street and Michigan Avenue, walked against a red light screaming to the pesky reporter's, *"Why don't you guys quit abusing people"* before jumping into a cab to make his escape.

Accardo's anger towards reporters was legendary. As the FBI listened in on a conversation between Murray Humphreys and Jackie Cerone, Cerone described Accardo and an incident with reporters:

Cerone	This newspaper reporter, Joe's been getting along pretty nice with them reporters. This one newspaper reporter for the American, turned around and said Mr. Accardo, I want to ask you something. Joe turned around and said you fuck, you dirty fuck, get away from me. Get away from me you dirty fuck. Clinton went over to Joe and said, quiet down. Joe turned to Clinton and says, 'I don't give a shit if they come out and give me 9-years.' This dirty fuck, he says, 'comes to my house when I was out of town, and muscled his way into my house, and was taking pictures of my kids.' He says, 'you rotten fuck,' so Bukovich, one of the investigators, says, 'you know Mr. Accardo, you're right. He is a fuck. I gotta agrees with you.' He says 'listen, I don't mind if you pick on me, don't pick on my kids.'
Humphreys	In his house? I'd like to catch them doing that.

Cerone	Both out of town. This guy went to the house, no one answered, so he went around to the back, and took pictures of the kids, and no one knew it.
Humphreys	Oh, they should have broken both of his legs, you know, a little later. Joe shouldn't have used that language, though.
Cerone	He says, 'I wish he was a little younger, I'd punch him right between the eyes.'
Humphreys	Well, you see, something like that. If I'd have known about that, we could have pulled a sneak and broke both of that guys legs. After a long time, see. They'd know how it happened, but they couldn't prove anything.
Cerone	I told Joe, when you're up there, be nice. We know what they are, but be nice. That press, they'll kill you. If you're nice, they can't print nothing.

Near then end of the 1950's Tony Accardo needed a break. After an incident in October 1959, Tony Accardo's son, Anthony Ross Jr., was involved in an automobile accident when the car he was driving smashed into a light pole at Mannheim Road and Grand Avenue. No one was hurt but Tony Accardo needed to get away.

In October and November 1959 Chicago newspapers picked up on a story that Tony Accardo and his wife were vacationing throughout Europe with Anthony DeGrazia and his wife, Henrietta. DeGrazia was a Lieutenant in the Chicago Police Department. Newspaper reporters in Italy snapped photos of the DeGrazia's and the Accardo's walking around seeing the sights together. As soon as the airplane landed in Chicago, reporters, photographers, customs agents and Chicago police big shots were waiting to welcome home one of their own. Once DeGrazia noticed all the attention was directed at him, he became so worried that he hid in one of the women's bathrooms. But it turned out to be a bad hiding place because a Chicago police Captain found him and informed him that he was suspended from the police force effective immediately for conduct unbecoming a policeman. DeGrazia was placed in front of the city's Civil Service Commission to answer questions why a Chicago Police Lieutenant was vacationing with the leader of the Chicago mob.

DeGrazia had told the committee that he first met a young Tony Accardo when he, Accardo, was 18 years old. DeGrazia would visit Accardo's father Frank at his shoe repair shop at Ada Street and Grand Avenue. He even told the committee that Tony Accardo was an usher at DeGrazia's wedding in 1927. The committee also wanted to know why directly across the hall from DeGrazia's hotel room in Italy was a John Roberts. John Roberts, aka Roberto, was a Chicago Heights minor character who had syndicate connections and was closely aliened with mob boss Frank LaPorte. Roberts's brother Dominic Roberts, aka Dom Roberto, was deported from the United States during the prohibition era as a bootlegger.

DeGrazia's life as a police officer had its ups and downs. He became a patrolman on June 7, 1922 and thirteen days later he was fired from the Chicago Police Department because he allegedly had been arrested for rape. On June 23, 1922 he was restored to his policeman job when he was cleared of the rape charge but the fifteen men he was arrested with for the same charge all went to prison. Other offenses in his career were in 1924 when he was charged with neglect of duty for receiving a bribe in a shakedown. He was cleared of the charge. In 1934 he was charged with conduct unbecoming an officer and willful mistreatment of a person when he allowed a poker game to operate in his district. Once again he was cleared of those charges. In 1940 he was suspended for three days for neglect of duty.

FBI agents listened as Murray Humphreys stated that DeGrazia "must" resign and that Tony Accardo should not take the stand because he would be dragged through the mud. He said that DeGrazia should get sick in order to prevent his appearance and to postpone the hearing. Humphreys even said he would provide the doctor who would attend to DeGrazia and that there were ways in which DeGrazia's temperature could be faked to show his illness.

DeGrazia's excuse for the European trip with Accardo was that he was not aware that Tony Accardo was a known hoodlum and the fact that he, Accardo, had never been convicted of a crime. He claimed he had read one or two stories about Accardo being in trouble with the law but said he did not always trust the newspapers as telling the truth. Tony Accardo did refuse to accept a subpoena on December 14 concerning the DeGrazia's hearing.

Murray Humphreys also talked about how John D'Arco, then First Ward Alderman, went to see Mayor Richard J. Daley to see if Daley could "help them out" concerning DeGrazia. However, Mayor Daley informed D'Arco that he was going to keep his hands off the situation and was not going to do anything for or against DeGrazia. Daley told D'Arco, *"It wouldn't do us any good if he gets back on. Too close to the election."*

DeGrazia explained that Tony Accardo had asked him and his wife to accompany them on the trip when the Beck family canceled on the Accardo's. The DeGrazia's took over the Beck's reservations. He said the Accardo's and he would stay in the same hotel but they would go their separate ways and the two families did not spend any time together despite the photographs taken of all four of them together seeing all the major sights in Rome. When asked why investigators discovered that DeGrazia paid for all of the hotel bills for both he and Accardo during the course of the five week trip, he did not have a good answer so he did not give one.

No one on the Civil Service Committee believed him and DeGrazia was fired from the Chicago Police Department in January 1960. A month later he filed a lawsuit to be reinstated but lost that hearing.

In September 1963 acting Circuit Court Judge William Eovaldi upheld the discharge of DeGrazia from the Chicago Police Department but he was allowed to keep his police pension.

Tony and Clarice Accardo arriving in Europe 1959

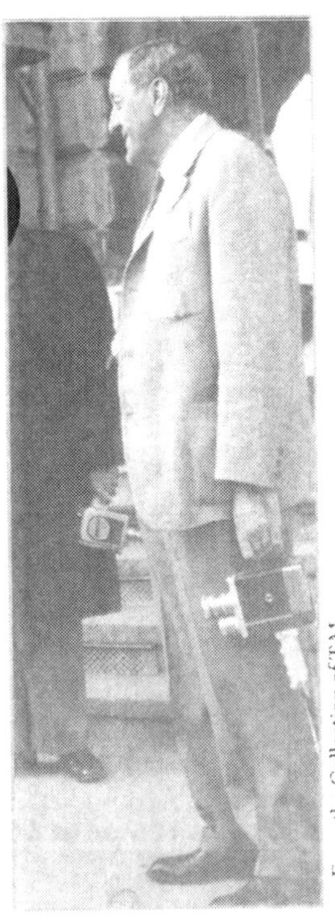

Spot Surveillance 1959

January 21, 1959 – Tony Accardo, Gus Alex and Marshall Caifano were observed in discussion at the Trade Winds Restaurant owned by Arthur Adler. Both Accardo and Alex were acting as arbiters in a dispute between Caifano and Sam Giancana.

March 1959 – Tony Accardo left for Miami, Florida to meet with Sam Giancana and other top mobsters. FBI agents found that Marie Accardo, Tony Accardo's daughter, was registered at the Thunderbird Hotel with a June Elwert from Chicago between the dates of March 9 thru March 28.

April 4, 1959 – Tony Accardo was observed at the wedding of Antoinette Giancana, daughter of Sam Giancana, held at the LaSalle Hotel in Chicago.

May 7, 1959 – Accardo meets Sam Battaglia and Joe "Black Joe" Amato at the Meo's Norwood House.

June 13, 1959 – Accardo, Sam Battaglia and Jackie Cerone were among a group of hoodlums observed in Waukesha, Wisconsin the day before the opening game of the 1958 World Series in Milwaukee, Wisconsin. The group visited the Fox Head Brewing Company and went to the Mohr's Mud Bath house for some mud baths.

July 4, 1959 – Tony Accardo observed at an un-named hoodlums July 4th party with William Daddono.

August 3, 1959 – Tony Accardo, Jackie Cerone, Gus Alex, Hy Godfrey, Frank Ferraro and Eddie Vogel hold a meeting at Celano's Tailor Shop on Michigan Avenue and discuss Mayor Richard J. Daley and some of his men. Accardo mentions he will be meeting Kan Jung Luke, an accountant from Honolulu, Hawaii who represented Martin Bromley, then a top hoodlum in Honolulu. A long discussion about each of their health scares of late. Accardo informed Alex that mob lawyer Sidney Korshak offered to provide a job for Accardo's daughter, Marie, as a switchboard operator in his law office at 134 North LaSalle Street for $300 a month pay. Later that night Accardo and Gus Alex attend the wake of Arthur X. Elrod, one-time Chicago Alderman of the 29th Ward and County Commissioner of Cook County Illinois. Arthur X. Elrod was a political power and mob associate.

September 8, 1959 – Tony Accardo and Sam Giancana met in Chicago to discuss the trip Giancana made to the East Coast and Las Vegas. Giancana met with Vito Genovese and Tom Luchese, both New York Mob bosses. Giancana told Accardo that the reason he went to the East Coast was because he was having difficulty in obtaining power in Las Vegas and the Tucson, Arizona area. Accardo is heard talking about mob boss Joseph Bonanno's move to Arizona saying, *"He has planted a flag in Tucson and claimed squatter's rights."* Apparently Tony Accardo was angry with this move since Arizona was always "open" territory and wanted to go to Tucson to tell Bonanno what he really thought about his actions. As for Las Vegas, Accardo told Giancana, *"That's a closed contact there, Tommy Brown (Luchese) and Steve Magaddino, that's the contact. They are all paisans. This is where you are in a position because there are three votes on your side too, you know, with Tommy Brown, but now you've increased it to what, ten? Twelve? Now you need seven for a majority and six for a standoff."* Accardo ended with telling Giancana he could count on New York mob boss Joe Profaci and Philadelphia mob boss Joe Ida as being on his side.

September 8, 1959 – Tony Accardo and Sam Giancana hold a meeting to discus individuals controlling various sections of the country as well as persons making up a "commission" and the number of votes necessary to control this commission. Accardo is heard saying, *"Philadelphia is Joe Ida, they made a new boss there, then the other one, the old underboss, had to make a new boss. Then a week later he turned around and made a new underboss, it's all fouled up (both laugh). Now there's no harm in that Mooney. It's just like straightening out something in your own vicinity, you understand."* Accardo receives a phone call from his sister asking how she can get her husband, Taiquin Simonelli, out. Accardo asked, *"Out of where?"* She replies, *"Out of the Cicero Police Department. The place got pinched."* Accardo told his sister, *"Don't worry, he'll get out, when the time comes."*

October 14, 1959 – Tony Accardo lands in London, England and stays at the Savoy Hotel.

October 16, 1959 – Tony Accardo lands in Paris, France and stays at the George V. Hotel.

October 22, 1959 – Tony Accardo's plane lands in Zurich, Switzerland and he stays at the Baur Au Lac Hotel.

October 25, 1959 – Accardo lands in Milan, Italy and stays at the Gallea Hotel.

October 27, 1959 – Accardo lands in Venice, Italy and stays at the Royal Danili

October 29, 1959 – Tony Accardo lands in Florence, Italy and stays at the Excelsior Hotel.

October 31, 1959 – Tony Accardo lands in Rome, Italy and stays at the Roma Excelsior Hotel.

November 8, 1959 – Tony Accardo lands in Nice, France and stays at the Negrescu Hotel.

November 11, 1959 –Tony Accardo lands in Barcelona, Spain and stays at the Ritz Hotel

November 13, 1959 – Accardo lands in Madrid, Spain and stays at the Ritz Hotel.

November 17, 1959 – Tony Accardo lands in Lisbon, Portugal and stays at the Avenida Hotel.

November 20, 1959 – Tony Accardo returns to the U. S. landing in New York and then on to Chicago.

December 1959- Tony and Clarice Accardo spend the holidays in Los Angeles, California. It was said that Tony Accardo was going to hide out until January 16, 1960 to avoid the Anthony DeGrazia civil service hearings.

December 24, 1959 – Mob associate Jimmy Celano sends Tony Accardo an artificial floral plant for Christmas.

At the end of 1959, FBI agents got a laugh while listening to one hidden microphone concerning Tony Accardo. Apparently Accardo's wife, Clarice, had been telling Tony Accardo that people like Murray Humphreys and Frank Ferraro were *"no good and none of his concern"* because he, Tony Accardo, was a "legit" man and a family man. Agents added at the end of the report that the bad part of that statement was that Tony Accardo believed Clarice and believed he was a legitimate person and not a mobster.

From the Collection of T.M.

Surveillance photo of Clarice Accardo

Chapter 24

Meet the Accardo Family

Authors Collection 2016 ©

Law enforcement spent a good amount of time finding out where the Accardo family came from. Tony Accardo's father, Francesco "Frank" Accardo died on December 29, 1949 in Miami, Florida. His mother Maria "Mary" Accardo lived most of her life as a housewife, she died in 1954.

Both of Tony Accardo's parents are buried at Mount Carmel Cemetery, in Hillside, Illinois.

Frank's and Mary's Known Addresses

129 Blue Island, Chicago (1904)
560 ½ Harrison Street, Chicago (1907-1909) (Address old numbering system of Chicago)
1357 West Harrison, Chicago (1910) (Same house, new numbering system for Chicago) (Now the University of Chicago, down the street from the U.I.C. Pavilion)
1000 Grand Avenue, Chicago (1911)
1353 Grand Avenue, Chicago (1911- 1928)
4949 Diversey Avenue Chicago (1928-1930's)
5724 North Meade Avenue, Chicago (1940's-1946)
1319 Broadway, Melrose Park, Illinois (1946-1947)
1126 South Monitor, Chicago (1954)

Tony Accardo's parents grave at Mt. Carmel Cemetery, Hillside, Illinois. The grave is with in 100 feet of Al Capone, Frank Nitti and Louis Campagna graves

Tony Accardo's Sisters

Bessie Meirs was born around 1911, and married Edward Meirs. Tony Accardo set Edward up as a bookie and lay-off man for the mob in the 1940's and 1950's. They lived on the first floor at 5724 North Meade Avenue, Chicago. Edward Meirs, born in 1902, died on October 19, 1952. Bessie then married Jack Piel, born August 11, 1915, died May 7, 1962. Bessie worked for the State of Illinois on the payroll of State Auditor Orville E. Hodge. Hodge was eventually sent to prison for embezzling state funds. In 1969 Bessie was exposed in the newspapers as a stenographer for James Tyndall, then a state chief forester, making $620 a month. Her political sponsor was Charles Bonk, who, when the story broke, withdrew his sponsorship the next day. Bessie was quoted as telling the newspaper, *"Just because I'm Tony's sister doesn't mean I'm his keeper."* She lived at 1500 South

Austin Boulevard in Cicero, Illinois. Bessie died in October 2002 and is buried at Queen of Heaven Mausoleum.

Martha Senese was born around 1913 and married Anthony Senese. Their son was Dominic Senese who became a Chicago labor leader and Nick Senese who was killed in March 1960.

Mary Simonelli was born around 1916 and married mobster Tarquin Simonelli.

There was information in an FBI report that a brother-in-law of Tony Accardo was named Tony Martin and he was placed in Local 110 on the Chicago Movie Projectionists Union. This information was never confirmed.

Brothers

John Phillip Accardo
Aka Johnnie
Born 1918

Know Addresses

1353 Grand Avenue, Chicago (1919)
1818 Lake Street, Melrose Park, Illinois (1946)
2139 North 75th Court, Elmwood Park, Illinois (1955)
506 E. Orchard Street, Arlington Heights, Illinois (1958)

Authors Collection 2016 ©
2139 North 75th Court, Elmwood Park as of 2014

John Accardo was Tony Accardo's younger brother who never really got involved in mob business. He was placed as a member of the Chicago Motion Picture Operators Union Local 110 and held jobs around Chicago as a projectionist. In 1955 John's name appeared in the investigation report as being at the wedding of John Moore's, aka Claude Maddox, daughter Patricia.

In 1956 John Accardo invoked the Fifth Amendment in refusing to testify before a Federal Grand Jury investigation for possible misuse of the welfare fund of Local

110. He was reported at the time to be making more than $600 a week during the horse racing season as a projectionist at Arlington and Sportsman's Park race tracks.

In October 1968 investigation reports state that Tony Accardo attended the wedding of his younger brother John, who married a 26-year-old blonde named Ann who was an officer of her father's printing supply company. Tony Accardo was the only Outfit member observed by the police at the wedding and the word on the street was that Accardo ordered all his Outfit pals to stay away so as not to cause "heat" on the wedding.

Martin Accardo

Tony Accardo had an older brother who was an active member of the Chicago Outfit. His name was Martin "Marty" Accardo. However, on the 1920 Census, his father filled out his son's name as his true first name, the name of Leonardi.

Martin's ex-wife once said that Martin and his brother Tony actually did not have that many business dealings with each other. She said that Tony Accardo had little respect for Martin's "business abilities" and Tony Accardo was somewhat known as a man who would not give Martin any money because he knew Martin was bad at business. However, despite that, the two were somewhat close brothers and it was said that Tony Accardo gave his brother a house in Chicago as a wedding gift in 1945. Martin's closest friends were mobsters Rocco Fischetti, Matthew Capone and Anthony Cosentino.

In 1930 Martin Accardo was working for a gangster by the name of John Matteis. Martin Accardo would go out on the streets of Chicago and find "clients" to purchase Matteis liquor. In April 1931 Martin Accardo and John Matteis went to the Sunnyside Inn on Waukegan Road near Glenview, Illinois to collect a bill for booze they had dropped off earlier. What Accardo and Matteis did not know was that the bartenders were undercover Prohibition agents. Both Accardo and Matteis had been attempting to compel a café operator to purchase Matteis's alcohol which lead to the two being arrested. A third member of the gang named Leo Schaffer was also arrested.

Martin Accardo, Leo Schaffer and John Matteis were found guilty and sent to Leavenworth Prison for conspiracy and violation of the Prohibition Act. Martin Accardo was sentenced on November 12, 1931 and entered Leavenworth on April 23, 1932 to serve a 2-year sentence. He was released on December 14, 1933.

Leo Schaffer was sentenced to 4 ½-years on November 12, 1931, entering prison on April 23, 1932 and being released on February 18, 1936. In 1961 he was sentenced once again for a crime and was sent to Terre Haute Prison in Indiana. John Matteis was given 4 ½ years, entering prison on November 12, 1931 and being released on April 23, 1932.

Authors Collection

Martin "Marty" Accardo

UNITED STATES PENITENITARY
LEAVENWORTH, KANSAS

19

Name John Matteis | Register No. 41440 | Color White

Alias -- | Civ. or Milty Civil

Crime Prohi-Poss-Trans-Conspy

Received Apr 23, 1932 | From ND-Ill-Chicago

Sentence 4½yrs | Fine, costs, etc. $1500.00 Com Yes
Costs: $214.05-Com yes

Date of Sentence November 12th 1931 | Sentence Begins April 23 1932

Maximum Term Expires Oct 22 1936 | Minimum term Expires Oct 10 1935

Good Time Allowed 378 days. | Occupation Salesman Age 33
Jan 18, 1899

Eligible for Parole Oct 22 1933 | Pleaded Not Guilty

Where Arrested Chicago Ill | When Apr 1931

How long in jail before trial On Bond | Nativity Italy

How Long in U. S. 24yrs | Final Natiz. pap. when and where obtained Obtained thru Parents-Act of Congress

Last entry date in U. S. 1908 | Where, how, what S. S. --

Passport? In whose poss. Parents

Father living? Yes | Mother living? Yes

If so, name and add. Michael-155 23 Ave Melrose Pk Ill | If so, name and add. Philomena-Same Address

Nativity of father Italy | Nativity of mother Italy

Father ever in U. S. Yes | Mother ever in U. S. Yes

Nearest relatives in native country. Full add. --

Nearest relatives in U. S. Full add. Father & Mother & Wife

Has alien any prop. in U. S. Full particulars No

Married Yes | Wife living Yes | Living with wife Yes | Boys -- | Girls --

Wife's name and address Pearl-155 23 Ave Melrose Park-~~Chicago~~ Illinois

In case of sickness or death, notify Parents-Same address

Education: Read Yes | Write Yes | Common School 8 | High -- | College --

Religion Catholic | Preference

Chew Tobacco No | Smoke Yes | Drink Yes | Use Narcotics No

residence CHICAGO ILLINOIS

(over)

John Matteis Prison Record

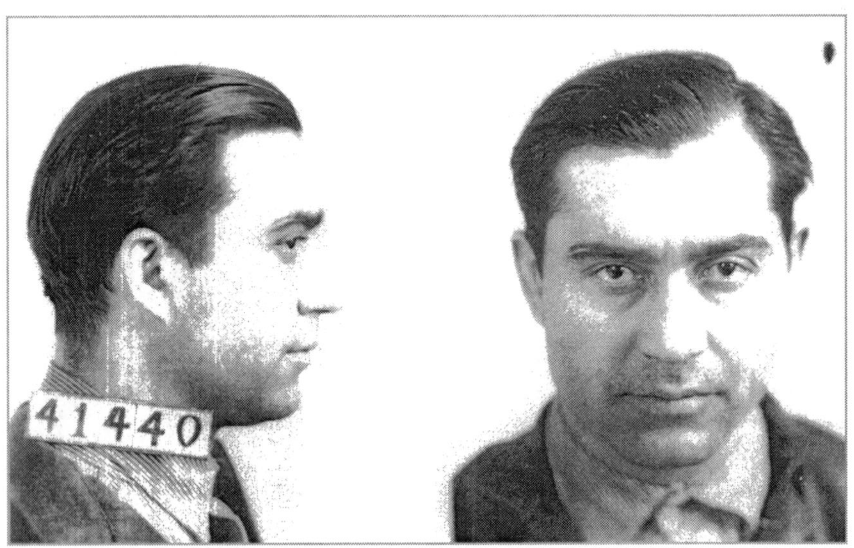

Mug shot photo of John Matteis

CERTIFICATE OF DISCHARGE OF POOR CONVICT.

UNITED STATES OF AMERICA, } ss.
District of Kansas

First Division

41440

THE UNITED STATES
vs.
John Matteis

CERTIFICATE OF DISCHARGE FROM IMPRISONMENT UNDER THE PROVISIONS OF SECTION 1042 OF THE REVISED STATUTES OF THE UNITED STATES.

It appearing to me, the undersigned United States Commissioner for said District, that John Matteis the above-named defendant has been imprisoned in the United States Penitentiary, Leavenworth, Kansas, for the period of thirty days, solely for the non-payment of a fine of $ 1500.00 and costs adjudged against him by the District Court of the United States for the District of at Chicago Illinois on the 12th day of November, 1931, for a violation of section of the Revised Statutes of the United States, that he is unable to pay same, and has complied with the requirements of the law:

IT IS THEREFORE ORDERED, that said John Matteis be discharged from further imprisonment on the 4th day of September, 19 35, and go hence without delay.

Given under my hand and seal this 4th day of September A. D. 1935

J.K.Codding
[SEAL] United States Commissioner as aforesaid.

41441

UNITED STATES PENITENTIARY
LEAVENWORTH, KANSAS

RECORD OF Leo Schaffer NO. 41441
Alias Leo Shaffer RN Color White
Crime Prohi-Poss-Trans-Conspy Military or Civil Civil
Sentence 4½ years -- months -- days
Fine $1500.00-Com yes Cost $214.05-Com yes
Received at Penitentiary Apr 23, 1932 From ND-Ill-Chicago
Date of Sentence Nov 12, 1931 Sentence begins Apr 23, 1932
Maximum term ends Oct 22, 1936 Minimum term ends ~~Oct 10, 1935~~ Jan 18, 1936
Good time allowed ~~378~~ 278-(100 days lost) days, Occupation Salesman Age 32 Years
Eligible to parole Oct 22, 1933
Action of parole board Denied November 5th.1933
LOST 100 DAYS GOOD TIME

41441

Trusty Appointment and Grades	Criminal History
3rd grade 11-1-33 2nd grade 1/29/34 1st grade 2/28/34 2nd grade 5/5/34 1st Grade 6/2/34 2nd grade 9/3/35 1st Grade 10/3/35	B of I reports CO.

(OVER)

DATE	VIOLATIONS	days lost
5-18-32	Violation of Prison Rules: Lazy. Shirks his work. Says he has plenty of time to work later. (LIENHARDT) To forfeit two weeks yard and amusement priviledges.	
10-11-33	Violation of Prison Rules: Oct. 10, 1933. Away from shop during working hours without permission. This man left Mach. shop at 3:20 P M He was away from the shop without a pass twice last week I found him loafing out by the ball park with out a pass and sent him back to work. (Addleman.) To forfeit 2 wks Yd. & Amusement privileges.	

-------*******--------

----------***************-----------

------*********-------

*****

Leo Schaffer's Prison Record

RECORD No. 41441-Schaffer

DATE	VIOLATIONS
11-1-33	Violation of Prison Rules: Oct. 25, 1933. Violating regulations governing inmate trust funds. This man received through the mails from his relatives in Chicago a Cashiers Check of a San Francisco Trust Company. It is now shown that this check for $50.00 represented money which was being transferred to Schaffer by Jacob Berman #41067 through an illegal conspiracy and in violation of above regulations. When questioned regarding the transaction Schaffer denied knowing Berman and when confronted with the evidence declined to discuss it. Dr. Sarasohn, Jewish Chaplain is authority for that these two inmates knew each other well and attended Jewish religious services together. (Mr. F. G. Zerbst, Warden.) Tried October 31, 1933 By Good Time Committee - Finding of the Court-Guilty. Penalty Imposed - Reduced to 3rd Grade and to forfeit 100 days good time. F. G. Zerbst, Warden.
5/5/34	Violation of Prison Rules: May 4, 1934. Having uneuthorized clothing. I found this man leaving the tailor shop with two pair of underwear shorts not regulation which had (according to the foreman tailor) apparently been made from hospital sheets. (R. Hazeltine, Guard) Placed in Isolation on restricted diet. And reduced to 2nd grade.
6-16-34	Violation of Prison Rules: June 15, 1934. 41441 was standing in door of tailor shop signaling an inmate in C Cell House. (Gd. H. P. Stites) To forfeit 2 wks yd and amusement privileges.
6-19-35	Violation of Prison Rules, June 16th.1935:- I found #41441,Shafer, in Jewish Chapel with about 4 lbs. of suger, 2 doz. cookies, a large cake, a pot of tea and six spoons on desk in chapel. All of this had evidently been taken from Kitchen.(Gd.Novinsky) To forfeit 2 wks yard and amusement priviliges.
~~XXXXX~~ 9/3/35	Violation of Prison Rules, September 1, 1935: #41441-Shaffer was loafing in the rear of laundry at 9.am.without a pass. (Guard H.P.Stites) Reduced to Second grade.

Leo Schaffer's Prison Record

August 21, 1959

Ben S. Meeker
Chief U. S. Probation Officer
Room 229, U. S. Courthouse.
Chicago 4, Illinois

ATTENTION: Jacob B. Barnett, U. S. Probation Officer

Dear Mr. Meeker: In Re: Martin Accardo, Our #41445-L
Leo Schaffer, Our #41441-L
John Matteis, Our #41440-L

Replying to your letter of August 14, this is to advise that the complete file of Martin Accardo, our #41445-L, was forwarded to the U. S. Penitentiary, Terre Haute, Indiana, on April 29, 1955, in which institution subject was then confined as Martin Accardo, #11700-TH.

In the case of Leo Schaffer, Our #41441-L, the usual Classification Material in this case is not available. Schaffer was sentenced on November 12, 1931, by the U. S. District Court, Chicago, Illinois, to serve a sentence of 4½ years for violation of the Prohibition Act. He was also given a Fine of $1500.00. He was received here on April 23, 1932, and discharged by Expiration of Sentence on February 18, 1936.

Concerning subject Schaffer, we are enclosing herewith, four photostatic copy of institutional records, which will give you additional information concerning him.

As to John Matteis, Our #41440-L, the usual Classification Material is not available. He was sentenced by the U. S. District Court, Chicago, Illinois, on November 12, 1931, to serve 4½ years, and a Committed Fine of $1500.00, for violation of the Prohibition Act. He was received here on April 23, 1932. He was discharged on September 4, 1935, by Expiration of Sentence. Photostatic copy of 8 miscellaneous records are enclosed for your information.

Respectfully,

CARL F. ZARTER
Administrative Assistant,
Classification and Parole

ENC:

Now, this is to command you the said Marshal forthwith to take said MARTIN ACCARDO and him safely transport to said U. S. Penitentiary and him there deliver to said Warden of said U. S. Penitentiary, with a copy of this writ; AND YOU the said Warden to receive said MARTIN ACCARDO and him keep and imprison in accordance with said sentence, or until he shall be otherwise discharged by due course of law.

WITNESS the Honorable JOHN P. BARNES
Judge of said Court, and the seal thereof, affixed at Chicago, Illinois *in said district, this* 22nd *day of* April, *19*32.

A TRUE COPY TEST
Charles N. Bates CLERK
April 22nd 1932

Clerk.

By
Deputy Clerk.

CERTIFICATE OF DISCHARGE OF POOR CONVICT

UNITED STATES OF AMERICA, } ss. 41445
District of Kansas
First Division

THE UNITED STATES
VS.
Martin Accardo

CERTIFICATE OF DISCHARGE FROM IMPRISONMENT UNDER THE PROVISIONS OF SECTION 1042 OF THE REVISED STATUTES OF THE UNITED STATES.

It appearing to me, the undersigned United States Commissioner for said District, that Martin Accardo the above-named defendant has been imprisoned in the U. S. Penitentiary, Leavenworth, Kansas, for the period of thirty days, solely for the non-payment of a fine of $ 1000.00 and costs $214.05 adjudged against him by the District Court of the United States for the District of Illinois, at Chicago on the 12th day of November, 1931, for a violation of section of the Revised Statutes of the United States, that he is unable to pay same, and has complied with the requirements of the law.

IT IS THEREFORE ORDERED, that said Martin Accardo be discharged from further imprisonment on the 14th day of December, 1933, and go hence without day.

Given under my hand and seal this 14th day of December, A. D. 1933

[SEAL] J. K. Codding United States Commissioner as aforesaid.

UNITED STATES OF AMERICA

Congress of the United States

To Martin Accardo

, Greeting:

Pursuant to lawful authority, YOU ARE HEREBY COMMANDED to appear before the Committee on SENATE COMMITTEE TO INVESTIGATE ORGANIZED CRIME IN INTERSTATE COMMERCE of the Senate of the United States, on June 21, 1951, at 9:30 o'clock A. m., at their committee room Federal Building 300 N. E. 1st Avenue, Miami, Florida, then and there to testify what you may know relative to the subject matters under consideration by said Committee.

and bring with you all records of your income and expense, copies of Federal income tax returns and records of ownership or interest in property both real and personal from 1945 to date.

Hereof fail not, as you will answer your default under the pains and penalties in such cases made and provided.

To Deputy U. S. Marshall to serve and return.

Given under my hand, by order of the Committee, this 9th day of June, in the year of our Lord one thousand nine hundred and 1951

Chairman, Committee on SENATE COMMITTEE TO INVESTIGATE ORGANIZED CRIME IN INTERSTATE COMMERCE

UNITED STATES DEPARTMENT OF JUSTICE
FEDERAL BUREAU OF INVESTIGATION
WASHINGTON 25, D. C.

1-4

For.32-32.M.W

The following is the record of FBI number 506 958

J. Edgar Hoover, Director.

CONTRIBUTOR OF FINGERPRINTS	NAME AND NUMBER	ARRESTED OR RECEIVED	CHARGE	DISPOSITION
USM Chicago, Ill.	Martin Accardo #--	4-28-31	Sec. 88, Title 18 NPA	pending
PD, Chicago, Ill.	Martin Accardo #240	4-28-31	suspect in a prohibition case	
PD Chicago, Ill.	Martin Accardo #C-33656	11-16-31	viol. Prohibition Act	4½ yrs and $1500.
USP Leavenworth, Kans.	Martin Accardo #41445	4-23-32	Prohibition-poss.-sale-trans.	2 yrs.; 12-14-33, exp.

* Represents notations unsupported by fingerprints in FBI files.

U. S. GOVERNMENT PRINTING OFFICE

NOTICE.—*This Record is furnished for official use only*

Martin Accardo's FBI Arrest Record

Tony Dark

UNITED STATES DEPARTMENT OF JUSTICE
FEDERAL BUREAU OF INVESTIGATION
WASHINGTON 25, D. C.

2

The following is the record of FBI number 506 958

J. Edgar Hoover, Director.

CONTRIBUTOR OF FINGERPRINTS	NAME AND NUMBER	ARRESTED OR RECEIVED	CHARGE	DISPOSITION
CC-PD North Chgo., Ill. Enclosure	This individual is identical with MARTIN ACCARDO, Chgo. PD #C-33656, subject of your letter dated September 11, 1948, which is attached.			

UNITED STATES DEPARTMENT OF JUSTICE
FEDERAL BUREAU OF INVESTIGATION
WASHINGTON 25, D. C.

3

The following is the record of FBI number 506958

J. Edgar Hoover, Director.

CONTRIBUTOR OF FINGERPRINTS	NAME AND NUMBER	ARRESTED OR RECEIVED	CHARGE	DISPOSITION
	Description:			

Description:

Color: white
Sex: male
Local Address: 1409 W. Erie St.,Chicago, Ill. (1931)
Date of birth: 30 in 1930
Place of birth: Chicago, Ill. and Italy
Height: 5 ft 8½ in
Weight: 160
Eyes: Brown
Hair: Black
Build: Medium
Complexion: medium dark

NOTICE.—This Record is furnished for official use only

CITY OF CHICAGO / DEPARTMENT OF POLICE 1121 South State Street Chicago 5, Illinois WAbash 2-4747
IDENTIFICATION SECTION

ARREST RECORD OF ACCARDO Martin

DATE

DATE OF BIRTH

C33656

NAME & ADDRESS	C.B. NO.	DATE OF ARREST	ARRESTING OFFICER & DIST.	CHARGE	DISPOSITION
Martin Accardo	C33656	Apr 25 32 U.S.P. Leavenworth Kans. #41445 fr. Chicago Ill. Viol. Prob. Act. 2 yrs. Judge Barnes. Apr 28 31 in Chicago, Ill. Susp. Prob. Viol. May 17 32 CCW Stricken Off. Judge Sullivan.			

I.R. NO.

FBI NO.

S.B. NO.

NAME (LAST) ACCARDO (FIRST) MARTIN (MIDDLE) SOC. SEC. NO. 350-03-6652 FILE NO.

NICKNAME OR ALIAS MARTIN RENN TYPE OF ACTIVITY I.R. NO. C-33656

HOME ADDRESS 1601 Westchester Blvd. CITY Westchester, Ill. HOME PHONE NO. F.B.I. NO.

BUSINESS ADDRESS CITY BUSINESS PHONE NO. TYPE OF BUSINESS

NEW ADDRESS CITY NEW PHONE NO. PHOTO REF. NO.

SEX Male RACE White DESCENT D.O.B. 63 yrs HEIGHT 5'8" WEIGHT 160 HAIR EYES

COMPLEXION PECULIARITIES, MARKS, SCARS, ETC.

ASSOCIATES FRANK SANTUCCI, VITO LOMBARDI CONSTANTINO DI STASIO

HANGOUTS

VEHICLE INFORMATION

CPD-38.351 (REV.2/62) FACE CARD SEE REVERSE SIDE FOR MISC. INFORMATION

Subject is observed only in leased vehicles. Subject was sentenced to the Penitentiary in 1931 with Leo Schaeffer and John Matties for violation of the National Prohibition Act. Subject claims to be a salesman for a Wholesale Grocery Firm. Reported to be involved in gambling in the Florida area. Subjects greates claim to fame is that he is the brother of the infamous Tony Accardo

Tony Dark

Martin Accardo married Rita Morley on July 30, 1945 in Chicago. She had been married five times to other men. Rita was born Orita Yelverton in Jackson, Mississippi on September 13, 1919. When she was 15 years old she ran away with a man named Lawrence Bass and had a daughter with him. Rita never lived with Bass and returned home to her mother without her daughter.

Rita's mother remarried a man named Al Morley and moved to Chicago. Rita followed in 1936 and legally changed her name to Rita Morley. In 1938 Rita married Joe Baxa and worked at the old Circle Club at 5534 W. Cermak Road in Cicero, Illinois as a bar hostess. The club was owned by "Swede" Johnson and had a large gambling operation in the back of the club. Often seen at the club were Louis Campagna, Jake Guzik, Tony Accardo and his brother Martin.

In 1944 Martin Accardo and Tony Jordan bought the Circle Club and brought in Arthur Becker to run the club while they ran the gambling. It was then that Rita and Martin began a romance. The two soon married.

In December 1945 Tony Jordan died and Martin bought his interest in the club from Jordan's widow with money he borrowed from Louis Campagna. Like all good mobsters Martin Accardo placed the interest of the club in the name of Rita Yelverton.

In the late 1940's Martin Accardo had worked out a situation so he could keep most of the money he made. Martin did not report his income from the Circle Club and had an arrangement with his good friend Tony Cosentino. Cosentino was the proprietor of O.K. Motors Incorporated and the deal was Martin Accardo would deliver him $600 a month in cash in exchange for a paycheck to show he worked for Cosentino and could use that as his only income to pay taxes on.

In 1947 Martin and his family moved and bought a home on 22nd Road, S.W. in Miami, Florida. A few months later he purchased an extravagant home at 217 Granada Blvd., Coral Gables, Florida. He put the house in the name of Rita Yelverton and listed his phone number in the name of Leo Martin.

After the death of his father, Martin began spending most of his time in Chicago while Rita was back in Miami. According to Rita, Martin became sullen and ill-tempered, threatened her, beat her and brandished one of his revolvers at her. She said she insisted the two go their own ways and on May 24, 1949 the two divorced in Dade County, Florida.

Rita was given custody of the two children and $300-mounth in child support. Martin demanded that Rita deed over to him the residences at 1217 Granada Blvd., Coral Gables and joint properties in Chicago at 1812 Austin Blvd. and a vacant lot in the Underwood section of Chicago. Martin was placing so much pressure on Rita that she had what she called a "complete breakdown" and was hospitalized for 2 months.

Soon after the divorce Rita married Dennis F. Shortridge and the two, with the children, lived in the Coral Gables house. The problem was Rita had never signed the deeds over to Martin so he held vigil of threats and harassments. Martin even moved into Rita's house and stayed overnight at times threatening to "kill them all" in the middle of the night while they slept. Rita said her new husband was "somewhat timid" about Martin and did nothing to defend her.

Rita and her new husband purchased a home at 2401 S.W. 9th Avenue in Miami, Florida to get away from Marin but that did not work. According to Rita, Martin moved into that house and frequently displayed his firearms and threatened to kill her and the kids. When he was not in the house, Martin would ride around the block for hours to keep the "heat" on her to sign the deeds over to him. She finally agreed to sign over the Coral Gables home and the two Chicago properties. Martin also made her sign a will which contained the provision that in the event of both Martin's and Rita's death the children would go to Tony Accardo and in the case of just her death, all of Rita' effects, personal and real estate, would go to Martin Accardo.

Rita's marriage to Shortridge ended and she quickly married Miami Police Officer Dallas Carroll in September 1950.

At the same time, Martin Accardo gave Harry Voiler $50,000 as an investment in the start up of the Miami Beach Morning Mail newspaper. The newspaper was a financial disaster. Harry Voiler was formerly from Chicago and was an ex-convict known to the mob as "too crooked and unreliable to deal with." Voiler used every trick he could think of to get money into the sinking business. He approached mobster Murray "The Camel" Humphreys who turned him down within seconds. He shopped around until one of the mob guys would "bite" on the deal and Martin Accardo did. He begged Martin to bring his brother Tony Accardo into the business; then asked if Tony Accardo would use his influence on the local movie theaters in Miami to purchase ads in the paper with threat of stink bombs tossed in the theater during every movie. Martin said no because he had not told his brother that he had gone into business with Voiler. When Tony Accardo did find out about the business, Tony was furious that Martin could have been so dumb as to have gone into business with Voiler. Tony told Martin that Voiler was strictly no good, and refused to aid in obtaining movie ads.

Voiler then tried to woo New York mob boss Frank Costello to get involved with the paper by writing a welcome story in the paper addressed to Costello when he arrived in Miami. Desperate, Voiler tried to convince Martin that they should stage a series of hold-ups and robberies to raise money, which Martin turned down. Martin knew he had been the victim of a "con job." In the end, a Reubin Clein struck a deal with Voiler and purchased the defunct paper and equipment.

Marin Accardo never took Rita marrying so soon after their divorce very well. He hatched a plot to get even. As the story goes, in 1950 Martin had to leave Miami because the "heat" was on and the government was looking to serve him a subpoena to appear before the Senate Crime Committee so he left to hide out in Chicago. On October 20, 1950 Martin sent his new girl friend Fleeta Iverson down to Miami to pick up his son, Martin Jr., and bring him back to Chicago for a visit. Rita and her new husband, Miami Police Officer Dallas Carroll, met Fleeta at the airport and they all went out to eat dinner.

Rita had actually introduced Fleeta to Martin while the two were going through difficulties. Fleeta Iverson, according to Rita, was a University of Miami student who was being kept by Edmund "The Baron" Henke, an elderly rogue who had been involved in some kind of fraud during World War II. After the trial, Fleeta left Henke for a wealthy Miami restaurant owner named Irving Moss. However, the very young Fleeta may have been a little too much fun for the elderly Moss since he died shortly after the two began dating. It was then that Rita introduced Fleeta to Martin and the two began to date.

After dinner and one or two alcoholic drinks they started home when Fleeta insisted they stop at the El Bolero night club because she wanted to meet a friend. The friend was a acquaintance of the man Fleeta used to live with. After a few drinks, Fleeta pretended she was upset over the way this man treated her and asked Rita to leave the club. Rita and her husband went outside and were waiting for Fleeta to come out when a Miami police squad car pulled up and the officer arrested Dallas Carroll. Rita went to the police station where she found her husband locked up and charged with being intoxicated and with assault and resisting arrest. The police chief asked Rita why she had called the police on her husband in the first place. While Rita and Dallas waited outside for Fleeta to come out of the club, Fleeta called the police saying she was Rita and wanted her husband arrested because he was drunk.

When Carroll was released on bond he was told by the Chief of Police that the charges would be dropped if Carroll gave his resignation from the police force. Martin Accardo had used his connections with the police chief in Miami to frame Carroll to get even with Rita.

Then it came time for Rita to get back at Martin for what he pulled. Rita went to the U.S. Senate investigators investigating organized crime and gave information on Martin's life in the Chicago Outfit, names, places, associates and stuff on his brother Tony Accardo's life. Rita also told investigators how the Italian Welfare Council of Chicago was completely under the control of the Chicago mob and was the mobsters official "club" where you either had to be a "made" mobster or had to be an "associate" of the mob to be inducted. She said all racketeers were assigned a set amount of money to contribute to the council and the amount sitting in the welfare "pot" was considerable. She said the council was set up for charity but that there was very little evidence of charitable activities or expenditures. She added that periodically meetings would be held by the council and all the big shot hoodlums would attend including men like Sam Giancana and Paul DeLucia. From what Rita could tell, the Italian Welfare Council of Chicago was just a front for the mob to store cash. Rita ended by saying Martin Accardo purchased a Welfare certificate in her name.

Rita Accardo's Italian Welfare Council 1946 Membership Certification

Known Officers listed in the Italian Welfare Council were:

John Lavezzorio (Director)
Frank Annunzio (Illinois Labor Director)*
Michael Notaro (Director)
Vincent Ferrara (Secretary)
Anthony Champagne (Lawyer)*
Adam Vignola (Council President)
Joseph Salerno (Council President)
Edward Bragno (Director)
Frank Aliotta (Director)
Joseph LaMantia (Director)
A. J. Lendino (Doctor)*
Louis Capparelli (Police Captian)*
Anthony DeJulio (Director)
Frank "Frankie X" Esposito (Union Boss)*
Joseph I. Bulger (Lawyer)*
Dario Toffenetti (Restaurant Owner)
John Sbarbaro (Judge)*
Vincent Russo (Treasurer)
Anthony Sorrentino (Council Director)
Eugene Chesrow (Doctor)*
Michael Fortino (Vice President)
Peter Fosco (Union Boss)*
John J. Lupe (Superior Judge)*
George Spatuzza (Director)
Frank Chesrow (Politician)*

* *Council Director*

Martin Accardo had been cited by the Senate Crime Commission for refusing to answer questions. Rita may have had the last laugh. In September 1954 Martin Accardo went on trial for tax evasion, which the government claimed he evaded $23,351 in income taxes for the years 1947, 1948 and 1949. How did the government know for sure? Their star witness against Martin was his ex-wife Rita. The government called Martin's bodyguard, who happened to be his brother-in-law, Taiquin "Queenie" Simonelli, as a witness but he disappeared. To find out where he was hiding the government subpoenaed Tarquin's wife and Martin's sister Mary. Queenie was hiding out.

In April 1955 Martin Accardo was sentenced to 3-years at Terre Haute prison for income tax evasion. As for Rita, she divorced Dallas Carroll and in September 1956 Carroll was listed as living in Cicero, Illinois and owned a café. That month Dallas Carroll had borrowed a car from a friend and was driving at Harlem Avenue and Riverside Drive in Berwyn, Illinois when a car pulled up next to him and shot him in the face with two shotgun blasts. The left side of his face was blown off completely. It was not known if it was a mob hit but police focused on Carroll's new wife who he had married in February 1956. His new wife's ex-husband had threatened her that she would be a widow in six months after she married Dallas Carroll.

Law enforcement kept an "eye" on Martin hoping they could find something that would tie him to his powerful brother. Among notes law enforcement had on Martin and his family were:

In April 1962, Martin Accardo was arrested with Frank Santucci, Vito Lombardi, and Constantino di Stasio for suspicion of possessing 500 stolen coins. Chicago burglary detectives noticed Santucci standing outside di Stasio's Lounge at 2409 N. Mannheim Road in Leyden Township and searched his car finding the 500 coins in his trunk. At that moment Martin Accardo and Vito Lombardi pulled up in their cars to meet with Santucci and were arrested. The coins were later identified by Rich Koch, who had his home robbed days earlier, as being his. The police found a screwdriver in Lombardi's car which matched one found in Koch's home that was left by the burglars. Santucci was charged with burglary, Lombardi was charged with possession of burglary tools, di Stasio and Accardo were charged with disorderly conduct.

In September 1962 an informant told the FBI that an alleged nephew of mob boss Tony Accardo, who was allegedly named Frank, possibly Martin's son, had allegedly purchased the Brass Lantern Restaurant and Bar which was located at 159th and Wood Street in Harvey, Illinois. This Frank's partner was a man who went by the name of Gilly and was a former alderman from the town of Harvey. The informant also alleged that the two men had purchased land near the Washington Park Race Track with the intention of building a dog racing track.

In November 1963, Martin Accardo was observed meeting with Chuckie English at the Armory Lounge. The two were discussing narcotics arrest made in Chicago by federal narcotics officers which included the arrest of mobster Americo De Pieto. Martin Accardo pointed out to English that his brother Tony Accardo was definitely against narcotics and those arrested were in "Trouble."

Throughout the 1960's, 70's, and 80's little was reported on Martin Accardo. It was reported that Martin Accardo died on October 10, 1992.

REGISTRATION CARD A-2467

Martin Accardo

1353 Grand Av. Chicago Cook Ill

18 March 19 1900

RACE

White ✓

U. S. CITIZEN

Citizen by Father's Naturalization Before Registrant's Majority ✓

PRESENT OCCUPATION — Teamster

EMPLOYER'S NAME — American Railway Express

PLACE OF EMPLOYMENT OR BUSINESS: 17th & Slate St. Chicago Cook Ill

NEAREST RELATIVE — Mary Accardo (mother) 1353 Grand Av. Chicago Cook Ill

I AFFIRM THAT I HAVE VERIFIED ABOVE ANSWERS AND THAT THEY ARE TRUE

Martin Accardo

12-2-11-C

REGISTRAR'S REPORT

DESCRIPTION OF REGISTRANT

HEIGHT			BUILD			COLOR OF EYES	COLOR OF HAIR
Tall	Medium	Short	Slender	Medium	Stout		
	✓			✓		Brown	Brown

29 Has person lost arm, leg, hand, eye, or is he obviously physically disqualified? (Specify.) No

30 I certify that my answers are true; that the person registered has read or has had read to him his own answers; that I have witnessed his signature or mark, and that all of his answers of which I have knowledge are true, except as follows:

K Clifford (Signature of Registrar)

Date of Registration

Chicago Local Board No. 39
955 Grand Ave., Chicago.

(STAMP OF LOCAL BOARD)

(The stamp of the Local Board having jurisdiction of the area in which the registrant has his permanent home shall be placed in this box.)

(OVER)

Martin Accardo's World War I Draft Cards

UNITED STATES DEPARTMENT OF JUSTICE
FEDERAL BUREAU OF INVESTIGATION
WASHINGTON 25, D.C.

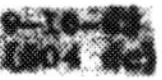

Director.

The following FBI record, NUMBER 506 958 , is furnished FO . OFFICIAL USE ONLY.

CONTRIBUTOR OF FINGERPRINTS	NAME AND NUMBER	ARRESTED OR RECEIVED	CHARGE	DISPOSITION
United States Marshal Chicago, Illinois	Martin Accardo #--	April 28, 1931	section 88, title 18, National Prohibition Act	pending two years on charge of liquor
Police Department Chicago, Illinois	Martin Accardo #240	April 28, 1931	suspect in a prohibition case	
Police Department Chicago, Illinois	Martin Accardo #C-33656	November 16, 1931	violation Prohibition Act	4½ years and $1500.
United States Penitentiary Leavenworth, Kansas	Martin Accardo #41445	April 23, 1932	Prohibition-possession-sale-transporting	2 years; December 14, 1933, expiration
United States Marshal, Chicago, Illinois	Martin Accardo #19142	August 13, 1951	contempt of Senate of United States	pending
United States Marshal, Miami, Florida	Martin Accardo #885-MCR	March 3, 1952	contempt	1 year, $1000. fine plus court costs
Sheriff's Office Miami, Florida	Martin Accardo #135984	March 5, 1952	hold for United States Marshal	
United States Marshal Chicago Illinois	Martin L. Accardo #55269	January 5, 1954	attempt to evade taxes	10-25-54 3 yr sent and $10,000 fine
Cook Co Jail Chgo Ill	Martin Accardo #168997	10-25-54	SKUSM	11-1-54 del'd to USM
US Pen Terre Haute Ind	Martin L. Accardo #117000	11-1-54	Income tax Evasion	3 yrs Conditional release 2-14-57
PD Chgo Ill	Martin L. Accardo #1154	4-17-62	inv of burg	

Information shown on this Identification Record represents data furnished FBI by fingerprint contributors. Where final disposition is not shown or further explanation of charge is desired, communicate with agency contributing those fingerprints.

Notations indicated by * are NOT based on fingerprints in FBI files but are listed only as investigative leads as being possibly identical with subject of this record.

U.S. GOVERNMENT PRINTING OFFICE : 1951—O-615915

Mob Boss

File Card

Martin Leonard Accardo
Real Name Leonardi Accardo
AKA Marty
Birth - March 18, 1900, Italy (World War I Registration says March 19, 1900 as birth date) Entering the United States in 1905 (That's what he told prison authorities; 1920 U.S. Censes says 1906)
Died - October 10, 1992 (DuPage County, Illinois)
Height 5'8 1/2"
Weight 167 pounds
Stocky Build
Brown Eyes
Brown Hair

Family

First Wife - Rita Yelverton (July 1945-May 29, 1949)
Second Wife - Mary Accardo
Son - Frank Accardo, age 14 in 1940 (Godparents Mr. & Mrs. Matthew Capone)
Son - Martin Leo Accardo Jr. (Son of Martin and Rita)
Daughter - Sandra Frances Accardo (Daughter of Martin and Rita)
Daughter – Mary Accardo, age 12 in 1940.
Girl Friend -Fleeta Iverson (1960's)

Known Professions

Teamster, American Railway Express Company, 17th & State Street, Chicago (1917-1918)
Driver for a plumbing supplies company (1919-1920's)
Chauffer (1920-1930's)
Cashier, Gambling Establishment (He said this to the 1940 Census taker)
Circle Club Tavern, 5534 W. Cermak Road in Cicero, Illinois (Owner) (1947)

Known Addresses

1353 Grand Avenue, Chicago (1917)
5950 West Wrightwood Avenue, Chicago (1930)
1409 Erie Street, Chicago (1931)
South 50th Avenue, Cicero, Illinois (1940)
2801 North Keating Avenue, Chicago (1944)
22nd Road, S.W., Miami, Florida (1947)
1217 Granada Blvd., Coral Gables, Florida (1947)
1812 Austin Blvd., Cicero, Illinois (1949)
Oak Park Arms Hotel, Oak Park, Illinois (1950)
2114 South Central Avenue, Chicago (1954)
2136 DeKalb, Chicago (1956)
1601 Westchester Blvd. Westchester, Illinois (1962)

Tony Dark

Known Cars

Oldsmobile, 2 door purchased from Mars Oldsmobile (1956)

Known Arrest Record

Date	Charge	Agency	Result
4-28-1931	Prohibition	CPD	U/K
11-16-1931	Prohibition	CPD	4 ½ Years Prison
4-23-1932	Prohibition Viol.	Feds	Prison
8-13-1951	Contempt	Feds	U/K
3-3-1952	Contempt	Miami S.D.	1 Year Prison
3-5-1952	Hold for Marshall	Feds	U/K
1-5-1954	Tax Evasion	Feds	3 Years Prison
10-25-1954	U/K	Feds	U/K
11-1-1954	Tax Evasion	Feds	U/K
4-17-1962	Invest. Burglary	CPD	Released

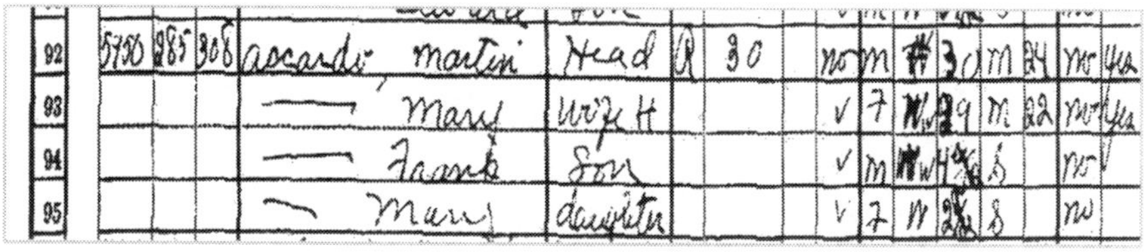

92	5790	285	308	Accardo, Martin	Head	R	30
93				— Mary	Wife H		
94				— Frank	Son		
95				— Mary	daughter		

Martin Accardo's 1930 Census Page

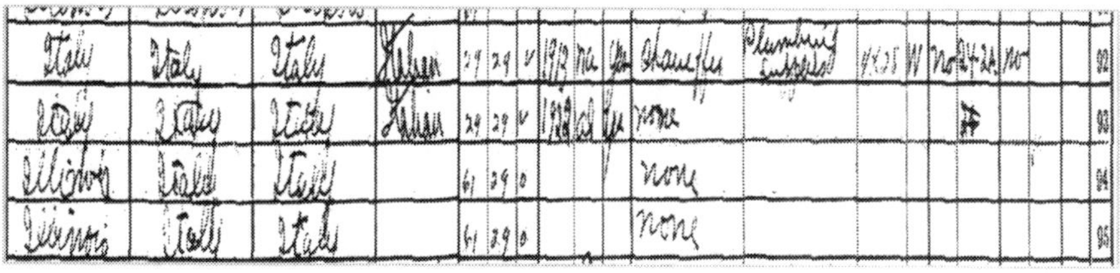

Italy	Italy	Italy	Italian	Chauffeur	Plumbing Supplies	92
Italy	Italy	Italy	Italian	none		93
[illegible]	Italy	Italy		none		94
[illegible]	Italy	Italy		none		95

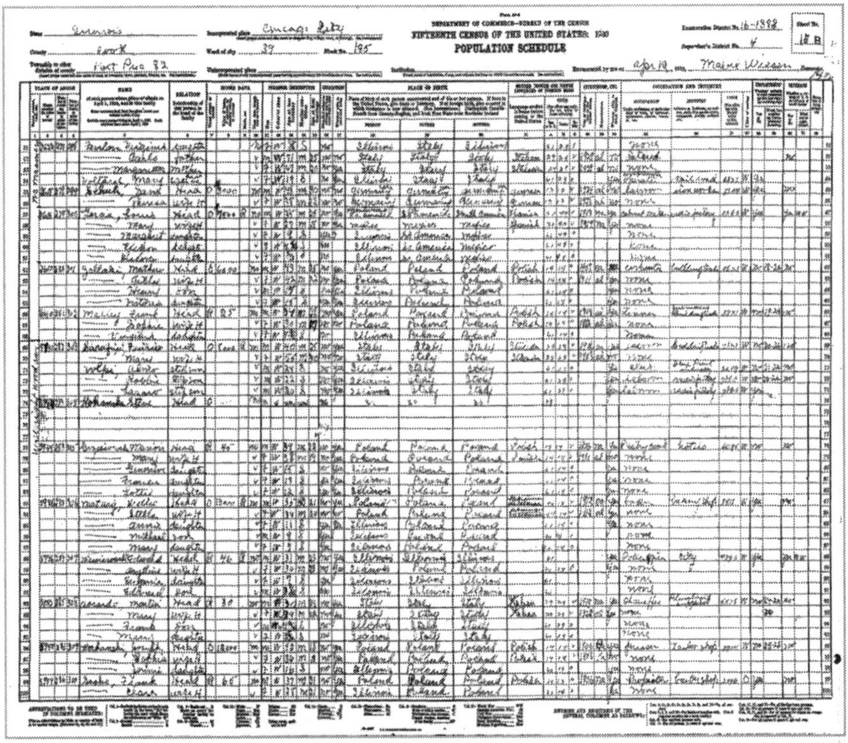

DEPARTMENT OF COMMERCE—BUREAU OF THE CENSUS
FIFTEENTH CENSUS OF THE UNITED STATES: 1930
POPULATION SCHEDULE

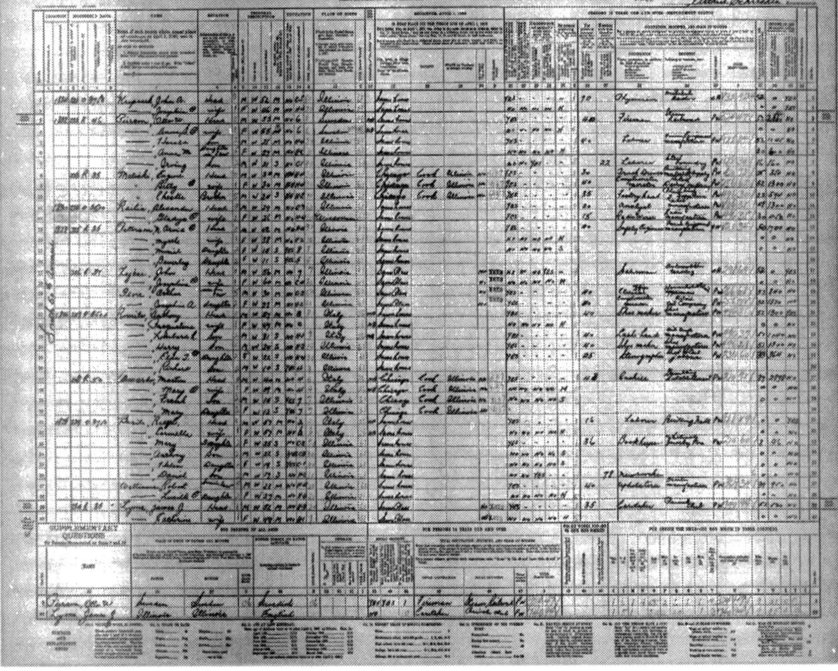
DEPARTMENT OF COMMERCE—BUREAU OF THE CENSUS
SIXTEENTH CENSUS OF THE UNITED STATES: 1940
POPULATION SCHEDULE

Martin Accardo's 1940 Census Page

27	2R 50	Accardo, Martin	Head	M	W	40	M	No	4	Italy
28		—, Mary O	wife	F	W	39	M	No	4	Italy
29		—, Frank	Son	M	W	14	S	Yes	7	Illinois
30		—, Mary	Daughter	F	W	12	S	Yes	7	Illinois

Chicago	Cook	Illinois	No	Yes	48	Cashier	Gambling Establishment	PW	52	2898
Chicago	Cook	Illinois	No	No No No No	H				0	0
Chicago	Cook	Illinois	No	No No No No	S				0	0
Chicago	Cook	Illinois	No							

Tony and Clarice Accardo's Children

Anthony Ross Accardo

Anthony Ross Accardo was the oldest son of Tony Accardo and was alleged to be adopted sometime around 1936. Often called Anthony Jr., he was alleged to take full advantage of his father's power and wealth when possible.

Marie Judith Accardo

Daughter Marie Accardo was born on July 3, 1939.

Linda Lee Accardo

Daughter Linda Accardo was born on January 14, 1941.

Joseph Accardo

Tony Accardo's youngest son Joseph Frank Accardo was alleged to be adopted by Tony and Clarice around 1946.

In April 5, 1963 Tony Accardo mentions his youngest son Joseph Accardo was graduating from the Valley Forge Military Academy and was awaiting an appointment to a Military Academy, hopefully, West Point. He was supposed to enter after graduation but Congressman Roland Libonati procrastinated on the application and the young Accardo had to wait a year.

One intelligent report stated that Joseph Accardo was working as a projectionist at Plitt Movie Theater in Stratford Square Mall in Bloomingdale, Illinois in the late 1980's. There he was working with other members of Outfit families such as the Giancana family, the Carlisi family and the grandson of Anthony "Tony X" Esposito.

Tony Accardo's Brother-in-law

Taiquin "Queenie" Simonelli

Tony Accardo's sister, Mary, married Taiquin Simonelli in the 1930's. His father, John Simonelli, was born in Italy in the town of Fuoggi and immigrated to America in 1899. In 1930 he wrote he was making a living working in a baker's shop and by 1943 he was listed as a broker. His mother was listed Angelina Zinlarelli, also from the town of Fuoggi, Italy. On the 1930 censes Taiquin's mother is not listed but his brothers, Albert and Mike, and sisters are. Tarquin was the seventh child in the family.

FIFTEENTH CENSUS OF THE UNITED STATES: 1930

POPULATION SCHEDULE

Taiquin Simonelli 1930 Census Page

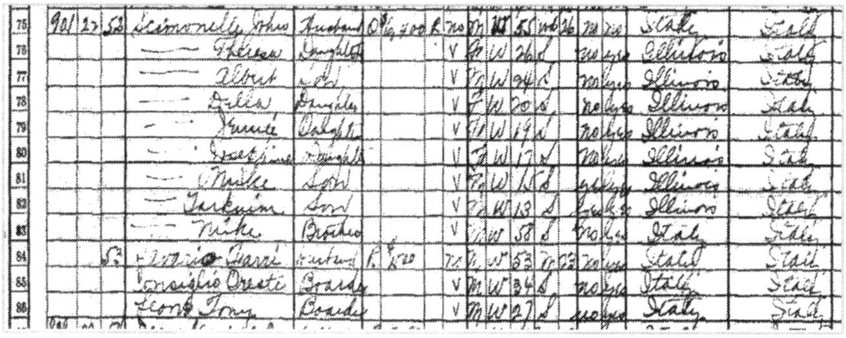

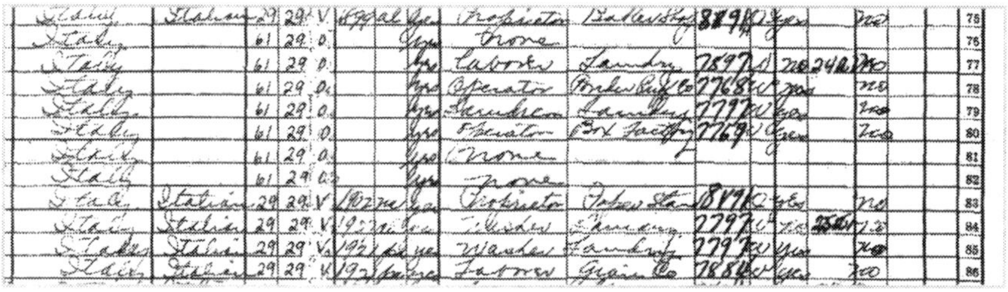

When FBI agents opened an FBI investigation on Tarquin Simonelli, they learned that his birth certificate had been filed on August 19, 1943 under what was legally called a "delayed birth certificate." For the times this was a common problem because many of the Italians born between 1900 and the 1920's were not required to file a birth certificate or many simply did not know how to because they did not speak or read English.

Taiquin "Queenie" Simonelli's childhood saw that he only made it to the 4th grade in school. The FBI knew this because in 1963 FBI agents listened in as Chuckie English and Queenie Simonelli watched the funeral of President John F. Kennedy at the Armory Lounge and the conversation came up as to what grades they finished. Simonelli said the 4th while English made it through all of grammar school. Simonelli often talked about his childhood while the FBI listened in on hidden microphones. He talked about being born on Ewing Street in Chicago and how he missed those days. Queenie got his start with the Outfit in the early days of the Capone Gang working for Rocco Fischetti at the Vernon Country Club. He would go on to work at all of Fischetti's gambling joints and his lucrative floating crap game.

In 1943 Queenie Simonelli was using the name T.J. Seno while using a car to pick up lay-off bets in the Chicago Loop area for the mob gambling operation at 4819 West Roosevelt Road in Cicero.

In 1950 Tony Accardo set Simonelli up in a job managing a horse book for Joseph "Fifkie" Corngold in Chicago. In 1955 Queenie was operating a crap game at 4812 East Cermak Road in Cicero, Illinois.

Around 1956 Simonelli was a partner with Frank "Sharkey" Eulo in a gambling operation. He was also listed as being associated with William "Willie Potatoes"

Daddono, Joseph "Pepe" Giancana and Dominic "Butch" Blasi on the west side of Chicago involved in "juice" loans and crap games.

On April 2, 1959 FBI agents were requested to speak to a syndicate burglar who was locked up in Cook County Jail on a burglary charge. This burglar, hoping to make some kind of deal to help him get out, gave the agents information on Sam Giancana and his activities. According to this burglar, Sam Giancana owned the Royal Café on Roosevelt Road in Cicero, where on the second floor this burglar would gamble and shoot "craps." On the first floor was a restaurant which according to this burglar was run by Tarquin "Queenie" Simonelli.

On September 7, 1959 Simonelli was arrested with mobsters Rocco Fischetti and Lester "Killer Kane" Kruse for running a dice game and gambling establishment at the old Viaduct Lounge, 4610 Cicero Avenue in Cicero, Illinois. Simonelli was charged with being the keeper of a gambling house. The "dice game" at the time was the biggest money maker for the Outfit, making ten's of thousands of dollars a night. When arrested, Queenie gave his name as Thomas Seno but police already knew who he really was. When mob boss Sam Giancana found out about the raid he swore to have the then Assistant State's Attorney in charge, John Stamos, fired from his job for heading the raid.

The next day FBI agents listened in on Sam Giancana and Tony Accardo as they talked about the raid and arrest. The conversation went as follows:

Giancana	They went over to one guy's house, the main guy, and he refused to go. Gimme a court order, he says, and I'll go. So they go see the second guy. He said, the best pinch you could ever want. So he took it. The state's attorney and everybody else in it. So they kidnap the guy, and bring him over to open it up. Mosler.
Accardo	That's a big outfit.
Giancana	Yeah.
Accardo	Well, you oughta sue them.
Giancana	Sure, you have to.
Accardo	Oughta sue the fucking state's attorney.
Giancana	The guy made a statement in front of Ferlic, what did you finally find in the place? Fuck the fucking cops, they come over there with machine guns and shotguns, and shit.
Accardo	And they kept them guys in the fucking can over night, too. I know, my sister called up, and said, how do I go about getting Queenie? I said, get him out of where? She said, out of the Cicero Police Department. The place got pinched. I said, don't worry, he'll get out, when the time comes. Did they get out yesterday or what?
Giancana	All day.

The charges against Tarquin Simonelli went nowhere. The charges had been nolle possessed due to lack of evidence.

By March 1960 Tarquin Simonelli was working as a "box man" with Rocco Fischetti running a "crap game" at Fischetti's new J & J Picnic Grove at 159th and Bell Avenue on Route 6 west of Will – Cook County Road.

A year later in 1961, investigators discovered that the Simonelli house at 601 Selbourne in Riverside, Illinois had two names on the mail box, T. C. Simonelli and Fred L. Carter. The phone number to the house was listed to a Fred L. Carter. The investigators asked the Riverside Police to find out who lived at the house. They contacted the investigator back saying it was the Simonelli family and no such person named Fred Carter lived there. The police officer did add that the Simonelli family *"is not what you would call reputable."* So the investigator looked at when the telephone number was listed which was in June 1958 to a Fred Carter, real estate broker at West Town Realty. In the intelligent files of the Chicago police Department the name Fred L. Carter was found and listed as an officer at the West Town Realty Company located at 334 South Pulaski Road. When the investigator arrived at the realty company, he interviewed some of the salesmen working there and each said that no one named Fred L. Carter had ever worked there or had anything to do with the place. Fred L. Carter was an alias of Tarquin Simonelli that he used when he needed to show that he was employed on applications or other incidents.

In October 1961 Simonelli was working at Club 66, located at 4139 South Harlem Avenue in Stickney, Illinois. This gambling operation had moved from the Prime Steak House which had been located at 3921 South Harlem Avenue.

FBI agents followed Tarquin often in 1962. They noticed that when he was not at the Armory Lounge he was at Maggio's Steak House at 7635 Roosevelt Road in Forest Park, just down the street from the Armory Lounge. There, Simonelli, Butch Blasi, Donald "Don Angel" Angelini, and Dom Cortina would meet and play cards. On occasion Sam Giancana would come and eat and hold meetings while playing cards in the basement.

Maggio's Steak House was owned by Freddie Maggio. He, his father Anthony "Buck" Maggio, and his brother Donald Maggio all worked to run the business. Freddie Maggio was a well-liked individual whose only interest in life was gambling, playing golf, and chasing women, in that order. He was a poor business owner and would gamble most of the money away by playing gin 8 hours a day or betting on golf at $50-a-hole. Simonelli, Blasi, Angelini and Cortina would use Maggio for everything they could without feeling bad. They rarely ever gave him any money for the non-stop booze they drank or food they ate. There was some form of gambling occurring at the steak house because FBI agents watched day after day as a runner would stop at the steak house and leave carrying large amounts of cash. Investigators believed Simonelli may have been running an operation from the steak house but failed to find anything. When the Cook County Sheriff's Office raided the steak house, they could find nothing-no money or phone lines-for bookmaking; just a few decks of cards.

In August 1962 Sam Giancana ordered Queenie Simonelli to make sure the word was out to all mob associates that all burglars and armed robbers living in Cicero would have to move out of that town. The rule had been in place a few years earlier but never enforced. The reason an irate Sam Giancana sent Simonelli out to make sure it was being enforced was a shipment of stolen women's garments had been recovered by the Illinois State's Attorney's Police in Cicero. This load of stolen merchandise had been stolen from Giancana's men by Cicero robbers before being recovered by police.

Queenie Simonelli's name often appeared in daily reports from Sam Giancana's Armory Lounge. There are many recordings of Simonelli hanging out with other mobsters. His most common associates listed by the FBI in 1963 were Dom "Butch" Blasi, Martin Accardo, John Matassa, Frank and Anthony "Tony X" Esposito, Joey Arcola, Charles English, Carmen Fanelli, John D'Arco Sr., Sam Giancana and Louis Briatta. Simonelli always had something to say, he liked to talk about everything, but not too much mob stuff. He was always kidding Butch Blasi that he was over sexed. Other days Butch Blasi, Chuckie English and Simonelli would shoot dice and bet money with each other, play cards, and discuss food.

One informant told the FBI in 1963 that Queenie Simonelli had good contacts but that he, Simonelli, was not smart enough or courageous enough to be involved in any criminal activities. However, also in that same year, an informant to the FBI whom they said always gave good information told them that Dom "Butch" Blasi and Tarquin "Queenie" Simonelli were both "made" men in the Outfit.

In 1963 he was used on occasion as an emissary to lesser hoodlums by Sam Giancana. In April 1963 Giancana sent Simonelli to Las Vegas, Los Angeles and Palm Springs where he made contact with Frank Sinatra to deliver a message from Giancana.

You think being in the mob is a glamorous and existing job? You may think differently. In July 1963 FBI agents watched as Sam Giancana ran the Outfit from a golf cart at the Fresh Meadows Golf Club located at Wolf Road and 22nd Avenue in Hillside, Illinois. Giancana would be driven around the golf course, golfing, by mobster Chuckie English while Butch Blasi and Simonelli would sit by the public telephone booths inside the club house making and accepting phone calls. FBI agents watched as Blasi and Simonelli would receive a phone call, run out to whichever golf hole Giancana was at, give him the message, receive a new message, and run back to the club house to make a call. The two would repeat this hour after hour, day after day, until Giancana was done with his 18 holes of golf. FBI agents added that on the 17th hole one day, Giancana shot his ball into the rough and while looking for it he turned to see what Chuckie English was doing. When he noticed English was not looking at him, he picked up his ball and tossed it onto the fair way. You can't trust mobsters with anything, not even a fair golf game.

Even though Simonelli was just a runner he had a dangerous job. In 1964 he was hit in the head by one of Sam Giancana's golf balls and was hospitalized for 10 days.

FBI agents listened in on December 10, 1963 on Simonelli, Dominic "Butch" Blasi, Sam "Moe" Giancana, Chuckie English, John Matassa and Joseph "Pepe" Giancana, who they called "Andy" the entire night. The conversation revolved around the kidnapping of Frank Sinatra Jr. and who could have done it. The meal was ham and beans and Dom "Butch" Blasi made a sarcastic comment as everyone was not paying attention to playing cards, *"Boy, I have a lot of fun, not playing this game."*

FBI agents had listened the entire month of November and December 1963 and every day Simonelli, Blasi and English were together, either playing cards or discussing mob operations and law enforcement. On the 22nd of December they discussed how the River Forest Police were out there every day writing down license plate numbers on all the cars parked around the Armory Lounge.

Other discussions revolved around how they were making plans to attend the final show of entertainer Keeley Smith at the Palmer House with their families. Keeley Smith was one of Sam Giancana's girlfriends while he was in a relationship with entertainer Phyllis McGuire. Agents listened in as Simonelli discussed the situation with Doris Fanelli, then front owner of the Armory Lounge for Giancana, and how McGuire allegedly berated, insulted and belittled Giancana about Smith being in Chicago with him. Simonelli hoped Giancana and Smith would stay together over Giancana and McGuire.

FBI agents also discovered that Simonelli was Giancana's contact man for Frank "Buster" Wortman in East St. Louis Illinois and St. Louis, Missouri. Wortman was the Outfit boss in downstate Illinois.

Simonelli conversation that will live on forever

Queenie Simonelli's conversations with Sam Giancana and Chuckie English about the killing of President John F. Kennedy will always live on as an important piece of American history. FBI agents listened in on November 25, 1963 as the three watched the re-play of the funeral on TV and listened for any clues that would link Giancana or the mob to the killing.

Chuckie English and Queenie discussed how the FBI would not be interested in them as much anymore and would be going after the Fair Play for Cuba and anything Lee Harvey Oswald was involved with. Queenie added, *"Don't have to worry about this fucking joint when he walks in no more. The FBI guys around won't see nothing no more. They'll be looking for some service guys now. They'll be looking for that pro-Castro guy."*

A conversation into the killing of Kennedy took place between English, Simonelli and Sam Giancana. Giancana mentioned to Simonelli that he had not yet seen the slow motion movie of Kennedy being shot.

Then Chuckie English began singing the song "The Caissons Go Rolling Along" as Kennedy's funeral moved down the street which sparked a discussion about the description of what was being seen on the TV, a cortege, a coffin and a caisson which asked the question as to what a caisson was. English sarcastically commented to Queenie that there couldn't be a war today without it being on TV. Chuckie asked if Kennedy's body was actually in the casket going down the street and said he believed that Kennedy was the first to be given the "eternal flame" in America.

Then the three began discussing how other foreign leaders looked at the funeral. Chuckie commented that Charles de Gaulle from France was the outstanding one. Queenie wondered if Italy had anyone present attending the funeral which Chuckie replied that Italy's second-in-command was there.

Then the discussion turned to how and where Kennedy was shot. Chuckie pointed out that the President got hit in the face which Queenie remarked that he got hit twice. Giancana added that he understood that "this guy" Oswald was after the governor (John Connelly of Texas) who had been hit by one of the bullets that passed through Kennedy. Chuckie commented about Oswald, *"This 24-year-old kid was an anarchist. He was a Marxist Communist."* Giancana added, *"This was a marksman who knew how to shoot,"* to which Chuckie and Simonelli agreed. Chuckie also said he believed that Oswald didn't have an accomplice or he (Oswald) would never have gone home for his jacket and acted as he did.

Chuckie then added, *"That guy with the bullet in his chest and dying killed the investigation, they don't know if he had any other contacts or what. He had to go the hard way."*

After silence and watching more of the funeral Chuckie English commented that the hardest job in the cortege was the solider holding the frisky horse. Giancana and Chuckie agreed that Kennedy's words *"Ask not what your country can do for you"* will become as immortal as the words *"agayn, agayn, and agayn"* which President Franklin D. Roosevelt once said. Then all three agreed Jacqueline Kennedy had held up splendidly during the funeral.

Giancana then wondered if Lyndon B. Johnson, then the Vice President of the Unites States, could in the time before the election make himself acceptable so that he could run for election. Chuckie replied that Johnson would have to get rid of Bob Kennedy in order to solidify the south again. Giancana added that it will be interesting to see what Johnson does in the matter of replacing the president's cabinet. The conversation ended with criticism of all of Kennedy's personal effects being moved out from the White House *"before he was even cold."* Chuckie added that had Kennedy been in office another five years he would have become a dictator.

Queenie Simonelli's name will forever be part of the assassination records on the killing of John F. Kennedy along with Tony Accardo, Sam Giancana and Paul DeLucia.

In 1964 FBI agents attempted to find out how Tarquin Simonelli was receiving an income. On his taxes he wrote he was a "gambler" and received $20,000 from gambling operations with an additional; $2,200 from rent of a two-story brick building at 1312 South Cicero Avenue in Chicago. That building housed the Show of Show lounge, a Cicero vice den housing striptease dancers selling drinks to customers. The lounge was stripped of its liquor license but continued to serve alcohol until they were caught.

By 1965 Tarquin Simonelli was no longer a messenger man for Sam Giancana but was now his handy-man running tasks.

He had a problem in May 1965 with Sam Giancana. FBI agents had noticed Tarquin Simonelli at the Armory Lounge almost every day in February and March of that year when Giancana was in Chicago. Then the agents noticed in April and May, Simonelli had stopped showing up and he had not been seen anywhere. When the agents investigated they discovered that Sam Giancana had ordered Simonelli to stay away from the Armory Lounge because he was always getting too drunk in the establishment. Giancana told him once his behavior improved he would be allowed back. So agents found out Simonelli had been appearing daily at "The Spot" restaurant which became his new base of operations. However, "The Spot" restaurant had burnt down on December 27th which was ruled an "accidental" fire. Some time later investigators learned that the building which housed "The Spot" restaurant was a bar and kitchen on one side of the building and another restaurant on the other side with a two-foot-thick firewall separating the two. The restaurant side had just been remodeled and carried no insurance but "the Spot" side was very old and carried a $20,000 insurance policy. In the fire, only the bar and kitchen burned down but there was no damage to the restaurant side. In the wreckage of the burned-down side, firemen found an old-time machine gun that had been hidden somewhere on the bar side.

In June 1965 Tarquin was running a dice game at A.R. Tavern located at 5900 W. Roosevelt Road. The game was known as "Queenie's game" and was considered a big and profitable game. Agents learned that running the game with Simonelli was another outfit member who used to be with Joey Aiuppa.

By June 1966 Sam Giancana had been locked away in prison for almost year and FBI agents had still not seen Tarquin Simonelli coming around the Armory Lounge any more. They went to one of their trusted informants and asked *"what happened to Queenie?"* The informant told the agents he had not seen Queenie anywhere and *"had almost forgotten about him since he has not seen him."* Another informant in July of that year said it was possible Queenie may have gone to Miami in January 1966 and stayed there.

Queenie did turn up in May 1967 back in Chicago when he was seen at the Whiskey A-Go-Go Club in Lyons, Illinois. The club was believed to be owned by Jackie Cerone.

In February 1968 agents learned that Queenie had been working out of the Dream Bar and the Town Review Club in Cicero. Simonelli was now under the direction of Joey Aiuppa, acting as a runner or go-for-boy and selling daily double race track tickets.

In October 1968 an FBI informant told the FBI that Queenie Simonelli was now working as a pit boss at the Stardust Hotel and Casino in Las Vegas. The informant also added that Queenie's son was also allegedly employed at the Stardust as a dealer. However, when FBI agents examined his tax records in the years between 1968 thru 1970 there was no listing of Tarquin Simonelli working anywhere.

The 1970's seemed to be a rough time for Queenie Simonelli. In April 1970 Tarquin was seen back golfing everyday with Dominic "Butch" Blasi at Fresh Meadows Golf Club. In September of that year an informant told the feds that Queenie went to the Oak Brook Drake Hotel which had a bar in the basement called "The Lodge" during the day where he would cabaret with girls.

One informant in September 1971 told the FBI that Queenie was working as a flagman with a road crew either for the State of Illinois or Cook County. He was reported to be making $50 to $60 a day. In August 1972 Tarquin Simonelli was listed as being a part-time carpenter at McCormick Place working for the United Exposition Service Company. At the time, McCormick Place was under control of the Chicago Outfit. Most likely Queenie was never working as a flagger on a road crew or a carpenter at McCormick Place but was rather put on the payrolls as a "ghost worker" just to receive a paycheck but not actually have to go to work.

In November 1972 the FBI decided that Tarquin "Queenie" Simonelli was not involved in any criminal activities and there was no further point in investigating him since he was in a retired state. He was still listed as a "made" member of the Chicago Outfit.

One of the last reports came in June 1975 when Queenie was arrested by the Chicago Police Department and charged with theft under $150. Tarquin Simonelli died on March 1, 1985 and was waked at the Chrastka Memorial Chapel in Berwyn, Illinois. He is interned at Queen of Heaven Cemetery in Hillside, Illinois.

Spot Surveillance

April 25, 1962 – Tarquin Simonelli is observed at the wedding of Jackie Cerone's son.

August 1, 1962 – Tarquin Simonelli was observed at the wake of Mary Cerone, Jackie Cerone's mother.

November 27, 1962 – Tarquin Simonelli is observed at the wake of Alfonso Serritella.

May 3, 1963 – Tarquin Simonelli is observed meeting with mobster Sam English and Dom "Butch" Blasi at the Amber Lite Club, 5534 W. Cermak Road, Cicero.

November 9, 1963 – Tarquin Simonelli is observed at the wake of Angelina Sortino, the mother of mob boss Frank Ferraro.

May 22, 1964 – Tarquin Simonelli was observed at the wake of mobster Mike Spranze.

February 7, 1965 – Tarquin Simonelli and Butch Blasi are observed at King's Bay Country Club in Miami, Florida.

On March 2, 1965, Tarquin Simonelli was observed meeting at Maggio's Lounge, 7635 West Roosevelt Road. There he met with James Calabrese, Sam "Spanky"

Orangios, Fern Nanducci and William Nelson. The day before, an Outfit meeting was held at Maggio's, headed by Dominic "Butch" Blasi, Carmen Carducci, George Andel, Richard Miller and Joseph Basco of Melrose Park.

March 3, 1965 – Tarquin Simonelli, Sam Giancana, Butch Blasi and Tony Tisci arrive at the Armory Lounge and hold meetings with many individuals until 3 a.m.

June 1965 –Tarquin Simonelli was observed back at the Armory Lounge meeting with Fifi Buccieri, Dominic "Butch" Blasi, and Marshall Caifano.

June 30, 1965 – Tarquin Simonelli was ejected from Sportsman's Park Race Track for being an associate of Sam Giancana's. He was listed as an "undesirable."

January 1966 – Tarquin Simonelli and Jackie Cerone are observed at King's Bay Country Club in Miami, Florida.

File Card

Authors Collection

Tarquin Simonelli
AKA Queenie
AKA Thomas Seno
AKA Fred L. Carter
AKA T. J. Seno
Born July 15, 1916
Died March 1, 1985
SS# 358-03-6716
DL# S55480016201
FBI # 438006
Chicago PD # 13688
Height 5'6"
Weigth 162 (1963)
Hair Black
Eyes Brown
First Wife Mary Accardo (Obituaries say wife's name was Gloria)
Height 5'2"
Weight 132 (1963)
Hair Brown
Eyes Brown
SS# 338-03-6399
Son John
Daughter Sheila

Known Addresses

901 South Laflin, Chicago (1926- 1940's)
5724 North Meade Avenue, Chicago (1946)
1126 South Monitor Street, Chicago (1947)
1922 S. Wenonah Avenue, Berwyn, Illinois (1954)
915 Franklin Avenue, River Forest (As of 1963 the Simonelli's were said to be living in the six room apartment guesthouse of the Accardo mansion)
601 Selbourne, Riverside, Illinois (1960's-1968)
5550 West Van Buren, Chicago (1961) (Gave this address during arrest in Indiana)
10620 Cermak Road, Apartment #2 W, Westchester, Illinois (Leased apartment at $260-a-month) (July 1968-1970's)

Known Vehicles of Simonelli

1961 Ford, Blue, License plate # KK 2283
1963 Pontiac 4-door Vista, License plate # 838387
1963 Pontiac royal blue Bonneville Sports Coupe, license plate # 838387
1965 New Orchid Pontiac Bonneville, license plate # 564817
1965 Pontiac grey and black, license plate # 828132
1968 Chevrolet Coupe
1968 Lincoln

Known Arrest Record

Date	Charge	Agency	
1926	Disorderly Conduct	Chicago PD	
1926	Disorderly Conduct	Chicago PD	
1-12-1936	Traffic Violation	Chicago PD	
1-22-1936	Traffic Violation	Chicago PD	
6-4-1937	Traffic Violation	Chicago PD	
2-27-1939	Disorderly Conduct	Chicago PD	
2-1939	Traffic Violation	Chicago PD	
2-1940	Investigation	Chicago PD	
9-6-1959	Gambling	Cook County States Atty.	
6-6-1960	Traffic Violation	Culver, Indiana	
6-11-1975	Theft	Chicago PD	$180 fine

CITY OF CHICAGO / **DEPARTMENT OF POLICE** 1121 South State Street Chicago 5, Illinois WAbash 2-4747
IDENTIFICATION SECTION

ARREST RECORD OF Simonelli, Tarquin

DATE 23 Aug 63

DATE OF BIRTH Aged 23 on 11 Jan 36

NAME & ADDRESS	C.B. NO.	DATE OF ARREST	ARRESTING OFFICER & DIST.	CHARGE	DISPOSITION
~~Tarquin Simonelli~~ 901 S. Laflin St. Chicago		~~11 Jan 36~~	~~Ofcr Lenert & Obrien~~	~~Susp.~~	~~Robbery~~
		21 Jan 36	Susp 22nd Dist		
		20 Feb 39	Susp 26th Dist		
		15 May 43	Susp 5-B		
Thomas Seno		6 Sep 59	States Atty Office, Inv.		

I.R. NO.

FBI NO.

S.B. NO.

CPD-22.466 (REV.3/62)

Here is a February 20, 1939 arrest photo of Tarquin Simonelli (listed as number 1 on Left) and an unknown mobster.

CONFIDENTIAL

NAME	:	SIMONELLI, TARQUIN 601 Selbourne North Riverside, Illinois
ALIASES	:	"Queenie" - Fred Carter - Thomas Sene
DESCRIPTION	:	M/W, D.O.B. 15 July 1916, 5'-5", 140 lbs. brown hair, brown eyes, Italian decent.
LOCALITIES FREQUENTED	:	Western Suburbs.
FAMILY BACKGROUND	:	Subject is a Brother In-Law to Tony Accardo. Wife: Mary Daughter: Shiela.
CRIMINAL ASSOCIATES	:	Tony Accardo; Sam Giancanna; Rocco Fischetti; Les Kruse; Gus Liebe; Phil Alderisio; Joe Glimco;
CRIMINAL HISTORY	:	Subject was arrested in 1936, suspicion of Robbery, Discharged. He has been arrested four times since. In 1959 he was arrested in a large gambling raid in a South West Suburb.
BUSINESS	:	Subject is alleged to have a financial interest in a South West Suburb lounge.
MODUS OPERANDI	:	The subject's past activities have been in the gambling field, predominantly in the suburban areas.

NAME (LAST)	(FIRST)	(MIDDLE)	SOC. SEC. NO.	FILE NO.
SIMONELLI	TARQUIN			

NICKNAME OR ALIAS	TYPE OF ACTIVITY	I.R. NO.
"Queenie"		

HOME ADDRESS	CITY	HOME PHONE NO.	F.B.I. NO.
601 Selbourne	No. Riverside, Ill		

BUSINESS ADDRESS	CITY	BUSINESS PHONE NO.	TYPE OF BUSINESS

NEW ADDRESS	CITY	NEW PHONE NO.	PHOTO REF. NO.

SEX	RACE	DESCENT	D.O.B.	HEIGHT	WEIGHT	HAIR	EYES
Male	White	Italian	7-15-16	5'5"	140	Brown	Brown

COMPLEXION — PECULIARITIES, MARKS, SCARS, ETC.

ASSOCIATES: Wife-Mary Accardo--Brother in law Anthony Accardo, Sam Giancanna

HANGOUTS: Maggio's Steak House

VEHICLE INFORMATION

CPD-36.331 (REV.2/62) FACE CARD — SEE REVERSE SIDE FOR MISC. INFORMATION

Subject at one time a bodyguard for Martin Accardo. He is known to have been picking up lay off bets in the loop. Known to be closely associated with the old Capone gang and was working at the Vernon Country Club when it was operated by Rocco Fischetti. Is said to be the operator of the Dream Lounge, 1312 S. Cicero Ave, Cicero, Ill

Taiquin Simonelli head stone at Queen of Heaven Cemetery

1-4 (Rev. 1-19-61)

UNITED STATES DEPARTMENT OF JUSTICE
FEDERAL BUREAU OF INVESTIGATION
WASHINGTON 25, D. C.

4-22-63

J. Edgar Hoover
Director.

The following FBI record, NUMBER none assigned, is furnished FOR OFFICIAL USE ONLY.

CONTRIBUTOR OF FINGERPRINTS	NAME AND NUMBER	ARRESTED OR RECEIVED	CHARGE	DISPOSITION
State's Atty's Off Chicago Ill	Thomas Seno #PI 313	FP 9-6-59	1. consp. (gamb) 2. keeper of gamb estab.	

1971

FEB-16-71 6485 00 H J -- 345 30.00

TARQUIN SIMONELLI
10620 CERMAK RD
WESTCHESTER ILL 60150

AV 142
560

PASSENGER CAR

164478F155400 COOK RIVERSO

1968 CHEVROLET COUPE 8 51.2

3554-8001-6201 358-03-6716

Tarquin Simonelli

51,2 HORSEPOWER REQUIRES PLATE FEE OF $30,00

C 318559

APPROVED

THE FOLLOWING QUESTIONS MUST BE ANSWERED.

YOUR LICENSE PLATES NOW SUSPENDED OR REVOKED? YES ☐ NO ☑

REGISTERED OWNER(S) DATE OF BIRTH? MO. July DAY 15 YEAR 1916

(SEAL)

029466 00128 41 $30.00 $30.00
A 211183
STATE OF ILLINOIS PAUL POWELL SECRETARY OF STATE

164478 F 155400 TITLE NO. C 318559

Chevrolet 1968 Imp. 2 Dr. H.T. 8

SIMONELLI, Tarquin

601 Selbourne

Riverside ILL 60546 Cook

Tarquin Simonelli 358-03-6716

CICERO STATE BANK
2446 South Cicero Avenue
Cicero Illinois 60650 $2,311.20

APPLICANT MUST SIGN FULL NAME
FOLLOW THE INSTRUCTIONS ON THE REVERSE SIDE

ALLEN CHEVROLET, INC.

THIS VEHICLE OPERATED FOR HIRE NOT FOR HIRE ☑

PRINT OR TYPEWRITE. USE BLACK INK ONLY

DO NOT SEND CURRENCY OR STAMPS

APPLICATION FOR CERTIFICATE OF TITLE

Tarquin Simonelli's Driver's License and FBI Rap Sheet

Tony Dark

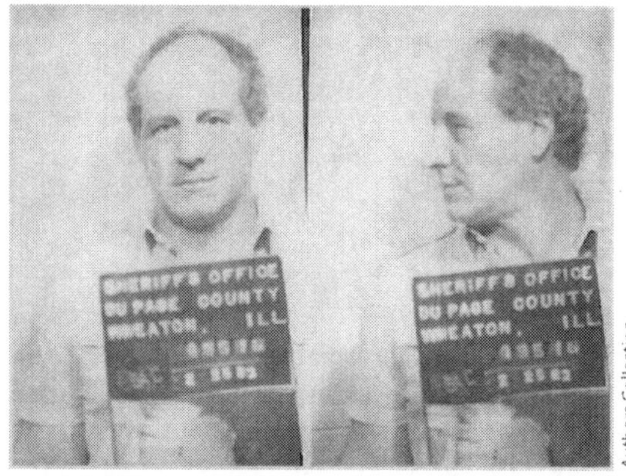

Authors Collection

In 1983 Tarquin's son, John Simonelli, aka Larry, was indicted by a DuPage County, Illinois grand jury on auto theft charges. John died in June 2013 at the age of 70.

In February 1984 Tarquin's daughter, Sheila Simonelli, was arrested in a FBI sting involving the attempted sale of $24 million dollars worth of stolen bonds at 25 cents on the dollar in an Oak Brook, Illinois hotel. Simonelli and her accomplices, William Doria, Vernon Seymour and Barbara and Daniel Kegg, were all arrested when the buyers turned out to be undercover FBI agents.

Sheila Simonelli had a two-shot Derringer pistol hidden in her bra. The bonds had been stolen from Kennedy International Airport in New York in 1973 and had been "buried" for 11 years waiting to be sold.

Simonelli, using the alias of Sheila Montalla, owned the Shelibar Lounge with the Kegg's, and Vernon Seymour was one of the help at the tavern. Sheila Simonelli pleaded guilty to charges of conspiracy and interstate transportation of stolen securities and was given a maximum sentence of 3 years in prison.

Tony Accardo's Sons-in-laws

Tony Accardo's son-in-law was Palmer Pyle, a one time professional football player who married Accardo's daughter Marie. At the time of their marriage in the early 1960's, Pyle was playing for the Baltimore Colts Football Team in Baltimore, Maryland. His brother was Mike Pyle was a former Chicago Bears lineman. They had three children, Craig, Eric and Cheryl.

William Palmer Pyle Jr.
Born June 6, 1937, Keokuk, Iowa
College Michigan State University
Position: Offensive Guard

Mob Boss

NFL Draft: 1960 / Round 6, Pick 72 / Played in 61 games / Started 15 games.
NFL Teams: Baltimore Colts (1960-1963)
Minnesota Vikings (1964)
Oakland Raiders (1966)

Accardo's Son-in-law Ernest Kumerow

Marie divorced Palmer Pyle and married Ernest Kumerow. Marie, and her three children all changed their last name to Kumerow. Ernest himself was once a baseball pitcher spending time in the minors. In 1982 Tony Accardo son-in-law Ernest Kumerow was chosen as president of Local 1001 of the Municipal Employees and Foreman Union of Chicago to replace outgoing mob president Joseph Spingola. In 1987 Kumerow was appointed as President of the Chicago District Council of Labor replacing mobster James Caporale. Many alleged that Kumerow was given both positions on orders from Tony Accardo.

FBI informant Mike Corbitt testified that he observed Ernest Kumerow, Tony Accardo and Joey Aiuppa holding a business meeting in a private dinning room on many occasions. Kumerow was also alleged to be observed meeting with mobsters Vince Solano, Pat Marcy, John Spano and John Serpico. When Tony Accardo died in 1994 Kumerow left the union and retired on a hefty pension. In 1997 Ernest Kumerow was listed by law enforcement as a alleged Chicago mob associate.

Ernest Kumerow son's and Accardo's grandson, Craig Kumerow, was placed in the Chicago District Council as a Delegate in 1989 and had a position as a field representative in Local 1001 until the early 2000's. Craig had been an Indiana Hoosier football player in the late 1970's and early 1980's.

Accardo's other grandson, Eric "Ernie" Kumerow, was born in 1965. Being 6-foot-7, 268-pounds, he was a standout football player at Oak Park High School and an all American linebacker at Ohio State University. In 1988 he was drafted in the first round of the NFL draft by the Miami Dolphins Football team. He was the 16th pick overall and put on the roster as a defensive end. After three seasons with the Dolphins he played one year with the Chicago Bears football team. His football career did not live up to expectations as he never started an NFL game and only recorded five quarterback sacks. He suffered a Achilles injury.

Intelligence reports stated that in November 1989 Eric and his sister, Cheryl Layne Kumerow, were arrested outside a Ft. Lauderdale nightclub. Police were called when a fight was reported at the Koz's bar. Eric, Cheryl and a friend named Robert Skelton, who was from Chicago, were arrested and charged with trespassing, while both Eric and Cheryl were charged with two felony counts of assaulting a police officer after allegedly punching one of the officers twice outside the club. Eric was also charged with resisting arrest. One eyewitness to the incident claimed the group, including the Kumerow's, was "drunk." Also with Eric at the bar was Dolphins defensive end John Bosa.

The Kumerow's put together a bank of lawyers to handle the situation. After posting bond, the Kumerow's agent, Herb Ruboy, said that the *"story as relayed by police is not true. Eric came to the rescue of a friend of his who was badly beaten at the bar. Eric was pounced on by about 10 bouncers and later by police officers."*

Months later Eric had been sentenced to 1 year probation after being charged with resisting an officer with violence. The plea also included Eric making a $1,000 contribution to a charity of his choice and performing 60 hours of community service.

F ④

BROWARD COUNTY

15738

COMPLAINT/AFFIDAVIT

SHADED FIELDS MUST BE ANSWERED IF DEFENDANT NOT IN CUSTODY

ARREST FORM 8123

10-29-54

ARRESTING OFFICERS: Cutler/ Sanders

CCN: 771/1011

UNIT: C 20 148

SHIFT: 3

DATE ARRESTED: 11-5-89

TIME ARREST: 2256

PLACE OF ARREST: 20 N Federal Hwy

NAME OF VICTIM: Koz's

ADDRESS: #20 N. Fed. Hwy Ft Laud.

COUNT NO	OFFENSES CHARGED		FS NO OR CAPIAS/WARRANT NO
1 & 2	Battery L.E.O.	Fel.	784.07
3	Trespass	Msd	810.09

PROBABLE CAUSE AFFIDAVIT

Before me this date personally appeared Cutler William M who being first duly sworn deposes and says that on the 5 day of Nov 19 89 at #20 N Federal Hwy the above named defendant committed the above offenses charged and the facts showing probable cause to believe same are as follows:

Responded to Koz's Bar at above location in reference to a fight in the parking lot. Def. was involved in a previous fight inside the bar and told to leave the property by the victim. The def. along with 5 to 6 others returned a short time later at which point these officers made contact with the group. The entire group were very aggitated , stating that they were going to " Get the guy" who haD STRUCK THEIR FRIEND. This officer attempted to stop the group at which time one subject began to fight with Officer Sanders. The def. then jumped on Officer Sanders back and began to strike him. Officer Cutler then attempted to remove the subject from the officers back, he was on the ground at which time she began striking Officer Cutler in the chest area and kicking my legs. The def. was placed under arrest and transported to Jail. Both Officer s received minor lacerations and bruises to arms, legs and chest area.

Sworn to and subscribed before me, this 6 day of November 19 89

I swear the above statement is correct and true to the best of my knowledge and belief

Mob Boss

Investigation reports state that Craig Kumerow had a brush with the law in 1995 which lead to his mug shot being taken. In 2001 both Craig and Eric "Ernie" Kumerow opened the Sportsplex Athletic Facility at 1400 Foundry Street in St. Charles, Illinois. The complex had two indoor fields that could be covered to hold soccer games, lacrosse games, flag football games, and large entertainment events. It was speculated the complex made over $300,000 a year.

In 2009 Craig Kumerow's son Colton was involved in a car accident in which one teenager was killed. The sports utility vehicle Colton was a passenger in lost control and went off a road and became wedged between two trees. It was reported and alleged that the driver of the vehicle's blood-alcohol level was determined to be three times over the legal limit. The driver also allegedly tested positive for marijuana. The Kumerow's were seeking $50,000 in a personal injury lawsuit at the time.

<u>File Card</u>

Craig J. Kumerow
Born in 1960
Wife Gina Cimino Kumerow
Son Colton Kumerow

Dominic Senese

Tony Accardo's sister Martha married Anthony Senese. In 1950 Anthony Senese was placed into Local 110 of the Motion Picture Union in Chicago as a projector operator by Tony Accardo.

There is a report that stated that they had two sons, and other reports stating they had 3 sons. One son was said to be named Frank Senese but no information was discovered. Another son named Nick Senese was said to be killed by a Puerto Rican in a barroom brawl at 3221 West 5th Avenue on March 5, 1960. Nick Senese was said to be speculating in real estate on the east side of Chicago which may have had a bearing on the fight and shooting that killed him. The last son named Dominic Senese was placed into Chicago union Local 703 of the Teamsters union as a business agent who had control of the Chicago Fulton Street Market.

Dominic "Big Banana" Senese was born in 1917 and was a $98,000-a-year labor union president. Dominic Senese began his career in the 1950's as a strong-arm enforcer for Joey Glimco in the Fulton market area of Chicago. A work agreement had to be kept at all times in the market between Teamsters and produce dealers. It was Senese's job to see that the trucks kept delivering his produce smoothly. With his good work ethics of following Glimco's orders, he was promoted to Secretary-Treasurer of Local 703. Incidents in Dom Senese's life linking him to organized crime and its figures are:

1) Dom Senese and Vic Conforti, another union boss hoodlum under Joey Glimco, were part owners in the Broadway Sheet Metal Works Company in which they held lucrative government subcontracts. With Broadway Sheet Metal Company being located at 1635 South Clinton Street in Chicago they were able to get 50 percent of all the sheet metal work on construction sites in Chicago. Another business Senese made a fortune with was Vernon Farm Products Company which supplied wholesale eggs to the Fulton Street Market area in Chicago. Other owners of that company were Conforti, Frank V. Pantaleo, and Dominic's brother, Frank Senese. Pantaleo was one of Charles "Cherry Nose" Gioe's guys in the construction business who had become close with Glimco. In 1952, Joey Glimco hired Pantaleo to build a new office at his headquarters. He was paid $85,325 for this work. During the McClellan Committee Senate hearings, an expert testified that the job should have cost no more than $35, 803.

2) In 1959, Dominick Senese was called to testify in a U.S. Senate Rackets Committee investigation of mob operations in the produce markets. Senese took the 5th Amendment to every question placed to him. Also questioned was Joseph Aiello, who was reported as head of the Chicago Hod Carriers union and Local B-18 of the Picture Frame Workers Union. Aiello and Michael Gaglione, president of the picture frame workers local, attended gangster funerals and other events and were often seen in the company of other mob labor union bosses such as James Caporale, Vince Solano Sr., and Frank and Anthony "Tony X" Esposito.

3) In 1961, Dominic Senese and his wife were subpoenaed to testify in a federal grand jury investigating alleged "sweetheart" contracts between the National Maintenance Company, a janitorial service, and McCormick Place. Other hoodlums who were subpoenaed were Louis Arger, who was being labeled as Gus Alex's cousin, Joe Pavelo, Ben Stein, an ex-convict close to Milwaukee Phil Alderisio, and Sylvester "Two Gun Pete" Washington, a saloon owner and one-time Chicago police officer who toted two guns and killed at least nine men in 18 years before retiring in 1951.

4) In June 1962 an informant for the FBI told agents that he was summoned to a meeting with "Outfit" people. Heading the meeting was Ben "Foggie" Fillichio who was acting as a representative for Tony Accardo. At the meeting the group questioned someone about their involvement in some situation and Dom Senese was seen whispering in Fillichio's ear in Italian that *"he was going to crack"* under questioning.

5) In 1963 mobster Manny Skar told one of the FBI's informants that Dominic Senese had threatened to kill him if a debt owed to Victor Conforti was not paid off. Conforti and Senese pursued Skar to Palm Springs and Beverly Hills in an attempt to collect the $35,000 owed to them. The problem was Skar did not have the money. Allegedly Skar had his wife Bea Skar, who was listed as an intimate friend of mob boss Sam Giancana, to intercede on Manny's behalf. It worked and Dominic Senese never threatened Skar again. However, in 1965 Dominic Senese and Victor Conforti were listed as prime suspects in Manny Skar's murder.

6) Some time in the 1960's mob lawyer Joseph Bulger and Dom Senese arranged a loan for $1 million dollars through James Hoffa's Teamsters Union for the Northlake Community Hospital in Northlake, Illinois. The deal went south when one of the original owners of the hospital, Dr. Giulio Bruni, was convicted and sent to prison for counterfeiting.

7) In 1966 an FBI informant with some stature in the Chicago Outfit told the FBI that Dominic Senese had become the "right-hand-man" of mobster Joey Glimco. Because of this, Dom Senese was "made" and was scouted to be a "rapidly progressing" person in the Outfit.

8) In 1967 Dom Senese had a meeting with an Outfit associate who was acting as an informant for the FBI. Senese tried to convince this informant to purchase a load of stolen cosmetics which he had just received. The informant passed.

Dominic Senese remained in his union position throughout the years without any obstacles in his way. In 1975, the Joint Italian American Civic Committee of Chicago named Dominic Senese man of the year.

Dominic had most of his family on the payroll of Teamsters unions in the 1970's. One was a Joe Senese, which one report lists him as a nephew of Dominic, who was a business agent in Chicago Local 710 of the Teamsters union in the 1970's. He represented the office worker segment of membership in Local 710. Joe Senese had once worked for Specter Freight Lines. He died of a heart attack in 1976.

In 1979 and 1983 Dominic Senese ran for president of the Teamster Local Council 25 and lost both times to Louis Peick. Peick was a tough labor leader who on occasion would resist mob wishes in the labor field even though he was very close to mob labor union bosses. Mob associate William T. Hogan Sr. replaced Peick in 1986.

In 1985 Senese was observed meeting with mob associate Ben Stein concerning their partnership in a maintenance company. Senese was in the middle of taking over the South Water Market area in Chicago. He was also involved in washing mob money using the Chicago Mercantile Exchange.

On January 23, 1988, Dominic Senese was leaving his posh home in the exclusive Saddle Brook Chase subdivision in Oak Brook when he stopped his car at his security gate to open it. Once Senese was outside the car, a mob assassin jumped out of the bushes and put a shotgun to Senese's face pulling the trigger. The blast took off the lower part of his face and knocked him back into his Lincoln Town car. The mob assassin shot once more blowing out the side window. Believing his job was complete, the assassin fled, but Senese was not dead, in fact he was able to drive back to his house where his wife Sadie called the authorities. Senese was taken to Loyola University Medical Center where he stayed for more that three weeks. He had to have plastic surgery to repair the damage from the shotgun blast but once out, he returned to work at the union offices with bodyguards and a nurse by his side.

FBI agents believed that Dominic Senese and then top mob boss Joseph Ferriola who was running the day-to-day operations of the outfit, had problems with each other and Ferriola did not like how Senese was running his union in the produce markets. Ferriola was a neighbor of Senese's in Oak Brook.

A few weeks after the attack reports suggested that Senese had cut a deal with the Chicago Outfit to call off the contract on his life. The alleged deal was that he would retire from the union and leave Chicago once his health allowed him to do so. It was learned that the mob assassin had fled to Florida after he bungled the mob hit on Senese. He was reported to be a top member of the Cicero mob under the direction of Ferriola and an outfit bookie.

It was alleged that Dominic's son, Lucien, might have been involved in the planning of the attack on his father because he would have benefited from it. However nothing was ever proved. Lucien Senese had started out as a truck driver until he took over as Secretary-Treasurer of Local 703 in 1983. Dominic made him a $98,000-a-year union official and heir apparent to the union presidency.

FBI agents testified that in 1987 they went to Senese and told him that his life was in danger but Senese ignored them. After the attempt on his life, he ignored the deal he may have made with the Outfit and was re-elected as president over challengers William Romondi, former vice president of Local 703, and Chuck Plaia. Romondi complained that the election was rigged and that Senese used strong-arm tactics to intimidate voters, handed out envelopes of money, and refused to count the votes of members who worked for the Chicago Park District. He also accused Lucien Senese of physically attacking him by punching him in the mouth and swinging his knee at his groin. Because Romondi ran against Senese, after the election, Senese stripped Romondi of all his union power. Romondi switched to Local 738.

Neither Dominic nor his son Lucien got the message with the murder attempt. On September 6, 1990, Lucien left his girlfriend's home in Little Italy and walked to his car. Once inside he tried to start the car but it would not start, instead, it exploded sending the entire back of the car flying in every direction. Lucien made his way out of the car with his clothes on fire and his skin dripping off his body. Residents came running to the scene but all they could do was put the fire out on Lucien clothes. He was taken to Cook County Hospital and lived.

Newspaper reports stated that Lucien was known as a loudmouth bully who was always upsetting his father and brother Joseph.

One week before the explosion, a federal judge ordered Dominic Senese to give up his position in the Teamsters because of his organized crime ties. The National Teamsters Union entered into a consent decree with the government in 1989 to appoint three administrators to take control of union affairs. As a result, Dominic Senese was expelled from the union on July 13.

His son was allegedly slated to take his father's place as president. However, it was alleged the up-and-coming mobsters of the day back then feared Lucien was just going to take orders from his father and ignore mob bosses so they ordered him killed or scared away for good.

During the investigation as to who planted the bomb, it was learned that the day before Lucien had sent a letter to the international union complaining that Teamsters Local 738, its Secretary-Treasurer Peter Agliata, son-in-law to Joseph Ferriola, and William Romondi were meddling in the Local 703 election and organizing activities. The bomb may have been in retaliation for the trouble Lucien was causing. The case may still be open today.

Joe Fosco, a descendant of mobsters, and writer for the America News Post, wrote that Dom Senese would smoke an entire carton of cigarettes in one day. Fosco added the reason for the shooting of Senese was that Senese and mob boss Sam Carlisie were in a power struggle over financial issues relating to a produce company. Fosco alleged that Carlisie and alleged mob underboss John "No Noise" DiFronzo made plans to have Senese killed. Allegedly Anthony "The Hatch" Chiaramonti, Anthony "Little Tony" Zizzo, Rudy Fratto Jr. and Johnny Matassa Jr. were sent to perform the failed hit. To date, none of the above have ever been charged for this attempted murder. Years later Anthony Chiaramonti was killed in a mob hit and Anthony Zizzo disappeared and has never been found.

In 1990 Dominic Senese, Joseph Talerico, James Cozzo and Joseph Glimco Sr. were charged by investigating officers looking into union corruption. At the time Joey Glimco had a medical condition and was put off until he recovered.

Dominic Senese was charged with violating Article II of the International Brotherhood of Teamsters Union constitution by conducting himself in a manner un-becoming of a union official by belonging to and associating with members of La Cosa Nostra, such as mob bosses Joey Aiuppa and Jackie Cerone. A mob underboss in the Cleveland mob named Angelo Lonardo confirmed to FBI agents that Dominic Senese was a "made" member of the Chicago Outfit.

Joseph Talerico, a Business Agent in Chicago Teamsters Local 727, was charged by the union for refusing to answer a federal grand jury investigation into skimming of funds from a Las Vegas casino and knowingly associating with Chicago mobsters Joey Aiuppa and Philip Ponto.

James Cozzo, an Executive Coordinator of Chicago Local 786, was charged with being a member of La Cosa Nostra and knowingly associating with mob boss Joey "The Clown" Lombardo.

Dominic Senese died of natural causes on January 29, 1992 in his Oak Brook home. After his death, the family dynasty formed by Senese came crashing down. In April of 1993, the federal government issued a barred-for-life sentence for Lucien Senese and he was ousted just like his father and permanently barred from the I.B. of T. Members of his union were suing his brother Joseph. Allegedly Joseph had spent large amounts of union money, $483,000 in one year, to provide around the clock security so no one in the Outfit could get to him to hurt him. Vice President Frank Stroud sued to have Joe Senese pay the money back to the union.

Also disciplined were James Bertino and William Raimondi. Raimondi had been appointed as Local 703's vice president by Dominic Senese in 1978. Both were ordered suspended for two years for their suspected mob involvement in the union.

In October 2000 Lucien Senese fought for disability from the Teamsters pension fund claiming he was left disabled after the car bomb.

In 1981 a Joseph R. Senese, listed as Dominic's son, was listed as president of Local 707 of the National Production Workers Union representing 18,000 members. He was also president of Local 707 which represented the taxi drivers in Chicago. In 1981 during a cab workers strike, Joseph Senese's car was set on fire.

On January 19, 1991 Joseph Senese, Hosen Oshita, Donald Pirkins, and Robert Gifford of the Independent National Production Workers Union were ordered by the Department of Labor to pay back $140,000 to the union's insurance trust fund. They were accused of steering fraudulent dental insurance coverage to Consultants and Administrators Incorporated between 1983 and 1987. The company was run by Paul Fosco, son of one-time Laborers Union president Angelo Fosco and grandson of mob labor union boss Peter Fosco.

As of 2014, Joseph Senese was still a union boss for the National Production Workers Union controlling around 600 members. In a 2013 article it mentioned that Joseph Senese was paid $591,346 in 2012 for his role in controlling the National Production Workers Union. The article mentions that Senese issued hundreds of thousands of dollars in cash loans back to the union. It also alleged that Joseph continued for decades to spent large sums of union money on 24-hour-a-day security to protect him.

Most believed Dominic Senese's life was due to him being related to Tony Accardo. And they may be right.

COPY OF ARREST RECORD

SURNAME / GIVEN NAME AND MIDDLE INITIAL: SENESE, DOMINIC
ALIAS IN FULL:
ARRESTED BY: 27 DIST. BUR.
ADDRESS: 2118 Flournoy
BOOKED AT: 27 DIST. BUR.
MALE / FEMALE: Male
AGE: 24 | WEIGHT: 180 | HEIGHT: 5 " 10
MARKS, SCARS, ETC.:
COLOR: WHITE / NEGRO / OTHER
COMPLEXION: LIGHT / RUDDY / DARK — Dark
BUILD: SLENDER / MEDIUM / STOUT — Medium
COLOR OF EYES: BLACK / BLUE / BROWN / GRAY — Brown
COLOR OF HAIR: BLACK / GRAY / BROWN / BLONDE / RED / WHITE — Brown
MARRIED / SINGLE
NATIVITY
CITIZEN / NON CITIZEN
DATE AND PLACE OF BIRTH | OCCUPATION | SOCIAL SECURITY NO.
HOW LONG A RESIDENT OF CHICAGO? | WHERE EMPLOYED | WERE PRINTS TAKEN YES / NO
ADDRESS OF ARREST: 2748 Van Buren A.M. P.M. | GROUP PHOTO NO. | B. OF I. NO.
TIME AND DATE OF ARREST: A.M. P.M.
ARRESTING OFFICERS: Kelliher - Sloan - O'Keefe
CHARGES: Par 84 - Ch 38 (Burglary)
COMPLAINANT: L. Lavin
ADDRESS: 1155 North Cicero Ave.
HELD TO GRAND JURY | DATE | COURT BRANCH | JUDGE
BOND OF
COURT DISPOSITION: Sup until 6-7-50
DATE OF DISPOSITION: 11-2-49 | JUDGE: Drucker | COURT: 42

ADDITIONAL ARRESTS ON OTHER SIDE

445 F. J. Nenning & Son, Chicago

Anthony and Frances Cosentino

Anthony Cosentino is mentioned here because he was investigated as the first cousin of Tony Accardo. It was never determined by investigators if this was true or not, but Anthony and Frances Cosentino were the owners of O.K. Motor Service, a company that employed Tony Accardo and were very close to the Accardo family. Investigators speculated that the Cosentino's were somehow related to Accardo because of the amount of business steered their way by Accardo.

Their names are mentioned in 1939 when mobster Charles Gioe told investigators that he was a general manager of O.K. Motors in Chicago for seven years. Gioe claimed his duties were only routine office work and he frequently changed offices with the manager of the Milwaukee office. He added he had nothing to do with the truck or the garage and that the company performed local and long distance hauling by contracts.

One report stated that Frances Cosentino was a partner with Tony Accardo in O.K. Motors and was used as a front and as a pay-off spot for use by the Outfit.

A Chicago police report dated 10-29-1949 gave information that a Frank Accardo, with the alias of Frank M. Allen, living at 1812 S. Austin, was employed as an office manager of O.K. Motors and that he and his father operated the Circle Club at 5534 W. Cermak Road in Chicago. It was never determined who this Frank Accardo was but the Circle Club at that time was used as a gathering place by Tony Accardo and his brother Martin.

Investigators knew O.K. Motors was connected to mob operations because in 1949 the offices of O.K. Motors were receiving phone calls from mobster Mickey Cohen who controlled the mob in Los Angels, California.

A 1950 report stated that the first wife of one of the senior Cosentino's was married to the sister of Capone gangster Laurence "Dago" Mangano.

In September 1951 Anthony Cosentino and his wife, Grace, were beaten by three mask men. Anthony had been driving home from a relative's home when his car broke down in front of the home at 5948 Division Street in Chicago. He had pulled over and was fixing his car when he was attacked. The three masked men pounced on Anthony, using their fists, feet and a lead pipe knocking him unconscious. After the men attacked Cosentino they turned to Grace; while one of the men held Grace's one-year-old daughter, Antonio Lee, she began to scream causing panic among the thugs. One of the men turned and punched Grace in the face knocking her to the ground. The three men ran and jumped into a waiting car and sped away. Anthony suffered a fractured skull, deep cuts on his head and had most of his right ear severed.

It was learned by investigators that months earlier in May 1951 Anthony had told his wife that he was going out to purchase some soft drinks but didn't return. He had $1,500 in cash on him and left in his very expensive car. Authorities conducted a search at the horse stables he owned in Des Plaines, Illinois where he had several Palomino ponies but he was nowhere to be found. Several days later he returned and told the police he had been in Milwaukee, Wisconsin on business. Police found the story suspicious at the time. They concluded that the men who had attacked Cosentino in September had tampered with his car and followed him knowing the car would eventually break down so they could attack him. Since no one was robbed during the attack, police believed Anthony Cosentino was not being honest with them about why the men attacked him. Investigators never did get to the truth about the matter.

In 1952 Anthony Cosentino was subpoenaed to appear before a Chicago City Council Crime Committee. Once he took the stand for questioning he was quoted as saying that he did not know why he was being called. The panel explained to him it was because of his relationship with Tony Accardo. Cosentino had nothing to say on that matter.

Anthony Cosentino would spend Chicago winters at his up-scale home in Palm Springs. He was also given the key to the city in Palm Springs by the mayor in 1957.

In 1959 during Tony Accardo's tax trial Anthony Cosentino stormed out of the Federal Grand Jury room complaining that he was not being treated properly by the grand jury. He said he was an honest man and did not see why he had to go through this. Cosentino told reporters, *"In 1942 I borrowed $15,000 from Accardo. That was before Accardo was a big shot, he was nothing then. I soon* *found out that he wanted half of my company so I borrowed from somebody else and gave him his money back. He hasn't spoken to me since."* He continued, *"This is ridiculous, it's terrible, it's not justice. I brought in all the records I have. What do they want – blood? I asked them if they could investigate me without hauling me down here. Then the government attorney got up and made a big grandstand speech about me not cooperating."*

The government attorney did not believe Cosentino when they asked him to bring in all his records since 1948 and he did not. Cosentino told the court that a fire had destroyed all the records of the trucking firm in 1956 and that any papers that had to do with Accardo had also been destroyed.

In 1960 FBI agents overheard Jimmy Celano, a Chicago mob associate and close friend of Accardo's, discussing that Anthony Cosentino hauled all of the beer for the various distributors from Chicago breweries. He also mentioned that Cosentino had set him up in a few "nice deals" bringing in some good money.

Investigators found it suspicious that Consentino claims of having nothing to do with any mobsters were true. If that was the case, how did he manage two years later to get the exclusive highly pursued trucking rights on Schlitz Beer from Milwaukee to Chicago and St. Louis without help from people in power? Consentino had nothing to say.

Another story concerning a Cosentino occurred in the late 1960's when Tony Accardo helped Ursula Cosentino. Ursula was diagnosed with cancer and wanted to go to a cancer research hospital in New York City but was refused admission. So Cosentino turned to Tony Accardo for help. Accardo agreed and contacted a highly placed government official in Washington D.C. who secured admission for Cosentino. Ursula Cosentino registered her occupation as Vice President of O.K. Motor Service in Chicago. It was not known if she lived.

File Card

Anthony F. Cosentino
Born around 1897
Wife Grace Cosentino
Brother Frances Cosentino

Known Home Addresses

6039 Roscoe Street, Chicago (1930's)
906 Lathrop, River Forest, Illinois (1951)
1185 Tachevah Drive, Palm Springs, California (1955)
5075 N. Shore, Lincolnwood, Illinois (1959)

Known Businesses

O.K. Motor Service Garage, 361 North Morgan, Chicago (1931), 620 May Street, Chicago (1948) & 2513 W. Armitage, Chicago (1955)

Chapter 25

The 60'S

The new decade started off with Tony Accardo dealing with his tax case and trying to stay out of prison. A good distraction for Tony Accardo came on May 23, 1960.

Tony Accardo's daughter, Marie Judith Accardo, secretly married William Palmer Pyle Jr. at the Chicago County Building. The two were said to be living in a Ridgeview hotel at 901 Maple Avenue in Evanston, Illinois.

The two married after a long college romance at Michigan State University and were said to be heading to live in Baltimore where William Pyle Jr. was going to play professional football for the Baltimore Colts Football team.

William Pyle Jr.'s father was a city sales manager for Kraft Foods and lived at 1485 Scott Avenue in Winnetka, Illinois.

Anco Insurance Company was basically a way for the Chicago Outfit to make money by shaking down the business men in the Chicago Loop area under the image of being legit. The official officers listed for this corporation were one time First Ward Alderman and Democratic Ward Committeeman John D'Arco Sr.; Pat Marcy, then administrative assistant to the regular First Ward Organization; Benjamin "Buddy" Jacobson, then secretary of D'Arco and Treasurer; and Joseph Bernstein as the legal represent. However, it was known that Sam Giancana was the real owner.

Pat Marcy and John D'Arco would put certain pressures on some of the bigger business in the downtown area of Chicago known as the Chicago Loop area. One FBI informant said Pat Marcy once shut down a construction project building a motel in the Loop area and called the owner saying, *"Don't you know you can't build in the Loop without my permission?"* Marcy informed the owner that construction would not resume until he purchased Anco Insurance.

In 1963 Tony Accardo told Pat Marcy that Palmer Pyle was to be placed in the Anco Insurance Company and given a large salary. The discussion between Pat Marcy and Buddy Jacobson starts on the next page:

Rev. 12-13-58)

FBI

Date: 1/29/63

Transmit the following in ______________________
(Type in plain text or code)

Via AIRTEL AIR MAIL
(Priority or Method of Mailing)

TO: DIRECTOR, FBI

FROM: SAC, CHICAGO (92-350-SUB U)

SUBJECT: ACTIVITIES OF TOP HOODLUMS
CHICAGO DIVISION JUNE

DAILY SUMMARY

CG 6576-C* furnished the following information on 1/25/63 concerning activities within the First Ward Democratic organization offices. On that date, PAT MARCY met with BUDDY JACOBSON and discussed an interview that MARCY had with SAM GIANCANA during the morning of the 25th. The conversation is as follows:

MARCY: I met MOE (GIANCANA) this morning. We got a problem. JOE B (TONY ACCARDO) got ahold of him. JOE B wants to put his son-in-law on our insurance company as a salesman.

JACOBSON: Son-in-law? The football player?

MARCY: Yeah, his son-in-law. He says to me that JOE B wants to put his son-in-law, PYLE, to work, so he tells me, PAT, put him to work, let him work. I asked him what do I pay this guy, and he told me to give him 3 or 400 a week. I told him how can I give him that kind of money, I've got a (obs) manager that I don't even give him that kind of money. I said he'll disrupt the whole (obs) office. JOE still has a lot to say, don't think he doesn't.

JACOBSON: I told you that.

MARCY: So he said, naw, the guy will work, PAT. I said I know but I can't disrupt the whole office just for one guy. I told him, let me see what

3 - Bureau (RM)
1 - Chicago
MER:rmh
(4)

10 JAN 31 1963

Approved: ______________________ Sent ____________ M Per ____________
Special Agent in Charge

I can work out, let me give him a C note a week and I'll give him 50 dollars for expenses and he will make 150. He said, hell no, and then he started talking about other things, then I said, what are we going to do with this guy, MOE. I can't (obs) a whole office. Well, he said, give him 150 a week and 50 dollars a week for expenses. He told me to let BUDDY talk to JOE and let BUDDY explain to JOE what you have told me. If the guy comes in for more money, you got a manager that has been with you for 12 years and a new guy comes in here and makes more money than him. So we'll start him off at 150 plus 50 a week for expenses. I'd better call JOHN and tell him about it.

JACOBSON: Well, you know I've been thinking, and I'm really serious. I love you like I love my wife. I'm doing nothing here. I'd just as soon drop my share, honest to God.

MARCY: What share?

JACOBSON: My whole (obs) interest here.

MARCY: How could you?

JACOBSON: It would make everything happy.

MARCY: That ain't the point, if we got to put him on, what's the difference. The Government gets it in taxes anyway. That ain't my point. The point is, now I got to tell JOHN about it, right?

JACOBSON: I'll put it to JOE this way. JOE, it's a very impossible problem. PAT is doing a very stretching job when he is giving this man 200 a week, and if he did any more, it would disrupt the whole organization. We have a man that has been working with us for 12 years and he is not getting that kind of money. I'll tell him that PAT is doing everything in his might, but that it is not there.

MARCY: Tell him that it will (obs) up the office. Hell, it's no secret what this guy is going to get, the girl is going to make his check out, the manager knows what the checks are.

- 2 -

JACOBSON: I'll tell him that. But what I mean in all sincerity, anything that will hurt you, I'd want to be hurt and I tell you why. I know you are in like a brick (obs).

MARCY: I told him, now listen, MOE, you tell me what (obs) you want, you are the boss.

JACOBSON: That's smart.

MARCY: I said don't work around me. He said what do you mean. I said, you had a kid at the meetings, he said wait a minute, do you mean, he said, you mean FLANDO (ph). I said what are you going to do with him. I said don't keep me in the dark. He said here is what I want to do but keep it to yourself. I got the kid registered on Taylor Street. Does he know.........he said I want to put him in......spot, I told him to tell me, I said I'll put him in a precinct, we'll work it out, we'll let everybody know, then he said to me, I'm thinking of making FREDDIE (ROTI) the Senator. He says what do you think of FREDDIE, so I gave him a rap, I said, let me tell you about FREDDIE, I said, he sticks his nose in everybody's business. I said I told him once before to mind his (obs) business. I said the kid is a little backward, but I said as far as this, I can't rap him altogether, as far as taking an order, he will take an order. I said he won't do nothing unless he is told. He said what the (obs) does a Senator do anyhow. (They start whispering and PAT says:) I don't want to get in bad with MOE, JOE may crack to MOE that I was out there. I don't want MOE to think that I'm playing JOE. Tell JOE that PAT would give him 350 to 400 in a minute, instead of giving it to the government. I'd give it to him but the problem is I can't bring in a new guy and pay him more than I'm giving the manager.

JACOBSON: I know, I'll tell him. I think you handled it good with MOE.

MARCY: MOE said JOE wanted me to give him 500 a week and MOE said where the (obs) are they going to pay that kind of money. Then MOE said, we will

- 3 -

give him 250 to 300 a week and I told him that I can't. I explained it to him and he said, you're right. I said he only pays tax on 150 and the 50 expenses he don't pay tax on it. I've got to call JOHN now, I bet he will be mad now because I didn't wait till he got back to go out to see MOE.

JACOBSON: Tell him that it was an urgent call and you couldn't wait.

MARCY: I also told MOE that we had a chance to make some money, we got a chance to make a score. IRV WEINER, I says that the bail bond guys came in to see me. I said that we got to get ahold of PETE, PETE can make some money too, he says, what do they want to pay. I says theywant to pay 25,000. He said ask them for 50,000. I said that I can't ask them for 50 but wait and I'll see what I can do. I says now what do I give PETE. He said give PETE 5,000, he has to take care of them guys down there. I said I'll work it out with PETE, he said go ahead. Now the only thing I'm worried about is that how much heat I'm going to get with JOE's son-in-law. But I can't dog it. Wait a minute, I'll let you know what MOSS' salary is so you can tell JOE his salary.

(JACOBSON leaves)

From the above it is apparent that TONY ACCARDO has interceded with GIANCANA to have ACCARDO's son-in-law, PALMER PYLE, given employment with the Anco Insurance Company at a rate of about $400 per week. It is pointed out that PYLE is a professional football player, who plays with the Baltimore Colts of the National Football League. MARCY in turn has requested JACOBSON to talk with ACCARDO and explain to him the predicament that MARCY would be in if he was to hire PYLE at a salary that would be greater than that paid to PAUL MOSS, the manager of Anco Insurance Company, for the past 12 years.

Chicago has no knowledge at this time of the situation discussed by MARCY concerning the "bail bond guys" who according to MARCY have offered to pay $25,000 for some unknown favor. IRV WEINER, mentioned in this conversation, is a leading bail bondsman in the Chicago area and a close associate of many of Chicago's top hoodlums.

\- 4 -

FBI

Date: 1/31/63

Transmit the following in .... (Type in plain text or code)

Via AIRTEL AIR MAIL (Priority or Method of Mailing)

TO: DIRECTOR, FBI

FROM: SAC, CHICAGO (92-350-SUB U)

SUBJECT: ACTIVITIES OF TOP HOODLUMS CHICAGO DIVISION JUNE

DAILY SUMMARY

CG 6576-C* furnished the following information on 1/25/63 and 1/28/63 concerning activities occurring within the offices of the First Ward Democratic organization. During the morning of 1/25/63 PAT MARCY held a conference with PAUL MOSS, the Manager of the Anco Insurance Company, concerning the fact that Anco was going to have PALMER PYLE as an additional salesman for the company. As pointed out previously PYLE is the son-in-law of ANTHONY ACCARDO and is being placed in the firm on ACCARDO's request through SAM GIANCANA. The following is the discussion held between MARCY and MOSS:

MARCY: Listen, we're putting on an outside salesman. His name is PYLE (PALMER PYLE), he's a football player. You're going to have to teach him everything. He'll make a good salesman. This guy will work. He's got the presentation. We'll get him in here for an interview. Do you think that we should send him out with DON?

MOSS: First of all I want to ask something. How much overhead can you stand in that office?

MARCY: This is something that I got to do.

3 - Bureau (RM)
1 - Chicago
MER:rmh
(4)

FEB 2 1963

MOSS: Look, PAT, BUDDY (JACOBSON), I'm not worried about being hurt. It's just as well that I let you know how I feel. PAT, you're sitting on the books with $150,000. Your overhead is going higher. The bulk of your political contributions, and I'm no dummy, are coming out of Anco. Your salaries are not going down. Whenever something comes up Anco pays for it.

(PAT tells secretary to check Anco records for any checks made out on Anco for any politicians.)

MOSS: I'm concerned about whether this guy can carry his load. If he can't carry his own, I'll have to throw out DON.

MARCY: No, I don't want him in the office. He should have a lot of contacts. You assign his work to him every day.

MOSS: If this ends up with what amounts to a payroll job you are going to be doing everyone a disservice. I think you are going to hurt yourself. This is going to be newspaper story. But I'll lay you a bet that you are going to get a blast from the newspaper.

MARCY: We get them anyway.

MOSS: True. But where they have been intimating association all these years they are going to come right out and say this is the case. If it were up to me and the man wanted him to have a job I'd call up MORRIE ARKIN and say this is the situation. Put him in MARSH MACK (?), that's big enough to pick up a kid and train him.

MARCY: Listen, will you do it my way?

MOSS: What do you want to pay this man?

MARCY: We'll have to work it out. Now you are going to have to stay with this man for awhile. In my mind and in my heart I'm not doing anything wrong. He ain't this guy's son, he ain't in the family, he's his son-in-law.

- 2 -

MOSS: Look, what do I have to do with GARY. But they are giving it to my old man. He can't look anyone in the face. It's guilt through association.

MARCY: That was different.

MOSS: Well, it's your business, you do what you like. But if it reaches the point where you start destroying this business, I'm going to come in and tell you I'm leaving.

JACOBSON: Listen, we have to start this fellow at $150 and $50 expenses. We have obligations here MOSS. Without these fellows we wouldn't be here. Now we have to do this PAUL or we can put a lock on ourselves. Now what's the best alternative.

MOSS: You do what you have to. But you cannot keep the overhead that you have. At this rate you may have to take money from your own pocket to pay this fellow. Your business will only take so much expense.

MARCY: You don't know what you're talking about. Help me out.

(Secretary comes in and says that there was one check written on November 14th, 1962, to the 18th Ward Democratic Organization for $40.00. That was the only one during the year. Given instructions not to write any checks for any type of political organizations on Anco.)

MARCY: Now listen, we're getting some money next week from the Villa Venice. Now what we pay in taxes to the government, if we put this kid on, that's money we don't pay the government so it's not a burden on us. Now PAUL, let me give you a little background. When we started out in our business we got a lot of help. This is the only thing that they have ever asked. We're in business since 1951 and this is the only thing that they ever asked. We can't say no.

(Discussion regarding MOSS' salary - $18,000 a year gross)

- 3 -

CG 92-350

MARCY: I'm hoping that by taking in this kid we will triple our business. I'll tell you another thing. This guy wants his son-in-law to make a name. He don't want him to dog it.

MOSS: Well we are going to lose a thousand in cancellations within the next two months.

MARCY: Those fires?

MOSS: That's only part of it. These guys are all setting fire to their own places and blaming someone else for it. You know last year you had $33,000 in bad debts. I don't know that we can stand that much this year. (MOSS leaves)

From the above it would appear that MOSS is upset with the aspect of hiring PYLE for one reason that it will leave the company open to newspaper publicity linking syndicate figures with the Anco Insurance Company, a fact that, according to MOSS, has been hinted for years. From the above conversation and statements of MARCY and BUDDY JACOBSON there is little doubt but what the Chicago crime syndicate was responsible for Anco Insurance Company's inception and provided a large amount of help in getting the company started.

Apparently MOSS is from Gary, Indiana, originally and has relatives including his father still in the Gary area who have received some adverse publicity from the recent political scandals which occurred in the Gary area resulting in the jailing of Gary's former Mayor.

In regards to Tony Accardo's time with his mob pals, FBI agents recorded Murray Humphreys giving his opinion about Tony Accardo on November 3, 1960 after he is told to make a doctor's appointment for Accardo, *"That Joe, he does the damnest things. Baby stuff, like a 2-year-old. Next time he asks me, I'll tell him, go do it yourself, you jerk, what's this shit. You too spoiled to do it yourself? Can't even make a phone call. I'll holler at him. He used to tell me I was nutty cause I holler at him all the time."*

Spot Surveillance 1960

March 8, 1960 – Tony Accardo observed at the wake of his nephew Nicholas Senese.

April 4, 1960 – Tony Accardo, Frank Ferraro and Sam Giancana hold meetings at Celano's Tailor Shop to discuss a situation in Chicago were Outfit associates were found guilty of kiting checks to Chicago conventioneers.

Tony Dark

April 18, 1960 – Tony Accardo, Sam Giancana, Gus Alex, Frank Ferraro, Hy Godfrey and Murray Humphreys held a meeting at the Armory Lounge in Forest Park, Illinois to discuss mob operation on the west side of Chicago.

April 23, 1960 – Tony Accardo was observed at the Villa Venice with Sam Giancana, William Daddono and Fiore "Fifi" Buccieri attending the wedding of Sam Battaglia's daughter.

April 26, 1960 – Tony Accardo, Irvin Weiner, Gus Alex and mob lawyer Richard "Dick" Gorman meet to discuss Accardo's court case. Accardo asked if he needed permission of the court to leave the area. Accardo is heard saying, "*The last time I was indicted, I went to Bimini. Nobody said anything.*"

June 3, 1960 – Howard Beck, who owned a motion picture company in Germany, tells the FBI that he will be traveling to Germany with Tony Accardo and his wife soon. Accardo says he will visit his son who is in the Army and stationed at a U.S. Army base in Germany.

June 9, 1960 –Tony Accardo was observed eating dinner at the Imperial House on East Walton Street in Chicago with his wife and daughter.

September 3, 1960 – Tony Accardo, Joseph Glimco and Carmen Fanelli were observed together at the Armory Lounge holding a meeting.

September 15, 1960 – Tony Accardo, Murray Humphreys and Frank Ferraro held a meeting to discuss Accardo's income tax trial. It was decided that Humphreys and Ferraro would use a personal approach to the jury members to make sure Accardo was found not guilty.

October 26, 1960 – Tony Accardo, Frank LaPorte and Al Pilotto held a meeting at Jack Fagman's Store, 108 West Randolph Street.

November 15, 1960 – Tony Accardo, Jackie Cerone, Frank Ferraro, Sam Giancana, Gus Alex and Ralph Pierce were observed eating together at Pete Fish's Restaurant at 161 E. Ontario Street in Chicago.

November 16, 1960 – Tony Accardo, Gus Alex, Sam Giancana, Frank Ferraro and Murray Humphreys held a meeting at the St. Clair Hotel in Chicago.

December 4, 1960 – Tony Accardo is observed attending a meeting held at Ben Fillichio's home in River Forest. Attending were John Lardino, Jackie Cerone, Frank Granata Sr., John Cimitile and John Carrino.

December 31, 1960 – Tony and Clarice Accardo spend New Years Eve with Nancy DeLucia. Tony Accardo explains his night himself. He complains of the FBI listening in:

Hy Godfrey	Did you talk to Nancy?
Accardo	Yeah, New Years Eve. We drank two pitchers of Screwdrivers. We got all screwed up. We were gonna sit home and babysit. Joseph was gonna have a splash party. Then Clarice and I was gonna sit home. So I called Nancy, and said, we'll be over at 4:00 and have a drink, because we're gonna sit home and babysit. So we went to Lardino's, then Nancy's, we were gonna swing all around. So we got to Nancy's at ten o'clock. Then Ralph Cantonese (Chicago Police Captain) came in with Foggie's brother, without their wives. I just kept drinking.

Joseph Accardo

Authors Collection

In the late 1950's there was some confusion from time to time amongst law enforcement agents and investigators because information of a Joe Accardo, sometimes spelled Accardi, would come in that would not fit the profile of Tony Accardo. Since Tony Accardo often went by the name Joe and Joe Accardo used the name Anthony Accardo, information sometimes became mixed up. There was another lower echelon Chicago mobster by the name Joseph Accardo. There is some mention that law enforcement was never completely sure if Tony Accardo and Joe Accardo were related.

The lower echelon Joe Accardo, or Accardi, had been sent to prison in 1950 for burglary. The sentence had come months after he had beaten charges of rape and another burglary.

In 1959 Joe Accardi was involved in the Fifth Jack Club located at 3340 West Fifth Avenue and Jackson Boulevard in Chicago. The club was a gambling joint operated by the syndicate where Accardi was partners with Charles "Chuckie" English. In fact, Joe Accardi and his brother, Harry Accardi, who were the owners of the Fifth Jack Club, were under the "English Group" where Joe was at one point referred to as Chuckie English's right-hand man. However, FBI reports say that Joe Accardi was not a "made" member of the Outfit but worked for the Outfit.

In 1963 Joey Accardo was running a small "sneak" dice and card game under mobster Rocco Potenzo. The reason it was on a "sneak" basis was because there was too much "heat" from the "G" (FBI) to operate in the open. Potenza had to curtail his gambling operations and had to let go twenty-five of his operators but could not let go of Joey Accardo under Tony Accardo's orders.

Chicago, Illinois
May 14, 1959

In re: JOSEPH ACCARDI
814 W. Harrison St., Chicago, Ill.,
7124 W. 82nd St., Oak Lawn, Ill.

Summary:

Reference is made to the Norton I. Kretske, general file, at Chicago, Illinois, Bureau of Narcotics. This file contains a Chicago Sun Times clipping dated April 5, 1953 regarding the arrest of Joseph Accardi, and other persons in connection with the theft of 9 religious paintings from a Bardstown, Kentucky Cathedral. Norton Kretske, former Assistant United States Attorney was to be charged for concealment of stolen goods. Also arrested in connection with the above thefts were:

Albert Spagnola, Cleveland, Ohio (formerly of Chicago)
Jasper Joseph Aiello, Youngstown, Ohio
Ralph Lupi, Warren, Ohio
William L. Skally; William L. Russo (all Chicago)
Charles R. LaCamerra, Farrell, Pennsylvania
Gus Manotelli, and Joseph DePietro.

Harry Accardi, Joseph's brother, is listed as the proprietor 5th Jacks Club 3358 W. Jackson St., Chicago, Ill. Joseph Accardi's address is also given as 3340 W. 5th Chicago, Illinois.

No other information available in our files.

Gp. Photo 54084

NAME (LAST)	(FIRST)	(MIDDLE)	SOC. SEC. NO.	FILE NO.
ACCARDO	JOSEPH			

NICKNAME OR ALIAS:
TYPE OF ACTIVITY:
I.R. NO.:
HOME ADDRESS: 727 N. Hamlin Ave.
CITY:
HOME PHONE NO.:
F.B.I. NO.: 4-276-800
BUSINESS ADDRESS:
CITY:
BUSINESS PHONE NO.:
TYPE OF BUSINESS:
NEW ADDRESS:
CITY:
NEW PHONE NO.:
PHOTO REF. NO.: 54084

SEX	RACE	DESCENT	D.O.B.	HEIGHT	WEIGHT	HAIR	EYES
Male	White		1929	5'8"	225		

COMPLEXION:
PECULIARITIES; MARKS, SCARS, ETC.:

ASSOCIATES: Ray Jones, Phil Katz, Carl Cananda, Moe Lepari, Arohel Sayadian, Anthony Amendo, Benny Ognibene, ThomasCampione

HANGOUTS:

VEHICLE INFORMATION:

CPD-36.951 (REV.9/62) FACE CARD SEE REVERSE SIDE FOR MISC. INFORMATION

Subject has operated gambling spots in Cicero, Illinois. Has been arrested several times in vice and gambling raids. Subject may have an interest in Mike's Hot Dog Stand with Mike Lisciandrella.

CITY OF CHICAGO / DEPARTMENT OF POLICE 1121 South State Street Chicago 5, Illinois WAbash 2-4747
IDENTIFICATION SECTION

ARREST RECORD OF Joseph A Accardo M/W
DATE June 23, 1963
DATE OF BIRTH Nov. 17, 1927

35526

35526 I.R. NO. 427 6800 FBI NO. S.B. NO.

NAME & ADDRESS	C.B. NO.	DATE OF ARREST / ARRESTING OFFICER & DIST. / CHARGE / DISPOSITION
Joseph Accardo	NG	6 Sept. 1944 supervision 1 yr. Contrib.to delinq. Judge Bonelli Offs Berg. & Cover, Dist 29
	D33829	11 Mar. 1945 T.O.T. Juv Auth. V.S. 193-1 Offs Manus & McCarthy, Dist 35 Judge Drucker
		10 July 1946 Off Knapp Dist 36 Inv.
		7 Nov. 1946 Off Smicklas D.B. Inv.
		13 Nov. 1946 prob. 1 yr. & 30 days Co. Jail V.S. 492, Chap 38 Judge Braude.Offs O'Donnell & Glon D.B.
		4 Feb. 1948 Off Swarthwood Dist 36 Inv.
		14 Dec. 1948 Off Valanis D.B. Inv.
		2 Sept. 1949Off O'Donnell Dist 35 Inv.
Tony Accardo		12 Feb. 1950 Offs Blanchard & Bickler Dist 36- Inv.
" "	D75684	10 May 1950Off Nierman Dist 37 Burg. (1)Indicted Feb. term 1950 G.J.
Joe Accardo	D76560	21 Aug. 1950 Offs Thoma & Co. Dist 35Burg. find. not guilty & rape find. not guilty Judge Miner
		27 Aug. 1950 Off Fitzgerald & Co. D.B. **G.P.
Tony Accardo		13 Nov. 1950 sent. Joliet, Ill. Pen.#30452. Burg. 1-2 yrs. Plea Guilty. Judge Miner. DISCH May 26,1953 exp. of sent.
Joseph Accardo		12 Sept. 1956 Off Komie D.B. Inv.
" "	E-45087	10 April 1959 Off Hastings & Co. Comm. Off. G.P.
		4 May 1961 Off Spospff & Co. OCD (36) Inv.
		15 Oct. 1961 Off Nalepa & Co. Dist 38 - Inv.
" "	1296318	23 June 1963 OffOgonowski Dist 13- Patron Gambling
		28 June 1963 Gambling, 193-2 Motion to suppress susta & Disch. Judge Chelos

CAB D-22.466 (REV.3/62)

35526

Joseph Accardo CPD Mug shot photo

Authors Collection

Tony Dark

1961 saw Tony Accardo still involved with his tax case. Sam Giancana was at the height of his power running Chicago and the FBI was at the peak of its investigating mobsters.

On April 27, 1961 Tony Accardo's daughter Linda Lee married Michael A. Palermo, son (some reports list him as nephew) of mobster Nick Palermo at St. Luke's Catholic Church on Lathrop Avenue in River Forest. Reports on the wedding stated after the vows were exchanged some of the close guests attended a private champagne breakfast at Accardo's house. That night around 700 people attended the reception at Sam Giancana's Villa Venice on Milwaukee Road in Wheeling, Illinois. The guests were served a menu of beef tenderloin or chicken, Venetian tarts, a pineapple boat appetizer and it was all presented in front of a 7-foot-tall wedding cake. Each guest was allowed ONE glass of champagne unless you were a powerful politician or very high ranking mob boss. Then you could have another glass.

Chicago police were there watching and writing down names. Some of the names were:

James Adduci
Joey Aiuppa
Eugene Albano
Phil Alderisio
Gus Alex
Sam Alex
Jimmy Allegretti
Vincent Alo (New York)
William Aloisio
Joe Amato
Donald Angelini
Robert Ansani
Joseph Arnold
James Arrigo
Ross Aulelli
Frank Balistrieri (Milwaukee)
Sam Battaglia
Dominic "Butch" Blasi
Frank Bompensiero (San Diego)
Dom Brancato
Louis Briatta
Mike Briatta
Dr. Giulio Bruni
Angelo Bruno (Philadelphia)
Fiore "Fifi" Buccieri
Frank Buccieri
Russell Buffalino (Scranton)
Marshall Caifano
Albert Capone
Ralph "Bottles" Capone
Anthony Cardamone
Alfred Carfagno
Frank "Skids" Caruso Sr.
Jimmy Caruso
James Catuara
Jackie Cerone
Carl Civella (Kansas City)
Nick Civella (Kansas City)
Joe Colombo (New York)
Dom Cortina
Frank Costello (New York)
John Costello
Nick Costello
Francis Curry
William DaddonoMoe Dalitz (Las Vegas)
John D'Arco Sr.
John DeBiase
James DeGeorge (Wisconsin)
Rocco DeGrazio
Paul DeLucia
Rocco DeStefano
Sam DeStefano
Dom DiBella
Charles "Spec" DiCaro
Joseph DiVarco
Ralph Emery
Charles English
Sam English
Anthony Esposito Sr.
Frank Esposito
Joseph Esposito
Albert Frabotta
Frank Ferraro
Joseph Ferriola
Anthony Fillichio
Ben "Foggie" Fillichio
Michael Fillichio
Joe Fischetti
Rocco Fischetti
Johnny Formosa
Joseph Gagliano
Carlos Gambino (New York)

Mob Boss

Vito Genovese (New York)
Anthony Gianfrancesco
Sam Giancana
Joey Glimco
Hy Godfrey
Frank Granata Sr.
Frank Greco
Murray Humphreys
Rocky Infelice
Vince Inserro
Bill Kaplan
Les Kruse
Nick LaCata (Los Angeles)
Butch Landon
Meyer Lansky (New York)
Joe Laino
John Lardino
John LaRocca (Pittsburgh)
Frank LaPorte
Lou Lederer
Gus Liebe
Joseph "Ruffy" Liscaindrello
Joe Lombardo
Pat Manno
Carlo Marcello (New Orleans)
Pat Marcy
John Matassa Sr.
Alex Mazzone
Bill McGuire
James Mirro
Chuck Nicoletti
Nick Nitti
Dom Nuccio
Michael Oliver "AKA
Moses Olitski
Rocco Padulo Jr.
Nick Palermo
Dolly Pantone
Sam Pardy
Ray Patriarca (New England)
Lennie Patrick
Ralph Pierce
Al Pilotto
Tony Pinelli (Gary and Lake County Indiana mob boss)
Ross Prio
Rocco Potenzo
Rocco Prano
Joe Profaci (New York)
John Roselli
Frank Ruffalo (Wisconsin)
Peanuts Smaldone (Denver)
John Scalise (Cleveland)
Dom Senese
Dominic Sibilano
Joe Sica (San Fernando Valley)
Tarquin Simonelli
Fred "Juke Box" Smith
Vince Solano
Tony Spilotro
Joseph Spingola Sr.
Funzi Tieri (New York)Al Tocco
James Torello
Santo Trafficante (Tampa)
Eddie Vogel
Anthony Volpe
Harold Eugene Williams (Michigan)
John Wolek
David Yaras
Joe Zerilli (Detroit)

Nick Palermo was owner of Melrose Park Plumbing Company located at 1827 North 25th Avenue in Melrose Park, Illinois. In 1954 Nick Palermo was arrested in a raid on an apartment above his plumbing shop. Found where stolen art valued at $150,000 that was being stored up in a loft. The items had been stolen from the home of Oscar U. Zerk who lived in Kenosha, Wisconsin.

In 1957 Nick Palermo had lost a great deal of money to mob boss Sam Battaglia and Rocco DeGrazio. To pay this off, Palermo went to work for them operating a race wire room in the vicinity of 140 South 21st Street in Melrose Park.

In 1967 Nick Palermo used an Illinois state charter to submerge his identity behind a false corporation. The trick was an attempt to hide his underworld image after being indicted with mob boss Sam "Teetz" Battaglia on an interstate extortion charge by the FBI. Palermo attempted to place his Melrose Park Plumbing Company under his niece's and secretary's name so he could continue to receive contracting jobs from the City of Chicago. The indictment said that he and his mob pals threatened the president of a multimillion-dollar land development corporation with violence and hardship if the plumbing contracts for all their projects did not find their way into Palermo's hands.

Palermo's plan was to start a new company called Mayo Plumbing at the same address of his Melrose Park Company. Since Melrose Park Plumbing was never incorporated it was solely in Palermo's name. So he enlisted his son-in-law James Langone, who was married to his daughter Ann Marie; his brother John's daughter Helen Severino; and his long time secretary Mrs. Jean Buonomo to be the names used to charter the new company Mayo Plumbing. He spent $15,000 putting up new signs, painting all his trucks new colors with the new logo on them and had his charter set up by Illinois Secretary of State Paul Powell. However, he made two mistakes, he never changed the phone number and investigators still observed Nick Palermo arriving everyday at the offices of Mayo Plumbing.

Meantime Tony Accardo was on top of all political situations in the city regardless of what Sam Giancana was ordering. In 1961 it was disclosed that Tony Accardo used mob labor leader Peter Fosco as his liaison man between Accardo and persons of political prominence by handing gratuities in the form of flowers from Accardo to various persons. Peter Fosco would order the flowers to be sent to a designated individual and enclosed Accardo's card along with the flowers. The bill was paid by Fosco.

Peter Fosco and Accardo had become close friends around the time when Joseph "Diamond Joe" Esposito was shot to death at the end of the 1920's. Fosco had been Esposito's secretary and when Esposito was killed, Fosco took over Esposito's operations.

The Chicago Outfit was mostly under the control of Sam Giancana in 1961. In November of that year FBI agents listened in on Tony Accardo, Frank Ferraro and Gus Alex as Ferraro complained about Giancana's men, known as the "Twelfth Street Guys," consisting of Frank Eulo, Gus Kringas and Joseph "Pepe" Giancana and their gambling operations in Cicero. Ferraro complained that, "*Them guys out there won't answer to us, only to Moe.*"

Ferraro stated he could not go over Moe's head and Accardo added that they should come to him, Accardo, when Giancana is out of town but they don't. Accardo was concerned because many of the mob killings going on were related to people operating in Cicero and there was a separation of organization between the suburbs and city.

The FBI knew Accardo was definitely no longer calling the shots with the Giancana Outfit in Chicago. It was confirmed just how powerful Sam Giancana was in Las Vegas when in October of that year Tony Accardo was overheard asking Frank Ferraro if he thought he could ask Murray Humphreys for permission to have his son, Anthony Ross, open his travel agency in the Riviera Hotel in Las

Vegas. Tony Accardo was asking since he, Accardo, could never get a hold of Giancana to ask him himself.

Accardo sill had headaches concerning the syndicate. The FBI listened in as Tony Accardo and Frank Ferraro complained, becoming very upset with the fact that their big gambling game was closed down. Accardo and Gus Alex discussed that things were very different in the 1960's than in the late 1950's when they had three of four gambling joints operating in every town around Chicago. It was Alex's opinion that the reason they lost most of their operations was because they did not have any top police officials behind them in the 1960's as they did in the 1950's. He also added that all the newspaper publicity hurt gambling in the city.

Not to mention, the government was going after Accardo this time saying he owed over $3-million in back income taxes from a defunct Erie-Buffalo policy wheel he controlled with Sam Pardy and Tom Manno. Both Accardo and mobster Jake Guzik had made a contract in 1949 that they were each to receive twenty-five percent of the profits from the $5-million-dollar-a-year gambling operation. Accardo and Guzik were named as "consultants" for the wheel operations.

Pardy and Manno said during the hearings that they assumed the blame for part of the back taxes owed because they stole between $5,000 and $6,000 a month from the wheel and did not report any of it on their taxes. They both admitted in court that they stole that money from Accardo and Guzik, which in the mob meant their deaths. Both had already served time in prison for tax evasion from the wheel operations so they could not be tried again for admitting stealing the money. But, as it turned out, stealing the money had helped Accardo in this case. Some even speculated that both were ordered to say they stole the money by Accardo himself.

In 1961 Tony Accardo's name was revealed in an investigation into a Howard P. Willens. Back in 1955 Howard Willens was going to be given the position of law clerk in the Antitrust Division for the Government. Investigators found no derogatory information on him. In 1961 Willens had climbed the ladder in politics and was being considered for the position of attorney in the criminal division. With a position such as that, it is very important the attorney have no ties to a criminal organization who could control him. When FBI agents looked into Willens again, one piece of information was discovered that Willens somehow forgot to mention. His father Joseph Robert Willens had happened to be the next door neighbor of Tony Accardo, top mob boss of the Chicago Outfit. When Joseph Willens was interviewed for the job he denied any affiliation or association with any criminal organization, including having any kind of association with Tony Accardo.

Tony Dark

Spot Surveillance 1961

January 1, 1961 – Tony Accardo and Jimmy Celano were at Celano's Tailor Shop in Chicago. Accardo complained that he just returned from a vacation down in Hot Springs, Arkansas and it was *"cold as hell down there."* He was also there for the wedding of Ross Prio's daughter. Accardo is heard trying to get a reservation for a round trip ticket to New Orleans. Later Accardo meets with Phil Alderisio to discuss someone who transferred from Milwaukee to Chicago to work for mobster Frank LaPorte.

January 6, 1961 – Tony Accardo is observed at the Armory Lounge in conversation with Sam Giancana. Accardo is then driven home by a Frank Szafran.

January 13, 1961 – Chicago Police find Tony Accardo's car parked in front of the apartments at 20 E. Delaware in Chicago. Police watch as Accardo's wife exits the apartment and drives away with Tony Accardo.

January 1961 – Tony Accardo, John Lardino, Charles English and Joe Aiuppa attend a mob meeting held at the home of mobster Ben "Foggie" Fillichio concerning Chicago's "Juice" racket.

February 2, 1961 – Tony Accardo and Gus Alex hold a discussion. Gus Alex tells Accardo he doesn't understand why Sam Giancana holds all his meetings at the Armory Lounge with so much law enforcement watching, *"I don't know why he picks that joint for his meetings. They're all over the place. Scotland Yard a few weeks ago chased him all over the place."*

February 10, 1961 – Jimmy Celano and Murray Humphreys are at Celano's Tailor Shop discussing what happened to Tony Accardo the day before. While Accardo was at the tailor shop one of Sam Giancana's men who Celano called a "punk" came into the shop and introduced himself to Tony Accardo. Celano told Humphreys, *"Joe (Accardo) was here Monday morning, and there was a guy here. He is one of the punks that works for Mooney. So he shook hands with Joe and Joe was cordial, so Joe said, you gonna buy some clothes, and the guy said, yeah, if you'll buy them for me, and Joe got hot, and said who the fuck are you that I should buy you a suit of cloths? That boy Taglia, he should have better brains. He was here for a couple of hours, and when he left, Joe said, That punk shouldn't have said that to me, and I said, Joe, he was only kidding."*

March 17, 1961 – Tony Accardo attends the wake of murdered mobster Joseph "Crackers" Mendino at the Montclair Chapel at 6901 West Belmont in Chicago. Accardo and Jackie Cerone acted as pallbearers for Mendino.

April 1, 1961 – Police noticed a party at the home of Tony Accardo. Outside was an auto registered to Charles Nicoletti. This car had been part of a wholesale disappearance of cars from the Sterling-Harris Company in March 1961.

May 14, 1961 – Tony Accardo is seen being driven to the wake of John Sortino, brother of mob boss Frank Ferraro, at the Montclair Funeral Home on Belmont Avenue in Chicago.

July 10, 1961 – Tony Accardo, Jackie Cerone, Gus Alex, Jimmy Celano and Frank Ferraro are at Celano's Tailor Shop discussing who was going to be subpoenaed in a court case and discussing Teamster union boss Jimmy Hoffa. Frank Ferraro is heard saying, *"How about that Hoffa? That fucking Hoffa had really gone power crazy, ain't he? They gotta nail him."* Jackie Cerone replies, *"He's not going power crazy. He's just givin' them what they gave him."*

July 12, 1961 – Tony Accardo, Jackie Cerone, Gus Alex, Frank Ferraro and Hy Godfrey discuss the age of Accardo's jacket in a joking manner. Accardo claims it's new but Alex says it's the same damn jacket he has been wearing for eight years.

July 23, 1961 – Tony Accardo, Ben Fillichio and John Lardino are watched as they drive together to the wake of James Meo.

July 31, 1961 – Tony Accardo arrives at Celano's Tailor Shop and purchases some new clothes.

August 2, 1961 – Tony Accardo, Frank Ferraro, and Jackie Cerone are at Celano's Tailor Shop discussing that when Accardo moved into his mansion on Franklin Street in 1951 he was paying $2,400 in property taxes and in 1961 it was up to $4,300. He then discussed a situation between Anthony and Rocco DeGrazio and Anthony's Funeral Home.

August 16, 1961 – Tony Accardo, Frank Ferraro, Jimmy Celano and Nathan "Butch" Ladon are at Celano's Tailor Shop discussing the release of Paul DeLucia from prison. Accardo instructed Ladon on how to shake a surveillance by entering an unknown building, going downstairs where there is an exit leading onto Grand Avenue and how it will give the impression that Landon is still probably in the building.

August 21, 1961 – Tony Accardo and Hy Godfrey are discussing the death of a New York guy they knew. Accardo tells Godfrey to go and pay a bill that Accardo owes on his kids clothes. Later Accardo, Jackie Cerone, Frank Ferraro, Hy Godfrey, Mike Brodkin, Herb Barsy and Ralph Pierce have lunch in the Pittsfield Building Restaurant at 55 East Washington Street in Chicago which was owned by Morris Norman, a close friend of mobster Murray Humphreys.

August 28, 1961 – Tony Accardo, Frank Ferraro, Jackie Cerone, Ross Prio and Jimmy Celano are at Celano's Tailor Shop discussing barbequing techniques.

Accardo wants to barbeque a 700-pound steer cattle.

September 2, 1961 – Tony Accardo was observed attending the wedding reception of Jack Cerone Jr. held at the Tam O'Shanter Country Club in Niles, Illinois.

September 13, 1961 – Tony Accardo, Hy Godfrey and Jimmy Celano discuss how government agents are reviewing Celano's 1959 tax returns looking for mob money. Jackie Cerone arrives and tells how amazed he is about Rocco DeGrazio's Casa Madrid casino which is one hundred percent underground with tunnels running in every direction. The Casa Madrid was located in Melrose Park on the corner of Lake Street and 25th Avenue.

October 13, 1961 – Tony Accardo, Jackie Cerone, Gus Alex, Frank Ferraro and Hy Godfrey meet at Celano's Tailor Shop. Accardo spends most of the time talking about his son's new travel agency business at the Riviera Hotel and Casino in Las Vegas. Later Murray Humphreys arrived and Tony Accardo asks Humphreys for permission to open his son's business in the lobby of the Riviera. The FBI was confused as to why Accardo was asking Humphreys for permission.

October 18, 1961 – Tony Accardo, Jackie Cerone and Frank Ferraro hang out at Celano's Tailor Shop discussing FBI agents hanging around watching them. They also discussed the publicity concerning John D'Arco Sr. and the Italian Civic Committee to lodge complaints against the "persecution of Italians".

October 19, 1961 – Tony Accardo, Murray Humphreys, Rocco Fischetti and Frank Ferraro hold a lunch meeting.

October 20, 1961 – Tony Accardo and Jimmy Celano discuss furniture desks for Accardo's son.

October 30, 1961 – Tony Accardo, Leslie Kruse, Jackie Cerone and Cerone's nephew Patrick Cerone discuss how Jackie Cerone has trouble with his electric can opener and can not open a can of Polish ham. Accardo then tells Cerone he had Miss Cox, the secretary for mob lawyer Eugene Bernstein, contact the Secretary of State for him to obtain a new driver's license. Accardo is recorded as saying, *"One of these fucking days we'll do something that will be right, instead of going the fucking hard way all the time."* Accardo then discusses the Chicago Bears game against the Baltimore Colts because his son-in-law plays in Baltimore. Accardo doesn't think the plastic helmets are proper, *"They should be leather, with some kind of a cushion on the inside. Palmer probably didn't want to get hurt. Every time I saw him he was on his feet, not on his back, that means he wasn't workin."* Accardo ended by stating that he would never let any of this sons play football, *"worse than the fight game"* for getting hurt.

November 15, 1961 – Tony Accardo, Frank Ferraro, Hy Godfrey and Gus Alex discuss how crazy Robert Kennedy, brother of President John F. Kennedy, was. Accardo then complained that he, Accardo, always "helps" everyone's son when he can but when it is time to help his son no one will. They discuss how the young Accardo held a conference at the Armory Lounge and ate a wild duck dinner. Then Accardo complained about the arrest and problems mobster Sam DeStefano was causing for the Outfit.

November 20, 1961 – Tony Accardo, Gus Alex, Frank Ferraro, Hy Godfrey and Jimmy Celano play cards at Celano's Tailor Shop. Ferraro asks Accardo if he wants to get lunch and where he wants to eat. Accardo replies, *"Anyplace, as long as it's free."* Jackie Cerone enters and the group talks about Miami, Florida. Cerone says, *"Up at the Thunderbird (Motel) you can go and nobody will see you. They got a big master bath, and closet."* Accardo replies joking around, *"You gonna spend your time in the bathroom?"*

November 27, 1961 – Tony Accardo, Frank Ferraro, Lester Kruse, Jackie Cerone and Gus Alex met to discuss the re-opening of the "Big Game" in Chicago, which was at one time the most profitable gambling rackets the Outfit had. Tony Accardo was concerned that if the "Big Game" was not re-opened, Chicago would lose the "good" employees who would move out west to Las Vegas if the Outfit did not give them work. The final decision was Sam Giancana's who was out of town.

November 28, 1961 – Tony Accardo, Gus Alex, Jackie Cerone and Frank Ferraro hold a meeting, it was not known about what.

December 1, 1961 – Tony Accardo, Gus Alex, Hy Godfrey, Jackie Cerone and Nick Benedetto are at Celano's Tailor Shop discussing articles in the daily newspaper. Jimmy Celano walks in and Accardo is heard saying, *"What do you know, Mr. Salerno?"* Jimmy Celano corrects Accardo, *"Celano, Salerno is the butter cookies."* Accardo laughs, *"Ok, Mr. Celano."* The group discusses talking to Allen Dorfman in order to "get to" Jimmy Hoffa.

December 8, 1961 – Tony Accardo and Jackie Cerone are followed as they walk down Michigan Avenue, then turn on to Walton Street walking to Lake Shore Drive where Tom Kelly's Restaurant was located. The code word for meeting at Tom Kelly's Restaurant then was "meet at Murphy's."

December 26, 1961 – Tony Accardo, Jimmy Celano, Hy Godfrey, Frank Ferraro and Jackie Cerone are seen and heard at Celano's Tailor Shop discussing how Accardo was glad Christmas was over. Accardo gave his advice on what cannot be hidden from the IRS. Accardo also told Ferraro to send back a case of whiskey to someone unknown. They all went to eat at Lowenbrau Restaurant located at Chicago's lower Wacker drive three blocks from the tailor shop.

The year 1962 started out with the tax trial lingering over Tony Accardo's head again. His name surfaced in many reports mostly about what legitimate business he was alleged to be a partner in. Businesses like the Peter Epsteen Pontiac Dealership, Henry Susk Pontiac Dealership, Dominic's Supermarkets with Jack Cerone, and Austin Liquors with Louis Briatta and the Fillichio brothers.

1961 had been a disaster for the Outfit. In January 1962 FBI agents listening in on Sam Giancana complaining that the Outfit did not make any money during the past year.

The old scams were offered to Tony Accardo because they worked in the past. On September 25, 1962 a heavyweight boxing match known as the Liston-Patterson fight was held at Comiskey Park in Chicago. In March 1963 the FBI learned that Jackie Cerone, Sam Giancana and Tony Accardo received assurances from Liston's manager of his impending victory and a wager of $100,000 was placed on Liston by the trio with non-syndicate bookies. Charles "Sonny" Liston knocked out heavyweight champion of the world Floyd Patterson in the first round.

There were crazy stories coming out in the press concerning Accardo's future that made Accardo and his pals scratch the top of their heads in confusion. A weekly Spanish newspaper published in Tampa, Florida wrote a story stating that once Tony Accardo was convicted and had to start serving his prison sentence, then Florida mob boss Santo Trafficante, second in command of Chicago, would take over as top boss of the Chicago mob. While Tony Accardo and Paul DeLucia laughed at the story, Sam Giancana just smirked and shook his head. Even Santo Trafficante was confused since he had never been to Chicago.

On September 10, 1962 Tony Accardo's retrial for tax evasion commences at the Northern District of Illinois U. S. Court House before Judge Julius J. Hoffman. Accardo was seen having lunch with his attorney, Maurice Walsh, and mobsters Murray Humphreys and Jackie Cerone at Staley's Restaurant on Clark Street, one-half block from the Federal Court House, on a daily basis during his trial.

October 3, 1962, Tony Accardo was found not guilty of tax evasion. Once again the government failed to beat Tony Accardo. The jury deliberated for 2 hours and 29 minutes coming back with a not guilty verdict. One juror said the government had inconclusive evidence. The court stated that Accardo was denied a fair trial because of the press publicity during the trial.

When the not guilty was read out loud in court, Tony Accardo looked at his lawyer with a victory grin. They left the courthouse and headed back to his River Forest mansion for a celebration party.

After the acquittal, due to the strain of the income tax trial, Tony Accardo decided he needed ten days away from Chicago to relax. Accardo, Jackie Cerone, Sam Battaglia and Ralph Pierce made plans to head down south to Hot Springs, Arkansas to stay at the classy Arlington Hotel where they would enjoy hot baths and massages. However, the newspaper discovered the trip and Accardo, Battaglia and Cerone did not go. Only Ralph Pierce was spotted by the FBI in Hot Springs. The FBI noted that Accardo *"had done nothing except lie around the house and take an occasional drive"* since his acquittal in October 1962. The FBI watched as William "Willie Potatoes" Daddono personally delivered Accardo's monthly installment of his "cut" from the Chicago Mob to Accardo's front door.

In November 1962 the FBI received information that payoffs were made in the amount of $250,000 to two federal Judges in Chicago in 1961. The payment was so the judges could reverse the conviction of Accardo in the lower courts.

The trial also made Tony Accardo attempt to make himself more legit when he told his underlings that he wanted them to find four prestigious fronts (men) for a shopping center he wanted to build on five acres of vacant land Accardo owned in the Northwest suburbs.

In December 1962 the Feds discovered that Tony Accardo was instrumental in the removal of Chicago First Ward Alderman John D'Arco through his contacts with Sam Giancana. Giancana and D'Arco were discovered meeting together by FBI agent William Roemer Jr. Reportedly Tony Accardo had opposed D'Arco for some time because he felt that there were activities in the First Ward that were being withheld from the Outfit. D'Arco's executive secretary was Benjamin "Buddy" Jacobson, an old-time gangster from the 1920's and 30's, was very close to Tony Accardo. Every once in a while Jacobson acted as a liaison between Accardo and the First Ward and had tried to talk to Accardo about not replacing D'Arco. However, it did not work and D'Arco was out. One of the informants inside the First Ward offices said that D'Arco and mobster Pat Marcy, who was the real power behind the First Ward, held Accardo responsible for this action to replace D'Arco.

Other information stated that Sam Giancana took charge in the "dumping" of D'Arco because he, Giancana, was taking a stand on his own and not having it appear as if he was receiving orders or acting upon the advice of Tony Accardo.

Spot Surveillance 1962

January 10, 1962 – Tony Accardo, Paul DeLucia and Jackie Cerone met for a short time at Jimmy Celano's Tailor Shop to discuss the recent reversal by the U.S. Circuit Court of Appeals involving Accardo's conviction on income tax.

January 23, 1962 – Tony Accardo and Jackie Cerone stop by Celano's Tailor Shop and discuss how someone close to the Outfit wants a civil service job with the City of Chicago and both were doubtful this individual could obtain it because he had a criminal record. Gus Alex is there and a game of cards breaks out.

January 24, 1962 – Tony Accardo, Paul DeLucia, Jackie Cerone, Gus Alex and Jimmy Celano hold a conversation at Celano's Tailor Shop.

January 29, 1962 – Tony Accardo is heard discussing with Jackie Cerone how the city of Chicago will not hire anyone with a police record, on orders from Mayor Richard J. Daley.

February 19, 1962 – Tony Accardo is observed at the Thunderbird Motel in Miami, Florida sitting by the pool engaged in conversation with an unidentified couple.

Tony Dark

April 9, 1962 – Tony Accardo, Frank Ferraro, Jackie Cerone, Jimmy Celano and Paul DeLucia are together at Celano's Tailor Shop. Accardo is interested in purchasing a neck tie from Celano and complains that all Celano's ties are *"like a whore house, all the same price."*

May 25, 1962 – Tony Accardo and Jackie Cerone are observed at the wake of Carmen Fanelli, part owner of the mob's Armory Lounge.

August 1, 1962 – Tony Accardo is seen at the wake of Mary Rose Cerone, mother of Jackie Cerone held at Rago Brothers Funeral home at 624 N. Western Avenue in Chicago.

August 21, 1962 – Tony Accardo holds a meeting of hoodlums at the Sultan's Table Restaurant at the mob controlled Sahara Inn Motel in Schiller Park, Illinois.

September 5, 1962 – Tony Accardo and his wife attend a gathering at the Sahara Inn Motel. Once there Tony Accardo meets with a number of mobsters for a few hours. Included were Jackie Cerone and Anthony Ricci, aka Tony Gobels who came in from Miami Beach Florida. One informant told the feds that Ricci was considered a "has been" and took orders from the Chicago Outfit.

September 10, 11 & 12, 1962 – Tony Accardo was observed on these days having lunch with Jackie Cerone and Murray Humphreys at Staley's Restaurant located at Congress Parkway and Wells Street in Chicago.

September 19, 1962 – Tony Accardo accompanied by seven hoodlums attended a party at the Riviera Restaurant and Lounge at 6540 North Milwaukee in Niles, Illinois. Before Accardo's arrival, the entire restaurant was completely cleaned and all the staff was given white serving jackets to wear. Once Accardo arrived, the restaurant was locked up and closed to the public.

October 3, 1962 – Tony Accardo checks into the Dunes Hotel in Las Vegas, Nevada.

October 8, 1962 – Tony Accardo meet two hoodlums at the Allgauers Restaurant in the old Villa Modern Motel on Skokie Highway in Northbrook, Illinois. Purpose of the meeting was unknown.

November 9, 1962 – Tony Accardo and Ralph Pierce attend the wake of James "Jimmy the Swede" Johnson at the Marzullo Funeral Home on West Harrison Street.

December 5, 1962 – Tony Accardo, Paul DeLucia and their wives attend the wedding of Michael Briatta Jr. and Diane Marterie. Michael Jr. was the son of mobster Mike Briatta Sr. and Diane Marterie was the daughter of big band leader musician Ralph Marterie.

Mob Boss

In early 1963 the year started with Tony Accardo focusing on making more money in the form of opening businesses and new rackets. He also wanted to make sure his family had a legit income for years to come.

Tony Accardo had meetings with Paul DeLucia and Sam Giancana because Accardo was interested in buying a bowling alley and cocktail lounge in Rosemont, Illinois, for $500,000. On February 1, 1963, Tony Accardo and Paul DeLucia met with Rosemont Mayor Donald E. Stephens at the old Flamingo Motel in Rosemont. Accardo informed Stephens he was going to purchase the two businesses across the street from the new Thunderbolt Motel for $500,000 for his son-in-law Palmer Pyle to manage and Accardo wanted Stephens to guarantee a liquor license. Stephens agreed.

It was also learned in early 1963 that Accardo was partners with Chuckie English in the Lormar Distributing Company. It was said that both split the profits 50/50. Another company was the White Way Electric Company. When its owner Thomas Flannery died in 1962, the business became more "Outfit" owned than it was previously. Accardo and Sam Giancana always had a financial interest in the business when Flannery was alive. With Accardo and Giancana as partners came the ability to be the only company in Chicago that could work on holidays and Sundays without interference from the electrical unions. This company was given all the work on the Mob's motels known as the "Mannheim strip" located on Mannheim Road leading to O'Hare International Airport.

Tony Accardo and Paul DeLucia were the driving force behind the Chicago Outfit's move into Mexico to open up gambling operations. Accardo made a few trips to Mexico City to visit mobster Nick Circella, aka Nick Dean, who had been deported from the U.S. and was living in Mexico and was going to head all the gambling operations for the Outfit. In August 1963 Accardo gave Augie Circella, brother of Nick who was an operator of a Chicago burlesque house, $150,000 of "Outfit" money to be delivered to Nick in Mexico for the gambling setup. Augie Circella used an unknown woman to smuggle the cash into Mexico. Nick Circella was very interested in making these gambling operations work since he lost a considerable amount of money in a failed shrimp boat business in Mexico.

One informant told the FBI that when Accardo made one of his trips to Mexico in connection with this gambling operation he returned to Chicago a very sick man which lasted many weeks. Accardo believed he had been suffering from some type of intestinal poisoning.

In July 1963 FBI agents went to Plan-it Travel at 6931 North Oak Park Avenue, which was owned by Anthony Ross Accardo Jr. and Nick Nitti, to find out if Sam Giancana had made travel plans with that agency. Anthony Ross Accardo told the FBI that even though Giancana was his Godfather, he had never made any travel plans through his agency. Both Accardo and Nitti told the agents they would contact the FBI if he ever did. Which, they never did.

It was also reported around this time from an FBI informant that Tony Accardo had been adamant to his friends that he did not want any of his children following in his footsteps in regards to being involved in organized crime. That's when this informant told FBI agents that allegedly, unbeknownst to Tony Accardo, his son was allegedly using "muscle" tactics in his dealings. It was not reported if Tony Accardo ever discovered this.

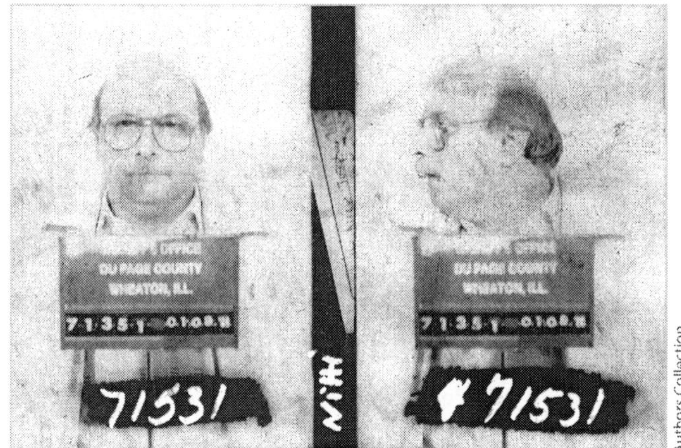

Nick Nitti's mug shot

Months later Tony Accardo sold his mansion at 915 Franklin Street to Fred J. Brunner, who at the time was the chairman of Brunner & Lay Incorporated, tool manufacturers, for around $200,000. Accardo and his wife moved into the seven room coach home behind the main house until his new residence was ready.

Accardo was going to hold an auction for all his furniture at the mansion and charge a $10 admission fee to keep the "riff raff" out of the auction. But once he learned that the IRS would be there to tax the admission fee and a herd of federal law enforcement agents would be in attendance he decided it was best to cancel that idea. His furnishings were moved to the Art Hanzel Galleries at 179 North Michigan Avenue where they were put in storage for a later auction.

Rumors flew in the newspapers as to where would Tony Accardo move. First it was a new home being built in Elmhurst, Illinois, and then it was a house in Barrington, Illinois, which had a private lake and hunting grounds.

Accardo's new house was a 16-room ranch style home, blocks away from his old house at 1407 N. Ashland Avenue, River Forest. Accardo purchased the home for between $100,000 and $160,000. There were ten rooms on the first floor with three rooms in the basement. Two family rooms, his and hers master suites, a private spa lined in cedar wood with a Jacuzzi and windows on three sides. The walls to the basement were over a foot wide of poured concrete with all the floors and walls either steel, concrete or brick. The outside of the house was covered with white Roman brick and orchard stone walls with a three-car garage.

On moving day in February 1964, Chicago Detectives sat and watched as Clarice Accardo bossed the movers as they carried out priceless antiques. First came an Elizabethan gold-plated love seat, followed by twin solid gold Italian floor lamps. A twin white marble nude statue supporting a flower pot was carried out along with a dozen gold candelabra. Movers struggled with a gray marble bench with two lovers entwined sculpted from a single block of Italian marble. Accardo was nowhere to be found during the move. As the news reporters and cameramen began to get too close Accardo's house, his brother-in-law Tarquin Simonelli began to chase and warn the reporters to stay off the property.

When the FBI went to see who was building this new home for Accardo, they discovered it was the Corbin Construction Company owned by Van Corbin, whose real name was Sam Panveno, an alleged cousin of mobster Frank LaPorte. Corbin was an associate of mobsters and was considered one of the "First Ward" cronies because he played poker often with Chicago First Ward political mobsters such as Pat Marcy, Charles Nicosia, John D'Arco, Louis Briatta, Ralph "Red" Ciangi and the Esposito brothers, Tony and Frankie X.

The sub-contractors for the house were the Melrose Park Heating Company whose owner was a close friend of Accardo's; the Melrose Park Plumbing Company owned by mobster Nick Palermo whose son was married to Accardo's daughter; and Frank Pantaleo construction business.

Van Corbin was not just a hanger-on to First Ward politicians; he was also a mob stooge. Corbin acted as a carrier of funds for Accardo from Chicago to Las Vegas and from Chicago to Miami, Florida. Years later Corbin fell out of favor with the Outfit. In July 1966 Van Corbin was shot to death as he stepped out of a Melrose Park motel he had been living in with his family.

Authors Collection 2016 ©

1407 N. Ashland Avenue, River Forest as of 2014

Spot Surveillance 1963

January 4, 1963 – Tony Accardo, Chuckie English and Jackie Cerone fly to Mexico City, Mexico and stay at the Hotel Maria Isabel, room 1417.

January 8, 1963 – Tony Accardo makes a side trip to Acapulco, Mexico and stays at the Hotel Caleta.

January 18, 1963 – Tony and Clarice Accardo return to Chicago from Mexico.

Tony Dark

January 20, 1963 – Tony Accardo, Charles "Chuckie" English, Bernie Glickman and their wives have dinner at the Armory Lounge. Accardo talks about his trip to Mexico, "When I came in, the guy at customs, said, you aren't declaring anything? I said, why should I? Mexico hasn't got anything I want." Later he talked about the food, "The best food there was in the hotel. The other joints were crummy. The meat was bad, even the fish was no good."

January 23, 1963 – Tony Accardo and Jackie Cerone had a dinner meeting at Salerno's Catering at 2910 North Avenue, Stone Park, Illinois. The purpose was unknown.

February 13, 1963 – Tony Accardo, Jackie Cerone, Frank "Skippy" Cerone and many other hoodlums gather at Salerno's Restaurant at 2910 North Avenue, Stone Park for a big secret meeting late at night.

March 13, 1963 – Several hoodlums arrive at Accardo's house and hold a meeting in the back yard. An apparently important discussion was being pursued but much of the conversation was in Italian and, on occasion, the tone of Accardo's voice became loud and heated.

April 5, 1963 - Paul DeLucia, Tony Accardo and Sam Giancana hold a meeting in Chicago. The three discuss politics in Chicago's old 25th Ward and Alderman Vito Marzullo.

April 22, 1963 – A rumor was running around town and appeared in a newspaper that Tony Accardo refused to sell his mansion at 915 Franklin Park to an African-American doctor. Accardo later referred to a lawyer if he could file a libel suit against the newspaper for printing that.

May 2, 1963 – Tony Accardo left Chicago for Las Vegas, Nevada.

June 25, 1963 – Tony Accardo and Paul DeLucia are observed arriving at the funeral of mobster Frank Russo in a rented car.

July 7, 1963 – Tony Accardo was observed inspecting the construction of the apartment building he was having built at 1829 Broadway in Melrose Park, Illinois.

Apartment Building at 1829 Broadway in Melrose Park as of 2014

July 8, 1963 – Tony Accardo was seen at O'Hare Airport. Tony Accardo leaves for Paris, France and stays at the George V Hotel. The Accardo party visited the Arc de Triomphe and ate at the Tour d' Argent, Chez Maxim, the Lido and Escargot in Les Halles. The party also visited the cabarets known as the Naturistes in Place Pigalle.

July 16, 1963 – Tony Accardo travels from Paris to Rome, Italy landing at Fiumicino Airport. He stayed at the Hotel Ambassador in Rome.

July 18, 1963 – Tony Accardo departs for Salerno, Italy.

July 19, 1963 – Tony Accardo takes a boat to Capri, Italy and then to Naples, Italy.

July 22, 1963 – Tony Accardo is seen in Venice, Italy and takes a train back to Rome.

July 27, 1963 – Tony Accardo returns to Chicago.

July 29, 1963 – Tony Accardo, Jackie Cerone, Frank Ferraro, Joey Glimco, Gus Alex, Hy Godfrey, Fred "Juke Box" Smith, Murray Humphreys, Ralph Pierce and mob lawyers Mike Brodkin and Eugene Bernstein hold a meeting at Stanley's Restaurant located on Congress Parkway in Chicago. It was believed that this meeting was to discuss the activities of Sam Giancana.

August 13, 1963 – Tony Accardo was seen meeting with mob labor union boss Louis Romano when Romano came back to Chicago from Florida where he was enjoying his retirement.

August 18, 1963 – Tony Accardo, Ross Prio and Frank LaPorte were together at the home of mobster Ben Fillichio discussing Outfit operations.

September 14, 1963 – Tony Accardo, Sam Giancana, Gus Alex, Paul DeLucia, Frank Ferraro, Jackie Cerone, Fifi Buccieri, William Aloisio, Phil Alderisio, Ben Fillichio, Ralph Cantonese and Murray Humphreys held a meeting at the wedding of Fillichio's son which was held in the Grand Ballroom of the Conrad Hilton Hotel in Chicago. It was not known what the meeting was for but Accardo used the 700-plus guests as a cover. The group retired to a suite reserved just for them to finish the meeting.

October 14, 1963 – Tony Accardo met Sam Giancana, Charles English and Butch Blasi at Armory Lounge. During this conversation Giancana became extremely agitated at the government for investigating his every move.

November 9, 1963 – Tony Accardo is observed standing in front of the Montclair Funeral home talking to Joseph LaBarbara and Joey Aiuppa. Accardo was attending the wake of Angelina Sortino, mother of mob boss Frank Ferraro.

December 13, 1963 – Tony Accardo was observed attending the wake of Phil Hoffberg, owner of the Hoffberg Insurance Company. Hoffberg and Accardo were very close friends and Hoffberg provided all of Accardo's car insurance.

The year 1964 became a first for Tony Accardo, for the first time in decades he was convicted of a crime. He was convicted of speeding and fined $15.

Tony Accardo was still handing conflicts between other mobsters in the Accardo faction. He had moved into his new home in February of that year and his name appeared in an investigation linking him as a financial backer of Sportsman's Park Race Track in Chicago and dog racing tracks in Hollywood and Miami, Florida, known as the Hollywood Kennel Club and the West Flagler Kennel Club.

The FBI had observed Sam "Mad Dog" DeStefano playing Gin Rummy with Tony Accardo and Jackie Cerone on a regular basis. It was figured out that Accardo was getting a "cut" of DeStefano's "juice" business. Sam DeStefano would pay his tribute money to Accardo at these games.

Accardo was also heavily into real estate purchase, having many acres of land in Hazel Crest, Illinois with mobster Joey Glimco. He built apartments and town homes in Franklin Park, Illinois called Howard Gardens. The FBI investigated to see if they could get Accardo for violating the Hobbs Act with all this land purchasing but that lead failed.

On June 10, 1964 Accardo's son, Anthony Ross Accardo, married Janet Marie Hawley at St. Vincent Ferrer Roman Catholic Church in River Forest, Illinois. Hawley was a former Miss Utah beauty queen who worked as an airline stewardess. Her father, Patrick Hawley, was the owner of a Utah cattle ranch.

Chuckie English was heard saying that there would be too much publicity on the affair and he was not going to attend. But he was going to send an envelope of money. Dominic "Butch" Blasi was overheard wanting to know if Chicago politicians were allowed at the wedding.

The wedding reception was held at Sam Giancana's Villa Venice. James "Turk" Torello was standing in the parking lot checking the reservations of the arriving guest while mobster Anthony "Pineapples" Eldorado was stationed at the main gate of the restaurant and lounge to make sure that the gates were open. Detectives noticed a car driven by a female would leave the parking lot and return with around 5 or 6 males in the car all hiding their faces. This car would repeat many times, bringing hoodlums and or politicians to the reception. The nephew of union mob boss Frank "Frankie the X" Esposito, orchestra and band leader Ralph Marterie provided the music for the reception.

Over 400 personal friends of the Accardo's gathered to celebrate the union. One incident which occurred at the wedding was when Gus Alex and the wife of mob lawyer Mike Brodkin got into a violent argument. Brodkin's wife, who was intoxicated, said several things to Alex, embarrassing everyone at the table. It became the "talked" about incident of the night in mob circles.

Known Mobsters seen at the Wedding

Phil Alderisio
Gus Alex
Jimmy Allegretti
Sam Battaglia
John Barone
Eugene Bernstein
Mike Brodkin
George Bravos
Nick Bravos
Marshall Caifano
Tony Campo
Dominic Caruso
Frank "Skids" Caruso
Joseph "Shoes" Caruso
James Catuara
Jackie Cerone
Patrick Cerone
Sam Cesario
Joseph Corngold
Francis Curry
William Daddono
Anthony DeGrazia
Paul DeLucia
Sam DiGiovanni
Joseph DiVarco
Sam English
Anthony Esposito Sr.
Frank Esposito
Joseph Esposito
Anthony Eldorado
Peter Epsteen
Rocco Fischetti
Frank Ferraro
Mike Fish
Albert Frabotta
Joseph Gagliano
Anthony Gianfrancesco
Joey Glimco
Frank Granata
Murray Humphreys
Vincent Inserro
John Lardino
James LaPietra
Frank LaPorte
Jerry Laurie
Ralph Marterie
Alfred Meo
William Messino
Charles Nicoletti
Nick Nitti
Frank Orlando
Ross Prio
Dominic Palermo
Tony Pinelli
Rago Brothers
Leo Rugendorf
Dominic Sibilano
Tarquin Simonelli
Henry Susk
James Torello
Frank Trumfio
Edward Vogel
Irvin Weiner

Business cars located around the church

5th Avenue Pontiac Sales, 900 South 5th Avenue, Maywood
Allen Tiling Company, 3232 North Elston Avenue, Chicago
Beutlich Inc., 7006 North Western Avenue, Chicago
Bruno's Super Service, 1801 North Harlem Avenue, Chicago
Chateau Livery Service, 600 North Parkside, Chicago
Chicus Barbeque, 1550 North Farewell, Milwaukee, Wisconsin
Chiwaukee Truck Lines, 1541 Stonegate Road, LaGrange Park
Continental Drill Company, 555 West Adams Street, Chicago
Co-Operative Music Company, 1723 Halsted Street, Chicago
D.F. Hedg Associate Inc., 8460 West Ogden Avenue, Lyons
Dick Fencl Chevrolet Inc., 600 West Madison Street, Chicago
Falson Electric Company, 1239 North Woodbine Avenue, Oak Park
Gerald Motors, 8201 Skokie Blvd., Skokie
Gourfain, Loeff & Adler, 35 East Wacker Drive, Chicago
Hartigan Olds & Cadillac, 8123 South Racine, Chicago
Mars Olds Inc., 5027 West Madison Street, Chicago
McHenry County Tobacco Company, 308 Lincoln, Fox River Grove
Melrose Park Plumbing, 1825 North 25th Avenue, Melrose Park
Melrose Park Electric Comp, 1915 W. Division Street, Melrose Park
M & C Motors 315 South Blvd, Oak Park
Mort Edidin Inc., 715 South 5th Avenue, Maywood
Nortell Olds, 1655 South Cicero Avenue, Cicero
Peacock Engr Company, 2865 Vogay Street, Northbrook
Standard Photo Supply Company, 43 East Chicago Avenue, Chicago
Sunset Restaurant, 125 North Clark Street, Chicago
Thorne Anderson Livery, 623 Drummond Place, Chicago
Union Clun Motor Livery, 1122 Balmoral, Chicago

Authors Collection 2016 ©

Photo's of St. Vincent Ferrer Roman Catholic Church in River Forest, Illinois where the Accardo wedding happened

In September 1964 Tony Accardo's physician Dr. Giulio Bruni from Northlake Hospital was arrested by secret service agents when they found counterfeit money in his possession. Bruni was on his way to visit his family in Italy. Bruni was convicted in federal court of conspiring to counterfeit 3 million dollars and was sentenced to five years in prison.

A month later Tony Accardo became a suspect in New York City when reports surfaced that Tony Accardo was seen in downtown Manhattan two days before the kidnapping of New York mob boss Joseph Bonanno.

Spot Surveillance 1964

March 14, 1964 – Tony Accardo and Frank Ferraro hold a private lunch meeting.

March 26, 1964 – Tony Accardo and Phil Alderisio are seen meeting in the lounge of the Drake Hotel in Chicago.

May 7, 1964 – Tony Accardo and Joey Aiuppa are seen meeting at the Thunderbird Motel in Miami, Florida.

May 8, 1964 – Tony Accardo, Joey Aiuppa, Rocco Potenzo, Joe Fischetti, Peter Sarnoff and Anthony Ricci, aka Tony Gobels, had dinner at the Lagoon Restaurant, 488 Sunny Isles, Miami Beach, Florida.

May 12, 1964 – Tony Accardo and crew go fishing off of the Bimini Island in the Bahamas.

June 10, 1964 – Tony Accardo's son's wedding reception was held at the Villa Venice Restaurant. FBI agents observed many mobsters like Murray Humphreys and Eugene Bernstein wearing fake rubber faces in order to hide their identities from law enforcement.

June 16, 1964 – Tony Accardo, Jackie Cerone and Albert Meo attended a luncheon at the Tam O'Shanter Golf Course in Niles, Illinois.

June 1964 – Tony Accardo and Sam Giancana meet at the Blue Horizon Motel at Belmont Avenue and River Road were they discussed the "juice" loan trial of Willie Messino and Joseph Gagliano. Both Accardo and Giancana had spent $65,000 trying to bribe the jury.

October 1964 – Tony Accardo is seen in Phoenix, Arizona meeting with unknown individuals.

October 27, 1964 – Tony Accardo observed by FBI agents standing in the Waldorf Astoria Hotel in New York City, New York.

November 6, 1964 – Tony Accardo, Ross Prio, Joseph DiVarco, and Sam Giancana had a meeting at the LaStrada Restaurant at 1531 North Wells Street in Chicago.

November 11, 1964 – Tony Accardo was observed meeting with Jackie Cerone, Chuck Meo and 12 unknown men, together at the Delta Airlines ticket counter at O'Hare Airport in Chicago.

The year 1965 was one the members of the Chicago mob wish they could have forgotten. The leadership of the Outfit fell apart. Tony Accardo focused on replacing Sam Giancana who was sent to jail for contempt of court.

The Chicago mob was in the middle of trying to take over the Italian bread industry in Chicago. Jackie Cerone and other hoodlums established the Yamo Bakery Company in Melrose Park, Illinois. This bakery specialized in Italian bread particularly small individual loaves that could be served in restaurants. They would undersell all their competitors by one-half cent per loaf, because they owned the unions that made all their competitors charge one cent per loaf to cover union cost for employees. Yamo did not use union workers and since they controlled the union, did not have to pay union wages.

In September 1965 Tony Accardo left for Italy to attend a meeting with Italian organized crime figures. Accardo then went to Salisbury, Rhodesia, Africa where it was thought he was on a three-week safari to hunt. The FBI was not sure what Accardo was up to. Once Tony Accardo returned to Chicago in November 1965, they found out by watching the local newscast. In Washington D.C. a FBI agent caught a local newscast stating that Prime Minister Ian Smith of Rhodesia, Africa made an announcement that he was laying the cornerstone for a large gambling casino.

FBI Agents discovered that when Tony Accardo returned from Africa he had given orders to Dominic "Butch" Blasi, who was then running the Armory Lounge for Sam Giancana, that he, Blasi, was now Accardo's main man for delivering messages to other mobsters in Chicago. FBI agents followed Blasi to see who orders were being sent out to and noticed that many were going to mob killer Fiore "Fifi" Buccieri. Buccieri was a Capo under Sam Giancana who had his own group of hoodlums and was never afraid or stood down to anyone in the mob. FBI agents were shocked when they noticed how Buccieri would "jump" and do what Accardo requested at lightning speed. Agents later found out that the reason Buccieri was so eager to do what Accardo wanted was because he, Buccieri, had told many of his fellow associates that the only person in this universe that he was afraid of was Tony Accardo.

Another sign Tony Accardo was attempting to make legitimate money for his family was when he invested $1.7 million into the construction of the then Bruni Memorial Hospital in Northlake, Illinois. The hospital was later changed to Northlake Community Hospital. He was also a partner in a jewelry store with Sam Giancana known as Towne Jewelers which was operated by Harold Lanoff.

Spot Surveillance 1965

May 1, 1965 – Tony Accardo lands in Miami, Florida and stays in the penthouse room of the Thunderbird Motel on Miami Beach.

May 4, 1965 – Tony Accardo meets with Joey Aiuppa and Anthony Ricci at the Thunderbird Motel coffee shop.

May 7, 1965 – Tony Accardo holds a large meeting at the Thunderbird Motel with many hoodlums in attendance.

May 10, 1965 – Tony Accardo returns to Chicago.

June 30, 1965 – Tony Accardo may have attended a wake in Kansas City, Missouri for mobster Louis Cangelose who was killed in a track racing accident on June 27, 1965. FBI agents in Kansas City believe they recognized Accardo from a photo. It was also believed that Accardo was seen at the home of mob boss Nick Civella while in Missouri.

July 1965 – Tony Accardo, Jackie Cerone and Sam Battaglia are seen meeting to discuss what should be done about Sam Giancana being sent to jail for Contempt of Court.

August 31, 1965 – Tony Accardo, Dominic "Butch" Blasi and Charles "Chuckie" English are seen entering the Armory Lounge in Forest Park to discuss Giancana's situation.

September 26, 1965 – Tony Accardo leaves for Italy and then on to Salisbury, Rhodesia, Africa to hunt animals on a three-week safari.

November 1, 1965 –Tony Accardo leaves Africa and lands in Rome Italy.

November 4, 1965 – Tony Accardo leaves Rome Italy and returns to Chicago.

December 3, 1965 – A doctor is rushed to the Accardo residence because Tony Accardo is suffering chest pains.

December 1965 – It was rumored that Tony Accardo was going to hide out in Florida with mobster Ben Fillichio over the holidays to avoid being subpoenaed by a federal grand jury.

In 1966 Sam Giancana was released from jail on his contempt of court charge and fled to Mexico because he was afraid he would be dragged back in front of a Grand Jury and be placed back in jail on a new contempt charge. That left the roll of day-to-day boss of the Chicago Outfit open and vacant. Once again Tony Accardo was calling the shots with Paul DeLucia and Jackie Cerone.

On the labor front, Tony Accardo and mobster Joey Aiuppa were still controlling all decisions made in Chicago's Motion Picture Operators Union Local 110. Both men were receiving large "cuts" from the union's treasury.

For Accardo, he and his chauffeur and bodyguard Joseph Caccione were watched as they would sit at Mare Antonio's Restaurant in Melrose Park, Illinois. There Accardo would hold his meetings. Joseph Caccione was born around 1910 and by the time he was Accardo's chauffeur he had already had three heart attacks.

Friday nights in 1966 centered around Accardo, Paul DeLucia, Jackie Cerone, Sam Battaglia and Ben Fillichio getting together at the home of someone whose name was unknown but was close to Paul Powell, Secretary of State of Illinois. This home was located on Van Buren Street, near Oak Park Avenue in Oak Park, Illinois. The discussion was mostly about business but it was an open invitation and many card games would break out.

Spot Surveillance 1966

March 16, 1966 – Ben Fillichio and Sam Battaglia are summoned to a meeting held at Tony Accardo's home. The meeting concerns a mob associate who is talking to the FBI and every one is "up in arms" that the information this person is providing will send them all to jail.

Tony Dark

April 30, 1966 – Tony Accardo travels to Miami Beach and is driven to the Thunderbird Motel by Tony Ricci.

May 6, 1966 – Tony Accardo, Anthony Ricci and three unknown males eat at Miami's Red Coach Grill.

May 9, 1966 – Tony Accardo, Ricci and two unknown males eat at the Rascal House in Miami Beach.

May 10, 1966 – Tony Accardo boards a chartered plane to Bimini, Bahama Islands with Joey Aiuppa on his annual fishing trip. Accardo later bragged that he caught 4 large tuna fish.

June 10, 1966 – U.S. Customs intercepts eighteen crates of animal skins, heads and parts shipped from South Rodesia, Africa to a taxidermist in Melrose Park, Illinois. Tony Accardo and Joey Aiuppa were listed as the people who killed these animals in Africa.

June 23, 1966 – Tony Accardo is observed at the wake of mobster Frank Roti.

November 2, 1966 – Tony Accardo is seen at Meo's Norwood Restaurant talking to the wife of Albert Meo.

November 12, 1966 – Tony Accardo is observed at a wedding held by the Palermo family at the Mar-Lac House in Oak Park. With Accardo were Joseph Bulger, Jackie Cerone, Sam Battaglia, Mayor of Melrose Park Chester Carson and attorney Francis Fanelli.

On June 18, 1967 Tony Accardo's mother, Mary Accardo, died at Oak Park Hospital, She was waked at the Montclair Funeral Home at 6901 Belmont Avenue in Chicago and buried at Mount Carmel Cemetery in Hillside, Illinois. Over 1,000 known hoodlums and politicians attended this wake and funeral. The only mobsters the FBI did not see attending were Paul DeLucia, Sam Giancana and Jackie Cerone. Even Fiore "Fifi" Buccieri, who had once been afraid of Accardo but got over it and had been making a power play on Accardo to take over control of the Outfit, attended and played nice causing no problems. Other mobster noticed at the wake were Joe "Caesar" DiVarco, Big Joe Arnold, Rocco Potenzo, Joey Aiuppa, Robert Ansani, Joseph Corngold, James "Turk" Torello, Ralph Pierce, Phil Alderisio, Irvin Weiner, Joey Glimco, Joe "Gags" Gagliano, Willie Messino, and Joe "Black Joe" Amato.

On August 28, 1967 a Chicago newspaper printed a story that Tony Accardo was being sued by his wife who charged him with desertion. In the article it stated that his wife requested child support for their children and a division of their property, government bonds, bank accounts, and businesses. Mrs. Accardo claimed her husband deserted her on August 16, 1967. Despite the newspaper story, it was never disclosed if the story was true or not.

Spot Surveillance 1967-1968

January 15, 1967 – Tony Accardo was seen arriving in Honolulu, Hawaii and staying at the most expensive hotel on the island of that time, the Kahala Hilton Hotel.

January 26, 1967- Tony Accardo returns to Chicago.

March 8, 1967 – Tony Accardo holds a meeting at El Greco's Restaurant on the North Side of Chicago.

April 10, 1967 – Informant says Tony Accardo was fishing off the Bahamas on this day but was observed by agents on April 12 back in Chicago.

June 22, 1967 – Tony Accardo was observed at the wake of his mother.

July 23, 1967 – Tony Accardo, William Daddono and Anthony Ricci were observed in Miami, Florida together.

August 27 & 28, 1967 – Tony Accardo, Jackie Cerone, Joseph DiVarco, Vince Solano and Joe Amato attend the 9th Annual Italian Golf Tournament at the South Hills Country Club near Racine, Wisconsin.

September 6, 1967 – Tony Accardo is observed at mobster Chuckie English's house at 1131 North Lathrop in River Forest to discuss business.

October 2, 1967 – Tony Accardo was observed by agents in New York City staying at the American Hotel.

November 28, 1967 – Tony Accardo, Jackie Cerone and Phil Alderisio hold a meting at Meo's Norwood House.

February 15, 1968 – Tony Accardo is observed at the Thunderbird Motel in Miami Beach, Florida meeting with former Chicago Mob Alderman John D'Arco Sr.

March 7, 1968 – Tony Accardo is observed at the wake of Michael Marchese held at Montclair Funeral Home in Chicago.

April 26, 1968 – Tony Accardo attended the wake of mobster Robert Ansani at the Rosewood Funeral home in Bellwood, Illinois.

June 27, 1968 – A group of Chicago syndicate members including Tony Accardo and Joseph DiVarco leave Chicago and fly to Isle Verde in Puerto Rico. They stayed at the Hotel Americana. They were observed attending a gathering at the El San Juan Hotel Corporation in San Juan, Puerto Rico to gamble and play golf.

November 5, 1968 – Tony Accardo, his wife Clarice, Nick Nitti and Anthony Ricci depart from O'Hare Airport heading to Europe.

November 9 & 10, 1968 – The Accardo's, Nick Nitti and Anthony Ricci were watched as they visited unknown people in Palermo, Italy. They stayed at the Hotel Villa Igea.

November 10, 1968 – The Accardo group traveled to Rome, Italy. They stayed at the Hotel Ambasciatori.

November 14, 1968 – The Accardo group traveled to Paris, France.

November 19, 1968 – The Accardo group returned from Europe.

The end of the 1960's was a welcomed event since there were not too many "good times" for the Chicago Outfit. For Tony Accardo, he had to deal with yet another investigation by the government.

In September 1968 another Federal Grand Jury investigating irregularities in the handling of funds from the Veteran's Park District, which his old mob lawyer Joseph Bulger used as his own personal bank account. The government placed immunity on Accardo to answer all questions, which he did, but the evidence against him was so weak that he was not held in contempt of court and released.

In June 1969 Rocco Culotta, one time park district treasurer, plead guilty to theft, conspiracy to commit theft and official misconduct. Four other Melrose Park men - Fred Maggio, Stanley Malinowski, Arthur Geiser and Joseph Fanelli - were found guilty and given three years probation. With Culotta pleading guilty, it spared another appearance for Tony Accardo before a grand jury. It was alleged that Culotta used park district funds to pay $2,000 of Tony Accardo's property taxes on his River Forest mansion.

FBI agents continued to watch Accardo every day in 1968. Every Friday, while in Chicago, he would go to Meo's Norwood House and have a lunch meeting with Paul DeLucia, Jackie Cerone and Phil Alderisio. They would meet in a private room in the back which opened into the main dinning room. Only Outfit people were ever allowed to eat in that room and only two waitresses that worked there were allowed to serve them. It just so happens every Friday at Meo's was a free fashion show showing off beautiful women in lace underwear.

On other days, many people came to visiting Accardo at his home, people like Frank Chesrow, who once controlled the Cook County Sanitation Department, was a frequent visitor to Accardo's home.

In November 1968 Tony Accardo and his wife Clarice went on a trip to Europe with mob boss Anthony Ricci and Nick Nitti, then the owner of Nitti Travel Company. Surveillance was set up in the countries they traveled to, including Rome, Milan, Palermo, Venice, and Paris. The Accardo group acted like tourists most of the time and the agents watching could not find anything suspicious about their activities.

FBI agents also discovered that Las Vegas entertainer Sammy Davis Jr. was working closely with Chicago hoodlums. A FBI report from February 1969 stated that Sammy Davis Jr. was allegedly broke, making $50,000-a-week and spending $75,000 a week. Because of this, he was acting as a go-between for Chicago hoodlums and the Blackstone Rangers. Tony Accardo was mentioned as being involved in this.

In 1969 Tony Accardo was attempting to handle a situation his right-hand man Jackie Cerone was involved in. Cerone was going to be on his way to prison and that meant Accardo was going to have to figure out who was going to run the day-to-day operations of the Outfit.

In March 1969 Jackie Cerone was released on bond and was granted permission from the courts to travel to Miami, Florida. What the courts did not know was he was going with Tony Accardo and Joey Aiuppa to attend a national La Costa Nostra meeting. Cerone was given the ok to leave Chicago by the courts saying he needed to have an operation on his hemorrhoids by the same doctor in Miami who performed the operation in 1962. When FBI agents investigated this doctor to see if it was true, the doctor did say Cerone came complaining that his rectum itched but it was only a rash and not the surgery Cerone told the court had to be performed.

The meeting was for all top mob bosses in every city to reorganize territories and confirm new promotions of mob bosses to the national council. It was two months after the death of mob boss Vito Genovese who died in prison and new leaders were chosen for the New York and Miami area.

There were also discussions about reopening gambling operations in Florida and new gambling operations in the Caribbean. Florida gambling was divided between Chicago, New York, Detroit and Cleveland. Santo Trafficante was chosen to remain mob boss of Florida since he took over the job two years earlier when mob boss Michael "Trigger Mike" Coppola died. Tony Accardo was in the company of Joey Aiuppa, Donald "Don Angel" Angelini, Jackie Cerone and his cousin Frank "Skippy" Cerone, Miami mobster Anthony Ricci, and New York mobsters Frank Martin, Joe Brown, then brother of the powerful deceased mob boss Tom Lucchese, Joe Colombo, Meyer Lansky and Carlos Gambino.

It was learned that both Paul DeLucia and Sam Giancana were on their way to Miami but found out about the subpoenas and turned around. Sam Giancana, who had been hiding out in South America, was making his was to Miami through San Juan. He made it to the Bahamas before turning away.

FBI agents gave this information to the Justice Department and issued subpoenas to mob chieftains in Miami to appear before a grand jury as to why they were all in Miami together. They all took the fifth to questioning.

In October 1969 Tony Accardo was using the name of M. Le Rack to try to throw off an investigator as he was hold up in a motel in Miami. He was holding his meetings with Tony Ricci to try and figure out what to do about running the day-to-day operations of the Outfit. The decade ended on a sour note for the mob.

The list of people subpoenaed in Miami

Tony Accardo (Chicago)
Jackie Cerone (Chicago)
Don Angeline (Chicago
Paul DeLucia (Chicago)
Sam Giancana (Chicago-Mexico)
Meyer Lansky (New York-Las Vegas)
Carlos Gambino (New York)
Anthony Ricci (New York-Miami-Pennsylvania)
Vincent "Jimmy Blue Eyes" Alo (New Jersey)
Anthony Civella (Kansas City)
Carl "Corky" Civella (Kansas City)

Spot Surveillance 1969

March 30, 1969 – Tony Accardo is in Miami, Florida attending a national La Costa Nostra conference. He is observed with Chicago mobster Joey Aiuppa, Jackie Cerone, his cousin Frank "Skippy" Cerone.

March 31, 1969- Tony Accardo and Tony Ricci were observed shopping at the Surfside shopping district. They then headed to the Castaways boat docks and then to eat at Rascal House Restaurant in Miami.

April 1, 1969 – Tony Accardo, Jackie Cerone, Donald Angelini and Tony Ricci are observed at the Castaways boat docks and later eating at the Rascal House Restaurant in Miami. Accardo was staying at the Thunderbird Motel.

April 2, 1969 – Tony Accardo and Tony Ricci were observed driving to the Le Café de Paris in Ft. Lauderdale, Florida with two females.

April 3, 1969 – Tony Accardo and Tony Ricci are observed at the Diplomat Country Club in Miami. Both were observed meeting with New York mob bosses Meyer Lansky and Vincent Alo.

April 20, 1969 – Tony Accardo is observed at the wedding reception of Vincent and Judith Guzaldo, son of mobster Phil Guzaldo, held at the Sheraton Blackstone Hotel in the Chicago Loop. Others in the company of Tony Accardo were Jackie Cerone, Charles and Sam English, William Messino and Joe "Gags" Gagliano.

May 5, 1969 – Tony and Clarice Accardo arrive at the Thunderbird Motel in Miami, Florida.

May 15, 1969 – Tony Accardo and a group of mobsters charter a plane to Bimini, Bahamas for a 10 day fishing trip aboard the Daddy 'O' boat. They stayed at the Big Game Fishing Club.

July 4, 1969 – Tony Accardo is observed at the wake of Dominic Alderisio, father of mobster Phil Alderisio. The wake was held at Montclair Funeral Home in Chicago.

October 23, 1969 – Tony Accardo and Nick Nitti arrive in Rome, Italy. They register at the Hotel Ambassador.

November 1, 1969 – Tony Accardo and Nick Nitti return from Europe.

November 3, 1969 - Accardo holds a meeting at Meo's Norwood House and meets with Milwaukee, Wisconsin mob associates.

November 11, 1969 – FBI agents spot Clarice Accardo in Las Vegas, Nevada with a friend. The two are on a pleasure trip and staying at the Stardust Hotel and Casino. She is seen in the company of Frank "Skippy" Cerone who is also in Las Vegas.

Authors Collection

Tony Accardo and mobster Anthony Ricci "Tony Gobels" walking down a street in the 1960's

Chapter 26

The King

In April 1970 Tony Accardo was indicted by a federal grand jury on two counts of having unregistered semi-automatic weapons in his home. Agents of the U.S. Treasury Department noticed during surveillance that a German Mouser machine gun pistol was hanging on the wall in Accardo's home. After obtaining a search warrant they raided Accardo's home. A search of the house turned up another weapon, a shotgun pistol. The guns were not registered in Accardo's name, his wife's name, or any of his son's names. Accardo faced a penalty of 10 years in prison for each gun. Accardo's son Joseph testified that the guns were his and that when he had turned 21 he was given the antique gun collection containing 50 guns. Two of the guns taken in the raid were from that collection. FBI agent watched as Tony Accardo, his son Anthony Ross, Paul DeLucia and Anthony Ricci discussed the legal options over lunch at Meo's Restaurant on April 23. In May 1971, Tony Accardo was acquitted of illegal possession of guns.

In 1972 Tony Accardo's routine consisted of meeting everyone he needed to meet with either at his home or at Meo's Restaurant or a place known as Phillipo's Restaurant. Once or twice a week mobsters Ross Prio and Dom DiBella would be observed having lunch with Accardo. Investigators also noticed that before Accardo would show up at Meo's Restaurant to eat and have a meeting Mario Gigante, Paul DeLucia's brother-in-law would arrive at Meo's alone and eat, spending his time looking around but would always leave Meo's before Accardo showed up. It was speculated Gigante was a look- out for Accardo to see if any surveillance could be recognized before Accardo held his meeting.

When Joey Aiuppa had to meet with Accardo, the meeting was always held at Accardo's home. Joey Aiuppa would always either be alone or in the company of mobster Larry Rassano. The meeting was always at 8:00 AM sharp.

Accardo was also observed meeting with Nick Nitti, Rocco Padulo Jr. and Bernard Bruno. Padulo Jr. was a freelance photographer who once worked for a Chicago newspaper. Around 1958 Tony Accardo and Padulo became friends and Padulo traveled with Accardo extensively on several trips to Europe and the Bahamas. Bernard Bruno was a Melrose Park attorney and close friend of both Tony Accardo and Sam Giancana. Both Bruno and Padulo were associated with other mobsters.

Spot Surveillance 1970 -1972

January 20, 1970 – Tony Accardo spends 4 days at a Chicago hospital for a bleeding ulcer. He had been suffering from the condition for a number of years.

May 3, 1972 – Tony Accardo, Paul DeLucia and Frank LaPorte hold a meeting.

June 1, 1972 – Tony Accardo leaves for his fishing vacation in Bimini, Bahamas.

November 1, 1972 – Tony Accardo is observed at the Hirsch's West End Funeral Home at 1340 West Otto, Chicago Heights, Illinois. He is attending the wake of mob boss Frank LaPorte. Accardo was observed sitting with Al Pilotto, Joey Aiuppa, James Catuara and Ralph Pierce.

In February 1973, FBI agents watched as Tony Accardo, Teamsters boss Frank Fitzsimons, mobsters Anthony Spilotro, Louis Rosanova and Marshall Caifano met together in Palm Springs for a meeting. It was believed the meeting concerned Las Vegas casinos.

Back in Chicago, Tony Accardo, Gus Alex and Joey Aiuppa sent word out that all mobsters were to shift many of their illegal operations out of Cook County and into the other counties around Chicago. The three were attempting to reorganize their operations after the death of Paul DeLucia.

Another problem facing Accardo was the fact that income to the middle and lower echelon of organized crime had diminished so drastically that these individuals had been pushing Accardo and Aiuppa to become involved in narcotics traffic which was the moneymaker of the 1970's. Up until that point, Accardo had refused the members of the Chicago mob to become involved in narcotics though most had secretly engaged in selling drugs. Because of this policy involving drugs, Accardo, Aiuppa and Gus Alex, the top three Chicago bosses at the time, had considerable difficulty in keeping the membership of organized crime in a pacified condition, causing a certain level of restlessness. Most of the lower echelon members had to scratch out a living involving some sort of legitimate work, whereas the middle level did their best to keep things together by becoming involved in financing legitimate businesses. For example, mobster Dominic "Butch" Blasi, once the right-hand man of mob boss Sam Giancana, opened a hot dog stand in Melrose Park with a partner to make a living.

In June 1973 Tony Accardo's home was under 24-hour surveillance by the River Forest Police. On June 4, 1973 the River Forest PD observed a 1973 Dark Blue Pontiac picking up Tony Accardo at his house. Police attempted to follow Accardo but the car used extreme evasive high speed tactics to lose them. However, detectives discovered that the person picking up Accardo was Sam Alex, brother of mob boss Gus Alex, which alarmed police. Sam Alex had been the Outfit's disciplinarian and "lord high executioner" and it was believed that Tony Accardo may have been involving Sam Alex to stop the rebellion by the "young turks" of the Outfit. Detectives believed this to be true since four days later Sam Alex once again was observed at Accardo's home meeting with Accardo and mob boss Joey Aiuppa. In all, Sam Alex's car was observed many times at Accardo's house within a three-week period. FBI agents sent word out to an informant in the Outfit who reported back that Sam Alex was "called in" back to Chicago by Accardo because there was some trouble in the Outfit and his services were needed.

According to the informant, the "troubles" Accardo was concerned about were the younger group of mobsters including Anthony Spilotro. The second concern for Accardo was of mobster Marshall Caifano, whose problems were more financial in nature. When Caifano was released from prison, he used "muscle" on several individuals who were very well situated with Tony Accardo. In the end, Accardo, Gus Alex, Joey Aiuppa and Sam Alex came to a decision that the "young blazers" would be allowed to go ahead and run any racket they had in mind; however, if they got into something unsanctioned by Accardo, they were all on their own, especially if they got caught. No Outfit money or connections would be used to help them get out of trouble. And because of Caifano, Accardo declared that if anyone was caught muscling in on any established source of revenue that was "Outfit" money, they would be "knocked off" regardless of what their position or situation was with the mob.

In December 1973 mob associate Richard Cain, who was a messenger for mob boss Sam Giancana after Giancana fled the United States in 1966, was murdered. During the investigation an informant said he heard that the money and contract for the hit on Cain came from the Outfit's "war chest" and the order came from "out west." The informant understood this to mean that "out west" meant Tony Accardo since Accardo was spending most of his time in Palm Springs, California. He added he figured the hit was a payout of $50,000 to $75,000 for the murder.

Spot Surveillance 1973

September 1973 – Tony Accardo and his wife were observed and followed as they toured Italy with Nick Nitti. After a law enforcement interview with Nitti, he said that he complained to Tony Accardo the entire trip as Italian police followed their every move. Nitti said he was told by Accardo to ignore the police and pretend that their surveillance did not bother them.

Accardo and Paul DeLucia had placed mobster Joey Aiuppa and Gus Alex in the role of day-to-day boss running daily operations after Jackie Cerone went away to prison. In January 1974 Tony Accardo left Chicago to spend the winter in Palm Springs, California where he rented a home under the name Tony Porter, which was his wife Clarice's maiden name, while Chicago's other mob boss Gus Alex left Chicago to spend the winter in Ft. Lauderdale, Florida. Both mobsters wanted to retire and were most reluctant to continue running the mob. But, due to their many contacts which they built up throughout the years had made them essential to the operations of organized crime in Chicago, they were stuck in their positions.

While in Palm Springs, Tony Accardo would spend most nights at an Italian restaurant and would often visit with old-time Capone gangster Joe Fusco. Fusco was a millionaire beer, wine and liquor distributor from Chicago who also spent his winters in Palm Springs. Accardo and Fusco had been friends since the early 1920's when both worked under Al Capone and Frank Nitti.

Known Capo's for Accardo as of 1974

Al Pilotto (Chicago Heights)
Joseph "Joey the Clown" Lombardo
James "Turk" Torello
Jackie Cerone

In May 1975 Tony Accardo returned to Chicago from Indian Wells California where he had spent the winter months. He was observed meeting with Gus Alex, lawyers Carl Walsh and Art Nesser. One of Accardo's sons was involved in a case wherein he was charged with making false statements on a loan application to a federally insured bank.

With the situation in the Outfit still in a bad place, one of its most famous gangsters was on his way out for good. In June 1975 Outfit boss Sam Giancana was killed in the basement of his Oak Park house. Many believe the order for his killing came from Tony Accardo, or, if he was asked for permission for the hit, gave the ok without a second thought. The one time heir-apparent to Accardo's empire, hand-picked by Accardo, had fallen so out of favor that his death meant nothing to the Outfit. Many believe the opposite, Giancana was killed to send a message to Tony Accardo that the old days were over and the old bosses were not safe anymore from the young and hungry mobsters.

When FBI agents interviewed newspaper reporter Jack Mabley, who had developed informants of his own in organized crime, informed the agents that he received an anonymous phone call claiming that Tony Accardo was going to be the next one to be killed and predicted his murder within six months of Giancana, unless Accardo gave in and turned power over to the "Young Turks" in the Outfit.

The "Young Turks" was a loosely knit band of fringe and dissident members of younger years in Chicago who felt that they were not receiving enough money from organized crime rackets and were attempting to obtain a greater piece of the action from the older leaders.

Spot Surveillance 1974 -1975

May 1974 – Tony Accardo was observed leaving Chicago just before the Memorial Day holiday. He was observed landing in Bimini where he fished for two to three weeks.

April 1975 – Tony Accardo returned to Chicago from spending the winter in Indian Wells, California.

April 8, 1975 – Tony Accardo is observed at the home of mobster Jackie Cerone in Elmwood Park.

May 4, 1975 – Tony Accardo is admitted to Mary of Nazareth Hospital for medical tests related to a stomach ailment and is released the next day. He is picked up from the hospital by Gus Alex.

It was a fact that if you drove by Tony Accardo's house at night and the light was right you could see through one of the picture windows from the street and see his collection of 15 rifles and 40 hand guns displayed on the wall. Some believed Accardo did this on purpose to make sure you understood that if you had a thought of burglarizing his home, think again, you would be killed.

Apparently, some of the younger mobsters in the Outfit did not get the message. In December 1977 five Chicago area burglars had a dumb idea. "*Let's break into Tony Accardo's mansion and steal all his jewels.*" So while the Accardo's were wintering in Palm Springs, California, the five men broke into Accardo's house at 1407 Ashland Avenue by bypassing Accardo's expensive alarm system using what they called a "black box" electronic device. Once the system was down, they went onto the roof of the house and used torches to cut through bars which secured the second-story bathroom. Once inside, the men ransacked the place searching for untold treasures. They found four wall safes which took many hours of carefully cutting into to break. Taken from the safe was a 70.20 carat diamond known as the "Idol's Eye" which dated back to the 1600's.

On January 6, 1978 at 4:00 pm Tony Accardo's housekeeper Michael Volpe, discovered that Accardo's residence had been burglarized. Volpe quickly telephoned mobster Nick Palermo who when he heard the news was extremely upset.

Tony Accardo arrived back in Chicago on January 7, and when police checked the phone records, Accardo contacted Joey Aiuppa to discuss the situation. In turn, Aiuppa contacted Jackie Cerone and the ball was rolling on figuring out who did this.

FBI agents reached out to Tony Accardo a few months after the break-in and he agreed to meet with them at his attorney's office at 39 South La Salle Street in Chicago. Tony Accardo, not very forthcoming, gave a different story of what occurred during the break-in.

The FBI report reads as follows, *"He (Accardo) acknowledged that a break-in had occurred at his residence in River Forest but stated that he could not recall what month in which the break-in had occurred. He did recall, however, that the break-in had occurred after Christmas of 1977. He preferred not to discuss how he learned of the break-in. He returned to River Forest from California by airplane the day after he was notified about the break-in, in order to determine what, if anything, had been taken by the burglars. The burglars obtained entry into his home by kicking in the rear door. The door had been taped together so that he could see it and was only fixed after he had seen it. He was asked if the means of entry appeared to be the work of a professional burglar and he replied that he did not know what a professional burglar's work would look like.*

Upon returning to River Forest, he conducted an inventory of his possessions and determined that nothing was missing and that there had been no damage done inside his home, except to the rear door. A drawer had been pulled out in his bedroom but this was the only indication that burglars had been in the home. The burglars left without leaving anything of theirs behind. No one was occupying his home at the time of the break-in.

There is an alarm system in his home that when triggered causes a bell to ring on the roof. The alarm has been shut off for some time because it malfunctioned in the past and was shut off at the time of the break-in. The alarm does not transmit a signal outside the premises. Since nothing was taken from his residence by the burglars, he did not report the matter to the police.

He was asked if he had any idea who burglarized his residence. He replied that he did not but that it may have been the FBI. He was informed by the interviewing agents that this was untrue.

Accardo was asked to comment on speculation appearing in the Chicago news media that the burglary of the Levinson's Jewelry Store in December, 1977, the burglary of his River Forest residence and the murders of the five men in January, 1978, were related. Accardo asked what type of questions the interviewing agents desired to ask concerning the information that had appeared in the news media and he was advised that the initial question would concern his relationship with the owner of Levinson's Jewelry Store. He stated that he did not wish to answer this question or any other questions about the information appearing in the news media connecting the Levinson burglary, the burglary at his home and the five murders. The interview was concluded at this point."

In the end, it turned out to be a bad career move for the five burglars. Their mutilated bodies began turning up between January 20 and February 20, 1978. As detectives tried to solve the murders, one of Tony Accardo's chauffeurs, Jerry Carusiello, was found murdered in Addison, Illinois in September 1979. At the time an informant told the FBI that Carusiello was given the "contracts" to kill the five burglars and then a "contract" was given to kill Carusiello due to his knowledge of the murders.

However, in the groundbreaking Family Secrets Trial in Chicago in 2007, the truth of the robbery came to light. It was said that these weren't stupid burglars daring to test faith to steal Accardo's treasures; it was an act to try to save their lives. Mob burglar John Mendell led a crew of thieves who had robbed Levinson's Jewelry Store of hundreds of thousands of dollars in jewels. The Levinson's Jewelers Store was located at 739 North Clark Street in Chicago. On December 18, 1977 Mendell and his crew used a "black box" to bypass the elaborate burglar alarm system to break into the store. Once inside, they used acetylene torches to burn open the wall safes containing the diamonds, watches and diamond rings. The take totaled $534,929.81 from the burglary. When Mendell found out the owner of Levinson's was a close friend of Tony Accardo's and that Accardo was pissed off, Mendell panicked and went into hiding. He took the stolen jewelry and hid it in the rafters of his business. Another rival group of mob burglars broke into Mendell's business and stole the Levinson jewelry from Mendell. The jewelry wound up in a walk-in vault in Accardo's home. So Mendell broke into Accardo's home to get the jewelry back.

John Mendell was lured to his death by mobster Ronald Jarrett, a trusted associate of Mendell's. Mendell was beaten and stabbed over and over with an ice pick by Jarrett, Frank Calabrese Sr., Nick Calabrese and Frank Saladino. Many years later, Ronald Jarrett would be shot dead in front of his house.

The men who robbed Accardo's home and were killed were Bernard Ryan, Steve Garcia, Vince Moretti, Donald Swanson, aka Donny Reno, John Mendell and John McDonald.

On November 10, 1978, FBI agents swarmed Accardo's house at 1407 Ashland Avenue because a long-time friend and houseman of Accardo's, Michael Volpe, had disappeared. Volpe had appeared before a federal grand jury investigating Outfit murders linked to the robbery of Accardo's home. Five days after Volpe testified he disappeared. Agents found in Accardo's home $275,000 in cash kept in a $50 and $100 bills in a fire proof compartment in the basement, a police scanner to listen in on police radio calls and a few guns.

They confiscated the money, a memo pad, scraps of papers which were mostly burned in the incinerator and a pair of gold cufflinks. They also noticed that the walls in the basement were lined with framed photographs of Accardo with many of his mob associates. There were photos of Accardo with Joseph DiVarco, Joey Aiuppa, James "Turk" Torello, Jackie Cerone, a few with Paul DeLucia and Joseph "The Clown" Lombardo. Many of the photos were of photographs depicting Accardo during his international travel, like his trips to Egypt, Italy and the Middle East. There were also many photos of Accardo and one of his attorneys, who FBI agents listed as suspected courier of illicit funds for Accardo. Tony Accardo eventually received his $275,000 in cash back from the FBI.

In February 1979 mobsters Nick Palermo and Dominic "Butch" Blasi were called before a federal grand jury to testify about the five burglars who were found murdered for robbing Accardo's home. Both Palermo and Blasi were given a choice; either appear and answer questions or report to jail. Both were granted immunity from prosecution in exchange for their testimony. Whatever was said in the hearing was not known.

In 1979 Tony Accardo spent much of the year going back and forth to Palm Springs. The winter in Chicago was bad, having one of its biggest blizzards on record. In honor of that, Tony Accardo used the last name of "Winter" on a flight from Chicago to California. It was discovered by a reporter who was accompanying then Chicago Mayor Jane Byrne, who was taking a 10-day vacation on the west coast after her April 3 victory in Chicago. The reporter had gotten up to use the restroom on the plane and as he was walking back noticed Tony Accardo sitting on the plane. After the plane landed in California and the passengers began leaving the plane Tony Accardo noticed the news media with cameras and reporters waiting by the exit of the tarmac. Accardo, unaware that Mayor Byrne had been on the plane with him, went into dodge mode thinking the media was there for him. Moments after he made his escape, he realized the media was not there for him so he quickly made his way out of the airport.

Back in Chicago, Tony Accardo attempted to purchase a $100,000 condominium in the exclusive Mission Hills Country Club Village near Northbrook, Illinois. When he applied for the condo he was told he was rejected because he was not wanted in that community. When he was told "no" it was learned that some of his children had also applied for condo's right next to the one he wanted to buy so he could make a secure area, with his neighbors being people he could trust 100 percent. What made Mission Hills so perfect to Accardo was that it was on a 150-acre development which had lavish security including uniformed guards at the entrance that would scrutinize visitors and it had additional guards roaming the grounds.

The reason Accardo was searching for a place to live stemmed from the event when FBI agents raided his house. Tony Accardo had attempted to have his house searched and swept the best he could after the FBI left but he was never convinced that some kind of electronic surveillance device had not been hidden in the home. He never felt safe there again and sold the home in September of 1979 for $487,500.

Spot Surveillance 1977-1979

March 31, 1977 – Tony Accardo attended the wedding of Dallas mob boss Joseph Camisi's son.

October 1977 – Tony Accardo, Joey Aiuppa, Anthony Spilotro and James "Turk" Torello held a meeting at a place called Tom's Resort. It was believed the meeting may have been to plan some mob murders.

November 16, 1978 – Tony Accardo, Joey Aiuppa and Jackie Cerone are observed at Rocky's Restaurant and lounge, 2212 West North Avenue in Melrose Park, Illinois. The three are holding a meeting while eating dinner. An FBI agent walks into the bar to watch, he observed Accardo commanding Aiuppa and Cerone to make phone calls and at one point, sent Cerone to walk around the bar looking at every person in the place to see if anyone looked like an undercover agent. Cerone did not catch the FBI agent inside. Some time later, Aiuppa and Cerone said their goodbye's to Accardo who was overheard saying to one of his bodyguards, "*Stand by the door until we are clear and see if any mother fucker follows us out.*" Once

Aiuppa and Cerone left the place, the bodyguard went and sat with Accardo before escorting him out of the restaurant.

December 9, 1978 – Clarice Accardo was observed in Indian Wells, California with her dog.

January 2, 1979 – Tony Accardo is watched as he met with an unknown individual in Indian Wells, California. The two ate lunch, drove around the area many times, always in deep conversation.

February 1979 – Tony Accardo is summoned to the California Attorney General's office to give a deposition in connection with a $55 million suit filed by Joseph Agosto in Las Vegas, against the Organized Crime Commission for listing him as an organized crime figure.

November 20, 1979 – Tony Accardo and Jackie Cerone are observed at Rosanova's Tailor Shop in Chicago.

November 28, 1979 – Tony Accardo was observed at the Walgreen's store on Lake Street in Oak Park. He is seated in the restaurant area of the store when he is met by Joey Aiuppa and Alfonso Tornabene. After the meeting, Aiuppa and Tornabene leave to meet with mob boss Angelo LaPietra.

Undercover photo of Tony Accardo and Jackie Cerone walking down the street in the 1970's

Chapter 27

Long Days Gone

A new decade, the decade of the drug dealer. Tony Accardo had always been against drugs being sold from the Outfit but he was not blind to reality. In January 1980 DEA and FBI agents received word that the talk from informants was that Tony Accardo may have become involved in narcotics, specifically cocaine.

The investigation actually dated back to November 1978, when Tony Accardo was listed as a subject in a DEA-FBI joint investigation into two organized crime associates in Chicago. The two were Edward Speice, a Chicago burglar and one-time henchman of mobster Sam DeStefano and Speice's boss, Anthony "Sonny" Esposito Jr., the son of mob labor union boss Anthony "Tony X" Esposito. In the early 1970's Sonny Esposito had been considered one of the top narcotic bosses of cocaine filtering into Chicago under the umbrella of the Outfit. In 1972 DEA agents sent a mob rat by the name of Charles "Chuckie" Crimaldi to set up Esposito which resulted in Esposito's arrest. By 1978 Anthony Accardo's name was being mentioned as having something to do with Esposito and Speice's operations involving narcotics. Sonny Esposito had also been close to some of the burglars that burglarized Accardo's home. It was said that Donald Swanson had actually given Sonny Esposito some of Accardo's loot to hide in his mother's garage in Melrose Park right after the burglary. It was not known if Accardo ever found out that information or Sonny may have been added to the "hit" list. By 1979 Sonny Esposito was ordered out of Chicago by mob bosses and banished to live in Brownsville, Texas. It was a take-it-or-die situation. There he became the Outfit's representative in the formation of a new country known as the Cherokee Nation. An island formed between the United States and Mexico after a hurricane reversed the Rio Grand River forming a large island. In this new country, which was to mint its own money, Sonny Esposito was to control all the gambling making sure the Outfit received its cut. The U.S. government stepped in and foiled all plans for this country.

In January 1981 reports came in that the Ceres Stevedoring Company which operated at the port of Montreal, Canada, had been linked to organized crime figures including Tony Accardo in Chicago. Investigations of this company leading back to the 1960's had revealed that warehouses owned by Ceres were under the control of the Chicago Outfit and had been used by men labeled as "Accardo's men" dealing in stolen goods. In 1970 large lots of illegal cargo was being sold as unclaimed goods at the port of Chicago. The investigation produced no charges against organized crime figures.

On June 3, 1981 Tony Accardo was indicted by a Federal Grand Jury in Miami, Florida along with Miami Mob boss Santo Trafficante. The indictment alleging union corruption and a kickback scheme was filed against Angelo Fosco, Tony Accardo, James Caporale, Al Pilotto, Seymour Gropman, Bernard Rubin, George Wuagneux, Salvatore Tricario, Louis Ostrer, John Giardiello and Terrence O'Sullivan. Others mentioned in the investigation but never charged were Joseph

Spingola, president of Chicago Local 1001 and the Chicago District Council, Vince Solano, president of Chicago's Hod Carriers Union Local 1, Edward T. Hanley, the Outfit's labor union boss and president of the Hotel and Restaurant Employees and Bartenders International Union, and Dominic Senese, nephew of Tony Accardo.

The charge was a one-count indictment for conspiracy to violate the federal anti-racketeering statute otherwise known as Racketeer Influenced and Corrupt Organizations Act or simply "RICO." The government's case focused on the allegation that the defendants conspired to receive kickbacks from various insurance or healthcare service provider representatives in exchange for exercising their influence with the union to obtain the union's health and insurance benefits contracts for the companies paying kickbacks.

The indictment alleged that Tony Accardo and a Joseph Hauser, held a meeting in 1974 between Accardo, Al Pilotto and Angelo Fosco. Accardo's plan was to make Hauser's insurance company the largest in the U.S. The profits were to be passed through Angelo Fosco's sons Paul Fosco's PF Agency. At the meeting it was indicated that Hauser was an associate of the Outfit. A year later in 1975 Tony Accardo met with Hauser to inform him that the union's insurance business would be controlled by the "Outfit" with Florida mob boss Santo Trafficante overseeing the southern portion while Accardo would handle the Midwest portion. The case was held in a southern District of Florida court.

On June 4, 1981 FBI agents went to Tony Accardo's condo at 1020 Harlem Avenue and knocked on the door at 8:15 in the morning. Tony Accardo answered the door and the FBI agent informed him that they had a bench warrant issued for his arrest and that he would be placed under arrest. FBI agents wrote that Accardo replied, *"Now what have I done?"* Agents informed him that the indictment was issued from the Federal Court in Miami, Florida. The agents then wrote they allowed Tony Accardo to lock up his condo and grab his cigarettes (English Ovals) before taking him to be booked. As they placed Tony Accardo in the agent's car, another car pulled up and parked near the condo. The agent noticed the man walking to Accardo's condo was Jackie Cerone. Cerone, not aware that Accardo was sitting in the agents' car, continued to walk to the condo when the arresting agent called Cerone over to the car. Casually, Cerone stopped and noticed his boss sitting in the car. Cerone walked up to the car when the agent informed him that Accardo was under arrest. Tony Accardo then told Cerone to give him $2,000 in cash which Jackie quickly pulled out of his pocket. The agents wrote that Cerone counted out twenty $100 bills and gave it to Accardo, putting twice that amount back into his pocket. Then Cerone asked Accardo if he had his heart medication with him, which he replied he did. The agent wrote that Jackie Cerone was very concerned about Accardo's health but when asked if he would like to accompany Accardo to the FBI building, he declined and walked back to his car. FBI agents noted that when Cerone reached his car he was checking all his pockets looking for something. Cerone had left his car keys on the roof of the agent's car.

Tony Accardo was taken to the FBI Chicago field office at 219 South Dearborn Avenue in Chicago where he was fingerprinted and photographed. Once Accardo was done getting photographed, agents walked him past mobster Al Pilotto who was on his way to be fingerprinted. Agents wrote that Pilotto's reaction to seeing Accardo was surprise and when he noticed Accardo he said, *"Oh, hi."* An unamused Accardo mumbled a reply as he was escorted to an interview room. FBI agents took Tony Accardo's wallet and made copies of everything in it. It contained:

1. Driver's License
2. Attorney card, Bruno and Orvino, 1607 Broadway, Melrose Park
3. Attorney card, 39-29 South LaSalle Street, Chicago
4. Certified Public Accountant, 77 west Washington Street, Chicago
5. Floridale Mobile Home, 2807 S.W. 15th Ave., Ft. Lauderdale, Florida
6. Attorney at Law, 10 South LaSalle Street, Suit 1400, Chicago
7. Prompt Pick Up and Delivery Service, Palm Springs
8. Photo of Clarice Accardo
9. Two photos of unknown males
10. Law Offices, Pribe and Beck, One Century Plaza, 2029 Century Park East, Los Angeles, California
11. American Express Card
12. Anco General Insurance Inc. 100 N. LaSalle Street, Chicago
13. Dairyland Insurance Company, Madison, Wisconsin
14. Voter's registration card, Illinois
15. Religious picture Prayer to St. Anthony of Padua
16. Religious picture Dear devout to St. Anthony
17. Blue Cross- Blue Shield insurance card
18. Health Insurance Social Security Act card
19. Physician & Surgeon, 6425 W. North Avenue, Oak Park / Central DuPage Hospital, Winfield, Illinois
20. Medallion, Jesus Immaculate Conception

Both Accardo and Pilotto were reunited once again in the prisoner elevator on their way to be turned over to the U.S. Marshalls. Once again, Pilotto tried to talk to Accardo but Accardo refused to acknowledge his presence. Pilotto should have gotten the hint from Accardo that day. Tony Accardo became so worried that Pilotto was going to testify against him he ordered him to be killed. A month later Pilotto was shot five times as he golfed at the Lincolnshire Country Club golf course in Crete, Illinois, However, Pilotto survived and still never ratted out Accardo or his friends. He was found guilty in the Miami case and sentenced to 20 years in prison.

Tony Accardo's bond was set at $100,000 with half being a personal-recognizance bond, meaning no cash had to be posted. Accardo's lawyer, Carl Walsh, went to the cashier's office in the Federal Building and produced fifty-one $100 bills, giving fifty of them to the cashier.

It was alleged that James Caporale was the one who gave Tony Accardo his "cut" of the money from the scam. He delivering it in a white envelope.

Angelo Fosco, Tony Accardo and Terrence O'Sullivan were acquitted. The eleven other defendants were all convicted and sentenced to various periods of incarceration. Some time later, it was alleged again that organized crime figures bribed a member of a Miami federal jury that had decided one of the nation's most significant labor racketeering cases. Two members close to the union informed the FBI that a juror had been paid $200,000 to vote for an acquittal. It was alleged that the bribe came from New England mobsters. The alleged bribe was to have Fosco, Accardo, O'Sullivan, and if possible, South Florida union officers John Giardiello and Salvatore Tricario found not guilty. It was determined that the allegations of jury tampering had been substantial.

Accardo attempted to claim $224,500 in lawyer fees on his taxes as a deduction from this case. Accardo claimed that the fees were deductible on the grounds that he had spent the money to prevent government confiscation of income-producing bank accounts. The U.S. Tax Court denied the claim by saying no one may ever claim legal fees as a deductible.

The Chicago mob in the 1980's saw a shadow of itself. Its leaders were old, its up-and-comers were not powerful and the law had the upper hand for the first time. When it came to Chicago mob situations Tony Accardo was very unhappy with the mob. One problem was the way the Outfits guys were running the South Side of Chicago. The solution was to have mob Capo Joseph Lombardo's west side crew move south to run things. Many other problems arose from that decision, but Tony Accardo was old and tired and did not care as much as he once did.

Tony Accardo spent ninety percent of his time at his Palm Springs home on Roadrunner Drive in Indian Wells, California. He maintained a condo in River Forest for when he was called back to Chicago on mob business. So many Chicago mobsters were staying in Palm Springs, California it was nicknamed Palm Springs Illinois by the police in California. Not just Accardo, but thirty-two Chicago mobsters like Joey Aiuppa, James "Turk" Torello and Frank Buccieri were pouring $50 million in to Palm Springs buying up land, businesses and old homes.

Tony Accardo, then listed as being worth well over $200 million dollars by the FBI, sat back, relaxed and collected his Social Security benefits check every month even though he never worked a real job.

When FBI agents approached him in the lobby of his Harlem Avenue condo building on July 28, 1982 the FBI agent tried to ask him some questions involving an extortion case against Joseph Lombardo and Allen Dorfman. Tony Accardo told the agents he did not know anything about it and that he was no longer in the "rackets" and was just interested in a quiet life and acquiring a good sun tan. He terminated the interview and walked out of the door.

In 1983 Tony Accardo was summoned before the Senate Governmental Affairs Permanent Subcommittee in Washington D.C. Also subpoenaed with Accardo were long-time mob political powerhouses Pat Marcy, John D'Arco Sr. and Edward Hanley. The sub-committee was investigating organized crime in the union and possible kickbacks and insurance scams performed by the union.

Reports said while recovering at St. Mary of Nazareth Hospital from lung cancer surgery, Tony Accardo received a post-surgery surprise, a subpoena. U.S. Senate investigators claimed that once Accardo found out he was going to be subpoenaed, he decided to check himself in to the hospital for a follow-up from his surgery. The committee knew Accardo would not be able to attend the hearing because of his health so they subpoenaed Accardo's attorney, Carl Walsh, to appear and explain why Accardo could not make it. Carl Walsh, the son of Maurice Walsh, who had once been Tony Accardo's lawyer also, was under scrutiny because he had been paid $100,000 over 10 years from the union but no one could say what he did to earn that money.

A year later in 1984 Tony Accardo was questioned by the Senate sub-committee about his position as boss of the Chicago mob. Accardo, hard of hearing and very old, told the committee, *"I have no control over anybody. I've never been a boss. I have no knowledge of a crime family in Chicago."* He was given immunity against prosecution to answer all questions placed before him and if he tried to use the 5th Amendment he would be found in contempt of court and placed in jail. When Accardo was told this he was unfazed as questioning began. Instead of taking the 5th, his reply too many of the questing was, *"On the advice of my attorney I refuse to answer, because I believe the question is based on illegal electronic surveillance."*

Senators began a civil contempt-of-congress charge against Accardo for refusing to answer 47 questions placed before him. When it was time for Accardo to appear again in April 1984, he checked himself back in to the Mayo Clinic in Minnesota, complaining of pain. When Carl Walsh went before the committee to explain when Accardo could appear, he told the court it was up to the doctors to release him and up to that point they had yet to find where the pain was coming from inside Accardo. Later Accardo's doctors told the committee that he needed to stay at the Mayo Clinic for physical therapy for a back ailment. It was later changed to a heart ailment and after 23 days in the hospital, Accardo was released.

The sub-committee demanded Tony Accardo fly to Washington to face the committee. However, they were informed that Accardo had suffered a head injury in a fall at his condominium in River Forest during a dizzy spell. He was taken to Oak Park Hospital and was given 8 stitches for a cut on the back of his head. He was then transferred to St. Mary of Nazareth Hospital in Chicago where he was admitted for "evaluation and observation." Once again, Tony Accardo informed the committee that he would not be able to appear before them. That was the 40th scheduled appearance for Accardo that he had to postpone.

However, investigators from the Illinois State's Attorney's office learned that when Tony Accardo was claiming to be too sick to appear before the committee, he was observed at the Illinois driver's testing facility taking a driver's test to renew his driver's license.

Enough was enough. Every dodge Tony Accardo tried to use to get out of answering the sub-committee's questions could not put off the committee from demanding he appear. In June 1984 Tony Accardo appeared once again before the sub-committee. This time he told the panel *"I've never been a boss"* when asked if he was the boss of the Chicago crime family. He admitted he knew Jackie Cerone and Joey Aiuppa and admitted he once knew Al Capone but it was nothing more than seeing and saying hello at the racetracks. When asked what Joey Aiuppa did for a living he replied, *"I didn't think it was any of my business"* which drew laughs from the senators. When asked what Jackie Cerone did for a living he replied,

"He's a golfer." When asked about Tony "The Ant" Spilotro he replied, *"I don't even know him."*

He told the committee that any kind of organized crime family in Chicago that he knew of was what he read in the newspapers. He also denied he ever ordered the death of anyone or even killed anyone. He told the committeemen that he was a tax-paying citizen who scraped up a modest life savings of $700,000 while mostly doing nothing illegal. One of the senators said after the hour-and-a-half session, *"It certainly appears strange that Accardo would know so many organized crime figures and never discuss organized crime with them."*

One of the last mug shots of Tony Accardo taken in the 1980's

Spot Surveillance 1980's

April 2, 1980 – Tony Accardo and mobster Nick Palermo are observed in conversation at Accardo's home.

July 10, 1980 – Tony Accardo and Jackie Cerone are observed in an animated conversation while standing at the east lobby of the Palmer House Hotel in Chicago.

September 15, 1980 – FBI agents investigate a top mob meeting being held at the Grand Hotel in Rome Italy. Tony Accardo, Joey Aiuppa, Dominic "Butch" Blasi and Jackie Cerone were summoned to this meeting.

October 1980 – An FBI informant told the FBI that Tony Accardo had a very close friend in the U.S. Congress. Congressman Frank Annunzio was named as Accardo's close friend and that Annunzio did whatever Tony Accardo asked him to do.

January 5, 1981 – Tony Accardo is observed in Las Vegas, Nevada.

March 1, 1981 – FBI agents noticed several cabs and limousines enter a garage at 2820 South Cicero Avenue. They noticed many well dressed men entering this building which house a company known as Belgo. FBI agents observe Tony Accardo as one of the men entering the building.

August 1983 – Tony Accardo has lung surgery at the Mayo Clinic in Rochester, Minnesota. Three days after surgery, Tony Accardo was walking around and out of intensive care.

May 25, 1984 – Tony Accardo is discharged from the hospital after an 11-day stay from fainting and cutting his head.

September 11, 1991 –Tony Accardo was observed at Austin Liquor Store in Highland Park, Illinois having lunch with Anthony "Facci" Fillichio.

Dubbed the "Last Super" photo of the Chicago Outfit taken in the summer of 1976 at Sicily Restaurant, 2743 N. Harlem Ave. In the photo are: (back row from left to right) Joey Aiuppa, Dom DiBella, Vince Solano, Al Pilotto, Jackie Cerone, Joey Lombardo (front row left to right) Tony Accardo, Joseph DiVarco, Joe Amato and James "Turk" Torello

In October 2000 Tony Accardo's ranch home in River Forest located at 1407 Ashland Avenue went on the market for $1.4 million dollars. His old home at 915 Franklin Avenue had sold for $1.9 million months earlier.

The ranch home had its share of bad luck once Accardo moved out. Accardo sold it to a doctor who went bankrupt in a divorce. Then a man who ran a bus company bought it only to lose it in bankruptcy and divorce. Then Bill and Marianna Tassaras purchased the house in 1990 and sold it for $1 million in 1995 after they went bankrupt. Years later the Tassaras's put Accardo's huge brass and pewter chandelier up for sale asking $15,000 for it.

During the last years of Accardo's life, he and Clarice lived on the 22-arce estate of his daughter and son-in-law Ernest Kumerow. The estate was named Willowgate which was located in an up-scale part of Barrington Hills, Illinois and the two lived in the cottage located on the grounds. The Kumerow's sold the estate in 1999 for $2.2 million dollars.

In the 1990's Accardo's son Anthony Ross won millions in the Illinois Lottery, what a charmed life. In 2003 Anthony Ross was reported as living in Greensboro, Georgia and made the news as he tried to sell 9 acres of property in Crystal Lake, Illinois for $900,000. The property housed dozens of rare wildflower species plants growing on a portion of the property that was worth preserving. Anthony Ross had sold a 9 acre parcel of land adjacent to the property to Metra, an Illinois train company who was going to build Crystal Lake's second train depot. Anthony Ross told the reporter he would be willing to work with the conservationists to save the wildflowers.

The 1990's began with Tony Accardo watching as three of his most trusted men in the Outfit were being prosecuted and facing prison time. His political bosses Pat Marcy and Fred Roti, who controlled most of the politicians in Chicago, were indicted and faced lengthy prison terms. The other was one of his most trusted "brains" in the Outfit who he had complete faith in with almost any mob decision. Gus Alex, the man who Accardo would not let retire because he knew Alex was one of the only "intelligent" men in the Outfit, was facing life in prison when Alex's lieutenant, also a friend of Accardo's, Lennie Patrick, turned government rat and testified against Alex. With all this on his mind Tony Accardo headed to his home in Palm Springs, California.

Even in his advanced old age, Tony Accardo was still in the thick of mob operations. One example was in September 1991 FBI agents watch as mobster Ben Fillichio dropped by at Accardo's Barrington Hills estate home. Fillichio pulled up to the house and exited his car carrying two pastry boxes. Some time later Accardo, Fillichio and another man walked out into the driveway carrying folding lawn chairs and sat down to continue their conversation. The conversation centered around a few days earlier when Tony Accardo attended a cancer research fundraiser. A few minutes after Accardo left the fundraiser a Chicago police officer showed up and began questioning people as to why Accardo was in attendance. Fillichio went to great lengths to convince Accardo that they were not followed to the fundraiser. Fillichio suggested that it was possible the telephone at that location was tapped. The unknown man was overheard saying, *"It's more than a coincidence that that policeman was there screwing around early Thursday morning."* Fillichio added, *"My friend was right, they must have been watching the place and saw you."*

The unknown man added, *"It was not the FBI, 219 Dearborn. He was a young guy, a dapper dresser."* The conversation turned to electronic surveillance. The unknown man was heard saying, *"There is a hearing on the twenty-third of September about how electronic surveillance took place. The judge had asked for all the FBI's files and if the government did illegal electronic surveillance, she will throw the case out."* Fillichio added, *"They got electronic equipment for a $140. They can tap any house, any phone."* The conversation continued after the unknown man went back into the house. To the agents it looked like Fillichio appeared to be explaining himself in an apologetic manner. Agents had a hard time hearing the conversation but they heard Accardo say, *"Bennie, Bennie, don't worry!"*

Then Clarice came outside and called out, *"You told me to remind you of something."* Startled, Tony Accardo responded as if he either didn't hear her or didn't know what she was talking about. Clarice then repeated, *"You told me to remind you of something,"* emphasizes the word "something" as though she either didn't want to say what it was or perhaps had not been told what this "something" was. Both Accardo and Fillichio stood up, folded the chairs and went back inside.

Sometime later Fillichio and the unknown person walked out of Accardo's home carrying a large heavy leather bag. Once inside his Cadillac, Fillichio opened the bag and pulled out two bundles of money secured together. Apparently this large leather bag was filled with cash. Fillichio then placed the money back in the bag and drove off.

The following day this Chicago detective paid a visit to Ben's brother Anthony "Facci" Fillichio to question him about his friendship with Tony Accardo and ask him why he was with Accardo almost every day. Facci admitted to the detective he was a close friend of Accardo's for 50 years and the two had homes near each other in Palm Springs, California.

At the time Anthony Fillichio was under investigation to see if the businesses he owned: a golf course named the Indian Valley Golf Club on Route 83 in Long Grove, Illinois; Austin Liquors in Deerfield; a strip mall; car wash in Glenview, and the Abam Corporation, were actually owned by him or if he was a front for the Chicago Outfit with Accardo holding a piece of them. Facci told the detectives that he was aware of Accardo's reputation and he, Facci, considered Tony Accardo a "classy" gentleman. Facci ended the interview by saying Accardo was in poor health and was in extreme constant pain from a deterioration of the spine and muscles in the neck area. Because of this condition Accardo was on painkillers night and day and was unable to sleep.

In the middle of May 1992 Tony Accardo and Clarice returned to Chicago from California and on May 14, Tony Accardo entered St. Mary of Nazareth Hospital Center in Chicago with heart problems.

On May 27, at 7:36PM Tony Accardo died from congestive heart failure, pneumonia, chronic obstructive pulmonary disease, and acute respiratory failure. He was 86-years old. His wake and funeral saw just immediate family members and a few close friends. The only made mobster mentioned attending the services was his old friend and mob boss, 86-year old Joe Amato.

Tony Accardo was placed in his private Italian marble room in the mausoleum at Queen of Heaven Cemetery in Hillside, Illinois. Tony Accardo and Paul DeLucia are in the same building, one floor apart for all of eternity. Clarice died in 2002.

From time to time, Tony Accardo's name surfaces in the news always in relation to organized crime stories and corruption. In one instance a niece of Tony Accardo was married to Fred Schreier, who was boss of Chicago's riggers union whose members work setting up trade shows and exhibits at Chicago's lakefront McCormick Place convention center. Schreier plead guilty to taking a bribe.

Both Paul DeLucia and Tony Accardo lived the American dream, but not with hard work or high education. They achieved it through killing, stealing and lying their way through life with deception, hate, and entitlement. They had the best life could offer and did it all with a clean conscience. In the life of a mob boss, it's not how much you have in the end, it's about how much you have by doing nothing for it and getting to enjoy it.

Tony Accardo private room at the Queen of Heaven Mausoleum in Hillside, Illinois

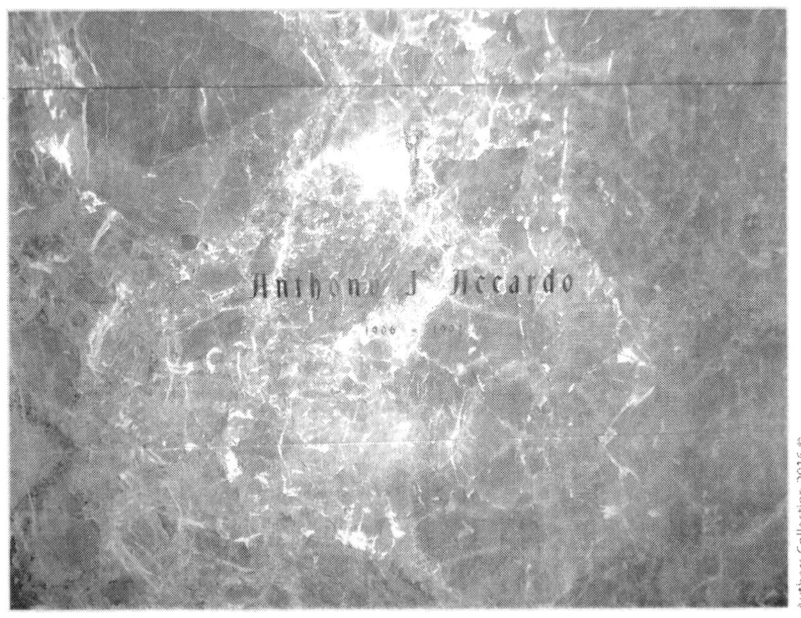

File Card

Anthony Joseph Accardo
Antonio Leonardo Accardo
AKA Joe Batters
AKA JB
AKA Tony Accardo
AKA The Big Tuna (Dubbed by the press after a photo of Accardo holding a "big tuna fish" was published)

Mob Boss

AKA Tony Arcado
AKA Tony Martin
AKA M. Le Rack
AKA M. Brown
AKA Mr. Winter
AKA Stone Face

Born April 28, 1906 (Chicago) (Birth record was not filed until February 1, 1954)
Baptism Certificate from Holy Guardian Angel Church in Chicago on May 13, 1906.
School records say he was born April 28, 1905 and April 8, 1905. Leavenworth information on Accardo's brother Martin stated that Tony Accardo was 28 years old in 1932 making Tony Accardo being born in 1904.
Died May 27, 1992 at St. Mary of Nazareth Hospital Center in Chicago of a heart attack Buried Queen of Heaven Mausoleum in Hillside, Illinois

Eyes Brown
Social Security # 360-14-0886
FBI # 1410106
Chicago P.D. # D-83436
DL # A263-0100-6121
Military Classification 4F
Tattoo of flying dove on back of his right hand
Named "Public Enemy" in Chicago on July 31, 1931

Wife's name Clarice Evelyn Porter, Born 12-10-1910 in Littleton, Illinois, Died November 18, 2002 / 5'4" in height / 145 pounds / Brown hair and brown eyes. Lived at 428 St. James in Chicago before marriage, with her father being Ross Porter. Her mother was Nettie McCloud. Both parents were born in Macomb, Illinois. Sister Irene Staggs, married to Harvey living at 1407 North Kellog, Galesburg, Illinois (1946). In 1969 a Glen Porter was reported as working as a floor man on the Las Vegas strip. Porter was listed as a brother-in-law of Tony Accardo and in November 1969 he was observed taking a taxi from Accardo's River Forest home to a hospital for a back problem.

Children

Anthony Ross Accardo (Adopted) (Godfather Sam Giancana) Born April 25, 1936 (Lived at 1322 Candlewood Hill, Northbrook, Illinois in 1973) (Married Janet Marie Hawley on June 10, 1964)
Marie Judith Accardo, Born July 3, 1939 (Married William Palmer Pyle Jr. on May 23, 1960 / Later married Ernest Kumerow)
Linda Lee Accardo, Born January 14, 1941 (Married Michael A. Palermo on April 27, 1961)
Joseph Frank Accardo (Adopted) Born November 30, 1946

Accardo's Known Servants

Janet Carrey, known as "Johnnie" Live-in maid (1940's)
Michael Volpe, houseman (1970's)

Accardo's Known Addresses

525 North Armor Street, Chicago (1910) (Not confirmed)
1126 South Monitor, Chicago (1906)
1353 Grand, Chicago, Illinois, 1916-1917
5724 North Meade Avenue, Chicago (1934)
1020 Pleasant Avenue, Oak Park, Illinois (1936)
1117 Grand Avenue, Chicago (1934-1937)
1402 Monroe Street, Chicago (1937-1941) (*12-room, 2-story brick home with an additional two-story brick building containing a three-car garage and apartment*)
1319 North 19th Avenue, Melrose Park, Illinois (1946) (*Home Accardo had built for his parents Frank and Mary Accardo. Lots were purchased for $1,500*)
1431 Ashland Avenue, River Forest, Illinois (1941-1951) (*10-room, 2-story brick residence) (Telephone number was Esterbrook 9-7205*)

Authors Collection 2016 ©

Photo as of 2014

1640 South Wesley Avenue, Oak Park, Illinois (1946)
9199 Collins Avenue, Surfside, Florida (1948-1950) *(Leased to Accardo by James Passanante, a slot machine and vending machine boss in Miami)*
6475 Allison Road, Miami Beach, Florida (1950) (*Winter home of Charles Fischetti which Accardo used to register his boat the "Clari-Jo*)
915 Franklin Avenue, River Forest Illinois (1951-1964) (*Bought 1951 for $125,000. 22 rooms, 6 master bedrooms, an indoor pool, 2 bowling alleys, a pipe organ, 6 bathrooms with gold plat fixtures, and a $10,000 (1958 price) bathtub carved out of a solid block of Mexican onyx. The servant quarters was a separate two-story brick building with an apartment above the 3-car garage*)
20 E. Delaware Street Chicago (*Accardo secret apartment 1962*)
1407 North Ashland, River Forest (February 12, 1964-September 1979) (Built in 1963 for $160,000 and sold for $487,500 in 1979. A brick ranch home with a 3-car garage, air-conditioning, 3 ½ baths, 5,100 sq. feet) (1969 real estate taxes $3,956) (Telephone number 366-9180)

Authors Collection 2016 ©

Anthony Accardo's Condo at 1417 Bonnie Brae Lane, River Forest

76775 San Piper Drive, Indian Wells, California (Rented 1975)
Condo Unit 2D at 1417 Bonnie Brae Lane, River Forest (1979)
(*Phone number 312-366-9180*) Photo on next page, as of 2014
Landers House Condo, Unit 137 at 1020 North Harlem Avenue, Chicago (1980) *(Between Chicago Avenue and Division on the west side of Harlem Avenue)*
76-841 Roadrunner, Indian Wells Condominium (*Twenty miles away from Palm Springs, California)* (1977-1980's)
86-341 Ground floor unit, Ca Condo, Roadrunners, Palm Springs, California (1983)
Cottage home at Willow Gate, 165 Algonquin Road, Barrington Hills, Illinois (1980's-1992)

Newspaper Quotes

"A husky, ill-tempered gang lord" (1958)

Alleged Businesses either owned or had interest in

O. K. Motor Service Incorporated, 620 N. May Street, Chicago (1930's)
Cigar Store in down town Chicago (1930's)
O. K. Trucking Service, 361 North Morgan Street Chicago (1942) (Accardo listed himself as general manager)
O. K Cartage Company, 1441 West Monroe, Chicago (1943)
O.K. Truck and Trailer Equipment Company, 2513 West Armitage, Chicago (1943)
Airport Cafe, Route 41, Glenview, Illinois (1950's)
Utility Engineering Company, 6142 West Roosevelt Road & 6201 Roosevelt Road (1956) (Owner acing as front man Anthony DePardo)
Cigar Store, 186 North Clark Street Chicago (1941)
A&L Sales Company, Kansas City, Missouri (1945)
Illinois Simplex Distributing Company (Juke Box Distributors) (1947)
Trotters Club, Melrose Park, Illinois (1949)
Super Club Milwaukee, Wisconsin (1950's)
Owl Club, 18 N. State Street, Calumet City, Illinois (1940's and 50's)

Tony Dark

Golden Bank Casino, Reno, Nevada (1953)
Tax Control Incorporated, 330 South Wells Street, Chicago (1957) (Alleged)
Balistrieri's Boxing Promotions, Wisconsin (1958)
Owner of the Heyworth Building, 29 East Madison Street Chicago, (1958) (Building rented to the Chicago Teamsters Union)
Mars Oldsmobile in Chicago (1959)
Plan-It Travel Company, 6931 North Oak Park, Oak Park, Illinois (1961)
Austin Liquors (1961)
Peter Epsteen Pontiac (1962)
Henry Suck Pontiac (1962)
Dominic's Finer Food's Supermarket, 6415 North Central Avenue, Chicago (1960's)
Lormar Distributing Company (1963)
White Way Electric Company (1963)
Sportsman's Park Race Track (1963)
Hollywood Kennel Club, Hollywood, Florida (1963-1964)
West Flagler Kennel Club, Miami, Florida (1964)
Howard Gardens Apartments and Town Home Development, Franklin Park, Illinois (1964)
Staley's Restaurant, Biltmore Hotel at Congress and Wells Street, Chicago Loop (1965)
Northlake Community Hospital, Northlake, Illinois (1965)
Findley Art Galleries Chicago (1965)
Petri Wine Company (1965)
Riverwoods Golf and Country Club, Riverwoods, Illinois (1965)
Towne Jewelers (1965)
Apollo Loan Company (1966)
Harlem-Irving Plaza Shopping Center (1966)
Old Cloister Inn, Willow Road (1966) (Alleged to have financed the purchase through his son-in-law)
Nitti Travel Bureau, (One location in Chicago and another in Forest Park, Illinois) (Alleged secrete ownership, business in Nick Nitti's name) (1970's)
Boat Rental Business, Miami, Florida (1980)

Known Illegal Operations

Body guard for Al Capone (1928)
Body guard for "Machine Gun" Jack McGurn (1931)
Handbook at 186-92 North Clark Street Chicago (1941)
Handbook and wire room at 192 N. Clark Street (1943)

Known Hangouts

Circus Café, 1857 North Avenue, Chicago (1920's)
Metropole Hotel, Chicago (1920's)

Hawthorn Inn, Cicero, Illinois (1920's)
Drum Cocktail Lounge, Chicago Loop area (1930's)
Valentine Barber Shop, 72 West Cermak Road Chicago (1943)
The Bomb Shelter Tavern, Chicago Avenue and Rush Street, Chicago (1943)
The Circle Bar, Cermak Road, Cicero (1943)
El Patio Club, Cermak Road, Cicero (1943)
Chicagoan Hotel, 67 West Madison Street, Chicago (1940's)
Kenna Cigar Store, 311 South Clark Street, Chicago (1940's)
First Ward Alderman's Office, 311 South Clark Street, Chicago (1944)
Meo's Norwood House, 1750 North Harlem Avenue Chicago (1958)
Northmoor Country Club, Kenilworth, Illinois (1964)
Riverwoods Country Club, Riverwoods, Illinois (1964)
Meo's Norwood House, Harlem & Lawrence Avenues, Harwood Heights, Illinois (1965)
Otto's Café, Forest Park, Illinois (1977)

Known Properties

4536 North Central Park Avenue, Chicago (1965)

Known Autos

1941 Cadillac sedan (License plate number 504516)
1946 Cadillac convertible
1946 Ford station wagon
1947 Cadillac, License plate number 736
1950 Cadillac convertible, yellow, License plate number 736
1955 Cadillac
1956 Chevy Tudor convertible 2-door, License plate number 915057 *(Under Clarice Accardo's name)*
1956 Mercedes-Benz 2-door coupe, red, butterfly doors which opened straight into the air, License plate number 915000
1957 Bel Air Chevrolet convertible, yellow bottom, white top 2-door. Total price fully loaded $2,945 from Allen Chevy Inc. at 6527 W. Roosevelt Road, Berwyn, Illinois *(Clarice Accardo's car)*
1957 Plymouth 4-door dark red Station wagon, dark red in color, purchased from Manhattan Motor Sales, 4660 W. Washington Blvd, Chicago (License plate number 736)
1957 Oldsmobile, License plate number 1135590 *(Issued to Joe Matia)*
1958 Belvedere four-door sports suburban station wagon
1962 Pontiac station wagon, red and white (License plate number 736)
1963 Pontiac station wagon, red over white in color (License plate number 736
1965 Pontiac station wagon
1967 Oldsmobile 98
1976 Oldsmobile (License plate number 736)

1978 Oldsmobile station wagon (License plate number 736)
In 1980 FBI wrote Tony Accardo like to only drive rented Oldsmobile's in the colors of red or white.

Known Boats

The ClariJo, Accardo's yacht in Miami, Florida (1951)

Best Accardo Quotes

"You always move so that you do not make a mistake. Once you make a mistake you get a slap in the face and one slap means another and another."

"Listen, for my kid, I'll go out and beg. I don't care if I put myself in the crank."

"The Salvation Army is the biggest racket of them all." (1-10-1961)

Personal greeting to other people

"What do you know" followed by the persons name. Example, *"What do you know Sam?"*

Tony Accardo's Known Arrest Record

Date	Charge	Agency	Result
3-22-1922	Motor Vehicle Law	CPD	Fine
5-31-1923	Disorderly Conduct	CPD	Fined $200
12-10-1923	General Purpose	CPD	Dismissed
1-3-1924	Disorderly Conduct	CPD	Dismissed
1-19-1924	Disorderly Conduct	CPD	Fined $10
4-7-1924	Disorderly Conduct	CPD	Fined $25
10-12-1924	Disorderly Conduct	CPD	Dismissed
11-16-1925	Motor Vehicle Law	CPD	Dismissed
1-5-1926	Disorderly Conduct	CPD	Dismissed
4-7-1926	Disorderly Conduct	CPD	Dismissed
3-3-1927	Disorderly Conduct	CPD	Dismissed
5-30-1927	Disorderly Conduct	CPD	Dismissed
10-13-1927	Disorderly Conduct	CPD	Dismissed
1-28-1928	Disorderly Conduct	CPD	Dismissed
2-1-1930	Concealed Weapon	CPD	Dismissed
2-1-1930	Murder Investigation	CPD	Released
3-1930	Arrested	Florida	Released
3-31-1930	Concealed Weapon	CPD	Stricken
6-24-1930	Bond Forfeited	CPD	Dismissed
7-29-1930	Concealed Weapon	CPD	Reinstated

Tony Accardo's Known Arrest Record Cont.

Date	Charge	Agency	Result
9-30-1930	General Principles	CPD	Released
11-12-1930	Aiello Murder	CPD	Released
11-12-1930	Disorderly Conduct	CPD	Dismissed
2-17-1931	Concealed Weapon	CPD	Released
5-10-1931	Disorderly Conduct	CPD	Dismissed
5-10-1931	Heitler Murder	CPD	Released
5-3-1932	Vagrancy	CPD	Not Guilty
3-4-1933	Carey Murder	CPD	Released
5-15-1933	Disorderly Conduct	CPD	Fined $25
8-1933	Investigation	CPD	Released
3-4-1943	General Principles	CPD	Dismissed
9-27-1943	Material Witness	Feds	Cook County Jail
1-3-1944	Conspiracy	CPD	Nolle Processed
2-16-1944	Investigation	CPD	Released
3-20-1944	Conspiracy	SAO	Nolle Processed
2-12-1945	Investigation	CPD	Released
1-13-1948	Conspiracy to Defraud	U.S. Marshal	Nolle Processed
7-13-1948	Conspiracy	U/K	U/K
6-23-1951	General Principles	CPD	Released
9-10-1952	U.S. Marshal	U.S. Marshal	Released
11-1960	False Tax Returns	IRS	Guilty,
	2 years prison, $5,000 fine (Reversed by Supreme Court in 1962)		
12-14-1963	Speeding	Oak Park PD	Fined $15
4-21-1970	Violation Firearms Act	U.S. Marshal	Not Guilty
6-4-1981	Rico Conspiracy	USM Chicago	Not Guilty
6-4-1981	Racketeering	FBI	Not Guilty

Tony Accardo at the 1983 Senate hearings

MARTIN H. KENNELLY
MAYOR

JOHN C. PRENDERGAST
COMMISSIONER

CHICAGO POLICE DEPARTMENT
OFFICE OF THE
BUREAU OF IDENTIFICATION
1121 S. STATE STREET
CHICAGO, 5 ILL.

NBB

October 6th, 1950. 19

Record of Anthony Accardo:

N.G.	Tony Accardo	- May 31, 1923, fined $200.00 & costs. V.S. 2655. Judge McKinley. Off. Hotho, 22nd Dist.
As	" "	- Jan. 19, 1924, fined $10.00 & costs. V.S. 2655. Judge Hosp. Offs, Kakacek & Cunningham, D.B.
As	" "	- Apr. 7, 1924, fined $25.00. V.S. 2655. Judge Borrelli. Offs. Eckert & J. Feeney, 19th Dist.
As	" "	- Feb. 1, 1930, Indicted by February Term 1930 Grand Jury. Concealed Weapons. Sergt. Drury & Howe, D.B.
As	" "	- Mar. 31, 1930, Stricken Off, Concealed Weapons. Judge J.J. Sullivan.
As	" "	- June 24, 1930, Bonds Forf. & Stricken Off. Concealed Weapons. Judge J.J. Sullivan.
As	" "	- July 29, 1930, Cause Reinstated. Concealed Weapons. Judge Normoyle.
C-25281	" "	- Sept. 30, 1930, G.P., arrested by Lieut. Mikes & Sq. 5-C, D.B.
As	" "	- May 15, 1933, fined $25.00 & costs. Dis. Cond. Judge McGarry. Off. Hanrahan, D.B.
D-23340	Anthony Accardo	- Mar. 4, 1943, G.P., arrested by Capt. Drury, Harlib & Gleason, 38th Dist.
D-27487	Tony Accardo	- Mar. 20, 1944, Nolle Prossed, Conspiracy. Judge De Sort. Deputy Sheriff Keenan, Cook County, Ill.
As	Anthony Accardo	- Feb. 12, 1945, Invest., arr. by Offs. McGuire, Weir & Sims, D.B.

FMN

Form D B 11 25M 1929

E.A. Evans
Chief Identification Inspector

Tony Accardo's 1940's Chicago Police Rap Sheet

NAME (LAST)	(FIRST)	(MIDDLE)	SOC. SEC. NO.	FILE NO.
ACCARDO	ANTHONY			

NICKNAME OR ALIAS	TYPE OF ACTIVITY	I.R. NO.
TONY JOE BATTERS	Syndicate Chief	

HOME ADDRESS	CITY	HOME PHONE NO.	F.B.I. NO.
915 Franklin Street	River Forest		1410106
BUSINESS ADDRESS	CITY	BUSINESS PHONE NO.	TYPE OF BUSINESS
NEW ADDRESS	CITY	NEW PHONE NO.	PHOTO REF. NO.

SEX	RACE	DESCENT	D.O.B.	HEIGHT	WEIGHT	HAIR	EYES
Male	White		4-28-06	5'9½	190		

COMPLEXION

PECULIARITIES; MARKS, SCARS, ETC.: Tattoo of a Flying Dove on back of right hand.

ASSOCIATES: MURRAY HUMPHREYS, JACK CERONE, SAM BATTAGLIA, SAM "MOONEY" GIANCANNA

HANGOUTS

VEHICLE INFORMATION: Mercedes Benz, Ill. 1963 915-000

CPD-38.351 (REV.9/52) FACE CARD SEE REVERSE SIDE FOR MISC. INFORMATION

The subject is considered as one of the Top Crime Syndicate Chieftains. Subject frequently uses leased transportation. His gangland association dates back to the Capone area. His police arrests have been numerous but he has never been sentenced to prison. Subject once gained entry under false pretenses to the Fed. Penitentiary at Ft. Leavenworth to visit inmates.

V. PHYSICAL DESCRIPTION:

Name	ANTHONY JOSEPH ACCARDO, alias TONY ACCARDO, JOE BATTERS
Age	40 (Born 4/28/06, Chicago)
Height	5' 9½"
Weight	195
Build	Heavy
Eyes	Hazel
Hair	Dark Chestnut
Complexion	Ruddy
Scars & Marks	Flying Dove on back of right hand Scars on back of left hand
Occupation	Gunman, gambler.
F.P.C.	31 W MO 4 W OI
Residence	1431 No. Ashland Avenue, River Forest, Ill.
Relatives	Married, wife's name unknown; ANTHONY ACCARDO, son, age app.9 MARIE ACCARDO, daughter, age app.6 LINDA ACCARDO, daughter, age app.4
Photograph	Two in file.

CONFIDENTIAL

NAME : ACCARDO, ANTHONY
915 Franklin Street (See Reverse Side of Sheet)
River Forest, Ill

ALIASES : "Joe Batters" "Tony" "Big Tuna"

DESCRIPTION : Male, White, Italian, 185 Lbs, Dark Complexion, Tattoo of a Dove on the base of the thumb on the right hand.

LOCALITIES FREQUENTED : Various locations in the City and Suburbs.

FAMILY BACKGROUND :

Wife:	Clarice Accardo
Brother:	Martin Accardo
Brother:	John Accardo
Son:	Anthony Ross Accardo, Jr.

CRIMINAL ASSOCIATES : Sam "Mooney" Giancanna, Murray "The Camel" Humphreys, Jack Cerone, Sam Battaglia, Joseph Fusco, Joseph Glimco, William Gold, Ross Prio, Joseph LaBarbera and numerous others prominently connected with the Crime Syndicate.

CRIMINAL ASSOCIATES : Sam "Mooney" Giancanna, Murray "The Camel" Humphreys, Jack Cerone, Sam Battaglia, Joseph Fusco, Joseph Glimco, William Gold, Ross Prio, Joseph LaBarbera and numerous others prominently connected with the Crime Syndicate.

CRIMINAL HISTORY : F.B.I. #1410106 I.R.# 83436
The subject's arrests have been numerous over the years but he has never been sentenced to prison. Subject once gained entry under false pretense to the Federal Penitentiary at Ft. Leavenworth, Kansas to visit inmates Paul Ricca and Louis Campagna.

BUSINESS : It was reported that the subject has had interests in the following: The Airport Cafe, in Glenview, Illinois; closed as a gambling den by the Sheriff's Police. The Plan-It-Traveling Agency, owned by the subject's son.

R-4 (Rev. 10-21-57)

UNITED STATES DEPARTMENT OF JUSTICE
FEDERAL BUREAU OF INVESTIGATION
WASHINGTON 25, D. C.

J. Edgar Hoover, Director.

1 410 105

The following FBI record, NUMBER 1 410 105, is furnished FOR OFFICIAL USE ONLY.

CONTRIBUTOR OF FINGERPRINTS	NAME AND NUMBER	ARRESTED OR RECEIVED	CHARGE	DISPOSITION
Police Department Chicago Illinois	Tony Accardo #C-25251	September 30, 1930	General principles	
United States Marshal Chicago Illinois	Anthony Accardo #8087	September 27, 1943	material witness	
Cook County Jail Chicago Illinois	Anthony Accardo #44469	September 27, 1943	remand post material witness	September 29, 1943 released to United States Marshal
United States Marshal Chicago Illinois	Anthony J. Accardo #15211	January 13, 1948	conspiracy to defraud	November 21. 1948 acquitted by Jury trial before Federal Judge at Chicago Illinois
Police Department Chicago Illinois	Anthony Accardo #D 834 36	June 3, 1951	General principles	
United States Marshal Washington District of Columbia	Anthoney J. Accardo #CR-1340-52	September 10, 1952	Section 192 T 2 United States C [illegible]	

Since neither fingerprints nor an identifying number which is indexed in our files accompanied your request, FBI cannot guarantee in any manner that this material concerns the individual in whom you are interested.

Notations indicated by * ARE NOT BASED ON FINGERPRINTS IN FBI files. The notations are based on data formerly furnished this Bureau concerning individuals of the same or similar names or aliases and ARE LISTED ONLY AS INVESTIGATIVE LEADS.

U. S. GOVERNMENT PRINTING OFFICE 1957 O—[illegible]

Tony Accardo's 1950's FBI Rap Sheet

Tony Dark

JOHN EDGAR HOOVER

Federal Bureau of Investigation
United States Department of Justice
Washington, D. C.

2 The following is the record of FBI number 1410106

J. E. Hoover
Director.

CONTRIBUTOR OF FINGERPRINTS	NAME AND NUMBER	ARRESTED OR RECEIVED	CHARGE	DISPOSITION

Tony Acardo, Chicago, Ill., 5-31-23, D.C.; $200. and costs.
Tony Acardo, Chicago, Ill., 1-19-24, D.C.; $10. and costs.
Tony Acardo, Chicago, Ill., 4-7-24, D.C.; $25. and costs.
Tony Acardo, Chicago, Ill., 2-1-30, C.C.W.; inlisted.
Tony Acardo, Chicago, Ill., 3-31-30, C.C.W.; stricken off.
Tony Acardo, Chicago, Ill., 5-24-30, C.W.; bond, forfeited and stricken off. 7-29-30, cause reinstated. Concealed weapons. 9-30-30, G. P., as #C-25251. (As on record sheet PD, Chicago, Ill.)
5-15-32, fined $25.00 and costs; dis. cond. (As on record she from PD, Chicago, Ill.)
As Anthony Accardo, D-23340, 3-4-43 G.P. (as app. on record sheet from PD, Chicago, Ill.)
As Tony Accardo, #D-27487, PD, Chicago, Ill., Conspiracy.

UNITED STATES DEPARTMENT OF JUSTICE
FEDERAL BUREAU OF INVESTIGATION
WASHINGTON 25, D. C.

J. Edgar Hoover
Director.

3 The following FBI record, NUMBER 1 410 106, is furnished FOR OFFICIAL USE ONLY.

CONTRIBUTOR OF FINGERPRINTS	NAME AND NUMBER	ARRESTED OR RECEIVED	CHARGE	DISPOSITION

DESCRIPTION:
race: white
sex: male
height: 5-9½
weight: 190
hair: black
eyes: brown
complexion: dark
build: heavy
birth: 4-28-06 Chgo Ill
criminal specialty: gangster
residences: in 1943 and 1948 1431 Ashland River Forest Ill; River Forest Ill in 1951
in 1952 915 Franklin, River Forest Ill
scars and marks: tatto "Bird" base of r thumb outer; several irregular scars on back of L hand
Aliases: Joe Batters, Anthony Joseph Accardo, Tony Arcado, Tony Vatters, Joseph Bulger

Since neither fingerprints nor an identifying number which is indexed in our files [illegible] [illegible] cannot [illegible] any manner [illegible] the individual in which you are interested.

Notations indicated by * ARE NOT BASED ON FINGERPRINTS IN FBI files. The notations are based on data formerly furnished this Bureau concerning individuals of the same or similar names or aliases and ARE LISTED ONLY AS INVESTIGATIVE LEADS.

1-31-80 137 CRY

MASTER
1-4 (Rev. 7-19-77)

MASTER

MASTER

UNITED STATES DEPARTMENT OF JUSTICE
FEDERAL BUREAU OF INVESTIGATION
IDENTIFICATION DIVISION
WASHINGTON, D. C. 20537

Sq 16

Use of the following FBI record, NUMBER 1 410 106 is REGULATED BY LAW. It is furnished FOR OFFICIAL USE ONLY and should ONLY BE USED FOR PURPOSE REQUESTED. When further explanation of arrest charge or disposition is needed, communicate directly with the agency that contributed the fingerprints.

CONTRIBUTOR OF FINGERPRINTS	NAME AND NUMBER	ARRESTED OR RECEIVED	CHARGE	DISPOSITION
United States Marshal Chicago, Illinois	Anthony Accardo 8087	September 27, 1943	Material Witness	
Cook County Jail Chicago, Illinois	Anthony Accardo 44469	September 27, 1943	Remand post Material Witness	September 29, 1943 Released to United States Marshal
United States Marshal Chicago, Illinois	Anthony J Accardo 15211	January 13, 1948	Conspiracy to defraud	November 21, 1948 Acquitted by Jury Trial before Federal Judge at Chicago, Illinois
United States Marshal Washington District Of Columbia	Anthoney J Accardo CR 1340 52	September 10, 1952	Section 192 Title 2 United States Code	

1-31-80 137 CRY

MASTER
1-4 (Rev. 7-19-77)

MASTER

MASTER

UNITED STATES DEPARTMENT OF JUSTICE
FEDERAL BUREAU OF INVESTIGATION
IDENTIFICATION DIVISION
WASHINGTON, D. C. 20537

2

Use of the following FBI record, NUMBER 1 410 106 is REGULATED BY LAW. It is furnished FOR OFFICIAL USE ONLY and should ONLY BE USED FOR PURPOSE REQUESTED. When further explanation of arrest charge or disposition is needed, communicate directly with the agency that contributed the fingerprints.

CONTRIBUTOR OF FINGERPRINTS	NAME AND NUMBER	ARRESTED OR RECEIVED	CHARGE	DISPOSITION
United States Marshal Chicago, Illinois	Anthony Joseph Accardo 61057	April 26, 1960	False income tax returns 3 counts	November 11, 1960 Found guilty all counts November 18, 1960 Sentenced to serve 2 years plus $5000 Fine on each of three counts indictment sentence consecutive acquitted October 3, 1962
United States Marshal Chicago, Illinois	Anthony Joseph Accardo 70760	April 21, 1970	Violation Federal Firearms Act	

5-5-58 204 JAM

UNITED STATES DEPARTMENT OF JUSTICE
FEDERAL BUREAU OF INVESTIGATION
WASHINGTON 25, D. C.

1-Bureau

J. Edgar Hoover
Director.

The following FBI record, NUMBER 1 410 106 , is furnished FOR OFFICIAL USE ONLY.

CONTRIBUTOR OF FINGERPRINTS	NAME AND NUMBER	ARRESTED OR RECEIVED	CHARGE	DISPOSITION
Federal Bureau of Investigation Chicago, Illinois	Anthony Accardo #--	September 27, 1943	material witness	released to United States Marshal

WANTED BY BUREAU: As Tony Accardo, location desired. Notify Division 6, Bureau per telephone call from there from December 15, 1950.
NO LONGER WANTED: As Tony Accardo, per telephone call from Division 6 January 6. 1951.
FLASH BY BUREAU: Anthony Joseph Accardo, if any information or inquiry received, notify Bureau Field Division, Chicago per information received January 20, 1958.

Where final disposition is not ... is us being possibly identical ...

MASTER
1-4 (Rev. 7-19-77)

MASTER

MASTER

UNITED STATES DEPARTMENT OF JUSTICE
FEDERAL BUREAU OF INVESTIGATION
IDENTIFICATION DIVISION
WASHINGTON, D. C. 20537

MAR 1 1983

1 410 106

Use of the following FBI record, NUMBER , is REGULATED BY LAW. It is furnished FOR OFFICIAL USE ONLY and should ONLY BE USED FOR PURPOSE REQUESTED. When further explanation of arrest charge or disposition is needed, communicate directly with the agency that contributed the fingerprints.

CONTRIBUTOR OF FINGERPRINTS	NAME AND NUMBER	ARRESTED OR RECEIVED	CHARGE	DISPOSITION
USM Chgo IL	Anthony J. Accardo 15211	1-13-48	Conspiracy to defraud	11-21-48 Acquitted by Jury Trial before Federal Judge at Chgo IL
USM Washington DC	Anthoney J. Accardo CR 1340 52	9-10-52	Section 192 Title 2 U.S. Code	
USM Chgo IL	Anthony Joseph Accardo 61057	4-26-60	False income tax returns 3 counts	11-11-60 found guilty all counts 11-18-60 sent to serve 2 yrs plus $5000 F on each of three counts indictment sent consecutive acquitted 10-3-62
USM Chgo IL	Anthony Joseph Accardo 70760	4-21-70	Violation Federal Firearms Act	
USM Chgo IL	Anthony Joseph Accardo 89274-024	6-4-81	RICO consp	
FBI Chicago IL	Anthony Joseph Accardo 183 214	6-1-81	T-18 USC Sec 1962 (d) prohibited racketeering activities	

U.S. GOVERNMENT PRINTING OFFICE : 1982 O - 371-581

Special Thanks

Many people assisted in writing this book. I would like to thank GramMarinator for all her help in writing this book. I would like to thank Frank Menalocino for his help in getting this book out. I would also like to thank Tina for being there everyday. A special thanks to Mar and T.M. for sharing there extensive research of files and photos. I can not forget the following people; James Kosik, Mickey "Baby Boom Boom" Washington, and William Davis at the National Archives. And last to the few people who worked hard getting information for this book and don't want your name printed, thank you. Contact Author at tonydark35@yahoo.com

References

Asbury, Herbert. Gem of the Prairie: An Informal History of the Chicago Underworld. Illinois: Northern Illinois University Press, 1986.

Brashler, William. The Don: The Life and Death of Sam Giancana, New York: Ballantine Books, 1977

Capone, Deirdre Marie. Uncle Al Capone, Recap Publishing Company 2015.

Dark, Tony, A Mob of His Own, Chicago: HoseHead Productions 2008.

Dark, Tony, The FBI Files Sam Giancana, Chicago: HoseHead Productions, 2004

Demaris, Ovid. Captive City: Chicago in Chains, New York: Lyle Stuart, 1969

Eghigian Jr. Mars, After Capone, The Life and World of Chicago Mob Boss Frank "The Enforcer" Nitti, Cumberland House Publishing 2006.

Kidner, John, Crimaldi: Contract Killer. Washington D.C. : Acropolis Books LTD, 1976

Kobler, John. Capone: The Life and World of Al Capone, New York: G.P. Putnam's Sons, 1971.

Landeace, John. Organized Crime in Chicago, Part 3 of Illinois Crime Survey, 1929

Napoli, Antonio. The Mob's Guys, Virtual Book Worm, 2004

Roemer, William F., Jr. Accardo: The Genuine Godfather. New York: DIF INC. 1995.

Roemer, William F., Jr. The Enforcer - Spilotro: The Chicago Mob's Man over Las Vegas, New York: Ive Books 1994.

Roemer, William F., Jr. Roemer: Man Against the Mob. New York: DIF INC. 1989.

Russo, Gus. The Outfit: The Role of Chicago's Underworld in the Shaping of Modern America, New York, and London: Bloomsbury, 2001.

Schoenberg, Robert J. Mr. Capone. New York: William Morrow and Company, 1992.

Many Different FBI Files

42-671	60-488
60-652	60-2149
63-619	72-39
94-519	63-1810
92-466	92-350

Other Sources

Chicago Police Intelligence Files, Photos and Records

Industrial and Commercial background for Planning Chicago, Published by Chicago Planning Commission, September 1942

Many personal interviews of people who wish not to be named

United States Senate Permanent Subcommittee on Investigations, Hearings on Organized Crime, March 4, 1983, Chicago Illinois.

Chicago Crime Commission: The New Faces of Organized Crime 1997.

Transcripts of the Independent Hearing Officer Laborers' International Union of North America. Trusteeship Proceedings of the Chicago District Council 1997.

Newspapers

America News Post, americannewspost.com, Articles by Joe Fusco

Chicago American
Chicago Daily News
Chicago Evening Post
Chicago Herald & Examiner
Chicago Herald-American
Chicago Sun
Chicago Sun-Times
Chicago Times
Chicago Today
Chicago Tribune

Also Available

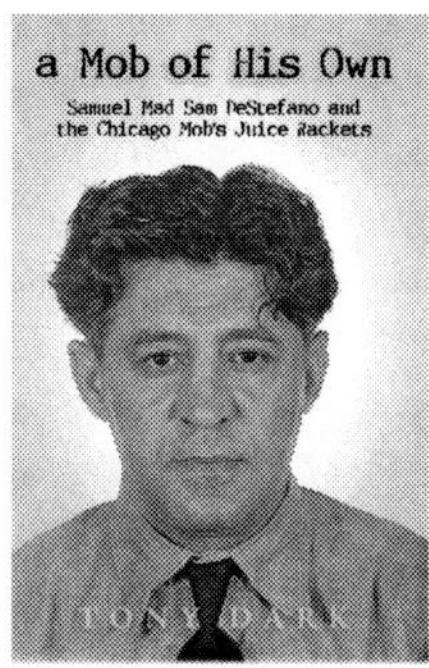

A Mob of His Own:

Mad Sam DeStefano and the Chicago

Mob's Juice Rackets

ISBN 978-0-615-17496-9

The FBI Files; Sam Giancana

ISNB# 978-0615127200

Index

CPSIA information can be obtained
at www.ICGtesting.com
Printed in the USA
LVOW10s1022280717
542988LV00016B/447/P

9 780985 11691